THEGREENGUIDE
Tuscany

Neptune Fountain, Piazza della Signoria, Firenze © ItalyGuides.it

General Manager	Cynthia Clayton Ochterbeck

The Green Guide **TUSCANY**

Editor	Jonathan P. Gilbert
Principal Writer	Melanie Renzulli
Production Manager	Natasha G. George
Cartographers	Alain Baldet, Michéle Cana, Peter Wrenn
Photo Editor	Yoshimi Kanazawa
Photo Researcher	Claudia Tate
Proofreader	Jenni Hairsine
Interior Design	Chris Bell
Layout	Nicole Jordan, Alison Rayner
Cover Design	Chris Bell, Christelle Le Déan
Cover Layout	Michelin Apa Publications Ltd.

Contact Us	The Green Guide
	Michelin Maps and Guides
	One Parkway South
	Greenville, SC 29615
	USA
	www.michelintravel.com
	Michelin Maps and Guides
	Hannay House
	39 Clarendon Road
	Watford, Herts WD17 1JA
	UK
	℘01923 205240
	www.ViaMichelin.com
	travelpubsales@uk.michelin.com

Special Sales	For information regarding bulk sales, customized editions and premium sales, please contact our Customer Service Departments:
	USA 1-800-432-6277
	UK 01923 205240
	Canada 1-800-361-8236

Note to the reader Addresses, phone numbers, opening hours and prices published in this guide are accurate at the time of press. We welcome corrections and suggestions that may assist us in preparing the next edition. While every effort is made to ensure that all information printed in this guide is correct and up-to-date, Michelin Apa Publications Ltd. accepts no liability for any direct, indirect or consequential losses howsoever caused so far as such can be excluded by law.

HOW TO USE THIS GUIDE

PLANNING YOUR TRIP
The blue-tabbed PLANNING YOUR TRIP section at the front of the guide gives you **ideas for your trip** and **practical information** to help you organise it. You'll find tours, practical information, a host of outdoor activities, a calendar of events, information on shopping, sightseeing, kids' activities and more.

INTRODUCTION
The orange-tabbed INTRODUCTION explores Tuscany's **Nature** and geology. The **History** section spans from the Etruscans to the modern day. The **Art and Culture** section covers architecture, art, literature and music, while the **Region Today** delves into modern Tuscany.

DISCOVERING
The green-tabbed DISCOVERING section features Principal Sights by region, featuring the most interesting local **Sights**, **Walking Tours**, nearby **Excursions**, and detailed **Driving Tours**. Admission prices shown are normally for a single adult.

ADDRESSES
We've selected the best hotels, restaurants, cafes, shops, nightlife and entertainment to fit all budgets. See the Legend on the cover flap for an explanation of the price categories. See the back of the guide for an index of hotels and restaurants.

Sidebars
Throughout the guide you will find blue, orange and green-coloured text boxes with lively anecdotes, detailed history and background information.

A Bit of Advice
Green advice boxes found in this guide contain practical tips and handy information relevant to the sight in the Discovering section.

STAR RATINGS★★★
Michelin has given star ratings for more than 100 years. If you're pressed for time, we recommend you visit the ★★★, or ★★ sights first:

★★★ **Highly recommended**
★★   **Recommended**
★   **Interesting**

MAPS
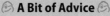
- Regional Driving Tours map, Principal Sights map.
- Region maps.
- Maps for major cities and villages.
- Local tour maps.

All maps in this guide are oriented north, unless otherwise indicated by a directional arrow. The term "Local Map" refers to a map within the chapter or Tourism Region. A complete list of the maps found in the guide appears at the back of this book.

Ingmar Wesemann/iStockphoto

PLANNING YOUR TRIP

INTRODUCTION TO TUSCANY

DISCOVERING TUSCANY

CONTENTS

Welcome to Tuscany

With its hilly countryside and high concentration of art, Tuscany is a region that inspires awe at every turn. Alpine peaks in the north feed rich river valleys where rows of vines and grains and pockets of olive trees add texture and order to the land. Tuscany's extensive coastline features major ports, idyllic beach coves and several islands. Meanwhile, breathtakingly beautiful cities–such as Renaissance Florence and medieval Siena–and bucolic villages, combine to make Tuscany one of Italy's most appealing destinations.

FLORENCE *(p88–181)*

Cradle of the Renaissance and former headquarters of one of Italy's most powerful families–the Medici–Florence is the capital of the region. Within its city limits are majestic buildings (Santa Maria del Fiore cathedral), troves of artistic treasures, both in the Uffizi Gallery and modest churches, vibrant markets and grand public squares. It merits a visit in one's lifetime.

Piazza Anfiteatro, Lucca

ItalyGuides.it

Santa Maria del Fiore, Florence

ItalyGuides.it

LUCCA AND NORTH OF THE ARNO *(p182–221)*

Enveloped by 16C walls, pretty Lucca boasts a pedestrian-friendly centre, unique religious architecture and the boyhood home of composer Giacomo Puccini. The town lies at the threshold of northern Tuscany, known for its Garfagnana woodlands and the Apuan Alps, where marble, especially at Carrara, has been quarried since Roman times. Natural hot springs (terme) and luxurious summer villas dot the immediate countryside around Lucca.

CHIANTI, SAN GIMIGNANO, METALLIFEROUS HILLS *(p222-249)*

The fertile subregion between Florence and Siena is the Chianti, which attracts visitors not only for its proximity to the famous cities, but for its eponymous wine, farmhouse inns and vivid green and blonde landscapes. San Gimignano, at once charming and austere, is a medieval "mini Manhattan" and lies in the rolling hills west of Chianti. South of San Gimignano, verdant pastures devolve into mineral-rich mining territory, an area known as the Metalliferous Hills.

Arco del Becci, San Gimignano

ItalyGuides.it

AREZZO (p250–273)

An illustrious artistic centre as early as Etruscan times, Arezzo is known primarily as the home of Piero della Francesca's astounding "Legend of the True Cross" fresco cycle, which is located in San Francesco church. Recently, Arezzo's fame has been eclipsed by Cortona, a lovely hilltown inhabited by numerous expats from Britain and North America. Beyond Arezzo lies the Casentino Forest, a quiet corner long favoured by the pious, including Saint Francis.

Palio delle Contrade, Siena

Mrohana/Dreamstime.com

SIENA (p274–299)

The heart of Humanist Tuscany lies in Siena, where the cityscape is little changed since medieval times. The compact centre consists of the elegant Palazzo Pubblico and the Piazza del Campo, site of the twice-yearly Palio horse race, a spectacle that breeds civic pride and attracts tourists in the thousands. An art city, Siena's Cathedral Precinct includes the Duomo, with its beautiful marble pavements, and multiple galleries showcasing early Sienese painting.

SIENESE HILLS AND THE SOUTH (p300–321)

Etruscan ruins at Murlo, medieval fortifications in Montalcino and Renaissance perfection in Pienza speak to the long history of civilisations in the land south of Siena. Yet nature rules much of southern Tuscany, with the vast Maremma plain covering a wide swath that includes diverse flora and fauna and endless farmland.

TUSCAN COAST (p322–357)

The Tuscan coastline runs approximately 400km/280mi along the Tyrhennian Sea from the slopes of the Alpi Apuane to the border with Lazio. The ports and villages along the shore have their own personalities, ranging from stylish beach resorts at Forte dei Marmi and Punta Ala to historic stretches along the Riviera degli Etruschi. The Tuscan Archipelago, which includes Elba, popular for its natural vistas as well as its historical link to Napoleon, makes up another 200km/124mi of coast.

PISA (p358–375)

The marvel that is the Leaning Tower makes up one piece of the Campo dei Miracoli, the "miraculous" set of religious buildings that is the centrepiece of Pisa. This university town on the Arno was once a maritime powerhouse, and its nautical heritage is reflected in its festivals, unusual Romanesque architecture and its lively, seaside demeanor.

Piazza dei Miracoli, Torre di Pisa

De Agostini Picture Library/Fototeca ENIT

Val d'Orcia, Tuscany
Ingmar Wesemann/iStockphoto

Michelin Driving Tours

DRIVING TOURS MAP

The map on the inside back cover charts the following routes.

1 THE GREAT CITIES

This itinerary takes in the major artistic centres of Tuscany, starting with **Florence**, where at least four days should be allowed to take in the sights. The Duomo, San Marco, the Palazzo Vecchio, the Uffizi, the Accademia, the Bargello, the Galleria Palatina in the Palazzo Pitti, the Boboli Gardens, the Cappelle Mediciee in the church of San Lorenzo, and the view from Piazzale Michelangelo are particularly noteworthy.

Heading towards the coast, the old centres of **Prato** and **Pistoia** are worth stopping for, prior to visiting **Lucca** with its fine city walls, and of course **Pisa** for the unforgettable sight of the Campo dei Miracoli. Turning back inland, the itinerary leads to the heartland of Tuscany and **San Gimignano**, famous for its many tower-houses.

Moving on, the next stop is **Siena**, pausing at **Monteriggioni**, as mentioned by Dante in the Divine Comedy. Return to Florence through the **Chianti** district.

2 ART AND NATURE AROUND THE MARBLE MOUNTAINS

The **Lunigiana** is celebrated for its castles and and Etruscan artefacts. Its rugged valleys open out as they drop down to the coast and the district of **Versilia**, dominated by the marble mountains that rise behind it.

The route continues towards **Pisa** and then **Lucca**, from where the **Garfagnana**, on the threshold of the **Parco delle Alpi Apuane**, is readily accessible. The famous Devil's Bridge at **Borgo a Mozzano** is steeped in folklore; continue to head north to return to the Lunigiana.

3 NORTH OF FLORENCE

This route covers the Apennine mountains on Tuscany's border with Emilia. Starting from **Florence**, the first stop is **Fiesole**, a favourite location for Renaissance artists and modern-day travellers alike: the route then enters the uplands of the **Mugello** district, once the favoured rural retreat of the Florentine merchant classes.

Returning towards Florence the itinerary takes in the **Villa Demidoff**, where Giovanni da Bologna's huge statue, the Appennino, may be seen in the gardens.

4 NATURE AND RELIGION: CASENTINO, PRATOMAGNO

From **Arezzo** the itinerary heads into the district of the Casentino, a place of seclusion long favoured by monks and hermits. Of particular note are **La Verna**, where St Francis would spend time in retreat with his followers, and **Camaldoli**, where the community and hermit traditions of monasticism exist side by side. Heading towards **Poppi**, a small detour leads to the charming church at **Romena**.

From **Poppi**, visible from some distance away on account of its forbidding castle, the route takes in **San Giovanni Valdarno** and **Gropina**, concluding a tour through some of Tuscany's most ruggedly beautiful landscapes, where the timeless atmosphere of spiritual devotion bubbles below the surface.

5 UPPER TIBER VALLEY TO THE CHIANA VALLEY

This route begins in **Arezzo** before proceeding to **Sansepolcro**, birthplace of Piero della Francesca. Following the border with Umbria leads you to **Monterchi** and the famous **Madonna del Parto**. Continuing the trip, the next stop is **Cortona**, perched on a hill and offering fine views of the Chiana valley and Lake Trasimeno.

A little to the south is the **Abbazia di Farneta**, worth visiting before

Landscape of Monticchiello near Pienza

B. Morandi/ MICHELIN

proceeding to **Chiusi** and then on to **Chianciano Terme** and **Montepulciano**, situated in a panoramic spot overlooking the countryside. Return to Arezzo along the Chiana valley.

6 SIENA AND ITS LANDSCAPE

Situated in the heart of Tuscany, **Siena** is a masterpiece in its own right with a history of splendour and bloodshed. From Siena the itinerary progresses to **Murlo** for a taste of Etruscan heritage, before reaching the medieval town of **Montalcino** and the nearby **Abbazia di S. Antimo**. The route then follows the **Val d'Orcia**, and the path of the Via Francigena, to reach **Pienza**, the quintessential "Ideal City of the Renaissance".
Continue to **Montepulciano** (& *see TOUR* 5) and visit the nearby Benedictine abbey of **Monte Oliveto Maggiore**. The final place of interest is **Asciano**, before returning to Siena.

7 METALLIFEROUS HILLS TO THE ISLE OF ELBA

Discover beautiful contrasts of scenery, from classic Tuscan rolling hills to the lunar landscape of the Metalliferous Hills, and fine coastal views.
Leaving **San Gimignano**, the route takes in **Volterra**, famous for its alabaster, and **Larderello**, where the roadside becomes lined by huge pipes and tubes, and the air is thick with the odour of sulphur.

Continuing towards the sea through countryside rich in Etruscan remains, the coast is finally reached at **Piombino**, the port of embarkation for the **Isle of Elba**. After returning to the mainland, the itinerary proceeds to **Massa Marittima**, which despite its name sits on a hill. The town has a fine Romanesque cathedral. The S 441 then leads to **San Galgano** with its delightful ruined abbey. The last leg of the trip takes in the fortified town of **Colle Alta Val d'Elsa** prior to returning to San Gimignano.

8 SOUTHERN TUSCANY

The **Maremma** district bordering Lazio is a rugged and unspoiled landscape with many wild boar. Along the coast are **Punta Ala**, **Castiglione della Pescaia** and the **Argentario**, with **Monte Amiata** rising behind. Lovers of archaeology will enjoy visiting **Vetulonia**, **Roselle**, **Ansedonia** (formerly Cosa), **Sovana** and the Archaeological Museum at **Grosseto**. In the tufa valleys nearby are the towns of **Pitigliano** and **Sorano**, seemingly untouched by the passage of time; finally the ancient spa of **Saturnia** is the ideal place to restore mind and body.
Information on the wide range of sporting activities available in Tuscany can be obtained from the **Servizio Turismo e Sport**, *26 Via di Novoli, 50127 Firenze.* &055 43 83 822/823.

11

When and Where to Go

Val d'Orcia

ROMA-OSLO/iStockphoto

WHEN TO GO

Tuscany is beautiful whatever the season, but the countryside is at its best in spring. March to June sees temperatures ranging from lows of 9°C (49°F) to highs of 19°C (67°F). The mild weather is ideal for touring, as well as more vigourous activities like biking and trekking. Travel at this time of year also means avoiding the mass tourism and soaring temperatures of high summer. While late June days can be glorious, with lows at 15°C (58°F) and highs at 26°C (78°F), low-lying Florence is particularly hot.

In summer many towns and villages stage traditional events or offer concerts and other outdoor entertainment. Autumn, which enjoys mild temperatures well into late October, brings fewer tourists than summer. The harvest season is particularly recommended for lovers of wine and truffles. Winter can be a trying time to travel in Tuscany, not only because the weather is unpredictable, but also because a number of lodgings close during the colder months. On the positive side, you can often find travel discounts if you choose to travel at this time.

WHERE TO GO
SHORT BREAKS

Florence, Siena and the Chianti
First-time travellers to Tuscany who wish to combine an art itinerary with fresh air should stay in Florence and Siena, leaving time for a tour of the Chianti countryside. In Florence, visitors should not miss the **Galleria degli Uffizi**, which requires almost a full day to appreciate the artistic treasures within. Michelangelo's *David* in the **Accademia** is another must-see and, of course, a visit to **Santa Maria del Fiore** and the **Piazza della Signoria** is essential. **Siena** merits a dedicated visit in its own right. Famed for the **Palio** horse race, this towered city is steeped in

Piazza della Signoria, Florence

ItalyGuides.it

Massa Marittima

vm/iStockphoto

medieval traditions and still retains an atmosphere of civic pride. A stroll around the shell-shaped **Piazza del Campo** and tour of the city's Duomo with its exquisite **pavements** is a chance to view the heart of medieval Tuscany.

Binding these two art cities is the **Chianti** countryside, lined with vines and olives, an ideal getaway for nature lovers and gastronomes. Follow up a tour of Florence and Siena's major sights with a daytrip or stay in Chianti. From Florence, take the route that passes through **Badia a Passignano**, **Castellina in Chianti** and **Greve in Chianti**, which is marked in yellow in the Chianti chapter. From Siena, the route (marked in orange) passes through **Radda in Chianti**, **Badia Coltibuono** and **Brolio** (💰*See CHIANTI*).

Religious Tuscany

The itinerary starts high in the Casentino forest, at the **monastery** and **hermitage** of Camaldoli.

Slightly to the south is the Santuario della **Verna**, where St Francis received the stigmata.

Continuing south to Arezzo and the Chiana valley, the next stop is the **Abbazia di Farneta**, a charming Romanesque church which, since 1937, has been the base for Don Sante Felice, a priest notable for his work in the field of archaeology, and who founded a remarkable museum here.

Heading towards Siena, the route passes the **Abbazia di Monte Oliveto Maggiore**, the mother house of the Olivetian order, with fine frescoes by Luca Signorelli (1498) and Sodoma (1505–08) chronicling the life of St Benedict. 30km south of Siena are the striking ruins of the **Abbazia di S. Galgano**, the earliest gothic church in Tuscany.

Close to Montalcino is the delightful **Abbazia di Sant'Antimo** standing in a quintessentially beautiful Tuscan landscape. It is worth lingering here to hear the Gregorian chant performed within this most elegant and harmonious interior.

Florence's "minor sights" and Lucchesia's villas

Any attempt to tackle the Uffizi in limited time can never do justice to the great masterpieces it displays. This itinerary offers an alternative for those already familiar with the major monuments of Florence, focusing instead on some of the smaller jewels which the city has to offer.

Close to Piazza della Signoria is the **Oratorio dei Buonomini**, bedecked in frescoes by the studio of Ghirlandaio. Not far from the Duomo, the **Palazzo Medici Riccardi** also has fine frescoes by Benozzo Gozzoli. The **Opificio delle Pietre Dure** near Via Alfani houses a rich collection of intricately carved precious stones. On the other side of the Arno, the church of S. Maria del Carmine includes the **Cappella Brancacci**, which is decorated with frescoes by Masaccio.

Leaving Florence and heading towards Lucca, the route takes in **Collodi**, famous for its associations with *Pinocchio*. Between Collodi and Lucca are numerous villas in the Lucchesia district. The itinerary concludes in the pleasant surroundings of the historic city of Lucca.

The Coast for History lovers

See TUSCAN COASTLINE.

From Versilia to the Maremma, the Tuscan coast offers panoramic views and a wealth of sites of artistic, historical and literary interest.

The **Versilia** hinterland is formed by the **Apuan Alps**.

Heading south, Pisa has the stunning Campo dei Miracoli, which includes the Leaning Tower.

Livorno marks the beginning of the **Etruscan Riviera**. Before heading on to **Populonia**, admirers of the Nobel winner Giosuè Carducci should stop at **Bolgheri** and **Castagneto Carducci**. The choice of resorts between Marina di Carrara and the Promontorio dell'Argentario is vast, both for campers and those in search of more comfortable accommodation.

Via Francigena

Marka/Alamy

The Medici Villa Trail

The Medici family, who ruled Florence and much of Tuscany during the Renaissance era, built lavish mansions and estates in the city and countryside, all of which were designed by the top artists and architects of the day. Beyond the **Palazzo Pitti** in Florence, the Medici commissioned Giuliano da Sangallo to build the Villa Medicea in **Poggio a Caiano** and Buontalenti to construct La Ferdinanda in **Artimino**. **Fiesole**, the hill town that rises above Florence, is home to the Villa Medici, realised by Michelozzo.

LONGER BREAKS

Arezzo, Siena and the Maremma

The landscape between Arezzo, Siena and the Maremma is the ideal backdrop for walking, cycling or riding. Make the most of the countryside by staying in an agriturismo; alternatively use Arezzo or Siena as a base from which to tour the area.

Siena's major sights are easily toured in a couple days, but the city and its province merit further exploration. In addition to being a good base from which to visit Chianti, Siena is near **San Gimignano**, another city of medieval towers, and **Pienza**, a Renaissance jewel worth a visit if time allows. In **Arezzo** are the peerless frescoes by Piero della Francesca in the church of San Francesco, and the fine Piazza Grande. Not far from here lie the towns of **Monte San Savino** and **Lucignano**, both of which are known for their splendid medieval centres. Heading towards the sea, it is worth stopping at the medieval town of **Massa Marittima** before joining the Via Aurelia and turning south towards the Parco Naturale della Maremma. Further south still, on the border with Lazio, **Pitigliano**, **Sorano** and **Sovana** are towns which appear to belong in another age.

Via Cassia near Siena

©Gimmi/Cuboimages/Photoshot

HISTORIC ROUTES

Via Francigena

www.viafrancigena.com.
Pilgrimage routes were principally popular at the beginning of the 11C, driven by a devotion to see the Holy Sites of Christianity. Pilgrims carried the emblems of the routes they travelled; on the Francigena they bore St Peter's key. You may have come across the logo of the Via Francigena, which depicts a pilgrim resembling a Roman statue, a little squat, with a cane in his hand and a bundle on his shoulder. The Via Francigena ran from Canterbury to Rome, with stops in the Tuscan towns of Lucca, San Gimignano, Siena and San Quirico, and was used by medieval pilgrims who managed to cover 20km/12.5 mi a day on foot.

Via Aurelia

Of ancient Roman origin, the Via Aurelia (S1) has linked Rome to Genoa since 109 BC. Construction began in 241 BC. It runs along the Tuscan coastline, from Marina di Carrara to Capalbio Stazione.

Via Cassia

Laid down in the 2C BC, this road runs through Etruria, linking Rome to Arezzo and then extending to Florence. The current S 2, which still bears the same name, links Rome and Florence.

TUSCAN WINE ROUTES

Viva Bacchus! What could be better than spending time among Tuscany's hills and vineyards, tasting prime vintages along the way? Tuscany has 14 dedicated wine routes, known in Italian as Le Strade del Vino. All of the routes have their own name and speciality and are accessible from the region's main tourist hubs (⌖*See CHIANTI and RIVIERA DEGLI ETRUSCHI*).

Province of Arezzo: Strada del Vino Terre di Arezzo.

Province of Florence: Strada del Vino Chianti Colli Fiorentini, Strada del Vino di Montespertoli, Strada dei Vini Chianti Rufina e Pomino.

Province of Grosseto: Strada del Vino Monteregio di Massa Marittima, Strada del Vino Colli di Maremma, Strada del Vino di Montecucco.

Province of Livorno: Strada del Vino Costa degli Etruschi.

Province of Lucca: Strada del Vino Colline Lucchesi e Montecarlo.

Province of Massa Carrara: Strada del Vino Colli di Candia e di Lunigiana.

Province of Prato: Strada Medicea dei Vini di Carmignano.

Province of Pisa: Strada del Vino delle Colline Pisane.

Province of Siena: Strada del Vino Vernaccia di San Gimignano, Strada del Vino di Montepulciano.

What to See and Do

OUTDOOR FUN

BEACHES

See TUSCAN COASTLINE.

From Marina di Carrara to the Argentario, Tuscany's coastline offers wide variety, from sandy beaches to more rugged settings.

Sandy beaches: Tuscany's most popular shore is the Riviera Versilia, which stretches from Marina di Carrara to Livorno. The sandy beaches, particularly at Forte dei Marmi, are ideal for families. Viareggio, the main city of the Versilia, is known for its nightlife and Carnevale (www.aptversilia.it). More sandy beaches are found south of Livorno to Piombino, along the gulf of Follonica and from Castiglione della Pescaia to Argentario.

Rocky coastline: The area just south of Livorno, from Baratti to Piombino, and the Argentario is known as the Etruscan Riviera (*Riviera degli Etruschi*). Beyond the pine groves that define the coast here are, as the name implies, towns and ruins of Etruscan origin, of which Ansedonia (formerly Cosa) is especially notable.

Islands: The Tuscan Archipelago includes the islands of Elba, Capraia and Giglio. Ports and harbours suitable for sailing craft are numerous. More information can be obtained from the Arcipelago Toscano website at www.aptelba.it.

BALLOONING

- **Chianti Balloon Club –** Castelnuovo Berardenga *0577 36 32 32.
- **Ballooning in Tuscany –** 17 Via dei Goti, Montisi (SI). *0577 72 55 17. www.ballooningintuscany.com.

CYCLING

Tuscany is a region well suited to touring by bicycle, although to date no dedicated cycle route network has been introduced. Access the website **www.cicloturismo-mtb.com** for suggested itineraries in the Maremma, Florence and surrounding area, the Apuan Alps, the Pescia area, the Sienese Hills, the Casentino area, and Siena and surrounding area, as well as links for cycling enthusiasts.

Several tour operators, including **www.cicloposse.com** and **www.ciclismoclassico.com**, will plan biking itineraries throughout Tuscany. Additionally, the Province of Siena tourist board has many suggestions for bike routes in Siena and the surrounding areas on its website at **www.terresienainbici.it**.

In Florence, **Florence by bike** offers interesting tours of the city.

GOLF

Tuscany has numerous good quality courses, from 18-hole courses to practice greens, most of which are open all year. A few popular golf clubs are listed below. More information can be obtained from **www.turismo. intoscana.it**.

- **Punta Ala Golf Club**, Punta Ala, Grosseto (near Piombino) *0564 92 21 21 www.puntaala.net/golf
- **Golf and Country Club Poggio dei Medici** Scarperia (25 km from Florence) *055 843 04 36 www.poggiodeimedici.com
- **Golf Club Ugolino** Grassina (15km from Florence) *055 23 01 009 www.golfugolino.it.

RIDING

Every province in Tuscany has at least a farm or park equipped for professional or casual horseback riding. Some well known horse centres are listed below.

For information about equestrian tourism throughout Tuscany, visit http://fitetrecantetoscana.it, the website for the Tuscany branch of the Italian Federation of Equestrian Tourism. See also the *Addresses* in each section of this guide.

Argentario

morenovel / Fotolia

- **Centro Equestre Ambasciador Arcidosso (Grosseto-near Monte Amiata)**
  ☎0339 18 36 923
  www.cavalloamiata.it
- **Tenuta San Rossore (pony trekking)**
  Centro Visite (near Pisa)
  ☎050 53 01 01, www.sanrossore.it
- **Club Ippico Fioralice (Riding school and pony trekking),** Fauglia (near Pisa)
  ☎050 65 91 01, www.fioralice.it
- **Centro Ippico "La Querce" Montemurlo (Prato)**
  ☎0574 68 21 38
  www.la-querce.it/interfaccia.htm
- **Associazione Provinciale dei Cavalieri Senesi**
  Siena, ☎33918 57530
  www.cavalierisenesi.it
- **Centro Ippico della Berardenga Castelnuovo Berardenga (Siena)**
  ☎0577 35 50 71
  www.chiantiriding.it

WALKING/HIKING

Walkers can obtain information from the main tourist offices and from the website www.terraditoscana.it.

🚶 Monte Amiata

One of Tuscany's most distsinctive geographic features, Monte Amiata is a dormant volcano in Tuscany's southeast. Its slopes are ideal for skiing and hiking, while the surrounding valleys enjoy a wealth of diverse flora and fauna, including thousands of hectares of nature reserves

Contact: **Agenzia per il Turismo dell'Amiata,** Via Adua, 25, 53021 Abbadia San Salvatore
☎0577 77 58 11
http://amiataturismo.info

🚶 Parco Nazionale Delle Foreste Casentinesi Monte Falterona e Campigna

This national park, which contains Tuscany's largest woodlands, has nine marked nature trails suitable for easy hikes. The La Verna and Camaldoli monasteries are also located here.

Contact: **Comunità Montana, Via Togliatti,** 45, 50032 Borgo San Lorenzo,
☎055 84 95 346
www.parcoforestecasentinesi.it

🚶 Isle of Elba

The island offers several hiking opportunities, from challenging treks along the northwest coast and up Monte Capanne, to rambles that explore Elba's rich mineral heritage. Hikes can also follow a route near Volterraio that leads to eagle nesting grounds. Many routes start in Marciana or Rio Elba. Maps of walking trails are available at newspaper kiosks on the island.

Contact: **Agenzia per il Turismo dell'Arcipelago Toscano,**

Isola d'Elba

De Agostini Picture Library/Fototeca ENIT

Calata Italia, 26, 57037, Portoferraio
℘0565 91 46 71
www.aptelba.it

🚶 Parco Naturale Della Maremma

Encompassing approximately 100 square kilometres, the Maremma parkland in southern Tuscany stretches from Principina a Mare to Talamone and from the coast to the Via Aurelia (S1) motorway. Its features include the Uccellina Mountains and a variety of ecosystems, including sandy shores, woodlands, marshes and even desert-like conditions. The park has mapped out 10 nature treks ranging from easy to difficult that pass by crumbled towers, caves and beautiful seaside panoramas. Some treks require guides and a few trails are closed during the hot, dry summer months.

Contact: **Centro Visite Alberese,**
℘0564 39 32 11
www.parco-maremma.it

🚶 Parco di Migliarino, San Rossore, Massaciuccoli

This park occupies undeveloped coast between Livorno and Viareggio, the estates of Migliarino and San Rossore and the area around Lake Massaciuccoli. Its main features are its wetlands, however, several guided walks are possible. Reserve guided tours by fax at least three days prior to visiting.

Contact: **Visitor Centre,**
Coltano, ℘050 98 90 84,
Fax 050 98 90 51
For Tenuta di San Rossore:
Centri Visite San Rossore, Loc.
Cascine Vecchie,
℘050 53 01 01, Fax 050 53 37 55
www.parks.it/parco.migliarino.
san.rossore

🚶 Mountains of Pistoia

The Montagne Pistoiese, the heart of the Apennine range in Tuscany, are easily discovered following the trails of the Ecomuseum, an open-air museum of six itineraries that explore the area's cultural and natural history. The Botanical Garden in Abetone is a highlight.

More Outdoors Contacts

AIGAE-Associazione Italiana Guide Ambientali Escursionistiche: Coordinamento provinciale c/o Maria Zuddas, 22 Via Fiume, 53036 Poggibonsi.
℘0577 98 29 23. www.gae.it.
CAI-Club Alpino Italiano:
95 Viale Mazzini, 53100 Siena.
℘0577 27 06 66. www.cai.it.
Parco Artistico Naturale e Culturale della Val d'Orcia:
33 Via Dante Alighieri, 53027 San Quirico d'Orcia. ℘0577 89 83 03.
www.parcodellavaldorcia.com.
WWF: 32 Via Campansi, 53100 Siena.
℘0577 45 159. www.wwf.org.

Contact: **Provincia di Pistoia -** Ufficio Cultura, &0573 97 461, Fax 0573 97 46 75 www.provincia.pistoia.it/ecomuseo

🏃 Prato and Surrounding Area

Easy and difficult treks are possible around the province of Prato, which includes the hilly terrain of Montalbano and Monteferrato and the mountainous Val di Bisenzio. Flora in the parks and protected areas include olive groves, chestnut trees and wild orchids.

Contact: **Club Alpino Italiano,** Sezione "E. Bertini", 8 Via dell'Altopascio, 59100 Prato. &0574 22 004 www.caiprato.it

🏃 Siena and Surrounding Area

Siena's province contains 11 nature reserves with well-marked routes where one can encounter rare flora and fauna and medieval ruins among the dense vegetation. The Provincial Tourist Board has also devised several easy and medium itineraries that explore the area's artistic heritage, from a 4km ramble around Monte Oliveto to a 9km hike in the San Gimignano countryside.

Contact: **Terre di Siena Tourist Information** &0577 28 05 51 www.terresiena.it

For the Nature Reserves: Ufficio Riserve Naturali, Villa Lodone, Via Sperandie &0577 24 14 16 www.riservenaturali.provincia.siena.it

SPAS

Tuscany has more spa towns than any other region of Italy. The springs have attracted visitors since time immemorial. Some are in the open air like the hot waterfall outside Terme di Saturnia; others have been channelled into elegant buildings offering hosts of medical treatments.

The charm and elegance of Chianciano, Saturnia (east of Grossetto) and Montecatini are known beyond the borders of Italy. These spas were at the height of their fame in the 19C and early 20C, when people took holidays in the elegant surroundings of fine architecture and landscaped gardens. A selection of these spa towns is shown on the **Places to Stay** map. The Italian Tourist Office (*see know before you go*) provides a complete list with supplementary information about the type of facilities available (drinking water, hot baths, mud baths, underground or surface baths, accommodation). In most centres a medical examination is necessary before embarking on certain types of treatment.

Terme di Saturnia

B. Morandi/ MICHELIN

19

Typical Tuscan produce

Vito Arcomano/Fototeca ENIT

More information can be obtained from the website: www.turismo.intoscana.it and from **Consorzio Terme di Toscana**, presso Terme di Chianciano, 12 Via delle Rose, 53042 Chianciano Terme (SI). ℘0578 68 111. www.termeditoscana.com

♦ **Terme di San Filippo**: Loc. S. Filippo, 23, Castiglione d'Orcia. ℘0577 87 29 82. www.termesanfilippo.it.

♦ **Terme di Chianciano Spa**: Via delle Rose. ℘0578 68 111. www.termechianciano.it.

♦ **Stabilimento Sillene**: Piazza G. Marconi, Chianciano Terme.

♦ **Centro di Fisiokinesiterapia e Rieducazione Motoria** Piazza G. Marconi, Chianciano Terme.

♦ **Centro di Medicina Estetica e Angiologia** Piazza G. Marconi, Chianciano Terme.

♦ **Centro Inalatorio** Via Roma, Chianciano Terme.

♦ **Sorgente Sant'Elena Spa** 112 Viale della Libertà, Chianciano Terme. ℘0578 31 141. www.termesantelena.it.

♦ **Bagni di Petriolo** Terme Salute, Ambiente Spa, Monticiano. ℘0577 75 71 04. www.termesaluteambiente.com.

♦ **Terme di Montepulciano Spa**

Sant'Albino di Montepulciano, 46 Via delle Terme. ℘0578 79 11. www.termemontepulciano.it.

♦ **Bagni delle Galleraie** Terme Salute, Loc. Le Galleraie, Radicondoli. ℘0577 79 31 51. www.termesaluteambiente.com

♦ **Stabilimento Termale Antica Querciolaia** 22 Via Trieste, Rapolano Terme, ℘0577 72 40 91. www.termeaq.it.

♦ **Terme S. Giovanni** Loc. Terme di S. Giovanni, Rapolano Terme. ℘0577 72 40 30.

♦ **Centro Termale Fonteverde:** Loc. Terme 1, San Casciano dei Bagni. ℘0578 58 023. www.termedisancascianobagni.it.

♦ **Terme di Bagno Vignoni** Piazza del Moretto, San Quirico d'Orcia. ℘0577 88 73 65. www.termedibagnovignoni.com.

👫 FOR KIDS

In this guide, sights of particular interest to children are indicated with a KIDS symbol (👫). Some attractions may offer discount fees for children. **Collodi** – The **Parco di Pinocchio** delights with oversize renderings of characters from the children's tale. **Florence** – The **Giardino di Boboli** provides fresh air and lots of space to move; **Museo Stibbert** features a stunning collection of armour. **Pisa** - The **Leaning Tower** will stir their imagination.

SHOPPING

Tuscany's craft industry is one of which it is justifiably proud. Traditional wares and souvenirs are widely available. In Florence, look for fine leather, especially at the Santa Croce Leather Workshop; discount leather accessories can be located in the San Lorenzo Market. Florence is also ideal for gold jewellery; the shops on the Ponte Vecchio specialise in gold, but may not offer the best prices.

Many craft items are also sold in the region's various monthly markets; Arezzo is particularly renowned for its antiques fair, which happens the last Sunday of each month and the preceding Saturday. Elsewhere in Tuscany, look for ceramics, marble souvenirs, wooden toys and hand-made paper.

- ◆ **Alabaster** – Crafted in Volterra and Pisa.
- ◆ **Paper and papier mâché** – Hand-crafted stationery can be found in many shops around Florence.
- ◆ **Ceramics and porcelain** – Ceramics are produced in Montelupo Fiorentino, Cafaggiolo (to the west and north of Florence). Porcelain can be found in Sesto Fiorentino.

Don't forget the vast array of Tuscan food products that make ideal souvenirs: **pasta**, **olive oil**, **artisanal vinegars** and **wine**.

Most shops open from 8.30/9am to 12.30/1pm and 3.30/4pm to 7.30/8pm, although in the centre of large towns and cities, shops usually remain open at lunchtime. Credit cards are accepted in most stores, with the exception of small food shops.

ANTIQUES FAIRS

Tuscany has many regular antiques fairs. Arezzo's is one of the best known in all Italy. All manner of items, from furniture to books and ceramics, is available. Bartering is expected.

- ◆ **Arezzo** – Not to be missed, this fair is held on the first Sunday and preceding Saturday of each month.
- ◆ **Florence** – Held on the last Sunday each month in Piazza dei Ciompi. The city also holds a biennial fair in Palazzo Corsini in odd-numbered years (www.mostraantiquariato.it).
- ◆ **Marina di Grosseto** – This bargain hunters' fair is held on the third weekend of each month.
- ◆ **Montelupo** – Annual event, third Sunday of October.
- ◆ **Montepulciano** – Held on the second Saturday and following Sunday of each month in Piazza Grande.
- ◆ **Orbetello** – Held during August, this antiques fair in the public gardens offers a wide range of collectors' items.

Poggio a Caiano – A monthly fair (*precise date varies, not held in Jul, Aug and Jan*) for antiques and collectibles held at the former Medici stables.

San Miniato – Antiques fair held on the first Sunday of each month except July and August. The second Sunday of the month sees an organic produce and craft market.

Siena – Collectors' fair focusing on stamps and coins held third Sunday of the month in Piazza del Mercato.

San Lorenzo Market, Florence

ItalyGuides.it

21

BOOKS

So much has been written about Tuscany, its history, culture, landscape and art that it is impossible to provide a concise list. The following has been compiled for readers who do not have unlimited time. The list focuses on works of easy reference, ample illustration, and classics that have captured the spirit of the region.

HISTORY

The Prince. Niccolò Machiavelli. (1532; 1996). Written during the reign of Lorenzo the Magnificent, this treatise on political thought is still relevant today.

The Merchant of Prato. Iris Origo. (1957). This biography of Francesco di Marco Datini provides compelling details of middle-class life in medieval Tuscany.

The House of Medici: Its Rise and Fall. Christopher Hibbert. (1982). A definitive guide to Tuscany's most powerful family, Hibbert's book chronicles the Medici influence in the 15C.

War in Val D'Orcia: An Italian War Diary, 1943–1944. Iris Origo. (1947). Origo's first-hand account of life at her Tuscan villa during World War II is a classic.

ART

Art and Architecture in Italy 1250–1400. John White. (1966; 1993). This hefty book is an excellent primer to the artworks of the Middle Ages and Renaissance era.

The Agony and the Ecstasy. Irving Stone. (1961; 2004). Stone attempts to relate the life, work and emotions of Michelangelo in this biographical novel.

Autobiography of Benvenuto Cellini. Benvenuto Cellini. (1728; 2006). One of the most celebrated autobiographies written by an artist, this book is a fascinating look at the goldsmith and sculptor's wild life during 16C Italy.

Brunelleschi's Dome. Ross King. (2001). King's look at the politics, rivalries and logistics behind the building of Florence's iconic dome is a quick and satisfying read.

GENERAL

The Stones of Florence. Mary McCarthy. (1956). This personal study of Florence is filled with insightful and often witty observations.

Under the Tuscan Sun. Frances Mayes. (1997). This memoir set in Cortona contains recipes and anecdotes about expat life in small town Tuscany.

Walking and Eating in Tuscany and Umbria. James Lasdun and Pia Davis. (1997). Sybaritic travellers will savour this book, which contains 40 gourmet rambles through the central Italian countryside.

COOKERY

Italian Food. Elizabeth David. (1954). The legendary British gourmand writes about the pleasures of Italian food and ingredients in a lively style.

Carluccio's Complete A–Z of Italian Food. Antonio Carluccio, Priscilla Carluccio. (2007) The popular London-based cook's guide to Italian cuisine features colourful illustrations and plenty of info on regional fare.

NOVELS

The Divine Comedy. Dante Alighieri. (1321). This epic book of verse about *Paradiso*, *Purgatorio* and *Inferno* is a standard of Italian literature.

The Decameron. Giovanni Boccaccio. (1353). The "100 stories" in this medieval Italian classic is set in Tuscany during the plague.

The Adventures of Pinocchio. Carlo Collodi. (1883). The original telling of this popular children's book is much darker than subsequent versions.

A Room with a View. EM Forster. (1908). A young English girl on holiday in Florence confronts the pleasures of travel and society's expectations in this satire.

Summer's Lease. John Mortimer. (1988). This novel details the joys and difficulties faced by an English family who let a Tuscan villa for the summer.

FILMS

The best films made in Tuscany are usually the work of Tuscan film-makers such as Mauro Bolognini, who was born in Pistoia in 1922, and the Taviani brothers, who were born in 1929 and 1931 in San Miniato.

The region is also a popular location for film-makers of other nationalities, and in recent years Tuscany has been the setting for a number of international films. Listed below are some of the best-known films made in Tuscany.

La Provinciale (1953). This story, adapted from a novel by Moravia, is set in provincial Tuscany near Lucca.

Lo Spadaccino di Siena (1962). This Franco-Italian production by Baccio Bandini is set in 17C Siena.

Vaghe Stelle dell'Orsa (1965). Luchino Visconti directed this film about Volterra and the balze.

Il Prato (1979). Despite the name, this Taviani brothers film is about San Gimignano and its towers.

La Notte di San Lorenzo (1982). Directed by the Taviani Brothers, this film is about an episode in the Second World War set in San Miniato (re-named San Lorenzo in the film), and which records the rural and agricultural life of the 1940s.

A Room with a View (1985). The adaptation by James Ivory of the novel by EM Forster is an exploration of Florence and the surrounding countryside by young English men and women early in the 20C.

Con Gli Occhi Chiusi (With Closed Eyes) (1994). Directed by Francesca Archibugi, this film is set in the Sienese countryside in the early 20C.

The English Patient (1996). Directed by Anthony Mingella, this film includes scenes set in Pienza and also the monastery of Sant'Anna in Camprena, in which the dying patient is nursed by Juliette Binoche.

La Vita è Bella (Life is Beautiful) (1997). With Roberto Benigni as producer and actor, this film is set initially around Arezzo and portrays a father struggling heroically to convince his young son (by inventng fanciful and humorous interpretations of events) that the concentration camp, to which they are deported, is a holiday camp and that each atrocity is make-believe.

Tea with Mussolini (1999). Directed by Franco Zeffirelli and starring Maggie Smith, Judi Dench and Joan Plowright, this film is based on Zeffirelli's childhood in Florence before and during WWII with a group of elderly British ladies.

Up at the Villa (1999). Set in Florence just prior to WWII, this adaptation of a W Somerset Maugham novella features Kristin Scott Thomas and Sean Penn.

Under the Tuscan Sun (2003). Starring Diane Lane, this film is set in Cortona, and based on the bestselling novel of the same name.

La Meglio Gioventù (The Best of Youth) (2003). Chronicling the lives of the members of an Italian family over four decades, this mini-series is set in Florence, Rome and other parts of Italy.

Calendar of Events

APRIL – MAY

CARNIVAL (SHROVE TUESDAY)
Viareggio – Procession of floats
Santa Croce sull'Arno –
Procession of floats

EASTER SUNDAY
Florence – Scoppio del Carro
(*see FLORENCE*)
Prato – Presentation of the
Holy Girdle (*see PRATO*)

2ND SUNDAY AFTER EASTER
San Miniato – Kite festival
(Festa degli aquiloni): kites are
flown from the fortress esplanade,
followed by a historic pageant and
the launch of a hot air balloon

1 MAY
Prato – Presentation of the
Holy Girdle (*see PRATO*)

4TH SUNDAY IN MAY
Massa Marittima – Balestro del
Girifalco (*see MASSA MARITTIMA*)

ASCENSION
Florence – Festa del grillo

MAY–JUNE

MAY
Florence –
Maggio Musicale Fiorentino:
month-long music festival.
www.maggiofiorentino.com.

17 JUN
Pisa – Historic regatta in honour
of St Ranieri

3RD SUNDAY IN JUN
San Quirico d'Orcia –
Festa del Barbarossa
(*see SAN QUIRICO D'ORCIA*)

PENULTIMATE SUNDAY IN JUN
Arezzo – Giostra del Saracino
(*see AREZZO*)

23 JUN, EVENING
San Miniato – St John's Day's
Bonfires (*see SAN MINIATO*)

24 JUN
Florence – Calcio Storico
Fiorentino: legendary football
tournament in the city's four main
squares (*see FIRENZE*).
www.calciostorico.it.

LAST SUNDAY IN JUN
Pisa – Gioco del Ponte (*see PISA*)

JULY

Siena – Siena Musical Week
(opera and chamber music).
www.sienasummermusic.org.

2 JUL
Siena – Palio delle Contrade:
historic horse race (*see SIENA*).
http://palio.comune.siena.it.

25 JUL
Pistola – Giostra dell'Orso
(*see PISTOIA*)

Saracen Joust, Arezzo

S. Chirol / MICHELIN

Longer Festivals

July–September – San Gimignano Summer Fair (Estate Sangimignanese): lyrical works, prose, ballet, concerts, cinema

July–August – Master classes given in Siena by famous soloists at the Accademia Chigiana.

Autumn–Winter – Busoni Piano Festival in empoli

AUGUST

TWO WEEKS IN AUG
Cortona – Tuscan Sun Festival. Based on the good life espoused in the novel and film, the cultural festival brings international musical and artistic talent to Cortona. www.tuscansunfestival.com.

2ND SUNDAY IN AUG
Massa Marittima – Balestro del Girifalco (&see MASSA MARITTIMA)

15 AUG
Prato – Presentation of the Holy Girdle (&see PRATO)

16 AUG
Siena – Palio delle Contrade: historic horse race (&see SIENA). http://palio.comune.siena.it.

LAST SUNDAY IN AUG
Montepulciano – Bravìo delle botti: two men from each district of the town push a heavy barrel uphill to the cathedral. The bravìo, or banner representing Montepulciano, is presented to the winners.

SEPTEMBER

SEPT EVERY OTHER YEAR
Pescia – Biennial Flower Show
1ST SUNDAY IN SEPT
Arezzo – Giostra del Saracino (&see AREZZO)
7 SEPT
Florence – Festa della Rificolona (&see FIRENZE)
8 SEPT
Prato– Presentation of the Holy Girdle to the congregation to celebrate the nativity of the Virgin Mary: large procession in period costume (&see PRATO)

13 SEPT
Lucca – Luminara di Santa Croce (&see LUCCA)
2ND SUNDAY IN SEPT
Sansepolcro – Crossbow tournament (&see SANSEPOLCRO)
LAST SUNDAY IN SEPT
Impruneta – Grape Festival: large procession of floats.

OCTOBER

3RD WEEK IN OCT
Impruneta – Fiera di San Luca (&see IMPRUNETA)
LAST SUNDAY IN OCT
Montalcino – Thrush Festival (Sagra del Tordo): historic pageant, costume ball (il Trescone), archery tournament and evening banquet at the fortress.

NOVEMBER

LAST 3 WEEKENDS IN NOV
San Miniato – Grand white truffle fair (&see SAN MINIATO)

DECEMBER

WEEKEND CLOSEST TO 8 DEC
San Quirico d'Orcia – Olive oil Fair
25 DEC
Prato – Presentation of the Holy Girdle (&see PRATO)

Palio delle Contrade, Siena

De Agostini Picture Library/Fototeca ENIT

Know Before You Go

USEFUL WEBSITES
General Tourism
+ www.turismo.intoscana.it
  Official website of the Tuscany Tourism Board.
Regional Tourist Sites
+ www.regione.toscana.it
  Official website of the government of Tuscany.
+ www.toscanacosta.it
  Official tourism website for the Tuscan coast, from Carrara to Grosseto and the islands.
+ www.comune.fi.it
  Official Florence website, with information on history and culture.
Wine lovers
+ www.vinit.net
  Where to buy and enjoy wine in Italy.
Mugello, Valdisieve, Chianti and Casentino:
+ www.terraditoscana.it
  Focuses on the towns of the interior.

CITY AND PROVINCIAL
+ **Arezzo**
  www.apt.arezzo.it
  www.comune.arezzo.it
+ **Florence**
  www.firenzeturismo.it
  www.comune.firenze.it
+ **Grosseto**
  www.provincia.grosseto.it
+ **Livorno**
  www.costadeglietruschi.it
  www.arcipelago.turismo.toscana.it
+ **Lucca**
  www.turismo.provincia.lucca.it
  www.comune.lucca.it
+ **Massa e Carrara**
  www.aptmassacarrara.it
+ **Pisa**
  www.pisa.turismo.toscana.it
  www.comune.pisa.it
+ **Pistoia**
  turismo.provincia.pistoia.it
  www.provincia.pistoia.it
+ **Prato**
  www.prato.turismo.toscana.it
  www.comune.prato.it
+ **Siena**
  www.terresiena.it
  www.comune.siena.it
  www.siena.turismo.it

TOURIST OFFICES
In addition to the tourist offices listed below, details of local information bureaux can be found at the beginning of each entry, indicated by the ⓘ symbol. In each of Tuscany's provincial capitals there is a tourist office either called APT (Azienda Promozione Turismo) or EPT (Ente Provinciale per il Turismo). The main towns of interest have an **Azienda Autonoma di Soggiorno, Cura e Turismo (AS)** at the Town Hall providing local information.

For information, brochures, maps and assistance in planning a trip to Italy, apply to the **ENIT (Ente nazionale italiano per il turismo)** in your country or consult the ENIT website: www.enit.it.

London
+ 1 Princes Street, London W1B 2AY.
  ✆020 7408 1254 or 0800 482 542 (*toll free from UK and Ireland*).
  24-hour Brochure Request Line:
  ✆090 65 508 925 (calls charged at premium rate)
New York
+ 630 Fifth Avenue, Suite 1565, New York NY 10111
  ✆212 245 4822/5618
Los Angeles
+ 12400 Wilshire Boulevard, Suite 550, Los Angeles CA 90025
  ✆310 820 1898/9807
Chicago
+ 500 North Michigan Avenue, Suite 2240, Chicago IL 60611
  ✆312 644 0990/0996
Toronto
+ 175 Bloor Street, Suite 907 South Tower, Toronto M4W 3R8
  ✆416 925 4882

INTERNATIONAL VISITORS
EMBASSIES AND CONSULATES
Italian Embassies
Great Britain
♦ 14 Three Kings' Yard,
London W1Y 2EH
☎ 020 7312 2200
Fax 020 7499 2283
www.amblondra.esteri.it

USA
♦ 3000 Whitehaven Street, NW
Washington, DC 20008
☎ 202 612 4400
Fax 202 518 2154
www.italyemb.org

Canada
♦ 275 Slater Street, 21st Floor,
Ottawa, Ontario, K1P 5H9
☎ 613 232 2401
Fax 613 233 1484
www.italyincanada.com

Italian Consulates
Great Britain
♦ 38 Eaton Place, London SW1X 8AN
☎ 020 7235 9371.
Fax 020 7823 1609
♦ Rodwell Tower, 111 Piccadilly,
Manchester M1 2HY
☎ 0161 236 9024
Fax 0161 236 5574
www.consmanchester.esteri.it
♦ 32 Melville Street,
Edinburgh EH3 7HA
☎ 0131 226 3631
Fax 0131 226 6260
www.consedimburgo.esteri.it

USA
♦ 690 Park Avenue,
New York, NY 10021
☎ 212 737 9100, Fax 212 249 4945
www.consnewyork.esteri.it
♦ 600 Atlantic Avenue, 17th Floor,
Boston, MA 02210
☎ 617 722 9201, Fax 617 722 9407
www.consboston.esteri.it
♦ 500 North Michigan Avenue,
Suite 1850, Chicago, IL 60611
☎ 312 467 1550, Fax 312 467 1335
www.conschicago.esteri.it
♦ Buhl Building, 535 Griswold,
Suite 1840, Detroit, MI 4822
☎ 313 963 8560, Fax 313 963 8180
www.consdetroit.esteri.it

♦ 1300 Post Oak Boulevard,
Suite 660, Houston, TX 77056
☎ 713 850 7520, Fax 713 850 9113
www.conshouston.esteri.it
♦ 12400 Wilshire Boulevard,
Suite 300, Los Angeles, CA 90025
☎ 310 820 0622, Fax 310 820 0727
www.conslosangeles.esteri.it
♦ 1200 Brickell Avenue,
Seventh Floor, Miami, FL 33131
☎ 305 374 6322, Fax 305 374 7945
www.consmiami.esteri.it
♦ 744 Broad Street, Suite 2800,
Newark, NJ 07102
☎ 973 643 1448, Fax 973 643 3043
www.consnewark.esteri.it
♦ 1026 Public Ledger Building,
100 South Sixth Street,
Philadelphia, PA 19106-3470
☎ 215 592 7329, Fax 215 592 9808
♦ 2590 Webster Street,
San Francisco, CA 94115
☎ 415 292 9210, Fax 415 931 7205
www.conssanfrancisco.esteri.it

Canada
♦ 3489 Drummond Street,
Montréal, Quebec, H3G 1X6
☎ 514 849 8351, Fax 514 499 9471
www.consmontreal.esteri.it
♦ 136 Beverley Street,
Toronto, Ontario, M5T 1Y5
☎ 416 977 1566, Fax 416 977 1119
www.constoronto.esteri.it
♦ 1970 Commerce Place,
10155-102 Street, T5J 4G8
Edmonton, Alberta
☎ 780 423 5153, Fax 780 423 5176
www.consedmonton.esteri.it
♦ Standard Building,
1100-510 West Hastings Street,
V6B 1L8 Vancouver, British Columbia
☎ 604 684 7288, Fax 604 685 4263
www.consvancouver.esteri.it

Foreign Embassies and Consulates in Italy
Australia
♦ Via Antonio Bosio 5
00198 Rome
☎ 06 85 27 21, Fax 06 8527 2300
www.italy.embassy.gov.au
Canada
♦ Via Zara 30
00198 Rome

☎06 44 59 81,
www.international.gc.ca/
canada-europa/italy/

Ireland
- Piazza di Campitelli 3,
00186 Rome
☎06 69 79 121, Fax 06 67 92 354

New Zealand
- Via Zara 28
00198 Rome
☎06 44 17 171
www.nzembassy.com

UK
- Via XX Settembre 80a
00187 Rome
☎06 4220 0001, Fax 06 48 73 324
www.britain.it
- Lungarno Corsini 2
50123 Florence
☎055 284 133

USA
- Via Veneto 119a
00187 Rome
☎06 46 741, Fax 06 48 82 672
http://rome.usembassy.gov
- Lungarno Amerigo Vespucci 38,
50123 Florence
☎055 239 8276
http://florence.usconsulate.gov

DOCUMENTS

Passport
European Union citizens traveling
from within the Schengen Zone only
need a national identity card to enter
Italy, while all others must have a valid
national passport. In case of loss or

DUTY-FREE ALLOWANCES WITHIN EU	
Spirits (whisky, gin, vodka etc)	10 litres
Fortified wines (vermouth, port etc)	20 litres
Wine (not more than 60 sparkling)	90 litres
Beer	110 litres
Cigarettes	3200
Cigarillos	400
Cigars	200
Smoking tobacco	3kg

theft, report to the embassy or consulate and the local police.

Visa
Entry visas are required by Australian,
New Zealand, Canadian and US
citizens (*if their intended stay exceeds
three months*). Apply to the Italian
Consulate (*visa issued same day; delay
if submitted by mail*). US citizens may
wish to read "A Safe Trip Abroad,"
which provides useful information
on visa requirements, customs
regulations and medical care for
international travelers. Consult
www.travel.state.gov for details.

Driving licence
*See GETTING THERE AND
GETTING AROUND.*

Car insurance
If you are bringing your own car
to Italy, an International Insurance
Certificate (Green Card), although no
longer a legal requirement, is the most
effective proof of insurance cover and
is internationally recognised by the
police and other authorities. This is
available from your insurer.

CUSTOMS
As of 30 June 1999, those traveling
between countries within the European Union can no longer purchase
"duty-free" goods. For further information, there is a free leaflet, **Duty
Paid**, available from HM Revenue
& Customs, Finchley Excise Advice
Centre, Berkeley House, 304 Regents
Park Road, London N3 2JY. ☎0845 010
9000. www.hmrc.gov.uk. The US Customs Service offers a free publication
for US citizens entitled *Know Before
You Go*. Consult www.customs.gov.

HEALTH
Visitors from EU countries should
apply to their own National Social
Security Offices for a **European
Health Insurance Card (EHIC)**, which
entitles them to medical treatment
under an EU Reciprocal Medical
Treatment arrangement. British
citizens should apply to the Depart-
ment of Health and Social Security.
Nationals of non-EU countries should

check that their insurance policy covers them specifically for overseas travel, including doctors' visits, medication and hospitalisation in Italy (in most cases you will probably have to take out supplementary medical insurance). American Express offers its cardholders a service called Global Assist to help in financial, legal, medical or personal emergencies. For further information, consult their website: www.americanexpress.com All prescription drugs should be clearly labelled, and it is recommended that you carry a copy of the prescription with you. A list of pharmacies open at night or on Sundays may be obtained from pharmacists' shops (*farmacia* – red cross sign). First Aid service (*pronto soccorso*) is available at airports, railway stations and in hospitals. Dial ℰ113 for police, Red Cross and emergency first aid.

ACCESSIBILITY

Many of the sights described in this guide are accessible to people with special needs. Sights marked with the ♿ symbol offer access for wheelchairs. Check beforehand by telephone. For further information contact the **Associazione Italiana Disabili**, Via S. Barnaba 29, 20122 Milan, ℰ02 55 01 75 64, and **CO.IN** (Consorzio Cooperative Integrate), Via Enrico Giglioli 54/A, Rome ℰ/Fax 06 71 29 011, 800 27 10 27 (*toll free for the Vacanze Serene service*). Visit the Web site at www.coinsociale.it/turismo.

Getting There Getting Around

BY AIR
AIRLINES

Many airlines fly direct to cities in Tuscany.

- **Alitalia**
  ℰ08705 448 259 (*from UK*)
  ℰ01 677 5171 (*from Ireland*)
  ℰ800 223 5730 (*toll free from US*)
  www.alitalia.com
- **American Airlines**
  ℰ800 433 7300 (*toll free from US*)
  www.aa.com
- **British Airways**
  ℰ0845 77 333 77 (*from UK*)
  ℰ800 AIRWAYS (*toll free from US*)
  www.britishairways.com
- **bmibaby**
  ℰ0870 264 2229 (*from UK*)
  www.bmibaby.com
- **Delta Airlines**
  ℰ800 221 1212 (*toll free from US*)
  www.delta.com
- **easyJet**
  ℰ0905 821 0905 (*from UK*)
  www.easyjet.om

- **Northwest Airlines**
  ℰ800 447 4747 (*toll free from US*)
  www.nwa.com
- **Ryanair**
  ℰ0871 246 0000 (*from UK*)
  www.ryanair.com
- **United Airlines**
  ℰ800 538 2929 (*toll free from US*)
  www.ual.com
- **US Airways**
  ℰ800 622 1015 (*toll free from US*)
  www.usairways.com

CHARTER FLIGHTS / PACKAGES

- **Citalia**
  ℰ020 8686 0677 (*from UK*)
  www.citalia.com
- **Florence Journeys**
  ℰ39 055 834 8998 (*from Italy*)
  www.florencejourneys.com
- **Horizon & Co.**
  ℰ800 387 2977 (*toll free from US*)
  www.horizon-co.com
- **The Magic of Italy**
  ℰ020 8939 5453 (*from UK*)
  www.magictravelgroup.co.uk
- **Maupintour**
  ℰ800 255 4266 (*toll free from US*)
  www.maupintour.com

- **Page and Moy**
  📞08700 10 62 12 (*from UK*)
  www.page-moy.co.uk
- **Perillo Tours**
  📞800 431 1515 (*toll free from US*)
  www.perillotours.com
- **Sophisticated Italy**
  📞39 02 481 96675 (*from Italy*)
  www.sophisticateditaly.com

AIRPORTS
Florence and Pisa both have international airports.

✈ **Florence – Aeroporto Amerigo Vespucci** (**Peretola**): Via del Termine 11. 📞055 30 61 300. www.aeroporto.firenze.it. Bus service to Florence city centre every 20min.

✈ **Pisa – Aeroporto Internazionale Galileo Galilei:** Via dell'Aeroporto. 📞050 500 707. www.pisa-airport.com. Regular rail link to Florence and direct access to A 12 (Pisa-Genova) and A11 (Pisa-Florence) motorways, and the Florence-Pisa-Livorno dual carriageway. Bus service to Pisa centre.

BY TRAIN
From London and the Channel ports there is rail service to many Italian towns, including high-speed passenger trains and motorail services. Rail passes offer unlimited travel and group travel tickets offer savings for parties on the Italian Railways network. Take the Eurostar to Paris to catch a sleeper train onwards; motorail is available from Paris and Calais (www.raileurope.co.uk).

- **Italian State Railway** –
  📞06 44101
  www.ferroviedellostato.it
- **Trenitalia** –
  📞89 20 21
  www.trenitalia.it
- **Rail Europe** –
  📞800-622-8600 (*toll free from US*)
  📞08448-484-064 (*from UK*)
  www.raileurope.com
  www.raileurope.co.uk

- **Eurostar** –
  📞0870 160 6600
  www.eurostar.co.uk

Tickets are also available from principal British and American rail travel centres and travel agencies. Travelling by rail is a particularly good way to reach the larger towns in Tuscany, especially Florence, as the rail stations there are within easy reach of the city centres.

BY CAR
MAPS
Use Michelin maps 719, 721 and 735 or the Michelin Atlas Europe to help you plan your route.
In addition, The Touring Club Italiano (TCI), Corso d'Italia 10, 20139 Milan (📞39 0285 2672), publishes a regional map series at 1:200 000.

DRIVING TO ITALY
Via France – Roads from France into Italy, with the exception of the Menton/Ventimiglia (Riviera) coast road, are dependent on Alpine passes and tunnels. The main roads go through the Montgenèvre pass, the Fréjus tunnel and Mont-Cenis pass, the Petit-Saint-Bernard pass and the Mont-Blanc tunnel.
Via Switzerland – Via Switzerland, three main routes are possible: through the tunnel or pass at Grand-Saint-Bernard, through the Simplon pass and through the St Gottard pass. If you're planning to drive through Switzerland, budget for the Swiss road tax (*vignette*). The *vignette* costs 40 Swiss francs and can be purchased at the border crossings, post offices, petrol stations, garages and cantonal motor registries, or in advance from the Swiss Centre, Swiss Court, London W1V 8EE. 📞020 7734 1921.
Via Germany and Austria – For those visitors driving through Germany and Austria, there is the Brenner pass south of Innsbruck. Remember that most of these tunnels or passes levy a toll.

DRIVING IN ITALY

Italian roads are excellent, and there is a wide network of motorways (*autostrade*); information on the Italian highway network is available at www.autostrade.it. Tuscany is served by three highways (A1, A11 and A12).

Driving licence

Nationals of European Union and North American countries require a valid national or home state **driving licence.** An **international driving licence** is useful because the information on it appears in nine languages. This is available in the US from the American Automobile Association for US$15 (*an application form can be found at www.aaa.com*) and in Canada from the Canadian Automobile Association for C$15 (*see www.caa.ca for details*). If you are bringing your own car into the country, you will need the vehicle registration papers.

Petrol

- *Gasolio = diesel.*
- *Super* = super leaded (98 octane).
- *Senza piombo* = premium unleaded petrol (95 octane).
- *Super Plus* or *Euro Plus* = super unleaded petrol (98 octane).

Petrol stations are usually open from 7am to 7pm. Many close at lunchtime (*between 12.30pm and 3pm*), on Sundays and public holidays, and many don't accept credit cards for payment.

Highway Code

The minimum driving age is 18 years of age. Traffic drives on the right. It is compulsory for the driver and front-seat passengers to wear seat belts, and seat belts must be worn in the back where they are fitted. Children under 12 must travel in the back seats, unless the front seat is fitted with a child restraint system. Full or dipped headlights must be switched on in poor visibility and at night; use side-lights only when a stationary vehicle is not clearly visible. Every car must carry a high visibility vest and red warning triangle.

In the event of a breakdown, the vest must be worn and a red warning triangle must be displayed in the road; these can be hired from the ACI offices at the frontier (deposit refunded).

Drivers should watch for unfamiliar road signs and take great care on the road, as many Italian drivers prefer using their horn to their brakes! At crossroads drivers coming from the right have priority.

Speed limits

- Built-up areas = 50kph/31mph
- Country roads = 90kph/55mph
- Motorways = 90kph/55mph (vehicles up to 1 000cc)
- Motorways = 130kph/80mph (vehicles over 1 100cc).

Road Tolls

Tolls are payable on most highways. Bear in mind that highway tolls can be paid in cash (*look for lanes with signs representing toll collectors*), with the Via Card (*look for lanes with the Via Card sign and blue stripes on the road surface*) and by credit card. Note that credit cards can also be used in Via Card lanes.

Road Signs

Highways (*autostrade* – subject to tolls) and dual carriageways (*superstrade*) are indicated by green signs; ordinary roads are indicated by blue signs and tourist sights by yellow signs.

Parking

In many large towns, the historical town centre is subject to traffic restrictions (*only authorized vehicles may enter*), indicated by large rectangular signs saying **"Zona a traffico limitato riservata ai veicoli autorizzati**." In this case, park your vehicle outside the town before proceeding on foot, as the streets are often very narrow and have no pavements or sidewalks.

GPS & Route Planning

Try Via Michelin's Sat Nav system, loaded with points of interest like hotels, restaurants and things to do and see from our guides.
Or, use the journey planner on **www.ViaMichelin.com** for all of the above and more.

Where to Stay and Eat

WHERE TO STAY
FOR EVERY BUDGET

The hotels and restaurants appearing in the Address Books in this guide were selected to suit all budgets (*see the Legend on the cover flap for a key to the price categories*). Budget accommodations (⊜) include campsites, youth hostels and modest but decent and well-located hotels and *pensioni* with double rooms for under €40 (under €60 in large cities). Restaurants in this category, without sacrificing quality, will charge less than €14 (less than €16 in large cities) for a three-course meal (including drinks). Those on a larger budget will find hotels of greater comfort and charm and better quality restaurants in the moderate range (⊜⊜ and ⊜⊜⊜). Rooms in this category will cost from €40 to €100 for a double (€60 to €130 in large cities) and expect to pay between €14 and €40 for a meal (€16 to €50 in large cities). For those in search of a truly memorable stay, luxury accommodations (⊜⊜⊜⊜, more than €100; in large cities, more than €130) include elegant hotels, B&Bs and guest farmhouses with a wide range of facilities, as well as enormous charm and atmosphere.

Restaurants in this category will satisfy the most demanding taste buds with prices to match (⊜⊜⊜⊜, more than €40; in large cities, more than €50).

BOOKING YOUR LODGINGS

Tuscany's popularity with tourists from all over the world makes booking in advance a sensible precaution, especially between April and October. Generally speaking, hotel prices are lower between November and March and many establishments offer discounted rates for weekend visits and short breaks.

Breakfast is usually included in the price but not in the case of some smaller establishments. For more information on accommodation in Tuscany, consult the websites listed in the *Know Before You Go* section of this guide.

HOTELS AND GUESTHOUSES

The distinction between hotel and guesthouse is not always apparent, but traditionally guesthouses are small family-run establishments, often forming part of a residential dwelling, offering simple standards of comfort and rooms without en suite bathrooms. Country guesthouses are usually rustic in feel, with terracotta floors and beamed or vaulted ceilings. Furnishings are usually a mix of antique pieces and country furniture in wood and wrought iron. Seaside establishments are

Agriturismo in Tuscany

©Paolo Cipriani/iStockphoto.com

more likely to be modern in style with a simple, functional feel.

In all cases, it is important to check prices by telephone before making a reservation, as rates may fluctuate depending on season and availability.

RURAL ACCOMMODATION

Rural guesthouses were originally conceived as an opportunity to combine accommodation and the chance to taste the products made on the farm (among them olive oil, wine, honey, vegetables and meat). In the last few years some regions of Italy have witnessed a huge growth in popularity of such guesthouses, some of which are as elegant as the best hotels, with prices to match. As a result, in some you will find a menu that makes use of the farm's own produce while in others you may be provided with a kitchenette in an apartment that will offer you complete independence; others still may only offer breakfast. The guesthouses included in the guide usually accept bookings for one night only, but in high season the majority prefer weekly stays or offer half or full board as well as requiring a minimum stay. Prices for the latter are only given when this formula is compulsory. Bear in mind that the majority of these rural guesthouses only have double rooms and prices shown here are based on two people sharing a double room. People travelling alone should try asking for a discount. In any case because of the ever-increasing popularity of this type of accommodation, it is advisable to book well in advance.

To get an idea of what is on offer consult www.agriturismo.regione.toscana.it, which has contact information for several farm holiday associations.

BED AND BREAKFAST

A varied category, where often the difference between a hotel and a bed and breakfast is indistinguishable. The house or apartment is also often the home of the hosts, who let out a few of their rooms (usually

Places to Stay Map
(🔍 see following pages)

Those interested in **cultural centres** should look for place names framed in green. For visitors on brief trips who want to stay in one of the many cities of artistic interest, destinations suitable for an **overnight stop** are underlined in green. Among the many other places to stay, look for areas shaded in green (nature parks) and for the symbols ♨ (**spas**), ⚓ (**seaside resort**) and ❄ (**winter sports resort**).

between one and three). Guests are usually required to stay for a minimum period and credit cards are not as widely accepted. Generally speaking a bed and breakfast offers a cozier atmosphere than a hotel at competitive prices.

Although the notion of "rooms to let" (*affitacamere*) does not have an entirely positive image in the collective imagination, Tuscany offers some delightful accommodation often, though not necessarily always, at very reasonable prices.

For more information, consult the Italian Bed & Breakfast website: www.bbitalia.it.

CAMPSITES

Campsites offer a value for money solution to accommodation near the most important cities, as well as the pleasures of fresh air and country living. They generally have a restaurant, bar and food shop and some have swimming pools. For less spartan travellers some sites have bungalows and caravans. Prices shown in the guide are daily rates for two people, one tent and one car.

An International Camping Carnet for caravans is useful, but not compulsory; it can be obtained from the motoring organisations or the **Camping and Caravanning Club**, Greenfields House, Westwood Way, Coventry CV4

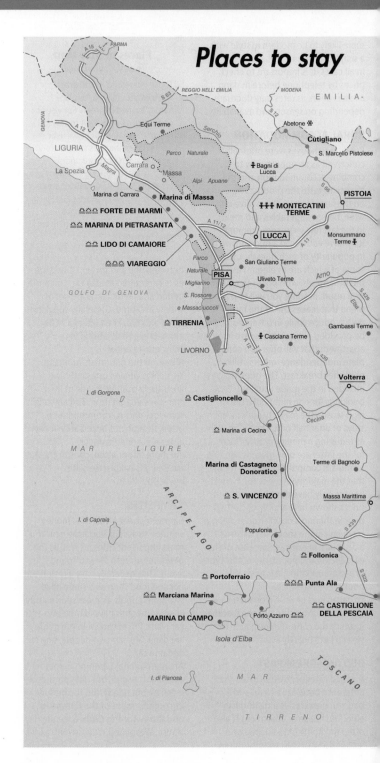

Places to stay

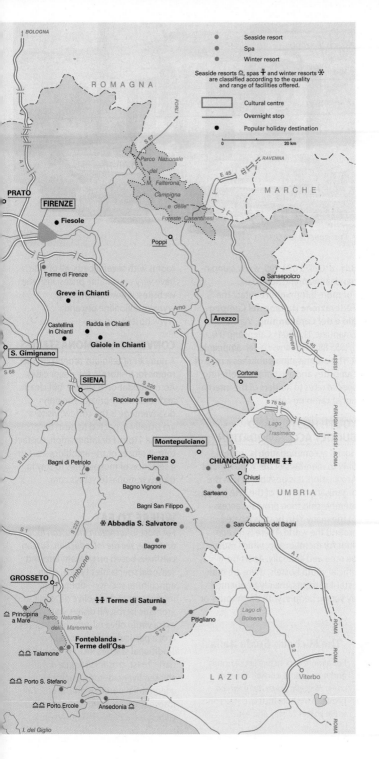

- Seaside resort
- Spa
- Winter resort

Seaside resorts ⌂, spas ✚ and winter resorts ❋ are classified according to the quality and range of facilities offered.

Cultural centre

Overnight stop

● Popular holiday destination

0   20 km

BOLOGNA

ROMAGNA

FORLI

S 67

RAVENNA

E 45

MARCHE

Parco Nazionale del M. Falterona, Campigna e delle Foreste Casentinesi

PRATO

FIRENZE

● Fiesole

Poppi

Sansepolcro

Terme di Firenze

A1

Arno

● Greve in Chianti

Arezzo

● Castellina in Chianti

● Radda in Chianti

Tevere

E 45

ASSISI

S. Gimignano

● Gaiole in Chianti

S 71

S 68

Cortona

SIENA

S 326

S 75 bis

S 73

Rapolano Terme

Lago Trasimeno

PERUGIA, ASSISI, ROMA

S 2

Montepulciano

S 441

Pienza

CHIANCIANO TERME ✚✚

Bagni di Petriolo

Chiusi

UMBRIA

Bagno Vignoni

Sarteano

Bagni San Filippo

S 223

❋ Abbadia S. Salvatore

San Casciano dei Bagni

S 1

Bagnore

A1

GROSSETO

Ombrone

✚✚ Terme di Saturnia

Lago di Bolsena

ROMA

⌂ Principina a Mare

Parco Naturale della Maremma

Pitigliano

S 74

S 2

⌂⌂ Talamone

Fonteblanda - Terme dell'Osa

ROMA

⌂⌂ Porto S. Stefano

LAZIO

Viterbo

⌂⌂ Porto Ercole

Ansedonia ⌂

I. del Giglio

35

Romantic Italian Osteria, Tuscany

t-lorien/iStockphoto

8JH. ℘02476 694 995. www.campin-
gandcaravanningclub.co.uk.
For more information contact the
**Federazione Italiana del Campeg-
gio e del Caravanning**, Via Vittorio
Emanuele 11, 50041 Calenzano (FI).
℘055 88 23 91. www.federcampeggio.
it. The organisation publishes a map of
campsites and a list of those offering
special rates to holders of the international camping card.

YOUTH HOSTELS AND BUDGET ACCOMMODATION

Hostel accommodation is available
only to members of the Youth Hostel
Association. It is possible to join the
organisation at any of the YHA hostels;
membership then provides access
to the many YHA hostels located
around the world. There is no age
limit for membership, which must
be renewed annually. Apart from
official youth hostels, there are many
establishments, mainly frequented
by young people, with dormitories or

rooms with several beds, all of which
have very reasonable prices. Visit the
websites: www.italiayhf.org,
www.ostellionline.org and
www.hostels-aig.org.

CONVENTS AND MONASTERIES

A number of religious orders provide
rooms for visitors in the major cities.
Accommodation is simple, but clean
and reasonably priced. The only
disadvantage is the curfew; visitors
are usually expected to be in by
around 11pm. For information, contact
tourist offices or the archdioceses. For
a selection of monasteries to stay in,
try www.monasterystays.com.

WHERE TO EAT

*For more information on Tuscan food
and wine, see the Introduction.* Tuscan
cuisine is based on peasant fare and
seasonal specialities typical of an
agricultural society – ubiquitous
ingredients include olive oil, garlic and
aromatic herbs. All dishes start with
extra virgin olive oil, which in Tuscany
is of a particularly high standard.
Traditional starters include *bruschette*,
garlic toast, *crostini di fegato di pollo*,
chicken liver croutons, *finocchiona*,
a fennel-flavoured salami, *prosciutto
toscano*, a cured ham and *lardo di
colonnata*, a highly flavoured pork

The Michelin Guide Italia

For a more exhaustive list of hotels
and restaurants, consult the red-
cover *Michelin Guide Italia,* which
provides a whole host of details on
great places to stay and eat.

meat. Among popular first course dishes are *minestra di farro*, a barley soup, *le pappardelle alla lepre o al cinghiale,* pasta in hare or wild boar sauce, and *zuppa di crostacei alla versigliese*, a seafood broth, while second courses include *cacciucco alla livornese*, a rich fish stew, *scottiglia*, a meat casserole with slices of garlic bread, *bistecca alla fiorentina*, T-bone steak, *arista di maiale*, roast pork, *pollo* or *coniglio alla cacciatora,* chicken or rabbit with mushrooms, *fritto dell'aia*, mixed grill and *misto di pesce*, seafood platter. To finish the meal, try *cantucci di Prato,* almond biscuits, *panforte* and *ricciarelli di Siena*, classic Sienese confectionery, *castagnaccio* and *necci con ricotta*, chestnut specialities. Traditional Tuscan cuisine is the dominant cuisine of the region. Alternatives are scarce, but Chinese, Indian, Japanese and Mexican restaurants can be found as well. Restaurant opening times vary, but generally they are open for lunch from 12.30pm to 2.30pm and for dinner from 7.30pm to 11pm. Service is usually included, but it is customary to leave a tip in proportion to customer satisfaction. Restaurants where service is not included, a rarity, are brought to the reader's attention; after the price of the meal an appropriate percentage for a tip is suggested. By law bread and the cover charge should be included in the price, but in some *trattorie* and especially in *pizzerie*, they are calculated separately. Given the significance of viticulture in the region, reference must be made to Tuscany's most famous wines: Chianti (produced throughout the region), Chianti Classico (from between Florence and Siena), Carmignano (from the Prato hills), Brunello and Rosso from Montalcino, Vino Nobile from Montepulciano and, from the Maremma, Morellino di Scansano and the small yet prestigious vineyard of Bolgheri. Among the few memorable whites, Vernaccia di San Gimignano is particularly noteworthy.

RESTAURANTS, TRATTORIE AND OSTERIE

Although the distinction between these different types of restaurants is not as obvious as it once was, in general, a **ristorante** offers elegant cuisine and service, while a **trattoria** or **osteria** is more likely to be a family-run establishment serving home-made dishes in a more relaxed, informal atmosphere. In typical trattorie, the waiter or owner will often tell you what dishes of the day are on offer; While this is usually a good choice, make sure that you know how much you are paying ahead of time to avoid any unpleasant shocks when the bill arrives! (A list is usually available; if in doubt, ask to see it.) Be wary of choosing the tourist menu, which usually has very limited choice. Trattorie used to have almost exclusively house wine on offer (served by the carafe), but you can now expect to find a proper wine list which often has a good selection of local wines.

WINE BARS

Given the region's heritage of viticulture, it is not surprising that wine bars (*enoteche*) are becoming increasingly popular in Tuscany. Like osterie, they often have a kitchen and serve daily specials and light starters as well as a choice of wines by the glass or bottle.

Bigpressphoto/Dreamstime.com

Wine bar

Basic Information

COMMUNICATIONS

The telephone service is organised by TELECOM ITALIA (formerly SIP). Each office has public booths where the customer pays for units used (*scatti*) at the counter after the call. *Reduced rates operate after 6.30pm and are even less between 10pm and 8am.*

Phonecards

Phonecards (*schede telefoniche*) are sold in denominations of €1, €2.50, €5 and €8 and are supplied by CIT offices and post offices as well as tobacconists (sign bearing a white T on a black background).

Public Phones

Telephone boxes may be operated by telephone cards (sold in post offices and tobacconists) and by telephone credit cards. To make a call: lift the receiver, insert payment, await dialling signal, punch in the required number and wait for a response.

TELEPHONES

When making a call within Italy, the area code (e.g. 055 for Florence) is always used, both from outside and within the city you are calling. For international calls dial 00 plus the following country codes:

- ♦ ☎ 61 for Australia
- ♦ ☎ 1 for Canada
- ♦ ☎ 44 for the UK
- ♦ ☎ 1 for the USA
- ♦ ☎ 64 for New Zealand

If calling from outside the country, the international code for Italy is 39. Dial the full area code, even when making an international call; for example, when calling Florence from the UK, dial 00 39 055, followed by the correspondent's number.

Useful Numbers

(👜 *See "Emergencies"*)

☎ **176:** International Directory Enquiries. Provides phone numbers

outside of Italy in English and Italian. Note that calls to this number are subject to a charge.

☎ **170:** Operator Assisted International Calls. Note that calls to this number are subject to a charge.

DISCOUNTS

ACCOMMODATION

👜Visitors trying to keep costs down will find information on budget accommodation (*pensioni*, youth hostels, campsites, convents and monasteries) in the *WHERE TO STAY* section.

TRAVEL

By Train

The **Carta Prima** (€67.14, valid for a year) gives card-holders a 20% discount on first-class travel throughout Italy. This card is valid for the card-holder only and is non-transferrable. The **Carta Amicotreno** (€51.13, valid for a year) gives a 50% discount on some local trains and a 20% discount on many medium- and long-distance trains and is ideal for travellers spending an extended period in Italy, doing most of their travelling by rail. Certain restrictions apply to days of travel. Concessions also apply to a companion travelling with the card-holder.

By Air

Alitalia has various special offers for passengers buying their ticket one, two or three weeks before departure. The airline also offers special weekend rates for travellers departing on a Saturday and returning on a Sunday of the same weekend (*tipo corto*) and for the same type of ticket, but valid for a month (*tipo lungo*).

YOUTHS (UNDER-26)

By Train – The **Carta Verde** (€25.82, valid for a year) gives young people a 20% discount in both first and second class, on all trains within Italy, including fast Eurocity trains and Eurostar. This card is valid for the card-holder only and is non-transferrable.

By Air

Discounted rates exist for young people aged between 12 and 26 (under 26 on the day of departure).

SENIOR CITIZENS

By Train

For travellers over 60 years of age, the **Carta d'Argento** (€25.82, valid for a year) offers 20% off in first and second class on the Italian section of all routes, including Eurocity trains and Eurostar (non-transferrable).

By Air

Senior citizens aged 60 or over are also eligible for discounts on some airlines, and senior citizens who are at least 65 on the day of travel are entitled to a 10% discount on some tariffs.

FAMILIES AND SMALL GROUPS

By Train

Families and groups of at least three people and no more than five are entitled to a 20% discount in both first and second class if they are travelling together. Children aged between 4 and 12 travel at half-price of the discounted fare and children under 4 travel free. This discount is available on all trains, including the Italian sections of Eurocity trains and on Eurostar, although it is not valid in July and August, or during the Easter and Christmas holiday periods.

By Air

Families qualify for discounted tickets on certain airlines if they fulfil the following conditions: the family must travel together and must comprise at least four people, with a maximum of two adults and a minimum of two children (between the ages of two and eleven). At least one of the adults must be a parent of the children, while the second adult does not necessarily need to be related to the family.

ELECTRICITY

The voltage is 220AC, 50 cycles per second; the sockets are for two-pin plugs. It is therefore advisable to take an adaptor for hairdryers, shavers, computers, etc.

EMERGENCIES

- **113**: General emergency services (*soccorso pubblico di emergenza*); to be called in cases of real danger.
- **112:** Police (*carabinieri*). Calls are free.
- **115**: Fire Brigade (*vigili del fuoco*). Calls are free.
- **118**: Emergency Health Services (*emergenza sanitaria*). Calls are free.
- **1515**: Forest Fire Service. Environmental emergencies. Calls are free.
- **803 116**: Automobile Club d'Italia Emergency Breakdown Service. Calls are free.

MAIL/POST

Opening Hours – Post offices are open 8am–2pm on weekdays, 8.30am–noon on Saturday. Stamps are also sold at tobacconists (*tabacchi*) that display a black *valori bollati* sign outside.

Stamps

- Stamps for letters or postcards cost €0.45.
- Express service stamps (*posta prioritaria*) cost €0.62.

MONEY

The unit of currency is the **euro**, which is issued in notes (€5, €10, €20, €50, €100, €200 and €500) and in coins (1 cent, 2 cents, 5 cents, 10 cents, 20 cents, 50 cents, €1 and €2). (*see Notes and Coins.*)

Banks – Banks are usually open Monday to Friday, 8.30am–1.30pm and 2.30pm–4pm. Some branches are open in city centres and shopping centres on Saturday mornings; almost all are closed on Saturdays, Sundays and public holidays. Most hotels will change travelers' cheques. Money can be changed in post offices (except travellers' cheques), money-changing bureaux and at railway stations and airports. Commission is always charged.

Credit Cards – Payment by credit card is widespread in shops, hotels and restaurants and also some petrol stations. *The Michelin Guide Italia* and

The Michelin Guide Europe offer a selection of hotels and restaurants for Italy and Europe. Included in the recommendations is practical information, such as opening and closing hours, prices and accepted credit cards.

NEWSPAPERS
The Florentine daily **La Nazione** is the most widely read paper in Tuscany.

PHARMACIES/CHEMISTS
These are identified by a red and white cross. When closed, each will advertise the names of the pharmacy on duty and a list of doctors on call.

PUBLIC HOLIDAYS
Museums and other **monuments** are usually closed on Mondays and public holidays. **Churches** are often closed at lunchtime and cannot be visited during services. The following are days when museums and other monuments may be closed or vary their hours of admission:

- 1 January
- 6 January (Epiphany)
- Good Friday, Easter Day and Easter Monday
- 25 April (anniversary of the 1945 liberation)
- 1 May
- 2 June (Republic Day)
- 15 August ("Ferragosto")
- 1 November (All Saints)
- 8 December (Immaculate Conception)
- 25 and 26 December

Each town celebrates the feast day of its patron saint (details at tourist offices).

SIGHTSEEING
See the "Discovering Tuscany" section of the guide for information on admission times and charges for museums and monuments.

Due to fluctuations in the cost of living and the constant change in opening times as well as possible closures for restoration work, admission times and charges listed in this guide are subject to change without prior notice.

Visitors are advised to phone ahead or, where applicable, to check the websites of sights they wish to visit to confirm opening times.

The admission prices indicated are for single adults; discounts for children, students, persons over 60 or large groups should be requested on site and be verified by proper identification. For nationals of European Union member countries many institutions provide free admission to visitors under 18 and over 65 with proof of identification, and a 50% discount for visitors under 25 years of age. Many museums require visitors to leave bags and backpacks in a luggage deposit area at the museum entrance.

Taking photos with a flash is usually forbidden.

During **National Heritage Week** (Settimana dei Beni Culturali), which takes place at a different time each year, access to state-run sights is free of charge. Visit www.beniculturali.it.

Churches and chapels are usually open from 8am to noon and from 2pm to dusk. Visitors should dress in a manner deemed appropriate when entering a place of worship – sleeveless or low-cut tops, short miniskirts or skimpy shorts and bare feet are not appropriate.

Visitors are not admitted during services. It's best to visit churches in the morning, when the natural light provides better illumination of the works of art; also churches are occasionally forced to close in the afternoons due to lack of staff. When visits to museums, churches or other sites are accompanied by a custodian, it is customary to leave a donation.

TIME
In winter, standard time is Greenwich Mean Time + 1 hour (*ora solare*).
In summer, the clocks go forward an hour to give Italian Summer Time (*ora legale*, GMT + 2 hours) from the last weekend in March to the last weekend in October.

Useful Words and Phrases

PHRASES

Potrebbe aiutarmi?/aiuto
Can you help me?/help
Dove posso trovare...?
Where can I find...?
...la strada per...
...the road to...
Sto cercando...
I'm looking for...
Parla inglese?
Do you speak English?
Come si chiama quella cosa in italiano?
What is this called in Italian?
Potrebbe parlare più lentamente?
Could you speak more slowly?
Ho bisogno.../Vorrei...
I need.../I would like...
Questo non funziona.
This doesn't work.
Non ho ordinato questo.
I did not order this.
Mi sono perso/a.
I am lost.
Vorrei prenotare (una camera).
I would like to reserve (a room).
Che ora è?
What time is it?
Non capisco.
I don't understand.
Il mio bagaglio non è arrivato.
My luggage has not arrived.
Si può visitare (il museo)?
May one visit (the museum)?
Non lo so.
I don't know.
Mi piace.../Mi dispiace...
I like.../I don't like...
Dove posso prendere i biglietti per...?
Where can i buy tickets for...?

VOCABULARY

on the Road/ In Town

	Translation
acqua potabile	drinking water
ai treni	to the trains
a sinistra/destra	to the left/right
aperto	open
ascensore	elevator
autostrada	motorway
banchina	pavement
binario	(railway) platform
corso	boulevard
discesa	descent
dogana	customs
fermata	(bus-) stop
fiume	river
ingresso	entrance
lavori in corso	men at work
neve	snow
passaggio a livello	level crossing
passo	pass
pericolo	danger
piazza, largo	square, place
piazzale	esplanade
spingere	push
stazione	station
stretto	narrow
tirare	pull
uscita	exit, way out
viale	avenue
vietato	prohibited

Sightseeing

	Translation
abbazia	abbey, monastery
affreschi	frescoes
arazzi	tapestries
arca	monumental tomb
biblioteca	library
cappella	chapel
casa	house
cascata	waterfall
castello	castle
cenacolo	The Last Supper
chiesa	church

Name that Century

In Italian the following terms are used for the centuries between the 13C and the 20C:

Duecento	1200s	13C
Trecento	1300s	14C
Quattrocento	1400s	15C
Cinquecento	1500s	16C
Seicento	1600s	17C
Settecento	1700s	18C
Ottocento	1800s	19C
Novecento	1900s	20C

chiostro	cloisters
chiuso	closed
città	town
convento	convent
cortile	courtyard
dintorni	environs
duomo	cathedral
entrata libera	free admission
facciata	façade
funivia	cablecar
fuori servizio	out of order
giardini	gardens
gole	gorges
lago	lake
lagotto	altar frontal
occupato	busy (in use, engaged)
orari	(opening) hours
passeggiata	walk, promenade
piano	floor, storey
pinacoteca	picture gallery
pulpito	pulpit
quadro	picture
rivolgersi a	to apply to
rocca	feudal castle
rovine, ruderi	ruins
sagrestia	sacristy
scala	stairway
scavi	excavations
seggiovia	chairlift
spiaggia	beach
tesoro	treasure
torre, torazzo	tower
visite guidate	guided tour
vista	view

Everyday

	Translation
si, no	yes, no
Signore	Sir
Signora	Madam
Signorina	Miss
oggi	today
ieri	yesterday
domani mattina	tomorrow morning
mattina	morning
sera	evening
pomeriggio	afternoon
per favore	please

grazie tante	thank you very much
mi scusi	excuse me
basta	enough
buon giorno	good morning
arrivederci	goodbye
quanto?	how much?
dove? quando?	where? when?
dov'è?	where is?
much, little	molto, poco
più, meno	more, less
tutto, tutti	all
grande	large
piccolo	small
caro	dear

Numbers

	Translation
0	zero
1	uno
2	due
3	tre
4	quattro
5	cinque
6	sei
7	sette
8	otto
9	nove
10	dieci
11	undici
12	dodici
13	tredici
14	quattordici
15	quindici
16	sedici
17	diciasette
18	diciotto
19	diciannove
20	venti
30	trenta
40	quaranta
50	cinquanta
60	sessanta
70	settanta
80	ottanta
90	novanta
100	cento
1 000	mille
5 000	cinquemila
10 000	diecimila

CONVERSION TABLES

Weights and Measures

🇪🇺	🇺🇸	🇬🇧	
1 kilogram (kg)	**2.2 pounds (lb)**	**2.2 pounds**	*To convert*
6.35 kilograms	14 pounds	1 stone (st)	*kilograms*
0.45 kilograms	16 ounces (oz)	16 ounces	*to pounds,*
1 metric ton (tn)	**1.1 tons**	**1.1 tons**	*multiply by 2.2*
1 litre (l)	**2.11 pints (pt)**	**1.76 pints**	*To convert litres*
3.79 litres	1 gallon (gal)	0.83 gallon	*to gallons, multiply*
4.55 litres	1.20 gallon	1 gallon	*by 0.26 (US)*
			or 0.22 (UK)
1 hectare (ha)	**2.47 acres**	**2.47 acres**	*To convert*
1 sq. kilometre	**0.38 sq. miles**	**0.38 sq. miles**	*hectares to*
(km²)	**(sq.mi.)**		*acres, multiply*
			by 2.4
1 centimetre (cm)	**0.39 inches (in)**	**0.39 inches**	*To convert metres*
1 metre (m)	**3.28 feet (ft) or 39.37 inches**		*to feet, multiply*
	or 1.09 yards (yd)		*by 3.28; for*
			kilometres to miles,
1 kilometre (km)	**0.62 miles (mi)**	**0.62 miles**	*multiply by 0.6*

Clothing

Women	🇪🇺	🇺🇸	🇬🇧
	35	4	2½
	36	5	3½
	37	6	4½
Shoes	38	7	5½
	39	8	6½
	40	9	7½
	41	10	8½
	36	6	8
	38	8	10
Dresses	40	10	12
& suits	42	12	14
	44	14	16
	46	16	18
	36	06	30
	38	08	32
Blouses &	40	10	34
sweaters	42	12	36
	44	14	38
	46	16	40

Men	🇪🇺	🇺🇸	🇬🇧
	40	7½	7
	41	8½	8
	42	9½	9
Shoes	43	10½	10
	44	11½	11
	45	12½	12
	46	13½	13
	46	36	36
	48	38	38
Suits	50	40	40
	52	42	42
	54	44	44
	56	46	48
	37	14½	14½
	38	15	15
Shirts	39	15½	15½
	40	15¾	15¾
	41	16	16
	42	16½	16½

Sizes often vary depending on the designer. These equivalents are given for guidance only.

Speed

KPH	10	30	50	70	80	90	100	110	120	130
MPH	6	19	31	43	50	56	62	68	75	81

Temperature

Celsius	(°C)	0°	5°	10°	15°	20°	25°	30°	40°	60°	80°	100°
Fahrenheit	(°F)	32°	41°	50°	59°	68°	77°	86°	104°	140°	176°	212°

To convert Celsius into Fahrenheit, multiply °C by 9, divide by 5, and add 32.
To convert Fahrenheit into Celsius, subtract 32 from °F, multiply by 5, and divide by 9.
NB: Conversion factors on this page are approximate.

Sunflower field, Tuscany
Kjell Brynildsen/iStockphoto

Tuscany Today

Though much of Tuscany still appears to be firmly rooted in the 15C, the region suffers from many modern maladies. Overcrowding, from tourists and the accompanying industry, plus an influx of immigrants looking for work within, has led to increased traffic and housing shortages in and around the cities. Light, air, and noise pollution are also threatening the distinctive landscape, historic buildings and quiet idylls that drive the Tuscan tourist trade. But, as one of the most prosperous and organised regions in the country, Tuscany is well positioned to address and overcome the challenges that the 21st century has presented.

POPULATION

Tuscany's population is approximately 3.7 million, with almost one-third of inhabitants concentrated in the Province of Florence. Tuscany is Italy's fifth-largest region, but currently ranks ninth (out of twenty) in terms of population density. Within the region, the tiny Province of Prato has the highest population density, with approximately 675 inhabitants per square kilometre. Conversely, the Province of Grosseto, Tuscany's largest, claims about 50 inhabitants per square kilometre. Foreign residents, including immigrants from Asia and Africa and nationals from Great Britain and the United States, account for almost eight percent of the population.

Like the rest of Italy, Tuscany has an aging population, with death rates outpacing birth rates. Most recent yearly statistics from 2007 show approximately 8,000 more deaths than births in the region.

LIFESTYLE

The Tuscan way of life has long been a source of envy among visitors. Not only do Tuscans enjoy a per capita income higher than most other Italians, but also a lifestyle that cannot be measured by money and goods. Much of the Tuscan way of life depends on taking the time to enjoy simple pleasures, such as spending time with family, preparing and eating a meal, savouring a glass of wine or taking an evening stroll (*passegiata*).

Most elements of a Tuscan's everyday life can still be sourced locally. But factors such as traffic, pollution, globalisation–which is nudging out small family-run businesses–and an ever-growing expat population, are reshaping Tuscan demographics, and as a result, the region's way of life.

RELIGION

Tuscany's religious makeup reflects national trends; about 90 percent of the population is Catholic. Only about one-third of Tuscan Catholics attend mass regularly.

There are long-standing Jewish communities in Florence, Livorno, Pisa and Siena and its province, but their numbers are dwindling. Protestant, Muslim and Buddhist communities are prevalent in cities, which have higher immigrant and expat populations.

SPORT

Football (*calcio*) reigns supreme throughout Italy, and Tuscany is no different. Every city and most large towns have a local squad, some of which are successful enough to play in the Serie A, Italy's premier football league. Regular contenders include Fiorentina, Livorno and Empoli.

Each year in Florence, rival neighbourhoods gather to play Calcio Storico, a historic form of the sport dating back to the 16C (see FLORENCE). Jousting and archery are two other traditional sports that are celebrated each year in festivals in the region (see PLANNING YOUR TRIP).

MEDIA

Behind Rome and Milan, Florence is a major media hub for Italy. The national newspaper *La Nazione* is headquartered here and several English language periodicals are produced in Florence. The region has also become a popular film location (see PLANNING YOUR TRIP).

Table at an agriturismo

Lara Pessina/MICHELIN

ECONOMY

Endowed with a wondrous landscape and a dizzying cultural and artistic patrimony, Tuscany is at the heart of Italy's giant tourism industry. Tuscany is one of Italy's largest regions and one of Europe's wealthiest.

The region accounts for approximately seven percent of Italy's GDP and its unemployment rate is below the national average. Italy's national economy has stagnated in recent years, due in part to the lack of labour and pension reforms necessary to address high unemployment in one of the world's most rapidly aging societies. Tuscany, however, maintains a highly diverse, competitive economy, centred on textiles, leather and apparel, jewellery, footwear, petrochemicals, agriculture and, of course, tourism.

While Milan is the centre of Italy's world-renowned fashion industry, Florence is a fashion mecca in its own right.

The venerable houses of Salvatore Ferragamo and Emilio Pucci, along with numerous up-and-coming designers, are headquartered here and depend on the region's vast network of small, artisinal producers for both inspiration and supply. In addition to design, petro-chemical plants and auto and steel factories employ thousands near the coastal towns of Livorno and Piombino.

Expertise in emerging sectors, such as biotechnology and nanotechnology, increasingly contributes to the region's economic growth and the development of its universities, in Florence and Pisa. The region continues to be a leading centre of agricultural production, notably of olive oil and fine wines, which command almost limitless demand on world markets.

GOVERNMENT

Tuscany is divided into ten provinces: Arezzo, Florence, Grosseto, Livorno, Lucca, Massa-Carrara, Pisa, Pistoia, Prato and Siena. Each province (*provincia*) provides centralised governance to cities and towns (*comuni*), while the regional capital is Florence.

Politically, citizens of Tuscany tend to lean towards the left. The region is perpetually a stronghold of the centre-left Democratic Party, which supported–unsuccessfully so–the candidacy of Walter Veltroni over Silvio Berlusconi in the 2008 national elections.

FOOD AND DRINK

Typified by its simplicity, Tuscan cooking gives pride of place to the fine quality of the abundant local produce.

It was Catherine de' Medici who introduced the pleasures of the table to France upon her marriage to Henri II. This event marked the beginning of modern European cookery and gastronomic culture. She also introduced the fork and table napkin to court life, so that the behaviour of the guests would be as refined and elegant as the dishes they ate.

"FIASCO"

The traditional Chianti bottle was the fiasco, a bulbous shaped flask; it was originally made by glass blowing, with a long neck and a perfectly spherical bottom, like a large glass globe. This characteristic shape was hidden by the straw container that enveloped the bottle and made it stable. Today, it has been replaced by a bottle of more classic shape, similar to the one used for the wines of Bordeaux.

Like the Tuscan landscape, the specialities of the Tuscan table exhibit a serene sense of harmony. The opportunity to taste them in situ, accompanied by Tuscan wines, is an experience that cannot be reproduced elsewhere.

By local tradition, people waiting to be served in a Tuscan restaurant begin by tasting savory **crostini**, crusty slices of bread topped with large white haricot beans, cooked al fiasco (in a bottle) or, more commonly, spread with poultry liver paté or one of the numerous local variations made from game or mushrooms.

There is an abundance of wild mushrooms in Tuscany, of many different species and all of excellent quality. The great variety of vegetables provides a wide range of interesting dishes such as fried artichokes, vegetable flans and soups (minestrone and aquacotta). Pork products include the strongly-flavoured uncooked Parma ham, which is traditionally sliced by hand with a knife, and **finocchiona**, a cooked sausage flavoured with wild fennel seeds. Among the cheeses are **pecorino** (sometimes also known as cacio) which is made solely from the milk of a ewe (pecora in Italian). It is eaten at various stages of maturity but never before it has ripened for at least eight months.

The best known of all the traditional hot hors d'œuvres (primi) are **pappa al pomodoro** and **ribollita**. The former consists of croutons cooked in herb-flavoured stock to which are added sieved tomatoes; the croutons are left to cook until the bread becomes soft, hence the name pappa. The latter is a bean and cabbage stew which derives its name from the fact that it used to be reboiled and served on several successive days. Other hot hors d'œuvres are fish soups, such as the famous Livorno-style **cacciucco**.

In Tuscany, as elsewhere in Italy, pasta is cooked in a variety of ways and makes a good start to a meal; a most unusual pasta dish is pappardelle with hare sauce. A typical dish in La Lunigiana is pasta served with olive oil and pecorino or with pesto (testaroli).

The queen of regional fare is Florentine-style steak (bistecca alla Fiorentina) better-known quite simply as **La Fiorentina**, which consists of a thick slice of tender beef cut from the sirloin and fillet (about 400g per person) and usually grilled. Among typical Tuscan main courses (secondi) are Tuscan **tripe** and **fried lamb**, **chicken** and **eel**.

A variety of sweets provide a fitting end to a meal – from simple **cantucci**, almond-flavoured biscuits that are traditionally accompanied by Vin Santo, to the **castagnaccio**, a cake made with chestnut flour, and **brigidini** from Pistoia, small waffles cooked in moulds heated over a flame.

The famous **panforte** of Siena used to be eaten only at Christmas. It is made from a recipe faithfully handed down since the 13C, which consists of a blend of cocoa, walnuts, hazelnuts, almonds, spices and crystallised fruit.

WINE

It is known from documents and works of art that wine has been made in Tuscany for many centuries; it was the Etruscans who introduced wine into Gaul. Throughout the region the seasons of the year are marked by the activities and rituals involved in wine production.

It was in Tuscany that the first attempts were made to standardise the criteria for granting a title to good quality wine produced in a specific region (denominazione di origine controllata). Edicts promulgated in the 18C expressed the intention of controlling production in the Chianti and Carmignano areas. Almost one-half of the region is now covered in vineyards whose names appear in the registers of the various regions; the map names the main *denominazione di origine*.

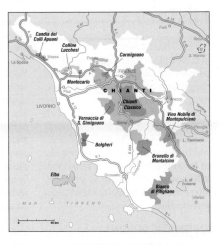

Chianti

Chianti is a red wine produced in the districts around Arezzo, Florence, Pisa, Pistoia and Siena, and the Chianti vineyard is the largest in Tuscany as regards acreage and production. The characteristics of the soil and other conditions vary considerably from one sector to another and the wine produced in them is equally different.

The blends of grapes are, however, the same – *Sangiovese, Canaiolo Nero, Trebbiano Toscano* and *Malvasia del Chianti* – and they produce a deep ruby red wine with a heady bouquet, the ideal accompaniment for Tuscan cooking.

The word *classico* is reserved for wine produced in the district straddling the provinces of Florence and Siena. This is the region famous in the Middle Ages for the Chianti League (*see CHIANTI*). The **Chianti Classico** consortium, which was set up in 1924 to control production, took over the League's emblem, the black cockerel (*gallo nero*) and began to reproduce it on the wine bottles. Gradually the emblem became synonymous with *classico* wines.

A second consortium was founded in opposition to Chianti, under the general name of **Chianti Putto** and the emblem of a cherub, to act as an umbrella organisation for the other *denominazione* – Montalbano, Rufina, Colli Fiorentini, Colli Senesi, Colli Aretini and Colline Pisane; the title is granted only to wines produced with grapes harvested and made into wine within the respective areas.

Heady Reds

Another prestigious wine is **Brunello di Montalcino** which cannot be sold under this name unless it has aged for four years or, in the case of the *riserva*, for five years. Brunello, like Chianti, is a DOCG (*denominazione di origine controllata e garantita*). Its alcohol content usually exceeds 12%.

The famous **Nobile di Montepulciano** is said to have acquired its name not only because of its sophistication but also because it was produced directly by local noble families. It requires a great deal of care during production and the wine itself should be left to age for a long time.

Tignanello and **Sassicaia** are good table wines.

White Wines

Although most Tuscan wines are red, some white wines provide a pleasant surprise. Among them is **Vernaccia di San Gimignano**, which is characteristically dry and was one of the first wines to be classified as a fine wine.

Vin Santo is an excellent dessert wine produced from semi-crushed grapes left for several months on wooden slats until over-ripe so that the juice has evaporated and the sugar content is concentrated. The grapes are then crushed, and the wine is aged for at least three years in sealed casks. It is traditionally drunk with biscuits called cantucci. It is usually made with white Malvasia or Trebbiano grapes, but there is also a red Vin Santo.

History

THE ETRUSCANS

In c. 1000 BC, Indo-European-speaking peoples from the North settled in what corresponds approximately to Tuscany today, as well as the North of Latium and Umbria. These new arrivals were skilled in the use of iron, and practised ritual cremation of their dead. This civilization, which seems to have spread northwards as far as the Po Plain, was called the **Villanovan** culture and was named after a town near Bologna, where it was first identified.

ENIGMATIC ORIGINS

It was long believed that the Etruscans came from Asia Minor. This at least was the view expressed by Herodotus, who described them as Lydians fleeing from their famine-stricken country in a mass exodus led by the King's son, Tyrrhenos, after whom the Tyrrhenian Sea was named. This hypothesis is born out by; the Orientalising character of their art throughout the 8–7C BC; their divination-based religion; and their language, which bore no resemblance to any of the other Indo-European languages spoken in the region at the time, but which had some similarities with Aegean dialects. However, other experts have found evidence of the presence of this Mediterranean tribe in the Italian peninsula long before the Indo-European invasions.

Even if the reason for the development of the Etruscan civilization remains unclear, the explanation of a sudden mass influx of people has been dismissed. Nowadays it is thought that Etruscan trends in art and philosophy spread as a result of trade, especially with the East and also with the arrival of various ethnic groups.

ETRUSCAN ECONOMY

The spread of the Etruscan civilization was based largely on the success of its traders who distributed the products made by its many craftsmen and farmers to destinations near and far. Etruria was not only rich in metal deposits, but also a fertile land, abundantly watered by the numerous streams and rivers rising in the Apennines. The mining of ore – iron, lead, copper and tin – and the related craftworks, were based mostly in northern Etruria. The southern part of the country developed an agrarian economy and the Maremma was extensively drained during this period. The two main products, much prized by the Mediterranean people, were olive oil and wine; the latter was a luxury beverage introduced into Gaul by the Etruscans during the 7–6C BC. This agrarian economy made possible the accumulation of surplus wealth, permitting the introduction of Hellenistic art, traded in return for ceramics and other crafts. This probably paved the way for the arrival of Greek artists who introduced monumental painting, evidence of which can be seen in the magnificent painted tombs situated in present-day Lazio (Roman Latium).

HISTORY AND CULTURE

Etruscan Expansion

The Etruscans appeared in central Italy in the 8C BC. Their power and civilization reached a peak in the 6C but began to fall into decline during the following century, until they were eventually absorbed by Rome.

Correctly speaking, **Etruria**, or as it is sometimes called, Tyrrhenian Etruria, covered the area bounded to the east by the Apennines, to the south by the Tiber and to the north by the Arno. With their powerful fleet of ships, the Etruscans soon established commercial links with the East (Greece, Cyprus, Syria), Gaul, Spain and Africa (Carthage), exporting Tuscan iron and copper, and importing fabrics, jewellery, ivory and ceramics.

The Etruscans sought to extend their domination southwards where, during the second half of the 7C, they occupied the Latin country, settling on the site of Rome which, for over a century, was governed by the Tarquinian dynasty of Etruscan kings. Early in the 6C they ventured into Campania, making Capua one of their main strongholds, but clashing with the Greeks who had settled in southern Italy (known as Magna Graecia) and from whom they were unable to capture Cumae. In the late 6C they spread north throughout much of the Po Plain, founding Bologna (then known as Felsina) and the port of Spina, from where they could control trade in the Adriatic. Their 'empire' stretched as far as Corsica, where they occupied the east coast after winning the Battle of Alalia (now Aleria) c. 540 BC.

It was during the 6C that Etruria reached the height of its influence and power as regards territorial expansion, trading relations, the quality of its artistic expression and the spread of its civilization. During this period Etruria formed a federation of City States, in which each state was called a *lucumonia* (from *lucumon* meaning a person exercising a priestly or regal function). Their fall was in fact hastened by their failure to combine their military might against their enemies. In theory at least there were 12 cities but it is difficult to know which were part of the federation since the list seems to have varied.

In the late 6C Tarquinius Superbus, the last Etruscan King of Rome, was driven from power and in the early 7C the Etruscans were cut off from Campania. They made a vain attempt to reach the region by sea but suffered a crushing defeat at the hands of the Greeks off Cumae. Threatened by the Celts in the North, who invaded the Po Valley in the early 4C, and in almost constant conflict with Rome, the Etruscans saw their cities fall one by one during the 3C in the face of the growing power of Rome. The fall of their religious capital Volsinii (now Orvieto in Umbria) in 265 BC marked the end of their period of independence. After submitting to the new masters of the peninsula, Etruria shared the fortunes of Rome and was granted official recognition in 90 BC.

Archaeological finds and Greek and Latin texts in which the Etruscan civilization is mentioned, have enabled modern specialists to define the boundaries of Etruria with some accuracy. However, there is no known Etruscan literature. The Etruscan language can be read without difficulty, as the Etruscans adopted the Greek alphabet in the 7C in order to facilitate trading relations, but its structure and the meaning of certain terms remain obscure.

Life on earth and after death

The Etruscan civilization was characterised by extreme refinement and great cruelty. The people delighted in luxury, adorning themselves with jewellery and rich clothing and surrounding themselves with beautiful furniture and precious objects. They enjoyed dancing and music so much that many activities were carried out to the sound of a musical instrument. On the other hand it is known that funerals were occasionally accompanied by human sacrifices, and it seems that some of the bloody spectacles which later became popular in Rome, such as gladiatorial combat, were inherited from Etruscan funeral rites.

The Etruscan gods bore a strong resemblance to those of the Greeks. They displayed great faith in divination, through the study of animal entrails (*haruspices*) and the flight of birds (*auspices*) and practised cremation or burial according to time and place. Like most ancient peoples, they believed in life after death for which sacrifices and offerings were required.

ETRUSCAN ART

Most of the remains that have been found are related to funerary art.

In its early phase (8C) the art form seems to have been strongly influenced by the Orient, from which it borrowed its decorative motifs.

Etruscan art reached the peak of its creative excellence from the 7C to the mid-5C BC. This period saw the arrival of Greek pottery in Etruria, the construction of most of the temples, the execution of the famous paintings in Tarquinia in Lazio, and the production of the most highly-accomplished bronzeware and the finest sarcophagi.

During the troubled period of the Roman conquest, Etruscan art lost its strength and character; from the 3C onwards it entered its Hellenistic phase.

Once Etruscan art had been assimilated by the Romans in the 1C BC, it appeared to lose all individuality.

Town Planning and Architecture

Etruscans usually founded their urban communities on a hill near a plain watered by a river or stream so that they could farm the land. They protected their towns with huge walls such as those at Roselle, and were remarkable technicians, excelling in bridge building and in the provision of water to towns and field irrigation.

Few Etruscan buildings have withstood the passage of time. The materials used in their construction were relatively fragile, but a few arches and monumental gateways, bonded with huge blocks of stone, have survived.

The Etruscans knew how to build semicircular arches and passed on their knowledge to the Romans. Their temples were rectangular in shape and raised above ground level. A flight of steps led up to the entrance which was preceded by a colonnade.

On the outskirts of the towns were vast graveyards, forming veritable cities of the dead, including streets and, in some places, squares. The graves were shaped like temples, houses or simple barrows. In volcanic areas they were hollowed out of the tufa cliffs.

Etruscan styles of housing were reflected in the funerary architecture, which has survived in greater quantity, and most of the available information comes from excavations on the sites of aristocratic residences, as in Murlo. Apparently the mansions were built around an atrium flanked by colonnaded porticoes, a style that was later used in Roman houses.

Sculpture and Bronzework

Etruscan sculptors did not use marble but preferred clay, often painting it in vivid colours or adorning it with gold leaf. The great period of Etruscan sculpture was the 6C BC when statuary was an important element in the decoration of temples and even aristocratic residences.

Decorative plaques and friezes, ornamented with animals, banqueting scenes and processions, were made for the same purpose, as were countless antefixes.

Figurative sculpture gave rise to votive statues that were smaller than life-size but represented the deceased in their earthly lives (a warrior in battle, a woman washing, etc). Busts of people are more unusual but, despite the stylised features, they are strikingly realistic owing to the intensity of the facial expressions. Large protruding eyes and enigmatic smiles are characteristic of Etruscan art, as are the famous figures on the sarcophagi, reclining in the manner of guests at a banquet.

The Etruscans excelled in bronzework. Owing to the extensive copper deposits in Tuscany, bronzeware was a major part of the trading economy from the late 7C onwards. Etruscan bronzes, both utilitarian and merely decorative, were highly prized by the Greeks and Romans. The bronze was rolled for dishes, mirrors and fibulae, but cast for votive statuettes and statues. The decorative elements were engraved or raised in relief using the *repoussé* technique.

Under the influence of the Orientals and Greeks, Etruscan bronzes reached perfection during the second half of the 6C and the first third of the 5C, but retained some of their own specific characteristics, such as the marked elongation of the outlines. The end of the 5C, when the Hellenistic influence was particularly strong, is the date of the masterpiece of animal statuary, the Chimera of Arezzo (*now in the Museo Archeologico in Florence*). Thereafter, bronze sculptors turned their attention more to the production of monumental statues. During the Hellenistic period there was no longer an authentically Etruscan art form. The famous Arringatore (*also in the Museo Archeologico in Florence*) has a somewhat dramatic realism that foreshadows Roman art.

Painting

The splendid remains of Etruscan painting were all found in the graveyards of southern Etruria, which is now in Lazio. The paintings were reserved for the wealthiest members of society. They underline the economic schism between the mining area of the North, where people enjoyed an average standard of living, and the richer, agricultural South. Although no examples of Etruscan art have been found in

Funerary urn, Museo Archeologico, Chiusi

Tuscany, the paintings prove that Etruscan artists knew and mastered all the various forms of art. The paintings are a precious record of the everyday life and beliefs of the Etruscan people.

In the burial chambers within the graveyards, the paintings were designed to remind the deceased of earthly pleasures. These included games, music, dancing, hunting and, more importantly, banqueting, which was traditionally the main subject.

Artists used the fresco technique, applying colours (ochre, a red made with iron oxides; white, produced from lime; coal black; and lapis lazuli blue) on a wet limewash that "fixed" the colours.

The so-called "archaic" style (6C BC) covered a wide range of topics. During the "classical" period (first half of the 5C), an austere Attic style predominated. Its main features were banqueting scenes, almost to the exclusion of any other subject, less obvious shading, very sophisticated drawing techniques and extreme attention to detail. In the second half of the 5C and during the 4C, outlines were gradually replaced by spots of colour. Here again, Etruscan artists showed a heightened sense of movement.

Pottery and Jewellery

The Etruscans made pottery in **bucchero**, a terracotta produced from black paste. Their products, most of them linked to the consumption of wine, included amphorae, wine pitchers, two-handled drinking cups and goblets. Buccheroware first appeared in about 670 AD in Cerveteri and was

initially characterised by its pure lines and total lack of decoration. Later it was decorated with motifs picked out in dotted lines. Eventually the pottery became more complex in both form and ornamentation and consisted of two types – lightly embossed (*bucchero sottile*) and heavily embossed (*bucchero pesante*). The former was decorated with friezes of repetitive motifs inspired by Greek bronze vases with a similar sheen. The second group, which appeared after the 7C, had more sophisticated shapes and was heavier. Pieces were decorated with a single figurative scene in relief.

Greek pottery was enormously popular in Etruria. It was imported in huge quantities and reproduced so that today, it is sometimes difficult to tell which of the many kraters, drinking-cups and pitchers in graves were Greek and which were produced locally.

In the 5C the artists produced superb cinerary chests (built to contain the ashes of the deceased). Some of them were shaped like animals (zoomorphic); others were shaped like human figures (anthropomorphic). All were decorated with geometric motifs reminiscent of Inca or Aztec pottery.

⌂ *Major events are shown in italics.*

ANTIQUITY – ETRURIA

753 BC – Legendary date of the founding of Rome by Romulus.

Late 8C – Emergence of **Etruscans** in central Italy.

2nd half of 7C – Occupation of the Latin country by Etruscans.

Late 7C–Late 6C – Rome governed by sovereigns from Etruria (Tarquin dynasty), whose reign marked the height of Etruscan expansion.

509 – Fall of Tarquinius Superbus. Beginning of the decline of Etruscan power. Founding of the Roman Republic.

3C – Etruscan submission to Roman rule. Volterra conquered in 295. Perugia and Arezzo rallied to the Roman camp in 294. Fall of Etruria's religious capital, Volsinii (now Orvieto in Umbria) in 265 and the end of Etruscan independence.

AD 330 – Byzantium chosen by Constantine the Great as the capital of the Roman Empire and renamed Constantinople in his honour.

395 – Division of the Roman Empire into the Eastern and Western Empires with Constantinople and Rome as their respective capitals.

476 – Fall of the Western Roman Empire.

DARK AGES AND FOREIGN INVASIONS

568 – Occupation by Lombards (from Northern Europe) of the Po Plain (Lombardy is named after them) and of Tuscany,

Umbria and Puglia and Campania in the south. Foundation of duchies; Tuscany centred on the Duchy of Lucca.
Weakening of Byzantine authority over its empire. Beginning of a period of co-operation with the Kingdom of Lombardy.

570–774 – Long and violent occupation of Tuscany by the Lombards.

751 – Surrender of Ravenna.

752 – Rome threatened by the Lombards. Appeal by the Pope to Pepin the Short, King of the Franks.

756 – Undertaking by Pepin the Short to restore the States occupied by the Lombards to the Pope, marking the beginning of the Pope's temporal power and the birth of Papal States that were to be of major importance in Italian history until the 19C.

774 – Defeat of the Lombards by Charlemagne (son of Pepin the Short). Tuscany under Carolingian rule. Lucca the centre of the new Marches of Tuscany.

9C – Break-up of the Carolingian Empire, causing anarchy in Italy and the founding of rival states.

951 – Intervention in Italy by King Otto I of Saxony at the request of the Pope.

962 – Coronation of Otto I as Emperor by the Pope; founding of the **Holy Roman Empire**. Emperor claims exclusive right to appoint the clergy.

THE CHURCH VS. HOLY ROMAN EMPEROR

In the late 11C, in defiance of the Holy Roman Emperor's growing stranglehold on the Papacy, Gregory VII decreed (1075–76) that no member of the clergy could be appointed to a parish or diocese by a layman, and he excommunicated Emperor Henry IV. This gave rise to the **Investiture Controversy**, the source of a lengthy dispute between Papacy and

Greek Ceramics

Much prized by the Etruscans, Greek vases were decorated with scenes in which mythology and daily life are closely linked; main characteristics vary from one period to another.

Corinthian ceramics, which were usually pale in colour and decorated with exquisite miniatures in the Oriental style constituting either a single subject or a frieze, were replaced in the 7C by Attic pottery produced in Athens. The decoration consisted originally of black figures set against a red background and then, from 530 BC onwards, of red figures against a glazed black background; within the figures, the lines and motifs were no longer incised but were painted on with a brush; eyes were shown facing forwards even when the face was shown in profile. By the beginning of the 5C this style had made Athens the main centre of pottery production. In the following century, in Athens and Magna Graecia, exuberant floral motifs and scrolls were painted on the glazed black background in white, yellow and dark red, surrounding a single figure.

Heavy jewellery, often made of gold and showing a high level of skill and sophistication, was worn by both men and women. As craftsmen, Etruscan goldsmiths were unrivalled, and they perfected the delicate technique of filigree work and granulation that had been developed at the end of the third millennium in Troy and later in Greece. The tiny grains of gold were several hundredths of a millimetre in diameter; the method used to produce them has been lost.

Empire, constituting the background to a whole era of Italian history.

This period saw the rise of the **Communes** (*comune*), whose role was to become a determining factor in the political life of medieval Italy.

THE COMMUNES

The struggle between imperial power and the Papacy, in which both protagonists attempted to foster support from various cities by granting them privileges, was one of the major reasons for the spectacular development of Italian towns in the late 11C. The Crusades and ensuing economic prosperity, especially in Pisa, further accentuated the expansion, creating an unprecedented boom in trade and industry (principally silk and wool), and resulting in the birth of a new merchant class.

The Communes flourished, and their existence, which was finally officially recognised by both Pope and Emperor, considerably altered political life in northern and central medieval Italy, including Tuscany, changing the face of numerous towns.

The Commune, a self-governing association of citizens, was marked by an unarmed takeover of power by the gentry and wealthy middle classes at the expense of the great feudal landowning nobility. As the prosperity of the towns grew, so the merchants and less wealthy classes of society gained power. The nobles meanwhile were gradually excluded from positions of authority.

In the early years, the Communes were governed by **consuls**, elected by an assembly, who held executive and judicial powers. Later, Frederick Barbarossa appointed a magistrate (*podestà*) as the direct representative of imperial power for each town under imperial rule. In principal, this magistrate came from outside the town and acted as the head of the army and an arbitrator in legal matters. However, like the consuls, he had no legislative power.

When the influence acquired by the craft guilds (*arti*) led to an administrative restructuring of towns and cities and the empowerment of the "popular" classes, a **captain of the people** (*capitano del popolo*), monitored by an increasingly influential assembly, was appointed to govern the town jointly with the magistrate. In the end the *podestà* was replaced by the *capitano*.

The Communes took advantage of the struggle between Church and Empire, adding to its complexity, and the Emperor was faced in many instances with violent hostility. All towns took sides in the controversy between the Pope and the Emperor, some fluctuating by choice or by coercion between the factions. In the furious clashes that set Italian towns and cities against one another, economic rivalries and individual enmities accounted for much of the fighting.

Despite these upheavals, the country experienced a major economic and artistic boom during the 13C and the first half of the 14C, stimulated by the power of the Communes which had become not only busy trading towns but also important artistic centres. Universities were founded in Siena, Pisa and Florence, and gained fame throughout Europe. Through Danté the Italian language acquired a glory that was never to wane.

The break-up of the Communes was provoked by the Black Death (1348), which was followed by sporadic outbreaks of plague during the second half of the 14C, by endemic fighting between neighbouring towns and by internal conflict within the towns.

1115 – Death of Countess Matilda, Marchioness of Tuscany. Tuscany bequeathed by her to the Papacy as a final gesture after half a century of supporting the Pope.

1122 – Investiture Controversy brought to an end by the Concordat of Worms, which gave the Pope the upper hand.

1125 – Annexation of Fiesole by Florence, marking the beginning of Florentine expansion in Tuscany.

1152 – Crisis of succession in Germany in which the supporters of the House of Bavaria oppose the supporters of the House of Swabia. Election of Frederick of Hohenstaufen, otherwise known as Frederick Barbarossa, supported by the House of Swabia.

1155 – Coronation in Italy by the Pope of Frederick Barbarossa as Emperor and Barbarossa's attempt to impose his rule throughout the whole of Italy. Renewal of the struggle between the Papacy and the Empire, complicated by the growing hostility of the Communes. Appointment by Frederick of a magistrate (*podestà*) to control the Communes that he had forced into submission.

1227–50 – New episode in the struggle led by Pope Gregory IX and Pope Innocent IV against Frederick II of Swabia (grandson of Frederick Barbarossa), crowned King of Sicily in 1194 and Holy Roman Emperor in 1220. New victory for the Papacy in 1245; excommunication and dismissal of the Emperor by the Pope.

CRISIS BETWEEN POPE AND EMPIRE

1250 – Death of Frederick II, marking the beginning of a period of strife.

1251 – Founding of a federation of Tuscan Ghibelline towns, headed by Pisa and Siena.

1260 – Attempt by King Manfred of Sicily, the legitimised bastard son of Frederick, to conquer the peninsula with the support of the Ghibelline towns. After being defeated at **Montaperti**, Florence, traditionally a Guelf city, which had already been Ghibelline for 13 years during the rule of Frederick II, again support the Ghibelline faction for a short period.

1263–66 – Appeal by the Pope to Charles of Anjou (brother of Louis IX, King of France) who defeated Manfred at Benevento (Campania) in 1266. Death of Manfred in battle and the establishment of the Anjou dynasty in Sicily and Naples, subjecting Italy to a period of French control.

1284 – Defeat of Pisa by Genoa at the **Battle of Meloria** causing Pisa to lose Sardinia and Corsica and its supremacy over the Mediterranean.

1289 – **Battle of Campaldino** near Poppi, quashing Ghibelline hopes.

Late 13C – Siena overtaken by Florence as a banking centre and the largest city in Tuscany. The 14C saw a decline in the power of the Communes and in Florence, as elsewhere in Italy, the rise of great families such as the Medici.

The collapse of imperial rule was followed by an erosion of the power of the Papacy, which was faced with grave difficulties. Italy was in crisis. Foreign influence began to make itself felt within the country, first through the French and later through the Aragonese, both of whom were fighting to gain control of the South. Florence exerted huge power and only Pisa, Lucca and Siena still managed to retain their independence.

1300 – Division in Florence between the **Black Guelfs**, who support foreign intervention, and the **White Guelfs**, who advocate total independence in the name of freedom.

1301 – Annexation of Pistoia by Florence.

1309 – Removal of the papacy to Avignon to escape the unrest in Rome.

1328 – Appeal for support by the Ghibellines to Louis of Bavaria; failure of his intervention marking the end of German claims in Italy.

1348 – Death of almost one-half of the urban population from the Black Death, which sweeps through Italy and spread throughout Europe.

1361 – Annexation of Volterra by Florence.

1377 – Return of the Papacy to Rome at the instigation of Petrarch and Catherine of Siena.

1378 – **Revolt of the Ciompi**: The lower classes, among them the *ciompi* (wool carders), suffers increasing economic hardship during the 14C. The rebellion of this section of society, led by the wool carder Michele di Lando, briefly bring to power one of the most democratic governments in Florentine history, in which all classes of society are represented. Within four years, however, the dominance of the major guilds is restored and the more conservative elements in Florentine society are back in power.

1378–1417 – **Great Western Schism:** Papal reinstatement in Rome opposed by the antipope resident in Avignon and a second antipope in Pisa (1409).

1384 – Annexation of Arezzo by Florence.

15C – TUSCAN RENAISSANCE

In the 15C Italy experienced a remarkable increase in economic and artistic activity. The medieval era drew to a close and was replaced by the Renaissance which blossomed in Florence, the city of the Medici, which became a glittering incarnation of a golden age.

1406 – Conquest of Pisa by Florence.

1434 – Beginning of the Medici oligarchy in Florence, with the arrival in power of Cosimo the Elder (*see FIRENZE*).

1454 – Political stability in Italy between the great rival States of Milan, Florence, Rome and Naples guaranteed by the **Treaty of Lodi**, which is vigilantly upheld by Lorenzo the

Magnificent, ruler of Florence from 1469.

1494 – Policy of interference in Italian affairs resumed by Charles VIII of France, thus putting the new stability in jeopardy. After a triumphant welcome in Pisa and benign indifference in Florence, he passes through Siena, marches on Rome and enters Naples but was soon forced to retreat.

His campaign marks the beginning of the Italian wars, which are later resumed by Louis XII, with the same lack of success.

1494–98 – Republic briefly established in Florence by Savonarola.

GRAND DUCHY OF TUSCANY

The **16C** was marked by the rivalry between France and Spain that turned Italy into a battlefield as the two great powers struggled for overall control of Europe. Florence was overtaken by Rome as a centre of artistic creativity in the reigns of the great Pope, Julius II (1503–13) and the Medici Pope Leo X (1513–21).

1508–26 – François I of France at war in northern Italy; victorious at Marignano but forced to renounce his claim to Italy after defeat at Pavia.

1527 – Italy attacked by Emperor Charles V. The power of the Holy See diminished by the sack of Rome.
Reinstatement of Alessandro Medici, the Emperor's son-in-law, in Florence which became a duchy (1532).

1545–63 – Council of Trent leading to the Counter-Reformation (or Catholic Reformation).

1555 – French claims in Italy temporarily brought to an end by the failure of the campaign launched by Henri II, whose supporters were defeated by the Emperor's forces at the Siege of Siena.
Siena forced to submit by Cosimo I, protégé of Charles V. Unification of Tuscany completed, except for Lucca, Piombino and the Garrison State (the five strongholds controlled by the Spanish: Ansedonia, Orbetello, Porto Ercole, Porto Santo Stefano, Porto Longone).

1559 – Treaty of Cateau-Cambrésis marking the end of the Italian Campaign and the beginning of Spanish domination. Central Italy sandwiched between territories subject to foreign rule; the Duchy of Milan under France to the north; and southern Italy, Sicily and

Guelfs And Ghibellines

The names Guelf and Ghibelline (Guelfi and Ghibellini in Italian), which came into use in Florence in 1215, are derived from the names of the two great German families who disputed the throne of the Holy Roman Emperor in the 12C. The Ghibellines were the supporters of the lords of Waiblingen, the cradle of the House of Swabia and therefore of the Hohenstaufen dynasty. The Guelfs, who were rivals of the Hohenstaufen family and therefore supporters of the Pope, were members of the Welf dynasty (House of Bavaria). The later division into White Guelfs and Black Guelfs was confined to Florence.

In the 13C the Investiture Controversy was replaced by the issue of primacy between Pope and Emperor. The zeal of the Guelf faction was stimulated by the preaching of the new religious orders (Minor Friars of St Francis of Assisi, Dominicans).

Sardinia under Spain to the south.

1569 – Tuscany made a **grand duchy** under the absolute rule of Cosimo I.

In the **17C** Italy was in decline and ceased to be the object of dispute between Spain and France during the reign of Louis XIV.

In the **18C** the rulers of a number of Italian States instituted a form of "Enlightened Despotism", a concept which was spreading throughout Europe from France. It was best embodied in Italy by Grand Duke Peter Leopold of Tuscany (1765–90), son of Maria Theresa of Austria, who based his style of government on the most innovatory theories of the day. The **Treaty of Utrecht** (1713) marked the end of Spanish domination and the beginning of Austrian control. In the ensuing years, however, Italy remained a bone of contention between the Habsburgs and the Spanish Bourbons.

1737 – End of the Medici line. Grand Duchy of Tuscany granted by the Austrians to François of Lorraine, husband of Maria Theresa and future Emperor of Austria. Under this dynasty, Florence and Tuscany experienced reform and progress.

NAPOLEONIC EMPIRE

1769–99 – Napoleonic campaign ending in the Peace of Campo Formio (1797) by which France annexed Italy. Occupation of Florence.

Early 1800s – The early 19C saw the annexation of territory by Napoleon and Italians experienced their first period of unity under governmental and military institutions similar to those established in France.

The Marzocco

This figure of a seated lion, gripping the Florentine heraldic lily in its front paw, symbolises the political power of Florence. It can be seen in the main square of every town and village governed by the city of the Medici and is an impressive testimony to the authority of Florentine rule. It gets its name from Mars, the god of war, represented by an ancient statue erected at the entrance to the Ponte Vecchio in Florence in the Middle Ages. The statue was destroyed by the floodwaters of the Arno in 1333 and replaced by the townspeople in 1420, in memory of its predecessor, by Donatello's everlasting sculpture of a lion, named *Marzocco* (little Mars). In 1810 it was moved to the Piazza della Signoria. The original is now in the Museo del Bargello.

1800–01 – Second Napoleonic campaign; founding of an Italian Republic; Tuscany became the Kingdom of Etruria.

1805–06 – Napoleon, now Emperor of France, proclaimed himself King of Italy, and appointed his stepson Eugène de Beauharnais as Viceroy, and gave his sister Élisa control over the newly-formed duchies of Lucca and Piombino. The Kingdom of Naples was ruled initially by his brother Joseph and later by Murat.

1809–11 – As Grand Duchess of Tuscany, Élisa moved to Florence. Annexation of the Isle of Elba by France.

1814–15 – Collapse of the Napoleonic Empire. The **Congress of Vienna** marked the end of the French occupation of Italy and confirmed the hegemony of Austria, which ruled the North and Centre of the country, including the Grand Duchy of Tuscany. When the Duchy was returned to the House of Lorraine, it was expanded to include the Isle of Elba and the Principality of Piombino. The Duchy of Lucca was granted to the Spanish infanta, Maria Luísa of Bourbon.

RISORGIMENTO

Following the Congress of Vienna, Italy was again divided and subject to the rule of absolute monarchs. An ideological movement began to develop based on a policy of liberalism combined with increasing patriotic awareness.

The movement known as **Risorgimento** (from *risorgere* meaning to rise again) was originally led by a cultured elite that was greatly influenced by Romantic ideals. It was later taken over by the liberal and moderate middle classes.

An initial phase of brutally quashed revolts reached a climax in the confusion of the 1848 revolution, which ended in failure. This was followed by a period of diplomacy, during which the spiritual leader and driving force was Cavour, resulting in the unification of Italy in 1870.

1831 onwards – After a number of riots throughout Italy, the rebels band together under **Mazzini**, whose "Young Italy" movement attracted numerous Freemasons and former members of the Carboneria, a secret society originating in France, which spreads to central and northern Italy from Naples, where it opposes Murat's regime. It is particularly successful in France, where Napoleon III is one of its followers who are known as Carbonari.

1848–49 – Introduction by a number of sovereigns, including the Grand Duke of Tuscany, of reforms aimed at establishing a degree of liberalism; increase in the number of rebellions.

February 1849 – Republics proclaimed by Mazzini's followers in Rome and Tuscany (the latter lasting only six months) after declaring the abolition of the temporal power of the Pope and expelling Grand Duke Leopold from Florence. From 1850 the inflexibility of Mazzini gave way to more moderate theories advocating political solutions.

1850 – Mechanization of the textile industry in Prato.

1852 – **Cavour** enters the political limelight as President of the Council.

1859 – Napoleon III launches a military campaign, marked by Franco-Piedmontese victories over the Austrians at Magenta and Solferino.

1860 – Decisive year for Italian unification. Unification with Piedmont of the Grand Duchy of Tuscany, the Duchy of Parma and Modena and the Duchy of Emilia and Romagna. In return for these concessions, Nice and Savoy granted to Napoleon III under the Treaty of Turin.

Unification with Piedmont of southern Italy through the Expedition of the Thousand Volunteers (Red-shirts) under the command of **Garibaldi**, who landed in Sicily and Naples. Only the Papal States and Venetia unaffected by the unification process.

14 March 1861 – Victor Emmanuel II of Savoy proclaimed King of Italy with the capital in Turin.

1865–70 – Capital transferred from Turin to Florence; final transfer to Rome in 1870 after conquest by Piedmontese troops.

TUSCANY WITHIN UNIFIED ITALY

1905 – Resumption and expansion of the scheme for draining the Maremma region, which was initially launched by the Dukes of Lorraine in the 19C; resulting in the almost complete eradication of malaria.

1915–18 – First World War

1919 – Earthquake in the Mugello region.

1929 – Industrial and mining activity in Tuscany is badly hit by the economic recession.

1940–45 – Second World War

1943 – Central Italy, particularly Tuscany, becomes a huge battlefield disputed between the Germans in northern Italy and the Allies in southern Italy (they land in Sicily in July). Major bombing raids on Pisa, Livorno and Grosseto, hence their modern appearance today. German bombing raid on Florence, which destroyed all the bridges except the Ponte Vecchio.

July 1944 – Pisa comes under artillery attack, setting fire to the Camposanto.

12 August 1944 – Florence liberated by the Allies.

2 June 1946 – Italy becomes a Republic, with Tuscany voting massively in favour.

1948 – Italy divides into 20 self-governing administrative regions, including Tuscany which is sub-divided into nine provinces – Arezzo, Florence, Grosseto, Livorno, Lucca, Massa-Carrara, Pisa, Pistoia and Siena.

1966 – River Arno floods, causing extensive damage, especially in Florence, where certain works of art were damaged beyond repair.

1986 – Florence voted European City of Culture.

1988 – Cars banished from the centre of major cities such as Florence, Siena, Lucca and Volterra.

1992 – Establishment of the Apuan Alps Natural Park following approval by the Tuscany Regional Council in 1985.

27 May 1993 – Bomb attack on the Uffizi Gallery in Florence causes the destruction of three paintings and varying degrees of damage to numerous works of art.

1993 – Council of Europe environmental protection award received by the Maremma Nature Reserve.

1994 – Addition of the Province of Prato to the nine existing provinces.

2000 – Catholic Jubilee brings thousands of pilgrims to Italy and Tuscany.

2001 December – Pisa's Leaning Tower reopens after 12-year renovation.

2002 January – Italy officially replaces the lira with the euro.

2004 September – 500th anniversary of Michelangelo's *David*, which underwent a controversial two-year cleaning from 2002–2004.

29 October 2004 – The Val d'Orcia landscape added to UNESCO's World Heritage Site list.

2 April 2005 – Death of Pope John Paul II.

19 April 2005 – Cardinal Joseph Ratzinger elected Pope, choosing the name Pope Benedict XVI.

July 2006 – Italy wins the World Cup football championship.

2007 – Prime Minister Romano Prodi resigns after a no-confidence vote.

April 2008 – Silvio Berlusconi is re-elected as Prime Minister.

Ponte Vecchio in Florence damaged by the 1966 floods

©Raffaello Bencini/World Illustrated/Photoshot

Art and Architecture

THREE CITIES, THREE TRENDS

From the 11C onwards in Tuscany, as elsewhere in central and northern Italy, the Communes played an important part in local history. Three of them – Pisa, Siena and Florence – were in conflict until the 15C when Florence, the city of the Medici, succeeded in acquiring a degree of control over the region as a whole. During this period, political rivalries and subdivisions had major repercussions on the Arts. Each city developed its own forms and style, influencing only its immediate neighbourhood and nearby towns.

Pisa, fascinated by the oriental splendors brought back by its seafarers and travellers, created unusual architectural forms showing a frenetic desire for ornamentation. Alternating bands of green and white marble were combined with rows of arcading on façades in which almost every feature was carved or inset with marble or ceramic motifs.

Siena, on the other hand, favoured Gothic architecture and continued to prefer the delights of its lyrical gentleness throughout the 15C. Sienese architecture, painting and sculpture show a search for delicate, floral beauty imbued with a great sense of freshness. Sienese art may sometimes be rather affected, but it is always lively. It may be tender or petulantly joyful, but never austere or dogmatic.

Although **Florence** also showed a liking for multi-coloured marble decoration during the Romanesque period, it was always a city of haughty rigour, of sobriety akin to austerity, and of intellectual perfection. Florence's painters' natural tendencies led to transcriptions of reality, with accurate drawing and definitions of a rigorous form of perspective. The sensual nature of light and voluptuous colours – features that bring warmth to a scene or a landscape – did not interest the artists of Florence, who differed in this respect from the Venetians. Their sole aim was to represent the truth, sublimated only to the representation of perfect beauty. This is the purpose of the famous **sfumato** technique (*see ARCHITECTURE GLOSSARY*) of Leonardo da Vinci, which was not intended as a means of transmitting a feeling, but rather as a subliminal way of muting outlines and colours in accordance with the distance between the artist and his subject.

Despite this diversity in the creative arts, Tuscany found a fundamental unity in these three trends – an intellectual view of art that appealed to the head rather than the heart, a beauty perfect in its forms and its tangible reality.

MEDIEVAL ARCHITECTURE

The growth of trade in the 11C and 12C brought with it a universal transformation in Tuscany. Economic changes and the relative prosperity that followed led to the building of numerous churches. Most of them were fairly modest affairs; parish churches (*pieve*), often built in isolated settings. Examples of these may be found in the Garfagnana, Lunigiana, Casentino or Pratomagno regions. Modest or grand, all testify to the emerging importance of Romanesque art and architecture in Tuscany; a more ornate and more universally adopted style than elsewhere in Italy.

The Middle Ages, between the 11C and 14C, also saw the establishment of numerous monasteries. These belonged to the traditional orders, such as the Benedictines or Cistercians, as well as the new mendicant (supported through charitable donation) orders, such as the Dominicans and Franciscans. The first Franciscan communities were founded in the neighbouring region of Umbria, and two of their monasteries in Tuscany were set up by St Francis himself: Le Celle near Cortona and La Verna, east of Florence, where he received the stigmata. Several new orders came into being in Tuscany itself during this period – the Vallombrosans and the Hermit Monks of Camaldoli in the 11C, the Servites, an order founded on Monte Senario, in the 13C and the Olivetan Order founded on Monte Oliveto Maggiore in the 14C.

Self-Portrait by Leonardo da Vinci

World Illustrated/Photoshot

Renaissance Man

It was in Tuscany that the Renaissance artist was born; a person who was inherently able to work in almost all art forms with the same degree of talent, a multi faceted Humanist who, in many cases, was versed in all the disciplines of human knowledge. Giotto, an artist who worked in the early 14C, was also an architect and town planner. He was followed by men such as Verrocchio, painter, sculptor and decorator; the Pollaiolo brothers, Antonio and Piero, who were painters and sculptors; Francesco di Giorgio Martini from Siena, architect, sculptor, painter, bronze-founder, decorator and engineer; Sansovino the sculptor and architect. The two most important artists were Michelangelo, sculptor, painter, architect, town planner and man of letters, and Leonardo da Vinci, painter, sculptor, engraver, architect, engineer and also musician and poet. This long list of outstanding all-rounders could also include Piero della Francesca. Research into perspective and optics led this remarkable painter, towards the end of his life, to write two treatises on perspective and geometry. It was this eclecticism that led to major advances in the technical aspects of each art form. Architects were concerned with beauty, but were also engineers, faced with the difficulties of translating their visions into physical reality; the marriage of the two was impressively achieved in the dome designed by Brunelleschi for Florence's Duomo. Although some artists concentrated on a single art form, they were in constant contact with their colleagues and, through their mutual admiration they learned from their respective discoveries. The painter Masaccio – a friend of Donatello and Brunelleschi – expressed volume with a fullness more usually found in the works of sculptors, and was the first to master the scientific use of perspective, as applied in architecture.

Through this blossoming of creative personalities, the concept of the "artist" achieved reality in Tuscany, replacing the anonymous craftsman of medieval times and marking a major turning point in the history of art.

The Last Supper by Leonardo da Vinci

De Agostini Picture Library/Fototeca ENIT

*Gothic windows, Palazzo Salimbeni, Siena*one artist

B. Juge/ MICHELIN

Wall Flowers

It was in Tuscany that the idea was first mooted of wall decoration that defines the wall itself and consequently the space behind it.

In Europe, the uniform façade – in which the doors, windows and stone bonding are set in static geometric lines – was first employed in Florence. The same may be said of the harmonious courtyards of Florence, designed around the symmetry of the four façades. The staircase was removed to the interior of the building so that it no longer disturbed the unity created by the architect.

This search for symmetry in the façade of a building was soon to spread to urban planning. Monuments were no longer considered in isolation; they had to harmonise with their surroundings within the available space.

As prominent features, street corners required careful decoration. This might be a loggia for trading purposes, a monumental shield, or a niche. A long façade facing the street used the rhythm of repeating features to articulate the perspective. Squares had to be treated so as to incorporate the existing buildings into a harmonious whole; in the case of a new square, such as the central square in Pienza, uniformity was the desired effect. This architectural sensibility has had an enormous impact on European designs ever since.

Façades became such an obsession in Florence that numerous churches are devoid of any decorative features because of a lack of agreement on, or the necessary funding for, the final masterpiece; San Lorenzo and Santo Spirito have totally plain façades and Santa Maria del Fiore and Santa Croce are fronted with 19C pastiches.

Interiors were not neglected and in large buildings they were used as decorative space. While Byzantium used mosaics, and the countries to the north used lavish stained-glass windows and tapestries, Tuscany employed the skills of its fresco painters.

Façade of San Michele, Lucca, a fine example of Pisan Romanesque style.

G. Bludzin/ MICHELIN

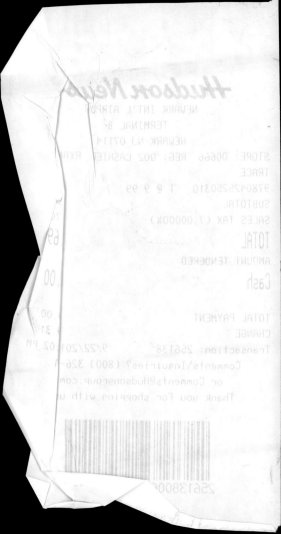

NEWARK INT'L AIRPORT
TERMINAL B
NEWARK NJ 07114
STORE: 00666   REG: 002 CASHIER: RYAN
TRACE
9780425250310   1 @ 9.99   9.
SUBTOTAL
SALES TAX (7.00000%)

TOTAL

AMOUNT TENDERED

Cash

TOTAL PAYMENT
CHANGE
Transaction: 256138   9/22/2012 2 PM
    Comments\Inquiries? (800) 326-77
      or Comments@Hudsongroup.com
    Thank you for shopping with us.

2561380066600209222

The spate of building in the countryside soon saw Tuscany's hilltops fortified, with small towns encircled by walls, or with fortresses or castles, such as Monteriggioni, Montalcino or Radicofani. More fortresses were built in the Orcia Valley (Montecchio, Poppi, etc).

In the towns, cathedrals and a large number of churches were built (or rebuilt), including new Franciscan friaries and Dominican monasteries. The aristocracy began to build houses with overhanging upper storeys and tower-houses. Street corners were enhanced with loggias used for trading activities and, to counterbalance the religious power of the church, an administrative building was erected in the town centre (*palazzo comunale or palazzo del podestà*).

ROMANESQUE RELIGIOUS ARCHITECTURE

The main feature of Romanesque architecture was its simplicity (except in Pisa, which is a special case, see below). The materials used included brick, timber and often irregular shapes of local stone. The buildings were modest in size – a *pieve* is, by definition, a small parish church designed for the people. The layout was simple. The basilica design dating from the palaeo-Christian era remained as popular here as elsewhere in Italy and the nave, sometimes flanked by aisles, extended into a single or sometimes a triple apse, often without a projecting transept. The roof was plain, the rafters being visible in most of the churches. The colours provided little contrast; a harmonious blend of brown, pale yellow or grey stonework unbroken by the vivid brilliance of a stained-glass window. In most cases the window openings were screened by a sheet of alabaster or marble which let in a pale, eerie light.

EXTERNAL INFLUENCES

Apart from the traditional **palaeo-Christian** elements that could be seen throughout Italy (basilica-type layout, rafters, a separate bell tower or none at all), Tuscan architecture incorporated elements from Burgundy. Much of this is owed to the influence, from the end of the 10C onwards, of the Benedictine Abbey of Cluny, and from Lombardy, where the large cities had a unique style of architecture.

The **Burgundian influence** saw the inclusion of a crypt; a re-introduction of a custom earlier established in the palaeo-Christian era. Crypts are evident in the Benedictine monasteries of the day; San Salvatore on Mount Amiata, Farneta Abbey or San Miniato in Florence. The use of the Latin Cross design was also common to Benedictine buildings, such as San Salvatore, Farneta and San Bruzio near Magliano. In Sant'Antimo, which was a Cistercian monastery, the influence of Cluny is obvious in the radiating chancel chapels, the marked difference in height between the nave and the aisles, and in some of the carvings like the narrative capitals.

Benedictine monastic life was comparatively limited in Tuscany, owing to the reservations of the region's bishops, and to the founding in Tuscany of austere religious communities – the Vallombrosans and the Congregation of Camaldoli – which required strict obedience to the Rule of St Benedict. The result was a restrained approach to Benedictine architecture.

Evidence of the **Lombard style** may be found in a few architectural works in Tuscany; arched friezes on the upper sections of buildings and on bell towers; pilaster strips; niches (San Piero a Grado, Sant'Antimo, Gropina, Sant'Appiano in the Chianti region, the parish church in Artimino); the use of single, sometimes clustered, pillars (San Donato in Poggio, San Quirico in Orcia, Sovana, Lucca Cathedral porch); pillars alternating with columns (Sant'Antimo, Gropina, Santa Maria della Pieve in Arezzo); splayed entrances (San Quirico in Orcia, Satreano, Pieve di Corsignano); and even the presence of a lantern-tower above the dome over the transept crossing (Asciano).

The Lombard style used more **trans-Alpine** features, an influence that spread along the Via Francigena and had particular influence in southern Tuscany

Religious Architecture

San Miniato al Monte (12C), Florence

The church of San Miniato is a perfect example of Florentine Romanesque Architecture, reminiscent of the Baptistery probably dating from the 11C.

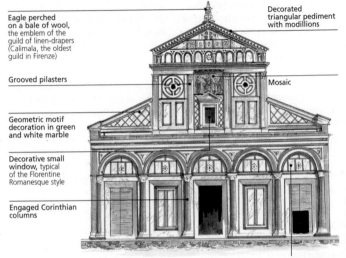

Eagle perched on a bale of wool, the emblem of the guild of linen-drapers (Calimala, the oldest guild in Firenze)

Grooved pilasters

Geometric motif decoration in green and white marble

Decorative small window, typical of the Florentine Romanesque style

Engaged Corinthian columns

Decorated triangular pediment with modillions

Mosaic

Semicircular arcading

R. Corbel/ MICHELIN

– details such as the use of multifoiled oculi, dentil arching, the exceptional use in Sovana Cathedral of quadripartite vaulting (despite the absence of any other Gothic feature), and the appearance of a non load-bearing arch combined with roof rafters in **San Miniato al Monte** in Florence.

From the second half of the 11C onwards these foreign influences began to wane in the face of the increasing popularity of local designs that showed a high degree of inventiveness.

PISAN ROMANESQUE

Through their contacts with Christians in the Middle East and their knowledge of Islamic art forms, the Pisans developed a highly ornate style that reached its peak in Piazza dei Miracoli, where the baptistery, cathedral, bell tower (the **Leaning Tower**) and Camposanto are laid out like a theatrical stage set.

The Pisan Romanesque style includes; green and white striped marble façades with blind arcading, open-work galleries and inset diamond-shaped decoration on the main façades; a colonnade

separating the nave and aisles; and the general use externally and internally of elevated arches.

The Pisan Romanesque style enjoyed enormous success in areas subjected to Pisan influence, but is perhaps best encapsulated in the Campo dei Miracoli in Pisa itself, designed by the architect Buscheto. The features of this style can be seen, to a greater or lesser extent, in the Pistoia and Prato districts, in and around Lucca, in the dioceses of Volterra and Massa Marittima, and as far south as Siena. Siena Cathedral, which is decorated with alternating bands of coloured marble, was begun in the Romanesque period.

FLORENTINE ROMANESQUE

The two main examples of this style, which was prevalent in Florence from the 11C to the 13C, are the Baptistery and the church of San Miniato al Monte in Florence. Both were strongly marked by the palaeo-Christian tradition, and both are outstanding for their classical design, pure volumes and rigorous geometric structure and decoration. Their

Leaning Tower (12C), Pisa

The Leaning Tower, the symbol of Pisa, is universally known for its famous tilt. It is a cylindrical bell tower in the style of the towers in Byzantium and is attributed to Bonanno Pisano.

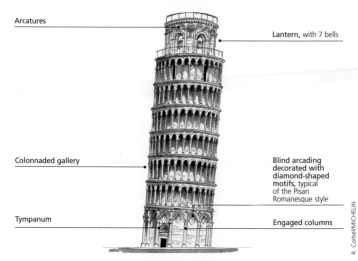

Arcatures

Lantern, with 7 bells

Colonnaded gallery

Blind arcading decorated with diamond-shaped motifs, typical of the Pisan Romanesque style

Tympanum

Engaged columns

R. Corbel/MICHELIN

façades consist of smooth white marble inset with linear motifs in coloured marble. This style was also used in the buildings in the Badia in Fiesole and in the church in Empoli, as well as in the decoration of religious furnishings such as ambos, fonts and pulpits, including the one in San Giovanni Maggiore (near Scarperia). The rational structural geometry of these buildings, which consisted of nothing more than simple volumes, can be seen in churches in areas under Florentine control, such as San Donato in Poggio.

GOTHIC ARCHITECTURE

Religious – The Gothic style came from northern Europe and had little success in Italy where it was seen as a form of political submission to the Holy Roman Emperor and was therefore referred to scathingly as "of the Goths" (*gotico*). The style was introduced by the Cistercians – exemplified in the abbey of San Galgano – adopted by the Franciscans, after the building of the basilica in Assisi, and later used by the Dominicans. During the 13C and 14C, the latter orders built churches in urban centres. Pointed

Loggia della Signoria (end 14C), Firenze

The loggia is a beautiful example of Gothic architecture, much admired and imitated (most notably in Munich). It was constructed to accommodate the members of the Signoria during official ceremonies.

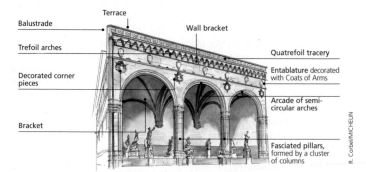

Terrace

Balustrade

Wall bracket

Trefoil arches

Quatrefoil tracery

Decorated corner pieces

Entablature decorated with Coats of Arms

Arcade of semi-circular arches

Bracket

Fasciated pillars, formed by a cluster of columns

R. Corbel/MICHELIN

Duomo or Santa Maria del Fiore (end 13C-15C), Firenze

The commission to build a replacement for the cathedral of Santa Reparata was given to the renowned architect, Arnolfo di Cambio (c 1245-1302) and, although work began in 1296, the cathedral was not consecrated until 1436. Giotto's bell tower was built between 1334 and 1359; Brunelleschi's dome between 1420 and 1434. This grandiose ensemble is a masterpiece of architectural balance.

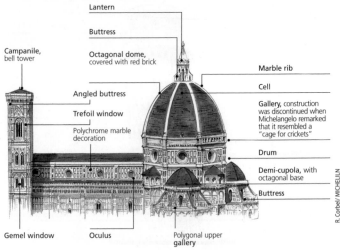

Lantern

Buttress

Campanile, bell tower

Octagonal dome, covered with red brick

Marble rib

Cell

Angled buttress

Gallery, construction was discontinued when Michelangelo remarked that it resembled a "cage for crickets"

Trefoil window

Polychrome marble decoration

Drum

Demi-cupola, with octagonal base

Buttress

Gemel window

Oculus

Polygonal upper gallery

R. Corbel/ MICHELIN

and ogive arches enabled them to erect more spacious buildings, which in many instances had single naves (San Domenico and San Francesco in Siena) so that even the poorest members of the congregation could see everything that was going on in the House of God. In most of the other religious buildings of the time, the Gothic style affected only the decoration and not the structure. In Pisa, the Gothic lancet windows (15C) in the Camposanto are framed by tall semicircular arches, while Santa Maria della Spina is a gem of stone-cutting, full of gables, pinnacles and niches. It is, however, in Florence and Siena that the major buildings from this period are to be found.

Siena Cathedral was started in the 13C as a Romanesque church with nave and aisles, semicircular arches, black and white striped façades in the Pisan style, and a dome on squinches. In 1284 Giovanni Pisano remodelled the façade in the Gothic style with deep doorways beneath gables, towers with piers and pinnacles, and a plethora of sculptures, mosaics and marble insets. In the 14C, a baptistery dedicated to John the Baptist (San Giovanni) was built underneath,

once the apse had been extended above street level and supported on ogive arches. From 1339 onwards, a project was launched to enlarge the cathedral, in which the older building would have become the transept of the new one, creating the largest Gothic building in Tuscany, had the work been completed (&see SIENA). The vast size of the project explains the extreme simplicity of the churches belonging to the mendicant orders in Siena; all of the effort and the funding went into the structure of the cathedral, to the detriment of any other work.

In **Florence**, on the other hand, it was the Dominican monastery of Santa Maria Novella that marked the introduction of the Gothic style in the last quarter of the 13C. The vast church, with nave and aisles roofed with ogive vaulting, was laid out like a basilica with a flat east end. Shortly afterwards, the Franciscans built a church, Santa Croce, in which the nave was separated from the aisles by great ribbed arches, although the roof was still constructed of traditional palaeo-Christian rafters.

The most unusual building is the Cathedral of Santa Maria del Fiore in which the

Palazzo del Podesta e Museo Nazionale del Bargello (13C), Florence

The palazzo was built 50 years before the Palazzo Vecchio and originally housed the Capitano del Popolo, who represented the working classes within the Florentine government, then the Podestà, the first magistrate who held executive and judicial powers. In 1574 the building became the residence of the Chief of Police (called Bargello) and part of it was turned into a prison.

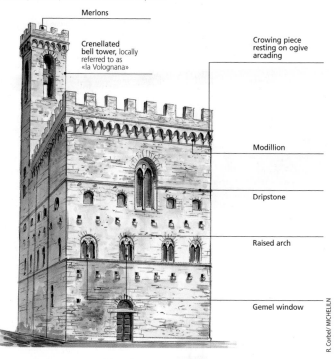

Merlons

Crenellated bell tower, locally referred to as «la Volognana»

Crowing piece resting on ogive arcading

Modillion

Dripstone

Raised arch

Gemel window

R. Corbel/ MICHELLIN

nave and aisles are almost of the same height. Its main features are its powerful design and its simplicity, and the obvious determination to create a vast interior devoid of luxury. It is the horizontal lines, rather than the vertical, that are emphasised, although verticality was a dominant feature of Gothic architecture. The same principle is at work in the interior of Santa Maria Novella, which is decorated with horizontal bands, and in Santa Croce, where a gallery along the upper section of the wall breaks the vertical lines.

In Florence, therefore, Gothic architecture was revised and adapted to suit a rational and modest feeling that did not easily express itself in a style profuse with slender decorative features.

Secular – Lay architecture was far more open to the Gothic influence than that of Tuscany's places of worship.

The Palazzo Vecchio in **Florence**, which has all the austerity of a fortress in its almost windowless lower section, has an upper section decorated with double windows, machicolations, crenellations and a fine projecting tower. The example of the Palazzo Vecchio was followed by the Bargello, which also has a tower.

In **Siena**, the Palazzo del Pubblico consists of a central section flanked by two lower sections. Its many windows give it a lightness echoed in the tall Mangia Tower.

All over Tuscany are other palazzi (del Popolo, or del Podestà) decorated with crenellations and mansions built for wealthy patricians with delightful double or tripartite bays. It was also during this period, the 13C and 14C, that towns such as Siena, San Gimignano, Volterra, Cortona and Arezzo acquired the appearance they have retained to this day.

The Tower-houses of San Gimignano

In the 12C and 13C, dozens of feudal towers were built in many Italian towns by the powerful families. They were mostly uninhabited but served as a safe place of refuge in times of danger.

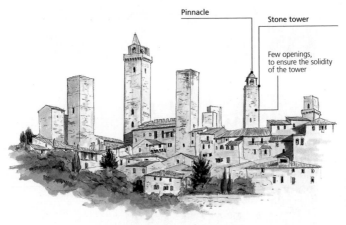

Pinnacle

Stone tower

Few openings, to ensure the solidity of the tower

R. Corbel/MICHELIN

Palazzo Pubblico (end 13C-14C), Siena

This is one of the finest vernacular buildings in Italy. It is exceptionally elegant and austere and it constitutes a synthesis of all the characteristics of the Sienese Gothic style. It served as a model for most of the other palaces in the city.

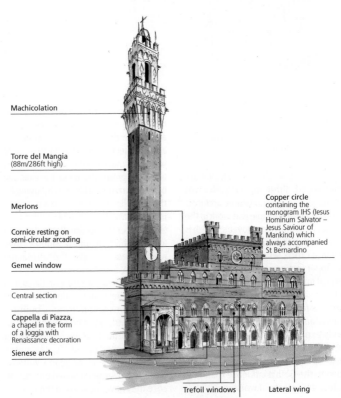

Machicolation

Torre del Mangia
(88m/286ft high)

Merlons

Cornice resting on semi-circular arcading

Gemel window

Central section

Cappella di Piazza, a chapel in the form of a loggia with Renaissance decoration

Sienese arch

Copper circle containing the monogram IHS (Iesus Hominum Salvator – Jesus Saviour of Mankind) which always accompanied St Bernardino

Trefoil windows

Lateral wing

Coat of Arms of the Medici

R. Corbel/MICHELIN

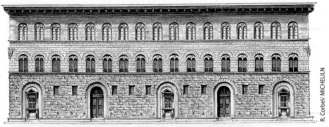

Palazzo Medici-Riccardi

R. Corbel/ MICHELIN

MEDIEVAL ART
PAINTING

Tuscan painting had strong links with Greek and Byzantine art. During the 12C a new trend developed in Pisa and Lucca, of displaying a Crucifix in the sanctuary or in the transept crossing. There were two types of Crucifix; one showed Christ in Triumph, a hieratic and serene representation; the other depicted the Passion of Christ, his body twisted and contorted with pain. An example of the former is the Crucifix by **Berlinghieri** painted for Lucca Cathedral c. 1220–30. The latter type was promoted by **Giunta Pisano**, who began to emphasise the pathos of Christ's Passion in the 1240s, and by the success of the sermons preached by the Franciscans, whose founder died in 1226.

Giunta adapted the Greco-Byzantine style to suit the new form of iconography, whereas **Margaritone of Arezzo** developed a degree of sensitivity and gentleness in his works, especially in the representation of St Francis himself. This trend towards Greek-style icons died out when the artists working on the decoration of the interior of the Baptistery in Florence expressed their skills in mosaics. **Cimabue**, who had worked on the enormous basilica in Assisi at the end of the 13C, showed a new approach within the traditional Byzantine forms. He succeeded in giving his figures an expressiveness that could not fail to move the congregation and induce feelings of tenderness. In addition to several Crucifixes, he painted many *Maestà* – paintings of the Madonna and Child seated on a throne and often surrounded by angels and saints – a tender subject popular in Florence and Siena. **Giotto** also painted Maestà, as did **Duccio di Buoninsegna** in Siena. The Sienese School (*see SIENA*) in which the leading figures in the 14C were Simone Martini and the Lorenzetti brothers, played a vital role in the **International Gothic** style. This was the most decorative, refined and florid trend of the Late Gothic period, practised by exponents in Paris, Avignon and Prague.

SCULPTURE

A number of works produced in Pisa in the mid-13C had a very real importance for medieval sculpture in Tuscany and even in Italy as a whole. There were promising beginnings – the ambo made by **Guglielmo** (12C) for Pisa Cathedral, and works that revealed the Lombard influence such as the figure of St Martin on the west front of Lucca Cathedral (13C).

The real initiator of the new trend was **Nicola Pisano**, who carved the pulpit for the Baptistery in Pisa in 1260. His powerful style combined Romanesque lions supporting the columns of the pulpit with Gothic trefoiled arches and low reliefs which were copies of Classical architecture. Pisano turned resolutely towards the Gothic style in the pulpit for Siena Cathedral, which he carved between 1266 and 1268.

From the 13C on, this type of furnishing became increasingly commonplace throughout Tuscany. In Pistoia in 1270 **Fra Guglielmo** carved the pulpit set against a wall in San Giovanni Fuorcivitas, and in 1301 **Giovanni Pisano**, Nicola's son, carved the hexagonal pulpit for Sant'Andrea. Giovanni Pisano

Façade of the Holy Trinity Church (1593-1594), Florence

The façade of the Romanesque church built in the 11C can be seen incorporated into the current façade. It was revealed by restoration work carried out at the end of the last century. The Baroque façade by Bernardo Buontalenti (1536-1608) was added in the late 16C. The extremely austere, slender interior is a fine example of the beginnings of Gothic architecture in Florence.

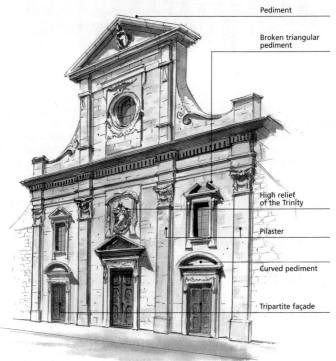

Pediment

Broken triangular pediment

High relief of the Trinity

Pilaster

Curved pediment

Tripartite façade

R. Corbel/MICHELIN

also worked on Prato Cathedral, on the façade of Siena Cathedral, the chancel of Massa Marittima Cathedral, and carved the huge pulpit (1302–12) – supported on ten columns and a central pillar – for Pisa Cathedral. His pupils included Goro di Gregorio, who made a name for himself with the sarcophagus of St Cerbone in Massa Marittima Cathedral, but the best known of all was **Tino di Camaino** from Siena who carved the tomb of Henry VII of Luxemburg (⚘*now in the Museo dell'Opera del Duomo in Pisa*).

The next generation continued to work in a style that was increasingly detached from architecture: sculptors acquired greater finesse in their use of the chisel and relied less on an impression of strength and force. In Florence **Andrea da Pontedera**, better known as Pisano, created the first of the three

bronze doors of the Baptistery (1336) and **Orcagna** carved the Orsanmichele tabernacle (1352–59).

THE RENAISSANCE

During the days of the Communes, the arts flourished in all the politically strong towns and cities in Tuscany. However, in the 15C, the beginning of Florentine domination in the region led to a centralisation of artistic development in the city of the Medici (⚘*see FLORENCE*). The concurrent blossoming of the arts was encouraged by the social climate. The city's economic and financial prosperity, the patronage of its aristocracy and the development of intellectual and philosophical thought, all coincided at a time when ancient ruins were being uncovered in Rome. From then on, the influence of ancient Roman civilization

Frescos on the walls and ceiling of the Scrovegni Chapel

De Agostini Picture Library/Fototeca ENIT

Gifted Graffiti

The fresco technique could be used to cover the entire surface of a wall and also the vaulting or ceiling above. The Tuscan fresco painters used the whole wall as their canvas, rather than as a mere surround for a single, isolated piece of ornamentation. The same principle was in some cases applied to the decoration of the floor.

The tableaux marble pavement of Siena Cathedral, and the coloured marble floors, walls and ceilings of the Princes' Chapel in San Lorenzo in Florence, are prime examples. This technique of wall painting takes its name from the Italian *affresco,* meaning fresh, and involves painting a mural on a fresh coat of plaster. As the underlayer dries, it absorbs and fixes the colours, causing the surface to solidify, protecting the wall from water and changes of temperature, and thus from damage over the centuries. The preparation of the plaster base was very important. The wall was sprinkled with water and covered with a rough base (*arricio*) consisting of one-fifth lime and four-fifths sand. This helped the paint to dry and kept it separate from the wall. It was on this rough base that the preliminary drawing was made.

As paper was uncommon and very expensive until the 15C, the underdrawing was done on the wall itself using a reddish-brown pigment called sinopia (see PISA). In later years, when paper became more readily available, the drawing was made separately and worked up to scale on a "cartoon" with the outlines of the drawing marked by perforations. The cartoon was held up against the wall, and the outline was transferred to the wall by passing lamp-black across the holes. The drawing could then be recreated on the wall from the black dots.

Two Techniques

There are two fresco painting techniques; *buon fresco* and *fresco a secco.* In *buon fresco,* paint was applied to damp *intonaco*; this was applied in sections known as *giornata* – the amount of surface that the artist could paint in a day. The *giornata,* which can be identified on some frescoes, varied in size according to the difficulty of the work. As the *intonaco* covered the original drawing, the artist had to work using the rest of the composition as a point of reference or he could again make use of the cartoon on the fresh plasterwork. In *fresco a secco,* the paint is applied either on top of dry *buon fresco,* or on dry *intonaco.* Unfortunately *fresco a secco* does not stand the test of time as well as *buon fresco.*

Small areas of the rough base were then covered with a thin mixture of sand and lime (*intonaco*), in which lime predominated, so that the surface crystallised when drying. This layer was smoothed and polished and remained fresh for just six to seven hours.

The fresco technique required painters to work swiftly, with great discipline. There was little room for error and the time limitations, particularly with *buon fresco,* required the detail to be painted in sections before the artist had a working overview. What's more, the fresco had to be painted from top to bottom lest the painting process of one *giornata* ruined the work of previous days.

Cappella dei Pazzi (1430-c 1460), Firenze

One of the most exquisite of the designs attributed to Brunelleschi. The artist worked on the chapel until 1445, the year before his death, but it was not completed until c 1460. In this chapel Brunelleschi raised to perfection the architectural ideal that he had already expressed in the old sacristy in San Lorenzo. All the architectural features are emphasised by the grey of the *pietra serena* which stands out against the white pebble-dash in a manner that is strict yet elegant.

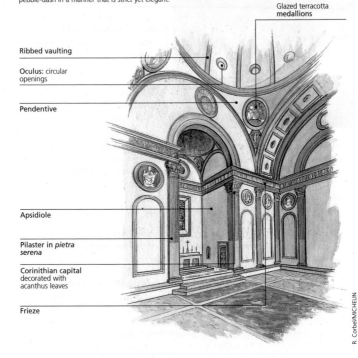

Glazed terracotta medallions

Ribbed vaulting

Oculus: circular openings

Pendentive

Apsidiole

Pilaster in *pietra serena*

Corinithian capital decorated with acanthus leaves

Frieze

R. Corbel/MICHELIN

was seen in every field of art and knowledge, leading to what was known as the Renaissance; a taste for Classical rather than Gothic aesthetics, a preference for mythology and lay subjects as well as the religious; and for tangible and mathematically-measurable reality rather than symbolism. This change in aesthetic values in Florence soon embraced the entire region, before spreading to the rest of Italy and Europe.

ARCHITECTURE

Brunelleschi made various trips to Rome to study the ancient Roman remains and to gain an insight into Classical art and architecture. His career was based solely in Florence, where he revolutionised every feature of architecture (&see FLORENCE). The Old Sacristy in San Lorenzo (designed 1421–28) and the Pazzi Chapel in Santa Croce (designed c. 1430) had a major impact because

of their domes. A number of churches followed their example and were laid out like a Greek Cross. Examples include the Santa Maria delle Carceri in Prato, which was begun in 1485 and designed by Guiliano da Sangallo; the Santa Maria del Calcinaio in Cortona, designed by Francesco di Giorgio Martini from Siena; the San Biagio in Montepulciano (built from 1518 to 1545 by da Sangallo the Elder, Guiliano's brother); and Santa Maria Nuova in Cortona, designed by Vasari.

In the field of **secular architecture** this period saw the building of **mansions** in towns and cities and **villas** in the country. Michelozzo (1396–1472), who designed the Palazzo Medici in Florence, worked in Pistoia, Montepulciano and Volterra. Guiliano da Sangallo (1443–1516) designed the Medici villa in Poggio a Caiano, which in its day was the only villa to be surrounded by a garden and park. The

Architecture A–Z

Ambo: small pulpit at the entrance to the chancel from which the Gospel or Epistle was read.

Archivolt: arch moulding over an arcade or upper section of a doorway.

Barrel vaulting: a vault produced by a continuous semicircular arch.

Bucchero: Etruscan pottery; black and shiny.

Cappella: chapel.

Ciborium: a canopy (baldaquin) over an altar.

Cortile: interior courtyard of a palace.

Duomo: cathedral.

Ecce Homo: Latin for "Behold the Man"; Jesus wearing the crown of thorns.

Entablature: The section at the top of a colonnade consisting of: architrave (flat section resting on the capitals of a colonnade), frieze (decorated with carvings) and cornice (top section).

Fresco: mural painting applied over a fresh undercoat of plaster.

Gable: triangular part of an end wall carrying a sloping roof; also applied to the steeply-pitched pediments of Gothic architecture.

Greek cross: a cross floorplan with four arms of equal length.

Lesena (Lombard bands): decorative band of pilasters joined at the top by an arched frieze.

Low relief: bas-relief, carved figures slightly projecting from their background.

Maestà: Madonna in majesty, often enthroned holding Infant Jesus.

Mascaron: medallion carved in the form of a human head.

Mannerism: artistic style, mainly Italian (mid–late 16C), which broke traditional rules, to express powerful emotion.

Merlon: part of a crowning parapet between two crenellations.

Modillion: small console supporting a cornice.

Oculus: round window.

Ogee arch: a pointed arch of double curvature: Cyma Recta (convex lower curve, concave upper curve), Cyma Reversa (vice versa).

Order: system in Classical architecture ensuring a unity of style characterised by its columns (base, shaft, capital) and entablature: Doric (capitals with mouldings – the Tuscan Doric order is a simplified version), Ionic (capitals with volutes), Corinthian (capitals with acanthus leaves) and Composite, derived from Corinthian but more complex.

Pala: Italian term for altarpiece or reredos.

Palazzo: town house usually belonging to the head of a noble family; the word derives from the Palatine Hill in Rome where the Caesars resided and came to mean the residence of a person in authority.

Pediment: ornament in Classical architecture (usually triangular or semicircular) above a door or window.

Piano nobile: the principal floor of a palazzo raised one storey above ground level.

Pietà: Lamenting Virgin with the dead Christ.

Pietra serena: blue-grey stone from the quarries north of Florence.

Pieve: Romanesque parish church.

Polyptych: a painted or carved work consisting of more than three folding leaves or panels (diptych: 2 panels; triptych: 3 panels).

Portico: covered gallery with vaulting supported by columns.

Predella: panelled base of an altarpiece.

Pulpitum: front section of the stage in an antique theatre.

Reredos: ornamental structure on the wall behind and above an altar in a church; French for "behind the back".

Rustication: rough textured dressed stone.

Sfumato: atmospheric impression of perspective (invented by Leonardo da Vinci); outlines and backgrounds are blurred in a light haze.

Squinch: the projecting part of a vault supporting the vertical thrust of an overhanging section in each corner of a square tower; allows the transition from square to octagon.

Stele: a Greek word meaning an upright carved tombstone (1.50m/5ft high) carved in low relief.

Tempera: a painting technique; pigments are ground down and bound usually by means of an egg-based preparation. The technique was replaced by oil.

Tondo: a circular picture, fashionable in Italy in the mid-15C.

Trompe l'œil: two-dimensional painted decoration giving a 3D illusion of relief and perspective.

Tympanum: section above a door (or window) between the lintel and archivolt.

Volute: spiral scroll architectural ornament.

Sagrestia Nuova (1st half of 15C), San Lorenzo, Florence

Michelangelo was commissioned in 1521 by Cardinal Giuliano, the future Pope Clement VII, to build this funeral chapel, which was designed to house the tombs of the Medici family.

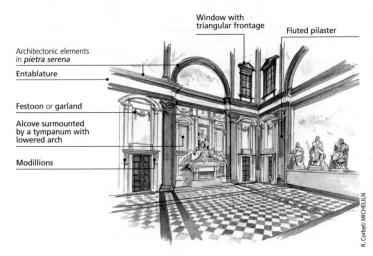

- Window with triangular frontage
- Fluted pilaster
- Architectonic elements in *pietra serena*
- Entablature
- Festoon or garland
- Alcove surmounted by a tympanum with lowered arch
- Modillions

R. Corbel/ MICHELIN

main entrance was embellished with a central portico capped by a pediment, like an ancient Roman temple. This was the first majestic country villa (see TUS-CAN VILLAS).

During this period some of the towns and cities acquired their own specific character. Florence, of course, owes much to the 15C. Pienza was the setting for the first modern town planning project (1459) designed by **Bernardo Rossellino** (1409–64), who worked with Alberti on the Palazzo Rucellai in Florence; the central square was flanked by the cathedral, the bishop's palace, the patron's palace, the people's palace and a huge well. In Montepulciano the town was renovated and given a Renaissance character by Michelozzo, Antonio da Sangallo and Vignola. The finest buildings in the main street of Monte San Savino are the work of **Sansovino**, a brilliant architect who was born in the town, as his pseudonym suggests.

SCULPTURE AND PAINTING

An impressive number of artists working in these two fields came from Florence (see FLORENCE), but in the 15C the whole Tuscan region became involved in the Renaissance movement. Although

Siena followed its own course until the 16C, it was the birthplace of **Jacopo della Quercia** (1374–1438), the inventive sculptor who created, among other works, the tomb of Ilaria del Carretto in Lucca and the Fonte Gaia in Piazza del Campo in Siena. **Francesco di Giorgio Martini** (1439–1502), painter, sculptor and architect, was born in Siena, although his main architectural works are in Urbino and in Pesaro in the Marches; **Baldassare Peruzzi** (1481–1536), who spent most of his career in Rome, was also a native of Siena.

Arezzo and Cortona were the birthplaces of two very great painters – **Piero della Francesca** (1416–92), who worked on the fresco cycle in the church of San Francesco (see AREZZO), and one of his pupils, **Luca Signorelli** (1450–1523), whose drawing techniques were powerful and incisive and who created most of the decoration in the cloisters in Monte Oliveto Maggiore. Filippino Lippi (1457–1504) was born in Prato where his father, Fra Filippo Lippi (1406–69) had painted the frescoes in the cathedral. Lucca was the birthplace of **Matteo Civitali** (1436–1501), sculptor and architect who worked on St Voult's Chapel in Lucca Cathedral, in the manner of Alberti.

The Uffizi Gallery is housed in a building commissioned in 1560 by Cosimo I for the offices ('uffizi) of the Medici administration. Giorgio Vasari (1511-74) designed this unusual building in late-Renaissance style on the site of a Romanesque church.

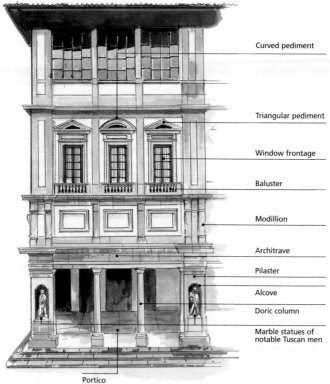

Curved pediment

Triangular pediment

Window frontage

Baluster

Modillion

Architrave

Pilaster

Alcove

Doric column

Marble statues of notable Tuscan men

Portico

R. Corbel/ MICHELIN

The Boboli Gardens, Florence

The gardens were begun in 1549 when Cosimo I commissioned the architect, sculptor and landscape gardener, Nicolo Pericoli alias Tribolo, to convert the hill behind the Pitti Palace into a vast garden. The park is a fine example of an Italian terraced garden with many different perspectives, interspersed with ramps, flights of steps and terraces and dotted with statues and fountains.

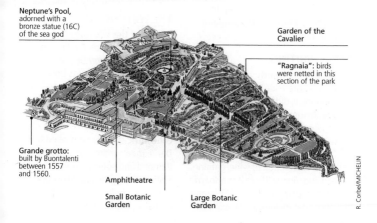

Neptune's Pool, adorned with a bronze statue (16C) of the sea god

Garden of the Cavalier

"Ragnaia": birds were netted in this section of the park

Grande grotto: built by Buontalenti between 1557 and 1560.

Amphitheatre

Small Botanic Garden

Large Botanic Garden

R. Corbel/MICHELIN

MODERN TIMES

In the 15C a few Florentine artists left the city and began to work elsewhere in Tuscany; Benozzo Gozzoli worked on the cathedral in San Gimignano and on the Camposanto in Pisa; others including Donatello and Alberti moved to neighbouring regions such as Umbria and the Marches. In the 16C the movement away from the city gathered pace. Florence had lost its political importance, while the artists she attracted moved to the new artistic centres of the day. Raphael, Michelangelo, Filippino Lippi, Giuliano and Antonio da Sangallo and others went to Rome; Leonardo da Vinci to Lombardy initially; Sangallo the Younger and Sansovino to Venetia; and Leonardo da Vinci (later), Cellini and Rosso Fiorentino to France.

In the centuries that followed, Tuscany seemed to be exhausted and provided very little in the way of new talent or artistic trends. The end of the 19C, was however marked by the Florentine Verist movement of the **Macchiaioli**, who can be compared with the French Impressionists. The 20C produced **Amadeo Modigliani**, a native of Livorno, famous for his elongated portraits and figure studies, as well as his involvement in the Paris School; and **Marino Marini**, the Florentine painter and sculptor.

In the 19C the golden age of Tuscany was rediscovered and its spontaneity, freshness and search for an ideal were promoted by the German **Nazareans**, a group nicknamed by the Florentines for their Bohemian lifestyle. There were also the English **Pre-Raphaelites**, such as Rossetti or Burne-Jones, who showed a marked preference for the Italian Primitives dating from the period before Raphael, hence their name.

Literature

Tuscany is considered the birthplace of the Italian language, and the literary sphere has, to some extent, eclipsed all others. In the Middle Ages Latin was the only written language – there was no literature in the vernacular. The appearance of poetry written in the Tuscan dialect was the first, and earliest, example of an attempt to preserve one of the many dialects spoken in the Italian peninsula. It was the first step to ensure that it became the language of all of Italy.

EARLY WRITING

From the 13C onwards various literary trends co-existed side by side. There was the allegorical, didactic style of Dante's teacher, **Brunetto Latini** (c. 1220–95). There were burlesque chronicles like those produced by **Cecco Angiolieri** (c. 1260–c. 1312) from Siena whose sonnets are a celebration of wine, gaming, women and money. There was also lyric verse inspired by the poetry of Sicily and Provence of which the greatest exponent was **Guittone d'Arezzo** (c. 1235–94). The most famous of all the schools of poetry during the 13C was the one that used what Dante called the **gentle new style** (*dolce stil nuovo*). The main poets in this movement, who opposed the earlier tradition by singing of platonic and spiritual love in verse, were **Guido Guinizzelli** (c. 1235–76) and **Guido Cavalcanti** (c. 1255–1300) – who was a Guelf and was immortalised in the *Inferno* in the *Divine Comedy* – and Dante himself.

THE WRITINGS OF DANTE

Author of the *Vita Nuova*, chronicling his love for Beatrice, the *Rime*, the *Convivio* and *De Vulgari Eloquentia*, **Dante Alighieri** (1265–1321) is best remembered for his allegorical poem of the afterlife, the *Divine Comedy*. Guided by Virgil in Hell and Purgatory and by Beatrice in Heaven, which consists of nine concentric spheres controlled by God, Dante meets many dead people, some damned and some among the chosen. Their sufferings or joys are proportionate to their behaviour during their time on Earth. It is a racy review of human nature, based on medieval imagery, and also an interesting source of historical detail. Dante, a supporter of the White Guelf faction (see HISTORY), played an active part in the politics of Florence and was appointed prior in 1300. In 1302 he was forced into exile by his opponents, the Black Guelfs, and spent the remainder of his life travelling throughout Italy until he died in Ravenna.

Machiavelli

The works of **Niccolò Machiavelli** (1469–1527), particularly *Il Principe* ("The Prince") remain of interest to scholars. He asserted that the fortunes of the state depended on a strong sovereign counterbalancing the individualistic and disordered aspirations of its citizenry.

15C–20C

The 15C was marked by the preaching of **St Bernardino of Siena** (1380–1444) and **Savonarola** (1452–98), whose campaign against the corruption of the Church was his downfall. **Leonardo da Vinci** (1452–1519) advocated scientific humanism, laying the foundations for the advances in the sciences in the 16C. **Lorenzo the Magnificent**, the epitomy of the Renaissance prince, wrote poetry and surrounded himself with philosophers such as Giovanni Pico della Mirandola and poets such as **Poliziano** (1454–94), who was born in Montepulciano. In the 16C, the *Galateo* by **Giovanni della Casa** (1503–56) laid down the etiquette then observed in every court in Europe.

In poetry **Michelangelo** (1475–1564) expressed, with the same vigour that characterises his sculptures and paintings, his torments as a man and an artist, his neo-platonistic stirrings of the heart and his later search for God. In the field of comedy, **Pietro Aretino** (1492–1556), who was born in Arezzo, produced distinguished, elegantly satirical works for numerous patrons. **Benvenuto Cellini** (1500–71), the goldsmith and sculptor who was also attracted to writing, was the first to publish an autobiography describing his life as an artist and a passionate and bellicose adventurer. **Francesco Guicciardini** (1483–1540), a Florentine diplomat, expressed his ideas in measured and carefully objective terms in his political and historical works. **Giorgio Vasari** was the forerunner of art historians through his valuable work entitled *The Lives of the Most Eminent Italian Painters, Architects and Sculptors*.

The 16C also saw the founding of the **Accademia della Crusca** (see CASTELLO), which began work on a dictionary of the Italian language in 1591.

The last of the great figures in the most intense period of creativity and inventiveness in the artistic and intellectual history of Tuscany was **Galileo** (1564–1642), who was born in Pisa. By referring to Archimedes rather than Aristotle, he made a distinction between the scientific approach to matter and the theological or philosophical approach.

In the 19C few names stand out in the literary field. Carlo Lorenzini (1826–90) achieved worldwide fame with **Pinocchio**, which he wrote under the name of Collodi, his birthplace. The first Italian to be awarded the Nobel prize, **Giosué Carducci** (1835–1907), spent his youth in Tuscany; in his *Odi Barbare* he attempted to recreate the metre of the ancient poetry which he preferred. **Curzio Malaparte** was the penname of Kurt Suckert (1898–1957) from Prato, author of *The Skin* and a writer who described post-war Italian society in the crudest of terms. Neo-realist **Vasco Pratolini** (1913–91) described everyday life in Florence, his birthplace, depicting the wealthy middle classes and people of more modest means involved in great historic events and in their own private love affairs.

The Tuscan countryside often served as the backdrop to the novels of **Carlo Cassola** (1917–87). **Indro Montanelli** worked as a journalist on *Il Corriere della Sera*, the great national daily, before becoming founder and managing director of *Il Giornale* (until 1994) and later of *La Voce*.

Music

With a few notable exceptions, Tuscany is relatively poor in musical terms compared with other Italian regions and cities.

16C: EARLY COMPOSITIONS AND MELODRAMA

Galileo's father, **Vincenzo Galilei** (c. 1520–91), was one of the first Tuscan musicians. He was a member of the *Crusca* Academy and well versed in the theory of music. He composed madrigals and pieces for the lute, and set the 23 *canti* of Dante's *Inferno* to music, although it has not survived.

Giulio Caccini (c. 1550–1618) devoted himself to *recitar cantando* at the court of the Medici. With the assistance of **Jacopo Peri** (1561–1633), another musician patronised by the Medici, he composed one of the first melodramas, *Eurydice*, which was presented at the Pitti Palace in 1600 for the marriage of Maria de' Medici and Henri IV of France.

Melodrama was in fact invented by the **Camerata fiorentina**, also known as the **Camerata de' Bardi**, a group which met at the house of Count Giovanni Bardi del Vernio and included both men of letters and others such as Vincenzo Galilei, Jacopo Peri, Giulio Caccini and Emilio de' Cavalieri, a Roman composer in the service of Cardinal Ferdinand Medici, who was in charge of entertainment at the court of the Grand Duke. The Camerata advocated a return to Greek tragedy.

In the same field Antonio Cesti (1623–69), a Franciscan monk, composed grandiose theatrical pieces, much acclaimed abroad.

17C AND 18C: FOREIGN RECOGNITION

Pistoia was the birthplace of **Bernardo Pasquini** (1637–1710), who, although little known as a player of the clavecin, was also an organist and composed many works – toccatas, partitas, suites, concertos and sonatas.

Much better known is **Jean-Baptiste Lully**, who was born in Florence in 1632. At the age of 13 he left Italy for Paris, where he died in 1687. He was composer at the court of Louis XIV and collaborated with Molière to create comedies interspersed with ballet, such as *Le Bourgeois Gentilhomme* and *Psyché*. Lully also composed many lyrical tragedies.

In his wake came the great Tuscan musicians who often worked outside their own country. **Francesco Maria Veracini** (1690–1768), a great violinist from Florence, who composed sonatas for solo violin and base continuo, was also active in Venice, Pisa, Turin, London, Düsseldorf, Dresden, and in Bohemia.

The composer and cellist, **Luigi Boccherini** (1743–1805) was born in Lucca but also worked in Vienna and Madrid. As a composer he favoured string quintets but he also wrote 30 symphonies, which include *La Maison du Diable* in D minor.

19C AND 20C: OPERA TO PIANO

In the 19C Tuscany contributed to the verist trend explored by Verdi through the works of **Giacomo Puccini** (1858–1924) who brought to it his own personal style. Born in Lucca and a resident of Torre del Lago from 1891, Puccini drew inspiration from his turbulent professional and emotional life to compose masterpieces such as the operas *La Bohème, Tosca, Madame Butterfly* and *Turandot.*

The neighbouring town of Livorno (Leghorn) was the birthplace of **Pietro Mascagni** (1863–1945), who was a teacher of harmony before his major work, *Cavalleria Rusticana*, won the Sonzogno competition, awarded by a publishing house.

Ferruccio Busoni (1866–1924), born in Empoli, was a composer and a pianist of great talent. He gained a certain recognition for his transcriptions of Bach for piano such as *La Ciaccona* taken from the 2nd partita for violin.

Florentine **Mario Castelnuovo-Tedesco** (1895–1968) began his career composing piano pieces and operas. He is renowned, however, for his guitar compositions, which number nearly 100.

Nature

The name Tuscany, first used in the 10C, is derived from the Latin word Tuscia, which was employed from the 3C onwards to describe the region situated between the Tiber and the Arno then known as Etruria, the territory of the Etruscans (who were also known as Tusci). Mountains, hills, inland basins and low coastal plains with varied types of soil are dotted across this mainly highland region, which has some of the largest stretches of woodland in Italy and an abundance of rivers and streams that run down the western slopes of the Apennines and into the Mediterranean.

LANDSCAPE

The northeastern boundary of Tuscany is clearly defined by the curve of the Apennines across the Italian peninsula, from Liguria on the Tyrrhenian coast of the Mediterranean Sea, to the Adriatic coast. This backbone of hills forms a watershed. The geological relief on the northern slopes (where the foothills lie perpendicular to the central ridge) is fairly simple but on the south-facing Tuscan side, there is a series of secondary ranges (low mountains and hills) lying parallel to the main range, creating valleys and inland basins containing the region's major cities such as Florence, Siena and Arezzo.

Like the Apennines, these low mountains are comparatively young, dating

only from the Tertiary or Caenozoic eras (65 to 2 million years ago), and consist predominantly of clay and schist, the one exception being the hard and immaculate marble of the **Apuan Alps**. The soil of this region is soft and susceptible to erosion by violent rainstorms, which often lead to the flooding of roads, fields and villages near the river beds, frequently causing dramatic landslides (*frane*) and deep gorges (*calanchi*), which alternate with the crags (*balze*) caused by erosion in the Volterra region. Less extensive landslides have formed jagged peaks (*crete*) among the hills of the Siena region and the Orcia Valley.

Countless rivers and streams rise in the Tuscan Apennines, where the highest peak is **Mount Cimone** (alt 2 165m/ 7 103ft). The range is fringed by small lush valleys – (from north to south) the **Lunigiana** region traversed by the River Magra; the **Garfagnana** region watered by the Serchio; the **Mugello** region containing the Sieve (a tributary of the Arno); the **Casentino** region traversed by the upper reaches of the Arno; the north end of the **Val Tiberina**, where the River Tiber (*Tevere*) rises on the border with Umbria.

Further from the Apennine backbone are folds of soft sandstone and schist forming a series of uplands that vary in appearance from the gently-rolling Florentine countryside to the bare limestone peaks of the Sienese Hills.

A number of rivers – Elsa, Cecina, Ombrone – also rise in these upland regions.

Countryside near Pienza
B. Morandi/ MICHELIN

Near the coast the landscape opens out into a wide coastal plain, formed mainly by alluvial deposits from Tuscany's rivers. The Tuscan Archipelago and Monte Argentario peninsula are the last outcrops of the Apennine folds extending into the sea.

The chief delights of the Tuscan countryside are its great variety, its human scale and its abundant vegetation – from the coniferous forests of the high mountains to the olive groves, vineyards and verdant pastures in the valleys.

ARNO BASIN

The River Arno (241km/150mi long), the major Tuscan river, rises on Mount Falterona on the border with Romagna and irrigates the alluvial land on either side of its long course. After flowing through the **Casentino** region, it skirts the south end of the **Pratomagno** range in a deep meander where it is joined, not far from Arezzo, by the fast-flowing Chiana River (one section of which has been canalised – Maestro Canal). The river then flows north through the **Upper Arno Valley** (*Valdarno Superiore*), its course bounded to the west by the Chianti Hills.

When the river reaches Florence, the valley suddenly opens out into the **Lower Arno Valley** (*Valdarno Inferiore*), widening until it reaches the sea. Most of the agricultural and industrial activity is concentrated in this area; it is also the most densely-populated part of the region. The main sectors of employment are intensive and specialised farming (especially around Pistoia, where the maritime climate has favoured the planting of huge nurseries producing fruit trees and house plants), chemical industries and glass-making in Pisa, textiles in Prato and engineering in Florence (where there is still an industrial infrastructure based on old crafts – leather goods, shoes, etc).

APUAN ALPS

The Apuan Alps north of the Arno glisten with the white marble that made the name "Carrara" so famous.

Blocks and slabs of this marble can be seen piled high on the wharves of Marina di Carrara.

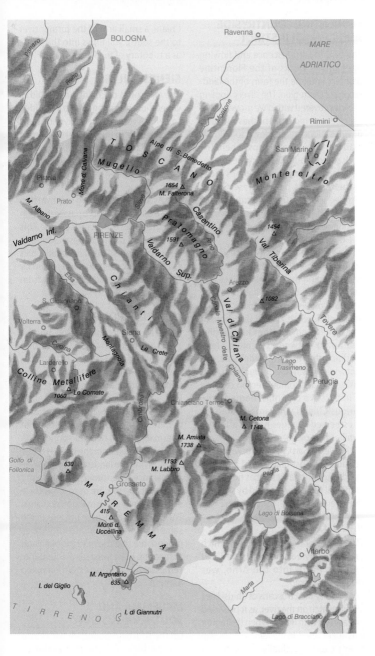

At the foot of the mountains lies the splendid sandy shoreline of **Versilia.** From June to September the packed rows of beach furniture stretch as far as the eye can see. Viareggio is undoubtedly the most popular resort.

The very mild climate is ideal for flower growing.

At the southern end of this flat coastal area lies Livorno (Leghorn), the only real commercial port in Tuscany, with major shipyards and oil refineries.

FLORENTINE COUNTRYSIDE AND CHIANTI DISTRICT

The serenity, irridescence and flowing lines of the works of the Florentine painters emulate the form of the landscapes of this region. The silvery rippling hillsides covered with olive groves, interspersed with mulberry bushes and rows of vines, slope gently down to fields of maize or corn. The hilltops, where the dark slender outlines of cypress trees occasionally contrast with clumps of oak or chestnut trees, provide the setting for fortified villages such as Monteriggioni or for majestic old farmhouses (*villas*) dominated by a large central tower used as a dovecot.

A hazy mist often hangs over the region, sometimes persisting throughout the day, softening the distant outlines and drawing a veil of pearly light over the brightly coloured, rolling hills.

South of Florence, on the threshold of southern Tuscany, rise the **Chianti Hills**, extending between the main Siena road and the Autostrada del Sole, the motorway which runs through the Arno Valley. This welcoming region consists of impressive clay hills, home to the famous Chianti vineyards, producers of esteemed vintages named after the families that own them.

To the west is San Gimignano, which has remained almost unchanged since the Middle Ages. Today it still has numerous medieval towers, identified by some as the forerunners of the skyscraper.

VAL DI CHIANA

The course of the River Chiana, which originally flowed south into the Tiber and not north into the Arno, was reversed in the 16C.

In Antiquity the Etruscans of Chiusi kept a close watch on the river, as it provided an easy link with Rome. When the region was abandoned in the Middle Ages, the river's course gradually blocked with alluvial deposits and stagnated. The Chiana Valley then turned into a vast and unhealthy area of marshland.

In 1551 most of the water was drained off through a canal (Canale Maestro Chiana) that ran north into the Arno. The Chiani, a small arm of the former river to the south, still flows into the Tiber, as a tributary of the Paglia.

SIENESE HILLS

The hills south of Chianti are devoid of vegetation, revealing their pale golden soil which turns to grey beyond Siena. This city is set in the heart of this serene pastoral landscape. Like Florence and Pisa, Siena, the home of the Palio horse race, constitutes a major tourist attraction.

The Asciano road leading southwest to Monte Oliveto Maggiore passes through strange limestone landscapes. This is the region of the Sienese *Crete*, line upon line of desolate, arid, chalky hills streaked with deep ravines created by the surface water draining down from the peaks.

METALLIFEROUS HILLS

Between the Florence region and the sea is a zone of low, squat yet forbidding hills. As their name suggests, they are rich in iron ore and also contain deposits of other minerals such as lead, copper, zinc. In the area around Larderello, white steam from the borax (a mineral used in the production of pharmaceuticals) rich hot springs (*soffioni*), is emitted from the bowels of the earth, giving the landscape a dreamlike appearance. The springs, which colour the landscape red, are used to produce electricity in geothermal power plants. The **Isle of Elba** offshore belongs to the same mountain chain. Its iron mines produce ore that is sent to the mainland to feed the blast furnaces of Piombino. Ferries to the island leave from Piombino harbour.

MAREMMA AND SOUTHERN TUSCANY

On the southern boundary with Lazio are the first volcanic mountains of central Italy, the highest being **Monte Amiata** (1 738m/5 702ft). The mountains are rich in cinnabar, which is used to produce mercury.

The austere landscape provides the backdrop to the **Maremma**, a region

Olives and Olive Oil

One of the main features of the countryside in Tuscany is the olive tree. Olive oil is always in abundant supply and of excellent quality; no table is ever without it.

According to custom, the olive harvest, known locally as the *brucatura*, takes place on the Day of the Dead at the beginning of November. The first olives, which are picked from the tree by hand, are for the table. The fruit picked up off the ground in nets is pressed using millstones. Only the oil obtained from this type of pressing, which does not include the addition of chemicals and complies with the statutory manufacturing regulations, can be classed as extra-virgin (extra vergine).

Tuscan olive oil is green. In most cases it is unfiltered and should be used within 18 months of harvesting. Its characteristic piquant flavour, which is sometimes erroneously considered a defect, is in fact proof of the freshness and strength of the oil.

of melancholy beauty, erstwhile land of evil spells and dark legends but now an area of quiet rusticity. It has herds of horses and buffalo, once raised there in the wild under the watchful eye of herdsmen (*butteri*). Under the agrarian reforms introduced in 1950, these regions, which were formerly the property of a few big city landowners, benefited from land improvement which completely altered their appearance. They were reallocated to farmers from other regions, whose farmsteads are now dotted across the area.

The land is cultivated in a more rational manner (cereal and fodder crops, market-gardening, rice, sunflowers) and modern farming co-operatives have been set up in the region. Cattle are raised for dairy products, supplying cities such as Florence or Rome, and sheep farming has produced a delicious ewe's milk cheese called *pecorino*.

TUSCAN VILLAS

Tuscany's villas date mainly from the Renaissance period and were once aristocratic residences. They were purchased or built by the members of such prestigious families as the Medici, Rospigliosi, Chigi or Ricasoli. They provided a retreat during hot summer days from the stifling heat of the cities like Florence, Pistoia, Lucca, Siena, where the families spent the rest of the year.

Most of them are fairly simply and rigorously designed and all had huge gardens, some of them to magnificent designs. They regained popularity in the 17C when many were extended and lavishly decorated with internal frescoes. The plainest villas are to be found in the countryside around Florence where some still have their medieval structure. Around Lucca on the other hand, the façades were embellished with loggias and wide bays, sculptures and balustrades, in the 17C. In the Siena district the villas blend into the countryside, underlining their simple design through the use of natural materials, such as undressed brick and stone.

FLORA AND FAUNA

Tuscany is the most densely wooded region in Italy. The forests (approximately 1 000 000ha/2 471 000 acres) contain an extremely wide variety of vegetation, from subtropical species in certain coastal areas and on the islands to alpine plants on the upper slopes of the Apennines.

TERRACED VEGETATION

Near the sea, pine trees reign supreme, spreading out into expanses of well-protected forests (Versilian and Etruscan Rivieras and the Maremma). Two varieties predominate; the **maritime pine**, which has a conical head and long straight trunk; and the **umbrella pine** with its flattened crown. The umbrella pine has been cultivated since ancient times for its edible oil-bearing pine kernels.

The **cypress** has been widely planted for its ornamental appearance and usage as a windshield for crops. It can be found in the lower regions of the Mugello Valley, the Sienese Hills, the Orcia Valley and, more especially, on the hills of the Chianti region of which it is one of the symbols, together with the vine and the olive tree.

For many centuries, the low-altitude areas were covered in coppices, artificially maintained woodlands. Many coppices have now declined after some 30 years of neglect, giving way to *macchia* vegetation consisting of trees and shrubs, mostly evergreens, such as the **holm oak,** or sub-evergreen species, like the **cork oak**. The dark or grey-green foliage and twisted trunks of the trees give the landscape an untamed appearance. The *macchia* vegetation also includes a wide range of thorny and aromatic bushes with tough, glossy leaves such as heather, bramble, butcher's broom (knee-holly), hawthorn, juniper and rosemary. In places where the *macchia* itself peters out, there is a poorer version of the vegetation known as *gariga*, which is generally found in particularly arid areas where plants such as lentiscus, myrtle, cistus and rosemary are able to survive.

Growing near these plants are agaves and prickly pears (common on the Isle of Elba), both of which were imported from the Americas in the 16C.

In the low-lying areas there is a significant amount of natural pastureland and meadow, as well as land devoted to cereal crops, market gardening, vegetable farming and horticulture. Intensive farming extends up to the limit beyond which olive trees will not grow (alt 600–700m/1 970–2 300ft). Together with **vines**, **olive trees** are the main plants on the hillsides. They are grown for the production of table olives and olive oil.

Chestnut trees, which can grow at altitudes of up to 1 000m/3 280ft, can be found throughout Tuscany, particularly in the woodland on the Isle of Elba, in the Mugello Region and on Monti Pisani and Monte Amiata. The thickest chestnut groves are to be found in the Mugello and Casentino Regions.

Beeches and **fir trees** mark the upper tree line (altitude 1 000–1 700m/3 280–5 580ft) on Monte Amiata and the Apennines. Magnificent coniferous forests cover the area around Camaldoli, Vallombrosa and Abetone. Beeches can be found growing alongside numerous other varieties such as maple, ash, hornbeam, poplar and the Turkey Oak.

PADÙLE

In Tuscany, a swamp (*palude*) is called padùle (inversion of the final consonants). Although the swamps have all but disappeared as a result of land improvement in unhealthy areas, the region still includes the Padùle di Raspollino (northwest of Grosseto), the Padùle di Fuccecchio (between Florence and Pisa) and the entire area around the Massaciuccoli Lake, which is considered locally as a **padùle**.

Sweet chestnut tree

R. Corbel/ MICHELIN

Olive

R. Corbel/ MICHELIN

FAUNA

Tuscany has retained a wide variety of fauna. However, here as elsewhere, wildlife is under threat from hunting, pollution and the impact of technological progress. The creation of nature reserves has been counter-balanced by the recent reclamation of former marshland. Native species have declined as their natural habitat has been eroded.

Among the **large mammals**, wolves can still be found in the Apennines and the upper valley of the Tiber. Stags, imported from Syria during the era of the grand dukes, survive in the Casentino Valley and in the Maremma region along with other members of the deer family. There are also very large numbers of deer in the pine forests of San Rossore, Migliarino, Capalbio and Monte Argentario.

The wild goat, an endangered species in Tuscany, survives only on the island of Montecristo where it is highly protected. The wild boar, the emblem of the Maremma, inhabits many areas of scrubland and pine forest in Tuscany. It plays an important role in keeping vegetation under control.

The most common **small mammals** in the region are the hare and the wild rabbit, which is particularly prolific. The fox, their main predator, is capable of adapting to all types of environment. In the dunes of the Maremma region in particular, wild rabbits are preyed upon by polecats, weasels, martens and stone martens and even a number of nocturnal birds of prey. Indeed it is the presence of large numbers of rabbits that ensures the survival of these predators. The pine forests are also home to martens and stone martens as well as hedgehogs, porcupines and badgers. Wildcats and polecats can be seen in the shrubby rocky areas of the Maremma region.

The otter lives in the swamps (*paduli*) and on the banks of the major rivers, co-existing with the Old World beaver. For a long time the otter was prized for its fur but it is now an endangered species as a result of land development along the river banks. Beavers, on the other hand, have adapted to such changes.

Owing to its varied relief and abundance of rivers and streams, Tuscany harbours numerous **species of birds**, including migrants such as passerines (thrushes, swallows, magpies, nightingales, kingfishers), birds of prey (golden eagles, falcons, buzzards, kites, owls), web-footed species (cormorants, mallard ducks, wild geese) and waders (herons, cranes, egrets, storks).

Livestock Farming includes the white beef cattle of the Val di Chiana, a long-established breed known as *chianina*; its extremely tender meat is famous throughout Italy.

Cypress

Umbrella Pine

R. Corbel/ MICHELIN

Brunelleschi's Santa Maria del Fiore and the view of Florence
B. Pérousse/ MICHELIN

FLORENCE★★★ *Firenze*

Florence has reigned as one of Italy's most prestigious cities since the 15C. It was here that the first flames of Humanism and the Renaissance were ignited. Florence is the birthplace of Dante, the cradle of the Italian language and was the proving ground for many of history's most notable painters, sculptors and architects, including Michelangelo and Leonardo da Vinci.

Florence's austere beauty and narrow streets are ill-suited to dense traffic. Those who succeed in forgetting the hustle and bustle will find a rich offering of museums, churches, and mansions filled with countless masterpieces and wonderful shops. It has been said that the god who created Florence's famous **countryside★★★** – one of the most noble and subtle landscapes anywhere – must have been a Florentine artist.

THE CITY TODAY

Florence has long depended on its legacy as the birthplace of the Renaissance for marketing itself, particularly to the millions of foreign tourists who swarm its streets and fill its coffers year after year. But the city's dependence on tourism has also meant a reduction in the native population, who for the last decade has been relocating to the suburbs to escape the crowds. Now, as the global economic downturn takes effect, Florentines are wondering whether it was wise to forsake the future for the past. In 2008, Florence saw its tourism numbers drop by almost half as more American and British visitors stayed home. The tourism slump has also resulted in layoffs in the hospitality industry as well as the shuttering of traditional businesses, from boutiques to butcher shops. How Florence emerges from this crisis may depend on its leadership. The summer 2009 mayoral election brought the youthful Matteo Renzi to the Palazzo Vecchio; the previous mayor had ruled since 1999.

A BIT OF HISTORY
Roman Origins

The Italiots are said to have settled on the site of Florence between the 10C and 8C BC. They were soon outnumbered by the Etruscans, who preferred the hilltops of Fiesole. In 59 BC Julius Caesar founded a colony on the riverbank to control the Arno crossing and the traffic along the Via Flaminia, the road which ran north from Rome to Gaul. The colony was set up in the spring; its name, Florentia, was reminiscent of floral games (*ludi florales*) or flower fields (*arva florentia*).

The Rise of a City

Florence rose to a position of power in Tuscany fairly late in the city's history. For many years Fiesole and later Lucca were predominant. Early in the

Campanile, Duomo and Palazzo Vecchio mark the city's skyline

B. Juge/ MICHELIN

11C Count Ugo, Marquess of Tuscany, transferred his residence from Lucca to Florence, where he built an abbey.

In the second half of the century, Countess Matilda, who supported Pope Gregory VII in his struggle against the Holy Roman Emperor, ruled this area. During this period Florence began to acquire power and influence. When Matilda died in 1115 the city had already gained a degree of independence which was to increase during the 12C. It was at this time that the two Romanesque masterpieces, the Church of San Miniato al Monte and the Baptistery, were built. It was also at this time (1125) that Florence annihilated its rival, Fiesole. A more important contemporary event was the addition of a third class of citizen – the wealthy merchants who provided the city with an extraordinary level of prosperity, which endured for several centuries.

The Middle Ages

The Power of Money – As trades and crafts began to develop, their practitioners were organised into influential **guilds** (*arti*), which were to form the basis of legislative power when Florence declared itself a Free Commune in the late 12C.

In the 13C the city enjoyed an extraordinary level of economic development, owing to its wool and, later, its silk industries. Officially it had seven "Major Guilds", five "Medium Guilds" and nine "Minor Guilds" (see p93).

In the following century the weavers' guild (*Arte della Lana*), whose mansion can still be seen near the Church of Orsanmichele, and the guild whose members finished imported cloth (*Arte di Calimala*), employed between them approximately one-third of the city's population and exported fine quality cloth to all the major trading centres in Europe. Indeed, its reputation spread as far as the Middle East.

In addition to the craftsmen and merchants, a third category of Florentines did much to increase the wealth of the city. Following in the footsteps of the Lombard and Jewish moneylenders,

Florentine **bankers** became famous throughout Europe. In 1269 they instigated the very first bills of exchange, which were to give considerable impetus to trade in Florence and Europe. At almost the same period they minted the famous gold florin, which bore the Florentine lily on one side and the effigy of the city's patron saint, John the Baptist, on the other. This coin was to become international currency until it was overtaken in the late 15C by the Venetian ducat.

The banking tradition was continued by the Bardi Peruzzi, who advanced enormous sums of money to King Edward III of England at the beginning of the Hundred Years War. They were joined in the world of finance by the Pitti, Strozzi, Pazzi and Medici.

Internal Strife – Guelfs and Ghibellines – The economic "miracle" was all the more amazing given the violent feuds that raged not only between Florence and other major towns in Tuscany but also between various Florentine factions within the city.

It was in the 13C that the Guelfs, supporters of the Pope, and the Ghibellines, supporters of the Holy Roman Emperor, first appeared on the scene. At first the Guelfs were victorious but the Ghibellines set up alliances with other cities that were opposed to Florence, in particular with Siena, and defeated the Guelfs at Montaperti (⚲ see CHIANTI) in 1260. Despite their crushing defeat, the Guelfs regained their strength and in 1266 they defeated the Ghibellines and returned to Florence.

Under the Guelfs the city became a republic with a democratic constitution ruled from the Palazzo Vecchio by a government mainly composed of representatives (*Priori*) of the guilds.

Divisions then began to appear between Black and White Guelfs, with the latter breaking away from the Papacy. Owing to this tragic development, Dante, a member of the White Guelf faction, was banished for life from his native city in January 1302.

In 1348 the Plague killed more than one-half of the population of Florence, thus putting an end to internal strife.

The Medici

In the 14C several members of the land-owning Medici family moved to Florence. Although all of them were little-known merchants and modest money-changers, this family was to give the city its leaders for the next three centuries. The Medici also played a vital part in shaping the city's destiny, and several of them were influential in the world of literature, the arts and the sciences.

The Century of the Medici – Giovanni di Bicci, a prosperous banker and founder of the dynasty, became a leading citizen in his home town by the time he died in 1429. His son, **Cosimo the Elder**, the "Great Merchant of Florence", was then aged 40. He turned the family enterprise into the largest of its kind in Florence, gave the wool and silk industries an "international" dimension and conducted the bank's activities on a European scale. When he came to power, the prosperity of Florence had enabled the city to gain control of several towns in Tuscany and, with the surrender of Pisa in 1406, Florence became a maritime power. This was a golden era for Florence.

Although Cosimo never held any official position, he acted like a statesman, virtually ruling the city for 30 years. His greatest merit, however, remains his active participation in the arts. He was a major patron and encouraged the spread of Humanism by attracting to his circle the very best of Florentine intellectuals and artists, including Brunelleschi, Donatello, the della Robbias, Paolo Uccello, Filippo Lippi, Andrea del Castagno, Benozzo Gozzoli and Fra Angelico. He set up the Platonic Academy and a number of libraries including the famous Laurenziana Library. He had a great love of building and he commissioned numerous major constructions or improvements. When he died in 1464, the Florentines had the inscription *Pater Patriae* (Father of his Country) engraved on his tomb.

His son, Piero I, also known as **Piero il Gottoso** (Peter the Gouty), was a sickly man who had inherited neither his father's political skills nor his business acumen and he survived him for only five years. His marriage to Lucrezia Tornabuoni, however, allied the Medici dynasty to one of the greatest families in Florence.

Piero's eldest son, **Lorenzo the Magnificent** (1449–92), was the most famous of the Medici. Although he was only 20 when his father died, he began to direct the affairs of Florence in accordance with the family tradition. He ruled like a prince, was outstanding for his skilful diplomacy and, like his grandfather, he succeeded in maintaining the dominant position of Florence in Italy and the balance of power between the Papacy and the various States. And, as a lover of the arts and a talented writer of verse, he was a supreme example of a Renaissance man. On the other hand, he proved to be less than able in managing the commercial and banking business, and this led to the ruin of the Medici financial empire. The death of Lorenzo the Magnificent in 1492 marked the end of the "century of

The "Guilds" in Florence in the Late 13C

The classification of the craft guilds into three categories (major, middle and minor) took place from 1282 to 1293. Initially there was only one guild, for merchants, named after the street where they conducted their business – Calimala. Gradually various crafts set up their own guilds, each with its own coat of arms; the arms below are those of the major craft guilds.

Leading merchants

Wool-workers

Silk-workers

Money-changers

Doctors and apothecaries

Furriers

Magistrates and lawyers

The five middle guilds were swordsmiths and armor-makers; locksmiths; shoemakers; harness-makers and saddlers; tanners and curriers.

The nine minor guilds were linen-drapers and clothiers; blacksmiths; masons and carpenters; joiners; oven-men and bakers; butchers; wine merchants; oil merchants; hoteliers.

the Medici" but also the beginning of a new era of discovery.

Savonarola – Girolamo Savonarola (1452–98), a Dominican monk from Ferrara who became prior of St Mark's monastery, was to cause the downfall of the Medici by taking advantage of a difficult period when the people of Florence were faced with crumbling republican institutions, and France and Spain were at war for control of Europe. The fanatical, ascetic monk gained power in 1493, when he preached a terrifying and powerful sermon from the pulpit of the cathedral, denouncing the pleasures of the senses and love of the arts. Savonarola was also a critic of the papacy of Alexander VI, and frequently cited it for corruption.

In 1497 Savonarola organised a "bonfire of vanities" in Piazza della Signoria.

Masks, wigs, musical instruments, books of poetry and works of art perished in the flames. Not long after that episode, the Pope excommunicated Savonarola and convinced the Florentine government to condemn the monk to death. In 1498, Savonarola himself was burned at the stake on the very spot where the bonfire had taken place.

The Return of the Medici

After several popular uprisings and several short-lived attempts to govern, the Medici officially returned to power in Florence in 1530, supported by Charles V, the Holy Roman Emperor.

Alessandro, Lorenzo's grandson, took the title of Duke of Florence but he was murdered in 1537 by his cousin Lorenzino, a member of the cadet branch of the Medici family. It was this branch of

93

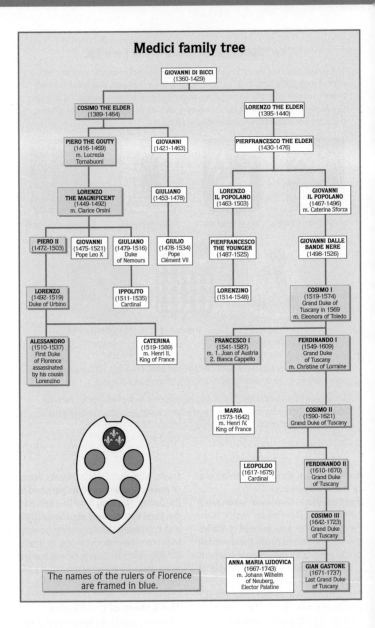

Medici family tree

The names of the rulers of Florence are framed in blue.

the family, descended from Giovanni de' Bicci, that was to regain power.

Cosimo I (1519–74) was the son of the military leader (*condottiere*), Giovanni dalle Bande Nere (John of the Black Bands, who was the great-grandson of Cosimo the Elder's brother). He was only 18 years old when he took power but his statesman-like qualities soon became

apparent. His was an authoritarian regime both in terms of administration and policy. Yet he gave Florence back the sparkle that it had lost and brought it renewed prosperity. He created a Tuscan state, keeping the reigns of government firmly in his own hands.

In 1555 he defeated Siena, thus achieving (except for Lucca) the unification of

Tuscany, which became a Grand Duchy in 1569. He also sought to protect his State from external predators such as Charles V, Philip II of Spain and the Papacy. Following in the tradition set by the senior branch of the family, he became a patron of the arts and he extended his protection to sculptors such as Giovanni da Bologna and Benvenuto Cellini and to the painter Bronzino. In 1539 he married the daughter of the Viceroy of Naples, **Eleonora of Toledo**, an intelligent and beautiful woman, whose portrait was painted by Vasari and Bronzino.

The first of their 11 children to reign was **Francesco I** (1541–87) who was more enthusiastic about science and alchemy than political power. He married Joan of Austria, daughter of Emperor Maximilian, and they had one daughter, Maria, the future Queen of France.

His younger brother, **Ferdinando I** (1549–1609), was the last enterprising member of the Medici family. He ensured the prosperity of the State by marrying the French princess, Christine of Lorraine, but his male descendants could not prevent the decline of the Grand Duchy of Tuscany. The last in the female line of this extraordinary family was Anna Maria Ludovica. Upon her death in 1743, she bequeathed the Medici family's vast art collection to Florence.

The Post-Medici Period

The Grand Duchy passed to the Princes of Lorraine, who continued in possession until the arrival of Napoleon in 1799. He renamed Tuscany the Kingdom of Etruria and made Florence its capital (1801–07) before turning the city into the main town in the French *département* of Arno (1807–09). Finally he restored the Grand Duchy and placed his sister, Elsa, at its head. She was forced to flee from Florence in 1814.

Lorraine then regained possession and the Prince of Lorraine remained Grand Duke of Tuscany until 1859.

In 1860 Florence was conquered by the House of Savoy and integrated into the Kingdom of Italy, of which it was the capital from 1865 to 1870.

ART & ARCHITECTURE
Florentine Painting

From the 13C to the 16C, Florence saw an extraordinary development of the visual arts, which reached its apotheosis during the century of the Medici.

The characteristics of the Florentine School are the search for beauty of form, a preoccupation with evoking an idealised natural environment, a preference for balanced composition and the importance of perspective.

Glimmerings of the Renaissance – The first painter to point Florentine and Tuscan art in this direction was **Cimabue** (1240–1302). He gave his paintings greater humanity through the facial expressions of his figures and by modelling their bodies to give an impression of volume. His pupil and successor was **Giotto** (1266–1337), whose aim was to represent volume in real space and to paint whole scenes (rather than a *Maestà* or a Crucifixion). His figures were draped with grand garments to create a solid mass. And, the gesture and visual expression in his paintings were intended to emphasise the central point in a composition. Among his successors were **Taddeo Gaddi**, **Maso di Banco** (also known as Giottino) and **Bernardo Daddi**.

A Return to Older Values – In the second half of the 14C, every level of society, including art, was affected by the period of crisis which followed the ravages of the Plague in 1348. When **Andrea da Firenze** painted the frescoes in the Spanish Chapel (in the cloisters of Santa Maria Novella) c. 1365, he opted for a style of composition that was no longer realistic and narrative but dogmatic and extremely animated, typical of the 13C.

Very few paintings survive from **Orcagna**, who worked from 1344 to 1368, but he used the same basic concepts in his works, such as the reredos in Santa Maria Novella. In the late 14C the narrative style returned, embellished with the beauty of the international Gothic movement which was popular in Siena. **Agnolo Gaddi** (c. 1345–96), Taddeo's son, and **Lorenzo Monaco**

(c. 1370–post 1422) worked in the same style. Monaco, who was a Camaldolite monk in Florence, began by illuminating manuscripts before painting altarpieces in which he expressed a blandness that was typical of the Gothic period. **Masolino da Panicale** (1383–1447), Masaccio's master, who was faithful to the decorative techniques of the Sienese School, gave greater importance to the representation of volume and space.

Perspective, Volume and Structure: a Design Revolution – A precursor of the technique of foreshortening, **Masaccio** (1401–28) undertook a study of space and the play of light across volume. Assisted by his friend, Brunelleschi, he was the first person to define a rigorous, scientific form of architectural perspective.

This determination to express the structure of volume reached its height with **Paolo Uccello** (1397–1475) and **Andrea del Castagno** (1423–57). Uccello reduced form to its purest expression, drowning it in light until he achieved an almost abstract use of colour. This is evident in his frescoes in the Chiostro Verde in Santa Maria Novella and his reredos depicting the *Battle of San Romano* in the Uffizi Gallery. These two artists, who both possessed superb drawing skills, created *trompe-l'oeil* sculptures (see *SANTA MARIA DEL FIORE and the UFFIZI GALLERY*).

Painters of Light and Colour – Some painters who adopted the technique of spatial construction continued to make use of pastel shades, detailed ornamentation or dense composition. The arrival of **Domenico Veneziano** (c. 1400–61) from Venice c. 1435 helped them to find a middle course between the stolid drawings of the Early Renaissance and the Gothic-style mannerisms of the heirs of the 14C. He showed the artists of Florence how to use oils and organise space. In this way he reinforced the style of those painters who inclined towards more gentle representations, such as the Dominican monk **Fra Angelico** (1387–1455), who used the new architectural vocabulary to create a very fresh approach to aesthetics.

Narrative Artists – The quietly graceful, descriptive trend led a number of artists to explore the field of narrative painting. From his teacher, Fra Angelico, **Benozzo Gozzoli** (1420–97) inherited a taste for luminous colours, exquisite detail and strong compositions buzzing with activity. Then came **Domenico Ghirlandaio** (1449–94), who excelled in the descriptive style and became a chronicler of Florentine society during the last quarter of the 15C. The arrival in Florence in 1482 of the Portinari triptych by Flemish artist Hugo Van der Goes (*Uffizi Gallery*) had a profound effect on other artists of the day. Apart from the technique of oil painting, of which they had until then seen very few examples, the most outstanding feature of the work was the realism of the figures and the background.

Among those who made even less use of colour than Ghirlandaio were **Antonio Pollaiolo** (1431–98) and his brother, **Piero** (1443–96). Antonio had a vigorous drawing technique, and was interested in conveying a sense of movement and illustrating physical and spiritual contortions. Even the backgrounds of his paintings were filled with sinuous movement, so that his compositions give an impression of great dynamism.

Painters of Grace – The last artistic trend in the 15C focused on ethereal beauty filled with a sense of purity, innocence and delicacy. The artist who was the precursor of this trend was **Filippo Lippi** (1406–69), a monk and pupil of Masaccio, who completed his master's cycle of frescoes in the Brancacci Chapel in Santa Maria del Carmine. His portraits of the Virgin Mary dressed in transparent veils are precursors of works by his pupil, Sandro Botticelli, who taught Lippi's son, **Filippino Lippi** (1459–1504). The apogee (and also the decline) of the Early Renaissance was marked by **Botticelli** (1444–1510). The main feature of his work is its sensuality but the artistic experience of the century in which he lived is also evident in his fine, incisive drawing, his sense of background and landscape and the studied poses of his figures draped in flimsy garments, with veils fluttering in a gentle breeze.

Masters of the High Renaissance – Although the High Renaissance reached maturity in Rome, it was in the artist studios in Florence that it first took root. **Leonardo da Vinci** (1452–1519) began learning his craft in the studio of the painter and bronze sculptor Verrocchio; **Michelangelo** (1475–1564) was one of Ghirlandaio's pupils; and **Raphael** (1483–1520) came from Urbino to follow his master, **Perugino**.

Leonardo, who came from the nearby town Vinci, was particularly successful in synthesising the art forms developed by his predecessors while enriching the art of painting with his knowledge of various scientific disciplines. His paintings (*Uffizi Gallery, Room 15*) are designed to express perfect beauty rendered through technical mastery. There is perfection in the landscape, the composition, the balance of colours and the architectural and atmospheric perspective (through the use of *sfumato*, which blurs outlines and suffuses backgrounds in a bluish light). Only Michelangelo could rival him, although he was convinced that the supreme art form was sculpture rather than painting. Raphael followed the example of these masters and sought consummate beauty, first in the manner of Perugino using softness and balance, then through the use of Leonardo's *sfumato* technique and finally by acquiring Michelangelo's knowledge of anatomy and vigorous creative skills.

Classicism and Mannerism – Although overshadowed by Leonardo da Vinci and Raphael, **Fra Bartolomeo** (1475–1517), a Dominican and follower of Savonarola, and **Andrea del Sarto** (1486–1531) – from Florence–represented Florentine Classicism, the final expression of the real Renaissance. Del Sarto was a brilliant colourist and, like Fra Bartolomeo, very fond of *sfumato*. He paved the way for Mannerism by showing an interest in some of his works in the expression of feelings (*The Last Supper* in San Salvi). The torments of the soul became more important than the ideal of beauty and the corresponding impression of timelessness.

His pupil, **Pontormo** (1494–1556), gave full vent to his natural anxiety in tormented works. This generation of artists was enormously affected by the paintings of Michelangelo, who painted the ceiling of the Sistine Chapel between 1508 and 1512. The power of his human figures, their sculpture-like positions and his vivid colours were all imitated. The result depended on the sensitivity of the artist.

Rosso Fiorentino (1494–1540) revealed his morbid anxiety in tortured works, elongated figures and strident colours. The second generation of Mannerists moved away from this uncontrolled sensitivity and, conversely, restricted themselves to a solemnity that was almost painful. **Bronzino** (1503–72), who was trained by Pontormo, was official portrait painter to the Grand Duchy after 1539. His vigorous, rather cold drawings and vivid colours show the continuing influence of the major artistic figure of the day, Michelangelo.

Vasari, who chronicled Italian art from Cimabue to his own time, was court painter to the Medici and created all the grand decors in the Palazzo Vecchio, including the allegories and the historical and mythological paintings.

Architecture and Sculpture

The architects of the day created a style based on restrained grandeur. The proportions were harmonious and the decor in religious buildings consisted of geometric motifs picked out in coloured marble while the mansions were decorated with rustication and projecting cornices.

The Middle Ages – Both the magnificent Baptistery and the Church of San Miniato al Monte date from the Romanesque period. Their simple layouts and harmonious geometric decor of coloured marble made them reference works for the movement known as the Pre-Renaissance.

The appearance of the city as it is today owes something to the Gothic style. The blossoming of new religious orders led to several Gothic-style buildings, including Santa Maria Novella for the Dominicans, Santa Croce for the Franciscans, Santa Annunziata for the Servites, Ognissanti for the Humiliati, Santo Spirito for the Augustinians, Holy Trinity for the Vallombrosians and Santa Maria del Carmine for the Carmelites. There were three main architectural designers in the Gothic period. **Arnolfo di Cambio** (c. 1250–1302) created the initial plans for the cathedral and, according to Vasari, for Santa Croce; he was also director of works at the Palazzo Vecchio between 1299 and 1302. **Giotto** built the bell tower (from 1334 onwards). **Orcagna** (1308–68), a pupil of Arnolfo di Cambio and Giotto, was the designer of the Tabernacle in Orsanmichele, a building on which work began in 1336 and which marked the beginnings of an architectural style in which prestige and decoration took precedence over utility. The Loggia della Signoria with its extremely wide arches is a fine example of this style.

Blossoming of the Renaissance – The beginning of this new era in Florence can, for the sake of convenience, be dated to 1401. This was the year in which **Lorenzo Ghiberti** (1378–1455) and Filippo Brunelleschi, among others, took part in the competition to choose the designer of the second doorway to the Baptistery (*see Battistero*). When Ghiberti was chosen, Brunelleschi felt constrained to give up sculpture, although he had trained as a goldsmith. Ghiberti was later chosen to design the third doorway, which Michelangelo called the Gate of Paradise because of its great beauty.

Following his failure to secure the commission, **Brunelleschi** (1377–1446) left for Rome and returned there several times in the following years. He became an enthusiast for Classical architecture, for the ruins of ancient Rome and for their gigantic scale. He was the first person to understand these structures and to adapt his findings to the needs of his day. The work that revealed his talent and the extent of his knowledge was the dome of Florence Cathedral (*see Duomo*). Nobody else at the beginning of the 15C would have been capable of erecting such a dome without the support of flying buttresses. Brunelleschi, whose building technique was rational and based on calculation and mathematical perspective, is considered the founder of modern architecture.

Leon Battista Alberti (1404–72) was the other great architect of the early 15C. He was a scholar and a humanist who wrote a number of treatises on painting, sculpture and architecture. Alberti shared with Brunelleschi a love of simple geometric forms, as is evident in his design for the west front of Santa Maria Novella. It is inscribed within a square and its details are structured around this motif. The Rucellai Palace in Florence is also his work.

A friend of both of the previous artists, especially Brunelleschi with whom he travelled to Rome, was the sculptor **Donatello** (1386–1466). He revolutionised Gothic art by refusing the easy, contemporary stereotypes of draped clothing, gentle movement and serene expressions, and created a great variety of characters, including the young David (*in the Bargello*), Judith and Holofernes (*Palazzo Vecchio*) and Mary Magdalen (*Museo dell'Opera del Duomo*).

Golden Age of the Florentine Renaissance – The second half of the century saw the development and blossoming of the forms which had originally been championed by Brunelleschi, Alberti and Donatello. In architecture, **Michelozzo** (1396–1472) made popular in vernacular buildings the forms used by his master, Brunelleschi. He was appointed architect to the Medici and built their mansion in Florence. Michelozzo inspired **Benedetto da Maiano**, another sculptor, who built the Strozzi Palace, and **Giuliano da Sangallo** (1445–1516), who designed the sacristy in Santo Spirito.

Donatello inspired a number of artists, including his contemporaries. **Luca della Robbia** (1400–82) also sought realism in his human figures, but he tended to idealise them, preferring greater flexibility and modesty to the sharpness of his rival. This difference

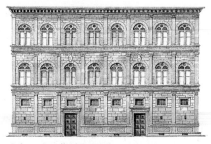

Palazzo Rucellai (1446–51)

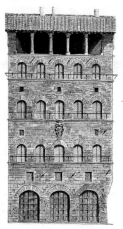

Palazzo Davanzati (14C)

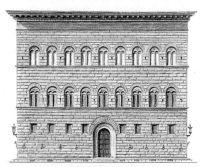

Palazzo Strozzi (1489–1504)

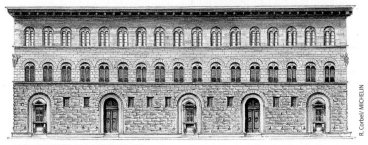

Palazzo Medici-Riccardi (1444–59)

R. Corbel/ MICHELIN

is obvious in the two *cantorie* – one by Donatello, the other by Luca (*now in the Museo dell'Opera del Duomo*). The popularity of high reliefs by Luca della Robbia – in azure blue and white glazed earthenware dotted with yellow and green – established the reputation of his workshop and was perpetuated by his descendants, Andrea (1436–1524) and Giovanni (1446–1527).

Many artists working in or around the middle of the century in emulation of Donatello showed little interest in monumental sculpture. **Desiderio da**

Settignano (1428–64) created some magnificent low reliefs. He died young, leaving the way open for **Mino da Fiesole** (c. 1430–84) and **Benedetto da Maiano** (1422–97), who created the pulpit in Santa Croce; both were famous for their work in marble.

In contrast to this trend in which flexibility was all-important, **Antonio Pollaiuolo** and **Verrocchio** (both of them painters and sculptors) and their pupils were attracted by vigor, energy and muscular strength, which they expressed in bronze.

Michelangelo – At the end of the century, owing to the political upheavals following the death of Lorenzo the Magnificent, Florence entered a period of uncertainty which was perfectly translated by the passionate personality of Michelangelo. Michelangelo's creations exhibited great realism and seem to be throbbing with inner life. Examples of his genius include his proud *David* (*original in the Galleria dell'Accademia*), his drunken *Bacchus* (*in the Bargello*), his gentle *Virgin Mary and Staircase* (*in the Casa Buonarroti*) and his *Pietà* (*in the Museo dell'Opera del Duomo*).

In architecture also, he breathed life into space by revolutionising the formalism of the Classical repertory. He divided up pediments and included empty niches in the new sacristy in San Lorenzo. In the entrance hall to the Laurenziana Library, he treated the internal walls as if they were external and designed the staircase in three parts so that it occupied almost all the floor space. He appropriated Brunelleschi's techniques but used them only to give greater freedom to the dynamics of space.

Florentine Mannerism – Michelangelo had such a strong personality that most artists were influenced by him. The most interesting was **Ammannati** (1511–92) who worked for Cosimo I from 1555 onwards. He designed the courtyard (*cortile*) and the façade of the Pitti Palace; he also designed the Santa Trinita Bridge with its elegant, flattened arches and sculpted the Neptune Fountain in Piazza della Signoria. He often worked with Vasari (1511–74), the architect and painter who supervised work on the Uffizi.

The best of all the late 16C Florentine architects was **Bernardo Buontalenti** (1536–1608) who succeeded Vasari at the Uffizi, designed the west front of Santa Trinita and drew up the project for the Belvedere Fort.

Among the sculptors, **Baccio Bandinelli** (1488–1560) carried over into the 16C a taste for well-balanced, ordered, Classical statues. His *Hercules and Cacus* stands opposite Michelangelo's *David* in Piazza della Signoria.

Benvenuto Cellini (1500–71), who produced a dazzling autobiography describing his life as an adventurer, was a fervent admirer of Michelangelo. Although principally a goldsmith, he also created bronzes of great impact, in which he managed to combine the many facets of his talent (*Perseus* in the Loggia della Signoria, and a *Bust of Cosimo I* in the Bargello).

Giovanni da Bologna (1529–1608), also known as Giambologna, arrived in Florence from Rome in 1555. His refined talents combined incisive gracefulness with a disciplined academic approach. From this time on, however, Florence began to lose its artists. In the 16C the new beacon was Rome and it was this city which attracted the finest talents of the day. Over the next few centuries, the Medici city lived in the reflection of its past glories but never again succeeded in bringing together the miraculous combination of rapid economic expansion, financial power, aristocratic patrons and a wealth of talented artists, unequalled since the days of Athens' greatness.

The Florentine House

Towers of the 13C – The economic boom that began in the 13C led to numerous wooden structures being replaced with stone buildings, although **medieval Florentine houses** were still designed to meet the same requirements – the ground floor constituted the workplace (workshop or shop) and the family lived on the upper storeys, which could be increased if and when more space was needed. The nobility, who began arriving in the city from their estates in the 11C, habitually commissioned the building of **towers** based, in the early days at least, on the design of their castle keeps. Common interests then brought these nobles and members of the wealthy middle classes from the same district together in "tower communities" which strongly defended each other if they came under

Santa Reparata and the Scoppio Del Carro

Although the present cathedral was dedicated to Santa Maria del Fiore, the people of Florence retained a place in their hearts for Reparata, the patron saint of the earlier cathedral. According to legend, when she was beheaded in Palestine at the age of 12, a dove flew out of her body to heaven. Some people claim that this story inspired the metal dove which flies out of the cathedral on Easter Day to set off the cartload of fireworks.

attack or fell into dispute with a rival clan. Their towers (up to 70m/230ft high) were interconnected by external wooden galleries. The political upheavals of the 13C led to the destruction of a number of these towers, first those of the Guelfs from 1260 onwards and then, after the victorious return of the Guelfs in 1266, those of their enemy, the Ghibellines. Very few towers – there were said to have been 150 in Florence – have survived to the present day, apart from the bases, which were often used as the foundations for new buildings. From the 14C onwards, the noblemen abandoned their towers in favour of more elegant mansions.

The 14C/ Late Middle Ages – The **traditional 14C palazzo** was still capped with battlements and consisted of four main wings surrounding a courtyard (*cortile*) from which an outside staircase led to the upper storeys. On the street front the upper floors were separated by a narrow cornice which, for aesthetic purposes, was set on a level with the window ledges rather than the floors as this gave greater emphasis to the windows. No particular attention, however, was paid to the regularity and symmetry of the façades, nor was any attempt made to conceal the bonding and this gave the residences a fortress-like appearance.

The ground floor or one corner of the mansion was often used for the family's business activities and was therefore built with a **loggia**. Sometimes a loggia was sited nearby rather than incorporated into the walls of the *palazzo*.

The 15C: Pride in Harmony – The leading families of the 15C took advantage

of their amassed fortunes and a period of greater peace to build themselves new residences to match their reputation. Their **mansions** usually consisted of three storeys, still divided by narrow cornices. The ground floor contained small square windows and one or more large doorways, whereas the two upper floors were built with majestic arched windows divided by mullions or colonnettes. As in the previous century, the windows were supported by intermediate cornices. Classical features were introduced, including superimposed pilasters (Palazzo Rucellai) or imposing terminal cornices (Palazzo Medici and Palazzo Strozzi).

Some buildings retained the traditional heavily rusticated stonework throughout the façade (Strozzi and Pitti Palaces); on others, it was restricted to the ground floor, with the masonry becoming gradually smoother on the upper storeys (Palazzo Medici and Palazzo Gondi). As in previous centuries, windows were faced with stone.

Just as the street fronts complied with well-balanced proportions, emphasis was placed on the harmony of the inner courtyard. The staircase was located inside one of the main wings, which meant that all four sides of the courtyard could be embellished with regular colonnades in the style of cloisters. Some of the mansions began to have their own gardens.

History Preserved – Over the next few centuries, owing to a decline in the influence of Florence, the city centre at least was saved from new building projects and the old architectural heritage was preserved.

Scoppio del carro

rete civica comune di Firenze, www.comune.fi.it

Events, Festivals

Scoppio del Carro

The Explosion of the Cart is held each Easter Sunday in Piazza del Duomo. It dates from 1101, the year in which a crusader returned from Jerusalem with three stones from Christ's tomb. The stones produced sparks that were used to re-light the lamps extinguished on Good Friday. From the 16C onwards the sparks began to light larger and larger "lamps" until the event acquired its present form. A wooden cart (6m/20ft high), known as *Il Brindellone*, is drawn through the streets by four oxen with gilded horns and hooves; it is accompanied by a procession of people dressed in Renaissance costume, comprising a standard-bearer, representatives of the four districts of the city and the teams participating in the historic football match (*calcio storico, see opposite*). On arrival in the square in front of the cathedral, the cart is unhitched; from the high altar in the cathedral a dove "flies" along a wire to the cart and sets off a cascade of fireworks (*scoppio del carro*). Then a young child draws lots to determine the order of play for the semi-finals of the football (*calcio*).

Calcio Storico Fiorentino

Calcio is the name given to a sort of football played in 16C costume – the first match is on the Feast of St John the Baptist (24 June) and the two others on the following days. The matches are played by teams from the four districts of the city. The Greens represent San Giovanni (the Baptistery and Duomo), the Reds

Teams collide in the Calcio Storico Fiorentino

Maurizio Degl'Innocenti/Corbis

Santa Maria Novella, the Blues Santa
Croce and the Whites Santo Spirito.
The game has no precise rules and is
a combination of football, rugby and
wrestling. It is descended from the
ball games played by the Romans in
Florentia, in which the objective was
to carry the ball into the goal of the
opposing team.

The tradition was perpetuated into
the Middle Ages when the town
council was obliged to impose
restrictions on the unruly players and
their fans who invaded the streets
and squares, disturbing the other citizens well into the night. The present
game commemorates a match played
on 17 February 1530 when the city,
which was under siege by the Holy
Roman Emperor, Charles V, dared to
demonstrate its defiance despite its
privations, celebrating Carnival with
much noise and clamour. Charles V
was eventually victorious but the
match went down in history. At the
end of the 18C the game went out
of fashion but, on the occasion of
the fourth centenary in 1930, the
festivities were revived and the tradition has continued unbroken except
during the Second World War.

The event begins with a huge procession of 530 players dressed in period
costume, representing every sector
of 16C Florentine society. To the
sound of trumpets and drums and
with standards flying in the wind,
the procession sets off from Santa
Maria Novella to the square in front
of Santa Croce, which is covered with
sand for the occasion of the match.
The kick-off is given by a blast on a
culverin, which is also sounded each
time a goal is scored.

Play lasts for 50 minutes. The teams
each have 27 players – four goalkeep-
ers, three backs, five half-backs
and 15 forwards. The winning team
receives a white calf which used to
be cut up on the spot for the ensuing
banquet. Nowadays the calf is sold
but the banquet still takes place.

Rificolona

Thefinalml... / Dreamstime.com

Rificolona

This festival takes place on the
evening of 7 September, the eve of
the Feast of the Birth of the Virgin.
The tradition probably dates from the
days when peasants from outlying
country and mountain districts used
to travel to Florence for the festival,
hoping to sell their produce at the
fair which was held at that time. The
long distances travelled by some of
these visitors meant they spent
several days on the road and had to
carry lanterns when it was dark. The
Florentines may have been thinking
of these old-fashioned lights when
they created the first paper lanterns
(*rificolone*). The lights, which were
originally in the shape of dolls, consisted of a candle shaded by the doll's
skirt, carried high in the air on the top
of a long pole. Later the shape of the
lanterns changed and people began
to hang them in the windows of their
houses.

Among the other traditional festivals
are the **May Music Festival** (Maggio
Musicale) consisting of concerts,
operas and ballets in the Teatro
Comunale, and the **Trofeo Marzocco**
when groups perform in Piazza Santa
Croce in May in a standard or pennant competition.

Souvenir stand outside the Duomo

R. Mattes/ MICHELIN

WHEN TO GO

To take full advantage of all that the city has to offer, it is best to avoid the summer months when the heat is stifling and when many of the locals are away on holiday. The best times of year to visit Florence are spring and autumn but it is advisable to book accommodation one or two months in advance.

▶ **Population:** 376,662.

Michelin Map: Atlas P 37, map 563 – K 15 and map 735 fold 14, 15.

Info: Via Cavour 1. ℘055 29 08 32. www.firenzeturismo.it.

Location: Florence's admirable setting★★ on the banks of the Arno has inspired countless artists and writers. The city is close to a main junction of two motorways – the A1 and the A11 (Firenze-mare).

Kids: Kid-sized, interactive exhibits at Musei dei Ragazzi; exploring Giardino di Boboli; medieval armour at Museo Stibbert.

Parking: Parking regulations in the town centre are strict – between 7.30am and 6.30pm access is limited to those with special passes. It is therefore advisable to walk or take the bus and park the car in the Fortezza da Basso or at Santa Maria Novella Railway Station. Contact Firenze Parcheggi, ℘055 50 01 994. www.firenzeparcheggi.it.

USEFUL CONTACTS

TOURIST INFORMATION: Central Office, **Azienda di Promozione Turistica** (**APT**), *Via Manzoni 16 (office not open to callers in person). Fax 055 23 46 286. www.firenzeturismo.it.*
For information in person:
Via Cavour 1r. ℘*055 29 08 32.*
Piazza Stazione (marquee).
℘*055 21 22 45.*
Borgo Santa Croce 29r. ℘*055 23 40 444.*
TRAVEL FOR THE DISABLED: Call the Ufficio Assistenza Disabili, near Santa Maria Novella train station,
℘*055 23 52 275.*

24HR PHARMACY: At Santa Maria Novella railway station, ℘*055 21 67 61. Molteni: Via dei Calzaiuoli 7r,* ℘*055 21 54 72 and 055 28 94 90; and in Piazza San Giovanni 20r,* ℘*055 21 13 43.*

LOST PROPERTY: *Via Circondaria 17b. Open Mon–Fri 9am–1pm.*
℘*055 32 83 942*

CONSULATES: UK – *Lungarno Corsini 2.* ℘*055 21 25 94, 055 28 74 49, 055 28 41 33.*
USA – *Lungarno Vespucci 38.* ℘*055 239 82 76, 055 21 76 05, 055 28 02 61, 055 28 40 88 .*
Post and telecommunications
Via Pellicceria 3 (near Piazza della Repubblica) is the office which deals with poste restante mail. At this office there is also a telephone operator service until midnight, although Florence is well supplied with card phones. There is another post office in Via Pietrapiana 53/55.

GETTING ABOUT

Florence is such a rich city that it takes at least four days just to see the main sights. The principal buildings and museums are nearly all in the city centre and fairly close to one another.

BUSES: A bus map, published by the bus company (ATAF), can be seen at the bus station next to Santa Maria Novella Railway Station. Tickets are sold here and also in town in shops displaying the ATAF sticker and in tobacconists' shops (indicated by a rectangular blue or black sign bearing a white "T"). Leaflets showing only the bus routes which are useful to tourists are available from the tourist office. The ATAF website provides useful information at www.ataf.net.

The main routes are:
Lines 12 and 13 going to the Colli and the Piazzale Michelanagelo; *Line 7* going from the station to Fiesole; *Line 10* going from the station to Settignano; *Line 17* going from the station to the youth hostel.
Ticket prices – €1 (ticket valid for 1hr permitting changes), €1.80 (3 hr); €3.90 (4 tickets valid for 1hr); €4 (valid for 24hr); €5.70 (valid for 2 days); €7.20 (valid for 3 days); €12 (valid for 7 days).
TAXIS: To call a taxi call ℘055 42 42, 055 43 90 or 055 47 98.
CAR HIRE: Cars can be hired at the airport or in town at one of the following agencies: **Avis**, *Borgo Ognissanti 128r.* ℘055 21 36 29, 055 23 98 826. **Italy by Car**, *Borgo Ognissanti 134r.* ℘055 28 71 61, 055 30 04 13 (*at the airport*). Fax 055 29 30 21.
Europcar, *Borgo Ognissanti 53r.* ℘055 29 04 37.
Hertz, *Via Maso Finiguerra 33r.* ℘055 23 98 205.

BICYCLES: Cycling is one of the best ways to see Florence and to bypass the permanent traffic congestion. Bicycles can be rented at some hotels or from **Florence by bike** (*Via S*

MICHELIN

Don't Miss

Florence is so full of art that travellers risk falling prey to the condition known as Stendhalismo, a term attributed to the writer Stendhal, who was so mesmerised by the beauty of Florence that he almost fainted. A type of traveller's nervosa, Stendhalismo mostly strikes visitors who have difficulties prioritizing a visit.
For those travellers who must see absolutely everything, the following sites are recommended:

- Piazza del Duomo (p108–110)
- Galleria degli Uffizi (p126–132)
- Palazzo Vecchio (p121–125))
- Michelangelo's works at the Galleria dell'Accademia (p159–160 and in the Museo del Bargello (p115–118)
- San Lorenzo and the Tombs.
- Fra Angelico's works in the Museo di San Marco (p162–163)
- Ghirlandaio frescoes in Santa Maria Novella (p151–156)
- Frescoes by Masolino, Masaccio and Filippino Lippi in the Cappella Brancacci in Santa Maria del Carmine (p143–145)

Zanobi 120r/122r, www.florencebybike. it) which has a range of different types of bicycles and scooters for hire (in summer only) and provides guided cycle tours of the city and the surrounding district.

STREET NUMBERS: The street numbering system in Florence can be somewhat anarchic, but it does follow a certain logic.
There are two entirely independent sequences of street numbers: red indicates a commercial building (noted with an "r"), and blue or black a residential one. To complicate matters further, letters sometimes accompany these numbers (a, b or c).

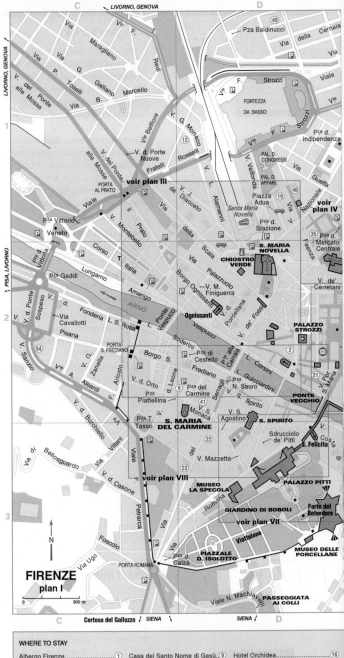

FIRENZE
plan I

0   300 m

WHERE TO STAY

Albergo Firenze.....................①	Casa del Santo Nome di Gesù..⑨	Hotel Orchidea.....................⑯
Albergo Scoti.......................②	Casa del SS. Rosario...........⑫	Hotel Palazzo vecchio..............⑲
Bed & Breakfast Dei Mori........④	Hotel Cimabue.....................⑬	Hotel Torre Guelfa................㉑
Campeggio Michelangelo...........⑦	Hotel Collodi.......................⑭	Istituto Gould ....㉒
Casa della Madonna del Rosario..⑧	Hotel Fiorino.......................⑮	Istituto Pio X Artigianelli.........㉓

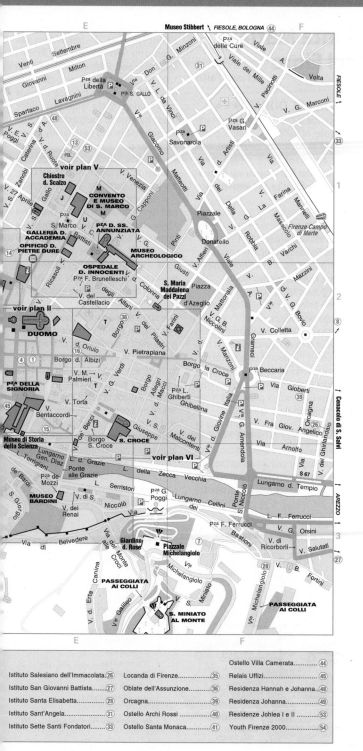

Museo Stibbert \ FIESOLE, BOLOGNA 44

Santa Maria del Fiore

Art and Faith

PIAZZA DEL DUOMO★★★

At the centre of the city stands a remarkable group of buildings in white, green and pink marble: the cathedral, bell tower and Baptistery, which mark the transition from medieval Florentine architecture to the Renaissance period.

Duomo★★★

🕐*Open Mon–Sat 10am–5pm (3.30pm Thu and 1st Sat in the month, 4.45pm other Sat), Sun and Hols 1.30pm –4.45pm. Guided tour available. Crypt:* 🕐*Open 10am–5pm.* 🕐*Closed: see dome below.* ℘*055 23 02 885. www.operaduomo.firenze.it.*

The **cathedral** is a symbol of the wealth and power of Florence in the 13C and 14C, and is one of the largest Christian buildings in the world. Its dedication to **Santa Maria del Fiore** recalls the golden rose that Pope Eugenius IV presented at the consecration of the cathedral.

The cathedral was built on the site of the Romanesque cathedral of Santa Reparata, which was deemed too modest a building for such an important city as medieval Florence. Its construction mobilised the resources of the city for almost 150 years. The commission was given to the renowned architect, Arnolfo di Cambio, and, although work began in 1296, the cathedral was not consecrated until 1436. During this time considerable modifications to the initial plans were made by Arnolfo's successors, Giotto, Andrea Pisano and particularly Francesco Talenti.

The building, which is mainly Gothic, is a striking example of the original character of this particular style in Florence. A marquetry design of multi-coloured marble in typical Florentine style forms the geometrical decoration of the stone courses. The west front designed by Arnolfo di Cambio was demolished in 1588 without ever being completed. It was replaced in the late 19C by the existing front, a complex imitation of the Gothic style.

The huge **dome**★★★ (🕐*see below*), an integral part of the Florentine landscape, is the most beautiful part of the building. It is the work of Filippo Brunelleschi. In 1420 he solved the problem of how to roof the vast sanctuary, by designing a roof made of two flattened domes linked by a complex network of arches and buttresses. The construction of the gigantic dome, erected without any apparent support, aroused enormous admiration and enthusiasm in Florence at the time. For almost 15 years the building site, with its hoists designed

DUOMO-CŒUR MÉDIÉVAL-SIGNORIA-OFFICES

Plan II

0   200 m

WHERE TO EAT

Cantinetta dei Verrazzano..............②
La Cattedrale..............................④
Le Mossacce..............................⑥
Trattoria Anita............................⑧
Trattoria I Chè Cé Cé....................⑩
Trattoria Nella............................⑫
Vini e Vecchi Sapori.....................⑭

Museo della Casa Fiorentina Antica.........**M**

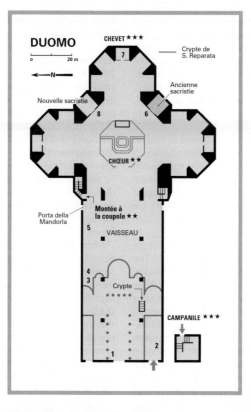

by Brunelleschi himself and capable of moving blocks of stone weighing over three tonnes, was an unprecedented sight for the Florentine people.

Exterior

Starting on the south side, walk round the cathedral anticlockwise. From the south side there is a striking view of the building, including its amazing marble marquetry. The **east end**★★★ is remarkably extensive consisting of three polygonal apses radiating from the transept crossing, that, together with the dome, form a complex yet superbly well-balanced composition.

On the north side of the building is the **Mandorla Door**, surmounted by a mandorla containing a carving of the *Virgin Mary of the Assumption* by Nanni di Banco in the early 15C. The mosaic work on the tympanum (1490) depicting the *Annunciation* is the work of Domenico Ghirlandaio.

Nave

After the lavish ornamentation of the exterior the nave is surprisingly plain. The stained-glass windows of the west end, especially the central rose window depicting the *Assumption of the Virgin Mary*, were based on drawings by Lorenzo Ghiberti. The tomb of Bishop Antonio d'Orso, who died in 1321, was carved by the Sienese sculptor, Tino di Camaino, who produced a number of famous monumental tombs during the Gothic period. A fragment of the original work (**1**) (*left of the centre door*) shows the deceased asleep and seated, above a sarcophagus.

In the first bay of the south aisle, just above the place where his tomb was discovered in the crypt (&see below) in 1972, is a portrait of Brunelleschi (**2**) (*first medallion on the right on entering*) carved by one of his pupils.

In the north aisle are two frescoes containing equestrian sculptures in honour of two military men (*condottieri*) who hired their services to Florence; the first one (**3**) is of Nicolò da Tolentino by Andrea del Castagno (1456) and the second one (**4**) is of Giovanni Acuto by Paolo Uccello (1436). Another fresco (**5**), painted by Domenico Michelino in 1465, depicts Dante explaining his *Divine Comedy* to the city of Florence, which is represented by its cathedral as it was in the 15C; the fresco illustrates the "geography" of the other world as imagined by the poet – the pit of Hell, the mountain of Purgatory and the heavenly ranks of Paradise. The aisles are lit by remarkable 14C stained-glass windows.

Sanctuary★★

It is here that the true grandeur of the building can best be appreciated. The huge octagonal sanctuary is enclosed by an elegant marble screen erected in the mid-16C. From it radiate three vast apses forming a trefoil, each one containing five chapels. Above rises the breathtaking **dome★★★** (50m/162ft in diameter at its base and 91m/296ft high), which is decorated with a huge fresco depicting *The Last Judgement*; it was begun by Vasari, who worked on it from 1572 to 1574, but it required a further five years' work by Federico Zuccari before it was finished in 1579. Over the high altar

The Double Pope

It may come as something of a surprise to learn that the Baptistery in Florence contains the tomb of Pope Alexander V's successor, John XXIII, who died in 1419. He was elected Pope by the Cardinals but his serious political blunders and flight from Rome caused him to be deposed in favour of Martin V. It was not until the 20C that a new Pope took the name of John and, having occupied the throne of St Peter with dignity, went down in history as the 23rd Pope of this name (the ordinal was deemed not to have been previously attributed).

hangs a wooden crucifix by Benedetto da Maiano (late 15C).

The tympanum above the door on the right leading to the Old Sacristy (*Sacrestia Vecchia*) (**6**) is decorated with a terracotta *Ascension* by Luca della Robbia. Beneath the altar (**7**) in the axial chapel lies the tomb of St Zanobi, the first Bishop of Florence. This remarkable work by Lorenzo Ghiberti consists of bronze reliefs depicting scenes from the saint's life. On either side of the altar are two delightful white glazed terracotta angel candle-bearers by Luca della Robbia. Their faces recall those of the adolescents in the famous *"Cantoria"* by the same artist now in the museum (🅖 *see below*).

The door of the New Sanctuary (*Sacrestia Nuova*), symmetrically opposite the Old Sacristy, is also surmounted by a tympanum decorated by Luca della Robbia (**8**) depicting the **Resurrection★** in light shades of blue. It was in the New Sacristy that Lorenzo the Magnificent took refuge when attacked by two monks involved in the Pazzi Conspiracy. In this dramatic episode, the Pazzi, great rivals of the Medici, mounted a conspiracy in the name of lost freedoms and were supported by the Pope.

The Pazzi attempt-ed to assassinate Lorenzo Medici in the cathedral during the Elevation at the Easter Mass on Sunday 26 April 1478. He was attacked by the monks but was only wounded and took refuge in the New Sacristy; his brother, Giuliano, was killed. Lorenzo then instigated a cruel and merciless repression against the Pazzi.

Skilful lighting shows off (*through a partition*) the **marquetry cabinets★** which reach halfway up the walls of the room and were produced in the second half of the 15C, mainly by Benedetto and Giuliano da Maiano. The splendid bronze door panels depicting figures of the Evangelists and Prophets are also worthy of note.

Dome★★

Access via the north aisle. 463 steps; 45min. 🕐*Open Mon–Sat 8.30am–7pm (5.40pm Sat, 4pm 1st Sat in the month); last admission 40min before closing.*

🕐*Closed Maundy Thu–Easter Sun, 24 Jun, Sun and Hols.* 🎫€6. 📞*055 23 02 885; www.operaduomo.firenze.it.*
The narrow gallery overlooking the chancel provides a breathtaking **view**★★ down into the cathedral and also a close-up view of the remarkable **stained-glass windows**★ in the oculi of the drum. They were produced in the first half of the 15C and are based on sketches made by the leading figures of the time – Ghiberti, Donatello, Paolo Uccello and Andrea del Sarto.

From the staircase leading to the top of the dome, which is constructed between the two vaults, there is an interesting view of the structural features. The final section, which is very steep and close against the wall, is the most spectacular. It leads to the exterior at the foot of the lantern turret which was Brunelleschi's last work and not set in place until after his death. From here there is a magnificent **panoramic view**★★ of Florence.

Santa Reparata's Crypt
Staircase by the first pillar on the south side of the nave. The crypt is all that remains of an earlier Romanesque church (13C–14C), which was discovered during excavation work in 1966. It had itself been created through the conversion of a palaeo-Christian basilica (5C–6C) and was demolished during the construction of the present cathedral.

The place where Brunelleschi's tomb was discovered can be seen through an iron grille in an opening overlooking the uncovered section to the left of the staircase.

The structural features so far uncovered have made it possible to reconstitute the layout of the original cathedral (a nave and two aisles and a raised chancel above a crypt). A drawing (*in a showcase*) shows the relevant periods of construction of the different architectural features and the large fragments of mosaic flooring. The place where Brunelleschi's tomb was discovered can be seen through an iron grille in an opening overlooking the uncovered section to the left of the staircase.

Campanile★★★
🕐*Open 8.30am–7.30pm (6.50pm last admission).* 🕐*Closed Easter, 8 Sept, 25 Dec, 1 Jan.* 🎫€6. 📞*055 23 02 885. www.operaduomo.firenze.it.*
The slender **bell tower** (82m/267ft high) by Giotto is no less famous than Brunelleschi's dome. Its straight lines form a harmonious contrast with the curved structure of the dome.

The plans for and decoration of the bell tower were the work of Giotto, who was appointed to supervise work on the cathedral. Construction began in 1334 but only the decorated section of carved panels had been built by the time he died in 1337. Andrea Pisano and Francesco Talenti completed the building work between 1349 and 1360 and designed the traceried section of the bays.

Copies have replaced the original low reliefs in the bottom section of the building. The decoration was based on an overall design by Giotto. The first register was carved by Andrea Pisano and Luca della Robbia; the second by pupils of Andrea Pisano. The originals, together with the statues of Prophets and Sibyls, which once occupied the niches on the second floor, are in the Museo dell'Opera del Duomo (🔎*see p114*).

From the upper terrace (*414 steps to the top*) there is a fine **panoramic view**★★ of the cathedral and the city of Florence.

Battistero★★★
🕐*Open Mon–Sat noon–7pm (6.30pm last admission), Sun and Hols 8.30am–2pm (1.30pm last admission).* 🕐*Closed Easter, 24 Jun, 25 Dec, 1 Jan.* 🎫€3. ♿. 📞*055 23 02 885. www.operaduomo.firenze.it.*
This elegant octagonal **baptistery**, clad in white and dark-coloured marble, is highly representative of Florentine architecture. A Romanesque building, probably dating from the 11C, it nonetheless contains a number of Renaissance features (pilasters, capitals, triangular pediments, etc) typical of Florentine architecture, which had always drawn on Antiquity for inspiration.

Doors★★★

The bronze doors decorated with magnificent carved panels are famous throughout the world. Begun in 1330 by Andrea Pisano, the Gothic **South Door** (*now the entrance*) is the oldest. The 20 upper panels depict scenes from the life of St John the Baptist, patron saint of Florence. In the eight lower panels, the sculptor represented the Theological and Cardinal Virtues – (*left to right and top to bottom*) Hope, Faith, Fortitude, Temperance, Charity, Humility, Justice and Prudence.

The commission for the **North Door** (1403–24) was given to Lorenzo Ghiberti after a competition in which the city's greatest artists, including Brunelleschi, took part. Although he was working almost 100 years after Pisano, Ghiberti's work achieved a harmony with the other doors, by retaining the quatrefoil composition of Gothic tradition for the medallions. The eight lower panels depict the Evangelists and the Doctors of the Church. Above are scenes from the Life and Passion of Christ (*from bottom to top*) depicted with remarkable austerity, nobility and harmony of composition. Above the doorway is *St John the Baptist Preaching* (*early 16C*) by Rustici.

The **East Door** (*facing the cathedral*) is the most famous of all, the one which Michelangelo thought worthy to be called the **Gate of Paradise**. Between 1425 and 1452 Ghiberti, then at the peak of his talent, produced a masterpiece of sculpture and metalwork. The ten panels contain highly complex compositions illustrating episodes from the Old Testament executed with an abundance of characters in scenes that are remarkably lively, elegant and poetic.

Interior and Mosaics

The interior of the Baptistery (25m/82ft in diameter) comprises marble-clad walls and two orders of granite pilasters and columns, with gilded Corinthian capitals. The most striking feature, however, is the dome covered in sparkling **mosaics★★★** (*see infobox*).

Fine marble mosaics, some with motifs borrowed from oriental designs, form the pavement leading to the Gate of Paradise, which was originally the main entrance to the Baptistery.

To the right of the small apse (*scarsella*) is the tomb of the Antipope John XXIII, friend of Giovanni di Bicci (the father of Cosimo the Elder). It is a remarkable work produced in 1427 by Donatello, assisted by Michelozzo.

Mosaics★★★ of the Baptistery Dome

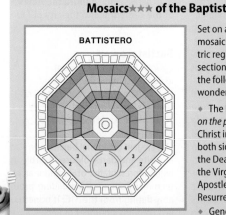

BATTISTERO

Set on a gold background, the mosaics are laid out in concentric registers covering the eight sections of the dome. They depict the following scenes, often in a wonderfully fresh manner.

◆ The Last Judgement (*in yellow on the plan*), consisting of the large Christ in Majesty (1), flanked on both sides by the Resurrection of the Dead with Heaven and Hell (2), the Virgin Mary with the Saints and Apostles (3) and the Angels of the Resurrection (4).

◆ Genesis (*pale pink*).

◆ Various choirs of angels or celestial hierarchies (*darker pink*).
◆ The Life of Joseph (*blue*).
◆ The Life of the Virgin Mary and Jesus (*light green*).
◆ The Life of St John the Baptist (*darker green*).

Part of Panel 1, depicting Adam and Eve

Thermos/Wikipedia/cc-by-3.0

Deciphering the Baptistery Doors ★★

Ghiberti's East Door, also known as the Gate of Paradise, depicts scenes from the Old Testament, and is an exceptional work of Renaissance sculpture.

Each register from top to bottom, including the left and right doors:

1   Creation of Adam and Eve, Original Sin. Adam and Eve expelled. Cain and Abel – Cain the laborer; Abel the shepherd; sacrifices made to God by the two brothers; Abel slain by Cain; the divine curse.

2   Story of Noah – the Flood; the rainbow sent as a sign of God's covenant with Noah; the drunkenness of Noah. Angels appearing to Abraham; his wife Sarah listening at the entrance of the tent; the sacrifice of Isaac.

3   Esau and his brother Jacob – Esau sent hunting by Isaac; Esau gives up his birthright to Jacob; Rebecca advises Jacob; God speaks to Rebecca; Jacob receives Isaac's blessing instead of Esau.
Joseph's life – (*top left*) Joseph sold by his brothers; (*bottom left*) discovery of the cup in Benjamin's sack; storing the corn after Joseph interprets Pharaoh's dream and predicts seven years of famine; Joseph seated on a throne is recognised by his family.

Part of Panel 2, depicting the Flood

Iillis photography / iStockphoto

4   Moses receives the Tables of the Law; in his absence the Hebrews at the foot of Mount Sinai fall into despair.
Joshua and the Fall of Jericho; (*above*) the people cross the dry River Jordan and pick up the stones of memory.

5   Saul and David – the battle against the Philistines led by Saul standing in a chariot; David beheads Goliath.
Meeting of King Solomon and the Queen of Sheba.

Part of Panel 3, depicting Jacob and Esau

A5506 / iStockphoto

113

Museo dell'Opera del Duomo★★

9 Piazza del Duomo. 🕐*Open Mon–Sat 9am–7.30pm (6.50pm last admission), Sun 9am–2pm (1.20pm last admission).* 🕐*Closed Easter, 25 Dec, 1 Jan.* ♿€6. ♿. 𝄞055 23 02 885; www.operaduomo.firenze.it.

A tour of the cathedral, bell tower and Baptistery would not be complete without a visit to the **Cathedral Museum**, which houses numerous sculptures and artefacts from the three buildings.

Ground Floor

The great hall situated behind the entrance is devoted to the west front of the cathedral, shown in a 16C drawing as it appeared shortly before it was demolished. The drawing is the work of Arnolfo di Cambio, who produced most of the sculptures decorating the cathedral. Other sculptors carved the monumental statues of the Evangelists (*against the entrance wall*), the most remarkable of which is *St Luke* by Nanni di Banco.

At the far end of the hall (*left*) there is a series of small rooms. The first contains some of the equipment used by Brunelleschi during the construction of the dome. The second room contains scale models of the dome and its lantern, in addition to the death mask of the great architect.

The first of the two rooms on the other side of the great hall contains various scale models proposed for the west front of the cathedral – by Buontalenti, Giovanni da Bologna and Giovanni de' Medici – as well as a collection of liturgical chants dating from the 16C. The second room contains part of the cathedral treasure.

Mezzanine Floor

Here is a **Pietà**★★ sculpted by Michelangelo at the age of 80. He intended it for his own tomb but left it unfinished because he was dissatisfied with the quality of the marble. He is supposed to have depicted himself as Nicodemus supporting the Virgin Mary and Christ. The figure of Mary Magdalen, added by one of Michelangelo's pupils, attempts to hold up the body as it sinks to the ground.

First Floor

The great hall houses the famous **cantorie**★★, choir galleries that once surmounted the doors of the sacristies in the cathedral. The more famous of the two (*left of the entrance*) is the one by Luca della Robbia (1431–38). These exquisitely carved reliefs are the first known works by the artist.

The gallery (1433–39) by Donatello (*opposite*) was also based on Classical low reliefs. Above the galleries is the famous statue of **Mary Magdalen**★ repenting, a late work (1455) by Donatello carved in wood.

In the same room is a group of statues that once adorned the bell tower. They include three more works by Donatello. Along the opposite wall are the prophets Jeremiah and Habakkuk, nicknamed *Zuccone* (pumpkin) because of the shape of his bald head.

The room to the left of the Cantoria room displays the admirable **low reliefs**★★ that once decorated the bell tower. The hexagonal ones, depicting various trades and activities, a number of characters from Antiquity and scenes from the Book of Genesis, were produced by Andrea Pisano and Luca della Robbia.

The room to the right of the Cantoria room contains the magnificent **silver altar**★★ from the Baptistery, a splendid example of Florentine gold and silversmithing from the 14C–15C, which combines Gothic and Renaissance style features and took over a century to produce. The story of John the Baptist was depicted on it by numerous artists, including Michelozzo, Antonio Pollaiolo and Verrocchio. The display cases on either side of the room contain the panels of the altar **frontal**★ from the Baptistery, a splendid silk and filigree embroidery worked with great skill and artistry, which depicts scenes from the life of John the Baptist and Jesus.

In the centre of the room are four original low reliefs from the Gate of Paradise in the Baptistery depicting the Creation, Cain and Abel, David and Goliath and the Story of Joseph.

Medieval Heart of Florence

🔊 *Map p108*

A short walk from Santa Maria del Fiore to the Piazza della Signora can easily fill a whole afternoon. Start from the apse of the cathedral. Before turning into Via del Proconsolo, glance at the 16C **Palazzo Niccolini**★ (*15 Via dei Servi*). In Via del Proconsolo make a brief detour into Via del Corso to admire **Palazzo Portinari** (*no 6, now the Banca Toscana*), and its 16C internal **courtyard**★. In Via del Proconsolo, at the corner of Borgo degli Albizzi, stands the late-15C **Palazzo Pazzi**★ (*no 10*) with twin windows.

BARGELLO PALACE★★★

1hr 30min. ⏱*Open 8.15am–1.50pm (1.20pm last admission). Guided tour (1hr; several languages) available.* ⏱*Closed 1st, 3rd, 5th Sun in the month, 2nd and 4th Mon in the month, Easter, 1 May, 25 Dec, 1 Jan.* ✎*€4.* ♿*.* ✆*055 23 88 606. www.polomuseale.firenze. it/bargello.*

This forbidding **palazzo**★ is a fine example of medieval vernacular architecture. The oldest part of the façade was built in the mid-13C and originally housed the Capitano del Popolo, who represented the working classes within the Florentine government, then the Podestà. The later part of the building was built in the Gothic style a century later.

In 1574 the building became the residence of the Chief of Police (called Bargello) and part of it was turned into a prison. Today the building houses the Bargello National Museum, which provides a valuable insight into Italian Renaissance sculpture and has a section devoted to the decorative arts.

The severity of the **courtyard**★★ is softened by a porch with wide arcades and a loggia reached by a picturesque outside staircase. In fact, this is one of the finest medieval courtyards in Italy. The coats of arms of the magistrates (*podeste*) who lived in the palace from the 14C to 16C provide a charming decoration. Condemned prisoners were put to death beside the well.

Works by 16C Tuscan sculptors have been placed along the galleries; the single statues and the impressive group standing against the wall opposite the entrance were once part of a fountain designed by Ammannati, the architect of the Pitti Palace, for the great Hall of the Five Hundred in the Palazzo Vecchio.

▷ *Start opposite the entrance at the far end of the gallery.*

Sala del Trecento

This 14C sculpture room contains the museum's few Gothic sculptures, including the *Madonna and Child* by Tino da Camaino (*against the left-hand wall*).

▷ *At the foot of the outside staircase.*

Sala di Michelangelo e della Scultura del Cinquecento

The Michelangelo and 16C Sculpture Room is mainly devoted to the two most contrasting artistic figures of the Florentine Renaissance.

There are four splendid Michelangelo sculptures (*left-hand bay*). The **Drunken**

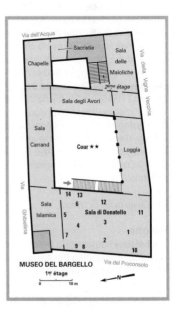

Bacchus group accompanied by a laughing satyr (1497–99) is an early work which still bears traces of Classical influences. In the famous **Tondo Pitti**, a large roundel representing the Madonna and Child with St John, carved between 1504 and 1506 for one of the members of the Pitti family, the artist seems to have transposed the *sfumato* style of Leonardo da Vinci into sculpture by creating roughly sketched reliefs. The powerful marble bust of **Brutus** (1540) also takes its inspiration from Roman statuary. The unfinished **David-Apollo** (c. 1530) (*further along*) seems captured midway between motion and immobility.

In contrast to the forceful artistry of Michelangelo, the work of **Benvenuto Cellini** is admired for its virtuosity and delicacy. The right-hand bay contains a number of his masterpieces. In the centre of the room stands the marble **Narcissus** with its slender forms and melancholy incurved lines. For many years it was one of the statues in the Boboli Gardens. Around the room are the bronze statuettes of Perseus, Mercury, Danae and her son Perseus, and Minerva and Jupiter, which once filled the niches of the pedestal supporting the famous Perseus in the Loggia della Signoria. On the wall is the original bronze plaque which decorated the base, representing **Perseus Delivering Andromeda**, a work treated with the gusto characteristic of the Mannerist style (graceful drapes, elegant slender bodies, flowing movement). The bronze bust of **Cosimo I** (1546) (*wall to the right of the door*) is an admirable portrait vigorously expressing cruelty, intelligence and energy; the decoration on the armour is worthy of a goldsmith. Also in this room is Danti's *Honour Triumphant over Falsehood*.

○ *Go up to the First Floor.*

Verone
The **balcony** houses works by Giovanni da Bologna, including the Allegory of Architecture in the centre, and remarkable bronze animals, which once adorned a grotto in the Villa di Castello's gardens.

○ *Entrance at top of outside staircase.*

Sala di Donatello
The vast high-ceilinged **Donatello Room** has the majestic appearance of the nave of a cathedral. Beneath the vaulting there is an outstanding **collection of works**★★★ by **Donatello**, (*○ see infobox on opposite page*) whose genius dominated the Early Italian Renaissance.

Sala Islamica
The **Islamic Art Room** is a testimony to Florence's trade links with the Middle East. It contains carpets, costumes and weaponry, cloth, ceramics, pewter and bronzeware, and ivories, some of which were collected by the Grand Dukes.

Sala Carrand
The **Carrand Room** houses a large part of the extensive collection bequeathed by Louis Carrand in the late 19C. The collection, mainly consisting of objets d'art, is also displayed in other parts of the palace. The room has a remarkable display of enamels including some from Limoges and the Rhineland, dating from the 12C and 13C (*first display case on the left*), 15C and 16C Venetian ware (*second group of display cases in the centre*) and Limoges ware dating from the 15C and 16C (*fourth display case on the left and last on the right*).

Sala degli Avori
The **Ivories Room** houses one of the most extensive collections of ivories in the world, with works dating from the 5C to 17C. Included in the displays are Italian ivories from the 14C and 15C and a splendid chess board made by the Burgundy School.

Sala delle Maioliche
The **Majolica Room** contains some spectacular bowls from Urbino (16C) with a highly elaborate combination of shapes, decorative motifs and colours (*display cases in front of the windows*), and some large white and brown Hispano-Moorish dishes (15C and 16C) with fine detail made in metallic shades.

Masterpieces of the Donatello Room★★★

There is a small lively bronze Cupid (1). The marble statue of **David** (2) is one of the artist's early works (1409) showing a realistic observation far removed from the Gothic tradition. The famous **"Marzocco"** (3), the Florence lion, whose paw rests on the city's shield, stood for many years in front of the Palazzo Vecchio. The bronze **David** (4) is a masterpiece dating from Donatello's more mature period. The splendid body, tensed yet carved in gentle relief, is the expression of an artistry that had reached the height of perfection. The imposing **St George** (5) (*in the niche in the end wall*) originally stood outside Orsanmichele.

The room also contains a number of other important works from the 15C, such as *St John the Baptist as a Child* (6) by **Desiderio da Settignano**, one of Donatello's most illustrious pupils. The touching *profile* (7), also of St John the Baptist as a child, has an exceptionally gentle quality. The artist learned from his master the technique of *schiacciato*: graduated flattened sculpture with slight relief. The delicate relief of the *Madonna and Child* (8) is another charming example of this style. Donatello's pupil, **Agostino di Duccio**, carved the *Madonna and Child with Angels* placed within a *pietra serena* surround (9). The room also contains a number of Madonnas and Child by **Luca della Robbia**. The *Madonna of the Rose Garden* (10) and *Madonna with Apple* (11) are among his most accomplished youthful, serene Madonnas.

Along the wall to the right of the doorway to the next room is a painting of St John the Baptist (12) by Francesco da Sangallo, and the two quatrefoil panels of the *Sacrifice of Isaac*, produced in 1401 for the competition to find the architect of the north door of the Baptistery. These panels were made by the winner, Lorenzo Ghiberti (13), and by Brunelleschi (14).

▶ *Go to the Second Floor. To the right of the first room is the Sala delle Armi.*

Sala delle Armi

The **armoury** contains a fine collection of mainly 16C–17C weapons and armour, most of which belonged to the Medici family.

The first display case against the left-hand wall contains a series of rifles and pistols decorated with fruit, animals and figures, all beautifully inset in ivory and mother-of-pearl. The remainder of the collection consists mainly of the state **armour of the Grand Dukes** of the Medici dynasty, including a number of splendid shields.

Sala di Giovanni della Robbia

This room houses a collection of works by the last of the three great della Robbia sculptors, the great-nephew of Luca. Giovanni della Robbia carried on the technique of glazed terracotta sculpture, extending it to larger and more complex compositions with greater variety of colour. A typical example of this development can be seen (*right of the door*) in the predella depicting Christ and the Saints. The same is true of the large Pietà in bold relief set against a landscape full of rocks, buildings, trees and horsemen, and the huge Nativity surrounded by two Apparitions of Jesus to Mary Magdalen (*Noli me Tangere*). Giovanni also created simpler and more tranquil compositions such as the tender *Madonna and Child with St John* (*wall opposite the door*).

Sala di Andrea della Robbia

Like his successor, Andrea della Robbia, nephew of Luca and father of Giovanni, also created some delicate and graceful Madonnas. His Madonnas and Child are embellished with heads of cherubs, flowers and foliage and are enlivened with bright colours. No less exquisite masterpieces, if only for the harmony of their composition, are **Our Lady of Architects** (*to the right of the window*), produced for the Guild of Masons and Carpenters, whose tools are depicted in the surrounding frieze, and his **Madonna with Cushion** (*to the left of the door*).

▷ *To the left.*

Sala del Verrocchio

The **Verrocchio Room** contains a collection of several sculptures by the Florentine artist who, as both painter and sculptor, was one of the leading figures of the Italian Renaissance. Near the centre of the room stands the famous bronze **David**, dating from c. 1465 and sculpted for the young Lorenzo the Magnificent and his brother, Giuliano, whom Verrocchio had befriended.

Against the wall opposite the windows, note the bust of a young woman holding a bunch of flowers. Her long hands are admired for their lifelike, aristocratic appearance, and there are very few rivals in the world of sculpture. The identity of the model remains a mystery (it may have been Lucrezia Donti, Lorenzo the Magnificent's mistress). Note also two delightful marble Madonnas and Child, which contrast sharply with the expressionism and dramatic character of works such as the polychrome terracotta *Resurrection* and *Death of Francesca Pitti-Tornabuoni*. Among the works by other sculptors of the late 15C, the most outstanding are: (*left of the door*) Francesco Laurana's bust of Battista Sforza, Duchess of Urbino and (*right of the door*) a number of sculptures by Mino da Fiesole, including a very fine medallion of the *Madonna and Child* and the remarkable portrait of *Rinaldo della Luna*.

The rooms at the far end on the left contain a collection of medallions. The first room contains a large bust of Costanza Bonarelli by Gianlorenzo Bernini (1589–1680).

Sala dei Bronzetti

The **Bronze Statuette Room** (*opposite the Verrocchio Room*) houses a large collection of bronze statuettes which were highly prized items of interior decoration among fashionable society in Renaissance Italy. These bronze statuettes were miniature replicas of either ancient statues (*the Laocoön*), contemporary works by Giovanni da Bologna or original creations from renowned artists' studios. There are also items in everyday use (mortars, ink-pots, candlesticks).

▷ *Opposite the Bargello, entrance in Via del Proconsolo or Via Dante.*

BADIA

This was the church of an ancient and very influential Benedictine abbey (*badia*), founded shortly before the year 1000 by Countess Willa, Marchioness of Tuscany. It was a centre of intense spiritual and intellectual activity throughout the Middle Ages.

It is believed that the building was extensively renovated in the late 13C by Arnolfo di Cambio. The elegant, hexagonal **bell tower**★, rebuilt between 1310 and 1330, is one of the finest bell towers in Florence and can be fully admired only from a distance.

The church underwent further restoration in 1627 and the present interior dates from this period. It is designed in the form of a Greek cross in an austere Baroque style and has a splendid carved wooden coffered **ceiling**★★.

The church contains a number of interesting Renaissance works, including a painting depicting the **Apparition of the Virgin** to St Bernarda by Filippo Lippi, in which the artist is said to have used his mistress and children as models for the Virgin Mary and angels, and an exquisite carved marble **relief**★★ by Mino da Fiesole, in which the youth and beauty of the characters (Madonna and Child, St Leonard and St Lawrence) are extremely moving. The church also has two elegant tombs★ carved by Mino da Fiesole. The two tombs are those of Bernardo Giugni (*south transept*), an eminent figure of the Florentine

Republic and Count Ugo (*north transept*), Marquess of Tuscany, who was a great benefactor of the Church and the son of the founder of the abbey.

▷ *Retrace your steps; turn left into Via Dante Alighieri; go to the corner with Via Santa Margherita.*

CASA DI DANTE

Via S Margherita 1 (corner of Via Dante Alighieri). ◔*Open Mar–Oct Wed–Mon 10am–6pm (2pm Sun, Hols); rest of the year 10am–4pm (2pm Sun, Hols).* ◔*Closed Christmas, New Year. Bookshop.* ◈€2.50. ✆*055 21 94 16. www.museocasadidante.it.*

The museum retraces the life of the poet from the origins of his family, members of the ancient Florentine aristocracy, to his official positions within the city and his years in exile. It also records Italian history and the position of Florence during Dante's lifetime, which were closely linked to his political preoccupations, as well as his major work, the *Divine Comedy*, and his platonic love for Beatrice Portinari, whose family lived in the same district and who was buried in the Church of Santa Margherita (*further up the street*).

In Via Dante (corner of Piazza S Martino) stand the remains of the 12C **Torre della Castagna**, where the representatives (*priori*) of the Guilds met before the construction of the Palazzo della Signoria.

▷ *Opposite is the Buonomini oratory.*

ORATORIO DEI BUONOMINI

This chapel belongs to the brotherhood of Buonomini di San Martino, which has looked after the "needy poor" (originally well-off families who had fallen from grace and were too ashamed to ask for charity), since 1441. Requests for help are still posted through the letter box marked *"per le istanze"*. When the Buonomini are unable to help with any more requests, a candle is lit by the door.

The beautiful **frescoes** inside the building date from the end of the 15C. They were painted by the workshop of Domenico Ghirlandaio, and possibly that of Filippino Lippi, and depict the story of St Martin and Works of Mercy.

▷ *Continue to Via dei Calzaiuoli.*

ORSANMICHELE

This unusually shaped church takes its name from a much older church dedicated to St Michael which was destroyed around 1240. It occupies a building that was initially a loggia used as a grain store. The loggia was partly destroyed by fire in 1304 and was rebuilt in 1337 in a Gothic-Renaissance style. In the late 14C the arcades were walled up and the height of the building was raised so that it could be used as a chapel. The upper storey, however, continued to be used until the 16C for the storage of food in case of famine. In 1569 Cosimo I set up the Deeds Office on the first floor. He also commissioned Buontalenti to construct an arched passage above street level between the rear of the building and the mansion of the Wool Merchants' Guild (*Arte della Lana*), in order to provide an access without having to pass through the chapel.

The **external** niches round the building are occupied by statues of the patron saints of the various guilds (*Arti*), which form a veritable museum of 14C–16C Florentine sculpture. On the side in Via dei Calzaiuoli (*from left to right*) are a bronze statue of *St John the Baptist* cast in 1416 by Lorenzo Ghiberti for the Drapers' Guild; a bronze group for which Verrocchio was commissioned in 1484 by the Merchants' Court depicting the

Four Saints by Nanni di Banco, in an external niche of the Orsanmichele

A5506 / iStockphoto

Disbelief of St Thomas (*missing*); and a bronze figure of *St Luke* made in 1562 by Giovanni da Bologna for the Guild of Judges and Notaries. On the side in Via Orsanmichele were *St Peter* (*missing*) carved in marble by Donatello in 1413 for the Butchers' Guild; *St Philip* (1410, *missing*) made for the Shoemakers; a group of four saints (1408) produced by Nanni di Banco for the Master Stoneworkers and Woodworkers; and a copy (*original in the Bargello*) of the famous *St George* by Donatello, created in 1416 for the Armour Merchants and Sword Cutlers. On the side in Via dell'Arte della Lana are the bronze statues of *St Matthew* and *St Stephen* produced by Ghiberti, the first in 1422 for the Money Changers and the second for the Wool Merchants in 1426; and *St Eligius* (1416, *missing*) by Nanni di Banco for the Blacksmiths. On the side in Via dei Lamberti are *St Mark* (1411–13) by Donatello; *St James* (*missing*) carved in marble for the Furriers' Guild; a Madonna and Child known as the *Madonna of the Rose* (1399) made for the Physicians and Apothecaries; and a bronze figure of *St John the Evangelist* cast by Baccio da Montelupo for the Silk Merchants in 1515.

The **interior** is a simple rectangular hall. It contains a splendid Gothic **tabernacle**★★, begun in 1329 by **Andrea Orcagna**.

▷ *Go along Via dei Calzaiuoli as far as Via della Condotta.*

MERCATO NUOVO★

In the 16C Cosimo I ordered the construction of this loggia with elegant Renaissance arcades in a district that had been occupied by traders and merchants since the Middle Ages. Its name, **New Market Loggia**, distinguished it from the old medieval marketplace which was demolished in the late 19C during the construction of Piazza della Repubblica. The loggia now houses a market selling Florentine craftwork including souvenirs, embroidery, lace, leather goods, *pietra dura* ware and gilded and painted wooden items. At the edge of the building, on the side

facing the Arno, stands the Porcellino ("piglet") Fountain. The bottom of the basin is strewn with coins that tourists traditionally throw into the fountain while making the wish that they may one day return to Florence.

▷ *Turn onto Via Porta Rossa.*

Palazzo Torrigiani (Hotel Porta Rossa) is a rare example of a mansion (14C) with well-conserved, corbelled upper storeys. Also in this street is the **Palazzo Davanzati**★ (14C).

MUSEO DELLA CASA FIORENTINA ANTICA★

Via di Porta Rossa 13. ⏰*Open daily 8.15am–1.50pm.* ⏰*Closed 2nd and 4th Sun and 1st, 3rd and 5th Mon of the month.* ☎*055 23 88 610. www.polomuseale.firenze.it/musei/davanzati.*

The **Old Florentine House Museum** is housed on the three floors of the **Palazzo Davanzati**★, a narrow, towering residence built in the 14C for a rich wool merchant and purchased in the 16C by the historian and man of letters, Bernardo Davanzati.

The building was superbly restored at the turn of the 20C and it contains a splendid collection of furniture (mainly Florentine or Tuscan from the 14C, 15C and 16C), tapestries, paintings, sculptures, ceramics, everyday objects and fabrics, most of which originate from the Bargello. The museum, part of which dates from medieval times, provides a vivid insight into what a rich Florentine residence would have looked like during the Renaissance period.

The first and second floors each comprise a dining room, bed chamber, lavatory and great hall – the hall on the first floor was used for family gatherings such as weddings, funerals etc, while the room on the second floor was reserved for the mistress of the house and contains a large Davanzati family tree.

▷ *Retrace your steps to the corner of Via Pellicceria; turn right and walk as far as Piazza di Parte Guelfa, where the Palazzo di Parte Guelfa (14C) stands.*

La Signoria

Art and Politics

🎧 *Map p108*

PIAZZA DELLA SIGNORIA★★

This was, and still is, the political centre of Florence set against the backcloth of the magnificent Palazzo Vecchio, the Loggia della Signoria and, in the wings, the Uffizi Gallery. It was created in the 13C when the victorious Guelfs razed to the ground the tower-houses belonging to the Ghibellines in the city centre. The numerous statues along the outside of the Palazzo Vecchio and the loggia make this a veritable open-air museum. In the middle of the square is an equestrian statue of Cosimo I–Duke of Florence 1537–1574 and a lavish patron of the arts–made in 1594 by Giovanni da Bologna. At the corner of the Palazzo Vecchio, the Neptune Fountain, whose local nickname is *Il Biancone,* is more impressive for its maritime gods, its elongated Mannerist-style nymphs and its bronze fawns than for its enormous marble statue of the sea god Neptune. The fountain was made by **Bartolomeo Ammannati**, assisted by Giovanni da Bologna, for the wedding in 1565 of Cosimo I's elder son with Joan of Austria. It was to some extent a challenge to the rigorous morality preached by the Dominican friar, Savonarola, who had constantly criticised the Medici style of government, as it was erected on the very spot where he was burned at the stake on 23 May 1498. In front of the fountain is a round slab marking the place of execution. Savonarola's death is commemorated every year in a ceremony known as the Fiorita.

Beside the steps up to the building (*left*) is the *Marzocco*, the lion of Florence gripping a heraldic lily, executed by Donatello (*original in the Bargello*). Beside it is an admirable copy of the famous group by the same artist representing **Judith and Holofernes**★ (*original in the Palazzo Vecchio*). Near the entrance is a huge marble statue of David, a copy of Michelangelo's famous work (*original in the Galleria dell'Accademia*).

Loggia della Signoria★★

The loggia was constructed at the end of the 14C to accommodate the members of the *Signoria* (*see below*) during official ceremonies. When later it was used as a guard room by Cosimo I's lancers (16C), it became known as the **Loggia dei Lanzi**. Although Gothic in design, it has wide semicircular arches built in the Florentine tradition, opening onto the square. An elegant decoration is provided by four shields representing the cardinal virtues, a band decorated with seven coats of arms which have been damaged, a graceful frieze of small trefoiled arches and a slender roof balustrade (*terrace accessible from the Uffizi during the high season only*).

Restored statues dating from the days of the ancient Romans and the Renaissance have been placed in the loggia. The admirable statue of **Perseus**★★★ brandishing the head of the Medusa (*front left*) was made between 1545 and 1553 by Benvenuto Cellini. The low relief depicting *Perseus Delivering Andromeda* is a copy (*original in the Bargello*). *Rape of the Sabine Women* (*right*) dates from 1583. *Hercules Slaying the Centaur, Nessus* (*behind*) (1599) is by Giovanni da Bologna.

Palazzo Vecchio★★ (Palazzo della Signoria)

2hr. 🕐*Open daily 9am–7pm, Thu and Hols 9am–2pm (last entry 1hr before closing).* 🕐*Closed Easter, 1 May, 15 Aug, 25 Dec, 1 Jan. Guided tour available. Restaurant. Bookshop.* ⊚⊚€6. €8 *combined ticket with Brancacci Chapel (*🎧*see Santa Maria del Carmine).* ♿*.* 📞*055 27 68 465. www.comune.fi.it.*

At the end of the 13C, Florence decided to build a city hall worthy of its importance, and it was probably Arnolfo di Cambio, the cathedral architect, who drew the design for the new city hall. The impressive mass of the palazzo, surmounted by an elegant belfry (94m/309ft high), dominates the square. It is in an austere Gothic style with an almost total absence of doors or windows on the lower level. On the upper storeys there are twin windows

121

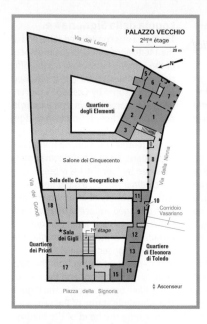

PALAZZO VECCHIO
2ème étage

Via dei Leoni

Quartiere
degli Elementi

Salone dei Cinquecento

Sala delle Carte Geografiche ★

Via della Ninna

Via dei Gondi

Corridoio
Vasariano

★ Sala
dei Gigli   1er étage

Quartiere
dei Priori

Quartiere
di Eleonora
di Toledo

Piazza della Signoria   ‡ Ascenseur

with trefoiled arches, machicolations, parapet walkways and crenellations. The merlons on the palazzo are Guelf and those on the tower are Ghibelline.

The building was designed to house the city government (**la Signoria**) composed of six representatives of the guilds (**priori delle Arti**), which held great power in Florence at that time, and a magistrate (*Gonfaloniere di Giustizia*) whose post combined judicial and mili-

Palazzo
Vecchio

C. Belloli/MICHELIN

tary authority. These officials were elected for only two months and, during their period of office, lived almost like recluses within the *palazzo*, where they worked, ate and slept. They were permitted to leave only for exceptional reasons. Dante lived there in 1300 as a member of the magistrature.

In the 16C Cosimo I made the building his residence and also adapted it to suit the lavish lifestyle of the grand-ducal court by enlarging it and making radical alterations to the interior. The work was supervised by Giorgio Vasari who, for almost 20 years, from 1555 until his death, was employed there as architect, painter and decorator. When Cosimo I left the building to his son and moved to the Pitti Palace, it became known as Palazzo Vecchio (Old Palace) instead of Palazzo della Signoria.

The luxurious, elegant Renaissance interior forms a striking contrast to the exterior. The **courtyard**★ with its tall portico was almost totally redesigned in the 15C by Michelozzo and was elegantly decorated a century later by Vasari, who added stuccowork on a gold background to the columns and painted grotesque figures on the vaulting. In the centre is a graceful fountain with a porphyry basin, surmounted by a small winged genius, a copy of a bronze by Verrocchio, which can be seen on the Juno Terrace inside the building.

▶ *To reach the first floor climb up the superb double staircase built by Vasari.*

Hall of the Five Hundred

The hall (*Salone dei Cinquecento*) is a gigantic chamber (1 200sq m/12 912sq ft in area, 18m/59ft high), built in 1495 during the days of the Republic instituted by Savonarola. It was designed to accommodate the Grand Council which had so many members (1500) that only one-third of their number could participate in the government of the city at any one time. Here Savonarola spoke in 1496, during his brief reign as master of

Florence, and here he was condemned to death two years later.

When the Medici returned to power, they used the hall as their audience chamber and also for receptions, including the one given to celebrate the marriage of Francesco and Joan of Austria.

The walls and **sumptuous coffered ceiling**★★ were decorated by Vasari and his assistants with allegories and scenes in honour of Florence and Cosimo I. He is depicted like a god in the central coffer, amidst a circle of cherubs and coats of arms representing the city's various guilds. Battle scenes cover the walls along the entire length of the chamber, in honour of the victories won by Florence, mainly over its two great rivals, Pisa and Siena.

Most of the sculptures placed along the walls were already in the chamber in the 16C. Among them (*left of the door opposite the entrance*) is *La Vittoria*, an admirable group representing Genius slaying Might. Michelangelo created this work for the tomb of Julius II but, as it was never finished, it was given to Cosimo I by Michelangelo's nephew.

Studiolo★★

Access to the right of the entrance. Visible from the door. ○━*No admission to the room itself.* The exquisite but visually challenging room was the study (studiolo) of Francesco I. Originally it could only be reached from his bedchamber via a small concealed door (*behind the bare panel to the right at the end of the room*). It has no external source of light, reflecting the solitary character of the prince and his taste for secrets.

It was Vasari who designed this tiny but elegant room. The walls themselves are covered in panels painted by several of the Florentine Mannerist painters. Using a symbolism that is often difficult to comprehend, they illustrated the myth of Prometheus (decoration on the ceiling), the four elements – Water, Air, Earth and Fire – or human enterprise, scientific discoveries and the mysteries of alchemy. The two portraits placed opposite each other at the ends of the room depict Francesco's parents,

For the Children...

The ♟♟**Museo dei Ragazzi** is aimed at children between the ages of three and six and houses a range of interactive displays, as well as hosting live events. The displays deal with themes such as light and shadow, Galileo's telescope and Torricelli's experiments on vacuum, while maintaining a link with the history of the palace and the city. ⊙*Open daily 9am–6pm* (*2pm Thu and Hols*). €*6.50 joint ticket with the Palazzo Vecchio. Information available about the different activities and prices.* ☎*055 27 68 224.*

Cosimo I and Eleonora of Toledo. Both were painted by Bronzino's studio.

Leo X's Apartments

Access from the Hall of the Five Hundred by the door opposite the Studiolo. ○━*Most of the rooms are not open to the public as they house the offices of the current mayor.* This wing of the palazzo was added in the 16C by Cosimo I. The rooms in Leo X's apartments were designed as reception rooms for the guests of the grand-ducal court. Their decoration glorified the merits of the Medici, each feature being dedicated to one illustrious member of the family. The decoration comprises not only a series of historical documents but also a veritable portrait gallery.

Leo X's Chamber, the largest chamber in Leo X's apartments bears his name and is dedicated to the son of Lorenzo the Magnificent who re-established the family's authority in Florence in 1512 and was elected Pope in 1513. He is depicted arriving in Piazza della Signoria during his visit to his birthplace two years later (*on the wall opposite the fireplace*).

❯ *Access to the second floor from this room.*

The second floor contains three suites of **apartments** (*quartieri*) – the Elements Apartments, Eleonora of Toledo's Apartments, and the Priors' Apartments (&*see infobox on following pages*).

Second Floor Apartments Tour

Refer to the floorplan.

Elements

These rooms, which are situated above Leo X's Apartments, were built at the same time and to an identical layout. The decoration, based on ancient mythology, was designed by Vasari using complex symbolism with the aim of exalting the virtues of Cosimo I.

The **Elements Chamber** (1) is named after the allegorical scenes in its decoration. On the walls are illustrations of Water (the Birth of Venus), Fire (Vulcan's forge) and Earth (Saturn receiving fruit). On the ceiling, in the rectangular coffer above the allegorical representation of Earth is Air (Apollo's chariot).

The **Ops and Cybele Chamber** (2) is dedicated to Ops, the Roman goddess of Abundance and Fertility, who is often assimilated with the Greek goddess, Cybele, mother of all the gods.

At the centre of the coffered ceiling of the **Ceres Chamber** (3) is Ceres, the goddess of harvests.

On the central coffer in the ceiling of the **Jupiter Chamber** (4) Vasari and his pupils described the mythical childhood of Jupiter.

The antechamber of the **Juno Terrace** (5) contains the small statue by Verrocchio of a winged Cupid holding a dolphin. It was designed to be placed in the entrance courtyard.

On the ceiling of the **Hercules Chamber** (6) are paintings of the *Twelve Labors of Hercules*. The central coffer shows Hercules as a child with his parents, Jupiter and Alcmene; he is strangling the serpents sent to kill him by Juno, Alcmene's rival.

The **Saturn Terrace** (7) looks out onto one of the most attractive stretches of countryside in the Florence district. In the centre of the ceiling is a painting of Saturn devouring his sons. The four triangular coffers contain representations of the Four Ages of Man. The 12 rectangular coffers round the edge are decorated with illustrations of the 12 hours of the day.

A **Gallery** (8) overlooks the Hall of the Five Hundred and gives a good idea of the exceptional height of the hall. Through the windows opposite there is a view of the cathedral dome and the Tuscan hills in the distance.

Priors'

These apartments were laid out a century earlier than the remainder of the palazzo, which was altered by Cosimo I.

The **Priors' Chapel** (16) was decorated in the late 15C by Rodolfo Ghirlandaio. It was here that the officials (*priori*) gathered to pray before making decisions of a legal nature, as is evident from the quotations from the Old and New Testaments contained in the series of panels round the walls.

The **Audience Chamber** (17), which was decorated in the second half of the 15C, has a sumptuous coffered ceiling by Giuliano da Maiano.

The **Lily Chamber**★ is one of the most beautiful chambers in the palazzo. It owes its name to the golden fleurs de lys on a blue background decorating its walls. This is not the Florentine lily, but the emblem of the King of France, with whom the Republic of Florence was on friendly terms. The superb gold and blue coffered **ceiling**★ was made, like the ceiling in the previous chamber, by Giuliano da Maiano (1478). The marquetry doors are decorated with portraits of Dante and Petrarch. The admirable sculpture entitled **Judith and Holofernes**★ by Donatello is displayed in this chamber.

Machiavelli worked in the **Cancelleria** (18) for his last 15 years in office as Secretary to the Chancery, playing a leading role in Florentine politics, until he was forced into exile following the return of the Medici in 1512. The room contains two portraits of Machiavelli – a terracotta bust and a posthumous painting by Santi di Tito.

The **Map Chamber**★, designed by Vasari for Cosimo I, was where the Medici kept their state dress and their valuables. The decoration on the cupboards, completed in the second half of the 16C, consists of a collection of maps of outstanding interest since all the areas of the world known at that time are shown. The enormous globe in the centre of the room dates from the same period.

On the left of the Palazzo Vecchio, in Via dei Gondi, on the corner with Piazza S Firenze, stands the **Palazzo Gondi**★ (1490), by Giuliano da Sangallo.

Eleonora of Toledo's

When Cosimo I came to live in the Palazzo della Signoria with his 18-year-old wife, he commissioned court architect Battista del Tasso to refurbish some of the austere apartments once occupied by the guild representatives (*priori*). A few years later, Vasari and Flemish artist Jan Van der Straet, better known as Lo Stradano, decorated the ceilings with scenes constituting a sort of hymn to femininity.

The **Green Chamber** (9), the only one on which Vasari did not work, was Eleonora's bedchamber. On the vaulting is a shield bearing the coats of arms of the Medici and the House of Toledo. This room opens into a tiny study (10) with a small window, used by the Duchess as her office (*scrittoio*). It also opens into her private chapel (11), which was decorated from 1541 to 1545 with scenes from the story of Moses by Bronzino. The artist is said to have taken Cosimo and Eleonora's eldest daughter as his model for the Virgin Mary in the *Annunciation*, which hangs on the back wall next (*right*) to the *Deposition from the Cross*.

Audience Chamber, Palazzo Vecchio

Gordon Pim (Toronto, Canada)

The **Sabine Chamber** (12) was used by Eleonora's ladies-in-waiting. On the ceiling is a painting of the Sabine women standing between their fathers and their Roman husbands to prevent the men fighting.

The **Esther Chamber** (13) contains an attractive 15C marble wash basin. Almost the entire ceiling is covered with a large coffer decorated with an illustration of Courage and Determination in the person of Esther, the Hebrew woman who succeeded in saving her people.

In the **Penelope Chamber** (14) the great central medallion is an exaltation of faithfulness symbolised by the wife of Ulysses dressed in 16C Florentine costume. In several places the Medici shield with its five roundels appears together with the chequerboard shield of the House of Toledo as well as the emblem of Cosimo I, the tortoise, a symbol of prudence, and a sail, which evokes a sense of opportunity.

The **Gualdrada Chamber** (15) is dedicated to Virtue, embodied in the young Florentine girl who gained fame in the 13C by refusing a kiss from Emperor Otto. The frieze below the ceiling contains a number of buildings in Florence which are easily recognisable.

The Uffizi★★★

Art for Art's Sake

♿Map p108

Set up by Grand Duke Francesco I de' Medici, the Uffizi Gallery contains the world's richest collection of Renaissance paintings and sculpture, including masterpieces by Botticelli, Raphael, Michelangelo and Caravaggio.

Reserve ahead to avoid long queues (☎€3). 2hr 30min for all rooms. ⏱*Open Tue–Sun 8.30am–7pm (Sat 10pm).* ⏱*Closed 1 May, 25 Dec, 1 Jan.* ☎*€6.50.* ♿. ✆*055 29 48 83.* *www.uffizi.firenze.it.*

The **Uffizi Gallery** is housed in a building commissioned in 1560 by Cosimo I for the offices (*uffizi*) of the Medici administration. Vasari designed this unusual building in late Renaissance style on the site of a Romanesque church. It consists of two long parallel wings joined at one end in a curve to form a kind of enclosed square like a courtyard, and extends from Piazza della Signoria to the Arno.

An aerial walkway, which is still visible, once linked the Palazzo Vecchio to the gallery and formed the top floor of the latter building.

In 1581 the east section of the gallery was laid out by Francesco I to house the works of art acquired by earlier generations and was opened to the public ten years later. The Medici collections represent a large part of the works of art which now make the Uffizi one of the world's leading art galleries.

The **ground floor** displays relics from the Romanesque church of San Pier Scheraggio, the former occupant of the site. There are a number of fresco portraits by Andrea del Castagno and a fine representation of the *Battle of San Martino*, painted in oils in 1936 by Corrado Cagli in the style of the famous *Battle of San Romano* by Paolo Uccello (*see Room 7*).

In the entrance to the gallery (*right*) hangs a large portrait of Anna Maria Ludovica, the last of the Medici who,

on her death in 1743, bequeathed to the City of Florence the extraordinary treasures acquired by her ancestors.

The monumental staircase built by Vasari leads to the top floor of the building. The lifts (*far right of the foyer*) are reserved for those with special needs.

East Wing – The long corridor displays Classical sculptures – sarcophagi, statues (mainly Roman copies of Greek works) and busts from the imperial era. The ceiling is decorated with grotesque figures.

West Wing — During the era of the Grand Dukes, this wing housed the Medici workshops, where craftsmen worked, producing *pietra dura* artefacts, miniatures and even perfumes, medicines, poisons and antidotes.

Terrace – From the cafeteria terrace, which is situated at the far end of the gallery overlooking the Loggia della Signoria, there is a superb view of the upper storeys of the Palazzo Vecchio. The terrace area used to be a garden with a fountain, where the Medici would come to listen to the musicians playing in the square.

The **rotunda** in front of the staircase contains a marble statue of a boar (Hellenistic, dating from the 3C BC) given to Cosimo I by Pope Paul IV. A bronze copy of the work, known as Porcellino, adorns the fountain in the Mercato Nuovo.

Corridoio Vasariano – (⏱*the Vasari Corridor is currently closed for restoration*) This gallery (1km/0.5mi long) was commissioned by Cosimo I so that he could pass unseen and apart from the crowds from the Palazzo Vecchio to the Pitti Palace. It was built by Vasari in 1565 and runs from the Uffizi, through the top storey of the buildings on the Ponte Vecchio, before penetrating the maze of houses on the south bank of the Arno.

The charm and beauty of this unusual location is enhanced by the view through the windows of Florence, the Arno and the surrounding hills.

The corridor forms a coda to the Uffizi galleries and is hung with 17C and 18C works and famous self-portraits. The first paintings are from the school of

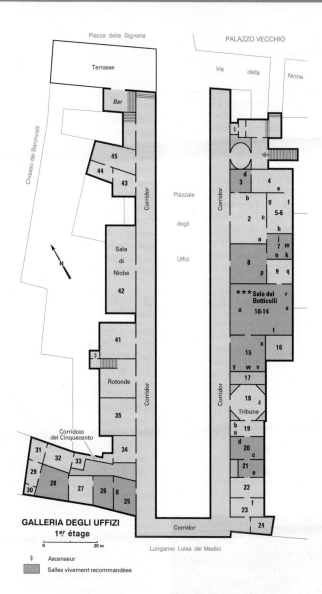

Piazza della Signoria

PALAZZO VECCHIO

Terrasse

Via   della   Ninna

Bar

Chiasso dei Baroncelli

Corridor

Piazzale

degli

Uffizi

Corridor

45

44

43

d
3

4

e

b

g

f

5-6

2   c

h

a

j
7   m

n   k

8

p   9   q

***Sala del
Botticelli

u   10-14

r

s

Sala
di
Niobe

42

t

N

41

15

x   16

y   w   v

Rotonde

17

Corridor

18   z

Tribune

35

Corridor

b   19

Corridoio
del Cinquecento

a

d   20

34

c

31

21

32   33

29

e

28   27   26   g   25

22

30

f   23

GALLERIA DEGLI UFFIZI
1er étage

24

Corridor

0   20 m

Lungarno Luisa de' Medici

Ascenseur

Salles vivement recommandées

Caravaggio (*Adoration of the Christ child* by Gherardo delle Notti), followed by works from other Italian schools – Bologna (Guido Reni, Albani, Guercino), Venice (Liss), Rome (Bamboccio), Tuscany (Lorenzo Lippi) and Naples (Salvator Rosa). The 17C Lombardy artists are represented by Giovanni Battista Crespi, and 18C Venetians by Bellotto and Rosalba Carriera. The French school is represented by La Tour, La Hyre and Boucher.

The section of the corridor above the Ponte Vecchio is lined by about a hundred self-portraits by Titian, Veronese, Rosalba Carriera and Correggio. The remaining section of the corridor is hung with portraits by Velázquez, Rubens, Élisabeth Vigée-Lebrun, Ingres, Delacroix and Chagall. It provides a view of the interior of the church of **Santa Felicità** and ends at the Pitti Palace, where Boboli Gardens begin.

Uffizi East Wing

The three large Madonnas in Majesty which dominate **Room 2** illustrate the main 13C and early 14C trends in Italian painting as it moved away from the Byzantine tradition. The painting (*far right*) by Cimabue (**a**) (c. 1280) is a composition in the early symmetrical style but it includes innovative features – decorative curved lines, the movement and a sense of humanity in the figure of the Virgin Mary and the expression on the faces of the prophets below the throne. The *Madonna Rucellai* (*left*) (**b**) (1285) is by the Sienese artist Duccio. In the Centre is Giotto's *Madonna* (**c**) (c. 1310), a Renaissance precursor, with its sense of perspective.

Room 3, which is devoted to the Sienese School of the 14C, contains Simone Martini's exquisite *Annunciation* (**d**) (1333). Martini was the first to illustrate this biblical scene, which was depicted so often over the following centuries, and his arrangement – angel on the left and the Virgin Mary on the right – became a model which was to be followed throughout history.

Room 4 contains 14C Florentine paintings, mainly by Giotto's pupils (Bernardo Daddi and Giottino, whose

Deposition (**e**) shows less dramatic effect than the works by his teacher, Taddeo Gaddi).

Rooms 5 to 6 house a collection of "International Gothic" works (late 14C–early 15C), a late exaggeration of the Gothic style which strives to reproduce nature in painstaking detail. The most brilliant representatives of this style were Lorenzo Monaco, whose style influenced Fra Angelico, and Gentile da Fabriano. Works by the first artist include the *Adoration of the Magi* (**f**) and a vivid *Coronation of the Virgin Mary* (**g**). The second of the two painters developed this art form to the ultimate in his sumptuous, dazzling *Adoration of the Magi* (**h**).

▷ *The following rooms are devoted to the Renaissance.*

Room 7 (the early years – 15C) is dominated by Paolo Uccello's famous *Battle of San Romano* (**j**), one panel of a huge triptych. The other sections are in the Louvre Museum in Paris and the National Gallery in London. By making daring use of foreshortening and reducing certain features (soldiers) to mere volume through the unusual use of colour (red horses), he set himself apart from his contemporaries and gave his work a modern, abstract character which has often led him to be considered as a distant precursor of Cubism.

During the Early Renaissance, two other painters focused their attention on conveying a sense of volume. The first of them was Masaccio, represented by a *Madonna and Child with St Anne* (**k**) painted in collaboration with Masolino, who worked on the Brancacci Chapel. The second was Piero della Francesca. Piero's powerful portrait (1465) of the Duke of Urbino, Federico da Montefeltro (**m**) and his wife, Battista Sforza, can be seen on an easel by a window. On the back of the work is a painting of the two nuptial chariots bringing the couple together.

Inside the Uffizi

Other artists from this period represented here are Domenico Veneziano, *Madonna surrounded by Saints* (n) and Fra Angelico, *Coronation of the Virgin* (*right of the entrance door*).

Room 8 contains a number of works by Filippo Lippi, an inspiration for Botticelli. On the wall between Rooms 8 and 9 is a delicate *Madonna and Child* (p) (1465), in which the Virgin Mary appears as a graceful young woman seated at her window.

Antonio Pollaiolo was the elder and more prominent of the two Pollaiolo brothers (second half of the 15C); **Room 9** contains one of his famous female portraits (*left by the window*). The large figures representing the theological and cardinal virtues were painted by Piero Pollaiolo.

The painting of Fortitude (*by the entrance to the next room*) is by Botticelli. The display case (q) contains four very small pictures – *The Labors of Hercules* by Antonio Pollaiolo and the *Story of Judith* by Botticelli.

The **Botticelli Room**★★★ (10–14) is the gallery's crowning glory. Apart from a series of world-famous pictures by the Renaissance master, it also contains splendid works indicating the reciprocal influence of Florentine painters and Flemish Primitives that accompanied the commercial exchanges of the 15C. Botticelli's major works (*from left to right*) include the **Madonna of the Magnificat** (r), a roundel including remarkable intricacy of detail and extraordinary harmony. From the peak of the artist's career comes the allegorical **Birth of Venus** (s) and (*next wall*) **Primavera** (t), undoubtedly the most representative examples of Botticelli's poetic lyricism and the idealism that characterised the Humanist culture favoured at the court of Lorenzo the Magnificent. In the **Birth of Venus**, a young woman expressing a melancholy and fragile grace emerges from a background of sea and sky painted in remarkably transparent cold tones; the artist is said to have represented the features of Simonetta Vespucci, mistress of Giuliano, the brother of Lorenzo the Magnificent.

Between the *Birth of Venus* and *Primavera* hang Botticelli's **Pallas and the Centaur** depicting Bestiality tamed by Thought, and his admirable **Madonna of the Pomegranate**, another roundel in which the artist displays a skill acquired from his contact with goldsmiths. The small picture next to it is the famous **Calumny**, a late work, which shows the development of the artist's skill. Next to *Primavera* is an *Adoration of the Magi* depicting several members of the Medici family. The character in yellow (*far right*) is said to be Botticelli.

The **Portinari Triptych** (u), opposite the *Birth of Venus*, is a masterpiece by Hugo Van der Goes. This skilfully structured work, painted in deep colours, reflects an Italian influence in the taste for huge compositions and life-size characters.

This technique, borrowed from the Flemish masters, can also be seen in *Adoration of the Magi*, a medallion painted in 1487 by Domenico Ghirlandaio (*left of the Portinari Triptych*).

The **Leonardo da Vinci Room** (**Room 15**) contains two of Leonardo's most famous paintings. **The Annunciation** (v) was painted during the artist's youth (c. 1475), and is traditional as regards its composition. As to the unfinished **Adoration of the Magi** (w) (1481), its triangular composition and the expressive faces of the figures make this a very unusual work for the late 15C. It is almost certain that Leonardo also painted the angel which can be seen in profile in the remarkable *Baptism of Christ* painted c. 1470 by his master, Verrocchio.

In Perugino's works, the peaceful and almost languid grace of the characters and their inherent sweetness hint at the influence that the artist was to have in later years on his pupil, Raphael. Note *Christ on the Mount of Olives* (x) and, opposite, *Madonna and Child between John the Baptist and St Sebastian* (y).

▷ *Return to the corridor.*

The **Tribune** (**Room 18**) is an octagonal room covered by a dome decorated in mother-of-pearl. It was built by Buontalenti for Francesco I, who wanted it to contain the most valuable items in his collections. Among the Roman sculptures, visitors can see the famous **Medici Venus** (z) inspired by Praxiteles.

Numerous portraits are hung around the room including several of the Medici family, such as Lorenzo the Magnificent by Vasari, Cosimo the Elder by Pontormo and a few works by Bronzino, the official painter of the Medici court.

In **Room 19** Umbrian Renaissance painting is mainly represented by Perugino. Note the portrait of the Florentine craftsman, Francesco delle Opere (a) and an indescribably melancholic portrait of an adolescent boy (b). The room also contains works by Signorelli and Piero di Cosimo's highly detailed *Perseus Delivering Andromeda* (*left of the door to the next room*).

Room 20 is devoted to the German Renaissance, represented here by its greatest masters. Dürer (1471–1528) made several visits to Venice where he was deeply influenced by the painting of Mantegna and Giovanni Bellini, as shown in his **Adoration of the Magi** (c). The famous **Adam and Eve** (d) by Cranach (1472–1553) is painted in a style that achieves extreme elegance through the elongated lines.

Venetian painting from the 15C and very early 16C is represented in **Room 21** by Giovanni Bellini (1435–1516) and his pupil Giorgione (1477–1510). This room also contains Bellini's famous **Sacred Allegory** (e).

Room 22 displays works by other leading German painters and a number of Flemish masters, including Albrecht Altdorfer (1480–1536), founder of the Danube School and one of the forefathers of landscape painting; Hans Holbein the Younger (1497–1543), official court painter to Henry VIII of England; and the Flemish painters Joos van Cleve (c. 1485–1540) and Van Orley (c. 1490–1540).

Room 23 is devoted to Correggio, whose painting makes unusually sensitive use of Leonardo da Vinci's *sfumato* technique. His *Adoration of the Infant Jesus* (f) heralded the beginnings of Mannerism.

Room 24, decorated during the 17C to house the Medici jewellery, contains a collection of medallions and miniature portraits.

From the corridor linking the two wings of the building, there is a fine **view** of the Ponte Vecchio (*foreground*) and across the River Arno to San Miniato on the hill.

Uffizi West Wing

Room 25 provides an introduction to the High Renaissance (16C) through work by **Michelangelo** and the Florentine School. The famous **Tondo Doni** (g) painted by Michelangelo in 1503, depicts the Holy Family against a background of young nudes. The contortion of the bodies paves the way for Mannerism and can be seen again in later works, especially in many of the figures within the Sistine Chapel.

Room 26 displays a number of works by Raphael. The famous **Madonna of the Goldfinch** (*left opposite the door*), painted c. 1506, is one of his most harmonious and most serene compositions. The room also contains a self-portrait of the artist (*right of the window*).

The large **Madonna delle Arpie** (*entrance wall*), who is named after the **Harpies** which decorate the pedestal on which the Virgin Mary is standing, is a majestic, somewhat academic work (1517) by **Andrea del Sarto**, the artist most representative of Florentine classicism.

Pontormo (1494–1556) was a leading figure in the Tuscan Mannerist movement. His *Supper at Emmaus* in **Room 27** (*right-hand wall*) reflects a restless melancholy.

Room 28 contains 16C Venetian paintings and displays a number of works by Titian including the **Venus of Urbino** (*right-hand wall*), one of the artist's late masterpieces (1538), and The **Flora**, painted c. 1515.

The following two rooms are dedicated to the 16C Emilian School. Parmigianino gave **Mannerism** a stylisation which originated in an extreme refinement and an even greater elongation of forms. **Room 29** displays the **Madonna with the Long Neck**.

The Ferrara-born artist Dosso Dossi (c. 1490–1542) constituted a link between the Emilian School and the Venetian School that had a profound influence on him (**Room 31**).

Room 32 contains works by the Venetians, including *Death of Adonis* by Sebastiano del Piombo (c. 1485–1547), who apprenticed with Giorgione and was influenced by Michelangelo.

The tiny "Cinquecento Corridor" (**Room 33**) leads to **Room 34** which contains a number of works by the Venetian painter Veronese (1528–88), who was influenced during his early career by the Emilian Mannerists.

Room 35 contains a number of portraits by Tintoretto (1518–94), in particular his **Leda and the Swan**.

The next section covers **17C Italian and European** works.

The Flemish School is represented in **Room 41** by Sustermans, Van Dyck and, in particular, a number of works by Rubens. He, more than any other Flemish painter, had extensive contacts with Italian artists (especially the Venetians).

The following large room, known as the **Niobe Room** (**Room 42**), was refurbished in the 18C in order to house Roman copies of a group statue representing Niobe and her children, carved in 4 BC by the Greek sculptor Scopas. Legend has it that Niobe mocked Leto, who had had only two children, Apollo and Artemis, by her husband, Zeus. In order to avenge their mother, the two sons killed Niobe's seven sons and seven daughters with their arrows. Niobe was so grief-stricken that Zeus granted her wish to be changed into a rock.

Room 43 is dedicated to **Caravaggio** (1573–1610). The artist was only 20 when he painted the famous **Adolescent Bacchus**. His painting of the *Sacrifice of Isaac*, where the sudden arrival of the angel seems to be taken from true life, is also a very early work yet a clear indication of the naturalistic style which was to have such considerable impact on 17C–18C European art. The striking head of Medusa, painted on a shield (*on an easel*), has a certain Baroque quality. Also displayed in the room (*right-hand wall*) is a splendid **Seascape** by Claude Lorrain (1600–82).

Room 44 displays 17C Flemish and Dutch painting, including works by Rembrandt (1606–69). On the end wall, there is a remarkable portrait of an old man and two self-portraits.

Room 45 contains 18C works from Spain, with two portraits by Goya (*left of the door*). There are also (*wall opposite the door*) Venetian paintings. The first two, executed with photographic accuracy, are by Canaletto (1697–1768) – *The Doges' Palace* and *The Grand Canal at the Rialto Bridge*. The second two are by Francesco Guardi (1712–93) and have an almost impressionistic feel, with their light brushstrokes and nuanced light.

Botticelli (1444–1510)

Botticelli was a pupil of Filippo Lippi and later Verrocchio. He was also an admirer of Pollaiolo. All three artists had a great influence on Botticelli, who retained the linearity and contour of Lippi, while showing, in his work, the energy characteristic of the other two. He remained indifferent, however, to the introduction of atmosphere into painting that Verrocchio had begun to explore. By the end of the 15C he was the greatest painter in Florence – he was among the artists called to Rome to paint the walls of the Sistine Chapel – and he mixed with the circle of neo-Platonist scholars, philosophers and writers at the court of Lorenzo the Magnificent. He revived the themes of Antiquity and painted mythological subjects – Venus, Pallas and the Centaur, Primavera (Spring) – bringing to them a tender lyricism that gave them an allegorical quality. He also painted numerous Madonnas and he excelled in introducing a sense of movement and rhythm to fabrics, veils, hair and limbs. The faces of his subjects are tilted rather systematically to one side in a somewhat Mannerist style.

The death of Lorenzo the Magnificent, the preaching of Savonarola and the future development of his artistic style, which through its exaggerated curves bordered on an affectation of the Gothic style, all conspired to push the artist from a state of extreme sensitivity to open doubt, as is shown in his *Calumny of Apelles*, a work drawn in such an incisive way that it arouses a feeling of distress. Although he embodies all that was best during the finest years of the century of the Medici, Botticelli failed to influence other artists because his originality was difficult to emulate.

De Agostini Picture Library/Fototeca ENIT

The Primavera

The scene takes place in Venus' garden. The goddess is in the centre of the composition, surrounded by orange trees and myrtle bushes. Above her flies Cupid, his arrow aimed at one of the three Graces, who are dancing with each other and are unaware of his presence.

To the left, Mercury disperses the clouds with his caduceus, while to the right the green-coloured Zephyr pursues the nymph Cloris. (Ovid recounts that after marrying the nymph Zephyr made her queen of the flowers.) Thus transformed, Flora scatters roses over the meadow. There have been many interpretations of this work, which could be seen as a portrayal of the metamorphosis of love. The shy and dreamy young woman about to be hit by the arrow could be Castitas, the girl to the left, Voluptas, and the third figure, Pulchritudo. Venus is a static figure, presiding over these games of love.

Mercury, who was thought to accompany souls to the next world, acted as a messenger between men and the gods; here he reaches up to the sky, as Castitas looks on. The harmony of the painting lies in its balanced composition: Mercury's upward motion is balanced by the figure of Zephyr at the opposite side of the painting, who stretches down towards the ground.

South Bank of the Arno

⌖*Maps pp134, 142*

PONTE VECCHIO★★

The **Old Bridge** is, in fact, the oldest bridge in Florence, and was built near where a Roman bridge once spanned the river carrying the road linking Rome to northern Italy. Over the centuries the bridge was destroyed on a number of occasions; the current structure dates only from 1345. In 1944 it was the only bridge in Florence to be spared by the Germans who, in order to block the advance of American troops approaching from the south, razed the surrounding old districts almost entirely to the ground. The Ponte Vecchio did, however, suffer extensive damage during the 1966 floods.

The arcades that initially lined the bridge housed the tanners' workshops and, later, the stalls of butchers for whom the river provided a handy "sewer". In the 16C, on the orders of Grand Duke Ferdinand II, the butchers were forced to make way for craftsmen whose activities were of a less insanitary and more decorative nature – jewellers and gold and silversmiths who built most of the tiny corbelled shops above the Arno, still occupied by craftsmen today. The shops attract a continuous flow of visitors, who come to browse or buy, and who throng the bridge during the summer season until late in the evening.

The esplanade in the middle of the bridge contains a bronze bust of the most famous goldsmith of all, Benvenuto Cellini, placed there in the 19C. From here, there is a fine **view** of the banks of the Arno and the succession of bridges that span it.

▶ *Walk towards the Palazzo Pitti, passing in front of the Church of Santa Felicità.*

Above the entrance porch is a sumptuous chamber, resembling a box at the theatre, where the Grand Dukes could attend Mass without ceremony, having entered from the Vasari Corridor.

The chapel (*immediately to the right of the entrance*), built in the early 15C by Brunelleschi, contains the famous **Deposition**★★ by Pontormo, painted in clear sharp tones with undulating, elongated forms in a style characteristic of Tuscan Mannerism.

PALAZZO PITTI★★

Half a day. ⌖*Map p134.* The **Pitti Palace** is a huge Renaissance palace built round three sides of a sloping square overlooked by the building's long, severe façade. Only the shading of the heavy rustication work softens the imposing architectural style and breaks up a unity verging on the monotonous.

For centuries the shop windows of the Ponte Vecchio have looked down onto the Arno flowing through Florence

B. Pérousse/ MICHELIN

Work began on the palace in 1458. It was designed for the Pitti, a family of influential merchants and bankers who were initially friends but later great rivals of the Medici. The building then consisted of no more than the section comprising the seven central bays. Several years later the Pitti family was financially ruined and the residence designed to outshine their rivals was left unfinished.

The palace was bought in 1549 by Eleonora of Toledo, wife of Cosimo I, and she turned it into a princely residence to which Cosimo I transferred his court c. 1560. The work of conversion was entrusted to the architect and sculptor Ammannati. The hillside was laid out as a magnificent garden but it was not until the 17C that the front of the building attained its current length (over 200m/650ft). The two projecting wings were added in the 18C.

The Pitti Palace provided the inspiration for the Palais du Luxembourg in Paris that was built by Marie de Médicis who as Maria de' Medici had lived in the Pitti Palace in her youth.

It is also a remarkably rich repository of works of art, furniture and priceless objects.

Galleria Palatina★★★

See the detailed tour on the following pages. The entrance is up the staircase designed by Ammannati (in the corner of the courtyard to the right of the entrance) Persons with special needs can access the lift near the courtyard. Open Tue–Sun 8.15am–6.50pm. Closed 1 May, 25 Dec, 1 Jan. Bookshop. €8.50 combined ticket with the Appartamenti Reali and Galleria d'Arte Moderna. ℘055 23 88 614. www.polomuseale.firenze.it.

The **Palatine Gallery** takes its name from the title of the last of the Medici, Anna Maria Ludovica (1667–1743), who was married to the Elector Palatine. The luxurious interior houses an outstanding collection of 16C, 17C and 18C works, including a series of **paintings★★★** by **Raphael** and **Titian**, which make the Pitti Palace one of the richest art galleries in the world. The works were collected from the 17C onwards by the Grand Dukes of the Medici family and later by the Grand Dukes of Lorraine. They are exhibited regardless of didactic or chronological order, as was the fashion of the great stately collections of the time.

Appartamenti Reali★

Access via the foyer of the Palatine Gallery. First Floor. Open Tue–Sun 8.15am–6.50pm. €8.50 combined ticket with the Galleria Palatina and Galleria d'Arte Moderna. ℘055 23 88 614. www.polomuseale.firenze.it.

The **Royal Apartments** extending from the centre of the façade to the end of

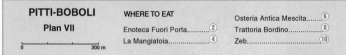

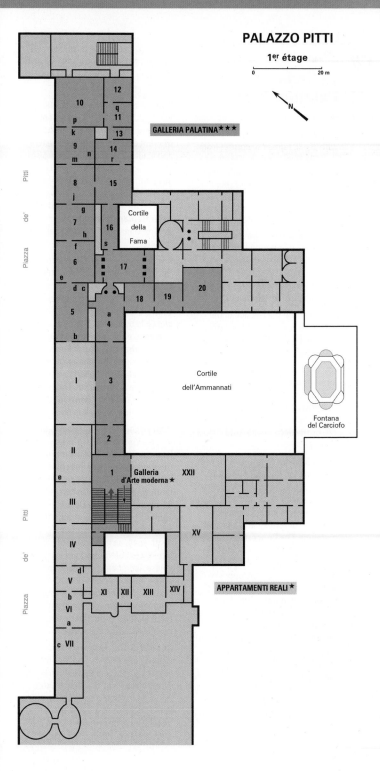

PALAZZO PITTI

1er étage

0   20 m

N

GALLERIA PALATINA ★★★

12
10
q
11
p
k
13
9
14
m   n
r
8   15
j
g
7   16   Cortile
h   della
f   s   Fama
6
e   17
d c
18   19   20
5
a
4
b
I   3   Cortile
dell'Ammannati
Fontana
del Carciofo
2
II
e   1   Galleria   XXII
d'Arte moderna ★
III
XV
IV
d
V
b   XI   XII   XIII   XIV
VI   APPARTAMENTI REALI ★
a
c VII

Galleria Palatina Tour

For an overview see preceding pages.

Room 3 (Statue Gallery), decorated with 2C–3C Roman sculptures from the Villa Medici in Rome, leads into **Room 4** (Castagnoli Room), which contains the remarkable **Table of the "Muses"** (in the centre is Apollo's chariot surrounded by the symbols of the nine Muses) (a), with some splendid inlaid work in *pietra dura*, executed during the first half of the 19C by the Florence Pietra Dura Workshop. Note also a large oil painting by Sodoma depicting the martyrdom of St Sebastian.

The rooms on the left side of the palace are named after the subjects of the mainly mythological scenes with which they are decorated.

The **decoration**★★ of the first five, formerly used by the Medici as reception rooms, includes sumptuous stuccowork, gold leaf and *trompe-l'oeil* paintings. It was designed in the 17C by the decorative artist Pietro da Cortona.

Room 5 (Venus Room) is hung with two large seascapes (*on opposite sides of the room*) by the Neapolitan artist, Salvator Rosa (1615–73). More importantly however, the room contains some of Titian's finest oil paintings. **The Concert** (b) is an early work painted under the influence of Giorgione, to whom it was long attributed. On the opposite wall hangs a powerful portrait of **Pietro Aretino** (c), writer and friend of Cosimo I, painted in 1545. The elegant female portrait known as **La Bella** (d) was painted c. 1536 for the Duke of Urbino; the mysterious model may perhaps have been the same woman who sat for the *Venus of Urbino* exhibited in the Uffizi Gallery. In the centre of the room is the *Italic Venus* (Paolina Borghese), an outstanding example of neo-Classical sculpture completed in 1811 by Antonio Canova, who was commissioned to undertake the work by Napoleon.

Room 6 (Apollo Room) contains Van Dyck's portrait of **Charles I of England** and his wife, **Henrietta of France** (e), daughter of Henri IV and Maria de' Medici. The room also contains other paintings by Titian, including a *Mary Magdalen* (*opposite corner*). Among his better-known works is the fascinating **Portrait of a Gentleman** (f) familiarly known as "The Man with Grey Eyes" painted c. 1540.

Room 7 (Mars Room. *Currently closed for ceiling restoration*; artworks temporarily housed in the Niche Room in the Appartamenti Reali) contains two examples of a *Madonna and Child* by Murillo. The paintings hang either side of the **Four Philosophers** (g), one of Rubens' last canvasses. The painter can be seen standing on the left and seated beside him is his brother. The large portrait of **Cardinal Bentivoglio** (h) is a splendid work by Van Dyck.

Room 8 (Jupiter Room) houses the famous **Veiled Lady** (La Velata) (j) by Raphael. *The Holy Family with Basket* (*right-hand corner*) by Rubens is a painting of an intimate rather than sacred nature. Also here is Fra Bartolomeo's moving *Deposition* (*opposite wall*). The painting, left unfinished on the artist-monk's death, gives an impression of balance reminiscent of the works of Perugino, whose *Adoration of the Child*, known as the "Madonna with Pouch" (*same wall by the window*), is a fine symmetrical composition in which religious feeling and poetic sensitivity combine in gentle harmony.

Room 9 (Saturn Room) contains eight oil paintings by Raphael, including two world-famous Madonnas. **The Madonna of the Grand Duke** (k), of which Grand Duke Ferdinand III of Lorraine was so enamoured that he refused to be separated from it, was painted c. 1505 in Florence.

At that time Raphael was influenced by both Michelangelo and Leonardo, borrowing from the latter the technique of *sfumato*. The **Madonna della Seggiola (m)** was painted a few years later and the artist, at the peak of his talent, uses a more subtle and varied palette. Note, too, several portraits by Raphael (Maddalena and Agnolo Doni) which show remarkable psychological intensity. Also worthy of note is a melancholy **Mary Magdalen (n)** painted by Perugino.

Room 10 (Iliad Room) is of particular interest for its series of portraits by Joost Sustermans (b. Antwerp 1597, d. Florence 1681) who was official portrait painter to the Medici. One of his most successful portraits is that of the young **Prince Waldemar-Christian of Denmark (p)**. Other outstanding works include an equestrian portrait of Philip IV of Spain by Velázquez (*left of the entrance*) and (*right of the door leading to the next room*) the *Woman Expecting a Child* (*La Gravida*) by Raphael.

Room 11 (Education of Jupiter) contains an astonishing *Sleeping Cupid* **(q)** painted by Caravaggio shortly before his death. Opposite hangs an admirable *Judith* by Florentine artist Cristofano Allori (1577–1621).

Room 12 (Stove Room) with its majolica flooring was formerly the bathroom in the ducal apartments. The large allegorical **scenes★★** depicting the four Ages of Man were painted between 1637 and 1640 by Pietro da Cortona.

Room 13, the small bathroom, was fitted out in the early 19C for Napoleon's sister, Elisa Baciocchi, who became Grand Duchess of Tuscany in 1809.

Room 14 (Ulysses Room) contains another famous Madonna by Raphael, the **Madonna of the Window** (Madonna dell'Impannata) **(r)**.

Room 15 (Prometheus Room) contains a *Madonna and Child* by Filippo Lippi (*right-hand side above the fireplace*) which is unusual in that it was

Portrait of Agnolo Doni by Raphael

Arte & Immagini srl/Corbis

set against a background depicting a familiar scene, an innovation which was followed by numerous artists in Florence. The interesting portrait (*next wall*) of a young man wearing the 15C Florentine headress (*mazzocchio*) was produced in Botticelli's studio.

Room 16 (Poccetti Gallery) contains a portrait by Rubens of the first Duke of Buckingham **(s)**, one of Charles I of England's favourites, and a magnificent table inlaid with *pietra dura* and semi-precious stones produced for Cosimo III in the Medici workshops in 1716.

Room 17 (Music Room), decorated in neo-Classical style, is embellished with eight cipolin marble columns. In the centre is a huge table with a Russian malachite top and superbly finished legs, a work dating from 1819 made by the French bronzesmith, Pierre-Philippe Thomire.

Rooms 18 and 19 (Allegory Room and Fine Arts Room) exhibit 16C–17C Italian paintings.

Room 20 (Hercules Room) was decorated in neo-Classical style by Giuseppe Cacialli early in the 19C. It contains a large Sèvres porcelain vase, embellished with gilt bronze by Thomire, and frescoes depicting the story of Hercules.

the right wing had always been used as state rooms or private apartments by Tuscany's three ruling families – the Medici, the Grand Dukes of Lorraine and the House of Savoy, sovereigns of Italy when Florence became the capital city (1865–70).

Room XXII (White Room) is the former palace ballroom. It is illuminated by 11 magnificent crystal chandeliers.

Room XV (Bona Room) is the largest room in the guest apartments. Ferdinando I commissioned Poccetti to depict his great military victories here. The room is named after the fresco on the right wall, illustrating the conquest in 1607 of Bona (now Annaba in Algeria).

Rooms XIV, XIII, XII, XI are located in a small apartment, decorated in 19C style. They comprise an antechamber (XIV), crimson reception room (XIII), study (XII) and bedchamber (XI) in which (*right of the door*) hangs a fine *Madonna and Child with St John the Baptist* by Andrea del Sarto.

Room VI (Parrot Room) gets its name from the design on the silk-hung walls. Above the doorways are the portraits of Henri IV of France (a) and his wife Maria de' Medici (b) by the Flemish artist, Frans Pourbus II (1569–1622), who painted the portraits of monarchs and grand dignitaries in all the courts of Europe.

Room VII (Yellow Room) contains a splendid ebony, ivory and alabaster **cabinet** (c) dating from the early 18C, which was produced by German and Dutch craftsmen in the Medici workshops.

Room V (Chapel) contains a tender *Madonna and Child* by the Florentine artist, Carlo Dolci. The painting is displayed in a sumptuous ebony and gilt bronze **frame** (d) embellished with *pietra dura* fruits, made in the Medici workshops in 1697 for Gian Gastone, the brother of Anna Maria Ludovica.

Room IV (Blue Room) has a finely decorated white and gold stucco ceiling.

Room III (Throne Room) looks exactly as it did when Victor Emmanuel II of Savoy became the first King of Italy. Beneath the baldequin is the gilded throne on which all the kings of Italy took the oath.

Room II (Green Room) contains another superb ebony and gilt bronze **cabinet** (e) with *pietra dura* inlay made in the late 17C in the ducal workshops. Beside it hangs a portrait of the young Louis XV by Rigaud. The room also contains a number of other French paintings.

Room I (Niche Room), aristocratic and formal, previously served as a dining room. The niches around the room contain classical statues which are copies of Roman and Greek works. The large full-length portraits of various members of the Medici family were painted by Sustermans.

Galleria d'Arte Moderna★

Above the Palatine Gallery. ⊙*Open Tue–Sun 8.15am–1.50pm.* ⊙*Closed 1 Jan, 1 May, 25 Dec.* ⊛*€8.50 combined ticket with the Galleria Palatina and Appartamenti Reali.* ♿. ✆*055 23 88 601. www.polomuseale.firenze.it.*

The **Gallery of Modern Art** is housed in a neo-Classical setting created for the Grand Dukes of Lorraine by the architect Poccianti. The gallery's rich collection of mainly Tuscan works from the late 18C to the early decades of the 20C is arranged according to the following themes: Historical Romantic painting, including *Samson* and *The Two Foscari* by Hayez; realism in Florence and Naples, including *Cloisters* by Abbati; Portraits from the period when Florence was capital of Italy; the Banti and Martelli collections; genre scenes from between the end of the Grand Duchy and the Unification of Italy, including *The Moneylender* by Induno; democracy and patriotism, among which is Fattori's *The Italian Camp after the Battle of Magenta* by Fattori; Stefano Ussi and the theme of the World Exhibition (note the carved, painted ceiling dating from the 17C in this and the next room; the Macchiaioli and other schools; landscape painting; naturalism in Tuscany; and Divisionism, Symbolism and social themes (Medardo Rosso).

The Macchiaioli

The most lively artistic expression during this period came from the "Macchiaioli", and the Galleria d'Arte Moderna owns an outstanding collection of their **works**★★. The movement, a contemporary of Impressionism, grew up in Florence in the mid-19C and breathed new life into painting, which had become entrenched in rigid academic conventions.

The Macchiaioli were enamoured of the truth and rejected subjects borrowed from mythology or the great historical paintings. Instead, they took their models directly from nature but they sought to give an impression of their subject rather than render an exact description. They generally painted small-sized works, translating reality by means of splashes ("macchie") of colour with light playing upon them.

The Livorno artist, **Giovanni Fattori** (1825–1908), a complex character with a nevertheless sober and vigorous style, and the more poetic **Silvestro Lega** (1826–95) were the movement's most illustrious members. **Telemaco Signorini** (1835–1901), who was also a controversial writer, moved away from the group to seek an even sharper sense of realism. **Adriano Cecioni** (1836–86), who was more of a sculptor than a painter, was the theorist and critic of the movement. **Giuseppe Abbati** (1836–68) gave a touch of seriousness to his works and his contemplation of nature is tinged with melancholy. The Ferrara artist, **Giovanni Boldini** (1842–1931), spent only a brief time with the Macchiaioli before going on to become a fashionable portrait painter, especially in Paris. The work of **Giuseppe de Nittis** (1846–84), who came from the Puglia region, is characterised by the use of typical Mediterranean colours. He also emigrated to Paris, where he enjoyed a career as a society painter.

Museo degli Argenti★★

♿ *See the detailed tour on the following page. Ground floor and mezzanine. The entrance is situated at the left of the Ammannati courtyard.* ◷*Open daily 8.15am–6.30pm (5.30pm Mar, Oct; 4.30pm Nov–Feb) (last entry 30min before closing).* ◷*Closed 1st and last Mon in the month, 1 Jan, 1 May, 25 Dec. Bar, restaurant, bbookshop.* ⬲*€6 combined ticket with the Museo delle Porcellane, Galleria del Costume and the Giardino di Boboli.* ✆*055 23 88 709. www.polomuseale.firenze.it/musei.*

The **Silver Museum** consists mainly of the treasures of the Medici family and House of Lorraine. Most of the exhibits were made in the workshops of Florence. The state rooms on the **Ground Floor** of the palace, which was used as the Grand Dukes' summer apartments, were lavishly decorated during the 17C, with mythological paintings, allegorical scenes in honour of the Medici and astonishing *trompe-l'oeil* architectural features.

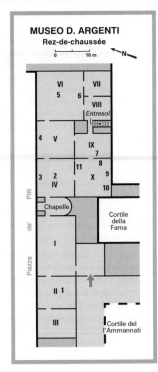

MUSEO D. ARGENTI
Rez-de-chaussée

Argenti Tour

Room I, Sala di Giovanni da San Giovanni, takes its name from the Tuscan painter who undertook its decoration in 1634 to celebrate the marriage of Ferdinand II to Vittoria della Rovere. The event is depicted in the main fresco on the ceiling.

Room II was formerly the bedchamber of the Grand Duchess. Some of the 16 cups and **ancient vases** (*one of the main central display cases*) (**1**) are examples of Roman art of the Later Empire and others of 14C Venetian art. Their magnificent gold and silver mounts bear the engraved monogram of Lorenzo – **LAVR.MED**.

The small 17C **chapel** leads to **Room IV** (Audience Room) with its *trompe l'oeil* architectural features; to **Room V** (Private Audience Room) where the ceiling depicts the *Triumph of Alexander*; and to **Room VI**. These three rooms contain some splendid pieces of ebony and *pietra dura* furniture dating from the late 16C and 17C, including a cabinet (*first room*) (**2**) made in Augusta and a prayer stool (**3**) from the Medici workshops in Florence. A blue and yellow chess board (*second room*) (**4**) was made in the same workshops in 1619. A large round porphyry table (*last room*) (**5**) is placed in the centre; the cabinet (*right*) (**6**), which dates from 1709, was a gift from Cosimo III to his daughter Anna Maria Ludovica.

Rooms VII and **VIII** house a very fine collection of German and Flemish **ivories** that once belonged to the Medici.

Room IX, formerly the Grand Duke's bedchamber, contains a fine **table** (**7**) with a splendid *pietra dura* inlaid top.

Room X, the **Crystal Room**, contains some of the museum's most valuable pieces. To the left of the door is the famous **lapis lazuli gourd** (**8**). The no less famous **Diana of Poitiers' Cup** (*next display case against the left-hand wall*) (**9**) is made of engraved rock crystal and was based on a design by Buontalenti. Exhibited in various display cases are an exceedingly elegant cup representing a dragon (**10**) (16C Milanese) and a splendid bird-shaped vase (**11**) bearing seven dragons' heads and encrusted with gems and pearls.

Mezzanine – *Access via the small staircase between Rooms VIII and IX on the plan.*

The Medici Treasure – Room XI (Cameo Room) – contains a large white onyx cameo (*central glass case*), bearing effigies of Cosimo I and members of his family. From the same period and origin is the *pietra dura* mosaic depicting Piazza della Signoria.

Room XII (Jewellery and Engraved Stone Room) contains the jewels of Anna Maria Ludovica. The most unusual collection in the museum is the late 16C and 17C Baroque jewellery and other small items made of pearl, gold and precious stones.

Ferdinand III's Treasure consists mainly of collections belonging to the Prince-Archbishops of Salzburg, brought to Florence in 1814 by Ferdinand III of Lorraine.

In **Room XIII** (*against the left-hand wall*) is an engraved silver altar front of the Madonna and Child.

Room XIV contains the sumptuous gold and silver-gilt tableware of the Prince-Archbishops, including enamelled pure gold cups decorated with grotesque figures and coats of arms.

The Medici Exotic Collections are exhibited in the last two rooms. Room XVI contains an unusual 16C Mexican mitre made of bird feathers depicting the Passion of Christ (*left of the door*) and a series of shell-shaped vases dating from the 16C–17C (*right-hand display case*). The second room contains *famille rouge* and *famille verte* Chinese porcelain in addition to blue-and-white ware, and a brightly coloured Chinese ceremonial dress with a strikingly modern appearance (first half of 17C).

Ocean Fountain in the Boboli Gardens

Galleria del Costume ★

Meridian Pavilion. Access by lift situated in the ticket office and staircase leading to the Palatine Gallery. ⏱*Open daily 8.15am–7.30pm (6.30pm Apr, May, Sept; 5.30pm Mar and Oct; 4.30pm Nov–Feb) (last entry 30min before closing).* ⏱*Closed 1st and last Mon in the month, 1 Jan, 1 May, 25 Dec.* ✆€6 combined ticket with the Museo degli Argenti, Museo delle Porcellane and the Giardino di Boboli. ♿. ✆055 23 88 763. www.polomuseale.firenze.it.

The **Costume Gallery** offers an insight into the history of fashion from the 18C to c. 1930 through its extensive collection of costumes, shoes, linen and accessories. There is a reconstruction of the burial clothes of Eleonora of Toledo and her husband, Cosimo I, based on the remnants found in their tomb.

Giardino di Boboli★

1hr 30min. ⏱*Open daily 8.15am–7.30pm (6.30pm Apr, May, Sept; 5.30pm Mar, Oct; 4.30pm Nov–Feb) (last entry 1hr before closing). Guided visits of the Grotta Grande available year-round.* ⏱*Closed 1st and last Mon in the month, 1 Jan, 1 May, 25 Dec. Bar, restaurant.* ✆€6 combined ticket with the Museo degli Argenti, Museo delle Porcellane and Galleria del Costume. ♿. ✆55 23 88 786. www.polomuseale.firenze.it.

The **Boboli Gardens** were begun in 1549 when Cosimo I commissioned Tribolo to convert the hill behind the Pitti Palace into a vast garden. Together with Ammannati's courtyard and the terrace, it was to be the setting for the lavish pageants held by the Grand Dukes. When Tribolo died the following year, he had only drawn up the plans. He was succeeded in 1550 by Ammannati then in 1583 by Buontalenti, both of whom added a number of refinements to the original design.

The park is a fine example of an Italian terraced garden with many different perspectives, interspersed with ramps, flights of steps and terraces and dotted with statues and fountains. The entrance is situated on the far side of the inner courtyard. The terrace is separated from the rear of the palace by the elegant Artichoke Fountain (*Carciofo*), built in 1641.

The 17C **amphitheatre** dominates the centre of the park. In 1841 the Royal House of Lorraine had a Roman granite basin and a 2C BC Egyptian obelisk from Thebes placed in the centre.

▷ *Walk towards the top of the hill; before reaching the first terrace, turn right into an uphill path which leads to a circle.*

This part of the gardens, covering the hillside, was not laid out until the early 17C. The long and steep **Viottolone**★ (*opposite*) descends majestically between a double row of age-old pines and cypress trees to the charming circular **Piazzale dell'Isolotto**★. At the centre is a round lake adorned with statues. In the middle of the lake is an island with orange and lemon trees and the Ocean Fountain, carved by Giovanni da Bologna in 1576.

On turning back towards the palace, visitors see **Neptune's Pool**, adorned with a bronze statue (16C) of the sea god and, on the following terrace, a statue of Plenty which was begun by Giovanni da Bologna and finished in 1636 by the Florentine, Pietro Tacca.

▶ *A short path (right) leads to the Porcelain Museum (below).*

The path (*left*) leads to the foot of the **Belvedere Fort** (*access now restricted by a gate*). Further down stands the **Kaffeehaus**, an extravagant and predominantly red edifice built by Zanobi del Rosse in 1776. From the bar patio, there is a **fine view**★ of Florence.

▶ *Walk back down towards the palace and turn right into the wide ramp.*

At the end is a path leading to the **Grotta Grande**, a fanciful creation designed mainly by Buontalenti (1587–97) and consisting of several chambers decorated with basins, statues, paintings, stalactites and a form of Rococo decoration depicting sheep, goats, shepherds, etc. The small **Bacchus Fountain** (*right near the exit*) includes a monstrous figure, one of Cosimo I's midgets, astride a tortoise.

Museo delle Porcellane★

Open daily 8.15am–7.30pm (6.30pm Apr, May, Sept; 5.30pm Mar and Oct; 4.30pm Nov–Feb) (last entry 30min before closing). Closed 1st and last Mon in the month, 1 Jan, 1 May, 25 Dec. €6 combined ticket with the Museo degli Argenti, Galleria del Costume and the Giardino di Boboli. ℘055 23 88 709.

The **Porcelain Museum** is comprised of three rooms.

The first room contains numerous porcelains from Sèvres, including a portrait of Napoleon (early 19C).

The second room is dedicated to Viennese porcelain from the 18C and early

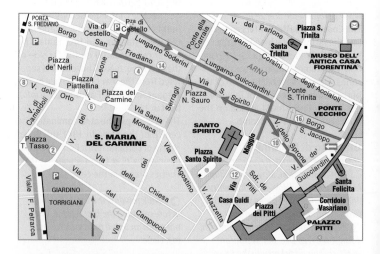

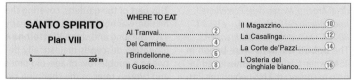

SANTO SPIRITO Plan VIII 0 200 m	WHERE TO EAT	
	Al Tranvai......② Del Carmine......④ l'Brindellonne......⑥ Il Guscio......⑧	Il Magazzino......⑩ La Casalinga......⑫ La Corte de'Pazzi......⑭ L'Osteria del cinghiale bianco......⑯

19C, with pieces brought to Florence by the Royal House of Lorraine.

The third room contains German ware from Frankenthal and Meissen.

▶ *Walk along Via Mazzetta towards Piazza S Spirito.*

On the SE corner stands the **Palazzo Guadagni**★, surmounted by a splendid loggia (1503) and attributed to Baccio d'Agnolo or Simone del Pollaiolo known as *Il Cronaca*.

ADDITIONAL SIGHTS
The tour marked on the Santo Spirito map explores the streets backing onto the Arno.

Chiesa di Santo Spirito★
⚠ *Santo Spirito is currently closed for restoration.*

This Renaissance **church** designed by Brunelleschi is situated at the end of a peaceful, shady square off the main tourist track. Building began in 1444 and had not progressed very far when the great man died two years later. Construction work on the modest façade continued until 1487 using the original plans, although a number of changes were made.

The building includes 38 small semi-circular chapels which, according to Brunelleschi's plans, were intended to be visible from the outside. The chapels open into the aisles through arches of the same height as those in the nave and it is this that gives the church its remarkably spacious character.

Santo Spirito contains numerous **works of art**★, including *Madonna of Succor* barring the path of a glowing red, cloven-hoofed devil, by an unknown 15C Florentine painter; Filippino Lippi's **Madonna and Child**; and the **Corbinelli Chapel** containing an ornate carved marble reredos dating from the early 16C by Andrea Sansovino.

The splendid **sacristy**★ *(entrance in north aisle by the door next to the second chapel)* is a monumental construction designed in 1489 by Giuliano da Sangallo in the spirit of Brunelleschi's designs.

Cenacolo di Santo Spirito
Left of the church – no 29. The fine Gothic hall with bare rafters is the **former refectory** of the Augustinian friary adjoining the church. One of its walls is covered by a large *Crucifixion*, a fresco painted c. 1360, and the remains of the *Last Supper* (*above*), which are attributed to Andrea Orcagna and Nardo di Cione.

The refectory also displays sculptures dating from the Romanesque to the Baroque periods, including a low relief (*end wall*) of St Maximus by Donatello.

▶ *Walk along Via S Agostino and then along Via S Monaca as far as S Maria del Carmine.*

Santa Maria del Carmine: The Brancacci Chapel★★★
Allow 15min. ⏱*Open Wed–Mon 10am –5pm, Sun 1pm–5pm (4.30pm last admission).* ⏱*Closed Tue, 16 Jul, 7 Jan. Reservations required.* ✎*€4, €8 combined ticket with the Palazzo Vecchio.* ✆*055 27 68 224.*

What makes this church so interesting is the extraordinary series of **frescoes**★★★ decorating the walls of the Brancacci Chapel at the end of the south transept. They were painted by three different artists and describe original sin and the life of St Peter; the latter subject was probably chosen because Florence had political links with the Papacy.

Michelangelo's Crucifix

In 1492, Michelangelo sculpted a wooden crucifix and gave it to the church of Santo Spirito in recognition of the services of the church's prior, who had helped him with his dissections in his study of anatomy.

According to the art historian Vasari, with this wooden crucifix, Michelangelo gave a hint of his future genius. At the time, the Crucifix was located above the master altar. After its restoration, it was placed in the sacristy.

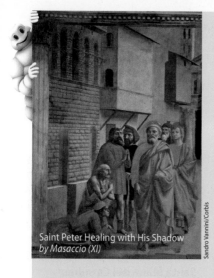

Saint Peter Healing with His Shadow
by Masaccio (XI)

Sandro Vannini/Corbis

The Brancacci frescoes★★★

Masolino da Panicale

Masolino was the first artist to be commissioned, in 1424, to undertake the decoration of the chapel built for the Brancacci, a family of silk merchants. Although the spirit of his work is still noticeably Gothic, as is obvious from his kindly, serene treatment of the subject matter, there is already an attempt to render perspective and volume. He was probably influenced in this respect by his pupil, Masaccio. On the upper section, he depicted the *Temptation of Adam and Eve* (**VII**), *St Peter raising Tabitha from the Dead* (**VI**) and *St Peter Preaching* (**III**).

Masaccio

This chapel is a fine example of the innovatory genius of this artist, who pointed the way forward to the Renaissance through his feeling for relief and expression. In 1427, shortly before his untimely death, he created this set of frescoes that are now considered one of the most consummate examples of Italian painting in existence.

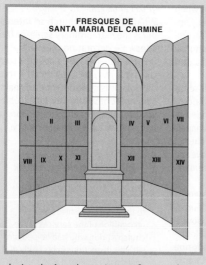

FRESQUES DE
SANTA MARIA DEL CARMINE

In his famous painting of **Adam and Eve being expelled from Paradise** (**I**), symmetrically opposite the *Temptation* painted by Masolino, he totally excluded idealism in order to express, with poignant intensity, the shame and despair of the figures. The light projected onto the scene and the splashes of shadow that conceal certain parts of the bodies and faces add to the dramatic effect and accentuate the impression of relief, giving the figures a striking reality.

The Tribute Money (**II**) depicts the Apostles as vigorous figures radiating supreme gravity. The fresco includes three episodes, reduced to their main elements. They show the tax-collector (*rear view*) at the Capernaum Gate, demanding payment of the toll from Jesus, who is showing Peter the water in which he will find the fish with the silver coin in its mouth (*central scene*). The Apostle takes the fish (*left*), then hands the coin to the tax-collector (*right*).

The Tribute Money *by Masaccio (II)*

Sandro Vannini/Corbis

Another fresco depicts *St Peter baptising* (**IV**) and *St Peter curing the lame man* (**V**). This scene was painted with Masolino, whose regular, more anecdotal style is obvious in the two elegant figures crossing the square.

The subjects treated by Masaccio (*on the lower register*) are *St Peter and St John giving alms* (**XII**), *St Peter curing the sick by the sole power of his shadow* (**XI**); and *St Peter on the episcopal throne* (**X**).

Filippino Lippi

The decoration of the chapel was still incomplete by the time Masaccio left for Rome. It was completed in 1481 by Filippino Lippi who painted the following scenes in an elegant style (*on the lower section of the wall*): *St Paul visiting St Peter in prison in Antioch* (**VIII**); *St Peter raising the Son of Theophilus, Prefect of Antioch, from the dead* (**IX**), a fresco that had been started by Masaccio; *St Peter set free by an Angel during his second term of imprisonment in Jerusalem* (**XIV**) and *St Peter and St Paul arguing with Simon Magus before the Emperor and the Crucifixion of St Peter* (**XIII**).

The two faces beside the altar piece are portraits of Masaccio and Masolino.

Masaccio (1401–28) and the Introduction of Volume in Painting

Masaccio died prematurely at the age of 27 after traveling to Rome with Donatello and Brunelleschi. He was to painting what his two friends were to sculpture and architecture. From the former, he acquired a taste for powerful figures, realistic expressions and heavy draped clothing; from the latter, he learned about perspective which he then applied not only to illustrations of buildings but also to human figures as in his frescoes in Santa Maria Novella. He discovered that light contained sculptural resources and concentrated on giving volume to his figures and improving his spatial layout, leaving aside the grace, ornamentation and excessive detail of the Gothic style. He paved the way for the Renaissance style in painting, and his works had a huge impact on successive generations because of their lifelike realism.

San Lorenzo District

Florence under Lorenzo de' Medici

Lorenzo de' Medici was a true patron of the arts and many creative projects were undertaken during his reign. Starting at San Lorenzo, this walk winds its way through the local market stalls.

SAN LORENZO★★★
Church★★

St Lawrence's Church is situated close to the Medici Palace (now the Palazzo Medici-Riccardi), and was formerly the Medici parish church, serving as their burial place for over three centuries.

Construction of the church was begun c. 1420 by Brunelleschi, who was commissioned to undertake the work by Giovanni di Bicci, Cosimo the Elder's father. Subsequent generations of the Medici family added their own embellishments.

As in the case of a number of other Florentine churches, the harsh façade never received the marble cladding included in the designs. The huge dome that caps the rear of the building is part of the Princes' Chapel (*see below*), which was added in the 17C.

For the interior Brunelleschi broke with Gothic conventions and introduced a style that became typical of the Florentine Renaissance. He adopted the traditional basilica layout – nave and two aisles – of the former building with 11C restorations, and combined its Romanesque semicircular arches with ancient Greek and Roman architectural features, such as Corinthian columns, fluted pilasters and cornices. San Lorenzo thus came to represent a new style of church with an austere, pure architectural design. The building has a coffered ceiling decorated, in the nave, with four reproductions of the Medici coat of arms. The barrel-vaulted aisles are flanked by shallow chapels surmounted by oculi.

In 1516 Pope Leo X, Lorenzo the Magnificent's son, commissioned Michelangelo to complete the east front that had been left unfinished on Brunelleschi's death in 1446. Michelangelo drew up a number of grandiose plans but only the inside was completed with a small gallery designed to display relics to the faithful.

In the *Marriage of the Virgin Mary* (**1**) (*second chapel on the right*) by the Mannerist painter, Rosso Fiorentino, the forms in the painting are gracefully elongated and the colours dazzlingly vivid. The delightful marble **relief**★ in the shape of a small temple (**2**) (*end of the south aisle*) was carved by Desiderio da Settignano.

SAN LORENZO

Plan IV

0   100 m

WHERE TO EAT

Ciro And Sons	②
Nerbone	④
Palle d'Oro	⑥
Trattoria Gozzi	⑧
Trattoria Mario	⑩

146

The work was inspired by Donatello and it formed the basis for the many such elegantly structured compositions with exquisite decorative effect called **tabernacles** (*tabernacoli*), which were produced in great numbers in Florence during the 15C. The work also shows a remarkable sense of perspective, one of the main features of Renaissance art.

The two **pulpits**★★ (**3** and **4**) are faced with splendid panels produced by Donatello during the last years of his life and completed after his death by his pupils. In front of the chancel is a large circular slab (**5**) with an inlay of multicoloured marble. In the corners of the surrounding square is the Medici coat of arms. This marks the spot above the crypt where Cosimo the Elder is buried.

The **Martelli chapel** (**6**) contains the **Annunciation**★ painted c. 1440 by Filippo Lippi, a work which is remarkable for the perspective in the arches, buildings and pergolas.

Sagrestia Vecchia★★

Work on the new church of San Lorenzo began with the **Old Sacristy**, which is considered to be one of the most successful achievements of the Early Renaissance. It was a joint project involving Brunelleschi, who was responsible for the architecture, and Donatello, who undertook the decoration. This square chapel, with its hemispherical dome on pendentives and various architectural features highlighted by grey *pietra serena* admirably conveys the well-proportioned unity of geometrical lines that are characteristic of Brunelleschi's style.

Donatello produced the cherubs comprising the frieze round the entablature, the polychrome medallions depicting the four Evangelists and scenes from the life of Saint John, and the remarkable bronze doors★ (**7**) containing 40 figures of Holy Martyrs and Apostles. He also designed the splendid traceried marble screen and the altar in the tiny domed apse. To the rear of the altar is a remark-

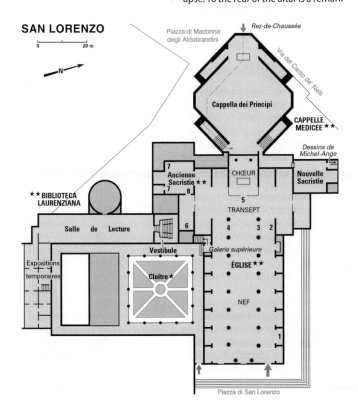

SAN LORENZO

0   20 m

N

Piazza di Madonna
degli Aldobrandini

Rez-de-Chaussée

Via del Canto de' Nelli

Cappella dei Principi

**CAPPELLE
MEDICEE** ★★

*Dessins de
Michel-Ange*

**7
Ancienne
Sacristie** ★★

CHŒUR

**Nouvelle
Sacristie**

7   8

★★ **BIBLIOTECA
LAURENZIANA**

5

TRANSEPT

Salle   de   Lecture

6

4   3   2

Expositions
temporaires

Vestibule

Galerie supérieure

ÉGLISE ★★

Cloître ★

NEF

1

Piazza di San Lorenzo

able triptych (*Madonna and Child*) by Taddeo Gaddi. In the centre of the room within the marble sarcophagus, which is capped by an altar table, lie Giovanni di Bicci and his wife Piccarda Bueri.

The elegant **tomb**★ (*left of the entrance*) (8) was produced in 1472 by Verrocchio, who was commissioned to undertake the work by Lorenzo the Magnificent and his brother Giuliano in honour of their father, Piero, and uncle, Giovanni. The lavish porphyry and bronze tomb is set in a bay connecting the sacristy to the adjoining chapel and is surmounted by an unusual trellis in which the mesh represents ropes. On a cabinet to the right of the door stands the terracotta bust of Lorenzo as an adolescent, a work attributed to Donatello.

Chiostro★ (Cloisters)

Entrance via the north aisle or by the doorway on the left of the façade.

The cloisters were built in the 15C in the elegant style of Brunelleschi. From just before the entrance to the cloisters a staircase leads up to the Laurenziana Library.

Biblioteca Medicea Laurenziana★★

Entrance via a staircase from the upper gallery of the cloisters. ◷*Open Tue, Wed, Thu 8am–5pm (Mon, Fri, Sat 2pm).* ◷*Closed Sun, Hols.* &. ℘*055 21 07 60. www.bml.firenze.sbn.it.*

The **Laurenziana Library** was founded in the 15C by Cosimo the Elder and considerably extended by Lorenzo the Magnificent, from whom it takes its name. It was not until the following century, in 1523, that Michelangelo was commissioned by Pope Clement VII (a member of the Medici family) to construct a dedicated building in the cloisters of San Lorenzo to house the library's priceless collection.

To decorate this exceptionally small yet disproportionately tall **vestibule**, the artist divided the walls into sections in an unusual way using architectural features that are normally found only on façades, while at the same time playing on the contrast between the white

surfaces and grey *pietra serena* relief. The unusual use of huge twin columns, heavy cornices on brackets and window frames set flat against the wall already heralds the Baroque era. This style is further emphasised by the volutes on the consoles and the splendid monumental three-flight **staircase**★★. Michelangelo left for Rome in 1534, where he settled permanently, and the staircase was left at the planning stage. It was completed in 1559 by the Mannerist architect, Ammannati, who used the original drawings and acted in accordance with the numerous instructions sent to him by Michelangelo from Rome.

Although the architectural style is more austere, the **Reading Room** has its own charm because of the strict geometrical lines that are systematically repeated along the whole length of the room, creating a remarkable sense of perspective. The desks and lavish coffered ceiling, carved in warm-coloured wood and shown off by skilful lighting, were both designed by Michelangelo. The fine terracotta flooring from the same period is by Tribolo (the designer of the Boboli gardens), who added decorative features reflecting the design of the ceiling.

A selection of the library's 10,000 manuscripts are exhibited in rotation. They include a 5C Virgil, a Horace annotated by Petrarch, Lorenzo the Magnificent's Book of Hours, Leonardo da Vinci's notebooks, a letter from Caterina de' Medici to Michelangelo, and manuscripts by Petrarch, Ariosto, Machiavelli and Michelangelo.

Cappelle Medicee★★

Entrance in Piazza della Madonna degli Aldobrandini. ◷*Open daily Apr–Nov 8.15am–5pm; rest of the year until 1.50pm.* ◷*Closed 1st, 3rd, 5th Mon in the month, 2nd and 4th Sun in the month, 1 Jan, 1 May, 25 Dec.* ◍€4. ℘*055 23 88 602. www.polomuseale. firenze.it/musei/cappellemedicee.*

The term **Medici Chapels** is used to refer to the **Cappella dei Principi** (Princes' Chapel) and the **Sagrestia Nuova** (New Sacristy). Entrance to the **Princes' Chapel** is by way of a huge crypt in which the Medici Grand Dukes were buried. The stone just in front of the staircase to the right marks the tomb of Anna Maria Ludovica, the last member of the dynasty.

The Princes' Chapel was built to immortalise the Grand Dukes for whom it was intended as a funeral chapel. The most immediately striking features of the building are its overwhelming proportions and severe appearance. It is octagonal in design with walls and floor faced with *pietra dura* and precious marble, an impressive piece of workmanship produced in the Medici Pietre Dure workshop. At the base of the walls are 16 coats of arms with lapis lazuli, coral and mother-of-pearl inlay representing the towns within the Grand Duchy of Tuscany. In this breathtaking mineral decor are the huge tombs, made of Oriental granite and green Corsican jasper, of Cosimo I (*left of the altar*) and his descendants, all of whom are buried below. The altar is also lavishly inlaid with *pietra dura*.

The **Sagrestia Nuova** is in fact a funeral chapel, designed to house **Le Tombe Medicee**★★★, the tombs of the Medici family. In 1521, Cardinal Giuliano, the future Pope Clement VII, commissioned Michelangelo to construct the New Sacristy. It was Michelangelo's first commission as an architect.

It is called the New Sacristy because it is symmetrically opposite the Old Sacristy and is reminiscent of the latter's architectural design. It uses the same grey *pietra serena* decoration, which forms a stark contrast with the pale-coloured marble and white walls. In the layout of windows, arches, cornices, niches and pediments – features that are mainly borrowed from Classical architecture – Michelangelo gives the spatial layout a new rhythm that conveys a touching solemnity.

In 1534, when Michelangelo left Florence for Rome, the work was unfinished and was not completed until 20 years later by Vasari and Ammannati. The sculptures on the **Medici Tombs** were also produced by Michelangelo. Closely combining his work as both sculptor and architect, the brilliant artist executed the famous tombs of the two members of the senior branch of the Medici family between 1526 and 1533. The monumental group was to be composed of four mausoleums but only two were in fact completed. On the right is the tomb of Giuliano, Duke of Nemours (son of Lorenzo the Magnificent), who died in 1516 at the age of 35. Giuliano is portrayed as a Roman Emperor holding the baton of an army commander on his knees. At his feet are the famous semi-reclining allegorical figures of **Day** (unfinished), conveying a powerful energy, and **Night**, sleeping in a pose of graceful abandon. Opposite is the tomb of Lorenzo, Duke of Urbino (the grandson of Lorenzo the Magnificent and father of Caterina de' Medici), who died in 1519 at the age of 27. He is shown in meditation and at his feet lie the other two famous statues depicting **Dusk**, in the guise of a melancholy old man, and **Dawn**, portrayed as a woman rising uneasily from her slumber. Each of these marble figures conveys a tragic grandeur and remarkable vigour. It is possible that the two idealised figures were intended to represent *Action* and *Thought* triumphing over Time which, through the different stages of life (symbolised by times of the day), leads man to his death.

The only work to be produced for the tomb of Lorenzo the Magnificent (*right of the entrance*) is the admirable *Madonna and Child*. Lorenzo, the most famous of the Medici, lies with his brother Giuliano in the plain sarcophagus below.

A small room beneath the chapel displays some mural **drawings**, attributed to Michelangelo, which were discovered in 1975. They may have been drawn during the few months the artist spent in hiding in the monastery of San Lorenzo, while being sought by the Medici for his part in the 1527 revolt that had driven the powerful family from Florence.

▷ *In nearby Via Cavour stands the Palazzo Medici-Riccardi.*

PALAZZO MEDICI-RICCARDI★★

(Medici Palace). Allow 30min. ◷*Open Thu–Tue 9am–7pm.* ◷*Closed 1 Jan, 25 Dec.* ✆€5. ♿. ☏*055 27 60 340. www.palazzo-medici.it*

The **Medici Palace**, the Medici family residence, was begun in 1444 on the orders of Cosimo the Elder to the design of his friend, Michelozzo. Cosimo did not, however, live in the building, which he deemed too large, until 1459; he died here five years later. His grandson, Lorenzo the Magnificent, held a princely court here, frequented by his poet, philosopher and artist friends. The building was also once the home of the young Caterina de' Medici, who became Queen of France.

In 1540 Cosimo I left the residence to settle in Piazza della Signoria. The mansion remained in the possession of the Medici family for another hundred years or so before being sold to the Riccardi. The noble building, which was considered the prototype for the aristocratic residences of the Florentine Renaissance, reflects a medieval austerity. Breaking with medieval tradition, however, Michelozzo structured the building around a fine courtyard with a tall portico. Between the arcades of the portico and the first floor, a string-course decorated with medallions carved in Donatello's workshop and depicting the Medici coat of arms or classical motifs, adds a graceful touch to the general architectural austerity.

Cappella★★★ (Chapel)

First floor. Entrance via the first staircase, on the left on entering Michelozzo's courtyard.

The tiny chapel with its rich gilt coffered ceiling and splendid marble flooring was designed by Michelozzo. The walls are decorated with **frescoes★★★**, painted in 1459 by **Benozzo Gozzoli**.

In a style that still echoes the influence of the international Gothic, the artist has produced a brilliant and picturesque illustration of Florentine life based on the theme of the **Procession of the Magi**. It was intended to honour the refined court of the Medici and to commemorate the Council, which met in Florence in 1439, and made a great contribution to the prestige of both the Medici and the city. The Three Kings, representing the ages of life, are portrayals of other major figures of contemporary society. At the head of the procession (*left-hand corner*) is the patriarch of Constantinople who died in Florence during the Council. Behind him, dressed in a splendid green and gold coat and Oriental headress, is the Byzantine Emperor John VIII Palaeologus (*wall opposite the altar – right of the entrance*). At the end (*right-hand wall*), clothed in a beige and gold jerkin and mounted on a palfrey (the harness bears the Medici coat of arms), is the young Lorenzo the Magnificent. Behind him on the white horse is his father, Piero I. In the middle of the group behind him is a self-portrait of Benozzo; his cap bears the inscription "Opus Benotii". Gozzoli's *Adoration of the Angels* is on the chancel walls.

Sala di Luca Giordano★★

Second floor. Entrance via the staircase (right), before Michelozzo's courtyard.

This bright and elegant gallery was built towards the end of the 17C, at the request of the Riccardi family. Its decoration of gilded stucco work alternating with mirrored panels is dazzling.

The room's crowning glory, however, is its barrel-vaulted ceiling decorated with a huge fresco painted in 1683 by the Neapolitan artist **Luca Giordano** (1632–1705). This fine exponent of Baroque decorative art earned the nickname "Luca Fa Presto" ("Luke works quickly") because of the extraordinary speed with which he executed his works. He learnt the art of grand decorative compositions and acquired his taste for light colours from his master, Piero da Cortona (who painted the ceilings in the Palatine Gallery in the Pitti Palace). Here the artist has depicted an **Apotheosis of the Second Medici Dynasty**. Above a frieze full of scenes borrowed from mythology, figures soar upwards into the clouds, while the use of foreshortening gives a sense of movement.

Santa Maria Novella District

SANTA MARIA NOVELLA★★

1hr. 🕐*Open Mon–Thu, Sat 9am–5pm (Hols 2pm).* ✆€2.50. *www.comune. fi.it/servizi_pubblici/arte/musei/b.htm.* The church and cloisters of Santa Maria Novella stand at the north end of the irregularly shaped **Piazza Santa Maria Novella**, which was laid out in the 14C. The south side is lined by the Renaissance arches of the long, slightly elevated **Loggia de San Paolo.**

In the Middle Ages the square was used for numerous tournaments and other pageants and from the mid-16C to the last century it hosted the Palio dei Cocchi, the chariot race held on St John's Day (24 June), which was introduced by Cosimo I and based on the two-horse chariot *(biga)* races of Ancient Rome. The Grand Dukes presided over the event from a canopied box set up on the steps of the loggia. The central area was divided into two tracks by a rope stretched between two wooden pyramids, which were replaced in the 17C by marble obelisks designed by Giovanni da Bologna.

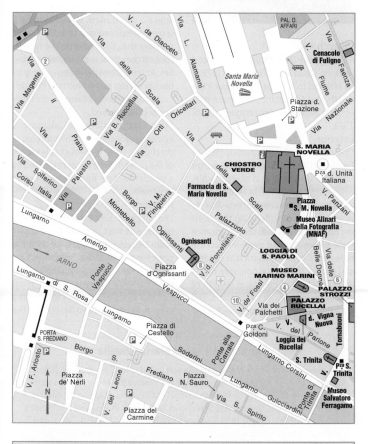

SANTA MARIA NOVELLA	WHERE TO EAT	
Plan III	Baldini...........................②	Osteria delle Belle Donne...⑥
	Il Latini............................④	Trattoria Sostanza-Troia.....⑧
0 ____ 200 m		Tre Merli.........................⑩

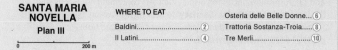

Santa Maria Novella

B. Morandi/ MICHELIN

Church★★

Although the Dominicans commenced work on Santa Maria Novella in 1279 in an attempt to heal the rift between the Guelfs and Ghibellines, the main part of the building was not completed until 1360.

Exterior

The lower part of the extremely elegant **façade** with its light geometrical design picked out in green and white marble, dates from the mid-14C. In 1458 the work was taken over by Leon Battista Alberti, who succeeded in blending the existing Gothic features with the Renaissance style by creating an overall structure based on simple forms such as squares and circles. The central doorway, pillars and the whole of the upper section of the façade were built to his plans. The remarkable voluted consoles in coloured marble marquetry were designed to fill the space between the aisles and the higher nave. This treatment was then adopted in a great number of Renaissance churches and in Baroque façades. Funding for the work was provided by the Rucellai, a rich family of merchants, whose dedicatory inscription – IOHANES.ORICELLARIVS.PAV.F.AN.SAL. MCCCLXX – adorns the pediment. The Rucellai coat of arms, a billowing sail, appears in the middle frieze. Above the twin recesses at each end of the façade there is a sundial (*right*) and an armillary sphere (*left*).

The small **cemetery** (*right* – ⚷ *closed to the public*), where Domenico Ghirlandaio was buried, is enclosed by a screen composed of a series of Gothic recesses that, like those on the façade, contain the remains of Florentine families. At the base of the recesses are marble sarcophagi carved with the People's Cross and the coats of arms of the families of the deceased.

From Piazza dell'Unità Italiana and Piazza della Stazione (*at the north end of the church*), there is a remarkable **view**★ of the powerful chevet, surmounted by a slender, austere Romanesque Gothic bell tower.

Interior

The interior of Santa Maria Novella was bright and vast (almost 100m/328ft long) because it was designed for the preaching of sermons. In architectural terms, it was strongly influenced by the Cistercian Gothic style. Its layout has the form of a Latin cross with a very short transept and flat chevet. The

Farmacia Di Santa Maria Novella

The **pharmacy of Santa Maria Novella** was founded in 1221 when the Dominicans first came to Florence. It has also sold spices since the 16C and their scents waft out into the street. The large shop is set out in an old chapel with ogival vaulting which was dedicated to St Nicholas. It was built in 1332 and redecorated in the neo-Gothic style in 1848. The room which opens on to the cloisters, now a herbalist shop selling a range of fragrant herbs, has stucco-work vaulting and 17C furnishings including display cabinets containing numerous stills. The frescoes in **St Nicholas' Sacristy** depict Christ's Passion. ⏱*Open by appointment Mon–Sat, 9.30am–7pm.* ⏱*Closed 26 Aug and Hols.* ♿. ☎*055 21 62 76; www.smnovella.it.*

outstanding feature of the interior is its austerity. The elegant, spacious nave is lined with arches that become narrower towards the chancel, thus accentuating the feeling of depth. There are alternating black and white archstones and the ogival vaulting in the nave and aisles is highlighted by geometrical designs, also in black and white.

Cloisters★

🕐 *Open Sat–Thu 9am–2pm.* 🕐 *Closed Hols. Guided tour available.* ⌾ *€5.* ℘ *055 28 21 87.* ♿. *http://giubileo. comune.fi.it.*

Chiostro Verde★

The **Green Cloisters** were built in the mid-14C in a style that was still Romanesque, with wide semicircular arches. The name refers to the predominant colour, green, of the decorative **frescoes**, which were painted c. 1430 by Paolo Uccello and his students, depicting scenes from Genesis. The frescoes on the wall between the cloisters and the church are the work of the master alone. They are painted in sombre tones and depict (*left to right*) scenes ranging from

the Creation to the story of Noah. Only two bays are still in good condition – the one (**9**), in which the creation of animal life, Adam and Eve and Original Sin are all clearly visible, and the one in the fourth bay (**10**), depicting the Flood (the storm is particularly interesting) and Noah's drunkenness.

Cappellone degli Spagnoli★★

North Gallery. Behind the elegant Gothic twin windows with multifoiled arches and delightful twisted columns, is the chapter house, which was built in the 14C. It is also known as the **Spanish Chapel** as in the 16C it was frequented by the courtiers of Eleonora of Toledo. The walls and vaulted roof are covered with highly complex symbolical **frescoes**★★ painted in vivid colours by Andrea di Bonaiuti, also known as **Andrea da Firenze**, between 1365 and 1370, in honour of the Dominicans.

Left-hand wall – The Triumph of Divine Wisdom and the Glorification of St Thomas Aquinas. On the vaulting is a representation of Pentecost (the dove of the Holy Ghost coming down to the Apostles who are grouped round the Virgin

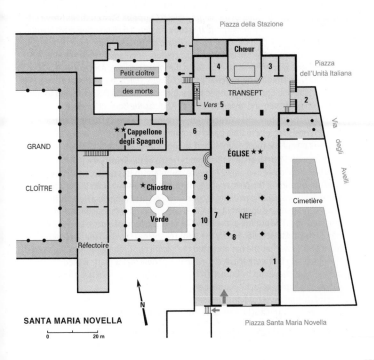

SANTA MARIA NOVELLA

Holy Trinity by Masaccio

©World Illustrated/Photoshot

Inside the Church

The **East aisle** contains the austere elegant tomb (1) (*second bay far right*) of the Blessed Villana delle Botti, a Dominican nun who died in 1361. Carved by Bernardo Rossellino almost one century later, it shows her recumbent figure lying beneath a canopy of flowing draperies.

At the end of the **East transept** above the altar in the raised **Ruccellai Chapel** (2) is Nino Pisano's sweetly smiling marble **Madonna and Child**★.

The **Filippo Strozzi Chapel** (3) is decorated throughout with **frescoes**★ painted by Filippino Lippi, who portrayed scenes from the life of St Philip and St John the Evangelist against a backdrop of exuberant architecture. The rich merchant to whom the chapel is dedicated and who commissioned the Palazzo Strozzi, one of the finest mansions in Florence, is buried in an ornate basalt sarcophagus.

The dazzling **frescoes**★★★ with which Domenico Ghirlandaio covered the walls of the **sanctuary** in 1485 at the request of Giovanni Tornabuoni are considered his finest work. In his illustration of the lives of the Virgin Mary (*left*) and St John the Baptist (*right*), he modelled his figures on members of the Tornabuoni family and their friends, and painted a brilliant and detailed picture of Florentine high society.

The **West transept** contains the **Gondi Chapel** (4) and its famous **Crucifix**★★ by Brunelleschi. The walls of the slightly raised **Cappella Strozzi di Mantova** (5) are decorated with unusually large **frescoes**★ painted by Florentine artist Nardo di Cione, c. 1357. Facing the entrance is a fresco of the Last Judgement; Hell (*right-hand wall*), depicted in dark, earthy colours, and Paradise (*left-hand wall*), with its light, golden tones, are based on the work by Dante. Above the altar is a Flamboyant Gothic **polyptych**★ in which Andrea Orcagna, Nardo di Cione's brother, showed Christ surrounded by seraphim handing St Peter the keys to the Kingdom of Heaven and giving St Thomas Aquinas the Book of Wisdom.

The **Sacristy** (6) contains a **Crucifixion**★ painted by Giotto. There is also a lavabo consisting of a marble basin surmounted by a glazed terracotta **niche**★ which is one of the most delightful of all Giovanni della Robbia's works.

Located in the **North aisle** is the famous fresco of the **Trinity**★★ (7), for which Masaccio needed only 27 days to complete. In this fresco, which is of vital importance in the history of art, the artist broke away from the attractive elegance of Gothic painting by painting God the Father in a Renaissance setting, holding the upright of the Cross and presenting the sacrifice of His crucified Son. The outline of the Holy Ghost in the form of a dove stands out on His chest. Christ is flanked by the Virgin Mary (her face and outstretched hand also show that she has accepted the sacrifice), St John and the donors, on their knees. In this work Masaccio made use of new mathematical theories on perspective, drawn up by Brunelleschi, and so achieved one of the finest and earliest examples of architectural perspective.

The marble pulpit (8) (*against the following pillar*) has decorations in gold leaf designed by Brunelleschi. The panels recount the story of the Virgin Mary.

Deciphering the Sanctuary frescoes

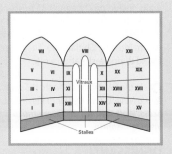

On the **left-hand wall** are (I) Joachim chased from the Temple because he has no children (the young man with the fine mop of hair to the left of the foreground is Giovanni Tornabuoni's son-in-law; the figure with hand on hip, in the group to the right, is said to be the artist himself; the Loggia di San Paolo is recognisable in the background); (II) The Birth of the Virgin Mary; (III) Mary being presented in the Temple; (IV) The marriage of the Virgin Mary; (V) The Adoration of the Magi (damaged); (VI) The Massacre of the Innocents; (VII) The Death of the Virgin Mary and (*above*) the Assumption.

On the **end wall** are (VIII) The Coronation of the Virgin Mary; (IX) St Dominic committing heretical and orthodox books to the flames; (X) St Peter the Martyr; (XI) The Annunciation; (XII) St John in the wilderness; (XIII and XIV) the patrons of the work, Giovanni Tornabuoni and his wife, Francesca Pitti, at prayer.

On the **right-hand wall** are (XV) The angel appearing to Zachariah; (XVI) The Visitation; (XVII) The birth of St John the Baptist; (XVIII) Zachariah, having lost the power of speech, is writing down the name to be given to his son; (XIX) St John the Baptist preaching; (XX) The Baptism of Christ; (XXI) Herod's feast.

Mary). Below them is a Dominican theologian personifying Catholic doctrine. He is sitting on a throne surrounded by the Wise Men of the Old and New Testaments, above whom are the Virtues. Through Roman Catholic doctrine, the Holy Spirit brings to life the Liberal and Sacred Arts, symbolised by 14 female figures sitting in Gothic niches with figures representing these disciplines at their feet.

Right-hand wall – The Triumph of the Church. Activities of the Dominicans.

On the vaulting is St Peter's boat, representing the Church. At the bottom of the wall, in front of a building that is one of the projects drawn by the artist for Florence Cathedral, are the Pope and the Holy Roman Emperor. In front of them (*left*) is a group consisting of representatives of religious orders and orders of chivalry. Among the group of Christian believers (*right*) is a standing figure, dressed in a great brown cloak, shown full face and said to be Cimabue. Beside him, depicted in profile and wearing a green hood, is Giotto. Boccaccio is further to the right, dressed in purple and holding a closed book. Above him, wearing a cloak and hood of white ermine, is Petrarch. The figure beside him, shown in profile and wearing a white cap, is Dante.

On the same register the Dominicans are shown (*right*) protecting the Faithful from attack by Sin. The name "Dominicans" comes from the Latin *Domini Canes* meaning the Hounds of God; they are therefore symbolised as dogs tearing to pieces heretics depicted as wolves.

Above them, being welcomed into Heaven, are the souls of believers who succumbed to mortal sin but who were saved through their Confession received by a Dominican. Only three sins are depicted: Avarice, Lust and Pride are sitting next to a woman playing a viol. The Faithful are shown contemplating the Almighty, who is surrounded by angels with the Virgin Mary in their midst (she is in the group on the left). At the foot of the throne is the Lamb of

Domenico Ghirlandaio (1449–94)

Ghirlandaio painted a large number of frescoes including the cycles in Santa Maria Novella and Santa Trinità, and the Last Supper scenes in the refectories of San Marco and Ognissanti. He ran a leading studio in which Michelangelo was a pupil. The main characteristics of his style are his sense of decoration, his taste for detail and his love of line and colour. His works depict the finery of the wealthy bourgeois society from whom most of his clients came. The portraits, costumes, headresses, buildings and furniture are all excellent descriptions of contemporary life in Florence.

God and the symbols of the Evangelists. **End wall** – The paintings (*left to right*) depict the climb up to Calvary, the Crucifixion and the descent into Hell. On the vaulting is the Resurrection. To the left of the tomb are the Holy Women who have come to embalm the Body of Christ. To the right, Christ appears to Mary Magdalen.

Entrance wall – This was not integrated into the overall decoration and was used to depict the first Dominican martyr – St Peter the Martyr. On the vaulting is the Ascension.

Chiostrino dei Morti (Little Cloisters of the Dead)

Right of the Spanish Chapel. The pavement and walls of these irregularly shaped cloisters and the small entrance gallery are almost entirely covered in gravestones.

Refectory

From the entrance lobby there is a view into the **Great Cloisters** (part of the Police College). The refectory and the room preceding it house the treasure of Santa Maria Novella – gold and silverware, reliquaries, frontals, vestments – and a number of frescoes that have been removed from the church

walls, including Orcagna's 35 busts of figures from the Old Testament which used to decorate the chancel before it was painted by Ghirlandaio. They were found during restoration work.

▶ *In the SW corner of Piazza di Santa Maria Novella turn right into Via della Scala. Walk towards the River Arno to visit Ognissanti.*

OGNISSANTI

Borgo Ognissanti 42. 🕒*Open daily 8am–12.30pm and 4.30pm–7.30pm.* 🕒*Closed Fri am.* ℘*055 28 47 27.*

All Saints' Church, which dates from the 13C, was completely rebuilt during the 17C, with the exception of the bell tower (13C–14C) standing on the south side. The Baroque façade was designed by Matteo Nigetti and is decorated with a glazed terracotta *Coronation of the Virgin Mary* produced in della Robbia's workshops (*lunette above the doorway*) and Florence's coat of arms characterised by its lily (*centre of the pediment*). The interior contains two frescoes by Domenico Ghirlandaio (*behind the second altar on the right*) depicting a *Descent from the Cross* and a *Virgin Mary of Mercy* protecting the members of the family of Amerigo Vespucci, the Florentine navigator, whose tombstone can be seen at the foot of the altar (*left*). It is interesting to compare Botticelli's fresco of St Augustine (*between the third and fourth altars*), with Ghirlandaio's fresco on the north wall of the nave opposite, portraying St Jerome, as both works were painted in 1480. Botticelli is buried in the south transept (*chapel on the right towards the entrance*) beneath a circular marble slab bearing the name Filipepi. The habit worn by St Francis of Assisi when he received the stigmata in September 1224 has been kept in the second chapel of the north transept since 1503.

Cenacolo (Old Refectory)

🕒*Open Mon, Tue, Sat 9am–noon.* 🕒*Closed 1 Jan, 1 May, 25 Dec.* ℘*055 28 47 27. www.polomuseale.firenze. it/musei/ognissanti. Off the cloisters on the south side of the church, access from the transept.*

The former refectory was decorated by Domenico Ghirlandaio in 1480 with a huge fresco of the **Last Supper**★, painted after his version in the Monastery of San Marco. Compared to the fresco in San Marco the Last Supper in Ognissanti conveys a greater sense of serenity and is more natural owing to the slightly more austere decor and the varied poses of the Apostles.

▶ *Walk upstream to the Carraia Bridge. Turn left towards the Museo Marino Marini.*

MUSEO MARINO MARINI★

Piazza San Pancrazio. ◷*Open Mon, Tue–Thu, Sat 10am–5pm.* ◷*Closed Hols.* ⊕€4. ♿. 𝄞*055 21 94 32. www.museomarinomarini.it.*

The Church of San Pancrazio now provides the setting for works by **Marino Marini** (1901–80), sculptor and painter, and has thereby regained the sense of space it lost when occupied by a succession of official departments after its deconsecration in 1808. The huge equestrian group *Aja* in the chancel is brilliantly lit through the glass construction replacing the apse which was destroyed. Sculptures, paintings, drawings and engravings show the artist's marked interest in the austere, static plastic art of ancient statuary onto which he grafted an anxiety typical of his day. The main themes represented are Woman, the Horseman and the Warrior.

▶ *Retrace your steps. At the corner turn left and walk into Via della Vigna Nuova towards the Palazzo Rucellai.*

PALAZZO RUCELLAI★★

18 Via della Vigna Nuova. ◷*Open by appointment only.* 𝄞*055 21 89 75.*

The mansion, built between 1446 and 1451 by Bernardo Rossellino to plans by Leon Battista Alberti, was constructed for Giovanni Rucellai, a member of a leading Florentine family. The Rucellai were related to the Strozzi and Medici and owed their name and fortune to

imports from the Orient of a lichen, Rocella (*oricella*), used to produce red dye. Their family emblem, a sail billowing in the wind, is depicted on a frieze on the first floor, on the loggia opposite and in Santa Maria Novella.

The mansion is the first example since Antiquity of a **façade** articulated by three orders superimposed. A rigorous sense of uniformity is created vertically by the alignment of pilasters and horizontally by the cornices that run along the top of each storey. The windows are set within these grid-like divisions against a background of slightly rusticated stonework, which contrasts greatly with the heavy rustication on the ground floor of the Palazzo Medici and throughout the façade of the Palazzo Strozzi, which dates from a later period.

Opposite stands the **loggia** that accompanied every notable family's residence. It is also attributed to Leon Battista Alberti. Although the bays are walled up, they have retained a certain elegance. Continue along Via della Vigna Nuova as far as Via Tornabuoni. Here are several typical Florentine mansions: **Palazzo Spini-Ferroni**★ (*no 2*) 13C with crenellations and **Palazzo Tornabuoni-Beacci** (*no 3*), a fine 14C mansion. After passing Piazza Strozzi, look at the **Palazzo dello Strozzino** (*no 7*), apparently a smaller replica (hence its name) of its prestigious neighbour, although it is an earlier building begun in 1458 by Michelozzo. Also look at the **Palazzo Larderel** (*no 19 – blue*), built by Dosio in 1580. In **Piazza degli Antinori** (*north end of Via Tornabuoni*), see the **Palazzo Antinori** (*no 3*), built 1461 to 1466, which is attributed to Giuliano da Sangallo.

PALAZZO STROZZI★★

Piazza Strozzi. ◷*Open during exhibitions only.* 𝄞*055 27 76 461. www.palazzostrozzi.org.*

This was the last of the great private mansions to be built during the Florentine Renaissance and it represents one of the period's finest achievements in terms of vernacular architecture.

A rich merchant named Filippo Strozzi commissioned Benedetto da Maiano, architect and sculptor, to design the building. By the time the patron symbolically laid the first stone of his residence on the 6 August 1489, the mansion of his rivals, the Medici – from which the Palazzo Strozzi draws much of its inspiration – had already been in existence for 30 years. In 1490, the year before he died, when building work had only just started, Filippo Strozzi commissioned another Florentine, Giuliano da Sangallo, to produce a scale model of his future residence. It was, however, a third architect, Simone di Pollaiolo, otherwise known as Il Cronaca, who eventually took charge of the work. He is responsible for the splendid stone cornice at the very top of the building.

The stately, elegant **courtyard** (*entrance in Piazza degli Strozzi*), surrounded by a high portico and overlooked by an open loggia on the upper floor in the Florentine tradition, is also the work of Cronaca.

The building was finished in 1504 and remained in the Strozzi family until 1937. It then underwent major restoration before becoming the headquarters of various cultural institutes. It is now the venue for the Biennial International Antiques Fair as well as numerous art exhibitions.

▶ *Walk south along Via Tornabuoni to Piazza S Trinità.*

On the corner with Via Delle Terme stands the **Palazzo Bartolini-Salimbeni** (1517–20), designed by Baccio d'Agnolo, with fine mullioned windows.

SANTA TRINITÀ

Piazza Santa Trinità. ◔*Open daily 8am–noon and 4pm–6pm.* ◔*Closed Sun morning.* ☏*055 21 69 12.*
Holy Trinity Church was built in the second half of the 14C. The Baroque façade by Buontalenti was added in the late 16C.

The extremely austere, slender interior is a fine example of the beginnings of Gothic architecture in Florence. The

façade of the Romanesque church built in the 11C can be seen incorporated into the current façade. The church's crypt also dates from this period.

The chapels contain some interesting works of art. The *Madonna in Majesty with Saints* (*third chapel in the south aisle*) is a 15C altarpiece by Neri di Bicci. The **Chapel of the Annunciation**★ (*fourth chapel*), enclosed by a fine 15C screen and decorated with Lorenzo Monaco's frescoes recounting the Life of the Virgin Mary, contains a fine Gothic altarpiece by the same artist depicting the Annunciation; the predella includes the Visitation, the Nativity, the Adoration of the Magi and the Flight into Egypt. The fifth chapel has an early 16C marble altar set in a splendid carved tempietto surround.

The main feature of interest in this church is, however, the decoration in the **Sassetti Chapel**★★ (*second chapel on the right in the south transept*) undertaken by Domenico Ghirlandaio in 1483. Using a technique he was later to employ in the chancel of Santa Maria Novella, the artist created a colourful portrait gallery of his contemporaries to depict episodes from the life of St Francis of Assisi. The vaulting is decorated with four splendid female figures representing Sibyls. The donors, Francesco Sassetti and his wife, are depicted kneeling. They both lie in the magnificent tombs with basalt sarcophagi, probably the work of Giuliano da Sangallo, on each side of the altar. Above is an *Adoration of the Shepherds*, another famous work by Domenico Ghirlandaio (1485) in which certain critics have observed the influence of the Portinari Triptych by Van der Goes (*now in the Uffizi*).

▶ *From the SE corner of Piazza S Trinità walk along Borgo SS. Apostoli.*

Here are (*no 10*) the **Case degli Acciaiuoli**, 15C; (*no 8*) **Palazzo Acciaiuolia** (*formerly Buondelmonti*), dating from 14C with an adjacent 13C tower; (*nos 17–19*) **Palazzo Usimbardi**, 16C; (*no 9*) **Palazzo Buondelmonti**, 14C–15C with restorations.

San Marco

Accademia to the Sinagoga

On this walk, history and art take precedence over less serious sightseeing, as there are many museums in this district. It is a good idea to choose according to one's preferences, as none of the museums can be seen in a hurry; it would take a whole day to visit all of them.

GALLERIA DELL'ACCADEMIA★★

30min. Via Ricasoli 58–60. ⏱*Open Tue–Sun 8.15am–6.50pm (6.20pm last admission).* ⏱*Closed 1 Jan, 1 May, 25 Dec.* ⬭*€6.50, €7 combined ticket with the Opificio delle Pietre Dure.* ♿*.* ✆*055 23 88 612. www.polomuseale. firenze.it.*

The Accademia is of exceptional interest for its collection of sculptures by Michelangelo. The gallery also houses an art collection of mainly Florentine works dating from the 13C–19C.

The first room contains paintings from the late 15C and early 16C, including a fine *Deposition* by Filippino Lippi and Perugino (*opposite the entrance*). The plaster cast group in the middle of the room is the model produced by Giovanni da Bologna for his *Rape of the Sabine Women* in the Loggia della Signoria.

Michelangelo Gallery★★★

On either side of the gallery are four of the famous **Slaves** (the other two are in the Louvre Museum in Paris), allegories for the soul imprisoned in the body, made for the tomb of Pope Julius II in Rome. A number of designs were produced for this mausoleum which was originally intended to include 40 huge statues and to be erected in the centre of St Peter's in Rome; the final version is in the Church of St Peter in Chains in Rome. In their contorted movements, the unfinished figures (1513–20) seem to be attempting to break free from the marble from which they emerge.

Flanked by the two Slaves (*right*) is St Matthew, part of a series of 12 statues of the Apostles that Michelangelo was commissioned to produce for the cathedral. This statue too is only roughly carved and the others were never produced.

The so-called **Palestrina Pietà**, together with the Pietà in the Museo dell'Opera del Duomo and the *Rondanini Pietà* in Milan, represents the final apotheosis of Michelangelo's art. The overdeveloped arms and torso and roughly carved legs, portrayed with unusual foreshortening, suggest the heaviness of Christ's dead body and illustrate the artist's remarkable knowledge of human anatomy.

At the end of the room stands the huge statue of **David**, in an apse that was

SAN MARCO
Plan V

0 _____ 200 m

WHERE TO EAT

Il Magnifico	②
Il Pirata	④
La Mescita	⑥
Pasticceria Robiglio	⑧
Pugi	⑩

specially built for the work in 1873. Michelangelo was 25 years old and already immensely famous when he carved this masterpiece (1501–04), one of his most famous sculptures, from an enormous block of marble that was considered to be unusable. The biblical hero who defeated the giant Goliath symbolised the determination of the Florentine Republic to defend its freedom in the face of its enemies. In contrast to older works, David is nervously poised for action with sling in hand, not yet experiencing the serenity and pride of victory. He stands with his body weight on his right leg to suggest, using the **"contrapposto"** technique, the tension arising immediately before movement. The artist also broke with tradition by portraying the character, not as a frail adolescent, but rather as a muscular young man whose consummate beauty makes him reminiscent of an Apollo from Antiquity. The statue was placed in front of the Palazzo Vecchio, where it remained until 1873.

Pinacoteca★ (Art Gallery)

The first of the three small adjoining rooms (*right of the main gallery*) displays the front panel of the famous **Adimari Chest** (*second bay on the right*) depicting the wedding celebrations held in Florence for one of the members of this aristocratic family; in the background are the Baptistery and surrounding houses.

The room also contains works providing a remarkable insight into the transition from Gothic to Renaissance art. In the first bay is the Gothic-style Virgin Mary with a girdle (*Madonna della Cintola*) flanked by St Francis and St Catherine of Alexandria, by Andrea di Giusto Manzini (first half of the 15C). The *Mystical Marriage of St Catherine* (*first bay opposite the entrance*), painted in the mid-15C by Mariotto di Cristoforo, retains a Gothic feeling, but the overall layout (rectangular form) and the sketched-in landscape in the far distance are characteristic of the Renaissance style. This evolution towards Renaissance art is illustrated in the two following rooms.

The third room contains two exquisite paintings by Botticelli: the famous **Madonna of the Sea** (actually of uncertain origin) and a delightful **Madonna and Child with the young St John and Angels**, a work displaying a wonderful freshness and tenderness.

In the continuation of the art gallery (*after the Michelangelo gallery*) is a statue of David flanked by 16C Italian paintings. The large *Deposition from the Cross* (*far right*) by Bronzino depicts in the background a descent from the cross. Alessandro Allori's *Annunciation* (*left*) unusually depicts the Virgin with her back almost turned towards the Archangel Gabriel and her hands raised as if she were already aware of her son's destiny, while at her feet, her book and embroidery form a fine still-life.

The **Gipsoteca** (Plasterwork Gallery) (*opposite end of the gallery*) contains works by two 19C sculptors, Bartolini and Pampaloni, professors at the Academy of Fine Arts. The plaster casts are the original models for marble sculptures.

The three rooms (*back towards the David gallery*) contain 13C–14C Tuscan paintings, including three eye-catching Crucifixion scenes. The first floor displays a collection of 14C–15C Tuscan paintings and a collection of icons.

▷ *Turn into nearby Via degli Alfani to the Opificio delle Pietre Dure.*

OPIFICIO DELLE PIETRE DURE★

Via degli Alfani 78. ◷*Open Mon–Sat 8.15am–2pm (7pm Thu).* ◷*Closed Hols.* ☞ *€2, €7 combined ticket with the Galleria dell'Accademia.* ♿. ℘*055 26 51 11. www.firenzemusei.it.*

The **Pietra Dura Workshop** upholds one of the grand traditions of Florentine craftwork. The art of working hard stone (*pietra dura*) which had been fairly popular during the days of ancient Rome and Greece, was brought back into fashion in the 15C by the Medici family. Lorenzo the Magnificent's liking for ancient objects made of semi-precious stones stimulated skills in restoration and reproduction which his successors maintained and diversified with similar enthusiasm. In the 16C Cosimo I and his son, Francesco I, brought artists to their court from all over Italy and other European countries. They included cameo carvers, rock crystal engravers, stone cutting specialists and goldsmiths. In Florence this period marked the beginning of the assembly (*commesso*) of hard stones, a form of mosaic in which the main feature is the juxtaposition of stones carved with such precision that the joins are invisible to the naked eye. The most commonly used stones were granite, porphyry, quartz, onyx and jasper, sometimes in conjunction with softer stones such as marble and alabaster.

In the early 17C the workshops were involved in the decoration of the Princes' Chapel in the church of San Lorenzo. Their innovations included the production of superb pieces of furniture (known as *stipi*) made of precious woods and decorated with rare stones. There are several examples in the Pitti Palace.

After three centuries of activity, the workshops began to decline in 1859 with the fall of the Grand Duchy of Tuscany. The formation of the museum in the late 19C was inspired by the work produced by the old workshops, one of which has been fitted up on the first floor.

The first exhibits in the **Museum** are decorated panels for cabinets (*stipi*), mosaics and reliefs in hard or soft stone (17C). The chief decorative motifs are **flowers, fruits and birds**, an obvious product of the naturalism cultivated by the Medici. The subjects chosen were particularly well adapted to this technique, where the bright colours of the stone stand out magnificently against the black marble background.

Ten panels have survived from the project of decorating the **Princes' Chapel** with *pietra dura* work. They depict landscapes (two of which evoke the Tuscan countryside) and scenes from the Bible (early 17C).

▷ *From Piazza San Marco walk westwards.*

CENACOLO DI SANT'APOLLONIA

Via XXVII Aprile 1. ○*Open daily 8.15am–1.50pm.* ○*Closed 1st, 3rd and 5th Sun in the month, 2nd and 4th Mon in the month, 1 May, 25 Dec, 1 Jan.* ℘*055 23 88 607. www.polomuseale. firenze.it/musei/apollonia.*

St Apollonia's Refectory, a large hall once used as a refectory by the nuns of this Camaldolese convent, is preceded by a small room containing a number of 15C Florentine paintings, including a *Madonna and Child surrounded by Saints* by Neri di Bicci, in which the Child is rather unusually depicted placing his hand inside his mother's bodice. The huge **Last Supper**★ covering one of the refectory walls is a masterpiece by Andrea del Castagno. The artist painted it towards the end of his very short life (c. 1450), at the same time as the other frescoes. It conveys great dramatic force because of the well structured framework, the abundance of mineral decoration, the relief achieved in the representation of the characters and the degree of realism. The depiction of the Passion of Christ (*above*), which shows the Crucifixion (*centre*), the Deposition (*right*) and the Resurrection (*left*), is painted in a freer style against a single landscape background.

CHIOSTRO DELLO SCALZO

Via Cavour 69. ○*Open Mon, Thu, Sat 8.15am–1.50pm.* ○*Closed 1 May, 25 Dec, 1 Jan.* ℘*055 23 88 604. www.polomuseale.firenze.it/musei/ chiostroscalzo.*

The **Scalzo Cloisters**, small and intimate, contain a cycle of frescoes by Andrea del Sarto. Two of the 12 scenes depicting the life of St John the Baptist, the patron saint of the cloisters, were completed by Franciabigio. Andrea del Sarto worked sporadically in the cloisters between 1512 to 1524. Interruptions in the work included a visit to the court of François I of France. The cycle is a fine example of his drawing skills and his gentle expressiveness.

▷ *Return to Piazza San Marco.*

CONVENTO E MUSEO DI SAN MARCO★★

Allow 1hr. Piazza San Marco 3. ○Open daily 8.15am–1.50pm (6.50pm Sat, 7pm Sun and Hols). ○Closed 1st, 3rd and 5th Sun in the month, 2nd and 4th Mon in the month, 1 Jan, 1 May, 25 Dec. ⊚€4. Bookshop. ⚲. ℘055 23 88 608. www.polomuseale.firenze.it.

St Mark's Convent adjoins the church of the same name and houses the museum which contains **works★★★** by **Fra Angelico**.

The convent was built for the Dominicans on the orders of Cosimo the Elder in 1436. It was his loyal friend and favorite architect, Michelozzo, who completed this extremely simple building in about seven years. Fra Angelico and Fra Bartolomeo, another artistic monk who also lived in the monastery but over half a century later, worked on its decoration. St Antoninus (1389–1459) and Savonarola were both priors of St Mark's.

Ground Floor

The elegant Renaissance **cloisters** in the shade of a huge cedar tree contain tympani decorated with frescoes (late 16C to early 17C) recounting the life of St Antoninus.

Ospizio

On the right, at the entrance to the cloisters. The **Former Hospitium** contains numerous altar paintings that rank among the Dominican's best-known works.

Although the large Descent from the Cross (*right of the entrance*) is a triptych of all Fra Angelico's works, it is the one that most reflects the spirit of the Renaissance – background of buildings and landscape, humanity in the attitudes and facial expressions.

In the famous **Last Judgement** (1425) (*next wall*) Fra Angelico combines elements inherited from the Gothic tradition – golden colouring, details treated with the delicacy of the miniaturists – with features characterising the spirit of the Renaissance – sense of perspective in the receding line of tombs and the semicircular composition, dramatic realism in the depiction of the open graves. The admirable series of small

panels (*farther along*), illustrating the Life of Christ, once covered the door of a church cabinet (*Armadio degli Argenti*). Among the scenes depicted (*from left to right*) against the exquisite backdrop of buildings and landscapes, the most outstanding include the Flight into Egypt, the Prayer on the Mount of Olives, the Kiss of Judas and the Arrest of Jesus. The tiny *Virgin with the Star* (*next pillar*) forms a stark contrast to the moving *Lamentation over the Body of Christ* (*farther along*).

The famous **Linaioli Madonna** (*far wall*), painted in 1433, was Fra Angelico's first public work, commissioned by the Linen Merchants' Guild to adorn a marble tabernacle. There is evidence of Masaccio's influence in the substance of the bodies and the feeling of space. The predella contains the Preaching of St Peter before St Mark, the Adoration of the Magi and the Martyrdom of St Mark.

One of the two tiny square panels (*towards the door against a pillar*) is a remarkable miniature depicting a *Coronation of the Virgin Mary*. Then comes the magnificent **Annalena Madonna**, named after the monastery for which it was painted. The small Gothic panel (*next pillar*) with two registers depicting the *Annunciation* and the *Adoration of the Magi* is also a masterpiece of miniature painting.

The **Lavabo Room** (*end of the next gallery on the right*) contains Fra Angelico's *Crucifixion between St Nicholas of Bari and St Francis*, which was extensively damaged by a flood in 1557. In the **main refectory** (*right*) the main wall is decorated with a huge fresco by Giovanni Antonio Sogliani depicting *St Dominic and his brother monks fed by the angels* (1536). Two rooms (*other side of the Lavabo Room*) contain works by Fra Bartolomeo and Alessio Baldovinetti.

Sala Capitolare

The **chapter house** leads off the gallery opposite the entrance containing a 15C bell. This bell has been an anti-Medici symbol ever since it was rung to call the people to defend Savonarola, then prior of St Mark's, when he was arrested in 1498.

The main wall of the room is covered with a huge, austere *Crucifixion* in which Fra Angelico depicted the people present at the historical event and the founder saints of the Dominican Order or saints who had links with the monastery (St Mark) and the Medici family (Saints Cosmas and Damian).

Refettorio Piccolo

Entrance from the small corridor on the left of the chapter house. The **Small Refectory** is decorated with Domenico Ghirlandaio's **Last Supper**★, which preceded a variation on the same subject painted by the artist in 1480 in the refectory in Ognissanti. Another room contains architectural fragments from central Florence.

First Floor

The monks' cells are all decorated with scenes portraying the Life of Christ and the Life of the Virgin Mary and the mysteries of the Christian religion. The artistic value of the works varies depending on whether they were executed by Fra Angelico or his assistants. These frescoes were intended to encourage the meditative contemplation of the monks rather than as altarpieces or tabernacles to impress the faithful.

Overlooking the staircase is a huge **Annunciation**★★★, one of the artist's masterpieces. The cells line three corridors under bare rafters.

Fra Angelico's finest frescoes (*left side of the corridor*) include a fresh, poetic *Apparition of Jesus to Mary Magdalen* (no 1), another admirable **Annunciation** (no 3), a *Christ on the Cross* (no 4), a *Transfiguration* (no 6), *Christ being mocked* (no 7), the *Holy Women at the Tomb* (no 8), a *Coronation of the Virgin* in which the colours seem to be absorbed by the light (no 9) and the *Presentation of Jesus in the Temple*, in which the reddish background is in fact an undercoat from which the actual colour has worn away (no 10).

The two cells (*end of the next corridor*) once occupied by Savonarola contain his missal, rosary, hair-shirt, Crucifix and (*small vestibule*) his ardent, obstinate and zealous portrait by Fra Bartolomeo whom he had converted.

▷ *Return to the staircase.*

St Antoninus' cell (no 31 *immediately to the left in the right-hand corridor*) contains his death mask and a number of his manuscripts.

The splendid **library**★ (*before the cell on the right*) is a bright, spacious room, containing three aisles with elegant arches, and is one of Michelozzo's most accomplished works.

The plaque (*near the entrance*) marks the place where Savonarola was arrested on the night of 8 April 1498. He was executed two months later in Piazza della Signoria.

His own cell (no 33) is decorated with the *Kiss of Judas* by Fra Angelico. The two adjoining cells (nos 38 and 39 far right), which were used by Cosimo the Elder, the monastery's munificent benefactor, during religious retreats, are decorated with *Christ on the Cross* (*first*) by Fra Angelico and an *Adoration of the Magi* (*second*).

▷ *From Piazza San Marco walk eastwards along Via Battisti.*

SANTISSIMA ANNUNZIATA★ (ANNUNCIATION)

This is the name of one of the prettiest squares in Florence and of one of the Florentine people's most beloved churches.

The Square★

Renaissance arcades run along three sides of this elegant square. At the far end (*approaching from the south*) stands the tall church porch and (*right*) the famous elevated portico of the Foundling Hospital. The portico of the Order of the Servants of Mary (*left*) was built to the same design by Antonio da Sangallo the Elder and Baccio d'Agnolo in the early 16C. In the middle of the square stands a bronze equestrian statue of Ferdinand I, the last work to be produced by Giovanni da Bologna. The square is also adorned with two delightful Baroque fountains made in 1629 by Pietro Tacca, who also worked on the completion of the equestrian statue that his master had left unfinished (d. 1608).

Fra Angelico

Fra Giovanni da Fiesole, better known by the name of Fra Angelico, was born in the latter years of the 14C in Vicchio, 30km/19mi northeast of Florence. He entered the Dominican Order in Fiesole and later came to St Mark's in Florence where he spent about ten years covering the walls of the cells and conventual rooms with edifying scenes designed to inspire meditation.

Through his art this modest monk achieved fame within his own lifetime. Pope Nicholas V called him to Rome and commissioned him to decorate the Papal chapel in the Vatican. Orvieto Cathedral has some admirable frescoes painted by him. He also produced numerous altarpieces. He died in 1455 during a visit to Rome and for several centuries bore the title "Blessed" (Beato) until he was eventually canonised in 1983.

His paintings are characterised by their serenity, tenderness and humility. Although he was deeply attached to the Gothic tradition and therefore often worked on triptychs, creating golden backgrounds and using the precious style of the miniaturist, he was also attracted by the new Renaissance theories, as is shown by a certain number of his works in which the figures are steeped in a sense of humanity and space is structured in such a way as to hint at perspective. His altar paintings and frescoes, however, which are true acts of faith, are impressive for the simple mysticism of his vision and the purity of line and colour. In many cases he worked with his pupil, Benozzo Gozzoli, and with Filippo Lippi, and it is sometimes difficult to distinguish what was actually painted by him.

The Church

🕐 Open daily 7.30am–12.30pm and 4-6.30pm. ☎ 055 26 61 81.
The church was built in 1250 for the Order of the Servants of Mary, founded in the 13C by St Filippo Benizzi. It was rebuilt in the 15C in the Renaissance style by Michelozzo.

It is preceded by cloisters (*Chiostrino dei Voti*), surrounded by a portico and covered with a glass roof, which was built between 1447 and 1452. Its decoration was begun in 1460 and continued sporadically over some 50 years. The restored **frescoes**★ portray a cycle (*right of the entrance*) painted by several artists, including Rosso Fiorentino, Pontormo and Andrea del Sarto, that relates to the Virgin Mary. The *Life of St Filippo Benizzi* (*last two walls*) is a cycle painted mainly by Andrea del Sarto.

The inside of the church, including the sumptuous coffered ceiling was lavishly renovated in the Baroque style during the 17C.

The marble chapel (*left after entering the church*) in the form of a small temple (*tempietto*) was built to plans by Michelozzo and designed to house the miraculous picture of the *Virgin of the Annunciation* which was said to have been completed by an angel after its artist fell asleep.

At the entrance to the choir on the wall (*right*) is a funerary monument to Monsignor Angelo Marzi Medici (1546) by Francisco da Sangallo; it is the first example in Italy of the renaissance of the Etruscan-style tomb where the dead man is shown reclining on one elbow on the coffin lid.

The choir in the form of a rotunda with nine radiating chapels is capped by a dome of impressive proportions (*to reach the dome follow the signs in the north transept to Sagrestia and Confessioni*). The Lady chapel, which was altered by Giovanni da Bologna to receive his own tomb, contains a bronze Crucifix of his own design. The large Resurrection (*next chapel on the left*) was painted c. 1550 by Bronzino. Andrea del Castagno painted the two frescoes (*last two chapels in the north aisle*) – the *Trinity* and *St Julian and the Savior*.

The **Cloisters of the Deceased** (*entrance in the north transept or by the doorway in the front of the church on the left-hand* *side beneath the porch*) are in the Renaissance style. The door (*at the end of the gallery opposite the street*) is surmounted by a famous fresco by Andrea del Sarto (*under glass*), the *Rest during the Flight into Egypt* (1525), known more familiarly as the **Virgin of the Sack**★ because of the magnificent sack on which St Joseph is leaning. The chapel of the Brotherhood of St Luke (*further along in the next gallery*), which belonged to an association founded in the 14C by Florentine artists, is the burial place of Benvenuto Cellini and Pontormo, among others.

OSPEDALE DEGLI INNOCENTI★

Piazza SS Annunziata 12. ⓞOpen 8.30am–7pm (2pm Sun). ⓞClosed Hols. €4 (gallery). ℘055 20 37 308.

The **Foundling Hospital**, one of the city's most popular institutions, was built in the early 15C to designs by Brunelleschi. The buildings are slightly elevated above the square and in front of them stands an elegant **portico**★★ consisting of nine semicircular arches set on very slender columns. This work was the first attempt to demonstrate the new theories formulated by Brunelleschi, and it marked the beginning of the era of great architectural achievements created during the Italian Renaissance. In 1463 Andrea della Robbia decorated the arches with a frieze of touchingly fresh **medallions**★★ depicting infants in swaddling clothes. The tiny window (*left beneath the portico*), which is now walled up and surrounded by a large door frame, recalls the wheel where, for four centuries until 1875, children were abandoned anonymously.

The small inner courtyard was also the work of Brunelleschi. The door at the end of the gallery on the left of the entrance is surmounted by Andrea della Robbia's graceful, flowing **Annunciation**★, a statue made of glazed terracotta.

The **art gallery** (*second floor*) specialises mainly in 14C–17C religious paintings. In the great hall (*right of the entrance*) are the **Coronation of the Virgin Mary**, a fine composition in warm tones (15C) by Neri di Bicci, and the *Madonna and Child*

Arcade of the Foundling Hospital by Brunelleschi

B. Juge/ MICHELIN

by Filippo Lippi. In the small adjoining room (*end wall*) hangs a huge **Adoration of the Magi** (1488) by Domenico Ghirlandaio. The fine *Virgin Mary with Saints* (*right wall*) painted in brilliant colours is by Piero di Cosimo. Beside it is an enamelled terracotta *Madonna and Child* by Luca della Robbia.

▶ *Walk eastwards along Via della Colonna.*

MUSEO ARCHEOLOGICO★★

Via della Colonna 38. ⓞOpen Wed, Fri, Sat, Sun 8.30am–2pm (7pm Tue, Thu); 2pm–7pm Mon. ⓞClosed 1 Jan, 1 May, 25 Dec. €4. ℘055 23 575. www.comune.firenze.it/soggetti/sat.

The museum contains numerous objects and works of art from many Etruscan settlement sites and graveyards, as well as extensive collections of items from ancient Egypt, Greece and Rome. On the landing of the first floor is a huge painting representing the Franco-Tuscan expedition to Egypt showing Ippolito Rosellini, the father of Italian Egyptology (*standing left*) and Jean-François Champollion (*seated in the central group*).

Most of the exhibits in the Egyptian collections come from Thebes (18th and 19th dynasties) and Saqqarah (26th to 30th dynasties).

Among the Etruscan funereal sculptures are cinerary urns, used only in the north of Etruria around Volterra, Chiusi and

Perugia. They contained the ashes of the deceased who were depicted on the lids in a seated or standing position (6C BC) or lying down at a banquet (from the 5C BC onwards). Men were depicted holding a chalice or horn, and women holding a mirror, fan or pomegranate. Among the sarcophagi, the Sarcophagus of the Amazons is outstanding for its interesting painted decoration.

The large collection of bronzes includes the **Chimera**★★, which dates from the first half of the 4C BC. It was discovered in 1553 in Arezzo and is thought to have been made by an Etruscan workshop in the Chiusi or Arezzo region. The mythical monster in the form of a lion with two extra heads – of a goat and a snake – bears a votive inscription on its front right paw. Another Etruscan statue called the *Arringatore*, an orator demanding silence, is thought to date from 100 to 80 BC because of its aristocratic Roman garb. The *Minerva* found in Arezzo in 1541 is said to be a Roman copy (1C BC) of a Greek variation on an original statue carved by Praxiteles (340–330 BC) of which more than 20 copies are known to date.

Among the extensive collection of ancient ceramics in the museum the most outstanding exhibit is the famous **François Vase**★★ named after the Florentine archaeologist who found its pieces between 1844 and 1845 scattered in an Etruscan grave near Chiusi. The vase, a superb example dating from 570 BC, indicates the popularity of Attic ceramics among the Etruscans. Its decoration includes hunting scenes, festivities and combats taken from Greek mythology, all showing remarkably skilful artwork.

▷ *Continue eastwards along Via della Colonna. Turn right into Via Borgo Pinti.*

Crocifissione del Perugino★
Borgo Pinti 58, access via the sacristy of Santa Maria Maddalena dei Pazzi (far right) and an underground passage.
🕐*Open Mon–Sat 9am–11.50am, 5pm–5.20pm and 6.10pm–6.50pm, Sun 9am–10.45am and 5pm–6.50pm.* ⊛€1. ℘*055 24 78 420.*

The Crucifixion by **Perugino** is a fresco he painted between 1493 and 1496 in the chapter house of the Benedictine convent of Santa Maria Maddalena dei Pazzi. The composition is divided into three pictures set within the arcades, and depicts (*left to right*) St Bernard and the Virgin Mary, Mary Magdalen at the foot of the cross and St John and St Benedict.

▷ *Return to the corner, turn right into Via della Colonna and right again into Via Farini.*

Sinagoga
Via Farini 4. 🕐*Open Sun–Fri 10am–5pm; rest of the year 10am–3pm.* 🕐*Closed Sat.* ⊛€3. ♿. ℘*055 23 46 654. www.fol.it/sinagoga.*

The Florence **Synagogue** was built between 1874 and 1882 and was based on the Byzantine Agia Sophia in Constantinople. The interior has a rich Moorish decoration including frescoes and mosaics, in addition to a superfluous pulpit in the Christian tradition. Part of the furniture originates from the two synagogues of the **old ghetto**, which was located near Piazza della Repubblica. The Jews of Florence lived in a ghetto between 1571 (with authorisation from Cosimo I) and 1848, the year in which the restrictions were abolished. It was gradually demolished in the late 19C.

WHERE TO EAT					
Acquacotta	(2)	Cibreo	(8)	Il Pizzaiuolo	(16)
Baccarossa	(4)	Darvish café	(10)	Osteria de' Macci	(18)
Boccadama	(6)	Del Fagioli	(12)	Ruth's	(20)
		Gilda	(14)	Vineria Cibreino	(22)

Santa Croce★★

Faith and Intrigue

Allow 1hr 30min. Piazza Santa Croce.
Open Apr–Oct 9am (3pm Sun and Hols)–6.30pm (5.30pm Sat–Sun and Hols). Rest of the year Mon–Fri 9am–12.30pm and 3pm–6.30pm, Sat 10am–12.30pm and 3pm–5.30pm, Sun and Hols 3pm–5.30pm. ℘055 24 46 19.

The white marble façade of the **Church of the Holy Cross** fills the east side of a vast square, **Piazza Santa Croce**, one of the oldest and most grandiose squares in the city. It still has several of its old houses – (*no 1 opposite the church*) Palazzo Serristori, built in the 15C; (*nos 21 and 22*) the early 17C Palazzo Antella decorated with frescoes and flanked (*left*) by an old similarly corbelled house. In the Middle Ages the people of Florence used to gather in this square. It was the site chosen by all the great Franciscan preachers including St Bernardino of Siena in the 15C. From the 16C onwards, one of major events in Florence, Calcio Storico Fiorentino, was staged in the square (*see Events and Festivals*).

This was one of the worst affected districts during the 1966 floods, and Santa Croce was one of the historic buildings of Florence which suffered most from the mud that reached a height of 3m/10ft inside the church and up to 5m/16ft in the cloisters.

Building began in 1295 to designs by Arnolfio di Cambio and was completed in the second half of the 14C, except for the present bell tower (the original bell tower collapsed in the 16C) and the neo-Gothic west front which dates only from the 19C. This is the Franciscan Order's church in Florence. It is a huge building (140m/459ft long and 40m/131ft wide) because it was designed for preaching. The Florentine Gothic interior is remarkably elegant. Because of the 276 gravestones set in the pavement and the lavish tombs contained in the church (most of them the tombs of famous men), Santa Croce has been nicknamed the "Italian Pantheon".

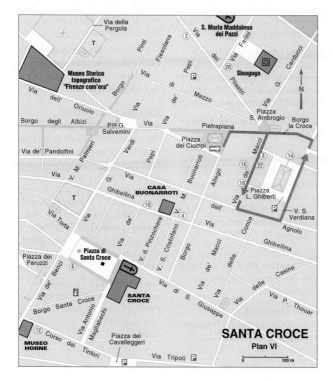

SANTA CROCE

Plan VI

0   100 m

Santa Croce Tour

South Aisle

The highly decorative *Madonna and Child* (1) (*against the first pillar*), carved by Antonio Rossellino in 1478, surmounts the tomb of Francesco Nori, who was killed during the Pazzi Conspiracy. The tomb of Michelangelo (2) (*opposite*) who died in 1564 was designed in 1570 (Rome also laid claim to his body) by Vasari, who also designed the great *Climb to Calvary* (3) above the next altar. The memorial to Dante (4)**,** who died in 1321 and is buried in Ravenna, dates from the 19C.

A monument by Canova (5) marks the tomb of Alfieri, an Italian playwright who died in Florence in 1803. Opposite is a superb marble **pulpit**★, carved with scenes from the life of St Francis in 1476 by Benedetto da Maiano.

Beyond the pulpit is a monument (6) to Machiavelli (d. 1572) dating from the late 18C. The allegorical figure representing Diplomacy is a reminder of his diplomatic missions.

Donatello's **Annunciation**★★ (7) (c. 1430) is one of the most harmonious examples of *tabernacoli*, a type of low relief set in a frame in the shape of a small classical temple.

For the **tomb of Leonardo Bruni**★★ (8), a Humanist and chancellor of the Florentine Republic, who died in 1444, Bernardo Rossellino created a new style of funereal architecture. It consisted of a sarcophagus bearing a sculpture of the recumbent figure of the deceased. Many tombs were created in this style during the Italian Renaissance.

Beside it is Rossini's tomb (9) (he died in 1868) and the tomb of Ugo Foscolo (1778–1827), one of the great poets of modern Italy (10)**.**

South Transept

Taddeo Gaddi painted the **frescoes**★ decorating the **Baroncelli Chapel** (11) from 1332 to 1338. They depict the Life of the Virgin Mary. On the altar is a fine **polyptych**★ representing the Coronation of the Virgin Mary.

Sacristy★

A Renaissance doorway created by Michelozzo leads into the **sacristy**, a fine 14C chamber which still has its painted rafters and one wall covered with frescoes. Inside one of the inlaid cupboards (15C–16C) is a reliquary containing the habit and belt of St Francis of Assisi.

The **Rinuccini Chapel** (12) (*opposite the door*) is decorated with **frescoes**★ recounting the Life of the Virgin Mary (*left*) and the life of Mary Magdalen (*right*). The scenes were drawn by Giovanni da Milano, one of Lombardy's main artists in the 14C, who became a citizen of Florence.

▷ *Beyond the Sacristy is a narrow passageway leading to the Leatherwork School.*

Medici Chapel (13)

⊶ *Closed but visible through a window in the door.*

The delightful **Medici Chapel** built by Michelozzo in 1434 contains a graceful terracotta **reredos**★ glazed by Andrea della Robbia.

Cappella Maggiore e Cappelle Adiacenti

The sanctuary is flanked by ten small chapels. The Giugni Chapel (14) contains the tomb of Giulia Clary, Joseph Bonaparte's wife (*right*) and the tomb of their daughter Charlotte Napoleon Bonaparte (*left*). The **Bardi Chapel** (15) is decorated with the admirable **Frescoes of the Life of St Francis**★★ (restored) which were painted c. 1320 by Giotto, recalling his famous frescoes in the basilica in Assisi.

The **sanctuary** (16) is decorated with **frescoes**★ telling the legend of the True Cross. They were painted in 1380 in a late Gothic style by Agnolo Gaddi.

The frescoes in the Pulci Chapel (17) were painted c. 1330 by Bernardo Daddi and his pupils.

North Transept

The **Bardi Chapel** (18) contains a shockingly realistic wooden **Crucifix**★★ by Donatello, a work that Brunelleschi wanted to surpass when he created his statue in Santa Maria Novella.

North Aisle

The **Tomb of Carlo Marsuppinia** (19), humanist and secretary to the Florentine Republic, who died in 1453, brought fame to its sculptor, Desiderio da Settignano.

Lorenzo Ghiberti (d. 1455) and his son, Vittorio, are buried opposite the fourth pillar (20). Galileo's tomb (21) (d. 1642) was built in the 18C.

Cloisters

These delightful 14C **cloisters** lead to the Pazzi Chapel (*at the end*) and the Santa Croce Museum (*to the right*). The closed gallery (*left*) contains a large and varied number of gravestones and tombs.

Cappella dei Pazzi★★

The **Pazzi Chapel**, one of the most exquisite of the designs generally attributed to Brunelleschi, was built for the Pazzi family, who were the main rivals of the Medici.

The interior is a masterpiece of Florentine Renaissance architecture owing to its unusual design, majestic proportions, purity of line and harmonious decoration.

Chiostro Grande

A superb Renaissance doorway opens into the **Great Cloisters**. The vast and elegantly proportioned construction was designed by Brunelleschi shortly before his death and completed in 1453.

Museo dell'Opera di Santa Croce (Santa Croce Museum)

⏱ *Open Mar–Oct daily 10am–7pm; rest of the year until 6pm.*
⏱ *Closed 1 Jan, 25 Dec.* ✆€4.
♿. ✆055 24 66 01.

The old Franciscan chapter house displays Cimabue's famous **Crucifixion**★ (22), which has been restored with exemplary care after the considerable damage it suffered during the floods in 1966.

The end wall is covered by a huge fresco representing the Last Supper; above is the Tree of the Cross (23), painted in the 14C by Taddeo Gaddi, to represent the genealogy of the Franciscans. Among the other remarkable exhibits are a gilded bronze statue of St Louis of Toulouse (24) by Donatello (*left*) and small fragments of frescoes by Orcagna found on the wall of the church but which had been concealed by restoration work carried out in the 16C by Vasari: (*left*) are fragments of *Hell*; (*right panel 3*) is a group of beggars that was once part of the *Triumph of Death*.

The rooms between the two cloisters contain underdrawings for frescoes (*sinopie*), 14C and 15C frescoes from the church and Tino da Camaino's tomb.

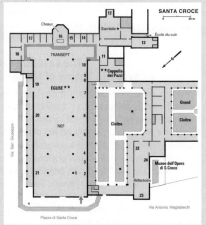

Other Museums

MUSEO LA SPECOLA★

Via Romana 17; at the top of the flight of steps on the left at the end of the street. ⏱*Open Thu–Tue 9am–1pm.* ⏱*Closed Hols and 24 Jun.* ⊗*€3, €9.30 to see the other sections of the Museo di Storia Naturale.* 🖉*055 22 88 251. www.specola.unifi.it.*

This natural history museum, which was founded in 1775 by Grand Duke Leopold, is named after the astronomical and meteorological observatory (*specola* in Italian) which was installed at the request of the Grand Duke. It houses an extensive zoological collection of vertebrates and invertebrates and over 600 amazingly lifelike **anatomical waxworks**.

MUSEO STIBBERT★

Via Federico Stibbert; take bus no 1 (Piazza dell'Unità d'Italia) or no 4 (Piazza della Stazione behind the chancel of Santa Maria Novella). ⏱*Open Mon–Thu 10am–1pm (Fri–Sun 6pm).* ⏱*Closed Hols. Audiovisual show. Bar. Bookshop.* ⊗*€4.* 🖉*055 47 55 20. www.museostibbert.it.*

The Stibbert Villa (19C) stands at the entrance to a small park. It now houses the huge art collections built up during the last century by Federico Stibbert, the Anglo-Italian Garibaldian hero.

The 57 rooms display a profusion of items: armour, sculptures, paintings, furniture, faïence, tapestries, embroi-dery, objects and costumes of varying origins and periods of history. The most outstanding of these are a malachite and gilded bronze table made by Thomire for King Jerome; Napoleonic memorabilia, including the coronation robes worn by Napoleon when he was crowned King of Italy and Murat's sabre; a *Madonna and Child* (*Room 32*) for many years attributed to Botticelli; and Venetian costumes from the 18C.

Special mention must be made of the hundreds of pieces of 🧍‍🧍**old armour**★★ worn by Tuscans, Turks, Moors, Spaniards, Indians, Japanese etc. Many of them are mounted on models of men and horses lined up in impressive processions (*mainly on the ground floor and the top storey*); the exhibit is guaranteed to stir the imaginations of older kids.

MUSEO BARDINI★

Piazza de' Mazzi 1. ⏱*Open Sat–Mon 11am–5pm.* 🖉*055 23 42 427. www.comune.fi.it*

The collections of this museum, displayed in a 19C mansion, include sculptures, stucco work, paintings, small bronzes and medals, Persian rugs (16C–17C), 18C Florentine tapestries, ceramics and old musical instruments. All were bequeathed to the city in 1922 by Stefano Bardini, a famous antique dealer, and all indicative of his eclectic taste.

The notable works here include a group representing *Charity* by Tino di Camaino (*Room 7*); a graceful relief of

The Last Supper, a Favourite Theme of Monastery Refectories

Monastery refectories (*cenacoli* in Italian) take their name from the Latin (cenaculum) meaning an eating room or, more specifically, the upper room where the Last Supper was held. It was usual for them to contain an illustration of this biblical scene as it was an important subject of meditation during meals.

Numerous works on this theme were produced in Florence. The 12 Apostles are usually portrayed seated in a row at a long table covered with a cloth, with Jesus in the centre and John by his side, bending towards him or leaning against his breast. Judas, without a halo, is almost always depicted alone in the foreground facing the others. Leonardo da Vinci was the first to interpret the scene with the 13 companions seated on the same side of the table (1495–97) in the refectory of Santa Maria delle Grazie in Milan.

Trial of Galileo, 1841. Museo di Storia della Scienza

World Illustrated/Photoshot

the *Madonna and Child* by a 15C Sienese artist and another *Madonna and Child* set within a mandorla with angels and cherubs (*both in Room 10*); an exquisite polychrome terracotta relief (*Room 14*) of the *Madonna and Child* by Donatello, a fine 15C inlaid ceiling (*Room 16*) and (*above the fireplace*) *St Michael the Archangel* painted on canvas by Antonio Pollaiolo.

MUSEO DI STORIA DELLA SCIENZA★

Open Jun–Oct Mon–Sat 9.30am–5pm (1pm Tue/Sat); rest of the year Mon, Wed–Sat 9.30am–5pm, Tue 9.30am–1pm, 2nd Sun in the month 10am–1pm. Closed Hols. €7.50. 055 29 34 93. www.imss.fi.it.

The museum, housed in the medieval **Palazzo Castellani**, displays a vast collection of ancient scientific instruments, many of which come from the collections built up by the Medici family and the Grand Dukes of Lorraine.

Rooms 1 to 3 on the **First Floor** contain 16C and 17C mathematical instruments. They include globes, armillary spheres, astrolabes, quadrants, sundials and compasses. The fourth room contains memorabilia relating to **Galileo** (1564–1642).

Rooms 5 and 6 deal with optics, a science that made huge progress in the 17C. The origins and development of the telescope, a prism and optical games are on display. Cosmography, the representation of the canopy of heavens, is illustrated in Room 7 by splendid terrestrial and celestial globes and armillary spheres.

Rooms 8 to 11 house a collection of observation and research instruments beginning with a microscope, invented in the 17C.

Room 12 on the **Second Floor** is devoted to clock mechanisms, which first appeared in the Western world in the 13C, and to clockwork figures which were very fashionable in the 18C.

Room 13 contains mathematical instruments and measuring devices which were perfected throughout the 18C and 19C, thereby paving the way for the extraordinary development of the precision instrument industry.

In Room 14 are 18C devices used to demonstrate electrical and magnetic phenomena, which were fairly recent discoveries at that time.

Room 15 describes the success of pneumatics and hydrostatics from the mid-17C to the end of the 18C.

Rooms 16 and 17 trace how mechanics also aroused a great deal of enthusiasm and consequently made huge strides forward throughout the 17C from Descartes to Newton.

Rooms 18, 19 and 20 all contain exhibits relating to the medical fields. Room 18 contains numerous surgical instruments and a very extensive collection of wax

171

and terracotta teaching aids used in obstetrics. Room 19 covers the history of pharmacy and Room 20 the origins of modern chemistry.

The last room contains weights, measures and balances.

▶ *Near Piazza dei Giudici note the Palazzo Castellani, 14C.*

MUSEO STORICO TOPOGRAFICO "FIRENZE COM'ERA"

Via Oriuolo 4. ⏰Open Fri–Wed 9am–1.30pm. ⊚€2.50. ♿. ☏055 26 16 545. www.comune.fi.it.

In the **Florence Historical Topographical Museum** paintings, engravings and old maps trace urban development in Florence and describe the history of its various districts from the Renaissance to the 19C. There is a fine series of lunettes representing the Medici villas created by Giusto Utens in Tuscany in 1599.

CASA BUONARROTI★

Via Ghibellina 70. ⏰Open Wed–Mon 9.30am–2pm. ⏰Closed Hols. ⊚€6.20. ☏055 24 17 52. www.casabuonarroti.it.

The **Buonarroti House** consists of a group of houses purchased in March 1508 by Michelangelo at the corner of Via Ghibellina. It is thought that he lived in one of them. When he moved to Rome in 1534, he sold the houses to his nephew, Leonardo, and left him the plans for alterations designed to convert the units into the present residence, in which Michelangelo never lived.

The building was sold to Florence City Council in 1858 by the last surviving member of the Buonarroti family.

The ground floor houses the collections of ancient Roman and Etruscan sculptures built up by the Buonarroti family. In the first room (*right of the hall*) are portraits of Michelangelo and a bronze sculpture of the artist, cast in two parts by Daniele da Volterra and Giovanni da Bologna.

On the first floor are works by Michelangelo, including the unfinished marble relief (*right of the door*) depicting the **Battle of the Centaurs** (before 1492) and the famous **Virgin Mary and Staircase** (1490–92). In the next room on the left are a large model of a statue of the river god, which was intended to decorate one of the two Medici tombs in San Lorenzo and a wooden scale model of the west front of the church.

The room behind the staircase contains rotating exhibitions of Michelangelo's works.

CENACOLO DI FULIGNO

Via Faenza 42. ⏰Open daily 9am–noon. ⏰Closed Easter, 15 Aug, 25 Dec. Donation welcome. ♿. ☏055 28 69 82.

This is the refectory of the former convent of Franciscan Tertiaries in Foligno. Its fresco of the **Last Supper**★ is attributed to Perugino and is said to date from slightly after 1491, the year in which Neri di Bicci, the artist originally commissioned for this work, died.

CENACOLO DI SAN SALVI★

Via San Salvi 16, to the east of the city. From Piazza Beccaria, take Via Vincenzo Gioberti and Via Aretina, its continuation on the other side of Piazza L B Alberti; turn left into Via San Salvi. By bus: take no 3 (Ponte Vecchio), no 6 (Duomo) or no 20 (San Marco); alight at Viale E De Amicis after the large bridge over the railway; after the bridge turn right into Via Tito Speri and right again into Via San Salvi. ⏰Open Tue–Sun 8am–2pm. ⏰Closed 1 Jan, 1 May, 25 Dec. ☏055 23 88 603.

The refectory of the former Monastery of San Salvi is preceded by a long gallery and two halls, containing altar paintings and works stylistically related to Andrea del Sarto. It was he who in c. 1520 painted the refectory's splendid **Last Supper**★★ inspired by the work of Leonardo da Vinci in Milan. The refectory also contains a *Noli me Tangere* by the same artist.

Outside Florence

🚗 DRIVING TOURS

See general map of Florence on Map 563, in the Road Atlas Italia or Europe, or in The Michelin Guide Italia.

I COLLI★★

This trip (about 1hr) is best done by car or bus, preferably in the morning, starting from Piazza F Ferrucci and returning to Via Porta Romana.

The splendid hillside route (Viale dei Colli), which is sub-divided into Viale Michelangelo (at the east end), Viale Galileo (in the middle) and Viale Machiavelli (at the west end), overlooks Florence from the south bank. It was built between 1865 and 1870 and its superb route was selected by the architect Giuseppe Poggi, who was in charge of urban improvement during the brief spell when Florence was the capital of the Kingdom of Italy. The road, which is lined with luxurious mansions, wends its way in wide curves across the hillside between two majestic rows of pines and cypresses.

Piazzale Michelangelo

From this vast esplanade overlooking the city, there is a magnificent **panoramic view**★★★ of Florence and the Appenines.

The memorial to Michelangelo, erected in 1875 in the centre of the square, is decorated with copies of some of the artist's most famous statues.

▶ *From Piazzale Michelangelo continue uphill away from the city along Via Galileo (part of Viale dei Colli).*

San Miniato al Monte★★

A steep flight of steps leads up to the church (left). The church of San Miniato was built in an outstandingly beautiful **setting**★★ overlooking Florence, at the top of a wide flight of steps commissioned by Poggi. It is flanked by a graveyard from which there is a view of the countryside, including the Boboli Gardens laid out on the hill below the Belvedere Fort which is distinguished by its 14C fortifications.

A Benedictine monastery was founded here in the 11C and its church is one of the finest examples of Florentine Romanesque architecture. It was built in memory of **St Minias**, who fell victim to the persecutions ordered in AD 250 by the Roman Emperor Decius. Minias, probably a Tuscan of humble origins who, according to popular belief, had already miraculously escaped a number of executions. When he had finally been beheaded, he crossed the River Arno holding his head in his hands, returning to die on the hillside where he had lived as a hermit (then known as Mons Florentinus).

The 12C **west front** is exceptionally elegant and is reminiscent of the Baptistery. On the left is the unfinished 16C bell tower. Michelangelo, who was commissioned to add fortifications to the hillside, decided to use the tower as a base for artillery when Florence was besieged in 1530 by the troops of Charles V in an attempt to re-establish the Medici.

Like the west front, the **Interior** is remarkable for the pleasing geometric combination of green and white marble. The superb pavement (1207), inset with white and black marble, is like a piece of lace.

The tiny **Crucifix Chapel** was built in 1447 on the orders of Pietro I to designs by Michelozzo. Its purpose was to house a miraculous Crucifix. The glazed terracotta coffering decorating the roof is by Luca della Robbia. Agnolo Gaddi painted the panels above the altar in the late 14C. In the centre, dressed in red, is St Minias.

The **Chapel of the Cardinal of Portugal**★ which was built in the 15C opens off the north aisle and is a fine example of Renaissance architecture, designed by one of Brunelleschi's pupils. It houses the tomb of James of Lusitania, Archbishop of Lisbon and nephew of the King of Portugal, who died in Florence in 1459.

The **pulpit**, and the **choir screen** against which it stands, form a superb **set of furnishings**★★ including some magnificent craftwork with inlays of white, green and pink marble dating from the early 13C.

Above the **apse** is a huge late 13C mosaic representing Christ giving His Benediction. He is flanked by the Virgin Mary and St Minias.

In the **sacristy**, Spinello Aretino painted **frescoes**★ in 1387 (restored) in a style reminiscent of that of Giotto; they illustrate the *Legend of St Benedict*.

The **crypt** includes seven aisles separated by a multitude of wonderful, slender columns crowned by Classical capitals. The altar contains the remains of St Minias.

The tour continues through a series of sweeping curves to the Porta Romana. Some way along this long avenue (*about 2km/1mi from Piazzale Michelangolo*) a narrow road (*one-way*) branches off to the right, leading down to **Forte del Belvedere** (*the road ends at Lungarno Torrigiani quay. Start from this quay if you wish to climb up to the Fort on foot*). The splendid **panoramic view**★★ provided many painters with inspiration.

COLLI ALTI SCENIC ROUTE★

26km/16mi from Florence by S65 (Bologna road); beyond Montorsoli turn left into the Monte Morello road.

The road climbs sharply at first and then winds across the southern slopes of Mount Morello, providing views (*south*) over Fiesole and Florence and the Arno Basin. The most extensive **view**★ extends over a considerable distance (3km/2mi) from Piazzale Leonardo da Vinci (6km/3.5mi beyond Montorsoli – alt 595m/1 952ft – *restaurant*). The view embraces Florence and the Arno Valley; in the background are the Chianti Hills (*south*) and the Prato plain (*west*).

Beyond the Gualdo Refuge (alt 428m/1 404ft) the road narrows and runs down a steep hillside in a series of bends with views through the pines of Prato and Sesto Fiorentino.

▶ *In Colonnata take the road to Sesto Fiorentino. In Quinto Alto turn left into Via Fratelli Rosselli, a long road.*

Tomba Etrusca della Montagnola★

Enquire at no 95. ⏱*Closed for restoration at the time of writing.*

The Etruscan tomb dates from the 7C or 6C BC and is interesting for its remarkable roofing systems concealed beneath an earth tumulus.

▶ *Continue to Sesto Fiorentino.*

Sesto Fiorentino★

The small town of Sesto Fiorentino is situated at the sixth (*sesto*) mile northwest of Florence. It has quite lost its medieval character since its industrial expansion based mainly on its reputation for the production of porcelain and ceramics.

Museo di Doccia★

Viale Pratese 31. ⏱*Open Tue, Thu, Sat, 9.30am–1pm and 3.30pm–6.30pm.* ⏱*Closed Hols, 11 Nov, Aug.* ⊚€5. ☏055 42 07 767. www.museodidoccia.it.

The prestigious Doccia porcelain works, which moved to Sesto in 1954, were founded by the Ginori in 1735 in the nearby town of Doccia. The collection displayed in the **museum** traces the changes in taste from 18C Baroque to the present day, and includes dinner services, vases, documents from the archives, wax and terracotta models.

Tour of Monte Senario★

38km/24mi N of Florence by S65 (Bologna road) following the same route as the previous tour as far as Montorsoli. From the Trespiano hill there are views (*right*) over Florence in the valley below, to Fiesole, followed by a few rare glimpses of the Mugnone Valley.

▶ *800m/875yd beyond the junction with the winding road (left) to Monte Morello turn right at the traffic lights into the villa entrance, a huge gate surmounted by two lions.*

Parco di Villa di Demidoff★

Near to Pratolino, 10km/6mi N of Florence. ○*Open Apr–Sept Thu–Sun 10am–8pm (8.30pm May–Jul); rest of the year Hols only 10am–6pm (7pm Oct).* ⚏€*2.50.* ℘*055 40 94 27. www. provincia.firenze.it/istcult/Demidoff/.*

Within this park, a masterpiece of Tuscan mannerism, used to stand the most luxurious of all the Medici villas, known as the **Villa di Pratolino**. Its present name is that of the prince who purchased the property in 1872.

Among the surviving traces of its past splendour is the huge statue of the **Appennino**★ by Giovanni da Bologna (1579–80) containing grottoes decorated with frescoes and fountains. To the right of the avenue is the chapel by Buontalenti.

▷ *Continue to Pratolino; turn right off S65 into the road to Bivigliano. At the following junction, where the road divides on a bend (before the junction with the road to Olmo), turn into the road up to Monte Senario.*

From the hilltop approach road there are some delightful views of the surrounding hills and the monastery glimpsed among the fir trees.

▷ *After 2.5km/1.5mi turn right; drive to the top of the hill (car park). A short private drive leads to the monastery.*

Convento del Monte Senario

Alt 817m/2 655ft. The **monastery** lies in a superb **setting**★★ on a wooded promontory above the Sieve Valley. It was founded in the 13C by the seven founding saints of the Order of the Servants of Mary. The monastery, which dates from the 17C and 18C, has a tiny **church** with an elegant Baroque interior and a few works of art including a 15C terracotta *Pietà* in the Chapel of the Apparition (*on the altar*).

▷ *On returning down the hill, turn right at the road junction towards Bivigliano (signposted).*

Bivigliano is a pleasant shady residential village near a fine pine wood. The road continues along delightful terraces above the Carza Valley.

▷ *From Pratolino take S65 to return to Florence.*

EXCURSION
Certosa del Galluzzo★★

6km/4mi S of Florence. On the west side of the road from Galluzzo to Siena. Allow 45min. Guided tour Tue–Sun 9am–noon and 3pm–6pm (5pm Oct-Mar). Donation to the guide. ℘*055 20 49 226.*

The **Galluzzo Charterhouse**, also known as the **Florence Charterhouse**, was founded in the 14C by the great Florentine banker, Niccolò Acciaiuoli. The Carthusian monks occupied the premises until 1957 and were succeeded a year later by a Cistercian community. A monumental staircase leads to the monastery buildings and to the Palazzo Acciaiuoli, which now houses an art gallery showcasing frescoes by Jacopo Pontormo (1523–25) that depict scenes from the Passion of Christ, originally in the cloisters.

The church was divided into two distinct sections to separate the lay brothers from the Carthusian monks. The Gothic Chapel of S Maria (*right*) leads to the underground chapels in which the members of the Acciaiuoli family are buried. The parlour (*left of the church*), where the monks were allowed one hour of recreation a week, leads into small cloisters and from there to the chapter house which contains the magnificent **tomb of Leonardo Buonafé** (1550) by Francesco di Giuliano da Sangallo and an intricately carved door (16C).

Round the great Renaissance **cloisters**, adorned with medallions by the della Robbias, are the 18 monastic cells (*one is open to the public*). The visit continues via the refectory, lay cloisters and guesthouse.

ADDRESSES

🏠 STAY

As one of the most attractive destinations in the world, Florence suffers from the peaceful invasion of tourists, especially between May and September. Visitors should book ahead as far as possible.

Prices are usually high and there is no particular district in Florence where cheaper accommodation is to be found; in fact the old historic centre contains hotels in every category. The only exception is the district around the Railway Station, which has several guesthouses often used by students. The noise and pollution caused by traffic is a constant problem in the town centre; although the centre is closed to traffic during the day, parking is very difficult. Obviously the pedestrian zones are the least noisy. Many hotels have double glazed windows but not air conditioning, so in summer one is obliged to choose between the heat and the noise.

The selection contains different types of accommodation, from small guesthouses with a few rooms and shared bathrooms to elegant hotels furnished with every comfort. Whatever your budget, if you are looking for a room with a view, you must expect to pay extra.

There is an impressive number of bars offering fast food, not to mention tourist restaurants. However, it is not easy to eat well in Florence and obtain value for money. The best hope is to look for a typical trattoria which offers traditional Florentine dishes such as tripe (*trippa*), bean and cabbage soup (*ribollita*), a tomato dish (*pappa al pomodoro*), and pasta.

😑 CONVENTS

A number of places to stay in Florence are managed by religious orders. Their rates are much less expensive, but the sole disadvantage is that the doors are locked at night (about 10.30pm), thus no late evenings on the town. Here's a selection:

Casa della Madonna del Rosario – *Via Capo di Mondo 44.* ℘*055 67 96 21. Fax 055 67 71 33.* 🛏. *32 rooms.*

Casa del Santo nome di Gesù – *Piazza del Carmine 21.* ℘*055 21 38 56. Fax 055 28 18 35.* 🛏. *26 rooms.*

Istituto Pio X Artigianelli – *V. Serragli 106.* ℘/*fax 055 22 50 44.* 🛏. *18 rooms.*

Istituto Gould – *Via dei Serragli 49.* ℘*55 21 53 63. Fax 055 28 02 74. www.istituto-gould.it/foresteria/.* 🛏. *41 rooms.*

Istituto Salesiano dell'Immacolata – *Via del Ghirlandaio 40.* ℘*055 62 300. Fax 055 62 30 282.* 🛏. *55 rooms.*

Sette Santi Fondatori – *Via dei Mille 11.* ℘*055 50 48 452. Fax 055 50 57 085.* 🛏. *65 rooms.*

Istituto Santa Elisabetta – *Viale Michelangelo 46.* ℘*055 68 11 884. Fax 055 68 11 884.* 🛏. *29 rooms.*

Oblate dell'Assunzione – *Borgo Pinti 15.* ℘*055 24 80 582. Fax 055 23 46 291.* 🛏. *30 rooms.*

Casa del SS. Rosario – *V. Guido Monaco 24.* ℘*055 32 11 71.* 🛏. *12 rooms.*

Istituto Sant'Angela – *V. Fra Bartolomeo 56.* ℘/*fax 055 57 22 32.* 🛏. *11 rooms.*

Istituto San Giovanni Battista – *V. di Ripoli 82.* ℘*055 68 02 394. Fax 055 68 02 394.* 🛏. *11 rooms.*

ACCOMMODATION

😑 **Ostello Villa Camerata** – *Viale Augusto Righi 2/4, zona Salviatino, 5km/3mi from the centre, towards Fiesole; bus 17.* ℘*055 60 14 51. Fax 055 60 13 00.* 🛏&. *322 beds.* The view of Fiesole from this address makes it hard to believe that it is in one of the busiest tourist cities in Italy. The 15C building has been converted into a hostel with bunk beds, shared bathrooms and a restaurant.

😑 **Ostello Santa Monaca** – *V. Santa Monaca 6 -* ℘*055 26 83 38. Fax 055 28 01 85. info@ostello.it.* 🛏. *114 beds.* Housed in a former 14C monastery, this professionally run cooperative is in the heart of the Oltrarno between Piazza Santo Spirito and Piazza del Carmine. Rooms contain from 4 to 20 beds and are accessed via charming corridors.

◎⚠ **Campeggio Michelangelo** –
*Viale Michelangelo 8, zona Piazzale
Michelangelo. ☏055 68 11 966. Fax 055
68 93 48. 240 sites.* This large campsite
is situated next to an olive grove, not
far from the city centre below Piazzale
Michelangelo. It is well equipped with an
open-air bar-restaurant and a mini-market for provisions. The tents and camper
vans are positioned on terraces which
descend to the bank of the River Arno.

◎ **Ostello Archi Rossi** – *Via Faenza 94r,
zona S Lorenzo. ☏055 29 08 04. Fax 055
23 02 601. Closed Dec. ⬦✕⬦. 97 beds
⬦.* Although a little old fashioned,
this a good place to stay owing to its
very central location and its pleasant
atmosphere.

◎◎ **Albergo Scoti** – *Via Tornabuoni
7 (2nd floor without lift), zona S Maria
Novella. ☏055 29 21 28. www.hotelscoti.
com. ⬦. 7 rooms. ⬦ €4.* The location in
elegant Via Tornabuoni and the frescoes
in the saloon give this Renaissance
mansion an aristocratic air tempered
by a hint of decadence. Small shared
bathrooms.

◎◎ **Youth Firenze 2000** – *Viale
Raffaello Sanzio 16, zona S Frediano.
☏55 23 35 558. Closed mid-Nov–mid-Dec.
⬦✕⬦. 76 beds/ double rooms. ⬦.*
Part hotel, part inn, this address is noted
for its spacious private bathrooms and
its very practical electronic keys, which
confer complete autonomy on the visitor. Only 15min on foot from the Ponte
Vecchio.

◎◎ **Hotel Orchidea** – *Borgo degli
Albizi 111 (1st floor without lift), zona
Duomo. ☏055 24 80 346. www.hotel
orchideaflorence.it. ⬦. 7 rooms. ⬦.*
The English owner has created a quiet,
family atmosphere on the first floor of
this old mansion in the historic town
centre. The spacious rooms have high
ceilings and simple decoration. Shared
bathrooms.

◎◎ **Residenza Hannah e Johanna** –
*Via Bonifacio Lupi 14. ☏055 48 18 96.
Fax 055 48 27 21. www.johanna.it. ⬦.
11 rooms. ⬦.* Well placed near Piazza
San Marco, this inn (also known as
Johanna I) provides a warm welcome
and reasonableprice. Breakfast is
delivered to the rooms.

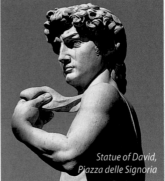
*Statue of David,
Piazza delle Signoria*

J. Malburet/ MICHELIN

◎◎ **Residenza Johanna** – *Via Cinque
Giornate 12, zona Fortezza da Basso.
☏055 47 33 77. www.johanna.it. ⬦.
6 double rooms. ⬦.* This small quiet
sister hotel to Hannah e Johanna is
appreciated for its welcoming atmosphere. The car park in the tiny courtyard
(a rare facility in Florence) compensates
for its isolated location (about 30min on
foot from the town centre).

◎◎ **Bed & Breakfast Dei Mori** –
*Via Dante Alighieri 12, zona Piazza della
Signoria. www.deimori.com. 12 rooms.
⬦.* This welcoming B&B, situated in a
15C mansion near the Cathedral, has a
classic ambience, created by painted
headboards and attention to romantic
detail.

◎◎ **Albergo Firenze** – *Piazza Donati 4,
zona Piazza Repubblica. ☏055 21 42 03.
Fax 055 21 23 70. www.hotelfirenzeflor-
ence.com. ⬦⬦. 60 rooms. ⬦.* The 13C
tower house belonging to the powerful
Donati family has been converted into a
hotel, offering welcoming public rooms
and modern, functional bedrooms at
a reasonable price, despite its location
near to Piazza della Repubblica.

◎◎◎ **Residenze Johlea I e II** –
*Via San Gallo 76/80, zona Piazza della
Libertà. ☏055 46 33 292. www.johanna.
it. ⬦. 12 rooms. ⬦.* These two addresses
are branches of a small chain of charming B&Bs offering elegance and comfort
in a homely and relaxed atmosphere.
See also Residenza Johanna I & II.

◎◎◎ **Locanda di Firenze** – *Via
Faenza 12 (3rd floor with no lift), zona S
Lorenzo. ☏055 28 43 40. Fax 055 28 43
52. 6 double rooms. ⬦.* Located on the

3rd floor of an old mansion, this inn is not far from San Lorenzo market. A retired university professor welcomes tourists as if they were guests in his own comfortable home.

Hotel Orcagna – *Via Orcagna 57, zona Piazza Beccaria.* ✆*055 66 99 59. Fax 055 66 99 59. 18 rooms.* ⌷. A warm welcome awaits in this simple family-run hotel with comfortable and well-maintained rooms. Bicycles can be hired here.

Hotel Fiorino – *Via Osteria del Guanto 6, zona Piazza della Signoria.* ✆*055 21 05 79. www.hotelfiorino.it. 23 rooms.* ⌷. If you are looking for a place to stay near the Uffizi, try this small family-run hotel. The large and airy rooms are plainly but suitably furnished.

Hotel Cimabue – *Via B Lupi 7, zona Piazza S Marco.* ✆*055 47 56 01. www.hotelcimabue.it. 16 rooms.* ⌷. Even if you cannot afford a suite or one of the bedrooms with frescoes on the ceiling, you will enjoy the spaciousness, remarkable furniture and the quiet family atmosphere.

Hotel La Scaletta – *Via Guicciardini 13 (1st floor with lift), zona Palazzo Pitti.* ✆*55 28 30 28. www.lascaletta.com. 13 rooms.* ⌷. The breakfast room and a reading room, with their old furniture, make you feel as if you were in a private house. There is a splendid roof terrace overlooking the historic town centre. The bedrooms are light and spacious.

Hotel Palazzo Vecchio – *Via Cennini 4, zona Stazione.* ✆*055 21 21 82. www.hotelpalazzo vecchio.it.* ♿. *25 rooms.* ⌷. This hotel, near the Palazzo dei Congressi, has huge attractively decorated bedrooms. The management extends warm welcomes to tourists as well as conference participants.

Residenza Apostoli – *Borgo Santi Apostoli 8 (1st floor), zona Ponte Vecchio.* ✆*055 28 84 32. www.residenza apostoli.it. 11 rooms.* ⌷. Not far from the Ponte Vecchio stands the 14C Palazzo del Siniscalco, offering pleasant and well-appointed rooms, furnished with taste and a few retro flourishes.

Relais Uffizi – *Chiasso de' Baroncelli-chiasso del Buco 16, zona Piazza della Signoria.* ✆*055 26 76 239. www.relaisuffizi.it. 10 rooms.* ⌷. If your budget allows, this is just the place you are looking for – a medieval Florentine palazzo with a welcoming, elegant ambience and a great room overlooking Piazza della Signoria.

⚘/ EAT

Restaurants are plotted on the maps on the preceding pages.

MAP: DUOMO/UFFIZI

Cantinetta da Verrazzano – *Via dei Tavolini 18/20r, zona p.za dalla Repubblica.* ✆*055 26 85 90. www.verrazzano.com. Closed Sun.* This small but sophisticated place has four strong points: its cooking, its wine, its desserts and its long hours. Wine from the Fattoria di Verrazzano is served by the glass.

La Cattedrale – *V. dell'Oriolo 61r.* ✆*055 21 69 18. Closed 25 Dec.* Near the Duomo, this small café offers snacks such as pizza, panini and bruschette.

Trattoria Anita – *V. del Parlascio 2r.* ✆*055 21 86 98. Closed Sun, 15 days in Aug. Reservations required.* This no-frills trattoria is frequented by tourists and locals, not only for its quick service and honest food, but also for wallet-friendly prices, including a set lunch Mon-Thu.

Trattoria I Chè Cé Cé – *V. Magalotti 11r.* ✆*055 21 65 89. Closed Sun.* Tuscan specialties served in a peaceful environment with informal service.

Trattoria Nella – *V. delle Terme 19r.* ✆*0552 18 925. Closed Sun.* This restaurant specialises in fish and seafood dishes prepared in the Tuscan way.

Vini e Vecchi Sapori – *Via dei Magazzini 3r, zona p.za della Signoria.* ✆*55 29 30 45. Closed Mon, Sun evening, two weeks in Aug.* ⌷. This welcoming, but tiny bar behind the Palazzo Vecchio offers a selection of appetising Florentine dishes and a choice of crostini, charcuteries and cheese. Be prepared to wait!

MAP: PITTI

☕ **Enoteca Fuori Porta** – *Via Monte alle Croci 10r, zona S. Niccolò.* ℘*055 23 42 483. www.fuoriporta.it. Closed Sun, 15 Aug, Easter, 25 Dec. Reservations required.* The young and enthusiastic owners of this well-stocked wine bar were among the first in Florence to offer good quality wine. Of the small dishes, do not miss the white beans on crostini.

☕ **La Mangiatoia** – *V. P.za S. Felice 8/10 r. ℘055 22 40 60. www.ristorantela-mangiatoia.it. Closed Mon.* Pizza, roast chicken, antipasti and a wide variety of other dishes are available. Dine in or take away.

☕ **Trattoria Bordino** – *V. Straciatella 9r. ℘055 21 30 48. Closed Sun.* Typical dishes from the Tuscan kitchen, from tripe to bistecca fiorentina, are served here.

MAP: SANTO SPIRITO

☕ **Al Tranvai** – *P.za Tasso 14r. ℘055 22 51 97. Closed Sat, Sun, 3 weeks in Aug. Reservations required.* This simple restaurant is arranged like a tram (tranvai) with tables running along the sides of the walls. Inventive Florentine fare is offered with friendly, attentive service.

☕ **La Casalinga** – *V. dei Michelozzi 9r. ℘055 21 86 24. Closed Sun, 3 weeks in Aug. Reservations required.* A few steps from the charming Piazza Santo Spirito, this large trattoria serves classic Tuscan dishes, from antipasti to desserts. Service is quick and courteous.

☕☕ **Café Cabiria** – *P.za S. Spirito 4r. ℘055 21 57 32. Closed Tue.* From breakfast to late night, this popular café has fare for any time of day: aperitifs, snacks, lunch and dinner.

☕☕ **Del Carmine** – *Piazza del Carmine 18r, zona S Frediano. ℘055 21 86 01. Closed Sun and 7–21 Aug. Reservations required.* This restaurant offers a variety of regional specialities and some fish dishes. In summer, outside tables are worth the wait.

☕☕ **La Corte de' Pazzi** – *Borgo San Frediano 26r. ℘055 23 81 569.* Traditional Tuscan cooking with some added flair, served up in a relaxing atmosphere.

☕☕ **L'Osteria del Cinghiale Bianco** – *Borgo San Jacopo 43r. www.cinghialebi-anco.it. ℘055 21 57 06. Closed Wed.*

Located on the ground floor of a 13C tower, this restaurant is a favourite among locals in the wealthy San Jacopo district. Rustic furnishings and exposed brick walls provide a casual backdrop for high quality, typical Tuscan fare.

☕☕☕ **Enoteca Pane e Vino** – *Via S Niccolò 70a/r. ℘55 24 76 956. Closed Sun and at midday and 7–21 Aug.* This wine bar on the south bank of the Arno combines rustic style with elegant attention to presentation. Traditional dishes are enhanced by imaginative detail.

☕☕☕ **Il Guscio** – *Via dell'Orto 49, zona S Frediano. ℘055 22 44 21. www.il-guscio. it. Closed Sun–Mon, 15 Aug, 25 Dec, 1 Jan. Reservations required.* Situated between San Frediano and Santo Spirito, this restaurant is frequented by those who appreciate typical Florentine cooking and carefully chosen wine. Dark wooden tables and attentive service make for pleasant and relaxing dining.

MAP: SAN LORENZO

☕ **Nerbone** – *Stand 292, Mercato di San Lorenzo. ℘055 21 99 49. Closed eve, Sun, 3 weeks in Aug.* 🍴. This deli stand in the San Lorenzo market has been feeding lunch to generations of Florentines since 1872. Lampredotto (cow's stomach) panini is a specialty, but they also have soups and other antipasti meats.

☕ **Trattoria Gozzi** – *P.za S. Lorenzo 8r. ℘055 28 19 41. Closed eve, Sun, Aug.* Set among the stands of the San Lorenzo Market, the Gozzi brothers' trattoria serves a hearty Tuscan lunch, including fish on Tue and Fri.

☕ **Trattoria Mario** – *V. Rosina 2r. ℘055 21 85 50. www.trattoria-mario.com. Closed eve, Sun, 3 weeks in Aug.* 🍴 ▤. Local workers and students crowd the tables of this trattoria at lunchtime to enjoy no-frills Florentine fare at low prices.

☕ **Palle d'Oro** – *Via Sant'Antonino 43/45. ℘055 28 83 83. Closed Sun and Aug.* Not far from the lively San Lorenzo market, this wine bar was started early in the 20C by the great grandfather of the present owners. On the menu are Tuscan specialities, rice dishes, pasta or, for those in a hurry, *panini* served at the bar.

⊝ **Ciro and Sons** – *V. del Giglio 28r.* ☏*055 28 96 94. www.ciroandsons. com.* Authentic Neopolitan-style pizza cooked in a wood-burning oven. 18C frescoes overlook the dining room.

MAP: SANTA MARIA NOVELLA

⊝ **Osteria Belle Donne** – *V. delle Belle Donne 16r.* ☏*0552 38 26 09. Closed lunch (summer), 2 weeks in Aug. Reservations required.* Florentines and tourists pack into this osteria for classic Tuscan food and a few surprises. Fresh vegetables are not only on the menu, but also a design statement. Lively.

⊝ **Trattoria Sostanza (Troia)** – *V. del Porcellana 25r.* ☏*055 21 26 91. Closed Sat, Sun, Aug, 10 days in Dec.* ✍. *Reservations required.* This Florentine institution, lovingly called "the trough" by locals, has existed at this location since 1932. Tuscan classics like ribollita and tripe.

⊝⊝ **Il Latini** – *Via dei Palchetti 6r.* ☏*055 21 09 16. Closed Mon, 24 Dec–5 Jan.* Locals and visitors find themselves side by side around the great wooden tables in this crowded restaurant, popular for its conviviality as much as its traditional local cooking.

⊝⊝🍽 **Baldini** – *Via il Prato 96r.* ☏*055 28 76 63. Closed Sat and sun eve; also Sun midday, Jul–Aug, 24 Dec–3 Jan, 1–20 Aug.* At this friendly trattoria, the dishes are authentic, whether local or not. This is a good place to try the traditional Fiorentina steak.

MAP: SAN MARCO

⊝ **Il Magnifico** – *V. Ricasoli 54.* ☏*055 23 98 413. Closed Sun May–Sep, Oct–Apr.* A nice place for a break not far from the Accademia. Panini and salads.

⊝ **La Mescita** – *V. degli Alfani 70r.* ☏*347 79 51 604. Closed Sun.* Ideal for grabbing a quick bite of crostini or panini. Chianti by the glass or *fiasco.*

MAP: SANTA CROCE

⊝ **Boccadama** – *P.za S.Croce 25/26r.* ☏*055 24 36 40. www.boccadama.it. Closed Mon eve.* Overlooking the beautiful Piazza Santa Croce, this is the place to go for a coffee, an aperitif or even a meal. Excellent wine cellar.

⊝ **Darvish Café** – *V. Ghibellina 76r.* ☏*055 39 00 702.* Kebabs, falafel and vegetarian appetisers are served in this small café. A spicy palate pleaser if you tire of Tuscan fare.

⊝⊝ **Acquacotta** – *V. dei Pilastri 51r.* ☏*055 24 29 07. Closed Mon.* This restaurant's dining room offers views of the kitchen, where chefs prepare traditional Tuscan dishes. Lunch is a good value.

⊝⊝ **Gilda** – *V. Ghiberti 40–41r.* ☏*055 23 43 835. Closed Sun.* Located near Sant'Ambrogio, this restaurant's ever-changing menu has appetising Tuscan and French dishes at reasonable prices. Eclectic decor.

⊝⊝ **Il Pizzaiuolo** – *V. de' Macci 113r.* ☏*055 24 11 71. Closed Sun. Reservations required.* This pizzeria is also a trattoria that specialises in Sardinian cuisine (fish and seafood).

⊝⊝ **Osteria de'Macci** – *V. de' Macci 77r.* ☏*055 24 12 26. Closed lunch.* ✍ 🖥. One of the best locales in Santa Croce. Inventive Tuscan cooking made with seasonal ingredients. Beef dishes are superb.

⊝⊝ **Ruth's** – *Via Farini 2, zona S Niccolò.* ☏*055 24 80 888.* ✍. *Reservations required.* This elegant restaurant next to the synagogue provides an opportunity to taste Kosher Jewish dishes to the strains of klezmer music.

⊝⊝🍽 **Vineria Cibreino** – *Via dei Macci 122r, zona Piazza Beccaria.* ☏*055 23 41 100.* ✍. *Reservations required.* This fashionable bistro is a branch of Cibreo (see below) and features delicious cooking and good wine.

⊝🍽 **Del Fagioli** – *Corso Tintori 47r, zona Santa Croce.* ☏*055 24 42 85. Closed Sat–Sun and Aug.* ✍. The friendly service and pleasant family atmosphere make for a very relaxing meal at this typical Tuscan trattoria.

⊝⊝🍽/ ⊝⊝🍽 **Baccarossa** – *V. Ghibellina 46/r.* ☏*055 24 06 20. www. baccarossa.it. Closed Mon, Sun lunch, 25–31 Jan, 25 Aug–7 Sep.* 🖥. *Reservations required.* Elegantly decorated with suffused light, antique wood and vibrant colours, this wine bar bistro has a pan-Mediterranean menu that includes pastas and desserts made on the premises.

🍽️🍷 **Cibreo** – *Via dei Macci 118r. 📞055 23 41 100. Closed Sun, Mon, 31 Dec–6 Jan and 26 Jul–6 Sept.* Not far from Sant'Ambrogio this elegant restaurant provides traditional dishes with a good choice of wine. Attentive but relaxed service.

🍽️ CAFÉS

Caffè Pitti – *Piazza Pitti 9. 📞055 23 99 863. Open 10am–1am.* It is worth spending a little time at one of this elegant, modern bar's outdoor tables if only to enjoy the panoramic view of the Palazzo Pitti.

Il Gelato di Vivoli – *Via Isola delle Stinche 7r. 📞055 29 23 34. www.vivoli.it. Closed Mon.* Ice cream connoisseurs would choose this little place, founded in 1930, as a good example of Italian flair.

🍷 BARS

Enoteca Gola e Cantina – *Piazza Pitti 16. 📞055 21 27 04. Open summer Tue–Sun 10am–1pm, 3pm–7pm. Closed winter Sun–Mon.* Situated in front of the Palazzo Pitti, this wine shop, which also sells books on wine, specialises in the great names among Tuscan wines.

Cantinetta Antinori – *Piazza degli Antinori 3, Palazzo Antinori. 📞055 29 22 34. Closed Sat, Sun.* Marquess Antinori invites you to his beautiful 15C mansion to taste his famous wine, including the Solaria, which has been judged the best in the world.

🎭 NIGHTLIFE

Jazz Club – *Via Nuova dei Caccini 3, corner of Via Borgo Pinti. 📞055 24 79 700 or 33 95 63 07 95 (Mobile). Closed Mon and Jun–Aug.* Jazz lovers meet at this most important jazz club for nightly performances, usually by Italian artists. Membership €5.

Meccano' – *Viale degli Olmi 1. 📞055 33 13 71. Closed Sun–Mon.* The biggest and best-known discotheque in Florence has several dance floors and a large garden, ideal for summer evenings. Techno, underground and progressive music.

Tenax – *Via Pratese 46. 📞055 30 81 60. Closed Mon and Jun–Sept.* As well as being a disco, Tenax is a concert hall during the week for alternative rock, both Italian and European. Thursday is house night.

🎭 PERFORMING ARTS

The local daily newspaper, *La Nazione*, prints the programme and starting times of all the shows in the city.

Box Office – *Via Alamanni 39r. 📞055 21 08 04. Open Mon 3.30pm–7.30pm, Tue–Sat 10am–7.30pm.* Make reservations at the Teatro della Pergola from the Tuesday before the concert.

Teatro Comunale – *Corso Italia 12. 📞 055 27 791. Open Tue–Fri 10am–4.30pm, Sat 10am–1pm.* Classical music concerts, opera and recitals are held every month in the various local houses – Teatro Verdi, Teatro Comunale and Teatro della Pergola.

Teatro Verdi – *Via Ghibellina 99. 📞55 21 23 20. www.teatroverdifirenze.it. Open Mon–Fri 10am–2pm and 4pm–7pm, Sat 10am–1pm.* Ticket Office opens 1hr before the beginning of the concert. (👉*see Teatro Comunale*).

ETI – *Teatro della Pergola, Via della Pergola 18. 📞055 22 641.* Ticket office opens 1hr before the beginning of the concert. (👉*see Teatro Comunale*).

🛒 SHOPPING

Florentines are great traders and there is no lack of choice. Popular items include:

Stationery, in Piazza della Signoria, Via de' Tornabuoni and Piazza Pitti;

Embroidery, in Borgo Ognissanti;

Leather goods, particularly at the leatherwork school (Scuola del cuoio di S. Croce);

Fashion, in Via de' Pucci and in Via de' Tornabuoni; and

Jewellery, in Via de' Tornabuoni and on the Ponte Vecchio.
For bargains, take a look at the stalls in San Lorenzo market, in Cascine (Tuesday) and the Flea Market (Piazza dei Ciompi).

Consisting of lush valleys staggered between mountain spurs, the area north of the Arno River has been a favourite haunt since ancient times. Etruscans, then Romans, settled in Fiesole, the splendid town that overlooks Florence. This territory is also where the Medici built their country estates, such as at Cerreto Guidi, Castello and Poggio a Caiano. Numerous other villas were built in and around Lucca in the second half of the 16C, during the city's boom years. Pistoia, the other major city in this sub-region of Tuscany, is largely industrial, but has a pristine medieval historic centre and cathedral. Sons of this area include composer Giacomo Puccini (Lucca), Leonardo da Vinci (Vinci) and Carlo Lorenzini (Collodi), author of *Pinocchio*.

The region, which includes sections of the provinces of Lucca and Florence and the entire province of Prato, stretches from the Tuscan-Emilian range of the Apennines and the Apuan Alps in the north to the northern bank of the Arno River in the south. The region is comprised of large swaths of parkland, including the Apuan Alps Park by Castelnuovo in Garfagnana, and the Mugello, a lush valley on Florence's outskirts.

This sub-region has a strong farming tradition, which includes the cultivation of vines and olives. *Farro* (spelt wheat) is a grain commonly grown here, especially in Garfagnana, and is processed for use in pasta and bread. The area also manufactures chestnut flour. Numerous farmhouses are open for farmstay (*agriturismo*) holidays here.

Conversely, there is also a large industrial presence. Industries in and around Pistoia include iron and steel works, vehicles, food production and firearms. The city is where the first pistol was manufactured, and thereby lent its name to the weapon. Prato is known for its textile industry.

Sports and nature enthusiasts will delight in skiing in Abetone, the racing circuit in the Mugello and the curative waters in the area's numerous spa towns, the most famous of which are Montecatini Terme, Monsummano Terme and Equi Terme.

The area has long been a playground for the wealthy and well-known. Many members of the Medici clan grew up here in the family's numeous country villas, and dignitaries, from royalty to diplomats, resided near Lucca. The English Romantic poets often visited the spa towns.

Music, both classical and modern, is an important component of this region's cultural heritage. Lucca is the birthplace of the composer Giacomo Puccini. Meanwhile, Pistoia is the site of the annual internationally acclaimed Pistoia Blues Festival.

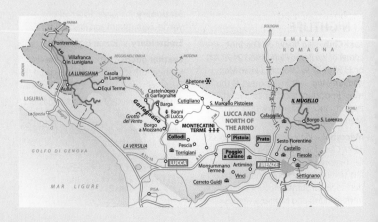

Lucca★★★
and nearby villas

This city, which was once a minor capital, contains some of the finest achievements of Pisan Romanesque architecture. Sheltered behind its ramparts, it has remained surprisingly lively and untouched by 20C town planning.

▶ **Population:** 85,484.
🖊 **Michelin Map:** Michelin Atlas p 36 and Map 563 – K 13 or Map 735 Fold 14.
▣ **Info:** Piazza S Maria 35 and Via Guidiccioni 2. ☎0583 91 99 31, 0583 91 991. www.luccatourist.it.
◖ **Location:** Lucca is situated on the major road from Florence to the sea, 74km/46mi from Florence and 20km/12mi from Viareggio.

A BIT OF HISTORY

The origins of the town of Lucca are remembered in its name, which comes from a Celto-Ligurian word, *Luk*, meaning "marshy place". It was colonised by Rome in the early 2C BC and still has the layout of a Roman military encampment, with streets intersecting at right angles along each side of two main perpendicular thoroughfares. It was already a large town when Caesar, Pompey and Crassus met there to form the First Triumvirate.

In the Middle Ages a network of narrow winding alleys and uneven squares was constructed within the Roman chequerboard plan; the amphitheatre was obliterated but the site reappeared with the construction of Piazza dell'Anfiteatro (🖊 *see below*).

In the 12–13C, after becoming a free town, Lucca continued to enjoy economic growth through producing and trading in silk. It experienced its period of greatest prosperity under the leadership of the great *condottiere*, **Castruccio Castracani** in the early 14C. It was at that time, when Lucca's merchants exported their famous silks throughout Europe and the Orient, that most of the churches were rebuilt and the splendid façades were constructed in the Pisan-Romanesque style. A number of imposing Gothic residences, some of which still have their towers, have survived.

Another major figure in local history was **Paolo Guinigi**, who came from a wealthy merchant family and was lord of the town in 1400.

During the **Renaissance**, in the second half of the 16C, Lucca abandoned its declining trade and industry and turned instead to **farming**. Its economic recovery was accompanied by intense architectural activity. Numerous villas (🖊 *see Excursions at the end of this chapter*) were built in the surrounding countryside. Construction began on the town walls but almost a century passed before they were completed. This period saw the construction of the many Renaissance façades that give the town its character today.

For a very short period in the early 19C, Lucca was a principality and life in the city was dominated by one woman, **Élisa Bonaparte**. She was crowned Princess of Lucca and Piombino by her brother, Napoleon, after his conquest of Italy. From 1805 to 1813, aided by her husband Félix Baciocchi, she ruled decisively and wisely over her principality and showed a remarkable talent for managing affairs.

THE CITY TODAY

An independent republic as late as 1799, Lucca was responsible for protecting itself from various rivals. Today, it is still completely enclosed within 16C and 17C gates, which have helped the city preserve its many medieval and Renaissance structures. An added benefit of the iconic fortifications is that Lucca's historic centre is closed off to cars, making it a paradise for pedestrians and bicyclists. A favourite pastime of the Lucchesi is a stroll or ride atop the ramparts, where there are tree-lined walkways and gardens.

🐾 WALKING TOUR

From Piazza San Michele take Via Fillungo to follow a short circular walk. Afterwards we suggest you make a tour of the town following the ancient walls. The streets and squares of **old Lucca**★ (*città vecchia*) have lost nothing of their harmonious medley of Gothic and Renaissance styles. They are steeped in charm through their palaces, noblemen's towers, shops, traceried entrances, coats of arms and wrought-ironwork. This walk starts at the **Piazza Napoleone**. Along the west side of the shaded **square** is the austere façade of the Palazzo Provinciale, which was begun in the 16C under the direction of the Florentine architect, Bartolomeo Ammannati.

Work your way north from here and you will find the **Via Fillungo**, an elegant shopping **street**. The Romanesque church of **San Cristoforo** (*right-hand side*), now deconsecrated, has a delightful entrance surmounted by a lintel carved with floral motifs and a fine rose window. Also in the same street is the 13C **Torre Civica delle Ore** (Civic Clock Tower).

Branching off to the left before the amphitheatre is Via degli Asili, home to the 17C **Palazzo Pfanner** (⟳ *not open to the public but the gardens can be seen from the ramparts*). Its former splendour can be detected in the monumental external flight of steps with arcades and balustrades and in the gardens laid out in the 18C against the backdrop of the rampart walk. Off to the right, the final section of Via Cesare Battisti is overlooked by the robust bell tower of **San Frediano**.

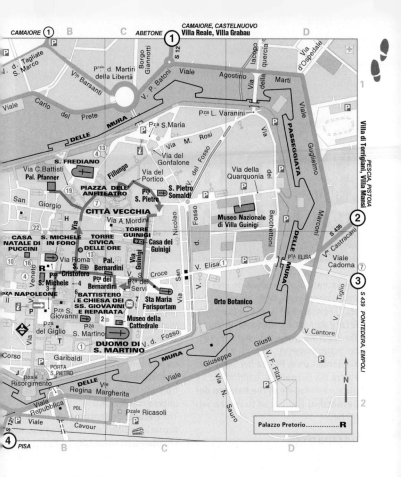

Piazza dell'Anfiteatro

Access through a vaulted alleyway from Via Fillungo. Passages beneath the houses lead into this unusual enclosed oval space, which occupies the site of an **amphitheatre** built by the Romans in the 2C. The amphitheatre fell into ruin during the Barbarian invasions and provided a large part of the building materials used during the Middle Ages to reconstruct the town's churches, particularly the marble used for the façades. It was not until 1830 that this space was laid out within the medieval quarter.

Close to the Piazza dell'Anfiteatro is the **Piazza San Pietro**, a small, irregularly-shaped square surrounded by stately 16C façades. It is overlooked by the two-tone bell tower of the 12C Romanesque church of **San Pietro Somaldi**. Its façade was completed in the 14C by

two registers of arcades in the Pisan tradition. The lintel above the central doorway depicts *Jesus handing St Peter the Keys of Heaven.*

Via Guinigi

This is one of the most picturesque **streets** in Lucca. **Casa dei Guingi** (no 29) is built of bricks and, above it, rises its famous tree-topped **tower**★ (*visible from the corner of Via S Andrea and Via delle Chiavi d'Oro*).

Santa Maria Forisportam

The name of the 13C **church** indicates that it was originally outside the Roman walls. The Pisan-style marble façade has three doors with architraves beautifully carved with floral and animal motifs. The lunette above the central doorway contains a *Coronation of the Virgin Mary* carved in low relief. The interior is Romanesque in style, with

185

Piazza dell' Anfiteatro

G. Bludzin / MICHELIN

the exception of the vaulting and the small dome which were added in the 16C. There are two works by Guercino: *St Lucy* (*last altar in the south aisle*) and *The Virgin Mary, St Francis and St Alexander* (*north transept*).

Via Santa Croce, Piazza dei Servi and Piazza dei Bernardini, overlooked by the austere façade of the **Palazzo dei Bernardini** (16C), lead to Piazza San Michele.

RAMPARTS★

The walls that give Lucca its characteristic appearance run right round the town (4km/2.5mi). They took the whole of the 16C and the first half of the 17C to complete and include 11 forward-projecting bastions (*baluardi*) connected by curtain walls (30m/100ft wide at the base). The walls originally included four gateways but in 1804 Élisa Baciocchi had a fifth opened on the east side, known as Élisa's Gate. The ramparts were planted with two rows of trees in the 19C and now form an unusual public park reserved for pedestrians and cyclists.

ART AND RELIGION
Duomo San Martino★★

Piazza San Martino. ◷*Open daily 7am–7pm (5pm winter).* &. ☎*0583 95 70 68. www.comune.lucca.it.*
Lucca **cathedral**, which is dedicated to St Martin, was first rebuilt in the 11C and its outside and interior were almost

completely redesigned in the 13C and 14C–15C respectively.

The splendid alternating white and green marble **façade**★★ is the work of the architect Guidetto da Como. This was the first example of Pisan Romanesque architecture in Lucca.

The **bell tower**★ (*campanile*), which dates from the 13C, displays a distinctive and impressive elegance.

The **decorative features**★ in the portico include pillars with colonnettes and sculptures, blind arcades picked out in red marble, a marble marquetry frieze, and narrative carvings. There are also scenes from the life of St Martin.

The **Interior** is Gothic in style. The inside wall of the façade contains a freely-carved Romanesque sculpture (1) depicting the famous scene of St Martin sharing his cloak. Above the second altar in the north aisle is a *Presentation of the Virgin Mary at the Temple* by Bronzino (2).

A little higher up stands a small private chapel in the form of an elegant temple (*tempietto*) built in 1484, during the Renaissance period, by **Matteo Civitali** (1436–1501), the local sculptor and architect, to house the **Volto Santo**. The **Large Crucifix**★, carved in wood blackened through age and bearing the figure of Jesus stiffly portrayed in a long tunic, dates from the late 11C.

The north transept contains the entrance to the Sanctuary chapel; above the altar is a *Madonna and Child flanked by*

St Stephen and St John the Baptist (**3**), painted in 1509 by the Florentine artist Fra Bartolomeo.

The sacristy (*south aisle*) contains a delightful brightly coloured *Madonna and Child surrounded by Saints* (**4**) (*above the altar*) by Domenico Ghirlandaio. The masterpiece, however, is the white marble **tomb of Ilaria del Carretto★★**, Paolo Guinigi's wife, who died in 1405. It is one of the purest examples of Italian funerary sculpture, produced in 1406 by the Sienese artist Jacopo della Quercia. ⏱*Open Mon–Sat 9.30am–6pm (5pm winter), Sun and Hols 9am–10am, 11.20am–11.50am and 1pm–6pm (5pm winter).* ⏱*Closed 1 Jan, Easter, 25 Dec.* ✆*€2, €5 combined ticket with Museo della Cattedrale and Battistero e Chiesa dei Santi Giovanni e Reparata.* ♿. ✆*0583 49 05 30. www.comune.lucca.it.*

The spectacular **Last Supper★** (**5**) (*above the altar in the third chapel of the south aisle*) is by Tintoretto.

The nearby **Museo della Cattedrale** contains church plate, paintings and carvings from the cathedral, including the statue of an apostle by Jacopo della Quercia and the ceremonial vestments used during the Volto Santo festival.

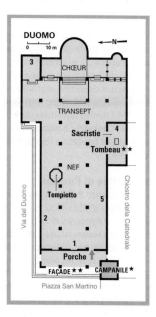

Piazza Antelminelli 5. ⏱*Open mid-Mar–Oct daily 10am–6pm; rest of the year Mon–Fri 10am–3pm (6pm Sat–Sun and Hols).* ⏱*Closed 1 Jan, Easter (mornings), 25 Dec.* ✆*€3, €5 combined ticket with Battistero e Chiesa dei Santi Giovanni e Reparata and tomb of Ilaria Del Carretto.* ♿. ✆*0583 49 05 30. www.museocattedralelucca.it.*

Battistero e Chiesa dei Santi Giovanni e Reparata★

Piazza San Giovanni. ⏱*Open mid-Mar–Oct daily 10am–6pm; rest of year Mon–Fri 10am–3pm (6pm Sat–Sun).* ⏱*Closed 1 Jan, 6 Jan, 28 Feb, Easter, 25 Dec.* ✆*€2.50, €5 ticket with Museo della Cattedrale and tomb of Ilaria Del Carretto.* ✆*0583 49 05 30. www.museocattedralelucca.it.*

Archaeological digs have resulted in the discovery of the remains of a Roman house and baths, in addition to the initial site and successive extensions of the **original cathedral** and **Baptistery**.

San Michele in Foro★★

Piazza San Michele. ⏱*Open daily 7.40am–noon and 3pm–6pm.* ✆*0583 48 459. www.comune.lucca.it.*

The **church**, built in the 12C–14C, stands in Piazza **San Michele**, on the site of the old Roman forum. It overlooks the square and is flanked by a massive bell tower built above the transept.

The 13C **façade★★** displays the most exuberant and delicate features produced by the Pisan Romanesque style, despite major restorations undertaken during the last century. The pediment is surmounted by a huge statue of St Michael slaying the dragon, flanked by two angel musicians.

The **Interior** is also Romanesque in style, except for the vaulting which replaced the timbered ceiling in the 16C.

Above the first altar in the south aisle is a white glazed terracotta **Madonna★** by Andrea della Robbia. The south transept contains a splendid vivid **painting★** by Filippino Lippi portraying St Roch, St Sebastian and St Jerome with St Helena.

San Michele in Foro

R. Mattes / MICHELIN

San Frediano★

Piazza San Frediano. ⏰*Open Mon–Sat 8.30am–noon and 3pm–5pm, Sun 10.30am–5pm.* ℘*0583 49 36 27. www.comune.lucca.it/l/39D1075C.htm.*
This Romanesque **church** was built in the 12C on the site of a basilica constructed in the 6C by St Frediano, Bishop of Lucca, to whom the miracle of the damming of the River Serchio is attributed.

The **façade** dates from the 13C. It is built of bare white stone that was originally used in the Roman amphitheatre.

Like the façade, the Romanesque basilica-shaped **Interior** has a simplicity that gives it a sense of nobility. The nave is lined with Classical columns crowned with splendid capitals, probably from the amphitheatre. The chapels added in the aisles in the 14C–15C broke up the overall harmony.

To the right of the entrance is an admirable 12C Romanesque **baptismal font**★ decorated with carved panels. Behind the font is a fine door surround, with an extremely graceful glazed terracotta **Annunciation** by Andrea della Robbia.

The **Trenta Chapel** (*first chapel coming back along the north aisle*) contains a Gothic marble **polyptych**★ portraying the Madonna and Child surrounded by saints, intricately carved by Jacopo della Quercia.

Pinacoteca

Via Galli Tassi 43. ⏰*Open Tue–Sun 8.30am–7.30pm, Sun and Hols 8.30am–1.30pm.* ⏰*Closed 1 Jan, 1 May, 25 Dec.* ⊕*€4, €6.50 combined ticket with Museo Nazionale di Villa Guinigi.* ♿. ℘*0583 55 570. www.comune.lucca.it.*
The **picture gallery** housed in the Palazzo Mansi (17C) displays large compositions by Italian painters including Veronese, Giordano, Bronzino, Pontormo (*Portrait of a Young Man*) and Tintoretto. There are also portraits and small paintings from Italy and abroad, particularly by the Flemish School.

A number of rooms in the **Apartments** display remarkable 17C–18C **decorative features**★. They include morning rooms in which the ceilings are painted with frescoes depicting mythological subjects and the walls hung with sumptuous 17C Flemish tapestries, and the 18C-style "Conjugal Chamber" with its canopied bed beneath a fresco of Eros and Psyche.

Casa Natale di Puccini

Corte San Lorenzo 9. ⏰*Currently closed for restoration.* ℘*0583 46 92 25. www.casanatalepuccini.it.*
This tiny **museum**, housed in Puccini's **birthplace**, has collections of the composer's letters, his piano, illustrations depicting the sets for some of his operas, portraits and postcards and other exhibits inspired by his works.

Museo Nazionale di Villa Guinigi

Via della Quarquonia. ⏱*Open Tue–Sat 8.30am–7.30pm (1.30pm Sun and Hols).* ⏱*Closed 1 Jan, 1 May, 25 Dec.* ✺€4, €6.50 combined ticket with Pinacoteca. ♿. ℘0583 49 60 33. www.comune.lucca.it.

This impressive Romanesque and Gothic brick building (built 1418) was once the country seat of Paolo Guinigi.

The **museum** displays archaeological finds from the region and offers a retrospective exhibition of local sculpture and paintings. There are also some splendid gold-embroidered **vestments** made of silk or silver thread in Lucca between the 15C and the 18C.

VILLAS

A number of nearby villas make pleasant daytrips from Lucca.

Villa Reale di Marlia *(8km/5mi N of Lucca by S 2; after 6km/4mi turn right towards Marlia (signposted) and cross the railway line; ℘0583 30 108. www.parcovillareale.it.)* is surrounded by magnificent 17C gardens★★. Visitors can stroll through the flower garden, lemon grove, grotto and parkland with its statues, niches, terraces and topiaried yew trees.

Nearby is the 16C neo-Classical **Villa Grabau** *(8km/5mi N of Lucca by S 12; Via di Matraia 269. ℘0583 40 60 98. www.villagrabau.it)*, which has been in the hands of the Grabau family since 1868. Fountains with bronze mascarons and white marble statues add to the elegant appearance of the **park★★**, which covers an area of 9ha/22 acres. The layout includes an outdoor theatre, an informal English garden, an Italian garden, a winter greenhouse and an unusual 17C–18C **Lemon House**.

The 16C rococo **Villa Torrigiani, Segromigno★** *(12km/7.5mi NE of Lucca by the Pescia road (Pesciatina); in Zone turn left to Segromigno in Monte. ℘0583 92 80 41. www.comune.capannori.lu.it)* was, in the 17C, a luxurious summer residence of Marquess Nicolao Santini, Ambassador of the Republic of Lucca to the papal court. The gardens are decorated with fountains, caves and grottoes.

Villa Mansi, Segromigno *(11km/7mi NE of Lucca by the same route as above for Villa Torrigiani; from Segromigno follow the signs. ℘0583 92 02 34. www.comune.capannori.lu.it)* is a superb 16C villa and has numerous statues on its façade. It stands in the middle of a huge **park★** with a large lake.

Legend of the True Cross

The Holy Face (**Volto Santo**) is the miraculous Crucifix worshipped in the Cathedral of San Martino. According to various traditions it was carved from memory by Nicodemus after the Entombment or his hand was guided by angels as he worked; that is why Christ's face is such a good likeness. The Volto Santo is said to have been washed up on the shores of Luni, north of Viareggio, in the 8C. The story as to how it arrived there differs; some say it was cast into the sea by Nicodemus himself, in obedience to an order from on high, while others believe that it was found by an Italian bishop on a pilgrimage to the Holy Land and that he left it to float with the tide. When the devout Christians of Luni and Lucca began to argue about ownership of the holy image, the Bishop of Lucca settled the matter by placing it on an ox cart and leaving the animals to decide on its destination; they headed towards Lucca.

In the Middle Ages the Volto Santo was famous far beyond Lucca. Its story was told by merchants from Lucca and soon spread to northern Europe.

The **Luminara di Santa Croce** *(evening of 13 Sept)* commemorates the mysterious arrival of the Volto Santo. The whole town joins with various religious orders from the region and representatives from other Tuscan towns, to take part in a huge procession that makes its way through the streets.

ADDRESSES

🛏 STAY

Ostello San Frediano – *Via della Cavallerizza 12. ℘0583 46 99 57. www.ostellolucca.it.* 🚫 ♿. *148 beds.* 🚭. This comfortable hostel within the old Real Collegio has spacious public rooms and a pretty little garden where you can relax after sightseeing in the historic old town.

Lucca in Villa – *Villa delle Tagliete 49, S Donato. ℘0583 58 28 80, Fax 0583 58 42 93. www.luccainvilla.it. 6 rooms.* 🅿. By the gates of the historic centre, this graciously renovated hotel has a kitchen available for guest use and bicycle hire on the premises.

Hotel Stipino – *Via Romana 95. ℘0583 49 50 77. www.hotelstipino.com. 20 rooms.* 🚭 *€10.* This well-run and well-maintained family hotel is on the edge of the town but not far from the centre.

Piccolo Hotel Puccini – *Via di Poggio 9. ℘0583 55 421. www.hotel puccini.com. 14 rooms.* 🚭 *€3.50.* Situated close to San Michele in Foro, this little hotel, with its pleasant and enthusiastic owners, is ideal for immersing yourself in local life.

Albergo San Martino – *Via Della Dogana 9. ℘0583 46 91 81. www.albergosanmartino.it.* ♿. *10 rooms.* 🚭. The high level of comfort and modern decor in this hotel near the cathedral are combined with young and enthusiastic owners who can provide guided tours on request.

Alla Corte degli Angeli – *V. degli Angeli 23. ℘0583 46 92 04. Fax 0583 99 19 89. www.allacortede gliangeli.com. 6 rooms.* - 🖥 🅿. A personalised touch, which includes painted walls in every room and fresh flowers in the breakfast room, is what makes this hotel in the heart of the city a true find.

🍴 EAT

Trattoria Da Guido – *Via Cesare Battisti 28. ℘0583 46 72 19. Closed Sun and Aug.* The mixed clientele of professionals, music students and tourists congregate in this charming little eating room to enjoy traditional Tuscan dishes.

Trattoria da Leo – *V. Tegrini 1. ℘0583 49 22 36. www.trattoriadaleo.it. Closed Sun.* 🚭. A few steps from S Michele in Foro, this lively trattoria serves large portions of simple local fare. Outdoor tables available in the warmer months.

Osteria Baralla – *Via Anfiteatro 5/7/9. ℘0583 44 02 40. Closed Sun, mid-Jan–mid-Feb. Reservations required.* Situated in the entrance to a medieval mansion, this restaurant's daily menu includes typical local dishes which can be savoured under the fine vaulted ceiling or in the smaller inner room.

Agli Orti di Via Elisa – *Via Elisa 17. ℘0583 49 12 41. Closed Wed lunch and 5–17 Jul.* This restaurant with the dynamic ambience of a bistro places an accent on grilled meats and a large range of specialities, from monster salads to pizzas.

Bucca di Sant' Antonio – *V. della Cervia 1-5. t 0583 55 881. Fax 0583 312 199. Closed Sun eve and Mon.* For more than half a century, this establishment has showcased local cuisine and products, including prosciutto, which doubles as decor in the dining room.

Ristorante All'Olivo – *P.za S. Quirico 1. t 0583 49 62 64. Fax 0583 49 31 29. www.ristoranteolivo. it. Closed Feb and Wed Jun-Sep.* This small, refined restaurant located on a picturesque piazza in the centre has a good selection of fish and meat dishes.

Puccini – *Corte Lorenzo 1. ℘0583 31 61 16. Fax 0583 31 60 31. Closed Tue, Wed lunch. Reservations required.* The speciality of this restaurant near Puccini's birthplace is fish, delivered daily from the Versilia.

Butterfly – *Strada statale 12 dell'Abetone, Località Marlia, 6 km north of Lucca. ℘/Fax 0583 30 75 73. www.ristorantebutterfly.it. Closed Wed, Hols lunch. Reservations required.* This family restaurant with an elegant atmosphere is situated within a 19C cottage with a lovely garden.

Abetone ✳
and local Tuscan Appenines

Occupying an attractive setting in the Tuscan Apennines, Abetone is one of the most famous winter resorts in central Italy. The mountain pass is indicated by two pyramid-shaped stones that serve as a reminder of the old border between the Grand Duchies of Tuscany and Modena. The town takes its name from one of the gigantic pines (abetone is the superlative form of abete meaning pine tree) that was chopped down in the 18C to make way for the Ximenes-Giardini road.

NEARBY
Cutigliano★
Alt 670m/2 178ft. 14km/9mi SE. Cutigliano, a delightful village built in terraces up the northern slopes of the Lima Valley, has become one of Tuscany's main winter sports resorts, owing to the **Doganaccia cable-car**.

The older buildings here include the **Palazzo Pretorio**. Its façade is decorated with the coats of arms of the Captains of the Mountain who, between the 14C and 18C, held legal and administrative authority over Cutigliano and the neighbouring hamlets. The church, known as the **Madonna di Piazza** (Our Lady on the Square) contains a superb altarfront by Andrea della Robbia.

San Marcello Pistoiese★
Alt 650m/2 112ft. 20km/12mi SE. The largest town in the Pistoia mountains is set in the middle of beautiful scenery. The district also includes the interesting hamlet of **Gavinana**, where, on 3 August 1530, the militiamen of the Republic of Florence, under the command of Francesco Ferrucci, valiantly resisted the troops of the Emperor Charles V. The battle is recalled in the nearby **Museo Ferrucciano**. (Open Jul–Aug daily 10am–12.30pm and 4.30pm–7pm; Sept–Jun Sat 3.30pm–6pm, Sun 10am–noon. €1.50; no charge 3 Aug 0573 62 12 89).

Nearby in Pian de' Termini is an **observatory** (Osservatorio Astronomico;

ADDRESSES

▶ **Population:** 718.
Michelin Map: Atlas p 33 and map 563 – J 13, 14 or Map 735 fold 14.
Info: Piazzale delle Piramidi, 51021 Abetone. 0573 60 231. Via Roma, 25, 51024 Cutigliano. 0573 68 029. Via Villa Vittoria, 129, San Marcello Pistoiese. 0573 63 01 45. www.abetoneapm.it.
Location: Abetone (alt 1 388m/4 511ft) is situated at the heart of the Tuscan Apennines, only 65km/40mi from Lucca and 51km/32mi from Pistoia. The numerous interlinked pistes make it possible to ski in several valleys: Sestaione, Lima, Scoltenna and Luce. The resort is strung out along the edge of a majestic forest (3 700ha/9 143 acres).
Kids: Older children will enjoy a ride on the Doganaccia cable car.
Don't Miss: The hamlets of Maresca and Gavinana.
Timing: After you've enjoyed skiing or summer activities, allow a full day to take an Excursion (below). Note that the observatory tours must be booked two days in advance.

Guided tour (1hr 30min) Tue and Thu–Sat (also Mon in summer) 9.30am–9pm. Closed Wed and 2nd week in Sept. €2.50. Book 2 days in advance at Biblioteca Comunale, Piazza Matteotti 159. 0573 62 12 89; www.gamp-pt.net).

Mammiano
Take the S 66 from San Marcello to Mammiano. The restored **suspension bridge** was built in 1922 to link the Mammiano metalworks with the villages on the opposite bank of the Lima river.

ADDRESSES

🏠 STAY

😊😊 **Albergo Regina** – *Via Uccelliera 5.*
℘0573 60 257. www.albergoregina.com.
Closed May–Jun and Oct–Nov. 26 rooms.
🛏 €5. Restaurant 😊😊.
The car park is immediately opposite
the entrance of this modest family
hotel, set in a central but quiet location.
Typical mountain ambience and warm
welcome.

🍴 EAT

😊😊 **Trattoria da Fagiolino** –
Via Carega 1, 51024 Cutigliano. ℘0573
68 014. Closed Nov . The delicious aroma
from the kitchen sharpens the appetite
before you reach the dining room of
this trattoria which serves generous
portions of good quality and carefully
prepared food. Game is on the menu
in the hunting season.

Artimino

Carmignano and Comeana's Etruscan Graves

The area around the high Artimino
hill was inhabited in the Palaeolithic
era. In the 7C BC an Etruscan town
was built on the site and probably
gained prosperity because of its
control of the natural trade routes
along the River Arno and River
Ombrone.

SIGHTS
Pieve di San Leonardo
Via della Chiesa, 19/A.
This Romanesque parish **church**, said to
have been commissioned by Countess
Matilda of Canossa in 1107, is unusual
in that it was partly built with materials
from the Etruscan graveyard, including
urns (some of them carved). The interior
has a nave and two aisles with ogival
vaulting.

Villa La Ferdinanda★
Via Papa Giovanni XXIII, 1. ⚿ *The inte-*
rior is not open to the public.
Grand Duke Ferdinando I commissioned
Buontalenti to design this vast **mansion**
towards the end of the 16C.
It stands in a dominant position in the
middle of a terrace (views south over the
Arno Valley to Florence and north over
Prato and Pistoia); the lawn is dotted
with amusing metal statues. In front of
the villa are double-spiral steps extending into a ramp leading straight to the
colonnaded balcony on the first floor.

🗺 **Michelin Map:** Atlas p37
and Map 563 – K 15.

ℹ **Info:** Piazza Vittorio
Emanuele II 1, 59015
Carmignano. ℘0558 71
24 68. www.carmignano
divino.prato.it.

▶ **Location:** Artimino is
situated a few miles S
of Poggio a Caiano
within the municipality
of Carmignano, about
20km/12mi W of Florence.
An acropolis probably stood
on the hill now occupied
by the Villa Ferdinanda.
Opposite the villa is the
village, which still has some
of its medieval walls.
The church stands further
down the hill.

Museo Archeologico
In the basement of the villa; entrance
behind the grand staircase.
The **archaeology museum** contains
all the items uncovered during a dig in
the area of the ancient **Etruscan** town,
including imported Greek vases, Etruscan buccheroware, coins, sculptures and
some interesting graveyard artefacts.
🕐*Open Apr–Sept Thu–Tue 9.30am–*
1pm (12.30pm Sun and Hols); Oct–Mar
Thu–Tue 9.30am–12.30pm (🕐closed
Hols). 👁*€4.* ♿. *℘055 87 18 124;*
www.carmignanodivino.prato.it.

EXCURSIONS
Etruscan Graves in Comeana★
4km/2.5mi NE. ○*Open 9am–2pm.*
○*Closed Sun and Hols.* ☎*055 87 19 741.*
The best preserved of these graves,
which date from the 7C BC, is the **Tomba
di Montefortini**★ (*43 Via di Montefortini*). It lies beneath a huge barrow,
now covered in trees, and consists of
a passage (*dromos*) (13m/43ft long), a
vestibule that used to be closed off by a
stone slab (still visible) and a rectangular
burial chamber. The unusual feature of
the grave is the continuous bracket running along the top of the walls, which
was used as a shelf for funeral articles.
This grave stands next to an older one
containing a circular burial chamber
(*closed to the public*). The **Boschetti
Grave** (*near the cemetery, to the left of
the Poggio-Caiano road*) is smaller and
only parts of its walls now remain.

Carmignano
6km/4mi N.
This small town, surrounded by vines
and olive trees, is home to the 16C
Church of San Michele.
Inside (*second altar on the right*) is a
splendid **Visitation**★★ by **Pontormo**.

Castello
and the Medici Villas

This village on the outskirts of
Florence is known for two villas that
once belonged to the Medici.

VISIT
Villa di Castello★
*NW in Castello (signposted). Large
semicircular car park in front of the
villa; the gardens are at the rear.*
Garden: ○*Open daily 8.15am–6.30pm
(Jun–Aug 7.30pm; Nov–Feb 4.30pm).*
○*Closed 2nd and 3rd Mon of the month
and 1 May, 25 Dec, 1 Jan.* ⊙*€2 combined ticket with the Villa della Petraia.*
&. ☎*055 45 47 91. www.polomuseale.
firenze.it.*
The villa (⊶ *not open to the public*)
was purchased by the Medici in 1477
and embellished by Lorenzo the Magnificent. As it was ransacked in 1527,
Duke Cosimo I commissioned Tribolo
to refurbish it and lay out the gardens.
Since 1974, the villa has housed the
Accademia della Crusca, the body set
up to maintain and protect the Italian
language.
The gardens include a large Italian-style
flowerbed set superbly in proportion
to Tribolo's beautiful central fountain.
There is also a grotto containing reproductions of Giambologna's animal statues. The original bronze sculptures are
in the Bargello Museum in Florence.

> ⚐ **Michelin Map:** Michelin
>   Atlas p 121 (plan of flor-
>   ence) and Map 563.
> ▯ **Info:** Via Cavour 1r, 50129
>   Firenze. ☎055 29 48 83.
> ▷ **Location:** Castello is
>   5km/3mi N of Florence
>   in the direction of Sesto
>   Fiorentino.

Villa della Petraia★
*NE in Castello at the end of Via della
Petraia (signposted).* ○*Open daily
9am–1hr before sunset (7.30pm
Jun–Aug).* ○*Closed 2nd and 3rd Mon
of the month; 1 May, 25 Dec, 1 Jan.*
⊙*€2 combined ticket with the Villa di
Castello.* ☎*055 45 26 91. www.polo
museale.firenze.it/musei/petraia.*
In 1576 Cardinal Ferdinand Medici commissioned the architect Buontalenti to
transform this former fortress into a villa
with gardens. Later, in the 19C, King Victor Emanuel II made the villa his summer
residence. During this time, the State
apartments, the courtyard and the
Renaissance portico were all glassed
in to create a ballroom. The **gardens**
(16C) consist of flowerbeds in front of
the villa and a wooded park at the rear.
On the right-hand side of the villa stands
a superb Tribolo fountain. Giambologna's admirable statue of Venus can be
seen on the first floor of the villa.

Cerreto Guidi★

This village grew up around the castle that once belonged to the Counts Guidi. The old estate passed into the hands of the Medici family, and was totally rebuilt by Cosimo I, c. 1560, to look as it does now. It was used as a hunting lodge for the Medici and their courtiers, but fell into decline after the tragic death of Cosimo I's daughter, Isabella Orsini, Duchess of Bracciano. The villa has since been restored.

▶ **Population:** 9,433.
🛈 **Michelin Map:** Atlas p 37 and Map 563 – K14.
🔢 **Info:** Via Santi Saccenti 57. ☎0571 55 671. www. prolococerretoguidi.it.
▶ **Location:** Cerreto Guidi is about 10km/6mi NW of Empoli. It stands on a hill among the delightful uplands southwest of Monte Albano.

VILLA MEDICEA★

Via dei Ponti Medicei, 7. 🕐*Open daily 8.15am–7pm (last admission 6.30pm).* 🕐*Closed 2nd and 3rd Mon of the month.* ⊚€2. ☎0571 55 707. *www.polomuseale.firenze.it.*
Buontalenti designed this austere hilltop **villa**. The approach is embellished by two majestic, monumental flights of brick steps, known as the *Ponti*. From the terrace there is a wonderful view of the Arno Valley hills and (*left*) of San Miniato and its high tower.

The entrance hall is hung with portraits (*right*) of Isabella Orsini and her husband and (*left*) of Bianca Cappello, wife of Francesco I Medici. On the first floor is the Medici portrait gallery. From the balcony (*loggia*), there is a delightful view of the garden and its pergola.

Collodi★★

Everything in this town set among rural hills, relates to the famous puppet Pinocchio, a storybook character created by Carlo Lorenzini (1826–90). The author took as his pen name the name of the village where his mother was born.

▶ **Population:** 9,433.
🛈 **Michelin Map:** Michelin Atlas p 36 and Map 563 – K 13 AND Map 735 Fold 14.
▶ **Location:** Situated between Lucca and Montecatini not far from S435.
👫 **Kids:** Kids will enjoy the Parco di Pinocchio.

VISIT

Castello Garzoni Garden★★

🕐*Open 9am to 1hr before sunset.* ☎0572 42 95 90.
The 17C **gardens**★★ are typical of exuberant Italian Baroque landscaping. The highly formal design includes terraced flowerbeds flanking flights of steps decorated with balustrades.

The 18C **castello**, built by the Marquesses of Garzoni, lords of Collodi, has a wide façade with coats of arms above the entrance. It was in the castello's kitchen where Lorenzini, the chef's nephew, began writing *Pinocchio*.

👫 Parco di Pinocchio★

Signposted. 🕐*Open daily 8.30am to sunset.* ⊚€6.75. ♿. ☎0572 42 93 42. *www.pinocchio.it .*
Inspired by the story of Pinocchio, this park is situated in a pine wood on the banks of the tumbling Pescia near the Villa Garzoni. The route, laid out in a winding trail with information panels recounting certain episodes from the puppet's adventures, is illustrated at intervals by bronze sculptures and other creations designed mostly by Emilio

Pinocchio, the Little Wooden Puppet

Since the 19C the story of Pinocchio has achieved international recognition, due in particular to numerous film adaptations, including Walt Disney's version in 1940. This outstanding classic of Italian children's literature is much more than a children's tale, however; it depicts life among the Italian provincial poor, imbued with resignation and pessimism. Indeed, the original story is far darker than the movies suggest.

ItalyGuides.it

Greco and Venturino Venture. At one interval, the path enters the jaws of the enormous shark that swallowed Geppetto. The trail ends in the Laboratory of Speech and Figures, which is devoted to temporary exhibitions of works and illustrations evoking the adventures of Pinocchio.

Fiesole★

and around

The Etruscans founded this city in the 7C or 6C BC, strategically built high in the hills with a healthy climate. Fiesole was the most important city in northern Etruria. It dominated its neighbor and rival Florence until the 12C.

A BIT OF HISTORY

The Etruscan town of Fiesole was the largest town in northern Etruria. The site had been chosen for its position on a rise commanding the routes which passed over the barrier of the Apennines (north) into the Arno Plain and continued south to Rome. This was, moreover, a healthier spot than the plain, which in those days consisted largely of swamps.

Within its mighty walls, Fiesole was a town of greater power and importance than Florence for several centuries. Sulla set up a colony of Veterans here c. 80 BC. In 63 BC the town rallied in support of Catiline, who sought refuge here before the battle of Pistoia, where he was fatally wounded. From then on the destiny of Fiesole was linked to that of Rome. New buildings were erected on the ruins of the Etruscan structures and the Roman town, known as Faesulae, with its temples, theatre and baths, became the main centre of the region. From the

▶ **Population:** 14,876.

◔ **Michelin Map:** Atlas p 37 and Map 563 – K 15 and Map 735 Fold 14, 15. For access, see plan of florence in the michelin italy atlas.

▤ **Infor:** Via Portigiani 3. ☏055 59 87 20. www.comune.fiesole.fi.it.

◐ **Location:** The road from Florence winds uphill to Fiesole through olive-clad slopes, past luxuriant gardens and long lines of cypress trees, so often depicted by the masters of the Italian Renaissance. Fiesole is 8km/5mi NE of Firenze.

◉ **Don't Miss:** The incomparable views of Florence and the countryside.

1C AD onwards it began to fall into a decline and was overtaken by Florence, its rival and neighbour. In 1125 Faesulae was finally conquered by Florence and almost razed to the ground.

🐾 WALKING TOUR

The centre of Fiesole is the vast, sloping **square**, which occupies the site of the old Roman Forum. On the north side stand an oratory, Santa Maria Prime-rana, with a late 16C portico and the small 14C and 15C **Palazzo Pretorio** bearing the coats of arms of the magistrates (*podeste*) whose residence it used to be. Opposite the cathedral entrance (*southwest corner*), a narrow and steep street, Via S Francesco, leads up to one of the heights, where the Acropolis of Faesulae stood in the Roman era. Half way up, turn left into the small public park for a fine **view**★★ of Florence; the park projects like a balcony, overlooking the Arno Basin spread out below.

○ *This walking tour begins on Via S Francesco and heads east to Piazza Mino, the main square. 10 min.*

Basilica di Sant'Alessandro

Via S Francesco. The **basilica** (c. 9C) was built on the site of a Roman temple that had been converted into a church by Theodoric (6C). The neo-Classical façade, added in 1815, is not inviting, but the austere interior has a certain nobility; its nave and aisles are separated by superb Roman columns reused from other, earlier buildings.

Convento di San Francesco★

Via S Francesco. ○Open (*services permitting*) *daily 9am–12.30pm and 1pm–6.30pm.* ℘*055 59 175.*
This very modest **friary**, which is admirably located on the highest part of the hill, has been occupied by Franciscans since the early 15C. The tiny 14C cloisters (*entrance to the right of the church*) are visible through a wrought-iron grille. On the first floor (*steps to the left of the grille*) are several of the tiny cells, furnished with plank bed, chest, desk and chair, where the friars used to live. One of them was occupied by **St Bernardino of Siena**, who was Prior here for a few years.
The adjacent **church**, built in the mid-14C but with major alterations from subsequent periods, still has its original early 15C Gothic façade decorated with a small multifoiled canopy of simple design that is utterly charming. The church contains a number of interest-

ing **paintings**★. On the south wall is an Immaculate Conception by Piero di Cosimo and, opposite it, an Annunciation by Raffaellino del Garbo.
The **Museo Missionario** (Franciscan Missions Museum – *access through the church*) contains a large collection of exhibits from the Orient (sculptures, paintings, clothing, porcelain) and a small archaeology section (artefacts excavated near the friary, Egyptian objects and a mummy found by missionaries in Egypt).

Duomo★ (Cathedral)

Piazza Mino da Fiesole. This is a Roman-esque **church**, started in the 11C and extended in the 13C and 14C. Between 1878 and 1883, it was subjected to a massive restoration programme during which the façade was rebuilt. It is surmounted by a bell tower erected in 1213 which was altered in the 18C by the addition of merlons and machicolations to look like a belfry.
The stark **interior**★ is laid out like a basilica with a chancel raised above the crypt supported on columns. Most of the capitals date from ancient times.
Above the west door is a polychrome glazed terracotta niche by Giovanni della Robbia containing a statue of St Romulus, Bishop of Fiesole, to whom the cathedral was dedicated. The Salutati chapel (*right of the chancel*) is decorated with frescoes by Cosimo Rosselli (15C) and contains two delightful **works**★ by Mino da Fiesole: the tomb and bust of Leonardo Salutati and a carved reredos representing the Virgin Mary in adoration with the young St John and other saints.

ZONA ARCHEOLOGICA

Museum; ⅃*archaeological zone.*
○*Open summer daily 9.30am–7pm. Apr and Oct 9.30am–6pm; rest of the year 9.30am–5pm.* ○*Closed Tue in winter, 25 Dec, 1 Jan. Joint ticket with Museo Bandini* ⅃⅄*€6.20; €14.50 (family ticket).* ⅃*.* ℘*055 59 477; www.ups. itpropart/museo-archeo-fiesole/.*
In an enchanting **setting**★ on a hillside clothed in cypress trees lie the **remains**

Favorite subject with Renaissance painters - Teatro Romano, Fiesole

G. Bludzin/MICHELIN

of several Etruscan and Roman buildings. The archaeological finds from the site have been placed in a small museum (*to the right of the entrance*).

Excavations

The **Roman theatre**★ (*teatro romano*) dates from 80 BC. It was buried for several centuries and was not excavated until the end of the 18C. Its 23 tiers of seats are well preserved; the central portion is set into the hillside and the first four rows were reserved for VIPs. At the foot of the tiers of seats is the semicircular orchestra, once paved with multicoloured marble. Behind the orchestra, on a slightly higher level, was the stage. The front curved inwards in the centre and was decorated with a frieze of carved marble reliefs, now in the museum. Behind the stage, in the base of the wall forming the backdrop, were the openings by which the actors made their entrances and exits.

To the left beyond the theatre was a small **Etruscan temple** (*tempietto etrusco*) built towards the end of the 4C BC. It was partly destroyed by fire; the remains were then integrated into a new building constructed during the days of Sulla. The rectangular layout of the building is still apparent, as are the steps leading up to it.

To the right are a few fragments of the **Etruscan walls**.

Opposite the temple and to the right of the theatre were the **baths** (*terme*) built by the Romans in the 1C AD. Three arches have been reconstructed. The baths were composed of an open-air section, consisting of two large rectangular swimming pools, the second of which had two basins, and at the rear, under cover, the hot baths (*caldarium*) where the floor was supported on small brick pillars around which hot air circulated (*hypocaust*).

Museo Archeologico★

The Archaeological Museum is organised by geography rather than chronology, thus objects from very different periods are presented together. Room I contains the items found during the restoration of the town walls. In the second room are funeral items excavated from the graves in an Etruscan necropolis, which was used in later years by the Romans. Here, displayed alone in a small glass case, is a cylindrical lead **urn**★ (*cista*), thought to date from the 3C or 4C AD, which was found to contain burnt bones and ashes. The third room contains objects from the Archaeology Zone, among which are antefixes (sort of gargoyle) in the shape of female figures and tiny bronze votive offerings, some of which are shaped like feet or legs; they date from the period prior to Roman colonisation. Against the wall at the end of the room is a row of fragments of the carved marble frieze which once decorated the stage in the theatre (games in honour of Dionysius).

The first room displays objects excavated in tombs found on the site of the main square and in the Archaeology Zone: bottles, iron belt ornaments dating from the 7C–8C, gold threads found on the arms and chest of a male burial, pearls from a necklace, and silver hairpins found beneath the skull of a female burial.

In the next two rooms the most outstanding exhibits are a tombstone typical of the Fiesole region (5C BC) decorated with an illustration of a funeral meal, a dance and an animal combat, several pieces of 6C BC black Etruscan buccheroware (cases 43 and 46), and vases from Apulia in Southern Italy dating from the 4C BC (cases 51 and 52).

The museum also houses the **Costantini Collection** of red and black figure Greek vases and Etruscan buccheroware.

Museo Bandini

⏱ *Open daily 9.30am–7pm (5pm winter).* ⏱ *Closed Tue in winter; 25 Dec, 1 Jan. Joint ticket with the Archaeological Museum and the Cappella di San Giacomo.* €6.20. ✆*055 59 477.*

The first floor features paintings from the 14C and 15C Tuscan School, including the Florentine School's Petrarch's Tri-

umphs: *The Triumph of Love and Chastity* and *The Triumph of Time and Religion.*

EXCURSIONS
Badia Fiesolana

3km/2mi SW of Fiesole.
Almost halfway down between Fiesole and Florence, turn right into the Via Badia dei Roccettini.

The Badia Fiesolana (Fiesole Abbey), which now hosts the European University Institute, was originally a Benedictine convent. The highly ornate decoration of the original Romanesque **façade**★, composed of geometric motifs in green and white marble has been rather strangely integrated into the newer 15C façade which was left unfinished on the death of Cosimo the Elder.

San Domenico di Fiesole

2.5km/2mi to the SW, beside the Florence road (left), just after the junction with Via Badia dei Roccettini.

Fra Angelico took his vows here, c. 1420, and spent several years in the adjacent monastery (*private*). The church contains his delicate but vividly coloured **painting**★ representing the Virgin Mary in Majesty surrounded by angels and saints (c. 1430); it was originally painted on a gold background and designed as a triptych, but the various parts were unified in 1501 by Lorenzo di Credi.

ADDRESSES

🏠STAY

🛏🍽 **Bed & Breakfast Le Cannelle** – *Via Gramsci 52/54/56.* ✆*055 59 78 336. www.lecannelle.com. 5 rooms.* 🍽. Great attention to detail has been employed in this sophisticated B&B, which is located not far from the town centre. Elegantly furnished in wood, each room has its own character. The gracious owner serves the ample breakfast.

🛏🍽 **Pensione Bencistà** – *Via Benedetto da Maiano 4.* ✆*055 59 163. www. bencista.com. 43 rooms; half board.* 🍽🍽. Enjoy the tranquillity of this old town house which is decorated with

period furnishings and set among the olive trees. The terrace and the large garden have panoramic views of Florence and the Arno Valley.

🛏🍽🍽 **Dino** – *Via Faentina 239.* ✆*055 54 89 32. www.hotel-dino.it. 18 rooms.* 🍽. In the verdant, peaceful hills, a short distance from the centre of Fiesole in the village of Olmo, this simple hotel has comfortable rooms with rustic furnishings.

🍴/EAT

🍽🍽 **India Ristorante Tandoori e Mughlai** – *Largo Gramsci 43.* ✆*055 59 99 00. Closed Tue. Reservations required.* If you tire of Tuscan cooking, try the contrasting savour of Tandoori and

Moghul cuisine. After visiting Florence or an evening at the Fiesole amphitheatre, treat yourself to an "alternative" meal in a different ambience.

🍴 **Osteria Carpe Diem** – *Via Mantellini 2/b. ☎055 59 95 95.* Two restaurants serving traditional Tuscan cooking share the same sign and the same courtyard. One is sophisticated, the other is less pretentious and less expensive.

🍴 **Ristorante Vinandro** – *P.za Mino 33. ☎055 59 121. Closed Mon.* Typical Tuscan cuisine that is both simple and delicious: tagliatelle, garganelli, carpaccio di manzo, ribollita. Large dining room with a pleasant atmosphere.

🚐 **TAKING A BREAK**

Caffè al no 5 di Piazza Mino – *Piazza Mino. ☎055 59 250.* This café in the main square (no 5) is the oldest in Fiesole, founded in 1908.

Garfagnana
Region

Inhabited since prehistoric times, this region is particularly interesting for its landscape and its geology. The rough configuration of the Apuan Alps is visibly different from the Apennines and the softer outline of the foothills.

🚗 **DRIVING TOUR**

This tour (50km/31mi) starts from Borgo a Mozzano, proceeds north and ends in Castelnuovo Garfagnana.

Borgo a Mozzano
This village on the road to Abetone attracts attention on account of its unusual Magdalen Bridge, **Ponte della Maddalena** (12C), spanning the River Serchio. Its name derives from the statue of Mary Magdalen, now conserved in the parish church. The bridge is also called the **Devil's Bridge** (Ponte del diavolo) because, according to legend, the builder asked the Devil to help him complete it. The Devil accepted in exchange for the first soul to cross the bridge. The builder managed to prevent a human soul from going to hell by ensuring that the first living thing to cross the bridge was a dog.

Barga
The town stands amid trees and vineyards in a delightful setting on a plateau

- 🐾 **Michelin Map:** Michelin Atlas p 32 and Map 563 – J 13 and Map 735 Fold 14.
- ⓘ **Info:** APT Garfagnana, Via Pascoli 44, 55032 Castelnuovo Garfagnana (Lucca). ☎0583 64 42 42. www.ingarfagnana.com.
- ▷ **Location:** The Garfagnana valley lies between the Apuan Alps and Abetone, and is easily reached from Lucca by the S12.

on the northern slopes of the Serchio Valley over which it had control during the Middle Ages. Its "castle" (*castello*) consists of the upper town, a medieval district of winding, steep and narrow streets behind the remains of the town walls. High above the upper town is an elegant **Duomo**. This superb Romanesque **cathedral** is built of white limestone. Its portal is flanked by two engaged columns, each crowned by a lion in the Lombard Romanesque style. From the terrace in front of the church there is a pleasant view over the rooftops of the upper town to the mountains on the horizon. Inside the cathedral, in front of the presbytery, which is closed off with coloured marble screens, is a superb 12C marble **ambo**★ decorated with low relief carvings (scenes from the Life of Mary and the Life of Christ). Other outstanding features of the cathedral include the eagle-lectern, the stoup decorated with carved heads and *St Christopher carrying the Child Jesus* (18C).

Castelvecchio Pascoli

5km/3mi W of Barga. The village is invariably linked in the Italian mind with the *Songs of Castelvecchio* composed by **Giovanni Pascoli** (1855–1912), a pupil of Carducci, who won five gold medals at the Latin poetry competition. In the middle of this quiet, rural landscape stands the **Casa di Giovanni Pascoli**. For 40 years it was maintained by the poet's sister, who is buried in the chapel in the same grave as her brother.
⊙*Open Apr–Oct Tue–Sun 10.30am–1pm and 3pm–6.45pm; rest of the year 9.30am–1pm and 2.30pm–5.15pm.*
⊙*Closed 25 Dec.* ⊛€3.10. ℘*0583 76 61 47. www.comune.larga.lu.it.*

▷ *Drive S for 4km/2.5mi to Gallicano, then 9km/6mi to Fornovolasco.*

Grotta del Vento

14km/9mi SW of Fornovolasco.
Guided tours (1hr) 10am–6pm; 2hr and 3hr tours available in summer only.
⊛*€6.30–€14.50.* ℘*0583 72 20 53. www.grottadelvento.it.*
The **Windy Cave** lies on a winding road bristling with sheer rocky cliffs and providing a breathtaking view down over the Calomini hermitage set in a wall of rock at an altitude of more than 100m/325ft.

The cave gets its name from the perceptible draught that can be felt at its mouth, caused by the difference in level between two natural ventilation holes. Inside the cave, the temperature is a steady 10.7°C/51°F. The "wind" is therefore sucked into the cave during the winter when the temperature outside is lower and, in summer, the phenomenon is reversed. Until the First World War, the cave had almost one sole purpose: it was used as a natural icebox. Potholers began to explore the cave in 1932. It contains interesting stalactites and stalagmites which are particularly bright because they are constantly covered in a film of water.

▷ *Return to Gallicano and continue 8km/5mi to Castelnuovo Garfagnana.*

Castelnuovo di Garfagnana

This small industrial town is the starting point for long-distance walks in the Apuan Alps Park (*www.parcapuane.it*). The most important buildings in the town are the 12C **Rocca Ariostesca**, which now houses a small archaeological museum, and the 16C **Duomo**, in which there are artworks attributed to Verocchio and Ghirlandaio. The village hosts a large market every Thursday.

Devil's Bridge near the town of Borgo a Mozzano

Lara Pessina / MICHELIN

La Lunigiana★
Region

This historical and geographical region with a backdrop of castles and Romanesque parish churches runs along the River Magra on the borders of Tuscany, Liguria and Emilia. Although it combines a number of different cultures, it still retains a strongly discernible character of its own.

- **Michelin Map:** Atlas p 32 and Map 563 – I-J, 11-12 or Map 735 Folds 13-14.
- **Info:** Viale Vespucci 23, 54037 Massa-Carrara. *0585 24 00 63. www. terredilunigiana.com.
- **Location:** La Lunigiana forms a thin strip of land along the course of the River Magra, between Tuscany, Liguria and Emilia.

🚗 DRIVING TOURS

1 FROM AULLA TO CASOLA IN LUNIGIANA

35km/22mi – about half a day

Aulla

The town is overlooked by the **Fortezza della Brunella**. This quadrangular fortress dates from the early 16C and is believed to have been built by Giovanni dalle Bande Nere. It now houses the **Natural History Museum**, which contains a reconstruction of the natural environments of La Lunigiana region, ranging from the caves to the Mediterranean scrub (*macchia*). *Via della Brunella.* ⏱*Open Apr–Sept Tue–Sun 9am–noon and 4pm–7pm; rest of the year Tue–Sun 9am–noon and 3pm–6pm. Parco Botanico Open daily 8.30am–7.30pm (6.30pm winter).* ⏱*Closed 1 Jan, 24–25 Dec, 31 Dec.* ☜*€3. *0187 40 02 52.*

▷ *Take S63 east. Beyond Rometta turn right into S445. On the outskirts of Gragnola follow the signs to Equi (south).*

Equi Terme

This **spa resort** with its sulphur-rich springs provides treatment for respiratory and skin disorders and bone and joint diseases. In addition to its therapeutic virtues, the locality is also of special archaeological and speleological interest.
The karst **caves** (⏱*open Jun–Sept Mon–Fri 10.30am–12.30pm and 2.30pm–7pm, Sat–Sun 10.30am–7pm, rest of the year by appointment only; *0347 58 17 347*) are open to the public and contain a wealth of stalactites and stalagmites. In some of their deep, rugged cavities, remains have been found showing evidence of human settlements in the Palaeolithic and Neolithic ages. There are also traces of the passage of cave bears.

▷ *Return to S445. Continue east towards Codiponte and Casola in La Lunigiana (Aulella Valley).*

Codiponte

Its main attraction is the Romanesque parish church (*pieve*) with Lombard-Carolingian decorative motifs. It has retained its old font.

Casola in Lunigiana

A stroll through the old village with its typical 15C–16C buildings is highly recommended.
The lone brick tower, the symbol of the city, once served as the belltower for the church of Santa Felicita, which has a rich Baroque interior.

"La Pieve"

The Italian word *pieve* is derived from the Latin *plebs*, meaning the common people, and is used to indicate the local place of worship – the parish church. These churches are often rich in symbolic carvings depicting both sin and redemption.

② AULLA TO PONTREMOLI
22km/13.5mi – about half a day

Aulla (&see above)

▷ *Take S62 north towards Pontremoli.*

Villafranca in Lunigiana
This small town is best known for its **Museo Etnografico★** (Ethnography Museum), which provides a clear illustration of the cultural identity of La Lunigiana's rural civilisation through numerous displays and audio-visual presentations. Exhibits include weights from the Roman era, wooden ex-voto statuettes, utensils for peeling chestnuts, looms, cheese moulds, butter churns, etc.
Via dei Mulini 1. ⏱*Open Jun–Sept Tue –Sun 9am–noon and 4pm–7pm (3pm–6pm Oct–Apr). Closed 1 Jan, Easter, 25 Dec.* ☞€2.50. ☎0187 49 34 17. www. comunevillafrancainlunigiana.it.

▷ *Continue north on S62.*

Filattiera
Beside the road stands the parish church, **Pieve di Sorano**, built in the Tuscan and Lombard style. The finest example of this architectural style can be seen in the splendid apse.

▷ *Continue north on S62 to Pontremoli.*

Pontremoli
Pontremoli lies at the confluence of the Rivers Magra and Verde. **Piagnaro Castle**, begun in the 10C, bears witness to the town's cultural history. It gets its name from the slate slabs (*piagne*) used to roof buildings in La Lunigiana region.
The castle houses the interesting **Museo delle statue-stele della Lunigiana** (⏱*open May–Sept Tue–Sun 9am–noon and 4pm–7pm (2pm–5pm winter);* ⏱*closed 25 Dec;* ☞€3; ☎0187 83 14 39; www.lunigiana.com), a collection of female anthropomorphic sculptures representing the Mediterranean mother goddess and symbol of fertility, and

Historical Note
La Lunigiana was first inhabited in Palaeolithic times. Later there were Etruscan settlements in the area and the Romans founded a 2 000-strong colony in the town of Luni (now in Liguria) from which the name La Lunigiana is derived. During the Middle Ages the region was still a single entity, under the authority of the bishop.

male sculptures whose weapons may be intended to indicate deified heroes or tribal chiefs. The statues are arranged in three groups and span a long period dating from the second millennium BC to the 5C BC.
The large bell tower (*campanone*), situated between Piazza della Repubblica and Piazza del Duomo, is the symbol of the town. It was once part of the wall known as the war-guard (*Cacciaguerra*), built in the 14C on the orders of Castruccio Castracani to separate the Guelf and Ghibelline districts of the town.

ADDRESSES

⏺/ EAT

☞ **Da Renato** – *Località Guinadi, 54027 Pontremoli. 10km/6mi NW of Pontremoli.* ☎0187 83 47 15. ⛔.
The woodland setting of the picturesque town of Guinadi explains the presence on the menu of this restaurant of specialities based on the local mushrooms; other typical dishes are wild boar stew accompanied by polenta, as well as diamond-shaped pasta (*testaroli*).

☞ **Alpi Apuane** – *Via Turati 155, 54020 Pallerone. 3km/2mi E of Aulla on S 63 towards Fivizzano.* ☎0187 41 80 45. *Closed Mon, last week in Jul to 1st week in Aug.* ⛔. *Booking essential.* People travel long distances to eat in this restaurant, which has been in the same family for 140 years; the purely traditional dishes are prepared by the owners themselves. The dining room is simple but elegant.

Montecatini Terme ⳩⳩⳩

and around

The therapeutic quality of the spring water here has been famous for centuries. It is used to treat metabolic disorders, liver, stomach and intestinal complaints and rheumatism. Numerous different therapies are used, including mud baths and balneotherapy, but the most common form of treatment is drinking the water straight from the spring. The town provides the ideal setting for an enjoyable break – with parks, entertainment and a racecourse. Though the Romans were aware of the town's thermal waters, it was an unpleasant, mosquito-infested place until the late 18C, when the Grand Duke of Tuscany commissioned several drainage improvement projects. Montecatini's heyday was in the 1920s, when many of the current facilities were built or enlarged, all in the art nouveau style.

ACCADEMIA D'ARTE

1.5km/1mi N of city centre. Viale Diaz 6.
Open summer Tue–Sun 10am–1pm and 3pm–7pm (2.30pm–6.30pm winter).
0572 77 33 17. www.accademia darteamontecatini.it.
This **modern art** gallery contains sculptures by Dupré, a dramatic fresco by Pietro Annigoni (Life), personal souvenirs of Verdi and Puccini and works by Guttuso, Primo Conti, Gentilini and Messina.

EXCURSIONS
Montecatini Alto

5km/3mi NE. This is a small but elegant hillside village overlooking the Nievole Valley. In 1315 it was the site of the meeting between Uguccione della Faggiuola, a member of the Ghibelline faction from Lucca, and Castruccio Castracani, a Ghibelline from Pisa. Together they defeated the Guelfs of Florence.
Piazza Giusti is made particularly attractive by the medieval tower known

▶ **Population:** 20,360.
⚙ **Michelin Map:** Michelin Atlas p 37 and Map 563 – K 14 and Map 735 Fold 14. Town plan in the michelin guide italia.
ℹ **Info:** Viale Verdi 66/a. ✆0572 77 22 44. www.montecatini. turismo.toscana.it.
▷ **Location:** Montecatini Terme is between Florence and Lucca on the motorway (autostrada Firenze-mare).

as Casa di Ugolino, the town houses, which are decorated with coats of arms, and the attractive cafe terraces.

Monsummano Terme ⳩

4km/2.5mi SE. Piazza Giusti 38.
Open Mon–Sat 8.30am–1pm (also Tue and Thu afternoon 2.30pm–5pm). Closed 1 Jan, 1 May, 25 Dec.
. ✆0572 95 09 60. www.comune. monsummano-terme.pt.it.
he **spa resort** of Monsummano is best known for providing therapy in its caves for the treatment of gout, arthritis and circulatory and respiratory diseases. It was also the birthplace of the Italian poet **Giuseppe Giusti** (1809–50), who is commemmorated by the memorial in the square and the nearby **Casa Giusti** national museum.

ADDRESSES

ⲩ STAY

⊖⊖ **La Pia** – *Via Montebello 30. ✆0572 78 600. www.lapiahotel.it. Closed Nov–9 Apr. 41 rooms. ⌲. Restaurant ⊖⊖.*
This well-run hotel's young proprietors cherish their guests. The rooms are simple but very clean and the home-style cooking is reserved for hotel residents only.

Typically intimate Italian square in Montecatini Alto

G. Bludzin/ MICHELIN

Villa Splendor – *Viale San Francesco d'Assisi 15.* ℘*0572 78 630. Fax 0572 78 216. 27 rooms.* 🚇. Restaurant. Located in a tranquil residential zone, this *pensione* is frequented by many return guests. The very simple rooms are equipped with bathrooms.

Grand Hotel e la Pace – *Via della Torretta 1.* ℘*0572 92 40. www.lhw.com/GrandHotelLa Pace.* 🏊. *138 rooms.* 🚇. *Restaurant*. If you have decided to do things in style, this historic and elegant 19C hotel is the place for you. Beautiful flower garden and heated swimming pool.

⛾ EAT

Da Marino – *Via Provinciale Lucchese 102, 51030 Serravalle Pistoiese, 5km/3mi NE of Montecatini Alto by S435.* ℘*0573 51 042. Closed Tue. Reservations suggested*. This restaurant is known locally for its steak alla fiorentina. There are other creative Tuscan dishes based on meat and fresh fish, and the home-made sweets must not be missed. Excellent selection of wine and liqueurs.

La Torre – *Piazza Giusti 8/9, Montecatini Alto, 5km/3mi NE of Montecatini Terme.* ℘*0572 70 650. Closed Tue*. For over 40 years the family owning this restaurant in the village square has welcomed guests with authentic cooking served with high-quality wines.

🍽 TAKING A BREAK

Bargilli – *Viale Grocco 2.* ℘*0572 79 459. Open Tue–Sun 9am–1pm and 3pm–8pm*. The almond cakes (*cialde*) of Montecatini are the speciality of the Bargilli family, who have been making them by hand since 1936.

Caffè Giusti – *Piazza Giuseppe Giusti 24.* ℘*0572 70 186. Open Thu–Tue 9am–midnight*. From the little tables outside in the square you can admire the view of the medieval towers or people-watch. Giusti also offers delicious snacks.

Voglia di Gelato – *Piazza Sestilio Campioni 6, 51010 Montecatini Alto.* ℘*0572 79 313. Open Fri–Wed 8.30am–1am*. The speciality here is the iced coffee cake (*semifreddo*), but you can choose from the 46 different flavours of ice cream.

🍸 GOING OUT

Le Panteraie – *Via delle Panteraie 26.* ℘*0572 71 958. www.lepanteraie.it. Open Wed–Sun 10.30pm–3.30am*. The great discotheque of Montecatini provides nightlife in the little spa town with its themed evenings. The Latin-American Club is equipped with a large swimming pool.

Il Mugello★

Region

As early as the 14C this delightful valley was popular with the Florentine aristocracy and wealthy middle classes as a summer resort, due to its mild climate, beautiful rolling hills, well-stocked forests and year-round lushness. The region was the birthplace of the Medici family and was particularly popular with Cosimo the Elder, who commissioned the construction of the Villa di Cafaggiolo (see p206).

The Mugello's idyllic landscape is ideal scenery for nature walks. It is best known, however, as the site of the Autodromo, used by Formula 2 and the Motorcycle Grand Prix racing circuits.

     Michelin Map: Atlas p 38 and Map 563 – J/K 15/16 or Map 735 Folds 14 and 15.

     Info: Via P. Togliatti 45, Borgo San Lorenzo. ℘055 84 52 71. http:// turismo.mugello.toscana.it.

     Location: The region of the River Sieve to the north of Florence.

🚗 DRIVING TOUR

By Hill and Dale
100km/62mi – allow about 5hr

Borgo San Lorenzo

Although badly damaged during the 1919 earthquake, Borgo San Lorenzo is nonetheless still the main town in the Mugello area. The Palazzo Pretorio in Piazza Garibaldi was reconstructed exactly as it had been, so too was the west front of the church of San Lorenzo, visible from the square.

The **church** dates from the 12C, but its unusual hexagonal bell tower dates from the 13C. The extremely bare interior contains a number of fine works by the Florentine School including a *Madonna and Child* attributed to Taddeo Gaddi (15C) and a fragment of a reredos depicting the face of the Virgin Mary, attributed to Giotto.

From Piazza Garibaldi the route to Piazza Cavour passes beneath the clock tower in Corso Matteotti. Just before **Porta Fiorentina** (14C) (*second street on the right*) there is a lane (*right*) which runs beside the old rounded town walls to Piazza Cavour.

▷ *Take R302 towards Faenza. After 3km/2mi turn left into the lane leading to the church (400m/433yd).*

San Giovanni Maggiore

This pretty little country **church** set behind an elegant arched portico and flanked by a graceful octagonal bell tower, contains a marble pulpit with symbolic inset motifs (vases) in black stone on all four sides.

▷ *Return to S302; continue towards Faenza; then turn left towards Grezzano and Scarperia.*

Autodromo Internazionale del Mugello (Mugello Motor Racing Track)
1km/0.5mi E of Scarperia.
The race track hosts Formula 2 races and motorcycle world championships.

Scarperia★

This is a small, well-maintained town with a thriving and traditional cutlery trade. It still has its splendid crenellated **Palazzo Pretorio**★★, built in the small central square in the early 14C to serve as a residence for the deputies of the Mugello region.

Opposite the Palazzo Pretorio stands the **church** which contains (*high altar*) two extremely delicate marble sculptures, the first a tabernacle by Mino da Fiesole and the second a tondo of the *Madonna and Child* by Benedetto da Maiano.

Just outside the church on the left side of the square is a small **oratory** known as the **Madonna di Piazza**. Inside is a Gothic shrine with wreathed columns containing a *Madonna and Child* by Jacopo del Casentino, which is held in great veneration by local people.

▷ *Take P503 north.*

The road climbs sharply up the range of hills on the north side of the Sieve Valley. The steep and winding road provides fine views south over the Mugello region before entering a wooded area. Further on, the road crosses the pass, Giogo di Scarperia, before heading down to Firenzuola, which is visible in the distance.

Firenzuola

Although Firenzuola was badly damaged during World War II, it has nevertheless retained its grid layout bisected by a picturesque thoroughfare lined with porticoes. At the southern end of the street is the Porta Fiorentina, surmounted by a pinnacle turret, and at the north end the Porta Bolognese.

▷ *From Porta Bolognese turn left into P503. After approx. 1.5km/1mi bear left into P116 towards Passo della Futa. At R65 junction turn right and continue approx. 100m/108yd.*

Cimitero di Guerra Tedesco

Beside the road (*left*) in the **German Military Cemetery** stands a huge, towering building erected in memory of the 30,653 German soldiers who were killed in this area during World War II.

▷ *Take S65 south towards Florence.*

The road soon crosses the pass (**Passo della Futa**) and then descends into the Sieve Valley through pine and beech trees. South of Montecarelli the view widens out to embrace the scenic Mugello Valley, bounded by gently rolling hills.

▷ *8km/5mi south of Montecarelli, at the crossroads after the right-hand turn to Barberino di Mugello, turn left towards Galliano. After 150m/162yd turn right to Bosco ai Frati.*

Bosco ai Frati

This Franciscan **friary** lies off the beaten track and retains the ideal of solitude, one of the basic tenets of the Franciscan Order. Cosimo the Elder commissioned Michelozzo to rebuild it between 1420 and 1428. In front of the church is a small porch with two columns crowned by capitals bearing the Medici coat of arms, which also appears on the tall façade.

▷ *Return to R65 and drive south.*

Villa di Cafaggiolo★

⚬━ *Not open to the public.* On the right-hand side of the road just before a bend stands the old Florentine **fortress** that Cosimo the Elder commissioned Michelozzo to convert into a country manor in 1451. The villa has retained the proud appearance conveyed by its central tower, fairly massive size and crown of battlements, which are now slightly obscured by the roofs erected over the old parapet walks. Lorenzo the Magnificent and his brother Giuliano spent part of their childhood here. The small town of Cafaggiolo was also famous in the 15C–16C for its majolica ware.

▷ *In south Cafaggiolo turn left at the second junction from the hamlet.*

San Piero a Sieve

San Piero is a small, relatively modern village overlooked to the west by **San Martino Fortress**, which was built on a high wooded hilltop by Buontalenti in the late 16C. It can be glimpsed on entering the village. From the high brick walls of the pentagonal fortress, there is a panoramic view of the Mugello Valley. The parish church in the village (*main street*) contains a magnificent glazed ceramic baptismal **font**★.

▷ *Take the road along the south bank of the Sieve. The road passes through superb scenery in the lush Mugello Valley, bounded by wooded hills.*

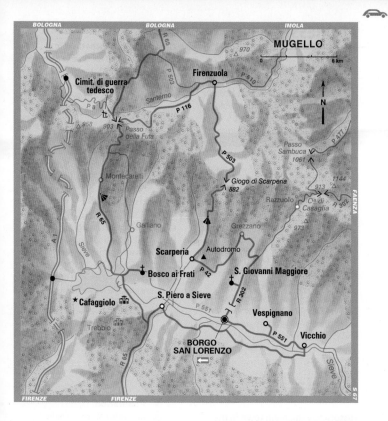

MUGELLO

Vicchio

A public park is laid out in the centre of the main square facing the loggia of the town hall (*municipio*).

▶ *Take Via Garibaldi; right on Piazza Giotto into Corso del Popolo.*

Benvenuto Cellini's house is where the famous sculptor spent his last 12 years. A raised terrace nearby offers a fine view over the rolling hillsides of the Mugello region.

The **Museo Comunale Beato Angelico** (*Piazzetta Don Milani*) is named after the Vicchio-born **Fra Angelico**; however, it contains no works from the Dominican artist. Instead, it is comprised of a collection of works of art from churches and religious buildings throughout the Mugello region, including a bust of St John the Baptist by Andrea della Robbia. ⓘ*Open Sat–Sun and Hols 10am–noon*

and 3pm–6pm; also open Thu summer. €2.50. ✆*055 84 39 224.*

▶ *From the main square opposite the town hall take the Gattaia road.*

On the outskirts of the village the road skirts a splendid purpose-built **lake**.

▶ *Take P551 west. After 3.5km/2mi turn right to Casa di Giotto (1km/0.5mi).*

Vespignano
(District of Vicchio)

Tradition has it that Giotto was born here c. 1266. **Casa di Giotto** (ⓘ*Open Thu 10am–1pm; Fri–Sun 10am–1pm, 3pm–7pm;* €4; *055-8439224; www. casadigiotto.com*), his birthplace, displays a number of documents relating to his life and works. There is a wonderful view of the Mugello Valley from the church overlooking the house.

ADDRESSES

🛏 STAY

😊🍴 **Azienda Agrituristica Poggio di Sotto** – *Via di Galliano 15/b, località Galliano di Mugello, 50031 Barberino di Mugello, 10km/6mi NW of Borgo S. Lorenzo. ℘055 84 28 447. agriturismo poggiodisotto@virgilio.it. Closed Feb. 9 rooms.* This comfortable farm offers spacious rooms decorated with taste in country style. Breakfast is served in the adjoining restaurant. Organised horse riding and mountain bike excursions are available.

😊🍴 **Casa Palmira** – *50032 Feriolo, 15km/9mi SW of Borgo San Lorenzo by S302. ℘055 84 09 749. www.casapalmira. it. Closed mid-Jan–mid-Mar. 🍴. 6 rooms. 🚗.* This fascinating medieval farm, surrounded by a beautiful garden, provides its guests with a warm welcome. The bedrooms are individual and contain fine old furniture.

🍽 EAT

😊🍴 **Badia di Moscheta** – *Via di Moscheta 8, 50033 Firenzuola, 8km/5mi S of Firenzola by S503 towards Giogo di Scarperia. ℘055 81 44 015. www.badia dimoscheta.com. Closed Mon afternoon, Tue. 🍴. Reservations suggested.* This farmhouse inn and restaurant is located at the heart of the little village. It prepares Emilian and Tuscan specialities such as potato pasta (*tordelli*) with mushroom sauce. In summer you could sit by the stream or in the shade of the gazebo, to rest after walking or horse riding.

😊🍴🍴 **Fattoria Il Palagio** – *Viale Dante 99/101, 50038 Scarperia. ℘055 84 63 76. www.fattoriailpalagio.com. Closed 2–25 Aug.* This 18C farmhouse is surrounded by a park. The country-style furniture and the menu, featuring steak and suckling pig, stress local tradition.

Pescia

Historically the main town in the Nievole Valley, Pescia was the object of dispute between Lucca, Pisa and Florence for many years. The town was founded in the 12C to link up the routes across the Apennines, and has retained traces of its past in a number of buildings of architectural interest, although it is better known throughout Europe for its horticulture. In keeping with this tradition, the town hosts a biennial flower show, a huge exhibition of cut flowers and ornamental plants.

VISIT
Porta Fiorentina
For visitors arriving from Pistoia, this **gate** is the starting point for a tour of the town. It was built in 1732 in honour of Gian Gastone de' Medici and is surmounted by the Medici coat of arms.
Duomo
This old parish **church**, built in AD 857, has been the seat of the bishop since

> ▶ **Population:** 17,913.
> 👤 **Michelin Map:** Michelin Atlas p 37 and Map 563 – K 14 or Map 735 Fold 14.
> ▶ **Location:** Piazza Mazzini 1. ℘0572 49 20. www.comune.pescia.pt.it.

1726. The bell tower is a massive structure. Despite its early origins, there is very little evidence of the existence of the cathedral before 1693 when it was completely refurbished. The west front dates from 1892. Opposite the building is the church of Santa Maria Maddalena.
Sant'Antonio Abate
The **church** stands near the cathedral and contains a 13C wooden carving depicting the *Deposition from the Cross*. The frescoes in the apse are attributed to Bicci di Lorenzo (1373–1452).
San Francesco
Past the hospital in Piazza San Francesco. The huge interior of the **church** contains an altarpiece depicting St Francis of

Assisi, who visited Pescia in 1211, and six illustrations of episodes from his life by Bonaventura Berlinghieri dating from 1235. Also worthy of note is the *St Anne Triptych*, the *Martyrdom of St Dorothy* and Brunelleschi's Cardini chapel dating from the 15C.

Beside the church are the monastery buildings, now used as the law courts. Opposite is the 18C **Affiliati Theatre**.

Palazzo dei Vicari
On the opposite side of the river.

This 12C building is now the town hall. It stands on the corner of Piazza Mazzini and is particularly attractive with its façade decorated with coats of arms. The council chambers are open to the public and contain the banner of Pescia surmounted by a dolphin, the municipal symbol.

On the other side of the square stands the **Oratory of Santi Pietro e Paolo**, also called the **Cappella della Madonna di Piè di Piazza**, built in 1447. The gilded wooden ceiling painted with a fresco of the Virgin dates from the 15C.

▷ *Continue towards Piazza Obizzi.*

San Stefano e San Niccolao
Records show that the **church** was in existence in 1068. A fine double staircase leads up to the entrance.

Nearby stands the building once occupied by the magistrate (Palazzo del Podestà, also called Palagio). It now houses the **Gipsoteca Libero Andreotti** (◷ *open Apr–Nov Fri–Sat 10am–1pm and 4pm–7pm, Wed, Sun and Hols 4pm–7pm; rest of the year 10am–1pm and 3pm–6pm, Wed, Sun and Hols 3pm–6pm; ℘0572 49 00 57; www.comune.pescia.pt.it*), a collection of 230 works by Andreotti, the local sculptor.

Pistoia★★

The very industrial town of Pistoia has a surprisingly old town centre with one of the most delightful medieval squares in Italy. The town is particularly proud of its 12C religious buildings, dating from the days when it was a free borough and enjoyed its greatest period of prosperity; the product of the work of its merchants and bankers.

▸ **Population:** 85,866.
⌖ **Michelin Map:** Michelin Atlas p 33 and Map 563 – K 14 or Map 735 Fold 14.
▯ **Info:** Piazza del Duomo (Palazzo dei Vescovi). ℘0573 21 622. www.provincia.pistoia.it.
▷ **Location:** Pistoia lies 36km/22mi from Florence by the Firenze-mare road.

PIAZZA DEL DUOMO★★

This vast **square** is attractive for its size and the layout of its main buildings, the largest religious and civil buildings in the city. The cathedral (*south side*) is preceded by its baptistery and flanked by the bell tower and the old **Bishop's Palace** (*Palazzo dei Vescovi*). Facing each other across the square are the town hall (*east*) linked to the cathedral by an archway and the Palazzo Pretorio (*west*). Set slightly back from the main line of buildings is a medieval tower, called the **Cataline Tower**. Its name recalls the fact that the famous Roman conspirator was

defeated and killed in 62 BC beneath the walls of Pistoia, then a Roman fortress. Each year in July the square is the setting for the **Bear Joust** (*Giostra dell'Orso*). Competitors dress in 14C costume and the best horsemen from the four urban districts (*rioni*) of medieval Pistoia ride at full speed at the target, held by a dummy shaped like a bear, and tilt at it with lances. In the adjacent square (*Piazza della Sala*) is the graceful **Pozzo del Leoncino**, a 15C well crowned by a lion cub (*leoncino*) resting its front left paw on the shield of Pistoia.

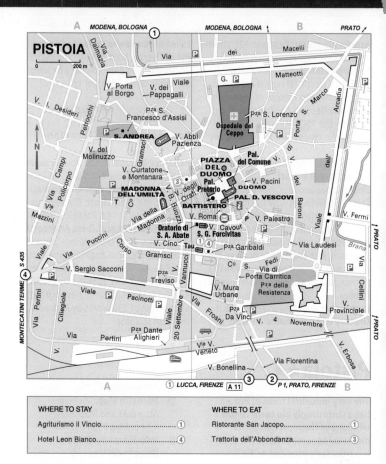

PISTOIA

0   200 m

MODENA, BOLOGNA   MODENA, BOLOGNA   PRATO

WHERE TO STAY		WHERE TO EAT	
Agriturismo il Vincio	①	Ristorante San Jacopo	①
Hotel Leon Bianco	④	Trattoria dell'Abbondanza	③

Duomo★

St James Altar: ◷*Open Mon–Sat 8am–9.30am, 10am–12.30pm and 3pm–6pm, Sun and Hols 11am–noon and 3pm–6pm.* ⊘€1.50. ℘0573 29 095. www.diocesi.pistoia.it.

The **cathedral** of San Zeno was destroyed by fire in 1108 and rebuilt in the 12C–13C but it continued to undergo major alterations until the 17C.

The marble-clad **west front**★ is a delightful combination of the very austere Pisan Romanesque style and the Florentine Renaissance style. The three upper tiers were added in 1300. The strange **bell tower** (almost 70m/227ft high) is also a combination of architectural styles, which date from the 13C to the 16C.

The **Interior**, which contains a Romanesque nave and a 17C Baroque chancel,

is most notable for the famous **St James Altar★★★** (*dossale di San Jacopo*), an outstanding example of the silversmith's craft. Made of *repoussé* and embossed silver, the altar includes 628 figures. The motifs on the altarpiece are set out around two large figures: St James (*sitting on a throne*) and Christ in Glory (*surrounded by cherubim and a choir of angels*). The front of the altar is covered with 12 episodes from the Life of Jesus and three scenes relating to St James. The nine small panels (*right*) show episodes from the Old Testament but the depiction of the life of St James (*left*) is the most outstanding part of the work. The chapel (*left of the chancel*) contains a very fine **Virgin Mary in Majesty★**, a tranquil piece of work in a subtle range of colours by Lorenzo di Credi, a pupil of Verrocchio.

Deciphering the St James Altar

Weighing nearly a tonne, the Altar of St James, dedicated to Pistoia's patron saint, is made almost entirely of silver. City elders commissioned the altar in 1287 in order to house a relic of St James that had been recovered from Santiago de Compostela in Spain, where the saint's remains are held. Work on the altar lasted almost 200 years and was carried out by numerous gold- and silversmiths, including Filippo Brunelleschi, to whom the figures of St Gregory and prophets Isaiah and Jeremiah are attributed. Because it took so long to complete, the altar contains Renaissance and Gothic stylistic elements. The altar consists of 628 figures, which were created using a *cire perdue* (lost wax) method, and scenes from the lives of Christ and his disciple, St James.

Martha de Jong-Lantink

Left Side	Altar Front	Right Side
St James and his brother, St John the Evangelist, answer the call	Annunciation and Visitation of the Virgin Mary	Creation of Adam and Eve
Their mother, Mary Salome, recommends them to Jesus	Birth of Jesus	Original sin: Adam and Eve expelled from the Garden of Eden
St James' apostolic mission	Christ in Glory, between the Virgin Mary and St James	Cain's crime and punishment
St James preaching	Procession of the Three Kings	Construction of Noah's Ark
His arrest	Adoration of the Magi	Noah and his family receiving the divine blessing; Sacrifice of Isaac
Trial and conviction of the saint	Massacre of the Innocents	Moses receives the Tablets of the Law on Mount Sinai and gives the Law to the Hebrews
St James baptises his accuser, who has been converted to Christianity	Judas' kiss	
	Crucifixion	
Martyrdom of St James	The Women at the tomb	David receives the divine blessing and is crowned king
His followers take his body to Spain	Christ appears to St Thomas	
	Ascension	Birth and presentation of the Virgin Mary in the Temple
	Presentation of Jesus in the Temple	
	St James preaching	Marriage of the Virgin Mary
	Conviction of St James	
	Martyrdom of St James	
	On the sides – the Prophets	

Battistero di San Giovanni in Corte

Battistero di San Giovanni in Corte★

⏰*Open Tue–Sat 9.30am–12.30pm and 3.30pm–6.30pm (rest of the year 4pm–7pm), Sun and Hols 9.30am–12.30pm.*
This octagonal Gothic **church** (14C), clad in alternating strips of white and green marble, was designed by Andrea Pisano. The main entrance has a tympanum decorated with a *Madonna and Child between St John the Baptist and St Peter*; the statues are attributed to Andrea Pisano's two sons, Nino and Tommaso. Below are small low reliefs depicting the martyrdom of St John the Baptist, including the scene of **Salome presenting the saint's head on a platter**.

Palazzo Pretorio

Formerly the Palazzo del Podestà, the palace was altered many times from the 14C to the 19C. The only traces that remain of the original building are the entrance, the Gothic double windows on the first floor and the staircase leading to the upper floor (*in the courtyard*).

Palazzo del Comune

This Gothic **town hall**, constructed between 1294 and 1385, has a massive **façade★** over arcades facing the square. In the centre of the façade and at the corners of the building is the Medici coat of arms with its six balls. The building was not linked to the cathedral by an archway until 1637. It is now the town hall, and also houses the **Municipal Museum**. In the centre of the courtyard is a huge bronze sculpture (1953)

from the *Miracoli* series, one of Marino Marini's most famous works.
The **Museo Civico** (⏰*Open Apr–Oct Tue, Thu–Sat 10am–6pm, Wed 4pm–7pm, Sun and Hols 11am–6pm; rest of the year Tue, Thu–Sat 10am–5pm, Wed 3pm–6pm, Sun and Hols 11am–5pm; ⏰closed 1 Jan, 1 May, 25 Dec.* ✎*€3.50, €6.50 combined ticket for all the town museums;* ♿*;* ☎*0573 37 12 96)* includes a collection of paintings and sculptures dating from the 13C to the 19C. On the first floor are a *St Francis* surrounded by scenes illustrating his life and posthumous miracles and four large Renaissance altarpieces illustrating the theme of the Holy Conversation. Two of them are by Florentine artists Lorenzo di Credi and Ridolfo del Ghirlandaio.
On the third floor, in the main reception room, are canvases dating mainly from the 17C–18C including a *Vision of St Jerome* painted by Piero Paolini who was strongly influenced by Caravaggio.

Palazzo dei Vescovi★

⏰*Open Tue, Thu–Fri 10am–1pm and 3.30pm–5pm. Guided tours available (in Italian).* ☎*0573 28 740. www.comune.pistoia.it.*
The tour gives an insight into the history of the **Bishop's Palace** (11C) and of the land on which it was built. The exhibits, including interesting remains of Roman town walls, remains from the Via Cassia, Etruscan funerary urns and Lombard vases were excavated during the restoration of the palace.
The tour includes a visit to the **cathedral museum** which has an extensive collection of church plate and vestments. Also worth a visit is the **sacristy** from which the treasure was stolen in the 13C by Vanni Fucci, as told by Dante in Song XXIV of his *Inferno*.
Beyond it is the **room★** containing works by Boldini (frescoes painted by the Macchiaolo painter from Ferrara) and the **Cappella San Niccolo** (13C) which is decorated with frescoes and bears inscriptions scratched on the walls by prisoners who were held there after the 15C when the chapel was deconsecrated and turned into a jail.

BEYOND THE PIAZZA
Ospedale del Ceppo

The name of this **hospital**, founded in 1277, means hollow tree trunk (*ceppo*), which was the vessel once used to receive offerings. Its portico is decorated with an admirable glazed terracotta **frieze**★★, which is one of the main sights of Pistoia. Created shortly before 1530 in the workshop of Giovanni della Robbia, the seven panels illustrate the *Seven Works of Mercy*. Between the panels are graceful female figures representing the Virtues of (*left to right*) Prudence, Faith, Charity, Hope and Justice. Medallions surrounded by garlands of leaves, fruit and flowers decorate the squinches between the arches. On the right-hand side is the Medici coat of arms with the emblem of Pistoia and its chequered motif beside it.

Sant'Andrea★

This attractive Pisan Romanesque **church** was built in the 8C but extensively altered in the 12C. The plain **interior**★★ consists of a tall and narrow nave, which is separated from the aisles by low arches with a narrow span. The columns are crowned by capitals with varied types of decoration.

A 15C marble niche carved with slender foliage (*beyond the first altar on the right*) contains a gilded wooden **Crucifix**★ by Giovanni Pisano.

The most outstanding feature in the church is Pisano's **pulpit**★★ made between 1298 and 1301. Designed to resemble the pulpits in the baptistery in Pisa and the cathedral in Siena, the hexagonal pulpit is covered with five marble panels depicting (*from left to right*): the *Annunciation* and the *Nativity;* the *Adoration of the Magi;* the *Massacre of the Innocents;* the *Crucifixion;* and the *Last Judgement.*

Madonna dell'Umiltà★

The huge dome of this octagonal basilica is reminiscent of Brunelleschi's dome in Florence. The Renaissance basilica was built to house the miraculous picture of the Virgin Mary of Humility, the patron saint of Pistoia.

Detail of the frieze by Giovanni della Robbia, Ospedale del Ceppo

L. Pessina/MICHELIN

South of Via Cavour

The Church of St John outside the Walls (**San Giovanni Fuorcivitas**) was built between the 12C and 14C. The **north wall**★, a long and spectacular striped façade, overlooks Via Cavour. The sombre interior is laid out in the form of a basilica, without aisles or apse. A niche to the left of the basin, which was partly the work of Giovanni Pisano, contains an all-white glazed terracotta sculpture of the **Visitation**★★ by Luca della Robbia.

The **pulpit**★ (*right-hand wall*) is a severe yet beautiful piece of work made in 1270 by Fra Guglielmo of Pisa. Its white marble panels depict the Life of Jesus and the Virgin Mary. Against the wall (*left of the altar*) is a polyptych of Mary surrounded by saints by Taddeo Gaddi (14C).

The small building near the church is the **Oratorio di Sant'Antonio Abate.** It was once connected to San Giovanni Fuorcivitas by an archway.

Nearby is the **Palazzo del Tau**. The word "Tau" refers to the letter "T" which appeared on the tunics and cloaks of monks of the Order of Hospitallers of St Anthony, who lived here in the 14C. It now houses the sculptures and drawings of the **Marino Marini Centre**. The Capella del Tau is a 14C **church** famous for its restored Gothic **frescoes**★ painted by local artists.

ADDRESSES

🛏 STAY

🌐🛏 **Hotel Leon Bianco** – *V. Panciatichi 2.* *🕾0573 26 675/ 676. www.hotelleon bianco.it. 30 rooms.* 🅿. Located near the Piazza del Duomo and 10 minutes from the train station in a fully renovated 14C inn, this hotel has comfortable rooms, all with en suite bathrooms.

🍴 EAT

🌐 **Ristorante S. Jacopo** – *V. Crispi 15. 🕾0573 27 786. www.ristorantesan jacopo.it.* Closed Sun eve, Mon. This centrally located restaurant features a dining room with a vaulted ceiling. Specialities of the menu are tradtional meat and fish dishes.

🌐🛏 **La Bottegaia** – *Via del Lastrone 20. 🕾0573 36 56 02. Closed Sun at noon, Mon, Aug.* 🖎. *Reservations suggested.* This restaurant uses only the best quality, locally sourced products. Cheese, desserts and hot and cold dishes are served in a pleasant ambience. Extensive choice of wines, including many famous names, with some served by the glass.

🌐🛏 **Rosticceria Francesco Gelli** – *Corso Gramsci 10. 🕾0573 22 216. Closed Sun evening, 16–31 Aug.* This little trattoria, a favourite with the people of Pistoia, is a boon to tourists looking for good food. The Gelli family deals in the most delicious Tuscan specialities.

🌐🛏 **Trattoria dell'Abbondanza** – *Via dell'Abbondanza 10/14. 🕾0573 36 80 37. Closed Wed, Thu at noon, 1–14 May, 12–16 Aug, 1–14 Oct.* 🖎. *Reservations suggested.* Serving traditional cooking charged at competitive prices, this popular trattoria has a pleasant and relaxing atmosphere.

☕ TAKING A BREAK

Caffè Valiani – *Via Cavour 55. 🕾0573 23 034. Open Wed–Mon 7am–1.30pm and 3.30pm–8.30pm.* This café, one of the oldest in Italy,is housed in the former oratory of Sant'Antonio Abate with vaulted ceilings decorated with 13C frescoes. Since 1881 the Valiani family has cherished the authenticity and charm of this historic building.

Gelateria di Paluzzi Maria Grazia & C – *Via Cavour 53. Open Tue–Sat 3.30pm– 10pm.* After many years in Australia, Dino prepares the best home-made ices in Pistoia in this minute shop, near the Church of San Giovanni Fuorcivitas.

🛒 SHOPPING

Bruno Corsini – *Piazza San Francesco 42. 🕾0573 20 138. Open Tue–Sat 9am–1pm and 3.30pm–7.30pm, Mon 3.30pm– 7.30pm. Closed Sun, 2 weeks in Aug.* The pride of Pistoia, which dates from 1372, is the tradition of sweets made in the shape of little hedgehogs (*riccio*), which used to be thrown to the crowds on feast days. In this family-run enterprise old-fashioned favourites such as aniseed sweets contrast with modern varieties made of almonds, hazelnuts and chocolate.

🏃 SPORT AND LEISURE

Giardino Zoologico – *V. di Pieve a Celle 160a, 4 km to the west of Pistoia. 🕾0573 91 12 19.* An oasis in the green valley of Vincio, the zoo is one of many breaks on offer in the Pistoia area.

EVENTS

Giostra dell'Orso – *P.za del Duomo.* 25 Jul. The best horsemen of the four medieval districts of Pistoia, dressed in costumes from the 13C, compete in a traditional jousting contest in which they try to spear a bear-shaped target (*orso*).

Pistoia Blues – *P.za del Duomo.* Beginning of Jul. www.comune.pistoia. it. A weeklong musical festival featuring major blues acts from around the world.

Duomo di Prato

Fabio Barni/Fotolia.com

Villa di **Poggio A Caiano**★★

Surrounded by pleasant gardens, the Villa of Poggio a Caiano was built in 1485 by Giuliano da Sangallo for Lorenzo the Magnificent.

VISIT

Piazza de Medici 14. ⏲*Open daily 8.15am–1hr before dusk.* ⏲*Closed 2nd and 3rd Mon in the month, 1 Jan, 1 May, 25 Dec.* ♿. ☏*055 87 70 12. www.polomuseale.firenze.it.*

Built in the classical style to a plan by Giuliano da Sangallo, this was the first example of a real Tuscan villa rather than a refurbished fortress. The style, which emphasised symmetry, became the hallmark of Renaissance villas.

Francesco I and his second wife **Bianca Cappello**, died here in 1587, probably of poison. Pope Leo X (son of Lorenzo the Magnificent) commissioned the magnificent drawing room on the first floor, where there is a strange coffered ceiling and frescoes by Andrea del Sarto, Franciabigio, Alessandro Allori and Pontormo. The latter created the delightful lunette fresco, based on a story from Ovid's *Metamorphoses*.

Elisa Bonaparte is rumoured to have had an affair with the famed violinist Paganini when she ived here in the early 19C. King Victor-Emmanuel II also lived here during the short time when Florence was the capital of Italy.

- 🎧 **Michelin Map:** Michelin Atlas p 37 and Map 563 – K 15 and Map 735 Fold 15.
- 🄸 **Info:** Comune di Poggio a Caiano. Via Cancellieri 4. ☏055 87 011. http://en.comune.poggio-a-caiano.po.it.
- ◖ **Location:** The villa of Poggio a Caiano is situated about 10km/6mi south of Prato on the A 11. Poggio a Caiano is also only a short distance – 15km/9mi – from Florence via the S 66.

Prato★★

Despite the peaceful atmosphere and provincial air of the central districts, Prato is the fourth-largest city in central Italy after Rome, Florence and Livorno. It is also one of the busiest and most highly industrialised. Its traditional wool industry was already producing cloth famous throughout Europe in the 13C. Today, it specialises in man-made fibres and fabrics, as well as "recycled" wools.

VISIT

The main sights all lie within the fortified town walls built in the 14C, beyond which the town did not extend until the beginning of the 20C.

Duomo★

The **cathedral**, which was built mainly in the 12C and 13C but which was con-

- ▸ **Population:** 172,473
- 🎧 **Michelin Map:** Michelin Atlas p 37 and Map 563 – K 15 or Map 735 Fold 14.
- 🄸 **Info:** Piazza delle Carceri 15. ☏0574 24 112. www.prato.turismo.toscana.it.
- ◖ **Location:** Prato is situated only 17km/10.6mi from Firenze and easily reached either by A1 Bologna–Firenze or by Firenze–mare motorway.
- ☺ **Don't Miss:** The opportunity to see the Virgin Mary's Holy Girdle (Sacro Cingolo), which is unveiled several times a year in Prato's Duomo.

Outdoor Pulpit by Michelozzo, Prato Cathedral

The elegant Gothic façade, which has an unusually tall central section, is partly clad in green marble and white stone. At the right-hand corner of the building is the famous circular **pulpit** with its fan-shaped canopy which was probably designed by Michelozzo in the early 15C so that the Holy Girdle could be shown to the congregation. Donatello, in whose studio Michelozzo was then employed, carved some remarkable decorative panels for the pulpit. The present panels are copies of the originals. A glazed terracotta *Madonna and Child* by Andrea della Robbia (1489) surmounts the entrance.

siderably extended in the 14C and the 15C, is a harmonious combination of Romanesque and Gothic styles.

The **Interior** is laid out with massive green marble columns supporting Romanesque arches emphasised by alternating strips of light and dark stone. The rafters were covered with vaulting in the 17C.

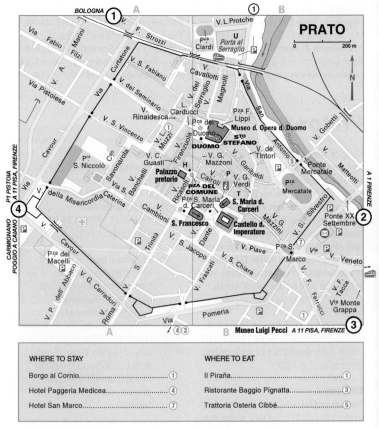

WHERE TO STAY		WHERE TO EAT	
Borgo al Cornio	①	Il Piraña	①
Hotel Paggeria Medicea	④	Ristorante Baggio Pignatta	③
Hotel San Marco	⑦	Trattoria Osteria Cibbé	⑤

At The Time of Communes

Prato, which means meadow, was originally the name of one of the districts which grew up outside the walls around a vast expanse of land used for markets. In the 11C this district finally took precedence over the others.

The town belonged to the Alberti, who were named Counts of Prato by the Holy Roman Emperor and who later possessed land throughout northern Tuscany. In the middle of the 12C the town became a free, democratically governed borough. In 1351, after many years of internal dissension and opposition to Florence in the rivalry between the Guelfs and Ghibellines, Prato came under Florentine rule and followed the fortunes of the larger city until the end of the 18C.

Prato was also a major centre of artistic activity, attracting several famous architects, sculptors and painters, who left a heritage of fine buildings and numerous works of art. It was the birthplace of **Filippino Lippi** (1457/8–1504), the son of Filippo, and more recently, of the writer, Curzio Malaparte.

Holy Girdle Chapel (*first chapel to the left*) was built in the late 14C to house the precious relic. The two very elegant bronze **screens**★ are decorated with roses, cherubim and animals. Between 1392 and 1395 Agnolo Gaddi and his pupils covered the walls of the chapel with frescoes. On the altar is the exquisite, tiny marble statue of the **Madonna and Child**★ known as the *Madonna della Cintola* carved by Giovanni Pisano towards the end of his life in 1317. The marble **pulpit**★ (*left-hand side*), shaped like a chalice, is by Mino da Fiesole and Antonio Rossellino (1473).

The touching **Virgin Mary with the Olive**★ (*Madonna dell'Ulivo*) (*end on the right-hand side*), set in a niche, is a terracotta statue made by Benedetto da Maiano (1480).

The **frescoes**★★ are one of Filippo Lippi's most accomplished pieces of work (1452–65). He used his mature talent to portray the lives of St Stephen and St John the Baptist with all the skill at his disposal in his search for light and perspective. The most famous scene depicts **Herod's Feast**★★★, and includes **Salome's Dance** with the same undulating lines, melancholic gentleness and ethereal grace that can be seen in the finest female figures painted by Botticelli, Filippo's famous pupil.

The Bocchineri Chapel (*first chapel on the right of the altar*) is decorated with **frescoes**★, that date from the first half of the 15C. Paolo Uccello began the work c. 1436, but it was completed by Andrea di Giusto, another Florentine and contemporary of the artist.

Museo dell'Opera del Duomo

Entrance via a recess to the left of the cathedral. ○*Open Wed–Mon 9.30am–12.30pm and 3pm–6.30pm, Sun and Hols 9.30am–2.30pm.* ○*Closed Easter, 1 Jan, 1 May, 15 Aug, 25 Dec.* ⊚€5, joint ticket with Spazi Museali Pratesi. ℘0574 29 339.

The few rooms in the **Cathedral Museum** are set out around a courtyard flanked on one side by the **arches**★ of delightful little Romanesque cloisters where the white marble of Carrara and the green marble of Prato combine to form charming geometric motifs above graceful white columns crowned by attractively-carved capitals.

A room opening directly off the courtyard contains the seven original **panels**★ from the outdoor pulpit. They were carved between 1428 and 1438 by Donatello and his pupils, and depict an exquisite circle of children dancing. Also in this room are the admirable coffer in the shape of a temple decorated with cherubim, a superb piece of Renaissance goldsmith's work designed to hold the Holy Girdle, and a charming painting of St Lucy, a composition painted by Filippino Lippi in his youth.

Palazzo Pretorio★

During the Middle Ages this was the residence of the Captain of the People (*Capitano del Popolo*) who held executive

An Artistic and Dissolute Monk

It was in Prato, where he was painting the frescoes in the cathedral, that Fra Filippo Lippi(1406–69), then aged 50, made the acquaintance of the delightful Lucrezia Buti, a nun in the convent to which he was chaplain. He had entered Holy Orders at the age of 15 but later left his monastery. He was captured by Barbary pirates and sold in Africa where his talents as an artist so amazed the Moors that they granted him his freedom. He returned to the monastic life until he fell in love with Lucrezia. Their son Filippino was born the following year. Despite the scandal, Cosimo the Elder obtained the Pope's permission for Lippi to be released from his vows. Filippo married Lucrezia whose smooth, angular face and delicate blonde hair he used time and again in his paintings of the *Madonna and Salome*. He was an unrepentant sinner and he is said to have died as a result of being poisoned by a jealous husband. A pupil of Lorenzo Monaco, Lippi was also strongly influenced by Masaccio. His paintings express grace and freshness and the main characteristics of this artist, who never painted anything but religious subjects, were his sincere inspiration, his natural, simplistic view, his pure lines and his subtle use of colours. In his early works Filippino used his father's style but his painting shows greater melancholy.

power. It is a tall rugged building resembling a fortress, standing in **Piazza del Comune**, a small square decorated with a graceful bronze fountain surmounted by a statue of Bacchus as a Child (*original in the Palazzo Pretorio*) by Ferdinando Tacca (1659).

Museo Civico

🕐 *Closed for refurbishment at the time of writing.* 📞 *0574 61 63 03. www.comune.prato.it/civico/.*
Located in the Palazzo Pretorio, this **museum** displays (*first floor*) a reconstruction of the small tabernacle known as the **Madonna del Mercatale** erected in 1498 by Filippino Lippi near the front door of the house of his mother. It has frescoes and a vaulted roof decorated with grotesque figures. The house was destroyed in a bombing raid in 1944, as were all the other houses in the square. The fresco, depicting the *Madonna and Child with Saints*, was miraculously spared. On the second floor, in the centre of the huge chamber with the fine ceiling of painted rafters, is the collection of 14C–15C Tuscan **polyptychs**★. The most outstanding exhibits are two works by Bernardo Daddi – the predella (1337) of the reredos which used to stand above the high altar in the cathedral and consisted of seven scenes telling the story of the Holy Girdle, and a *Madonna and*

Child with Sts Francis, Bartholomew, Barnabas and Catherine.
Giovanni de Milano, the Lombard artist who also worked in Florence, produced the great polyptych (1354) representing the *Virgin Mary in Majesty with Saints*. There is another *Madonna and Child with Angels and Saints* on a triptych attributed to Lorenzo Monaco, one of the most brilliant representatives of the "international Gothic" style. The *Madonna del Ceppo* (1453) is by Filippo Lippi.

Castello dell'Imperatore

Frederick II von Hohenstaufen ordered the construction of this mighty **imperial fortress** c. 1248 in order to strengthen the position of the Ghibelline faction. Built using a rigourous geometrical type of architecture and a square layout around a central courtyard, the fortress, which resembles other castles built to defend Frederick's territory in the Holy Roman Empire and the Kingdom of Sicily, is an anomaly in central and northern Italy.

Santa Maria delle Carceri

The **church** derives its name from a miraculous painting on the wall of the prison (*carcere*) that stood on the site before the church was built. This is an early Renaissance building and the exterior has never been completed. It was erected in the last few years of the 15C by Giuliano da Sangallo. The main characteristics of the **interior** are its austerity, geometric rigour and majestic proportions. *Pietra serena*, used to emphasise the architectural lines, contrasts with the light colours of the walls. Above the grooved pilasters is a graceful frieze of glazed white and blue terracotta by Andrea della Robbia, who also produced the four medallions of the Evangelists decorating the squinches between the arches.

San Francesco

Building began on this **church** in the late 13C. The tall façade striated with green marble was built in the early 14C; the triangular pediment dates from the Renaissance period. The chapter house, which is also known as the **Migliorati Chapel** (*access at the end of the nave to the right of the altar*) is lit by a Gothic window opening into the small 15C cloisters. It is decorated with **frescoes★** depicting the lives of the Apostles by Nicolò di Pietro Gerini, a Florentine artist who was influenced by Giotto's work.

Museo d'Arte Contemporanea Luigi Pecci

Viale della Repubblica 277. Bus 7 or 8. By car by T on the street plan and follow the signs. ◷*Open Wed–Mon 11am–7pm.* ◷*Closed 1 Jan, 1 May, 15 Aug, 24 Dec afternoon, 25 and 31 Dec. Guided tour (Italian and English) by appointment with Dipartimento Educazione,* ☎*0574 53 18 25.* ⊛*€5. Bar. Bookshop.* ♿. ☎*0574 5317. www.centropecci.it.*

The **Museum of Contemporary Art**, which has an interesting futuristic structure, houses works from modern Italian and international artists. It has temporary exhibitions, an educational service and a library.

Museo del Tessuto

Piazza Santa Chiara 24. ◷*Open Wed–Mon 10am–6pm.* ◷*Closed 1 Jan, 1 May, 25 Dec.* ⊛*€4.* ☎*0574 61 15 03. www.museodeltessuto.it.*

Prato's tradition as a producer of fine fabrics is on display at the Textile Museum. Modern in structure, the museum houses more than 600 remnants of antique and contemporary textiles from Europe, South America and India. The collection includes machinery and exhibits on dyeing.

ADDRESSES

🛏 STAY

⊜⊜ **Hotel San Marco** – *Piazza S. Marco 48.* ☎*0574 21 321. www.hotelsanmarcoprato.com. 40 rooms.* �. This hotel is close to the motorway and to the railway station and also to the historic town centre. The rooms are simply decorated and the buffet breakfast well-supplied.

🍴 EAT

⊜⊜ **Osteria Cibbé** – *Piazza Mercatale 49.* ☎*0574 60 75 09.* The décor – simple wooden or marble tables, covered with yellow paper covers – and the service at this osteria are unpretentious. The main dishes are based on the traditional cooking of the region.

⊜⊜⊜ **Enoteca Barni** – *Via Ferrucci 22.* ☎*0574 60 78 45. Closed Sat and Sun at midday, also 2–8 Jan and Aug.* This modern restaurant, run by young but experienced owners, has a limited menu at lunch (self-service) but features a full menu of creative cooking at dinner.

☕ TAKING A BREAK

Antonio Mattei – *Via Ricasoli 20/22.* ☎*574 25 756. Clsoed Mon and three weeks in Aug.* This is where the first *cantucci* were made in 1858. It is usual to dip these dry almond biscuits in Vin Santo or to eat them straight from the oven before they go dry and hard – a real delicacy.

Loggetti di Messeri Mario e Figlio – *Via Matteotti 11a/17.* ☎*0574 25 267. Closed Sun and in Aug.* This little bakery, founded in 1921, is well known to the people of Prato for its speciality – bread made with natural yeast and without salt, called *bozza pratese*.

Settignano★

Settignano is a small residential town steeped in memories of the past. It was here in the 15C that a large number of sculptors were born and that more modest stonecutters worked *pietra serena*, the bluish-grey stone used for so many of the architectural features in Florence. Michelangelo spent his childhood here among the stonecutters. The beauty of the stony hillsides was appreciated very early on by the great families of Florence who had superb villas built throughout this area. Boccaccio set the beginning of his *Decameron* in the grounds of a country house at the foot of the hill here. In the 19C the area was fashionable with English high society. In the 20C D'Annunzio chose this part of the world, where he himself had a villa, for his love affair with the great actress Eleonora Duse.

VISIT
Viale Gabriele D'Annunzio★

This long **avenue** winds out of Florence through **Coverciano** and up the hillside; the view reveals the beauty of the landscape and the magnificent country houses. Halfway up (*left of the road in a right-hand bend*) stands the **villa Contri di Mezzaratta**, set high above the valley. It attracts attention because of its

> ⚬ **Michelin Map:** Atlas p 37 and Map 563 – k 15.
> ▯ **Info:** Viale D'Annunzio. ℘055 26 54 321. www.settignano.com.
> ◐ **Location:** Settignano is situated in the hills northeast of Florence, not far from Fiesole.

crenellated tower and the neo-medieval features that were characteristic of the end of the 19C.

The road leads to the heart of the village, Piazza Tommaseo, and the small **Church of l'Assunta** which was built in the 15C and altered in the following century.

◐ *From the square take the very narrow Via di San Romano; turn right into Via Rossellino; when the street bears right, go straight on and park (right) in front of the villa.*

Villa Gamberaia: Gardens★

No 72; entrance on the right in front of a short vaulted passageway. ◐*Open daily 9.30am–6pm.* ◉€7.75. ℘055 69 72 05. www.villagamberaia.com.

The original building was erected in the 14C by Benedictines who worked the surrounding land. It was acquired in the 17C and turned into a plain quadrangular villa, soon embellished with magnificent gardens, which were laid out with immense artistry. On the south side below the loggia is a formal layout of topiary work in cypress, yew and box, redesigned at the beginning of the century; it is semicircular in shape and enclosed by a hedge of cypress trees pierced by arched openings; it ends in a terrace from which there is a fine panoramic view of the Arno Valley. On the east side the grassy walks are flanked by azaleas, camellias, hydrangeas and rhododendrons; there are groups of lemon trees in pots, grapefruit trees and mandarin trees, and also two grottoes decorated with shells, niches and statues.

Bernard Berenson (1868–1959)

American art historian and collector, Berenson lived for many years near Settignano in a villa, Villa I Tatti (*entrance in Via Vincigliata*), which he had restored. In his will he bequeathed the property to Harvard University as a Centre of Italian Renaissance Studies. His library is open to post-doctorate scholars and his collection of Italian paintings is shown by appointment to scholars with a letter of introduction.

Vinci★

It was near this village, not far from Monte Albano, in a landscape of olive trees and vines, that the genius Leonardo da Vinci was born in 1452.

VISIT

Perched on the hill of this medieval village is the 11C castle of the Counts Guidi, now the **Museo Leonardiano**★ (*open Mar–Oct Tue–Sun 9.30am–7pm (6pm Nov–Feb); €5; 0571 56 055; www.museoleonardiano.it*), which contains a collection of about 100 models of machinery built to the artist's plans and designs and exhibited on three floors. Among the models built according to the artist's innovative vision are (*ground floor*) a mechanical wing, a helicopter, a clock mechanism, a tank, a bronze smelting kiln, a speed guage for wind or water, a spotlight and a ventilator; (*first floor*) a bicycle, rack and pinion steering, a diver's breathing apparatus and a parachute. The second floor features temporary exhibits inspired by Leonardo's drawings and a small auditorium. Leonardo da Vinci was born into a gentle and harmonious **landscape**★★, composed of the silver-leafed olive groves, terraced plots, rounded hills on the horizon, enhanced by the transparent light. The house thought to have been his **birthplace** (*casa natale; 2.5km/1mi to the north of Vinci on the road to S Lucia and Faltognano; car park*

▶ **Population:** 13,964.

Michelin Map: Michelin Atlas p 37 and Map 563 – K 14 or Map 735 Fold 14.

Info: Via della Torre 11. 0571 56 80 12. www.prolocovinci.com.

Location: The little town of Vinci is 24km/15mi S of Pistoia by a scenic road and 10km/6mi N of Empoli.

50m/54yd; open Mar–Oct Tue–Sun 9.30am–7pm (6pm Nov–Feb); closed 25 Dec; 0571 56 519; www.museo leonardiano.it/anchiano.htm) has a few 15C features: the fireplace, the stone sink, the family coat of arms in the main room and the paving in the lower room.

Vinci
B. Morandi / MICHELIN

Leonardo da Vinci (1452–1519)

Leonardo was an illegitimate child, who took his name from the village of Vinci, where he was born. He was a creative genius whose "gaze was four centuries ahead of its time." Very early on in life, he showed a gift for drawing, painting and science. In 1469 he travelled to Florence where he studied painting with Verrocchio. Florence did not, however, enable him to exploit his many talents and in 1482, he moved to Milan. There he entered the service of Ludovico il Moro and worked in every conceivable sector as painter, sculptor, civil and military engineer, hydraulics engineer, town planner, musician, organiser of festivities and special events. At the same time, he continued his research into human anatomy, water, air, bird flight, physics and mechanical engineering. In 1499, owing to the fall of Ludovico il Moro, he was forced to leave Milan. Eventually, in 1516, after extensive travels, he found a patron worthy of his enormous intelligence, François I of France. He died in Amboise, France, in 1519.

Chianti presents one of Tuscany's most memorable landscapes. Its rolling hills fold over with silvery olive groves, slender cypress trees and rows of terraced grape vines. These vineyards, which produce *Chianti Classico* wine, have lent this pocket between Florence and Siena its name and its fame. Today, hundreds of vintners produce Chianti and other variants, making this area an obvious choice for wine lovers, as well as a picturesque setting for a driving tour. Beyond Chiantigiana is a land of fortified hilltowns much contested during the Middle Ages. San Gimignano, with its tower-houses, and Monteriggioni, completely confined within 13C walls, are among this region's most architecturally intriguing sights.

Chianti

Vito Arcomano / Fototeca ENIT

Chianti's earliest boundaries were between the towns of Castellina, Gaiole and Radda, which in 1384 joined to form the **Lega del Chianti** (the Chianti League), both a wine district and military alliance. One of the league's main objectives was to protect the name and manufacture of Chianti wine, thereby creating one of the world's first wine production codes. Over the years, the

Chianti-producing territory expanded and was officially redrawn in 1932 to include seven sub-regions, from Florence and Siena's hills to parts of the provinces of Pisa, Arezzo, Prato and Pistoia.

In addition to fine wines, Chianti and the hills between Florence and Siena have contributed to the artistic and architectural heritage of Tuscany. The city of **San Gimignano**, one of this subregion's most popular tourist destinations, is punctuated by 14 medieval tower-houses, the remnants of an early real estate frenzy between rival families. The towers and some marvellous frescoes, located in the Collegiata, have earned San Gimignano UNESCO World Heritage Site status.

Charming towns abound in this region. Colle di Val d'Elsa has views of the Elsa Valley and a historic centre consisting of Renaissance palazzi and medieval tower-houses. Impruneta is known for its terracotta works; Empoli for its glass-making; and San Miniato was once the Tuscan residence of the Holy Roman Emperors.

Another noteworthy town includes **Volterra**, which has an impressive collection of Etruscan relics at the Museo Etrusco Guarnacci and magnificent views of the Metalliferous Hills.

The **Metalliferous Hills** owe their name to the presence of iron, copper and pyrite mines, which give the countryside near Larderello a strange appearance. This was once a desolate area where the eerie puffs of smoke and often persistent smell of sulphur were sufficient to explain the sinister name of Devil's Valley (&see MASSA MARITTIMA).

Certaldo

Built of pink brick , the town of Certaldo is the probable birthplace of Giovanni Boccaccio, a major Italian writer during the Middle Ages. It was certainly the place where he spent the last few years of his life.

Magistrates' coats of arms on the Palazzo Pretorio, Certaldo

G.Budzin/ MICHELIN

TOWN

The **Casa-Museo del Boccaccio** (Boccaccio Museum) in the upper walled town has been rebuilt, having been almost totally destroyed during the war (✆closed for restorations at the time of going to press; ✆0571 66 42 08; www. casaboccaccio.it.)

▶ **Population:** 15,792.

Michelin Map: Michelin Atlas p 37 and Map 563– L 15 and Map 735 Fold 14.

Info: Via Giovanni Boccaccio 16. ✆0571 65 27 30. www.comune.certaldo.fi.it.

Location: Certaldo is 47km/29mi SW of Florence on S 429 and is set in the attractive Elsa Valley.

Higher up is the 13C Church of San Jacopo (St James); the cenotaph (*north wall*) was set up as a memorial to Boccaccio in 1503; the spot where he was buried was marked by a tombstone in 1954.

Nearby is the **Palazzo Pretorio**, which was rebuilt in the 16C. Its frontage is decorated with earthenware and marble coats of arms and it has an arcaded courtyard. (✆Open Apr–Oct daily 9.30am–1pm and 2pm–7.30pm; rest of the year 10.30am–12.30pm and 2pm–5pm. ✆Closed Mon in winter. ✆€2.50. ✆0571 66 12 19. www.comune.certaldo.fi.it.).

An Incomparable Storyteller (1313–75)

Boccaccio wrote commentaries on Dante's work and was a close friend of Petrarch, with whom he corresponded regularly for more than 20 years. A precursor of Humanism and recognised as the third "major figure" in medieval Italian literature, Boccaccio was born to a Frenchwoman of high birth who had a love affair with a merchant named Boccaccino di Chellino de Certaldo. While still an adolescent, he was sent to Naples as his father had decided that his son should follow him into business.

For 12 years he frequented the cultured court of Robert of Anjou and fell in love with the king's illegitimate daughter, Maria of Aquino, who has gone down in history under the charming nickname of Fiametta (little flame). The poet was a tender-hearted man, but he made light of everything and was typical of the 14C Italian bourgeoisie, loving the arts and pleasure. Boccaccio became a canon of the Church but he was cynical as well as gracious.

In Florence Boccaccio wrote his masterpiece the **Decameron** (*Ten Days*) in a clear and fast-moving style. The collection of 10 novelle was presented as the work of three youths and seven young girls who, during the outbreak of plague in Florence in 1348, sought refuge far from the town and decided to pass the time by telling each other a new story every day for ten days.

Decameron is a spirited and sometimes satirical work describing the charms of the Tuscan countryside and the cultured life that accompanied the development of Humanism. Several of the tales have parallels with Chaucer's *Canterbury Tales*; some were adapted for the screen by Pasolini.

Chianti ★★
Pesa Valley and Greve Valley

The soil of Chianti has been tilled for many centuries, as evidenced by the farmed and furrowed landscape of the region. Among the forests of chestnut, oak, pine and larch lie row-upon-row of vines and silver-green olive trees, forming a bright carpet on Chianti's gently sloping hillsides. Small villages, villas, an abbey, and a handful of elegant mansions and fine estates, blend harmoniously into a natural environment tamed by the hand of man.

A BIT OF HISTORY

The Chianti region is famous for its excellent wine (♨ *see INTRODUCTION*). The vineyards that produce it extend well beyond the boundaries of the geographical Chianti territory.

The central Chinati area, including Castellina, Gaiole and Radda (the three territories of the 13C Chianti League), produces Chianti Classico.

🚗 DRIVING TOURS

The three excursions described below all follow **Via Chiantigiana** (*R222*). Visitors doing a rapid tour of Tuscany, including Florence and Siena, are advised to travel from one city to the other along this road, which provides wonderful views of the local forests and vineyards.

The highway between Florence and Siena, known as the *Raccordo*, is particularly attractive in the Pesa and Staggia Valleys.

1 UP THE PESA VALLEY AND DOWN THE GREVE VALLEY

About 100km/62mi

▷ *From Florence take Via Senese going to Galluzzo (see the Florence area map in the Michelin Atlas Europe or Italy or on Michelin Map 563).*

Certosa del Galluzzo ★★
♨ *see FLORENCE*

- 🖢 **Michelin Map:** Michelin Atlas p 37 and Map 563– L 15, 16 and Map 735 Fold 14-15.
- ▤ **Info:** Via Rocca, Castellina in Chianti. ℘0577 74 06 20. Viale Giovanni da Verrazzano 59, Greve in Chianti. ℘055 85 46 287. Piazza Ferrucci 1, Radda in Chianti. ℘0577 73 84 94.
- ▷ **Location:** Chianti is the region between Florence and Siena. It is traversed from north to south by S222, known as the Via Chiantigiana.
- ⏱ **Timing:** Expect to spend one day per tour (*below*).

▷ *Take R2 to Siena rather than the superstrada or the Raccordo autostradale Firenze–Siena. South of Tavarnuzze, pass under the motorway. After about 1.5km/1mi turn right to Sant'Andrea in Percussina, crossing the River Greve.*

The first few miles are through forest, but the road gradually runs out from the trees and gives the first glimpses of the vines. In the hamlet of **Sant'Andrea in Percussina** (*left*) is the Albergaccio di Machiavelli, now a restaurant, where **Machiavelli** lived after being banished from Florence by the Medici. It was here that he wrote *The Prince* in 1513. He was not allowed to return to Florence until 1526, one year before his death.

San Casciano in Val di Pesa

Set on a hilltop, between the valleys of the Greve and the Pesa, this town still has some of its 14C and 16C town walls. From the tiny central square known as the Orazio Pierozzi (*junction of Via Roma and Via 4 Novembre*), Via Morrocchesi leads to **Chiesa della Misericordia**, a Romanesque-Gothic church (*later restoration*), which contains some interesting works by 14C and 15C Tuscan artists. Santa Maria del Gesù

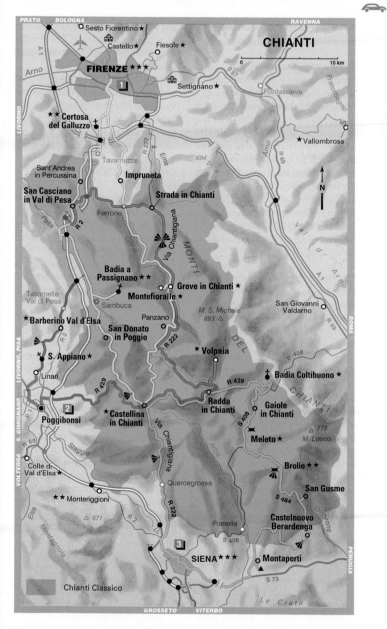

CHIANTI

0   10 km

Chianti Classico

(Map labels:)
PRATO · BOLOGNA · RAVENNA · Sesto Fiorentino ★ · Castello★ · Fiesole ★ · Settignano ★ · **FIRENZE** ★★★ · Arno · LIVORNO · ★★ Certosa del Galluzzo · Pontassieve · ★ Vallombrosa · Tavarnuzze · Ema · R 222 · 694 △ · Sant'Andrea in Percussina · Impruneta · Strada in Chianti · San Casciano in Val di Pesa · Ferrone · R 2 · Pesa · Val d'Arno · A 1 · Badia a Passignano ★★ · Tavarnelle Val d'Elsa · Montefioralle ★ · Greve in Chianti ★ · San Giovanni Valdarno · MONTI · Sambuca · Panzano · M. S. Michele 893 △ · ★ Barberino Val d'Elsa · San Donato in Poggio · R 222 · R 69 · ROMA · LIVORNO, PISA · R 2 · ★ S. Appiano ★ · Linari · ★ Volpaia · † Badia Coltibuono ★ · DEL · R 429 · R 429 · Radda in Chianti · Gaiole in Chianti · CHIANTI · S. GIMIGNANO · **2** · Poggibonsi · ★ Castellina in Chianti · Via Chiantigiana · S 408 · Meleto ★ · △ 778 M. Lucci · P 408 · Colle di Val d'Elsa · Staggia · Quercegrossa · R 222 · Brolio ★★ · San Gusme · VOLTERRA · R 68 · ★★ Monteriggioni · △ 671 · R 2 · Elsa · Montagnola · Pianella · S 484 · Castelnuovo Berardenga · Ombrone · PERUGIA · **3** · S 408 · **SIENA** ★★★ · Montaperti · ▲ · S 73 · GROSSETO · VITERBO · Le Crete

---

(*Via Roma*) contains a **Museo di Arte Sacra** (Museum of Sacred Art). Further on is the large public park, Piazza della Repubblica, flanked by the remainder of earlier fortifications including a 14C tower. From the terrace, there is a fine view over the Pesa Valley. (🕓*open May–Sept Sat 5pm–7.30pm, Sun and Hols 10am–12.30pm and 4.30pm–7.30pm; rest of the year Sat 4.30pm–7pm, Sun and Hols 10am–12.30pm and 4pm–7pm;* ✆*055 82 551*).

▶ *The road (R2) descends into the Pesa Valley and follows the course of the Tavarnuzze river for some distance. Before reaching Sambuca, turn left towards Badia a Passignano.*

Badia a Passignano★★

Donation welcome. For information ℘55 80 71 622. www.passignano.org.
This splendid **abbey** stands on the top of a gentle rise planted with vines and cypress trees. **St Giovanni Gualberto** founded Passignano in 1049 and died there in 1073; he is buried in the abbey. A flight of steps leads up to the church, the façade of which is surmounted by a 13C marble statue of St Michael the Archangel. The interior is decorated with 16C paintings by Domenico Cresti, who is known as Il Passignano in memory of his birthplace.

▶ *The road back towards the Pesa Valley crosses a landscape of coppices, olive groves, vineyards and fields of cereal crops. In the valley bottom the road skirts the old village of Sambuca before returning to the hilltops.*

🅿 *Park at the rear of the abbey.*

San Donato in Poggio

This partially fortified, medieval hilltop village was once part of an old castle. In the central square is the Palazzo Malaspina and a Renaissance water tank. Below the houses stands the **Parish Church of San Donato**, which dates from the second half of the 12C. The original basilica-like layout has survived. It comprises the nave, with pitched roof, and aisles ending in three apsidal chapels, with semicircular roofs. The crenellations of the bell tower betray its original defensive purpose.

The road to Castellina continues to cross vast stretches of countryside where the views are interrupted by copses and broom. From a bare hilltop (*7km/4mi from San Donato*) there is an extensive **view** (*right*) over the Elsa Valley and beyond.

Castellina in Chianti★

🎧*see Tour* 2
The road twists and turns as it descends into the Pesa Valley.
Panzano (*left*) is visible from some considerable distance because its church and bell tower stand on a rise.
The next stretch of Via Chiantigiana passes through a delightful succession of olive groves, vineyards, copses and rows of cypress trees.

Greve in Chianti★

The village, which is situated on the floor of the valley of the River Greve, centres on attractive Piazza Matteotti; it is bordered by irregularly shaped porticoes supporting flower-decked terraces. At the narrow end of the square stands the tiny church of Santa Croce, rebuilt in the 19C, also preceded by a portico. The interior of the church is in the Renaissance style. In the apsidal chapel beside the chancel (*north side*) there is a triptych (*left*) of the *Madonna and Child with Saints* and (*right*) a small *Annunciation* by Bicci di Lorenzo.

Chianti League

In 1384, Florence set up the Chianti League, a military alliance to counter the territorial expansionist policies of Siena. The League, which included the three territories (*terzieri*) of Castellina, Gaiole, and Radda, were administered by a magistrate (*podestà*), originally based in Castellina. In 1415 his offices were moved to Radda. In the middle of the 16C, when the Republic of Siena was annexed to the Grand Duchy of Tuscany, the League ceased to have any purpose.

Upon its formation, the League took as its emblem a black rooster (*gallo nero*), which was depicted later in Giorgio Vasari's ceiling painting in the Salone dei Cinquecento in the Palazzo Vecchio in Florence. Tuscan pride and tradition are such that the famous black rooster is now used by the wine consortium of Tuscany as a marketing symbol for Chianti Classico.

The road continues north beside the Greve, through fairly wild countryside. In Le Bolle bear left to Ferrone (the major road (S222) bears off right to Florence). North of Ferrone the road climbs up to Impruneta, lined with many trees – cypress, pine and oak.

Impruneta
see IMPRUNETA

2 HEART OF THE CHIANTI LEAGUE

From Poggibonsi (or San Gimignano): about 100km/62mi

Poggibonsi
This is a dynamic, modern town; its old town, however, is set slightly above the valley. In Piazza Cavour stands the small **Palazzo Pretorio**, decorated with coats of arms, dominated by a crenellated Gothic tower and surrounded by more recent buildings.

Pass through the industrial estate to reach the hills on the other side of the valley. Here the road gradually climbs the Chianti uplands, giving way to frequent bends in the road until reaching the crest, where it runs through stretches of woodland. There are a few magnificent views of the hills below, particularly in the last stretch before Castellina.

Castellina in Chianti★
At the end of the 13C the town was on the border between the territories of Florence and Siena. It often changed hands because of its strategic position between the river valleys of the Elsa, Pesa and Arbia.
At the entrance to the town, opposite the neo-Romanesque Church of San Salvatore, is the start of an unusual street, **Via delle Volte**★, which is vaulted along almost its entire length. It skirts the interior of the town walls. From the 16C onwards, when Tuscany was unified and became the Grand Duchy of the Medici, openings were made to give views of the wooded hillsides in the Chianti area.

At the end of the vaulted street, turn back along Via Ferruccio.

The impressive **Palazzo Ugolino** (*no 26*) has wine cellars dating from the Renaissance period. Opposite this *palazzo*, a narrow street climbs to the **Rocca**, the crenellated 15C castle; on the ground floor are two glass cabinets containing artefacts discovered in Poggino, the Etruscan graveyard in Fonteruoli (6C BC). From the second storey there is a panoramic view. (*Open Jun–Aug Thu–Sun 10am–12.30pm and 4.30pm–7pm*).

Radda in Chianti
An original member of the Chianti League, this medieval village became the main town in the League in 1415. It has retained one side of its town walls and its 15C town hall, which is decorated inside the double-arched porch with a fresco painted by the Florentine School.

West of Radda turn left into a minor road beside the Pesa to join R222 going north.

From Panzano to Greve
see Tour 1

From Greve continue north on S222.

The area between Greve and Strada contains some of the most attractive scenery in the Chianti region. The magnificent road follows the crest of the hills in several places, providing an extensive **panoramic view**★★ of the vineyards.

Strada in Chianti
In the past, travellers between Florence and the Chianti district would have had to pass through this village, hence its name (*strada* means road). All that the modern village has retained of its past is the Romanesque church of San Cristoforo.

Take the road west Via Ferrone.

San Casciano in Val di Pesa
see Tour 1

▶ *Take the motorway (superstrada) south towards Siena. As the road runs downhill, there is a fine view over the Pesa Valley. Turn right off the motorway at the Tavarnelle exit. South of Tavarnelle there is a view (right) over the Colli Fiorentini and (left) of the Pesa Valley.*

Barberino Val d'Elsa★

Barberino has now extended beyond the limits of the fortified hilltop village. The Porta Senese, the only gate in the 13C and 14C fortifications, leads into the main street, Via Francesco da Barberino. Further on is Piazza Barberini, flanked (*right*) by the Palazzo Pretorio. Beside it rises the simple east end of the church. From the church door there is an admirable view of the Pesa Valley.

▶ *On the outskirts of Barberino turn right off R2 to Sant'Appiano.*

The road to this hamlet provides some outstanding **views**★★ of the Colli Fiorentini, clothed in vineyards and olive groves.

Sant'Appiano★

🕐*Open Apr–Jul and Sept daily 4pm–7pm; rest of the year by appointment. ✆055 80 75 519.*
This pre-Romanesque church (10C–11C) has retained its original apse and part of the north aisle; its bell tower collapsed in 1171. The remainder of the church

was rebuilt in the late 12C. In front of the façade are four sandstone pillars, the remains of a separate octagonal baptistery that was demolished by an earthquake in the early 19C. Beside the church (*right*) is a set of buildings enclosing picturesque little cloisters which are reached via the **Antiquarium** at the rear of the building. After winding its way through woodland, the road provides a view of a promontory (*right*), crowned by the village of **Linari**.

▶ *Take the S429 to return to Poggibonsi.*

③ SIENA TO THE CHIANTI HILLS
About 100km/62mi

▶ *Between Siena and Castellina, the R222 passes through woods and very few vineyards. South of Quercegrossa, the road follows the contours of the land; then climbs, providing magnificent* **views**★★ *(left) over the Staggia Valley.*

Castellina in Chianti★
🕐*see Tour ②*

Radda in Chianti
🕐*see Tour ②*
East of Radda, a well-tended landscape of neat vineyards alternate with a succession of dark wooded hills.

Radda in Chianti

B. Morandi/ MICHELIN

> *At the junction of five roads follow Badia Coltibuono signs(900m/0.5mi).*

Badia Coltibuono★

This prosperous abbey was built in the 11C. It was, however, vacated by its monks in 1810, under a Napoleonic edict, and turned into a farm. The Romanesque church is devoid of aisles and surmounted by a crenellated bell tower; it and the neighouring buildings together give some idea of past grandeur. From the east end of the church there is a view over the middle reaches of the Arno to the wooded uplands of Pratomagno.

The winding road to Gaiole (*5km/3mi*) is flanked by dense woodland.

Gaiole in Chianti

This village is mainly a modern holiday resort in a small valley surrounded by vine-clad hillsides.

> *Take S408 south; after 2km/1mi turn left towards Meleto; after 400m/ 433yd turn right into a dirt track (700m/ 758yd).*

Castello di Meleto★

Private property. This is a fine example of a quadrangular medieval **castle** with round towers at the corners. It was built in the 12C and badly damaged during numerous attacks over the centuries, before being restored and turned into a stately residence in the 18C.

> *Continue south and east by S408 and S484. The Brolio district abounds in vines and olive trees.*

Brolio★★

1km/0.5mi from the entrance to the castle door. ○*Open summer daily 9am–noon and 3pm–6pm. Winter Sat–Thu 9am–noon and 2.30pm–5pm.* ○*Closed over Christmas period, 1 Jan.* €2.50. 0577 73 01. www.ricasoli.it. This huge crenellated **castle** has belonged to the Ricasoli family since the 11C. Its pentagonal fortifications, which include the first bastions ever built in Italy, were probably designed by **Giuliano da Sangallo**. From within the castle walls there is access to the gardens and the parapet walk.

The castle, which is still inhabited, underwent extensive restoration in the 19C. Beside it stands the Chapel of St Jacopo, which houses the Ricasoli family tomb in the crypt.

From the top of the walls (*south side*) there is a magnificent **view**★★★ over the Arbia Valley. In the distance beyond the towers of Siena is the high peak of Monte Amiata; to the west, downhill, are the buildings where the castle wine is produced.

> *Return by car to the valley following a dirt track (4km/2.5mi) that loops through the Brolio vineyards with the castle on the right.*

There are some fine views downhill over the castle.

> *Beyond the estate farm buildings, turn right into S484, which returns past the entrance to the estate.*

Between Brolio and San Gusme (*7km/4mi*) the country is still fairly wooded, except near San Gusme where it becomes more open.

> *Turn left off S484 into a narrow road (700m/758yd to the village).*

San Gusme

This stone-built farming village has retained its medieval character with outer walls, gateways and narrow streets.

From the village, there is an attractive view over the southern part of the province of Siena with Monte Amiata in the background.

The same view can be enjoyed from Castelnuovo Berardenga.

Castelnuovo Berardenga

The most southerly village in the Chianti region stands on a hilltop above the upper reaches of the River Ombrone. The road which skirts the village turns south towards the majestic **Villa Chigi**★, which was built in the early 19C on medieval foundations. It is surrounded by a beautiful **park** full of very old trees which can first be seen from the San Gusme road.

Next to a well-proportioned square with a central fountain is the Church of Santi Giusto e Clemente. Its main features are its neo-Classical portico and a small bell tower to one side.

It contains a *Madonna and Child with Angels* by Giovanni di Paolo (1426). ⊙*Open Sun and Hols 10am–8pm (5pm winter).* ℰ*0577 35 55 00.*

On the outskirts of Castelnuovo, there is a breathtaking **view**★★ over the gently rolling, bare hills of the Sienese countryside.

▶ *After 1.5km/1mi turn right to Pianella (not left to Montaperti as this road is unsurfaced). At the next junction (beyond a stud farm) turn left into the road to Siena.*

Montaperti (also Monteaperti)
It was near this village on 4 September 1260 that the famous battle took place in which the Ghibellines of Siena defeated the Guelfs of Florence. A memorial to the battle, a small pyramid flanked by cypress trees, stands on a prominence. *On the outskirts of the village opposite the war memorial turn left into a narrow dirt track (1.5km/1mi).*

▶ *Take S 73 west to return to Siena.*

ADDRESSES

🏠 STAY

⊜⊜ **Agriturismo Fattoria Castel-vecchi** – *53017 Radda in Chianti, 6km/4mi N of Radda in Chianti, towards Volpaia.* ℰ*0577 73 80 50. www.castelvecchi.com. 12 rooms.* 🍴 🛒. This 18C wine-making establishment offers well-appointed rooms and country-style suites. The swimming pool overlooks the wooded hills, which are gradually giving way to vineyards.

⊜⊜ **Casali della Aiola** – *Località l'Aiola, 53010 Vagliagli, 8km/5mi SW of Radda in Chianti on S222.* ℰ*0577 32 27 97. Fax 0577 32 25 09. Closed Dec–Feb. 8 rooms.* 🛒. This little farm is set among oak and chestnut woods and the occasional vineyard or olive grove. The country style is matched by elegant classic furniture. Do not miss visiting the cellars and the owner's residence.

⊜⊜ **Il Colombaio** – *Via Chiantigiana 29, 53011 Castellina, 1km/0.6mi N of Castellina in Chianti on S222.* ℰ*0577 74 04 44. www.albergoilcolombaio.it. 21 rooms.* 🛒. There is a peaceful and relaxed atmosphere about this stone-built farmhouse, which is a short walk from Castellina. The rooms have iron bedsteads, solid wood furniture and spacious en suite bathrooms

⊜⊜ **Podere Terreno** – *In Via della Volpaia, 53017 Radda in Chianti, 5.5km/3mi N of Radda in Chianti; 3km/2mi towards Firenze and then turn right.* ℰ*577 73 83 12. www.podereterreno.it. 7 rooms half board.* 🛒. This 16C farmhouse has terracotta tiles, chestnut beams and country furniture. The convivial atmosphere reaches its peak when the guests meet round the large dinner table. There is also a reading room.

🍴 EAT

⊜⊜ **Da Padellina** – *Corso del Popolo 54, 50027 Strada in Chianti.* ℰ*055 85 83 88. Closed Thu.* As well as serving local Chianti dishes, this restaurant is the headquarters of the Club Dante Alighieri and offers poetry readings of Dante's works.

⊜⊜ **Pietra Fitta** – *Località Pietrafitta 41, 53011 Castellina, 5km/3mi N of Castellina on S222 towards Firenze.* ℰ*0577 74 11 23. gaiagio@tin.it. Closed Thu. Reservations suggested.* Ideal for a snack or a leisurely Tuscan meal, this hotel restaurant has a relaxed atmosphere and country–style furnishings.

⊜⊜⊜ **Il Caminetto del Chianti** – *Viale della Montagnola 52, 50027 Strada in Chianti, 1km/0.6mi N of Greve in Chianti.* ℰ*055 85 88 909. Closed Tue, Wed lunch; early Jul to Aug.*

A comfortable restaurant on the old road between Florence and Chianti, offering typical local dishes.

🍽🍽🍽 **Badia a Coltibuono** – *Località Coltibuono, 53013 Gaiole in Chianti. ☎577 74 90 31. www.coltibuono.com. Closed Mon (except May–Oct), 10 Jan–1 Mar.* This classic restaurant in the old Abbey of Coltibuono offers Tuscan dishes prepared in the style of Lorenzo the Magnificent. In summer meals are served on the terrace, which offers a superb view of the hills.

🍷 BARS

Enoteca del Chianti Classico – *Piazza Santa Croce 8, Piazza Matteotti, 50022 Greve in Chianti. ☎055 85 32 97. Open summer daily 9.30am–1pm and 3pm–7.30pm. Closed Wed in winter.* One of the best wine merchants in the region has a selection of about 200 "Chianti Classico" DOCG vintages. The wines classed by year (some date from the 19C) are kept in five handsome vaulted cellars. Other Tuscan wines on offer are the famous Brunello di Montalcino, Nobile di Montepulciano and Vernaccia di San Gimignano.

Enoteca Baldi – *Piazza Bucciarelli 25, 50022 Greve in Chianti. ☎055 85 28 43. Closed 10 Jan–10 Feb.* This wine bar keeps a great range of red and white wines served by the glass. There are at least 800 bottles on offer, including French and Australian labels, but Tuscan wines are in the majority.

Castello di Verrazzano – *50022 Greve in Chianti. ☎055 85 42 43. Open Mon–Fri 11am–noon.* This was the birthplace of the famous explorer Verrazzano. Since 1960 this estate has belonged to the Cappellini family who have devoted themselves to the promotion of the several Sangiovese wines, a speciality of this fine vineyard.

Cennatoio Inter Vineas – *Via San Leolino 37, 50022 Greve in Chianti. ☎55 85 21 34. www.cennatoio.it. Open 9am–6pm; closed Nov–Easter.* Although it is difficult to find, this magnificent property is worth the effort for its exalted location

P. Bénet/ R. Holzbachova/ MICHELIN

and for the careful and original presentation of its wines. Try the velvety and well-balanced Etrusco.

Castello di Querceto – *Via Dudda 61, 50020 Lucolena, 14km/9mi W of Greve in Chianti. ☎055 85 921. querceto@ chiantipop.it. Open Mon–Sat 9am–6pm.* This crenellated castle, which has been owned by a French family for over 100 years, is superbly located in the centre of the Chianti district. It is not only the quality of the wine to which this great vineyard owes its fame but also the beauty of the property and its attendant peacocks.

Barone Ricasoli – *Via Cantine del Castello di Brolio, 10km/7mi S of Gaiole in Chianti towards Siena, 53013 Gaiole in Chianti. ☎577 74 90 66. www.ricasoli.it. Open summer daily 8am–7pm; winter Mon–Fri 8am–6pm.* The Ricasoli family, which has belonged to the nobility since 1141, was the first to define "Chianti Classico". In 1997 Francesco Ricasoli created "Castello di Broli", which is made with the best Sangiovese grapes.

Da Maria Cristina Diaz – *Località San Donatino 20, 53011 Castellina. ☎577 74 03 18. Open daily 8am–7pm.* Léo Ferré's last residence is rich in souvenirs but the best is the personality of Maria Diaz. Here, the quality of the wine and the olive oil is equally good.

Colle di Val d'Elsa★

The town has three districts (*terzieri*) divided into two distinct urban areas: Colle Bassa (*terziere di Piano*), which is in the valley beside the river Elsa, and Colle Alta (*terzieri di Castello e Borgo*), which clings to the hillside and has retained its 16C bastioned walls and fortified gate.

HIGH HILL (Colle Alta)

The town's main attractions are located on the upper hill (*Colle Alta*).

From Porta Vecchia (*north*) the road up to the castle (*castello*) runs south through the upper part of the town (*borgo*) be-neath one of the arches of the Palazzo Campana, a 16C mansion, and along the main street, Via del Castello, which is paved and bordered by 16C mansions and medieval tower-houses with truncated towers.

Piazza del Duomo

In Colle Alta, just beond the gates of Palazzo Campana.

The 17C **cathedral** has a neo-Classical façade, a robust quadrangular bell tower and interior furnishings in the Baroque style. Opposite the cathedral stands the Bishop's Palace, flanked by (*right*) the Palazzo Renieri and the former town hall (13C).

Beside the bell tower (*left*) stands the 14C Palazzo Pretorio, decorated with coats of arms; it now houses the **Museo Archeologico Bianchi Bandinelli** (🕐*Open Jun–Sept Tue–Fri 10am–noon and 5pm–7pm, Sat–Sun and Hols 10am–noon and 4.30pm–7.30pm; Oct–May Tue–Fri 3.30pm–5.30pm, Sat–Sun and Hols 10am–noon and 3.30pm–6.30pm;* ✆€3; ♿; ℘*0577 91 22 59*), which displays some interesting Etruscan collections. Next is the Palazzo Giusti, the Old Seminary (17C). From the southwest corner of the square a strange 14C and 15C street, Via delle Volte, leads down under the houses; it is arched-over for its entire length (*110m/120yd*).

> ▶ **Population:** 18,916.
> 🚑 **Michelin Map:** Michelin Atlas p 37 and Map 563 – L 15 and Map 735 Fold 14.
> ▯ **Info:** Via Campana, 43. ℘0577 92 27 91. www.terrediarnolfo.it.
> ⏵ **Location:** Colle di Val d'Elsa is 3km/2mi from the Florence Siena Motorway (*superstrada Firenze–Siena*) on S68 to Volterra.

Via del Castello

Access from Piazza del Duomo.

This **street** contains the **Palazzo dei Priori** (15C), now the **Museo Civico e d'Arte Sacra** (*Municipal and Sacred Art Museum;* ℘*0577 91 22 59. www.collevaldelsa.net*)), which displays 16C and 17C paintings by the Florentine and Sienese Schools and the tower-house that is said to be the birthplace of **Arnolfo di Cambio** (c. 1245–1302), the architect and sculptor who designed Florence Cathedral. From the nearest bastion, there is an extensive view over Colle Bassa, the Sienese Hills, the Chianti region and the surrounding countryside.

ADDRESSES

🛏 STAY

🍴 **Hotel Arnolfo** – *Via E Campana 8.* ℘*0577 92 20 20. www.hotelarnolfo.it. Closed 1–2 months in winter. 32 rooms.* ⌑. This hotel is housed in a 15C mansion with spacious and comfortable rooms, some of which have very high ceilings. During warmer months, breakfast is served out in the open air.

🛒 SHOPPING

Sandra Mezzetti Cristallerie – *Via Oberdan 13.* ℘*0577 92 03 95. Open Mon 3.30pm–8pm, Tue–Sat 9am–1pm and 3.30pm–8pm.* Here you will find the famous *calici degustazione* magnificent crystal goblets, suitable for every type of wine and made in Colle Val d'Elsa by CALP, the greatest glassmakers in Italy.

Empoli

and around

The town of Empoli has experienced massive development since the Second World War, especially in the glass-making and clothing industries. Once mainly agricultural, the region has now been largely taken over by the industrial suburbs.

A BIT OF HISTORY

After the defeat of Florence at Montaperti in 1260, a Ghibelline parliament was set up in Empoli to decide on the future of the Guelf capital. The Ghibellines were in favour of razing Florence to the ground in order to emphasise their enemy's defeat, but a passionate plea that the city should be spared was made by **Farinata degli Uberti**, the Ghibelline leader of Florence, who had been banished from Florence by the Guelfs in 1258 and was so delighted to return home that he could not bear his city's destruction. He died four years later, and when the Guelfs defeated the Ghibellines in 1266 and returned to power in Florence, they took their revenge by demolishing the Uberti houses and banishing the Uberti descendants.

PIAZZA FARINATA DEGLI UBERTI★

In the city centre, south of Via del Giglio. This **square** is one of the few surviving parts of the old town and its name commemorates **Farinata degli Uberti**, who persuaded the Ghibelline parliament assembled in Empoli in 1260 to spare Florence from destruction. The square is surrounded by a portico and decorated with a large central fountain erected in the 19C. Opposite the collegiate church is the **Palazzo Ghibellini**, where the famous parliament met.

The **Collegiata Sant'Andrea** has a delightful Romanesque **façade★**, built of white and green marble, which marks the westernmost limit of the use of the Florentine style. Only the lower arches are original. At the end of the tiny square to the right of the church is the **Museo della Collegiata★** (⊙*open Tue–Sun*

▶ **Population:** 43,887
⚲ **Michelin Map:** Michelin Atlas p 37 and Map 563 – K 14 and Map 735 Fold 14.
▤ **Info:** Via Giuseppe Del Papa 98. ☎0571 76 115. www.comune.empoli.fi.it.
◗ **Location:** Empoli lies in the fertile plain of the lower Arno Valley approximately 30km/19mi W of Florence on the Florence–Pisa motorway (superstrada Firenze–Pisa).

9am–noon and 4pm–7pm, also Jul Tue and Thu 9pm–11.30pm; ⊙*closed hols;* ⊜*€2.50;* ☎*0571 76 284; www.comune.empoli.fi.it),* which contains a superb collection of 14C–17C paintings and sculptures. There is a **fresco★** representing a *Pietà* by Masolino da Panicale, works by Filippo Lippi and Lorenzo Monaco, sculptures by Bernardo and Antonio Rossellino, and painted terracotta pieces by Andrea della Robbia (*upper floor in the cloisters*).

The visit continues with a guided tour of the **Church of Santo Stefano**, built by the Augustinians in the 14C in the Gothic style and reconstructed after the Second World War. It contains a reredos (*1st chapel in the north aisle*) by Bicci di Lorenzo of *St Nicholas of Tolentino protecting Empoli from the Black Death;* an emotive fresco (*tympanum of the door into the sacristy*) by Masolino of the *Madonna and Child;* an *Annunciation* (*Mercy Chapel near the sacristy*) by Bernardo Rossellino; traces of other frescoes by Masolino (*1st chapel in the south aisle*).

EXCURSIONS
Montelupo Fiorentino

7.5km/4.5mi E. The modern-looking village is the site of the **Museo Archeologico e della Ceramica★** (⊙*open Tue–Sun 9am–noon and 2.30pm–7pm;* ⊙*closed 1 Jan, 1 May, 15 Aug and 25 Dec;* ⊜*€2.50 or €4 for a combined ticket with entrance to all museums in Empoli and*

Vinci; bookshop; &; ℘057151 352; www.
montelupoceramica.firenze.it) housing
archaeological exhibits from Prehis-
tory to the Middle Ages and a fine set
of ceramics produced in Montelupo
between the 14C and the end of the
18C.

Pontorme

*1km/0.5mi E. Take the narrow street to
the left of the Firenze (Florence) road.*
This village was the birthplace of the
painter Jacopo Carrucci, better known
as **Il Pontormo**. The tiny brick Church of
San Michele contains two Saints painted
by the artist.

Castelfiorentino

18km S of Empoli.
This town, whose name means Florentine Castle, became the property of the
Bishop of Florence in the 12C. It was
here that Siena and Florence signed the
peace treaty after the Battle of Montaperti in 1260.

From **Piazza Gramsci**, a large square,
the Siena road leads to the brick-fronted
Church of San Francesco and then to
the **Church of Santa Verdiana**, one of
the most significant examples of early
18C architecture in Tuscany, standing at
the end of a superb esplanade of trees.
In the centre of the village, the **Rac-
colta Comunale d'Arte** (*no 41 Via Tilli*)
is a small art collection worth visiting
because it contains **frescoes★** and
underdrawings for frescoes (*sinopie*) by
Benozzo Gozzoli (1420–97). The painter's style is remarkably well represented
both in the frescoes of the Madonna
della Tosse Tabernacle, which depict
the *Virgin Mary, St John and Two Saints*,
the *Funeral of the Virgin Mary* and the
Assumption, and in the frescoes from the
Visitation Tabernacle, which also depict
scenes from the life of the Virgin Mary.
 Open Tue–Thu and Sat 4pm–7pm, Sun
and Hols 10am–noon and 4pm–7pm.
 Closed 1 May, 1 Jan. €1.50. &. ℘571
68 63 38.

Impruneta

Impruneta is a pretty little town
situated in the Chianti wine-growing
region and is traditionally renowned
for the manufacture of high-quality bricks, tiles and decorative
terracotta ware. It is a commonly
held belief that Brunelleschi ordered
Impruneta tiles for the roof of Florence Cathedral. The Fiera di San
Luca, organised each year around
the Feast Day of St Luke (18 October), is an ancient tradition that has
been famous for many centuries. In
the past, its horse, donkey and mule
fair attracted buyers from all over
Europe. Today the event consists
of a horse race and an exhibition of
agricultural machinery.

▶ **Population:** 14,785
 Michelin Map: Michelin
Atlas p 37 and Map 563 –
K 15 and Map 735 Fold 15.
 Info: Piazza Garibaldi.
℘055 23 13 729. www.
fabbricaimpruneta.it.
 Location: Impruneta is a
few miles S of Florence,
between the motorway
(superstrada Firenze-
Siena) and the S222.

TOWN

The centre of town is Piazza Buondelmonti, near which several of Impruneta's
old brickworks are located.

Santa Maria dell'Impruneta★

Piazza Buondelmonti. The **basilican
church** has a Renaissance portico with
five arches opening into the huge main
square. Little has survived from the
Romanesque period except the 13C bell
tower. Inside is a nave and on either side
of the choir are two private **chapels★★**
designed by Michelozzo to resemble the
one in Santissima Annunziata in Flor-

ence (1456). The south chapel is decorated with glazed ceramics by the della Robbias; the north chapel contains the famous portrait of the Virgin , which is thought to date from the 13C. The building was bombed in 1944 (*photographs in the Baptistery to the left of the entrance*) and was reconstructed using sections that were not destroyed.

Bell tower of Santa Maria dell'Impruneta
©Daniel Haller/Dreamstime.com

Museo del Tesoro

Next to Santa Maria dell'impruneta.
🕐*Open Jun–Sept Wed–Sun 10am–1pm (Sat–Sun also 4.30pm–8pm).* ∞€2.50. 📞*055 23 13 729.*
The **Treasury** contains the result of many centuries of devotion in the basilica to the Virgin Mary of Impruneta and the generosity of eminent Florentine families including the Medici: gold and silverware, reliquaries, church plate, numerous ex-votos dating from the 14C–19C and a fine collection of illuminated liturgical works (14C–16C).

Massa Marittima★★

and the Metalliferous Hills

The name Massa Marittima is believed by some to indicate that the territory formerly extended as far as the sea. This old medieval town stands on the last foothills of the Metalliferous Hills. Twice a year in May and August, Massa recalls the Middle Ages during the Balestro del Girifalco, an historic pageant featuring pennant-throwers in 14C costume.

> ▶ **Population:** 8,823
> 👣 **Michelin Map:** Michelin Atlas p 43 and Map 563 – M 14 and Map 735 Fold 14.
> ℹ **Info:** Via Parenti 22. 📞0566 90 27 56. www.massamarittima.info.
> ▶ **Location:** Massa Marittima is set in typical Tuscan landscape on the road between Follonica and Siena.
> 👁 **Don't Miss:** Massa Marittima's Pisan Romanesque Duomo.

PIAZZA GARIBALDI★★

In the city centre. The **square** is surrounded by three Romanesque buildings – the Palazzo del Podestà with double window bays, the town hall capped with merlons and the Duomo (cathedral).

Duomo★★

This majestic Pisan Romanesque **cathedral** was extended by Giovanni Pisano in 1287 and its façade was completed with a triple-pointed pediment.
Its fine **bell tower**★, which was formerly crenellated, now has four bellcotes and contains window bays increasing in number from ground floor to top. On the façade note the lintel above the central doorway depicting the life of St Cerbone, Bishop of Populonia from 570–573 and patron saint of the town, to whom the church is dedicated.
The **interior**, laid out in the style of a basilica, contains a marble low relief originating from a 3C Roman sarcophagus. The chapel (*north side of the chancel*) contains a *Virgin of the Graces* attributed to **Duccio di Buoninsegna** (c. 1255–c. 1318). The chancel houses St Cerbone's marble sarcophagus (*arca*), carved by Goro di Gregorio in 1324.

Palazzo del Podestà

This 13C building, formerly the residence of the most eminent magistrate (*podestà*), now houses the **Museo Archeologico** (Archaeology Museum) which contains an interesting *stele* from Vado all'Arancio, the only example found in Etruria of a style typical of northwest Tuscany and southern France, and Etruscan collections from the burial ground at Accesa Lake. *Piazza Garabaldi.* ⏰*Open Tue–Sun 10am–12.30pm and 3.30pm (3pm winter) to 7pm (5pm winter).* ⏰*Closed 1 Jan, 25 Dec.* €3. 📞*0566 90 22 89. www.coopcollinemetallifere.it/musei/archeologico.html.*

Museo della Miniera

Near Piazza Garibaldi. Guided tours only Apr–Sept Tue–Sun 10am–5.45pm. Rest of the year by appointment only. €5, *inlcudes entry to the Museo di Storia e Arte delle Miniere.* 📞*0566 90 22 89. www.coopcollinemetallifere.it/musei/miniera.html.*

The **Mining Museum** gives an insight into the mining of iron ore in the region, with a long gallery (700m/2,300ft) containing reconstructions of the various kinds of pit props (wood, iron, concrete) that were used in turn, and the recesses contain the trucks, machinery and tools used in mining.

PIAZZA MATTEOTTI

Città Nuova. Around this square, the heart of the "new city", are the fortifications of the Torre del Candeliere and the Fortezza dei Senesi.

Fortezza dei Senesi e Torre del Candeliere★

⏰*Open Apr–Oct Tue–Sun 10am–1pm and 3pm–6pm. Rest of the year Tue–Sun 11am–1pm and 2.30pm–4.30pm.* ⏰*Closed 1 Jan, 25 Dec.* €2.50. 📞*0566 90 22 89. www.coopcollinemetallifere.it.*

Massa is surrounded by 13C walls which were partly destroyed by the Sienese in 1337 and rebuilt by them during the 14C. The **Sienese fortress**, with its five towers, was built in 1335 and divides the town into two sections joined by the Porta alle

Duomo

G. Bludzin/ MICHELN

Silici. It is connected by an arch to the **tower** (Torre del Candeliere) (22m/72ft wide), which is all that remains of an earlier fortress built in 1228.

Museo di Storia e Arte delle Miniere

⏰*Open Apr–Oct Tue–Sun 3pm–5.30pm. Rest of the year by appointment only.* €1.50, €5 combined ticket with the Museo della Miniera. 📞*0566 90 22 89. www.coopcollinemetallifere.it.*

The **History and Art of Mining Museum** contains collections of tools, some of them dating from the Middle Ages, minerals, scale models of main mine shafts and documents illustrating the town's ancient mining industry.

METALIFFEROUS HILLS

Once the SR398 from the coast has passed the turning to Canneto, the scenery gradually becomes otherworldly as the jets of steam are captured by a power plant to produce electricity in the **Valle di Diavolo**. The surrealistic effect of this power plant is particularly noticeable in **Larderello**, a town which owes its name to Francesco de Larderel, who in 1818 began to extract boric acid from the "lagoons" of Montecerboli.

North of Larderello the panoramic road (*S439 between Massa Marittima and Volterra*) enters the heart of the Metalliferous Hills, passing through **Pomarance**, the birthplace of two painters, Cristoforo Roncalli (1552–1626) and Niccolò Circignani (c. 1530–92), each of whom is known as **Pomarancio**.

ADDRESSES

🏠 STAY

🛏️🛏️ **Podere Riparbella** – *Località Sopra Pian dei Mucini, 6km/4mi N of Massa Marittima on S441 towards Prato.* *📞0566 91 55 57. www.riparbella.com.* *🚪. 11 double rooms. 🍴.* Set in the countryside, this small family farm is notable for its organic produce, which is used to prepare creative home-cooked meals. The rooms are light and airy, with wooden furniture.

🛏️🛏️ **Azienda Agricola Agrituristica Fiordaliso** – *Podere Fiordaliso 69, 58020 Valpiana, 12.5km/8mi SW of Valpiana by S439. 📞0566 91 80 58. Fax 0566 91 80 49. Closed Nov–early Mar. 🏊. 7 rooms, half board available.* Not far from the sea, this modern property has comfortable country-style rooms, family cooking and a swimming pool situated by a small mountain lake.

🍴 EAT

🍽️ **Osteria da Tronca** – *Vicolo Porte 5. 📞0566 90 19 91. Closed Wed, 29 Dec–Feb.* The motto "I love wine so much that damned be those who eat the grapes" sets the tone of this establishment. Local cooking, unpretentious service and plenty to drink!

☕ TAKING A BREAK

I Tre Archi – *Piazza Duomo 7. 📞0566 90 22 74. Open Mon–Sat 10am–2am, Sun 5pm–3am. Closed Sept–Jun Mon.* This café, sheltered under old arches, has a terrace overlooking the main square.

🎉 EVENTS AND FESTIVALS

In May and August, during Massa's Balestro del Girifalco, people dressed in 14C costume give spectacular demonstrations of flag tossing accompanied by trumpet blasts and drum rolls.

Monteriggioni★★

Monteriggioni stands peacefully on top of one of the graceful hills north of Siena. It owes its picturesque beauty to the clear-cut outline of its enclosing wall and 14 square towers. The fortress was formerly a Ghibelline outpost, built by the Sienese in the early 13C, and was described by Dante in his "Divine Comedy".

VILLAGE

The **village**, which is totally contained within its walls, consists of a long main street running from south to north between the two gates (Porta Franca and Porta Senese) and passing along one side of the main square, Piazza Roma. The square is flanked (*east*) by the small Romanesque-Gothic church, Santa Maria Assunta, which was once used as a waypoint for pilgrims travelling the Via Francigena.

It is possible to walk along a small section of the defensive walls, next to which is a small museum displaying medieval armour.

▶ **Population:** 7,744

⌖ **Michelin Map:** Michelin Atlas p 37 and Map 563 – I 15 or Map 735 Fold 15.

🖼️ **Info:** Piazza Roma 23. 📞0577 30 48 10. www. monteriggioniturismo.it.

▶ **Location:** Monteriggioni lies only 15km/9mi from Siena. Its towers are visible from the Florence–Siena motorway.

🅿️ **Parking:** Traffic is restricted within the walls to residents and hotel guests only. Car park beside the approach road 5min on foot from the entrance. As the approach road beyond the car park is steep, it is not advisable to drive up to the village with a trailer or caravan in tow.

Entry is at Piazza Roma or Piazzetta Fontebranda (🎫€3.50 for museum and walkway.)

Abbazia di
San Galgano★★

The majestic and impressive ruins of this complex, set atop Monte Siepi, leave an indelible picture in the memory. The ruins consist of a Cistercian abbey and a hermitage built on the site where Saint Galgano died a pauper. The wayward knight lived out his last days on this hill after thrusting his sword into a stone – proof that here was where the Lord wished him to live as a hermit. Visitors can still see his legendary sword stuck in the rock.

VISIT
Abbey
2min on foot from car park; restoration in progress. ◷*Open daily 10am–dusk.* ✆*577 75 67 38.*
The unroofed **church** is flanked by one range of the cloister buildings – the chapter-house and the scriptorium. The Romanesque-Gothic abbey was built in honour of **St Galgano** (1148–81) between 1224 and 1288 by Cistercian monks from Casamari (*southeast of Rome*) and contained the earliest Gothic church in Tuscany which provided the inspiration for Siena Cathedral. A tour of the buildings reveals the traditional features of Cistercian architecture.

- ⌖ **Michelin Map:**
  Michelin Atlas p 43 and Map 563 – M 15.
- **Info:** Loc. San Galgano, Chiusdino. ✆0577 75 67 38. www.prolocochiusdino.it.
- ▶ **Location:** San Galgano is situated on the main road between Massa Marittima and Siena.

Eremo
Separate approach road and car park. The **hermitage**, which stands on the hill (200m/217yd from the abbey), is a strange 12C Romanesque rotunda with an amazing **dome** (1181–85) devoid of ribs. Its design was inspired by Etruscan and Roman tombs and it should be seen as an ideal link between Classicism and the Renaissance.
Its main feature is the 24 red-and-white brick and stone circles. The number is a multiple of 12, which has sacred connotations – the 12 Apostles and the 12 tribes of Israel. The church was built to house the body of Galgano Guidotti and the rock in which in 1180 he planted his sword, henceforth considered to be a Cross.

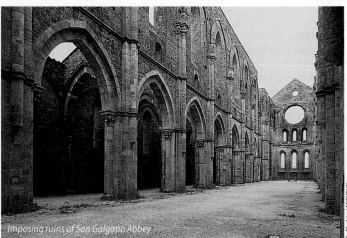
Imposing ruins of San Galgano Abbey

G. Bludzin / MICHELIN

San Gimignano★★★

and around

San Gimignano has all the charm of a small medieval town, and its mainly brick structures have been amazingly well preserved to the extent that the town's historic centre was declared a UN World Heritage Site. Within its walls are 14 grey stone towers that rise above the town like ancient skyscrapers.

A BIT OF HISTORY

Little is known about the origins of San Gimignano, a bishop who lived in Modena in the 4C, and the reasons that led the town to take his name are steeped in legend. The town became a free commune in the mid-12C and continued to prosper for 200 years, although it did not escape the rivalry between the Guelf and Ghibelline factions, which were represented in the town by the Ardinghelli and Salvucci families, respectively. The town supported the Pope and rallied to the side of Florence in her wars with Pisa, Siena, Pistoia, Arezzo, Volterra, etc. In 1353 the town took an oath of allegiance binding it to Florence.

A number of great painters from Siena and, later, Florence, worked in San Gimignano where they produced great masterpieces.

☙ WALKING TOUR

This walking tour follows the Via San Giovanni, which has plenty of shops, and Via San Matteo, lined with mansions and tower-houses.

Porta San Giovanni

The massive 13C **San Giovanni Gate** (*south side of the town*) with its barbican and Sienese arch, opens into the picturesque street (Via San Giovanni) which leads up past medieval houses to the central square.

Piazza della Cisterna★★

Piazza della Cisterna is an irregularly shaped area paved, in medieval style,

- ▸ **Population:** 7,027
- **Michelin Map:** Michelin Atlas p 37 and Map 563 – I 15 or Map 735 Fold 14.
- **Info:** Piazza Duomo 1. ✆0577 94 00 08. www.sangimignano.com.
- **Location:** San Gimignano is easily reached from Florence: take the north–south motorway south towards Siena; in Poggibonsi turn west and follow the signs to San Gimignano (13km/8mi from Poggibonsi).
- **Parking:** Public car parks are available on the outskirts of the town, as parking within the walls is restricted to residents of the town and certain hotels.
- **Don't Miss:** Views of the city from the medieval Torre Grossa and fresco cycles by Benozzo Gozzoli in Sant'Agostino and by Bartolo di Fredi in the Collegiata di Santa Maria Assunta.

with bricks forming a herringbone pattern. The square takes its name from the **well** (*cisterna*) which has occupied the centre of the space since the 13C.

Around it are austere buildings dating from the 13C–14C, some of them with towers. The 13C **Savestrini House** (*south side*) is now a hotel. At the entrance to Via del Castello (*east*) is the 14C **Palazzo Tortoli** which has two rows of Gothic twin windows.

Almost opposite is the **Devil's Tower** (*Torre del Diavolo*). The northwest corner of the square, which leads to Piazza del Duomo, dominated by the two **Ardinghelli Towers** named after the most influential Guelf family in the town.

Piazza del Duomo★★

The austere collegiate church, very old mansions (*palazzi*) and seven towers provide a majestic setting.

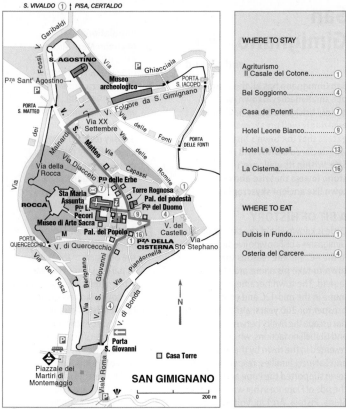

S. VIVALDO ① ↑ PISA, CERTALDO

SAN GIMIGNANO

⬜ Casa Torre

0   200 m

⑬ VOLTERRA ✗ SIENA, FIRENZE

Santa Maria Assunta (○*Open Apr–Oct 9.30am–7.30pm. Rest of the year 9.30am–5pm.* ○*Closed 16–31 Jan and 16–30 Nov.* ⊚*€3.50, €5.50 combined ticket with the Museo di Arte Sacra.* ✆*577 94 22 26. www. sangimignano.com)*, the cathedral of St Mary of the Assumption, is a 12C Romanesque building that was extended in the 15C by Giuliano da Maiano. In the 19C the west front underwent major restoration. The interior is covered in frescoes.

On the rear of the façade on the lower section of the wall (*coin box for lighting near the second pillar on the right*) the Florentine artist Benozzo Gozzoli has depicted the *Martyrdom of St Sebastian* (1465) flanked by two painted wooden statues representing the *Virgin Mary* and the *Angel of the Annunciation* carved c. 1420 by the Sienese sculptor Jacopo della Quercia. Above them another Sien-

ese artist, Taddeo di Bartolo, painted a *Last Judgement* (1393).

In the second half of the 14C, the north aisle was covered with a cycle of **frescoes**★ illustrating the major stories from the Old Testament by the Sienese artist, Bartolo di Fredi.

Influenced by Simone Martini and the Lorenzetti brothers, the artist illustrated the following scenes: top, the *Creation of the World*, the *Creation of Man*, *Adam in the Garden of Eden*, the *Creation of Eve* and the *Forbidden Fruit*. On the middle level, after two scenes which are no longer visible (*Adam and Eve being expelled from Paradise* and *Cain killing Abel*), there is the *Building of Noah's Ark*, the *Animals entering the Ark*, the *Departure of the Ark*, *Noah's Drunkenness*, the *Departure of Abraham* and *Lot, Lot taking Leave of Abraham*, *Joseph's Dream* and *Joseph being lowered down into a well*.

View of the city, San Gimignano

R. Mattes/MICHELIN

At the bottom, again beyond the first bay where the painting is now illegible (*Joseph having his Brothers Arrested*, and *Joseph Recognised by his Brothers*), there is *Moses and the Brazen Serpent*, *Pharaoh's Army being swept away by the Red Sea*, the *Jews Crossing the Red Sea*, *Moses on Mount Sinai*, *Satan receiving God's permission to tempt Job*, the *Murder of Job's Servants and the Stealing of his Animals*, the *Collapse of the House of Job*, *Job giving Thanks to God*, and *Job, in his illness, being comforted by his Friends*.

In the south aisle the *Life of Christ* is illustrated in a series of **frescoes**★★ by Barna da Siena, who worked in Simone Martini's studio. These frescoes, painted c. 1335–40, were produced before those by Bartolo di Fredi. If Vasari is to be believed, the artist died falling from scaffolding shortly before this work was completed. This cycle remains an essential part of the history of Italian Gothic painting, because of its sheer size.

The paintings depict (starting at the lunettes, top right) the *Annunciation*, the *Nativity*, the *Adoration of the Magi*, the *Circumcision*, the *Massacre of the Innocents* and the *Flight into Egypt*; (middle, from left to right) starting at the great Crucifixion, they represent *Jesus and the Doctors of the Law*, *Christ's Baptism*, *St Peter's Call*, the *Marriage in Cana*, the *Transfiguration*, *Lazarus being Raised from the Dead*, and *Christ's Entry into Jerusalem* (two panels); (lower level, from right to left) the *Last Supper*, *Judas receiving the Thirty Pieces of Silver*, the *Prayer on the Mount of Olives*, *Judas' Kiss*, *Jesus being brought before Caiaphas the High Priest*, the *Scourging*, the *Crown of Thorns* and the *Road up to Calvary*, ending with the *Crucifixion*. On the left of this great panel are (below) the *Disposition* (almost entirely missing), *Christ Descending into Hell* (badly damaged), and (above) the *Resurrection* (partly damaged) and *Pentecost*.

The **chapel, Cappella di Santa Fina** (*at the end of the south aisle*) is dedicated to the local saint, Serafina di Ciardi, a paralysed girl who died in 1254 at the age of 15. On the day of her death, all the bells began ringing and her bed was covered with flowers, as were the tops of the towers in the town.

In 1468 the townspeople commissioned Giuliano da Maiano to build this chapel in her honour. He produced this elegant chapel in which the harmonious marble and alabaster **altar**★ with its fine carvings and gold ornamentation was made by Giuliano's nephew, Benedetto. In 1475, Domenico Ghirlandaio painted some remarkable **frescoes**★ depicting the life of the saint; these paintings exhibit a less refined elegance than is evident in his masterpiece in Santa Maria

241

Novella in Florence, which he painted a few years later.

Piazza Luigi Pecori

Access via a vaulted passageway to the left of the collegiate church.

One side of this charming little square is lined by a portico, also known as the **Baptistery loggia**, which is all that remains of the 14C cloisters at the end of which Domenico Ghirlandaio painted a harmonious *Annunciation* fresco in 1482.

To the left of the vaulted passageway is a 13C palace housing two small museums. In the **Museo d'Arte Sacra** (⏲*Open Apr–Oct 9.30am–7.30pm; rest of the year 9.30am–5pm.* ⏲*Closed 16–31 Jan and 16–30 Nov.* ⊜*€3.50, €5.50 combined ticket with Collegiata di Santa Maria Assunta.* ℘*0577 94 00 08. www.sangimignano.com*) *(first floor)* the prize exhibits are a very expressive marble bust of Onofrio di Pietro by Benedetto da Maiano (c. 1493) *(first room)*, a wooden *Crucifix* by Giuliano da Maiano *(second room, in a glass case)* and the *Madonna and the Rose* set against a golden background by Bartolomeo di Fredi.

The single-roomed Museo Etrusco *(right of the staircase;* ⏲*Open Fri–Mon 11am–6pm.* ⏲*Closed Fri in winter.* ⊜*€4.* ♿. ℘*0577 94 00 08. www.sangimignano.com)* contains mainly funeral urns and pottery.

Palazzo del Popolo★

⏲*Open Nov–Feb 10am–5.30pm.* ⏲*Closed Mar–Oct.* ⊜*€5; €7.50 combined ticket for all museums.* ℘*0577 94 03 12. www.sangimignano.com.*

This building, which is called the People's Palace and also the Magistrate's Palace, dates from the 13C–14C and is surmounted by a tower (54m/176ft) (Torre Grossa). There is a small inner courtyard on two levels, flanked by a portico, with an octagonal well in the southwest corner.

The **museo civico★** *(access by the external staircase in the courtyard)* occupies the upper floors. The Grand Council Chamber, where Dante made a speech in 1300 and which overlooks Piazza del Duomo, is decorated with frescoes by the 14C Sienese School representing hunting scenes and Charles of Anjou, King of Naples. In 1317 Lippo Memmi, the Sienese primitive, painted a masterpiece entitled **Maestà**★ there, which was restored c. 1467 by Benozzo Gozzoli.

From the top of the **Torre Grossa** *(access by the staircase – 200 steps – to the right between the first and second floor)* there is an unusual **view**★★ of the towers and rooftops and the surrounding countryside. On the second floor, a small room *(left)* is decorated with frescoes depicting married life.

The other rooms *(right)* are hung with collections of paintings; most of them were the work of the 12C–15C Florentine and Sienese Schools. The museum's finest exhibit is an **Annunciation** by Filippino Lippi in the form of two rondels *(tondi)*. Also notable are two polyptychs by Taddeo di Bartolo *(Madonna and Child* and *Scenes from the Life of St Gimignano)*.

Palazzo del Podestà

The building on the east side of Piazza del Duomo dates from the 13C. It opens onto the square through a huge porch *(loggia)* with stone benches along each side, under a wide arch. It is surmounted by the mighty **Rognosa Tower** (51m/166ft high). To the left of the tower is the 13C Chigi Palace, which has its own tower beside it.

Sant'Agostino

At the northern end of the town stands this 13C Romanesque-Gothic church. Its chancel includes 17 **frescoes**★★, painted in 1464 and 1465 by Benozzo Gozzoli, one of the masters of the 15C in Florence. With his taste for intimate, personal details, the artist has depicted the life of St Augustine, the famous theologian.

The most outstanding scenes are *(bottom of the left-hand wall)* Augustine being taken to school by St Monica, his mother; *(bottom of the right-hand wall)* Augustine teaching philosophy in Rome and his Departure for Milan; *(lunette on the same wall)* his Funeral.

Tower House, Ghibellina

Tower Houses
(Case Torri)

It was in the 12C and 13C, when San Gimignano was a free borough, that the main buildings in the town were constructed. In the Middle Ages there were 70 towers but the number had dropped to 25 by the end of the 16C and only 14 have survived to the present day. Half of these, including the Torre Grossa (the tallest at 54m/177ft, which was built over the course of 11 years) and the Torre della Rognosa (one of the oldest, constructed around 1200) are located around the main square, Piazza del Duomo.

These feudal towers, designed like castle keeps, were built in many Italian towns by the great families during the struggle for supremacy between the **Guelfs** and **Ghibellines** and, later, between local tyrants. Two of the main rival families in San Gimignano were the Ardinghelli (Guelf) and Salvucci (Ghibelline). The latter's twin towers (*torri gemelli*) are iconic.

For reasons of prestige the nobility built as tall as they could. The holes that can still be seen in their walls are said to have been used in those days as supports for a network of footbridges linking the houses of allied families who could gather together quickly in one place in times of danger.

A more prosaic explanation is that the towers are a legacy of the period when San Gimignano was a major textile centre and held the secret of saffron yellow dye, which is produced from a particular variety of crocus. In order to fix the colour, the cloth had to be kept away from dust and sunshine and, as a higher price could be asked for the longer pieces of cloth, the rich cloth-producers are said to have been forced to build tall towers since the lack of space in the town prevented them from building horizontally. The holes in the walls would have been used to support the staircases attached to the exterior to avoid using up space in the interior.

Palazzo del Podestà

EXCURSIONS
San Vivaldo★
17km/11mi NW to Montaione.
It was to these woods in c. 1300 that Vivaldo Stricchi, a Franciscan lay brother from San Gimignano, withdrew to live the life of a hermit. He was found dead on 1 May 1320 beneath a chestnut tree. In 1500 the Franciscans established a community in the woods here to guard the saint's body.

Immediately after Vivaldo's death a small chapel was built; a **church** was constructed beside it in the 15C. The place where St Vivaldo's body was found is commemorated in the first chapel on the right. Above the altar is a gentle *Nativity* by Giovanni della Robbia.

Sacro Monte (Sacred Mount)
○*Open 9am–11.30am and 3pm–dusk.* ◎*Donations welcome.* ℘*0571 69 92 55.* Between c. 1500 and 1520, the Franciscans built 33 chapels of which only 17 are still standing. The chapels are miniature reproductions of the holy places in Jerusalem and all contain superb painted terracotta pieces, almost life size, depicting events from the New Testament which occurred between the Passion and Pentecost.

ADDRESSES

⌂ STAY

◎ **A La Casa de' Potenti** – *Piazza delle Erbe 10.* ℘*0577 94 31 90. http://casa deipotenti.com. 6 rooms.* ⌨.
This reasonably priced hotel, located in a 14C mansion, could not be nearer the centre of San Gimignano; some rooms look onto the square and have a fine view of the Cathedral.

◎◎ **Agriturismo Il Casale del Cotone** – *Via Cellone 59, 2.5km/1.5mi N of San Gimignano towards Certaldo.* ℘*0577 94 32 36. www.casaledelcotone.com. Closed Nov–Dec.* ⌨. *11 rooms.* ⌨.
This 18C farmhouse is a harmonious combination of old furniture and rustic art. Its isolated country setting guarantees a quiet holiday.

◎◎ **Bed & Breakfast Il Rosolaccio** – *Via San Benedetto 34, Località Capezzano, 8.5km5.2mi NE of San Gimignano towards Certaldo.* ℘*0577 94 44 65. www.rosolaccio. com. 6 rooms.* ⌨. *Restaurant* ◎◎. In this 18C farmhouse comfort is allied with tradition. Stylish rooms open into a common room with a large fireplace. From the swimming pool there is a panoramic view of the hills.

◎◎ **Agriturismo Podere Villuzza** – *Località Strada 25, 3.5km/2mi N of San Gimignano, towards Certaldo.* ℘*0577 94 05 85. www.poderevilluzza.it. Closed Dec–Feb.* ⌨. *6 rooms.* ⌨.
This country property has a fine view of the towers of San Gimignano and is ideal for a quiet stay. Language courses and excursions on horseback or mountain bike are available.

☍ EAT

◎◎ **Osteria del Carcere** – *Via del Castello 13.* ℘*0577 94 19 05. Closed Wed, Thu (only in winter), Jan–Feb.* ⌨.
This restaurant, near Piazza della Cisterna, has a menu which changes daily. The first class meat comes from the Panzano butcher in Chianti.

◎◎ **La Mandragola** – *Via Berignano 58.* ℘*0577 94 03 77. Closed Thu (winter only) and Nov. Reservations suggested.* When you tire of the usual tourist haunts, you will enjoy this local favourite, where the dishes are accompanied by local wines and served in the large and classically furnished room.

⌗ TAKING A BREAK
Caffè delle Erbe – *Via Diacceto 1.* ℘*577 90 70 83. Open Jun–Oct Wed–Mon 8am– midnight (8pm Nov–May).*
This is the most elegant and welcoming café in the town. Outside are small tables in the square.

Pasticceria Armando e Marcella – *Via San Giovanni 88.* ℘*0577 94 10 51. Open Apr–Oct daily 6am–8pm. Rest of the year Thu–Tue 6am–8pm.*
This café-patisserie in the main street offers a huge choice of cakes and an impressive array of chocolates.

San Miniato★

The charming town of San Miniato, which has retained its old appearance, stretches out along a hilltop forming an amphitheatre. Its name used to be followed by the words *al Tedesco* (of the German) because, from the 10C onwards, it was the official residence in Tuscany of the Holy Roman Emperors and the seat of imperial vicars. Its proud outline is visible from some distance, broken up at the very top by the tower on the fortress and supported on the northeast side by the huge brick buttresses of the San Francesco Monastery, which was built on the site of the 8C San Miniato Church. A few tower-houses and aristocratic mansions dating from the 15C, 16C and 17C also bear witness to a prosperous past.

TRADITIONS AND FESTIVALS

A number of ancient traditions have survived to the present day such as the bonfires lit for the Feast of St John (24 June), the shortest night of the year, when corn cobs and cloves of garlic are burnt on the hillsides around the town to ward off evil spirits. White truffles grow in these hills and they are picked during the autumn; this expensive fungus is the main item

- ▶ **Population:** 26,301
- **Michelin Map:** Michelin Atlas p 37 and Map 563 – K 14 and Map 735 Fold 14.
- **Info:** Piazza del Popolo 20. ℘0571 41 87 39. www.cittadisanminiato.it.
- **Location:** San Miniato is situated half way between Florence and Pisa just south of the motorway.

for sale at a large fair held during the last three weekends in November. Since 1947 San Miniato has been the centre of the Popular Drama Institute which stages an original dramatic work of a sacred or spiritual nature every year in July during the theatre festival. The authors of works performed in previous years have included TS Eliot, Julien Green, Thomas Mann, Elie Wiesel and Karol Wojtyla.

WALKING TOUR
Prato del Duomo

This includes a number of historic buildings. The **cathedral**, which dates from the 12C, incorporates an older machicolated bell tower, which was the defensive tower of the old castle. The cathedral has a Romanesque façade studded with a

San Miniato at daybreak
B. Morandi / MICHELIN

Santuario del Crocifisso

©Gimmi/Cuboimages/Photoshot

number of 13C ceramic bowls in the Pisan tradition, a style which can also be seen at San Piero a Grado near Pisa. The three doors date from the 15C.

The **Museo Diocesano di Arte Sacra** (*left of the cathedral;* ⊶ *closed for restoration*) contains paintings and sculptures from the 15C–19C by Filippo Lippi, Neri di Bicci, Cigoli and Verrocchio, as well as items of sacred art.

Opposite the cathedral is the **Bishop's Palace**, built in the 12C and initially used as the residence of the Captain of the citadel's militia. Later it was the residence of the *Signori Dodici* (the 12 magistrates of the town) and then of the Captain of

Brothers of the Cinema

In 1929 and 1931, respectively, the film directors Paolo and Vittorio Taviani were born in San Miniato. The inseperable brothers are renowned for using the Italian landscape, especially Puglia and Sicilia, as the backdrop for many of their films. But they reserved their backyard, Tuscany, for *Il Prato* (1979), which takes place in San Gimignano, *Good Morning, Babylon* (1987), initially set in Pisa, and for *The Night of San Lorenzo* (1982), a story about a painful episode of San Miniato history during the Second World War.

the People. Since 1622 it has been the bishop's residence.

The **Palazzo dei Vicari dell'Imperatore** (formerly the residence of the imperial vicars but now a hotel) is surmounted by a tower. It dates from the 12C and tradition has it that Countess Matilda of Tuscany was born there in 1046.

A narrow street between these two buildings leads to a tiny terrace from which there is a view of the rooftops of San Miniato and the Tuscan countryside. Below in **Piazza della Repubblica** is the **Palazzo del Seminario**★, a building with a concave façade decorated early in the 18C with frescoes and Latin aphorisms by the Fathers of the Church along the upper section; the lower part contains medieval shop fronts which have been partially preserved.

▷ *From the terrace to the left of the cathedral walk up the steep street and steps (15min return on foot).*

Spiazzo del Castello★

The brick tower on the flattened hilltop was rebuilt so that it was identical to the original, part of Frederick II's castle (*Rocca*) which was destroyed during World War II. From the esplanade there is a superb **panoramic view**★★ of San Miniato, the Arno Valley, the hills around Pisa, Pistoia and Florence, and the Appenine Mountains.

Santuario del Crocifisso

Behind the cathedral is the 17C **Crucifix Chapel** capped by a circular drum. The chapel contains a 10C Ottonian wooden Crucifix. A rather dramatic flight of steps leads to Via delle Vittime del Duomo.

▷ *Walk along Via delle Vittime del Duomo.*

Palazzo Comunale

The building contains frescoes by Giotto's School and a small church, **Chiesa del Loretino**, which has a precious altar made of marquetry with gilding and painting, a tabernacle painted by Lanfranco and 16C frescoes depicting the Life of Jesus.

Volterra★★

Volterra stands on a hill between the Cecina and Era Valleys, enclosed within Etruscan and medieval walls. It is set in an unusual and fascinating landscape★★. To the west the outline of the hill is broken by the grandiose crags★ (*balze*) caused by erosion and rock falls. West of the town are vast saltpans where table salt and soda are produced.

> ▸ **Population:** 11,686
> ↻ **Michelin Map:** Michelin Atlas p 37 and Map 563 – I 14 or Map 735 Fold 14.
> ▯ **Info:** Piazza dei Priori 20. ℘0588 87 25. www.comune.volterra.pi.it/english/.
> ◖ **Location:** Volterra is found on S68, which links Poggibonsi and Cecina.

🐾 WALKING TOUR
Piazza dei Priori★★

The **square** is flanked by austere and sober mansions. The **Palazzo Pretorio** (13C) has twin-bay windows. Beside it rises a massive crenellated tower, which owing to the wild boar on its upper section is called *Porcellino* (Piglet). Opposite stands the 13C **Palazzo dei Priori**, decorated with the emblems of Florentine magistrates.

◖ *Take Via Turazza (along left side of the Palazzo dei Priori).*

Duomo and Battistero★

The **cathedral** in picturesque Piazza S Giovanni, was built in the Pisan Romanesque style. The nave is divided from the aisles by 16C monolithic columns with capitals. The coffered ceiling represents Paradise with the saints of Volterra and (*above the sanctuary*) the Assumption of the Virgin Mary.

The Addolorata Chapel (*left*) contains the *Procession of the Magi*, a fresco by Benozzo Gozzoli (1420–97) serving as the background to a multicoloured terracotta crib by Zaccaria Zacchi da Volterra (1473–1544). Opposite is another polychrome terracotta work by Zacchi. In the south transept is a touching 13C **Deposition from the Cross**★★ made of polychrome, silvered and gilded poplar wood. It represents Christ, Nicodemus, Joseph of Arimathaea, Mary and John, and is one of the best-preserved groups of its day. The octagonal **Baptistery** dates from 1283. It has a marble doorway and one side decorated with white and green marble.

Porta all'Arco★ (Arch Gate)

This Etruscan archway, dating from the 4C BC, is built with huge quadrangular blocks of stone.

◖ *Return to Piazza dei Priori. Take the street which slopes north and turn right into Via Buomparenti.*

The street contains the remarkable Buonparenti 13C tower-houses, linked by a slender arch.

Palazzo Viti

Via dei Sarti 41. ◷*Open Apr–Nov daily 10am–1pm and 2.30pm–6pm; rest of the year by appointment only.* ⊜€3.50. ℘0588 84 047. www.palazzoviti.it.
This mansion houses collections belonging to the Viti family, who once owned the most famous stone, marble and alabaster factory in Volterra; the factory closed down in 1874. Giuseppe Viti was also a Vizier and Emir of Nepal. His beautiful Indian garments are exhibited in the museum, as are fine collections of Chinese drawings and porcelain.

Volterra

B. Morandi/ MICHELIN

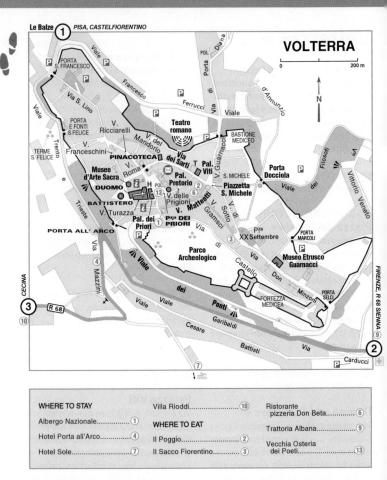

WHERE TO STAY	Villa Rioddi......................⑩	Ristorante pizzeria Don Beta..............⑥
Albergo Nazionale...............①	**WHERE TO EAT**	Trattoria Albana...................⑨
Hotel Porta all'Arco..............④	Il Poggio............................②	Vecchia Osteria dei Poeti............................⑬
Hotel Sole............................⑦	Il Sacco Fiorentino.............③	

Pinacoteca

Via dei Sarti 1, in the Palazzo Minucci-Solaini. ◷*Open mid-Mar–Nov daily 9am–7pm (1pm winter).* ◷*Closed 1 Jan, 25 Dec.* ⌾*€7, combined ticket with the Museo Etrusco Guarnacci.* ✆*0588 86 290. www.comune.volterra.pi.it.*
The **art gallery** has some interesing works of religious art by Tuscan masters of the 14C–17C – a *Madonna and Child* by Taddeo di Bartolo (c. 1362–1422); a superb Annunciation by Luca Signorelli (c. 1445–1523); a dramatic **Deposition from the Cross**★★ with stylised out-lines by Rosso Fiorentino (1495–1540); and a *Christ the Redeemer* by Domenico Ghirlandaio (1449–94).

▶ *Continue to Piazzetta San Michele.*

The Romanesque west front of the church of San Michele, which houses a *Madonna and Child* terracotta by Giovanni della Robbia, is flanked (*right*) by an unusual tower-house.

▶ *Walk down Via Guarnacci.*

Porta Fiorentina at the bottom of the street leads to the **Roman ruins** (*rovine romane*) which date from the 1C BC.

▶ *Return to Piazzetta San Michele and descend the long flight of steps in Via di Docciola.*

Porta di Docciola

The fortified gateway dates from the 13C. The Docciola Fountain was built in 1245.

▶ *Return up the steps to Piazzetta San Michele. Turn left into picturesque Via Matteotti and left again into Via Gramsci.*

The small church in Piazza XX Settembre contains a 16C terracotta *Assumption of the Virgin Mary* in the style of the della Robbias.

Museo Etrusco Guarnacci★

Via Don Minzoni 15. 🕐*Open mid-Mar–Nov daily 9am–7pm (2pm winter).* 🕐*Closed 1 Jan, 25 Dec.* 👓 *€7, combined ticket with the Pinacoteca.* ♿. *☎0588 86 347. www.comune.volterra.pi.it.*
The **Etruscan Museum** houses the **archaeological collection** and private library of Monsignor Mario Guarnacci, who bequeathed them to the town in 1761. His extensive collection includes Etruscan pieces ordered from the Vil-

lanovan period (8C BC) to the Hellenistic period (4C–1C BC), a time of extraordinary artistic creativity seen mainly in the tufa, alabaster and terracotta **cinerary urns**. Among the small bronze votive offerings is the famous **Ombra della sera** (*Evening Shadow*) (Room 22); it was named because of the elongated pose of the body.

Viale dei Ponti

This promenade provides superb **views**★★ over the Metalliferous Hills (✪*see COLLINE METALLIFERE*).
Above it is the Fortezza, an impressive piece of military architecture now used as a prison and consisting of the Rocca Vecchia (14C) and the Rocca Nuova built in 1472, which comprises a keep and four corner towers.

ADDRESSES

🛏 STAY

😊 **Hotel Sole** – *Via dei Cappuccini 10.* *☎0588 84 000. www.hotelsole volterra.it.* 🅿. *10 rooms.* 🍽. This family-run hotel, situated outside the walls, has large, very clean rooms. This is a good hotel for people touring by car and looking for somewhere quiet.

😊😊 **Villa Rioddi** – *Località Rioddi, 2km/1.2mi W of Volterra on S68.* *☎0588 88 053. www.hotelvillarioddi.it. Closed mid-Jan–early Mar and 10–30 Nov.* 🅿♿. *13 rooms.* 🍽. This refurbished 15C establishment has its own large garden and a panoramic view of the town and the Cecina Valley.

🍴 EAT

😊 **L'Incontro** – *Via Matteotti 18.* *☎0588 80 500. Closed Wed, 2nd week in Jan .* The panelled interior consists of a bar, where you can enjoy a wide range of home-made cakes, and another room where they serve cheese, sausages, soup, *bruschette* and wine by the glass.

😊 **Osteria di San Lorenzo** – *Via Massetana, loc. San Lorenzo, 5km/3mi SW of Volterra on S68 towards Saline di Volterra.* *☎0588 44 16 60. Closed Tue and 15 days in Jan.* Here, not far from Volterra, you can admire the lunar landscape of the old salt works.
The hostelry is open at midday and in the evenings and provides snacks at any hour.

🍸 TAKING A BREAK

Pizzicheria da Pina – *Via Gramsci 64.* *☎0588 87 394. Open 8am–8pm. Closed winter, Sun and Feb.* A well-kept, friendly establishment with a vaulted cellar where you can taste sausages and fine cheeses.

🛍 SHOPPING

Rossi – *Via del Mandorlo, 100m/110yds from Piazza dei Priori, towards Teatro Romano.* *☎0588 86 133. Open Mon–Fri 9.30am–1.15pm and 3pm–5pm, Sat 10am–12.30pm and 3pm–5pm, Sun 10am–12.30pm.* A workshop founded early in 20C with a well-established reputation for original creations and Etruscan reproductions, Rossi is now one of the best known craftsmen and his work is displayed in a small private museum.

AREZZO PROVINCE

Site of monasteries (at Camaldoli and Vallombrosa) as well as St. Francis' sanctuary at La Verna, the province of Arezzo presents a contemplative landscape of pine forests and seclusion dotted with parish churches (*pieve*). The area is better known, however, as being the home of Piero della Francesca. The early Renaissance artist was born in Sansepolcro, and his fresco cycle, "The Legend of the True Cross", considered one of the masterpieces of Renaissance painting, is in Arezzo's Basilica di San Francesco. Cortona, a charming hill town of medieval walls and Renaissance *palazzi* overlooking the Chiana Valley, lies south of Arezzo. It hosts the annual Tuscan Sun Festival, a major arts and music event spawned by the Frances Mayes bestseller.

Piazza Grande, Arezzo

Paolo Ghirotti/ Fototeca ENIT

Traversed by two major rivers – the Arno and the Tiber – Arezzo's province is one of lush valleys, in which grow olives, sugar beets, numerous grains and fields of sunflowers. Grapes, mostly of the Sangiovese variety, grow on the hills around the southern half of the province. Also in the south is the Val di Chiana, famous for its beef. In the north near the border with Emilia-Romagna is the heavily forested Casentino valley, home to the Camaldolese, Franciscan and the Vallombrosan religious orders.

The Etruscans were some of the first inhabitants here, with Arezzo (Arretium) and Cortona (Curtun) belonging to that civilisation's important League of Twelve Cities, or Dodecapolis. In Roman times, Arezzo was one of the largest cities in Italy, thanks to its production of Arretine pottery, highly prized throughout the Empire.

Arezzo, the capital, also flourished as a centre of art in the Middle Ages and Renaissance. Native son Giorgio Vasari constructed his *Logge* around the city's vast medieval Piazza Grande and also helped in the renovation of Santa Maria della Pieve. Meanwhile, Renaissance master Piero della Francesca's fresco cycle in the San Francesco Basilica, painted between 1452–1466, is the city's most popular attraction.

The Piero della Francesca trail continues in Sansepolcro, the artist's birthplace and site of his superb composition *Resurrection*.

Visitors who come to this less-travelled region of Tuscany will find proud medieval traditions, such as the Saracen Joust festival (Arezzo) and the Crossbow Tournament (Sansepolcro); and serene vistas, such as from Cortona's Piazza Garibaldi, and major works of art.

Good shopping can also be found here: a monthly antiques fair, one of Italy's oldest and largest, draws a large crowd of collectors to Arezzo's Piazza Grande.

Arezzo★★

As a supporter of the Ghibelline faction, Arezzo was involved in a long struggle against Guelf-leaning Florence before it merged with the latter larger town in 1384. During those days of conflict, Aretini built a large number of tower-houses, which now contribute to the picturesque aspect of the town.

A BIT OF HISTORY

After a period as one of the centres of Etruscan civilisation, Arretium became a prosperous Roman town famous for its production of "Aretine" vases. This type of pottery, invented by Aretine native Marcus Perennius, was made of very fine, reddish-brown, glazed clay. The major period of prosperity for this "industry" seems to have lasted for more than a century, between 30 BC and AD 40. Production spread from Arezzo to other towns in the peninsula and was exported throughout the Roman world from Gaul to Syria.

Long after the Roman period, the town was the birthplace of a number of major figures in the field of the arts: the Benedictine monk, **Guido of Arezzo** (c. 990–c. 1050), who was recognised as the in-ventor of a system of musical notation; the scholar and poet **Petrarch** (born 1304); the writer, **Pietro Aretino**, also known as **The Aretine** (born 1492); the painter and art historian, **Giorgio Vasari** (born 1511). The town owes it greatest claim to fame to **Piero della Francesca** (*see below*), who was born in Sansepolcro and produced most of his work in Arezzo.

FRESCOES
Piero della Francesca

Piero della Francesca (c. 1416–92), who divided his time mainly between his birthplace, Sansepolcro, the courts in Ferrara and Urbino, and Arezzo where he painted his masterpiece, was one of the most unusual and most outstanding representatives of the 15C, because of the austerity and powerful sincerity of his work. He was initially influenced

- ▶ **Population:** 91,729
- ⌚ **Michelin Map:** Michelin Atlas p 38 and Map 563 L 17 or Map 735 Fold 15.
- ℹ **Info:** Piazza della Repubblica 29; ℘0575 37 76 78. www.apt.arezzo.it.
- ◐ **Location:** Arezzo is 81km/50mi from Florence and 11km/7mi from the Florence-Rome motorway (autostrada Firenze–Roma). The old town is built in terraces on a hill crowned by a citadel. From the parapet walk of the citadel, there are a number of delightful views of the town and the surrounding countryside.
- ◎ **Don't Miss:** Piero della Francesco's frescoes in the church of San Francesco.

by the painters of the Sienese School and it was they who gave him his taste for harmonious colours and accurate drawing.

As a young man, he worked in Florence for more than five years with Domenico Veneziano, who taught him how to produce a soft, unreal light and use pale, light colours. During this period Masaccio taught him about perspective and its links with a rigorous form of geometry; Uccello gave him a feeling for volume in his paintings. It may have been his admiration for Flemish painting that led to his use of light and *chiaroscuro*, which give some of the details in his frescoes a strong resemblance to oil painting.

His statuesque, impassive figures have all the robustness and solidity of slow-moving peasant stock. His compositions are strongly structured and comply with geometric rules. When taken with his preference for soft colours, these characteristics produce an impression of balance and solemnity in his work. Piero spent almost all the last 20 years of his life writing two treatises, one on pictorial perspective and the other on the geometry of "pure forms".

Queen of Sheba before Solomon, detail of The Legend of the True Cross *by Piero della Francesca*

Frescoes ★★★ of San Francesco

The **frescoes**★★★ were painted by Piero della Francesca on the walls of the apse between 1452 and 1466 and are considered as one of the most outstanding examples of Renaissance painting in Tuscany. They illustrate the **Legend of the True Cross**, a common theme in Franciscan churches and friaries in the Middle Ages and were inspired by the 13C *Golden Legend* by Jacopo de Varagine.

The artist did not intend to follow the chronological order of the tale in any strict fashion. Instead, the work "reads" as follows:

I–Death of Adam (*right*) and his burial (*left*). Three seeds, from which will grow the Tree of the Cross, are being placed in his mouth by his son, Seth. The tree divides the scene in two.

II–Adoration of the sacred wood. The Queen of Sheba, having received a divine revelation, refuses to cross the bridge (*left*) which has been built with the sacred wood. After travelling to Jerusalem, she explains her vision to Solomon (*right*).

III–The sacred wood is moved and buried.

IV–The angel tells the

Virgin Mary of her Son's Crucifixion. This scene forms a central point in the story of the wood of the True Cross (before and after the Crucifixion) without depicting the central episode in the story.

V–On the eve of his battle with Maxentius who is disputing his claim to the imperial crown, Constantine (later to be the first Christian emperor) is advised by an angel in a dream to fight under the sign of the Cross. This is the first example of the use of chiaroscuro in Italian art.

VI–Constantine, brandishing the Cross, has defeated Maxentius at the Milvian Bridge (AD 312).

VII–The torture of the Jew. St Helena, Constantine's mother, while trying to trace the wood from the True Cross in Jerusalem, was told that only one Jew knew where the relic had been buried. As the man refused to speak, Helena had him dropped down a well where he remained for six days before agreeing to her request.

VIII–Empress Helena, aided by Judas, has the three Crosses excavated outside the walls of Jerusalem, which the artist depicts as an exotic version of Arezzo. The resurrection of a dead man (*right*) shows her which one was the Cross of Christ.

IX–Three hundred years later, Heraclius defeated the Persian King, Chosroes, who had stolen the Cross to decorate his throne.

X–Exaltation of the Cross, which is re-turned to Jerusalem by Heraclius.

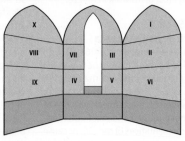

SAN FRANCESCO

Piazza San Francesco (at Via Cavour).
Open by appointment only Mon–Fri
9am–6.30pm (5.30pm winter), Sat
9am–5.30pm (5pm winter), Sun and
Hols 1-5.30pm (5pm, winter). Closed
13 Jun, 4 Oct. €4 + €1 booking fee.
*Contact the ticket office for a booking
number.* 0575 90 04 04 or 06 32 810;
www.pierodellafrancesca.it .

This is a vast **church**, designed for the
preaching of sermons and built in the
Gothic style in the 14C for the Franciscan
Order. It was altered in the 17C and 18C
but restoration work has now returned
it to its original austerity. The Franciscan
monks, as keepers of the Holy Places,
showed particular devotion to the True
Cross. They commissioned Piero della
Francesca to decorate the chancel of
the church.

Other Works of Art★ – Ancient frescoes
decorate the other walls – (*south wall*) an
Annunciation by Spinello Aretino (early
15C); (*south apsidal chapel*) the **Assumption Triptych** painted by Nicolo di Pietro Gerini in the early 15C; (*in front of the
main chapel*) a huge **Crucifix** painted on
wood, dating from the late 13C.
The oculus (*west wall*) is filled with a
superb stained-glass window, bearing
the coat of arms of the Berry region with
its fleur-de-lis, in which the artist, Guillaume de Marcillat, depicted St Francis
giving roses to Pope Honorius III, in the
middle of the month of January.

WALKING TOUR

Piazza Grande★

The **main square** is surrounded by
medieval houses, the Romanesque gal-
leried apse of Santa Maria della Pieve
(parish church), the late 18C Law Courts,
the part-Gothic part-Renaissance Palazzo della Fraternita and the 16C galleries (*Logge*), designed by Vasari.

Santa Maria della Pieve★

This superb Romanesque parish **church**
is crowned by a haughty campanile,
which, owing to its numerous double
bays (there are 40 of them in all), is called
the "One Hundred Holes". Construction
of the church began in the mid-12C and
was completed in the 14C. In the 16C
alterations were made, notably under
the direction of **Giorgio Vasari**. The
façade★★, which was inspired by the
Romanesque style used in Pisa, is very
ornate with three tiers of arcades supported by colonnettes, decorated with
a variety of motifs. The upper coving of
the central doorway is decorated with
witty representations of the 12 symbols
of the zodiac.
The interior includes a half-rounded
apse and a raised chancel in which the
pillars are decorated with capitals carved
with large human heads. Among the
works of art are two marble low reliefs
– *Epiphany*, of Byzantine origin (*rear of
the façade*) and *Nativity*, dating from the
13C (*wall in the north aisle*).

The Legend of the True Cross

This legend tells the story of the Cross on which Christ was crucified.

The legend starts with the death of Adam who, as he was dying, asked his
son Seth for holy oil. Seth is said to have placed three seeds from the Tree of
Knowledge under Adam's tongue. After Adam's death these seeds grew into the
tree cut down for the Cross on which Christ, the new Adam, was crucified.

The tree was then used to build a bridge, the holy significance of which was
recognised by the Queen of Sheba. She told Solomon of her prophecy that the
wood from the bridge would bring disgrace to the people of Israel. Solomon
ordered that the bridge be buried.

The legend goes on to recount how the three Crosses from Calvary were later
discovered by Helena, the mother of Emperor Constantine. The resurrection of a
dead man showed her which of the three was the Cross of Christ.

Stolen by the Persian King, Chosroes, the Cross was later retrieved by Heraclius,
who returned it to Jerusalem.

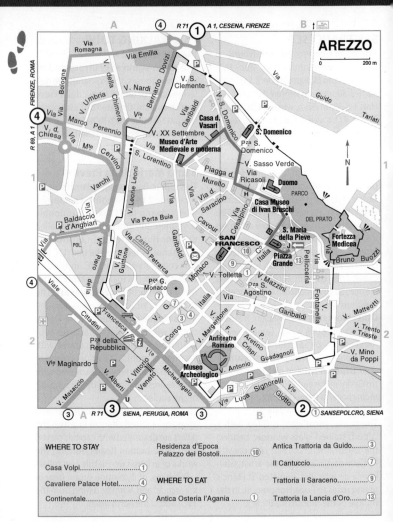

AREZZO

0 200 m

The High Altar includes a superb polyptych (1320–24) by Pietro Lorenzetti from Siena.

Via dei Pileati

This **street**, which runs along the façade of Santa Maria della Pieve, is a strange sight with its palaces, Gothic towers and old houses. On one corner overlooking a crossroads is the Palazzo Pretorio (14C–15C) covered with coats of arms of the magistrate (*podestà*).

Duomo

The **cathedral**, built from 1278 to 1511, has a neo-Gothic façade. On the south side is an attractive Romanesque-Gothic portal dating from the first half of the 14C. The cathedral contains some fine **works of art**★ including (*middle of the south aisle*) stained-glass windows by Marcillat; (*north aisle*) the tomb of Bishop Guido Tarlati and (*near the vestry*) the fresco by Piero della Francesca depicting *Mary Magdalen*; and (*behind the High Altar*) the 13C tomb of St Donatus.

▶ *Take Via Ricasoli and turn into Via Sasso Verde.*

San Domenico

This **church**, built in the Gothic style in the 13C, has an asymmetrical façade. It contains frescoes by the Duccio School, and by Spinello Aretino and his school. On the High Altar, there is an admirable **crucifix**★★ by Cimabue.

▷ *From Via S Domenico, turn left on Via XX Settembre.*

Casa del Vasari (Vasari's House)

🕐*Open Wed–Sat and Sun afternoon 8.30am–7.30pm (7pm last admission).* 🕐*Closed 1 May, 25 Dec, 1 Jan.* 📞*0575 40 90 40.*

The residence was luxuriously decorated in 1540 by **Giorgio Vasari** – painter, sculptor, architect and writer – whose multiplicity of talents made him a typical Renaissance Man. The house contains works by Tuscan Mannerist painters and a terracotta by Andrea Sansovino.

▷ *Via XX Settembre to Via S Lorentino.*

Museo Statale d'Arte Medievale e Moderna★

🕐*Open Tue–Sun 8.30am–7.30pm.* 🕐*Closed 1 May, 25 Dec, 1 Jan.* €4. 📞*0575 40 90 50.*

The **museum of medieval and modern art** is housed in the fully-furnished Palazzo Bruni-Ciocchi. It contains sculptures, gold and silverware and numerous paintings dating from the Middle Ages to the 19C. Early works include art by Luca Signorelli, Andrea della Robbia and Vasari. The 19C is represented by some of the main *Macchiaioli* artists such as Fattori and Signorini. The extensive range of exhibits also includes an outstanding collection of Renaissance **majolicaware**★★ from Umbria, 17C and 18C ceramics, glassware, weaponry, ivories and a large collection of coins.

VISIT

Museo Archeologico

Via Margaritone 10. 🕐*Open daily 8.30am–7.30 (7pm last admission).* 🕐*Closed 1 May, 25 Dec, 1 Jan.* €4. ♿. 📞*0575 20 882.* *www.archeologia.beniculturali. it/pages/atlante/S49.html.*

The **archaeological museum** stands adjacent to the oval **Roman amphitheatre** which dates from the 1C and 2C. It contains interesting collections of Etruscan and Roman bronze statuettes (from 6C BC to 3C AD), Greek vases (Euphronios' krater), Aretine vases andHellenistic and Roman ceramics.

Santa Maria delle Grazie

1km/0.6mi S by Viale Mecenate. This mid-15C **church** is preceded by a graceful, ethereal **portico**★ designed by Benedetto da Maiano (15C) from Florence. Inside, is a marble **reredos**★ by Andrea della Robbia framing a painting by Parri di Spinello (*Virgin Mary of Pity*).

ADDRESSES

🛏 STAY

🍽 **Casa Volpi** – *Via Simone Martini, 1.5 km SE of Arezzo towards Sansepolcro.* 📞*0575 35 43 64. www.casavolpi.it. Closed 1–15 Aug. 12 rooms. 🍴. Restaurant* 🍽. Set in a large peaceful park near the city gates, this 19C country home is elegantly decorated with beamed ceilings and frescoes. The superb terrace has a panoramic view of Arezzo.

🍽 **Badia di Pomaio** – *Località Badia di Pomaio, 4km/2.5mi on Via Guido Tarlati.* 📞*0575 37 14 07. www.badiadi-pomaio.it. 17 rooms.* 🅿 *Restaurant* 🍽. From the gardens and pool, you can enjoy a lovely view of Arezzo and its environs; indoors, every room has been renovated, taking great care to preserve the original style of the 16C abbey. The restaurant, located in the old wine cellars, offers a menu based on traditional regional fare.

🍽 **Cavaliere Palace Hotel** – *V. Madonna del Prato 83.* 📞*0575 26 836. Fax 0575 21 925. www.cavalierehotels. com. 27 rooms.* 🖥 🅿 *paid parking.* In the heart of the old city, this hotel has all the charm of an old inn, often at a discount rate.

⊜⊜🍽 **Hotel Continentale** – *P.za Guido Monaco 7.* ℘*0575 20 251. Fax 0575 35 04 85. www.hotelcontinentale.com. 76 rooms.* 🖥 🅿 *paid parking.*
This modern hotel in the city centre offers good quality for the price. Spacious rooms, including three suites.

♉ EAT

⊜⊜ **Antica Osteria l'Agania** –*Via Mazzini 10.* ℘*0575 29 53 81. Closed Mon.*
Near the Piero della Francesca frescoes, this modest family-style restaurant serves typical local dishes with Tuscan wines.

⊜⊜ **Il Cantuccio** – *V. Madonna del Prato 76, p.za Guido.* ℘*0575 26 830. Closed Wed.* 🖥. In this trattoria, you can sample traditional dishes in the vaulted dining hall.

⊜⊜🍽 **La Lancia d'Oro** – *P.za Grande 18-19.* ℘*0575 21 033. www.loggevasari.it. Closed 5–25 Nov, Sun in Jul-Aug, Mon rest of the year.* Located under the *logge* built by Vasari, this trattoria is especially pleasant in the summer, when one can dine at one of the outdoor tables.Typical Tuscan cuisine.

⊜⊜🍽 **Trattoria il Saraceno** – *Via Mazzini 6/a.* ℘*0575 27 644. Closed Wed, 7–25 Jan, 7–28 Jul .* This pleasant family restaurant offers authentic local dishes with plenty of good wine. There is also a good selection of pizzas cooked in a wood-burning oven.

🍴 TAKING A BREAK

Piazza Grande – Most of the antique shops are situated at the top of the town and particularly in this sunny square. To recover from the climb, take a break in the **Café Vasari** under the arches built by the great architect.

Caffè dei Costanti – *Piazza San Francesco 19/20.* ℘*0575 21 660. Open Tue–Sun 7am–midnight (7.30pm winter).* This popular café and cocktail bar, which opened in 1804, was immortalised by Benigni in his film *La vita è bella.*

Carraturo – *Corso Italia 61.* ℘*0575 35 57 57. Open Wed–Mon 7.30am–1am (7.30pm winter).* This tea room/bar offers aperitifs and magnificent cocktails. The 19C ambience is lively and full of good humour.

🎭 EVENTS AND FESTIVALS

Piazza Grande is the setting for the **Saracen Joust** (*Giostra del Saracino*) in which the best horsemen in Arezzo tilt with lances at a representation of a Saracen, accompanied by a huge procession of people dressed in 14C and 15C costume (*last Sunday in August and first Sunday in September*).

Arezzo's **Antiques Fair** takes place on the 1st Sunday and preceding Saturday of each month.

Anghiari

In 1440 a battle between the troops of Florence and Milan was fought on the wide Tiber Plain between Anghiari and Sansepolcro. As the latter were beaten, the town surrendered to Florence. Leonardo da Vinci memorialised the Battle of Anghiari in a commissioned work in the Hall of the Five Hundred in the Palazzo Vecchio (City Hall) in Florence.
The town occupies a picturesque site★ on the top of a hill; its narrow, winding, irregular streets running up and down the hillside, preserve their medieval charm.

▸ **Population:** 5,908
🕭 **Michelin Map:** Michelin Atlas p 38 and Map 563 – L 18 and Map 735 Fold 15.
🚩 **Info:** Via Matteotti 103; ℘0575 74 92 79. www.anghiari.it.
▶ **Location:** Anghiari is 8km/5mi from Sansepolcro.

TOWN
Perched on a hill overlooking the Tiber Valley, the walled city of Anghiari has a compact historic centre, most of which lies southwest of Corso Matteotti.

Museo Statale
di Palazzo Taglieschi★

Halfway along Via Garibaldi in a tiny triangular square. ◷*Open summer Tue–Sun 9am (11am Sun and Hols) to 7pm, winter 9am–7pm (1pm Sun and Hols).* ◷*Closed 1 May, 25 Dec, 1 Jan.* ⟁€2. ℘0575 78 80 01.

The **museum** housed in the 15C Taglieschi Palazzo contains mainly works of art and exhibits relating to popular traditions in the Upper Tiber Valley connected with aspects of domestic or religious life and farm work. There are pieces of Romanesque and Gothic architecture, fragments of frescoes, furniture, 15C and 16C paintings, and Renaissance sculptures including a superb painted *Madonna* by Jacopo della Quercia and a *Nativity* by the della Robbia school.

▷ *A few yards farther along Via Garibaldi, turn right and then left. In the square stands the town hall, easily recognisable by its many shields. Take the narrow street opposite leading to another small square.*

Chiesa di Badi★

This much-altered **church** dates from the Romanesque period. Its interior layout is unusual and asymmetrical. The decorative elements on one of the altars (*second to the left*), a fine example of Renaissance *pietra serena*, are said to be the work of Desiderio da Settignano.

Camaldoli★★

St Romuald chose this area, among the moutains of the vast Casentino Forest, as the location for the headquarters of the Camaldolese religious order in the 11C. It is comprised of a monastery, where communal life took place, and the hermitage, where the select group of reclusive monks lived. As a result, the two different aspects of the monk's life are harmoniously reflected in the architecture.

VISIT
Convento★

The **monastery** is impressively situated at the end of a dark valley flanked by slopes covered with pine trees.

Within the section that has been converted into accommodation, one may see an 11C portico in the courtyard and small 15C cloisters leading to a number of rooms and chapels.

The left-hand entrance in the façade opens into the 16C church. The Baroque interior includes several paintings by Vasari including a Deposition above the high altar. The monks' quarters are on the upper floor.

Round to the left of the building is the 15C **pharmacy**★★. Its origins can be

⚆ **Michelin Map:** Michelin Atlas p 38 and Map 563 – K 17 and Map 735 Fold 15 – Alt 816m/2 652ft.

▤ **Info:** www.camaldoli.it.

▷ **Location:** Camaldoli is 18km/11mi NE of Poppi, midway between Arezzo and Florence. The winding **road**★★ from Poppi (*18km/ 11mi*) provides views over the town, the castle and the Arno Valley before climbing the slopes of a small valley and passing through the forest.

traced to the 11C when the monks, having built a hospital, began to care for and treat the sick free of charge. Their hospital continued to function until the beginning of the 19C.

Eremo★★

Alt 1 027m/3 338ft.

The **Hermitage** is a veritable monastic village, consisting of some 20 small houses built between the 13C and 17C and enclosed by a wall. In front of the Hermitage are a few buildings open to the public. On the right of the inner courtyard is the superb 18C **church** with two bell towers and a façade decorated with statues. At the entrance is a fine low relief by Mino da Fiesole. The interior is decorated in the Neapolitan Baroque style, with a mixture of stuccowork, gold leaf, marble, paintings, wood carvings and statues, together with a number of older works. In St Anthony's Chapel (*left of the entrance to the rear*) there is a glazed earthenware figure (15C) by Andrea della Robbia. The apse is flanked by two marble **tabernacles**★★ (15C) by Desiderio da Settignano; the *Crucifixion* is attributed to Bronzino. Opposite the church is the tiny garden and St Romuald's cell, a small apartment with dark wainscoting laid out like the other monks' lodgings with a living room where the monk lived, slept and worked, a private chapel, a woodshed, a washing area and a store-room off a single corridor.

ADDRESSES

🛏 STAY

⊖ **Foresteria del Monastero di Camaldoli** – *Via Camaldoli.* ℘*0575 55 60 13. www.camaldoli.it.* 🖼 🛏. "Hospitality plays a central role in the Benedictine tradition" states a leaflet on the hermitage and monastery at Camaldoli. A stay here is for those interested in courses at the monastery (meditation, Hebrew) or in spending time on a personal retreat.

🍴 EAT

⊜⊜ **Il Cedro** – *Via di Camaldoli 20, 52010 Moggiona, 5km/3mi SW of Camaldoli.* ℘*0575 55 60 80. Closed Mon (except Jul–Aug), 25 Dec, 1 Jan.* 🖼. In the village, not far from the Camaldoli Monastery, sits this excellent provincial restaurant, simply furnished and family-run; the cooking is regional supplemented with mushrooms and truffles in season.

Castiglion Fiorentino

and Castello di Montecchio

Once the site of an Etruscan settlement, the town's first stronghold ("castiglion"), was built on the hilltop during the Barbarian invasions in the 5C. It was replaced in the 11C–12C by a citadel ("cassero") dominated by a slender tower.

TOWN

The streets of Castiglion radiate downhill from Piazzale del Cassero, location of the Pinacoteca. The Collegiata di San Giuliano lies at the eastern edge.

Pinacoteca★

Take the street to the right that climbs up behind the town hall. ⏱*Open Apr–Sept Tue–Sun 10am–12.30pm and 4pm–6.30pm; Oct–Mar 10am–12.30pm and 3.30pm–6pm.* ⏱*Closed 15 Aug, 25 Dec, 1 Jan.* ⊜*€2.50.* ℘*0575 65 74 66. http://musei.provincia.ar.it.*

▸ **Population:** 11,644
🈺 **Michelin Map:** Michelin Atlas p 44 and Map 563 – L17 and Map 735 Fold 15.
🈁 **Info:** Piazza Municipio 12. ℘0575 65 82 78. www.comune.castiglion fiorentino.ar.it.
◐ **Location:** Castiglion Fiorentino is 17 km/11mi S of Arezzo on S 71.

The **art gallery**, which is housed in the Chapel of Sant'Angelo next to the citadel, contains a number of valuable paintings, including two Umbrian Crucifixion scenes painted on wood and dating from the 13C and 14C, a painting of *St Francis of Assisi* by Margaritone of Arezzo (13C), a *Virgin Mary in Majesty* (14C) by Taddeo Gaddi and two reredos panels by Giovanni di Paolo (15C). There are also some superb pieces of church plate, including a bust-reliquary of St Ursula (14C Rhenish School), a Crucifix-reliquary from the Moselle (late 12C) and a French Crucifix dating from the second half of the 13C.

From the top room (*saletta della Torre*), there is a wonderful view of the Church of San Giuliano, the countryside and the mountains.

Collegiata di San Giuliano

This **church** contains a 17C carved wooden presbytery and a number of interesting works of art, including a painted earthenware *St Anthony Abbot* and an *Annunciation* from the della Robbia workshop, a *Virgin Mary in Majesty* by Bartolomeo della Gatta and *Mary and Joseph Adoring the Infant Jesus* by Lorenzo di Credi (15C).

The 16C **Chiesa del Gesù** (Church of Jesus) close to the collegiata has a fine Baroque interior.

Chiostro di San Francesco

These small **cloisters**, next to the uninspiring 13C Church of St Francis, were rebuilt in the 17C with an upper storey that forms a balcony with colonnettes. The cloisters are decorated with a series of frescoes (*in poor condition*) depicting the life of St Francis of Assisi.

EXCURSION
Castello di Montecchio★
3.5km/2mi S by S 71.

The **castle** stands on a rise on the east side of the road between Castiglion Fiorentino and Cortona. It is interesting for the size of its crenellated outer wall reinforced by eight small towers and for its keep (*30m/97ft*), which contained the main apartments. This was the largest fortress in the Chiana Valley, retaining its military importance until the 17C.

Chiesa di Gropina★

The church of San Pietro in Gropina dates from the first half of the 12C and is considered to be the first example of a Romanesque church in Tuscany. It stands on the lower slopes of the Pratomagno, slightly above the Arno Valley.

VISIT

Open daily 8am–noon and 3pm-5pm.
The **interior** is laid out in three aisles. The semicircular central apse has an external gallery with colonnettes; the central colonnettes are interconnected. The richly **carved decoration★** inside the church is unequalled anywhere else in Casentino. The capitals and ambo in the south aisle (the first to be completed) date from the second half of the 12C and are carved in an early Romanesque style still using flattened sculpture. The capitals in the north aisle are more highly sophisticated and are thought to be the work of Emilian workshops. The most interesting designs are: (*south side, starting from the entrance*

- **Michelin Map:** Michelin Atlas p 38 and Map 563 – L 16 and Map 735.
- **Location:** Gropina Church is located between Florence and Arezzo, 1.8km/1mi SE of Loro Ciuffenna (*signposted – S Giustino Valdarno*); after 1.2km/0.5mi turn right.

pillar) the sow, a symbol of the Church, suckling her litter; the knights-in-arms fighting the demon; the highly stylised vine stocks; the eagles crowning the ambo which is carved both in flattened relief and in the round; (*north side, third column*) the figures of Christ, St Peter and St Paul, Samson killing the lion, and St Ambrose presenting the new Law; (*fourth column*) the punishment of lust: a man being dragged by his beard and three women whose breasts are being bitten by dragons.

Below the church are remains from two previous churches dating from the 5C and the 8C; both can be visited via the stairs on the right aisle.

Cortona★★

Cortona occupies a remarkable site★★ on the steep slope overlooking the Chiana Valley. The town used to belong to the League of Twelve Etruscan Towns before coming under the control of Rome. It has retained its medieval town walls, commanded by a huge citadel (*fortezza*) that replaced the Etruscan precinct. Annexed to Florence in 1411, Cortona has barely changed since the Renaissance period, when some fine mansions (*palazzi*) and narrow, paved streets, mostly very steep, leading to irregularly shaped squares lined with arcades and public buildings.

ᴥ WALKING TOUR

Piazza Garibaldi

From the **square** there is a **view**★★ (*south*) to Lake Trasimeno and (*southwest*) over the Chiana Valley to Montepulciano. Continue along the pleasant **Via Nazionale**. This shopping street is lined with picturesque alleys. From **Vicolo Vagnucci** there is a delightful view of the countryside below.

Palazzo Comunale

The **town hall** building dates from the 13C but was completed in the 16C with a bell tower and a huge flight of steps

Narrow street in Cortona

Brigitta L. House/ MICHELIN

> **Population:** 22,436
> **Michelin Map:** Michelin Atlas p 44 and Map 563 – M 17 AND Map 735 Fold 15.
> **Info:** Via Nazionale 42; ℘0575 63 03 52. www.comunedicortona.it.
> **Location:** Cortona is just off S71 between Arezzo and Lake Trasimeno.
> **Don't Miss:** The views of the Chiana Valley and the Museo Diocesano.

leading up from Piazza della Repubblica. The **Sala del Consiglio**★ (Council Chamber) overlooks Piazza Signorelli, the site of the original town hall. The medieval character of the building is evident in the richly painted ceiling subdivided by wooden beams and the stone walls, one of which is decorated with a huge fresco. (◷*Open Mon–Sat 8am–1.30pm.* ◷*Closed 22 Feb and Hols.* ℘*0575 60 47 44*).

Palazzo Pretorio★

This 13C building is also known as Palazzo Casali in memory of its former owners who were the lords of the town. The frontage facing Piazza Signorelli dates from the early 17C but the right-hand wall decorated with the coats of arms of magistrates (*podeste*) is Gothic in origin. It houses the Museo dell'Accademia Etrusca (ℰ*see p262*).

▷ *Make a detour along Via Guelfa.*

The headquarters (*40 Via Guelfa*) of the **Centro Convegni S**. **Agostino** has a beautiful cloister. Each arch contains a fresco illustrating an episode in the life of St Augustine.

▷ *Return to Piazza della Repubblica and walk towards the cathedral.*

Piazza del Duomo

The **square** abutting the town walls provides an attractive view of the valley and the cemetery. The **cathedral** was origi-

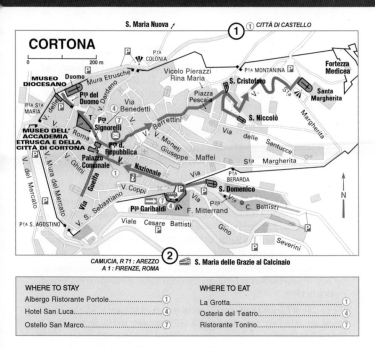

CORTONA

S. Maria delle Grazie al Calcinaio

WHERE TO STAY	
Albergo Ristorante Portole	①
Hotel San Luca	④
Ostello San Marco	⑦

WHERE TO EAT	
La Grotta	①
Osteria del Teatro	④
Ristorante Tonino	⑦

nally built in the Romanesque period, but was altered in the Renaissance.

San Cristoforo

This small, elongated **church**, which is said to date from the late 12C, is surmounted by a bellcote. The sacristy serves as the entrance. Inside there is a 14C fresco of the *Crucifixion*, the *Annunciation* and the *Ascension*.

San Niccolò

An elegant porch extends across the façade and down one side of the 15C **church**. The Baroque interior includes two works by Luca Signorelli: (*left of the entrance*) a fresco of the *Virgin Mary surrounded by the Saints* and (*on the High Altar*) the **Deposition of Christ**★.

Santuario di Santa Margherita

The **church**, which stands above the town, was built in the 19C, but the bell tower dates from the 17C. The interior contains (*left of the chancel*) the Gothic **tomb**★ of the saint (1362); the saint's body lies on view at the high altar; (*right of the chancel*) a moving representation of the *Crucifixion* (13C). From the esplanade there are some attractive

views★ of the town, the valley below and Lake Trasimeno. To the right of the terrace in front of the church is Via Santa Margharita decorated by Severini with mosaics representing the **Stations of the Cross**.

San Domenico

This early 15C Gothic **church** contains a *Madonna with Angels and Saints* by Luca Signorelli and a fresco by Fra Angelico of the *Madonna and Child between two Dominican Friars*. From the promenade opposite the church there are delightful views of Lake Trasimeno.

VISIT

Museo Diocesano★★

🕐*Open Tue–Sun 9.30am (10am Oct–Mar) to 1pm and 3.30 (3pm Nov–Mar) to 7pm (6pm Oct; 5pm Nov–Mar).* ⊕€4. 🕿*0575 62 830.*

Opposite the cathedral in the Chiesa del Gesù (Church of Jesus), which has a superb carved ceiling dating from 1536, are housed valuable collections of the **Diocesan Museum**.

Fra Angelico, who came to Cortona to paint, is represented by two of his best works – an **Annunciation**, very

261

Art in Cortona

Cortona began to attract artists in the 14C and the Sienese School proceeded to predominate until the arrival of Fra Angelico. The town's main claim to fame, however, is as the birthplace of a number of famous Old Masters. **Luca Signorelli** (1450–1523) was a painter who, through his dramatic temperament and sculpture-like forms, was a precursor of Michelangelo. He died when he fell from the scaffolding as he painted frescoes in the Villa Passerini (*east of Cortona*).

Among architects the most famous name is that of Domenico Bernabei (1508–49), known as **Boccador** (literally "Mouth of Gold"), who worked principally in France; at the age of 25 he was invited by King François I to Paris where he worked from 1533 to 1549 on the design of the City Hall.

Pietro da Cortona (1596–1669), painter and architect, was one of the great masters of the Roman Baroque style. He had a prodigious imagination and was a genius in interior decoration. His main works include the decoration of the Pitti Palace in Florence and the Barberini Palace in Rome and the façade of the Church of Santa Maria della Pace in Rome.

The painter **Gino Severini** (1883–1966) was born in Cortona and became one of the best representatives of Futurism, the great Italian avant-garde movement created in 1909.

The people of Cortona have a very special regard for St Francis, who set up a hermitage at Le Celle; for St Margaret, a 13C Magdalen; and for Brother Elias, St Francis' first friend and follower, who supervised the construction of the basilica in Assisi and is buried in Cortona, beneath the chancel in the church of San Francesco.

delicate, where the attention is drawn to the exchange of looks between the angel, conveying the will of God, and the Virgin Mary, exhibiting total submission; a **Madonna** surrounded by the Saints, which is more interesting for the tenderness on Mary's face than for the liveliness of the scenes from the life of St Dominic on the predella.

There are a number of superb paintings by the Sienese School – a *Madonna* by Duccio, a *Madonna with the Angels* and a huge *Crucifixion* by Pietro Lorenzetti (late 14C) and a triptych of the *Madonna and Child* (1434) (*restored*) by Sassetta. The museum also houses a carefully selected collection of works by the local painter Luca Signorelli, of which the best are the *Communion of the Apostles* and the *Deposition* in which the horror is heightened by the gentle landscape.

Among the sculptures is a fine 2C Roman sarcophagus with low reliefs (Lapiths and Centaurs). The former vestry displays church plate, including the Vagnucci reliquary made by Giusto da Firenze (1458).

The small lower church is covered in 16C frescoes based on designs by Vasari; it also contains an expressive painted terracotta *Pietà* dating from the same period.

Museo dell'Accademia Etrusca★

Open Apr–Oct Tue–Sun 10am–7pm (5pm Nov–Mar). Closed 25 Dec, 1 Jan. €4. 0575 63 72 35; www.accademia-etrusca.net.

The main central hall of the **museum** contains the most important exhibits, including an Etruscan bronze **oil lamp★★** (second half of the 4C BC). There is also a collection of bronze Etruscan and Roman statuettes, ceramics, and 15C Italian ivories. Among the paintings are works by Signorelli and his followers, a superb *Miracle of St Benedict* by Andrea Commodi (17C), a *Madonna* by Pinturicchio and a huge *Virgin and Child with Saints* by Pietro da Cortona (17C). The smaller rooms display an Egyptian collection, 14C paintings, a lapidary collection dating from Antiquity and funeral urns. The Severini Room contains the works donated to the town by this artist, including *The Gypsy Woman* (1905) and **Motherhood**★ (1906).

EXCURSIONS
Santa Maria del Calcinaio★★
3km/2mi S of Cortona by exit (2).
This church was built between 1485 and 1513 in the style of Brunelleschi, to designs by Francesco di Giorgio Martini of Siena. It is constructed of a dark-coloured stone and is admirable for the elegance and coherence of its overall design and its well-balanced proportions. The oculus in the façade contains an outstanding stained-glass window (1516) by Guillaume de Marcillat depicting the *Madonna of Mercy*.

Tanella di Pitagora
3km/2mi S of Cortona by exit (2); at the left-hand hairpin bend, continue straight on towards Arezzo.
The circular Etruscan **tomb**, which dates from the 4C BC, stands in a delightful setting surrounded by cypress trees. It is called the tomb of Pythagoras because of an age-old confusion between Cortona and Crotona; Pythagoras the mathematician lived in Crotona.

Le Celle
3.5km/2mi E of Cortona by exit (1); after 1.5km/1mi, at a right-hand bend, turn left into a narrow road.
On his return from Rome, after the Pope had officially recognised the Franciscan Order (1210), **St Francis** came to Cortona. He withdrew to Le Celle where he founded his first community. He chose this spot for its natural silence and austerity.

The **monastery** is occupied by Capuchins and retains the original chapel used by St Francis' first companions. Behind the altar is the tiny cell used by St Francis himself, to which he returned after receiving the stigmata in La Verna.

Abbazia di Farneta
15.5km/10mi SW of Cortona by exit S.
⏰*Open daily 9am–dusk. Museo archeologico-paleontologico by appointment only.* ✎*Donation welcome.* 📞*0575 61 00 10 (Monsignore Sante Felici).*
This austere T-shaped **church** was built by the Benedictines on the site of a Roman temple. The most interesting feature is the **crypt** (9C–10C), which has ribbed barrel vaulting and three multifoiled apsidal chapels supported by Roman columns from a variety of sources.
Since 1937, the abbey has been closely linked with the extraordinary personality of Don Sante Felici, a committed archaeologist with Tuscan roots who discovered the crypt, as well as numerous archaeological remains and fossils found at Farneta and the surrounding area, some of which can be seen in his **Museo-Antiquarium** (Archaeological and Palaeontological Museum).

ADDRESSES

🛏 STAY
🍽 **Ostello S. Marco** – *V. Maffei 57. 📞0575 60 13 92. Fax 0575 60 13 92. www.cortonahostel.com. Closed mid-Oct –mid-Mar.* 🍴. *80 beds.* With a young, international clientele, this is one of the most popular hostels in Tuscany. All essential comforts provided.

🍽🍽 **Albergo Ristorante Portole** – *V. Umbro Cortonese 36, 7km/4.3mi above Cortona in the direction of Città di Castello.* *📞0575 69 10 08. Fax 0575 69 10 35. www. portole. it. 20 rooms. Restaurant* 🍽🍽. 🅿. At 850m/2,788ft above sea level in a traditional Tuscan stone building, this hotel has comfortable rooms and splendid views over the Chiana Valley, Lake Trasimeno and Mount Amiata.

🍽🍽/🍽🍽🍽 **Hotel San Luca** – *P.za Garibaldi 1. 📞0575 63 04 60. Fax 0575 63 01 05. www.sanlucacortona.com. 60 rooms.* 🍽. In Cortona's historic centre, this is a modern hotel with an elegant interior. Rooms on the 4th and 5th floors offer the best views.

ⴾ EAT

☻☻ **La Grotta** – *Piazzetta Baldelli 3.* *🖉575 63 02 71. Closed Tue and Jan.* This small family-run trattoria serves local dishes. Its happy location, just off the main square in the pedestrian zone, makes it particularly attractive in the season.

☻☻ **Osteria del Teatro** – *Via Maffei 5.* *🖉0575 63 05 56. www.osteria-del-teatro.it. Closed Wed and 15 days in Nov. Reservations required.* There is a friendly atmosphere in this little restaurant, where the chefs emerge from time to time to serve their traditional tasty dishes.

🍴 TAKING A BREAK

Caffè degli Artisti – *Via Nazionale 18.* *🖉0575 60 12 37. Open 7am–2am. Closed Thu and Nov.* The secret of this café's success is good humour, the family atmosphere and the house cocktails!

La Saletta – *Via Nazionale 26/28.* *🖉575 60 33 66. www.caffelasaletta.it. Open May–Oct; closed Wed, Nov–Apr.* On Saturdays this comfortable and elegant wine bar puts on concerts of jazz and blues or classical guitar. A good place for a pleasant evening of music and wine.

Pasticceria Banchelli – *Via Nazionale 64. 🖉0575 60 31 78. www.banchelli.com. Open 7am–midnight (9pm winter).* This pastry shop is as well known for its gingerbread and Etruscan biscuits as for its home-made ices.

Tonino – *Piazza Garibaldi 1. 🖉0575 63 05 00. Open 12.30pm–2.30pm and 7.30pm–9.30pm.* At the end of the main street you will find a hotel-restaurant which, in between meal times, opens to non-residents its splendid terrace, overlooking the valley as far as Lake Trasimeno – a good opportunity for a photograph!

Lucignano

Lucignano is a peaceful village in the Val di Chiana. It has an unusual elongated shape as the main street rises in spirals before entering a picturesque maze of medieval streets.

VILLAGE

Backing onto the town walls are the remains of the 14C **castle** (*cassero*). Opposite stands the **collegiate church of San Michele** built in the late 16C. In front of the church is a beautifully designed staircase (in a poor state of repair). It is concave then convex in shape and set around an oval stairhead. Inside the church, the barrel vaulting is highlighted by the *pietra serena* of the pillars and arches. The monumental Baroque altar was designed by Andrea Pozzo.

The street running along the left side of the church leads to Piazza del Tribunale; at one end stands the small **Palazzo Comunale** decorated with coats of arms. The **museum** (☉*open summer Tue–Sun 10am–1pm and 2.30pm–6pm; rest of the*

▶ **Population:** 3,442
🜚 **Michelin Map:** Michelin Atlas p 44 and Map 563 – M 17 and Map 735 Fold 15.
🅘 **Info:** Piazza del Tribunale. 🖉0575 65 82 78. www. comune.lucignano.ar.it.
▶ **Location:** Lucignano lies between Arezzo and Siena, not far from the motorway (*autostrada Firenze-Roma*).

year afternoons only 2.30pm–5.30pm. ☻€3. 🖉0575 83 801) includes a number of Sienese paintings (13C–15C) and (*ground floor*) a remarkable gold gem-encrusted reliquary, which, owing to its shape, is known as the **Tree of St Francis**★★. It is a masterpiece produced in Sienese goldsmiths' shops during the 14C–15C.

The church of **San Francesco** (*right of the Palazzo Communale*) is a simple building with a harmonious Romanesque façade of alternating black and white stone.

Monte San Savino
and Santa Maria delle Vertighe

This medieval town was the birthplace of the sculptor and architect, Andrea Contucci, otherwise known as Sansovino (1470–1529). A thoroughfare lined with some fine historic buildings runs right through the town linking the two gates set within the walls of the old stronghold (*cassero*).

▶ **Population:** 8,087
Michelin Map: Michelin Atlas p 44 and Map 563 – M 17 or Map 735 Fold 15.
Info: Piazza Gamurrini 25. &0575 84 30 98. www.promontesansavino.it.
Location: Monte San Savino is 21km/13mi SW of Arezzo.

TOWN
The main monuments of this village, enclosed within four medieval gates, lie on or near Piazza Garmurrini.

Piazza G F Gamurrini
The **square** lies near the Porta Fiorentina and is marked by a 17C obelisk. Next to the old stronghold stands the humble 17C church of **Santa Chiara**. It contains two examples of terracotta ware by Sansovino – a group depicting *St Sebastian, St Lawrence and St Roch* and a *Madonna and Child between Four Saints*, glazed by Giovanni della Robbia.

Loggia dei Mercanti★
The lines of this majestic loggia, attributed to Sansovino (1518–20), are emphasized by the use of *pietra serena*. Its Corinthian capitals display great finesse.

Palazzo Comunale
The **mansion** stands opposite the loggia and was built for the Del Monte family by Sangallo the Elder between 1515 and 1517. It consists of a ground floor built in heavily rusticated stonework, supporting a well-structured *piano nobile*, including windows surmounted by alternating rounded and triangular pediments. The corner of the building is decorated with a fine coat of arms of the Del Monte family. The typical Renaissance courtyard contains two wells; the upper storey has mullioned windows.

Chiesa della Misericordi ★
This Romanesque **church** consists of a nave with wooden rafters. It was redecorated throughout in the Baroque style during the 17C–18C. The tomb immediately to the left of the main entrance was an early work by Sansovino (1498).

Palazzo Pretorio
This 14C building, formerly the **residence** of the Florentine magistrate (*podestà*), is decorated with the coats of arms of those who held the office.

Sant'Agostino
This 14C **church** (extended in the 16C–17C) is decorated with a fine Gothic doorway and a rose window with stained glass designed by Guillaume de Marcillat. Inside are a number of early 15C frescoes. To the left of the church is the entrance to small cloisters with semicircular arcades built to plans by Sansovino. Beyond them is the **Baptistery of San Giovanni**, which has a splendid door designed by the artist.

EXCURSION
Santuario di Santa Maria delle Vertighe
2km/1mi E.

A stand of chestnut trees flanks this 16C building, which was formerly a Marian church dating from the 11C. The nave and aisles, roofed with wooden rafters, incorporate the Romanesque chevet of the original chapel which was the subject of popular devotion. This ensured that the two successive portraits of the Virgin could be kept in their original setting. They consist of a fresco of the *Assumption* (partly preserved) which adorns the small oven-vaulted apse, and the **Virgin altarpiece**★ by Margaritone of Arezzo (13C), which became the subject of worship after being placed on a lower level in the 15C.

Poppi★

and Bibbiena

The arcaded streets of Poppi are dominated by the proud castle, once the property of the Counts Guidi. It is visible at a distance, nestling in the mountains that were once dear to Sts Francesco and Romualdo.

▶ **Population:** 5,822
ⓕ **Michelin Map:** Michelin Atlas p 38 and Map 563 – K 17 or Map 735 Fold 15.
🗒 **Info:** Via Cavour 11. ℘0575 52 96 82. www.comune.poppi.ar.it.
◖ **Location:** Formerly the main town in the Casentino district, Poppi dominates the Arno Valley. It is easily reached from Arezzo, 33km/20mi away by S 71.

UPPER TOWN

A long climb leads up to the entrance to the town, a gateway set among the houses. Overlooking the tiny Piazza Amerighi decorated with a central marble fountain is the Church of **Madonna del Morbo** (17C) capped by a dome and flanked by porticoes on three sides. **Via Cavour** (*opposite*), also lined with shady porticoes, leads to the right-hand side of the **Church of San Fedele**, built in the 13C by the monks of Vallombrosa.

Castello★

ⓒOpen daily 10am–6pm (7pm Jul–Aug); rest of the year Thu–Sun 10am–5pm. ∞€4. ℘0575 52 05 16. www.castellodipoppi.it.

At the top of the upper town beyond a tree-lined esplanade stands a 13C Gothic **castle** with trefoiled window bays, merlons, a barbican and keep. It was built for the *priori* and is now used as the town hall. In the strange **courtyard**★, which is decorated with coats of arms, stands a stone table (*at the rear*) from which justice used to be dispensed. Two rows of roofed wooden balconies and an outside staircase add to the impression of height. The rooms open to the public include the library (*first floor*), containing 20 000 books, some of which date from the 13C and 14C, and the great hall in which the ceiling beams still have their original painted decoration.

At the end of the chamber is a *tondo* representing a *Madonna and Child* by the Botticelli School and (*right of the door*) a glazed terracotta in the style of the della Robbias. The corner drawing room (*second floor*) has a wonderful fireplace (1512) bearing the coat of arms of the Marquess Gondi. The adjoining chapel is decorated with frescoes attributed to Taddeo Gaddi. From the windows of the drawing room there is a delightful view of the valley and the mountains north towards Camaldoli and east to La Verna.

Zoo

0.5km/0.3mi E of Poppi. ⓒOpen 9am–dusk. ∞€6. ⓕ. ℘0575 50 45 41. www.parcozoopoppi.it.

This pleasant zoo, devoted to European wildlife, is traversed by a tree-lined circular path round a central lake.

EXCURSION
Bibbiena

5km/3.1mi SE of Poppi on S 71.

Bibbiena used to extend no further than a hilltop; today it stretches down to the valley floor, making it the largest town in the Casentino area.

Cardinal **Bernardo Dovizi**, better known as **Cardinal Bibbiena** (1470–1520) was born here. He was secretary to Leo X and a friend of Raphael. He was also the author of *La Calandria* (1513), the first comedy in the history of Italian theatre. There had been no other examples of this type of theatre since the days of Ancient Rome, but from the 16C onwards it was to enjoy success throughout Europe.

The old town, perched right on the top of the hill in a position that guarantees a panoramic view, has sloping narrow streets and is steeped in the discreet charm typical of rugged, mountainous areas like this where ostentation is totally out of place.

Poppi Castle

B. Morandi/ MICHELIN

▶ *The first entrance is at the top of a long climb, to the left of a major crossroads. The town centre is signposted. Turn into Via Dovizi.*

Palazzo Dovizi★

26–28 Via Dovizi.

This is the **residence** commissioned by Bibbiena early in the 16C. It is an austere building with brick facing yet it has a certain air of elegance. The central doorway is surmounted by a coat of arms, and the loggia above the building adds a touch of ethereal originality.

The church of **San Lorenzo**, opposite the palace, was built in the 15C. Its natural stone frontage conceals an interior with a nave and two aisles laid out in a uniform Renaissance style in alternating greys and whites. The aisles are decorated with two glazed **terracotta sculptures★★** by the della Robbias. On the third altar to the right is the *Adoration of the Shepherds*; on the third to the left the *Deposition*.

San Lorenzo

This church, standing opposite the palace, was built in the 15C. Its natural stone frontage, austere like the façade of the palace, conceals a Renaissance interior.

▶ *Continue on Via Dovizi to Piazza Roma, where you will find the 16C Palazzo Comunale. Across the square turn into a narrow street and walk to the end.*

Piazza Tarlati

Turn left off the square.

The **square** was named after the Tarlati family, one of whose members, Pier Saccone, had one of the four towers of the fortress (*cassero*) built on this very spot. Very little remains today except the crenellated **Clock Tower** and, to the rear of the square, a wall linking the clock tower to a lower tower.

Opposite it is the **Church of Santi Ippolito e Donato**, built in the early 12C as a private chapel for the Tarlati castle. It is built in the Romanesque style and has an unusually wide transept crossing flanked by very short arms. The walls are covered with numerous frescoes dating from the 14C to 16C. On the south side just inside the door is a *Crucifixion* painted by the Master of San Polo in Rosso (13C) followed by a sculpture of the *Madonna and Child* (14C Tuscan School). In the north transept is a *Crucifixion* by the School of Giotto (second half of the 14C). The apse contains a triptych of the *Madonna and Child with Saints* by Bicci di Lorenzo (1435). In the south arm of the transept is a rare painting by Arcangelo di Cola da Camerino, **The Madonna and Child with Angels★**.

To the left of Piazza Tarlati is a terrace from which there is a superb **view★** of the valley with Poppi Castle (*right*) and the rolling wooded hills of Pratomagno in the background.

Romena★

Stia and Porciano

Romena lies within the administrative district of Pratovecchio (*2km/1mi north*), the neighbouring village that was the birthplace of Paolo Uccello, the artist who specialised in portraying volume and almost abstract compositions.

VILLAGE
Pieve di San Pietro★

For information and appointments
℘575 58 37 25 (Signora Alba Cipriani).
The road from Pratovecchio provides a view of the delightful **chevet of the church** and its two rows of decorative arcading. This is a particularly fine example of early 12C Romanesque architecture.

The church lost its first two bays and its original façade in the 17C as the result of a landslide. The interior consists of a nave and aisles with rafters supported on columns carved out of single blocks of stone and crowned with attractive carved capitals. The nave and aisles rise slightly towards the east end of the church. The central apse has attractive half-barrel vaulting.

▷ *A few yards to the left on the road back to Pratovecchio is a tarmac path leading to the castle.*

Castello★

⊶ *Closed. ℘335 12 20 930.*
The impressive ruins of **Romena Castle** stand on a hilltop overlooking the Casentino countryside. Built for Count Guidi and his descendants in the 11C, the castle now has only three of the original 14 towers – the keep, postern and prison.

This was the setting for an episode narrated by Dante in his *Inferno* (Song XXX, verses 46–90). A man named Master Adam minted counterfeit florins here (21 carats instead of 24) at the request of the Guidi. His crime was discovered and he was arrested and burnt at the stake in Florence in 1281, the statutory punishment for all counterfeiters.

⚙ **Michelin Map:**
Michelin Atlas p 38
and Map 563 – K 17.

▤ **Info:** Via di Rignano, Bibbiena. ℘0575 59 30 98. www.comune.bibbiena.ar.it.

▷ **Location:** A tiny hamlet in the upper Casentino Valley, Romena is located on the road between Arezzo and Florence over the Consuma Pass.

There is a magnificent **view**★★ of the picturesque ruins of the castle and its avenue of cypress trees from a point several hundred metres along the Poppi to Consuma road (S70).

EXCURSIONS
Stia

5km/3mi North.
This village lies at the confluence of the Stia and the Arno, which rises only a short distance away on Monte Falterona. It contains some relics of the time when it was known as Palagio.

In Piazza Bernardo Tanucci, an attractive but narrow and elongated square, stands the 12C church of **Santa Maria Assunta**, which has been much altered over the years. The Romanesque interior with its nave and two aisles, divided by columns with fine decorative capitals, contains a number of interesting **works of art**★. The triptych of the *Annunciation* (*first chapel on the right*) is by Bicci di Lorenzo (1414). There is a superb glazed terracotta tabernacle (*chapel to the right of the chancel*) by the Della Robbias and a 14C wooden *Crucifix* (*centre of the apse*). The *Madonna and Child* (*chapel to the left of the chancel*) is by Andrea della Robbia and the *Madonna and Child with two Angels* (*over the altar*) is by the Master of Varlungo. The early 15C painting of the *Assumption* (*above the altar in the north aisle*) is by the Master of Borgo alla Collina.

The ancient **castle** (*northeast of the village*), which belonged to the Guidi, has been totally restored in the neo-Gothic style popular in the late 19C. The **Museo d'Arte Contemporanea** (*second floor*) displays collections ranging from Futurism (1916) to the conceptual art of the present day.

The common characteristic of the artists represented is their love of Tuscany. *Palagio Fiorentino. Open by appointment only. 0575 58 22 96. www.comune.stia.ar.it.*

Porciano
1.7km/1mi on the outskirts of Stia on S556 to Londa. Turn right into a narrow

road which climbs the hill. From the top there are some fine views of the castle. The **castle** (*open mid-May to mid–Oct Sun and Hols 10am–noon and 2pm–7pm, rest of the year by appointment only; 0575 58 26 35; donation advised*) in Porciano, which was built c. 1000, is considered to be one of the earliest residences of the Counts Guidi. It is surrounded by the medieval village and has retained its impressive tower and a few stretches of outer wall. The ground floor houses a Museum of Rural Art. On the first floor is a collection of ceramics discovered during archaeological digs.

San Giovanni Valdarno
and Montevarchi

San Giovanni is one of the main industrial towns in the Arno Valley and is particularly famous for its steel works and the huge lignite mines in the vicinity. The first great painter of the Florentine Renaissance, Masaccio (d. 1428), was born here in 1401.

TOWN
San Giovanni is arranged around two central *piazze* - Piazza Cavour and Piazza Masaccio - between which stands the Palazzo Pretorio.

Palazzo Pretorio★
This building, which stands in the centre of the town, is emblazoned with the coats of arms of former magistrates (*podeste*). Said to have been designed by Arnolfo di Cambio, the building dates from the 13C and was altered during the Renaissance.

San Giovanni Battista
This early 14C **church** in Piazza Cavour stands opposite the main façade of the Palazzo Pretorio. It resembles its neighbour with its elegant portico decorated with glazed roundels (*tondi*) in the style of the della Robbias.

> ▶ **Population:** 17,122
> ⚲ **Michelin Map:** Atlas p 38 and Map 563 – I 16 or Map 735 Fold 15.
> ℹ **Info:** Piazza Cavour 3. 055 94 37 48. www.comune.san-giovanni-valdarno.ar.it.
> ▷ **Location:** San Gio-vanni Valdarno is about 40km/ 25mi from Florence on the motorway (A1) between Florence and Rome.

Santa Maria delle Grazie
Open Jun–Sept 11am–1pm and 4pm–6pm (7pm Sun and Hols). Rest of the year 10.30am–12.30pm and 3.30pm–5.30pm. Closed Wed, Sun morning and religious festivals. €2.50. 055 91 22 445.

Behind the Palazzo Pretorio stands this 15C **basilican church** with a 19C neo-Renaissance façade facing Piazza Masaccio. Beneath the porch is an *Assumption of the Virgin Mary*, a superb, vividly-coloured glazed ceramic by Giovanni della Robbia.

Inside the basilica, the high altar is decorated with the fresco of *Our Lady of Grace* (14C), from which the church takes its name. Behind the chancel is a small **museum** containing works by the Florentine School, mainly from the

15C–16C, including a superb **Annuncia-tion**★★ by Fra Angelico.

Oratorio di San Lorenzo
To the right on leaving the basilica.
The **chapel**, which is set behind a modest brick and stone façade, contains numerous 14C–15C frescoes and a reredos depicting the *Coronation of the Virgin Mary* by Giotto's School (*behind the high altar*).

EXCURSION
Montevarchi
5km/3mi SE. This village is famous throughout Tuscany for its market selling Arno Valley chickens and wine from the hillsides of Aretino. The streets in the historic old town form parallel arcs on each side of Via Roma. The 18C **Church of San Lorenzo** in Piazza Varchi (in the middle of Via Roma) supposedly contains an ampoule of breast milk from the Virgin Mary, kept in the tabernacle on the high altar.

Sansepolcro★
Monterchi and Caprese

This small industrial town, once the centre of the Buitoni pasta empire, is located in the centre of the Upper Tiber Valley. It is still enclosed within its walls and has numerous old houses dating from the Middle Ages to the 18C, an indication of its early and long-lasting prosperity. Its name recalls that in the 10C, two pilgrims returning from the Holy Land brought with them relics of the Holy Sepulchre, (*santo sepolcro*) and a chapel was built to contain them. A village then grew up around the chapel and was quite naturally given the name Borgo San Sepolcro, which over the years was simplified to Sansepolcro. This town was the birthplace of Piero della Francesca, who was born between 1415 and 1420, the son of a shoemaker. Although his name is connected with Arezzo, it was here that he spent part of his life and where he died in 1492. The town holds a crossbow competition (second Sunday in September) at which the competitors and all their companions are dressed in Renaissance costume.

✎ WALKING TOUR
Patrician Streets★
In the heart of the old town is a vast square, **Piazza Torre di Berta**, a popular meeting place. A medieval tower of the

▸ **Population:** 15,760
⏱ **Michelin Map:** Michelin Atlas p 39 and Map 563 – I 18 or Map 735 Fold 15.
🛈 **Info:** Piazza Garibaldi 2. ℘0575 74 05 36. www.sansepolcro.net.
◖ **Location:** Sansepolcro is situated on the border of Tuscany and Umbria on the motorway between Cesena and Perugia.
◉ **Don't Miss:** Piero della Francesca paintings in the Museo Civico.

same name used to stand in the centre but it was destroyed by a German shell during World War II.

Between the square and the very wide street, Via Matteotti, runs **Via XX Settembre**, which is almost entirely flanked by Gothic, Renaissance and Mannerist mansions (palazzi); it also contains a few truncated medieval towers. The section of road (*right*) contains some particularly fine examples (nos 127 and 131). In the intervening narrow alleyway, known as **Via Del Buon Umore**, the buildings are separated by five brick arches. The other section of Via XX Settembre contains some attractive shops and leads (*turn left into Via Luca Pacioli*) to the **Church of San Lorenzo**, where there is a superb **Deposition from the Cross**★ by the Mannerist artist Rosso Fiorentino.

Duomo
Via Matteotti.

The **Cathedral** of St John the Baptist
dates from the early 11C but has both
Romanesque features – plain interior
with nave and two aisles, and rafters
in the centre – and Gothic elements
– polygonal chancel. Its austere façade
has three coffered doorways and an
alabaster rose window. The square and
pointed bell tower was rebuilt in the 14C
in the Franciscan style and is similar to
the one belonging to the nearby Church
of San Francesco. **Palazzo delle Laudi**
(*left of the cathedral*), now the town hall,
has, like **Palazzo Aggiunti** (*opposite*), a
Mannerist design (late 16C–early 17C).

◗ *From Via Matteotti pass
through Porta della Pesa.*

Museo Civico★★
*Via Aggiunti 65, left of the Porta
della Pesa.* ◷Open Jun–Sept daily
*9am–1.30pm and 2.30pm–7.30pm.
Rest of the year 9.30pm–1pm and
2.30pm–6pm.* ✆€5. ℘0575 73 22 18.
www.sansepolcro.net.

The main attractions of the **museum**
are some admirable **paintings★★★** by
Piero della Francesca – the superb
triptych of the *Virgin Mary of Mercy*,
which shows echoes of Masaccio, especially in the Crucifixion, two fragments
of frescoes (*St Julian* and *St Ludovic*) and
a *Resurrection*, an impressive example of
his art reaching maturity. The museum
also houses works by artists born in
Sansepolcro – Santi di Tito, Matteo di
Giovanni, Raffaellino del Colle – and by
Bassano, Signorelli, and the della Robbia School.

◗ *Arrive at Piazza San Francesco.*

Piazza San Francesco
The **Church of San Francesco** (12C–
18C) with its pointed bell tower stands
opposite the **Church of Santa Maria
delle Grazie**, which is flanked by a small
loggia with two arches; the two tall coffers above the door are decorated with
skeletons and the brackets on the tympanum are supported by two skulls.

Duomo, Sansepolcro
Clodio / Dreamstime.com

In the street running along the right-
hand side of San Francesco is the **casa
di Piero della Francesca** (*no 71*). This
was the artist's home (15C).
On the outskirts of the town, towards
Perugia, are the remains of the Medici
fortress.

EXCURSIONS
Monterchi
17km/11mi S.

In Via della Reglia a little **exhibition
centre** (*spazio espositivo;* ◷*open Tue–
Sun 9am–1pm and 2pm–7pm (5pm
winter);* ✆€2.50; ℘0575 70 013) has
been established to house an unusual
work by Piero della Francesca, the
Virgin Mary giving Birth★ (*Madonna
del Parto*). This fresco, which has been
restored, was painted at more or less the
same time as the *Legend of the True Cross*
cycle in Arezzo and its majesty is reminiscent of the other work.

Caprese Michelangelo
*Take the motorway towards Cesena;
in Pieve Santo Stefano follow the sign
for Caprese Michelangelo (about
25km/15mi). Park at the top of the
village. A cobbled street (pedestrians
only) leads to the castle.*

The controversy as to whether Chiusi
della Verna or Caprese could claim
the honour of being the birthplace of
Michelangelo on 6 March 1475 was set-

tled in 1875 by the discovery of a copy of the artist's birth certificate – the original had been lost. It was mere chance that Michelangelo was born in Caprese, where his father, a magistrate (*podestà*) employed by Florence, had been posted. After his birth, Michelangelo was placed with a wet-nurse in Settignano, not far from Florence.

Casa di Michelangelo

The 14C castle contains **Casa del Podestà**, the magistrate's house, where Michelangelo's family lived. Coats of arms adorn the façade but the architectural style is modest. The house is now the **Museo Michelangiolesco** (Michelangelo Museum). On the ground floor are a few plaster casts and photographs showing the artist's sculptures and paintings. On the upper floor are reproductions of paintings illustrating his life. Michelangelo was probably born in the small room at the end of the corridor. ⊙*Open Apr–Oct Tue–Sun 11am–* 7pm; rest of the year 11am–5.30pm. ⊜€4. ℘575 79 37 76.

At the foot of the castle is the 13C Church of St John the Baptist (San Giovanni Battista), a small, modest building with bare stone walls, where Michelangelo is said to have been christened.

ADDRESSES

⊉/EAT

⊜⊜ **Il Convivio** – *Via Traversari.* ℘575 73 65 43. Closed Tue. Reservations suggested. This elegant restaurant, situated around old tower walls, serves exquisite Apennine cooking. Good wine list.

⊜⊜ **Da Ventura** – *Via Aggiunti 30.* ℘0575 74 25 60. Closed Sat, 8–20 Jan, 1–20 Aug. A traditional restaurant offering mushroom and truffle specialities in season. Rustic furnishings and a beautiful collection of cartoons on the walls create a familial atmosphere.

Vallombrosa★

Celebrated by Milton in *Paradise Lost*, Vallombrosa is known for its abbey, its natural beauty, its views, its magnificent pine forest and excursions in the Pratomagno range.

VISIT

The **monastery** was founded c. 1028 by **Giovanni Gualberto**, a young Florentine nobleman, with a companion and the two hermits they met when they retired to this place.

The Congregation of Vallombrosa was inspired by the Benedictines and was recognised in 1055 by Pope Victor II. Its founder was canonized in 1193. The monastery rapidly became influential because of the numerous gifts it received.

It was altered several times during the centuries and now looks as it did in the 16C–17C. Its noble white façade with regularly spaced windows framed in *pietra serena* was designed by Gherardo

- ⚷ **Michelin Map**: Michelin Atlas p 38 and Map 563 – K 16 or Map 735 Fold 15.
- ▣ **Info:** Piazzale Roma 7, Saltino. ℘055 862 003. www.vallombrosa.it.
- ▶ **Location:** Vallombrosa is situated about 10km/6mi S of the Consuma Pass (S70).

Silvani (1635–40). In front of the building is a walled courtyard, dominated by a tall 13C bell tower and (*right*) a 15C tower, the only surviving features of the earlier buildings.

The entrance leads to an inner courtyard and the church. Beneath the porch is a sculpture by Roberto Nardi (1990) titled *An Olive Tree for Peace*, depicting St John Gualberto and the wild game in Vallombrosa. The Baroque interior has a nave but no aisles. The *pietra serena* architrave beneath the organ loft dates from the Renaissance church.

Santuario della
Verna ★

In 1213 Count Cattani from Chiusi gave Monte Verna to St Francis, who settled there with his brothers and received the stigmata there in 1224. The sanctuary is now a popular place of pilgrimage, owing to its atmosphere of serenity and meditation and its dramatic site★★, perched on the edge of sheer limestone cliffs among pine, fir and beech trees.

- **Michelin Map:** Michelin Atlas p 38 and Map 563 – K 17 or Map 735 Fold 15.
- **Location:** The Sanctuary, which has its own hostel (℘0575 59 90 25), sits at an altitude of 1,128m/3,666ft 18km/11mi from San Stefano, 26km/16mi from Bibbiena and 22km/14mi from Rassina.

LIFE OF ST FRANCIS

Every day the Franciscan brothers process along the **Corridor of the Stigmata** on their way to the Chapel of the Stigmata. Halfway along the corridor is a door leading to the cave where St Francis used to sleep on a bare stone. The **Chapel of the Stigmata** was built to preserve the place where the miracle occurred. On the end wall is a **Crucifixion** by Andrea della Robbia. The 15C choir stalls are decorated with marquetry (restored in the late 19C) depicting the Saints, Popes and famous people who bore witness to St Francis' stigmata. The **church** contains two glazed terracotta pieces by Giovanni della Robbia (*on the screen dividing the church in two*) and a terracotta altarpiece (*high altar*) by Andrea della Robbia representing the *Assumption of the Virgin Mary*. From the square, a path (*88 steps*) leads down to a rock, **Sasso Spico**, where St Francis used to pray.

St Francis of Assisi (1182–1226)

Francis, who had a brilliant mind, was the son of a wealthy Italian linen merchant of Assisi and a French woman. As a young man, being fond of society and fired with chivalrous ideals, he lived the life of a rich merchant's son. In 1202 he was taken prisoner during a border dispute with Perugia. On his return to Assisi he fell victim to a serious fever; during his illness he was touched by grace and decided to devote his life to prayer and the poor, hence his nickname, the poor man (*il poverello*).

Francis had several visions of the Virgin Mary and Christ; the most famous one, when he received the stigmata, occurred at La Verna. He died in 1226, 16 years after setting up the Order of Minor Friars, a mendicant order, known as the Franciscans. Throughout his life of prayer and penitence, he attracted a large number of followers and he encouraged Clara, a young noble woman from Assisi, in her religious vocation; she founded the Order of Poor Clares. The real or legendary story of his life and the life of his followers was set down in an anonymous work in the 14C. It has now become famous and is called the *Fioretti*.

The simplicity of his lifestyle was evident in his language, which could be understood by even the poorest members of the community. This was the Umbrian vulgar, in which he wrote the *Canticle of the Creatures* (1224), one of the first great poems in the Italian language. As a lover of beauty and nature, preaching love of all living creatures, he celebrated the value of Joy in the service of God and was nicknamed "God's juggler". The same simplicity can be seen in the joy with which he invented new and efficient ways of saving souls. He probably touched the hearts of the common people most effectively with his promotion of the Christmas crib.

SIENA ★★★

Siena is a mystical, refined city of art and architecture with a passionate and generous soul, welcoming visitors with its motto inscribed above the Camollia Gate: *"Cor magis tibi Seni pandit"* or, "Siena opens its heart even wider to you". This Gothic city of yellow-brown buildings – the "burnt Sienna" of paint-boxes – has always held a unique fascination for visitors. Set on three steep hills of reddish clay and enclosed by extensive walls, the city is overlooked by the elegant tower of the Palazzo Pubblico and the black-and-white striped cathedral, which rise above the rooftops and are visible for miles. Siena is perhaps best known for the Il Palio horse races, held annually in the summer. These races carry on a medieval tradition of competitive rivalry between the city's neighbourhoods (🌏 *see p277*).

THE CITY TODAY

Though Siena has a youthful populace, thanks to its university, it has retained much of the culture and values espoused during medieval times. True Sienese are loyal first to *contrada* (🌏 *see opposite*), then city, then country. This civic pride is on display year-round, but most fervent during the twice-yearly Palio horse race, an event that has guaranteed Siena a prominent place on the tourist itinerary.

A BIT OF HISTORY
A City of Uncertain Origins

Nobody knows whether it was the Etruscans, the Gauls or the Romans who founded the original town. Legend has made up for the lack of sure historical fact and maintains that Siena was founded in the early days of the Roman era (8C BC) by Senius, son of Remus. This would explain the presence on the Sienese emblem of Romulus and Remus being suckled by the She-wolf. One fact, however, is certain: the site now occupied by the city was a small town in the days of the Republic of Rome and Caesar Augustus repopulated it (1C BC) by setting up a Roman colony here under the name of Sena Julia.

In the 12C Siena became an independent republic. Having prospered through its merchants and bankers, it became a threat to neighbouring Florence. At the same time political rivalry was rife between the two cities, Siena being a supporter of the Ghibelline faction while Florence supported the Guelfs. Until the 15C the history of the two cities, which had little in common, was marked by alternating success and failure. In 1230

▶ **Population:** 54,256

🚗 **Michelin Map:** Michelin Atlas p 44 and Map 563 – M 15/16 or Map 735 Fold 15.

ℹ️ **Info:** Piazza del Campo 56. ✆0577 28 05 51. www.terresiena.it.

▷ **Location:** Siena is located 68km/42mi south of Florence by the motorway ("Tangenziale") or 72km/45mi by Via Chiantigiana (S222) through Chianti.

🅿️ **Parking:** Paid parking lots are available in Via Esterna Fontebranda and Via Baldassare Peruzzi, and several lots are located near Fortezza Medicea. Rates start at €1 per hour.

😊 **Don't Miss:** The Piazza del Campo is one of the most famous squares in the world. It is the setting for the twice-annual race, the Palio delle Contrade. in the Piazza stands the Torre del Mangia, which affords stunning views of Siena and the Chianti Senese countryside. Siena's Cathedral Precinct, site of the magnificent Duomo, also should not be missed.

the Florentines besieged Siena and catapulted manure and donkeys over the town walls. In 1258 Siena breached a treaty it had signed with Florence and

GETTING THERE
BY RAIL
The railway station is on the north side of the city (*Piazza Fratelli Rosselli*). Siena is linked by rail to Florence, Rome (Via Chiusi) and seaside resorts as far south as Orbetello (Via Grossetto). The "**nature train**" (*treno natura*) runs a seasonal service on a special circular route through the surrounding country (Siena-Asciano-Monte Antico-Siena). Information is available from the Ufficio Accoglienza Clienti FS, *0577 20 74 13*.

BY COACH
There is a frequent coach service between **Florence and Siena** provided by TRAIN and SITA (*0577 20 42 45*) by the direct route (*1hr 15min*) or by the longer route Via Poggibonsi (*2hr 10min*); departures (morning and evening) from the coach station near Santa Maria Novella Railway Station in Florence and Piazza Gramsci in Siena.

As the bus station in Siena is nearer the city centre than the railway station and as the journey is swift and the cost moderate, it is more sensible to travel by bus than by train between Siena and Florence.

TO REACH THE CITY CENTRE
There is a bus service (5min) from the railway station in Piazza Fratelli Rosselli on the north side of the city to the centre (Piazza del Sale) – no 17 (station to centre) and no 2 (centre to station); also no 9 and no 10; do not take no 3 and no 15 as they go round the city but not into the centre. For information contact TRAIN, Piazza Gramsci, *0577 20 42 46*.

BY BICYCLE
For information contact Amici della Bicicletta di Siena, Via Campansi 32. *577 45 159. www.adbsiena.it.*

---

opened its gates to Ghibelline exiles. The most memorable episode in this long struggle took place on 4 September 1260, a dozen or more miles to the east in **Montaperti**, where the Ghibellines of Siena defeated the Guelfs of Florence. This period of unrest – from the middle of the 13C to the middle of the 14C – was nevertheless the heyday of Siena. It was then that the most prestigious public buildings were erected together with most of its palaces and patrician mansions.

The great plague which ravaged the Western world between 1348 and 1350 reduced the city's population by one-third. In the early years of the 15C internal struggles finally took the city into decline.

Although at first Siena accepted the peace-keeping role of Emperor Charles V and celebrated his arrival in the city in April 1536, the city then rebelled against his authority and placed itself under the protection of the King of France, Henry II. The town was besieged by imperial troops from early in 1554 to April 1555. Four years later Siena was annexed to the Grand Duchy of Tuscany governed by Cosimo I of Florence.

Administrative Structure
The medieval administrative structure has partly survived to this day. The three hills correspond to three urban districts: di Città, di Camollia and di San Martino. Each district (*terzo*) was divided into 59 sub-districts (**contrade**) or parishes of which 17 still exist. At the head of each sub-district is an official (*capitano*), who has administrative, judicial and territorial powers.

In the past the emblem of each district was borne on a standard or pennant which was the responsibility of the standard-bearer. Every citizen was required to take an oath of allegiance before the Cart of Freedom (*carroccio*), the symbol of the community, which was taken into battle.

These days the 17 *contrade* spend the entire year in preparation for the *Palio* (*see p277*). Each *contrada* has a centre containing a museum which displays the trophies it has won over the years, a church, a public fountain in the

Although the city has a coat of arms, its true face is reflected in the colours of the "contrade".

Wave

Shell

Porcupine

Eagle

Unicorn

Forest

Owl

Tortoise

Ram

She-wolf

Snail

Goose

Giraffe

Caterpillar

Panther

Panther

Tower

shape of its emblem, a band, stables and warehouses in which weapons used to be stored. Each also has its own local social life based on gastronomic evenings, dances and preparations for the *Palio*. The emblems of the 17 *contrade* represent one of the 17 virtues of Siena: the Porcupine symbolises sharpness, the She-wolf faithfulness, the Goose perspicacity, the Forest power, the Dragon ardour, the Giraffe elegance, the Wave joy, the Panther daring, the Eagle the willingness to fight, the Snail prudence, the Tower resistance, the Tortoise obstinacy, the Caterpillar skill, the Ram perseverance, the Owl finesse, the Shell discretion and the Unicorn science.

Palio delle Contrade

B. Morandi / MICHELIN

The "Palio delle Contrade"

The *palio* horse race, which dates from the 13C, is the most famous of its kind in Italy. The race is held twice a year on 2 July and 16 August, but only 10 "*contrade*" take part in each competition so the 17 must take turns to participate. During the days of preparation intrigue is rife and betting is heavy. The streets are draped in the colours of each "*contrada*," young people practise throwing the flag, the edge of the Piazza del Campo is covered with sand to form the race track and dangerous corners are protected with mattresses. The outer edge is lined with tiers of seats but the centre, from which anybody can watch the race free of charge, is left open. Feelings run very high in the last two days before the race, when there is a solemn drawing of lots in the Campo to see which horses are assigned to the participating "*contrade*." The animals are then carefully prepared; doping is allowed. If a horse dies, the "*contrada*" that it represented has to retire from the race but its standard, set at half-mast, is entitled to take part in the opening procession and the horse's hooves are solemnly carried on a silver tray. The jockeys (*fantini*) are accommodated within the *contrade* and watched day and night to ensure that they are not paid by a competitor to lose the race.

On the morning of the race a Mass is said in the church of each *contrada* and horse and rider are blessed. In the afternoon there is a lavish procession around the Campo involving all the representatives of the 17 *contrade* dressed in 15C costume and carrying their emblems while the flag-bearers (*alfieri*) skilfully brandish their pennants. Behind them come six black horses mounted by riders in mourning in memory of six *contrade* that no longer exist – the Viper, Rooster, Oak Tree, Sword, Bear and Lion – and that were probably taken over by more powerful *contrade*.

At the very end of the procession is the triumphal chariot, built to the design of the ancient *carroccio*. The town archers bring up the rear.

The high spot of the festival occurs at the end of the afternoon when the famous "*corsa al palio*" is run. This is a dangerous horse race in which no holds are barred and it is all over within a matter of minutes, the time it takes the jockeys to ride bareback three times round the Campo.

The winner receives the banner (*palio*), hence the name of the race. The banner bears a representation of the Virgin Mary which is painted by a leading artist especially for the occasion. After the race all the "*contrade*" continue the festivities in their streets and community centres where the dinner may be an occasion for feasting or bitterness, depending on the result.

SIENESE ART

Whereas Florence was a great Renaissance city, Siena enjoyed its main period of artistic development during the flowering of Gothic art and has remained very conservative in this respect. The Gothic style was expressed here in a manner that was particularly elegant, affected and expansive.

Architecture

Although most of the architects who worked in Siena were born elsewhere, the Gothic style which developed, particularly in vernacular buildings, has certain specific characteristics – the combined use of brick and stone; double-arched openings on the lower levels of buildings consisting of a pointed arch with surbased arch below and known as **Sienese arches**; an abundance of windows – usually triple bays with slender colonnettes and tympani; merlons supported by a frieze of small arches to cap the top of buildings.

Religious architecture in Siena also had its own characteristics. Like the west front of Orvieto cathedral (see *The Green Guide Italy*), which was designed by Sienese artist **Lorenzo Maitani**, the façade of Siena cathedral indicates the transition from the Tuscan Romanesque to the Flamboyant Gothic style.

Siena made its contribution to the Renaissance through a talented architect named **Francesco di Giorgio Martini** (1439–1502) who left very few traces of his artistry in the city of his birth but who worked in other towns in Tuscany, Umbria and the Marches, in particular in Urbino.

Sculpture

This art was originally a Pisan speciality and its greatest exponents were Nicola and Giovanni Pisano, who came to work in Siena, where they had a number of pupils.

Tino di Camaino, who was born in Siena c. 1280 and died in Naples in 1337, may have had a weaker personality than Giovanni, his master, but his talent was robust as well as delicate. He too worked on the cathedral where his

skills are most apparent in the complex tombs carved like reliquaries.

The leading figure, however, in Sienese sculpture in the 15C was **Jacopo della Quercia** (born c. 1371, d. 1438) who rivalled the greatest artists of the day and who competed with Brunelleschi and Ghiberti for the commission to design the doors for the Baptistery in Florence. He was trained in the Gothic tradition but was equally open to the Florentine Renaissance culture, and he combined both styles to produce a very personal synthesis. His austere and pure style was very different from the exquisite gracefulness which had been the main feature of Sienese work until that time.

Sienese School of Painting

It was mainly the Primitives in the 13C–14C who earned Siena its reputation as a major city of art. Filled with fervent but calm piety, they painted hieratic figures against golden and engraved backgrounds, initially in a style strictly inspired by Byzantine art. Their expressiveness is often closely akin to Mannerism.

The favourite subject of these artists was the *Madonna and Child*; it should be mentioned that for several centuries the people of Siena regarded the Virgin Mary as their supreme Saviour. There were so many representations of her in Siena in such similar attitudes that her image seems to have been mass-produced.

The first of the Sienese Primitives to make a name for himself was **Guido da Siena** who, in the second half of the 13C, produced a *Maestà* for the Palazzo Comunale.

It was, however, through **Duccio di Buoninsegna** that Siena made its brilliant entry into the pages of the history of art. The artist, who was born in Siena c. 1255 and died c. 1318, slipped from the Byzantine tradition to a new art form steeped in Gothic sensitivity. His works were still impregnated with Byzantine atmosphere but they include an exquisite sense of line and colour and show the naïve grace and Mannerist charm, together with the golden backgrounds inherited from Byzantine art, that were to characterise the Sienese School.

His pupil, **Simone Martini**, born c. 1285, was one of the great exponents of Gothic painting and his influence spread as far as Provence, Catalonia, Aragon, England, Flanders and Bohemia. He worked in the same style as his master but shed the constraints of Byzantine hieratic painting and tended instead towards a more natural art form.

Foremost among Simone Martini's pupils were **Lippo Memmi**, his brother-in-law and assistant, and **Barna da Siena** (died c. 1380) whose cycle of frescoes in the collegiate church in San Gimignano show pathos and great vivacity.

The **Lorenzetti** brothers, who were contemporaries of Simone Martini, both trained with Duccio and were influenced by the expressive, tormented works of Giovanni Pisano and the naturalistic and dramatic style of Giotto. The work of **Pietro** (born c. 1280), the elder of the brothers, was still close to the severity of Byzantine art but from Pisan sculpture he borrowed the way of depicting a Madonna seemingly linked to the Infant Jesus through a tender dialogue. **Ambrogio**, the younger brother, had a reputation for wisdom and was very well known in Siena. As a true Sienese, he painted several pictures of the Madonna and the Virgin Mary in Majesty but he was most famous for his "civilian" fresco cycle in the Palazzo Pubblico. Both the brothers died of the plague in 1348.

The techniques of these masters of Gothic painting were continued in the second half of the 14C and later by a number of lesser artists such as **Lippo Vanni**, **Luca di Tommé**, who was strongly influenced by Pietro Lorenzetti, **Bartolo di Fredi**, who also worked on the frescoes in the collegiate church of San Gimignano, and **Taddeo di Bartolo** (1362–1422).

The 15C brought attractive and in some cases innovatory artists. While Florence was moving towards the Renaissance, Sienese art maintained a fundamental link with Gothic values. **Lorenzo Monaco** (1370–c. 1425), a native of Siena, was still considered a major artist of his day in Florence, where he taught Fra Angelico, with compositions that have all the intricacy of a miniaturist and all the colours of an illuminated manuscript, making him one of the most brilliant exponents of the international Gothic style. **Giovanni di Paolo** (born c. 1403, died c. 1483) retained close ties with the Sienese tradition. Other artists, however, were more open to the Florentine influence. Stefano di Giovanni, also known as **Sassetta** (born c. 1400, died 1450) attempted to reproduce perspective while showing a benign ingenuity in his flowing figures and delightful harmonies of colour. His pupil, **Sano di Pietro** (1406–81), continued to pay minute attention to detail, and introduced a refreshingly new approach to the narrative aspect in his wonderful predellas.

It was Lorenzo di Pietro, better known as **Vecchietta** (born c. 1410, died in 1480), who was responsible for a real change in style. In close contact with the Florentines, he introduced perspective into Sienese painting and gave it a new form of vigour. His most famous pupil was **Matteo di Giovanni** (born c. 1430, died in 1495) who created elegantly refined paintings of the Madonna as well as dramatic works that were full of movement.

He also influenced **Francesco di Giorgio Martini**, whose paintings reveal the attention to perspective handed on from the Florentines. His main characteristic, though, was his typically Sienese lyricism and gentleness.

In the 16C **Pinturicchio** from Umbria settled in Siena (1502) and created the brilliant decoration for the Libreria Piccolomini (see below), thereby marking an artistic renaissance in the city. Siena was also the adopted home of **Il Sodoma** (1477–1549), Leonardo da Vinci's pupil who came originally from Lombardy. His works influenced the Sienese artist **Domenico Beccafumi** (born c. 1486, died c. 1551) and encouraged him to adopt the Mannerist style, of which he became one of the greatest exponents in Tuscany.

Piazza del Campo★★★

1hr 30min

The "Campo" is one of the most famous squares in the world, and the harmony of its buildings has rarely, if ever, been surpassed. It is a pink and white "shell" or "fan" set on a slight slope and is a consummate example of the "drawing room squares", which are one of the main sights in any Italian city, representing rather less the point of convergence of city streets and rather more an enclosure in which life and history are lived to the full. Since its establishment in the 13C as a marketplace, it was in the Campo over the centuries where the great proclamations were heard by the citizens, where the factions whose fighting tore the city apart confronted one another, and that St Bernardino addressed the people from a pulpit erected in front of the Palazzo Pubblico.

In the mid-14C the square was paved with bricks within an outer circle of cobblestones. On the southeast side, also in brick and stone, is the long façade of the Palazzo Pubblico. From its centre radiate eight white lines dividing the Campo into nine sections, which symbolise the government "of the Nine", the nine magistrates from among the craftsmen, traders and bankers who brought the city its greatest period of prosperity (1287–1355).

At the top of the square is the **Fonte Gaia** (Fountain of Joy), so-called because of the general joy that accompanied its inauguration in 1348. In 1419 it was decorated with marble panels by Jacopo della Quercia, which were replaced by copies in 1868. The originals are currently undergoing restoration and those finished are displayed in Santa Maria dell Scala.

Behind the fountain beneath a small tower (*right*) is the 13C Sansedoni Palace, which was extensively altered at the end of the 19C.

Palazzo Pubblico★★★

Open mid-Mar–Nov daily 10am–7pm; rest of the year 10am–5.30pm. €7, €10 joint ticket with Torre del Mangia. 0577 29 22 26. www.comune.siena.it/museocivico.

This is one of the finest vernacular buildings in Italy. It is exceptionally elegant and austere and it constitutes a synthesis of all the characteristics of the Sienese Gothic style. It served as a model for most of the other palaces in the city.

Construction began at the end of the 13C and by the middle of the following century, it was almost complete, except for the second floor of the two wings, which was added in 1680. The pale travertine used for the lower section contrasts sharply with the yellow ochre of the remainder of the building. The large number of doors and windows along the ground floor and the

Piazza del Campo

B. Morandi / MICHELIN

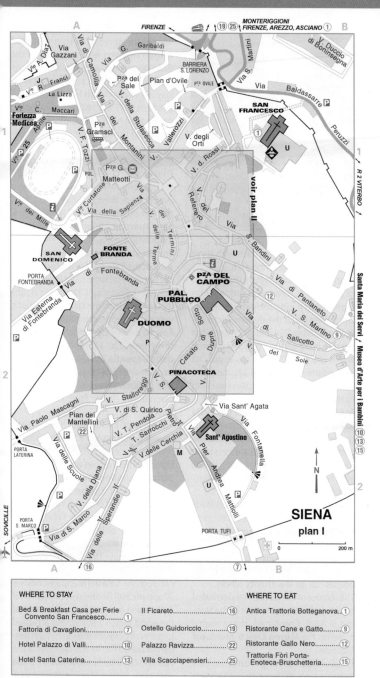

SIENA

plan I

0   200 m

voir plan II

WHERE TO STAY

Bed & Breakfast Casa per Ferie
Convento San Francesco.........①

Fattoria di Cavaglioni.................⑦

Hotel Palazzo di Valli.................⑩

Hotel Santa Caterina.................⑬

Il Ficareto..........................⑯

Ostello Guidoriccio.............⑲

Palazzo Ravizza.................㉒

Villa Scacciapensieri.........㉕

WHERE TO EAT

Antica Trattoria Botteganova..①

Ristorante Cane e Gatto.........⑨

Ristorante Gallo Nero............⑫

Trattoria Fòri Porta-
Enoteca-Bruschetteria.........⑮

slightly concave façade give an impression of lightness despite the size of the building. Two crenellated bell turrets, now empty, flank the top of the main building in the centre of which is a

huge copper circle containing Christ's monogram (IHS – *Iesus Hominum Salvator* – Jesus Saviour of Mankind) which always accompanied St Bernardino. The Sienese shield decorates the tympani of

Torre del Mangia'

the trefoiled windows, each with three bays beneath a relieving arch.

Soaring heavenwards from the east end of the façade, crowned with a white stone belfry elegantly designed by Lippo Memmi, is the slender **Torre del Mangia** (88m/286ft high). It took ten years to build and was only just finished when the Black Death broke out. Its name derives from the nickname of the first of the bellringers. Visitors can climb to the top of the tower (*see below*).

At the foot of the tower is the **Cappella di Piazza**, a chapel in the form of a loggia built in 1352 to express the gratitude of the people of Siena at the cessation of the plague. A century later it was altered and decorated in the Renaissance style.

The doorway (*right of the chapel*) leads into the narrow and austere courtyard, called the Magistrate's Court (*Cortile del Podestà*), of the Palazzo Pubblico.

The palace has been the seat of successive governments of Siena and still houses the local authority offices.

The interior of the palace was decorated by most of the great names in the Sienese School. Combined, these rooms make up the **Museo Civico** (Municipal Museum).

The **Sala de l Risorgimento** (6) gets its name from its decoration which was painted between 1886 and 1891 and which depicts the life of the first King of Italy, Victor Emmanuel II.

The **Sala di Balìa** (7) is also known as the **Priors' Chamber** because, from 1445, it

was the meeting place of the influential magistrates who were members of the *Balìa*, a very old Sienese institution. Its walls, vaulted ceiling and dividing archway are covered with frescoes.

Between 1405 and 1407 Spinello Aretino painted the highly descriptive frescoes depicting the struggle in the 12C between Pope Alexander III, who was born in Siena, and the Holy Roman Emperor, Frederick Barbarossa, in which the Pope was victorious. The most outstanding events were the naval battle in which the Venetians defeated the imperial navy (party wall with Room 8) and (opposite) the Pope's return to Rome.

The allegorical frescoes decorating the vault of the **Sala del Concistoro** (Council Chamber) (9) were painted c. 1530 by Domenico Beccafumi. The classical subjects all allude to the civic and patriotic virtues of the Sienese government.

Among the priceless pieces of gold and silver plate (12C–17C) in the **Vestibollo della Cappella** (Ante-Chapel) (10) is a small and intricately worked gold rose tree by Simone da Firenze, which was given to the city by Pope Pius II Piccolomini.

The **Cappella**★ (Chapel) has a superb wrought-iron **screen**★ which is said to have been designed by Jacopo della Quercia. The frescoes are by Taddeo di Bartolo narrating the *Life of the Virgin Mary* (1407–14). The backs of the choir **stalls**★★ consist of wonderful marquetry panels illustrating the Creed, which are the work of Domenico di Niccolo, assisted by Matteo Vanni, over five years (1425–29). Above the altar is a *Holy Family* by Il Sodoma.

Although the **Sala del Mappamondo**★★ (Mappamundi Room) was named after Ambrogio Lorenzetti's rotating map of the world, which was formerly attached to the wall beneath the equestrian portrait of Guido Riccio, it is famous for the two frescoes by Simone Martini. The admirable **Virgin Mary in Majesty**★★ seated beneath a canopy and flanked by the Apostles, angels and saints (a), is an unexpected sight in a vernacular building. It was the artist's first known work, created in 1315 but badly

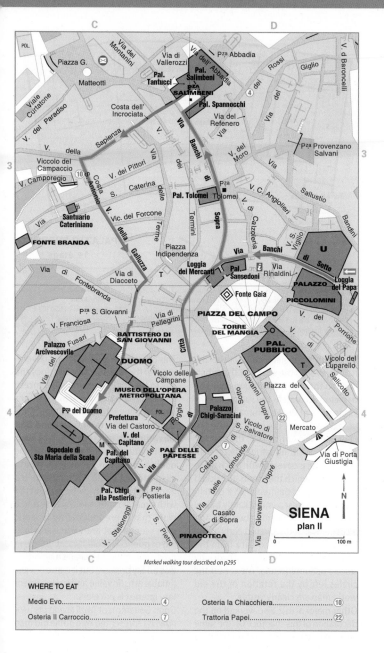

SIENA

plan II

0   100 m

Marked walking tour described on p295

WHERE TO EAT			
Medio Evo	④	Osteria la Chiacchiera	⑩
Osteria Il Carroccio	⑦	Trattoria Papei	㉒

damaged by the damp which has risen from a salt store below. It is unusual in that it was restored by the artist himself in 1321. The flowing composition, expressive faces, wonderfully fluid clothes, delicate colours and intricate decoration make this one of the most

graceful and poetic examples of work from the Sienese Gothic period.

Opposite it is the famous **equestrian portrait of Guido riccio da Fogliano**★★ (**b**). The Sienese General is portrayed between the two fortresses where he put down rebellions in 1328. Although

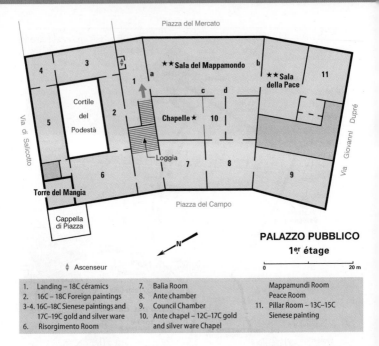

Piazza del Mercato

★★ Sala del Mappamondo   b

★★ Sala della Pace   11

Cortile del Podestà

Chapelle ★   10

Loggia

Torre del Mangia

Piazza del Campo

N

Ascenseur

PALAZZO PUBBLICO
1er étage

0   20 m

1.	Landing – 18C céramics	7.	Balìa Room		Mappamundi Room
2.	16C – 18C Foreign paintings	8.	Ante chamber		Peace Room
3-4.	16C–18C Sienese paintings and 17C–19C gold and silver ware	9.	Council Chamber	11.	Pillar Room – 13C–15C Sienese painting
6.	Risorgimento Room	10.	Ante chapel – 12C–17C gold and silver ware Chapel		

the Republic of Siena paid for the artist to travel to the scene of the rebellions so that the background could be depicted accurately, the rugged chalky landscapes of the Maremma area seem unreal because of the contrast with the inky blue sky. Conversely, the *Condottiere*, proudly sitting astride a horse that, like its rider, is covered with a rich piece of cloth on which the motifs are picked out in detail, is painted with a certain realism. The fresco immediately below the portrait, representing two men and a castle, was rediscovered early in the 1980s. It is thought to date from the early 14C and to be the last work by Duccio di Buoninsegna. The concentric circles left by the rotation of the old world map are clearly visible.

Other major artists also worked on the decoration of this chamber. On the same wall are two frescoes representing two saints painted by Il Sodoma. On one of the pillars St Catherine (**c**) was painted in 1461 by Vecchietta; on the next pillar (**d**) is St Bernardino painted by Sano di Pietro in 1460.

The **Sala della Pace**★★ (Peace Room) contains a number of priceless paintings, unfortunately in a very poor condition.

This chamber was used by the government of the Nine for their meetings and it is to them that Ambrogio Lorenzetti dedicated the two vast compositions painted between 1335 and 1340, illustrating the **Effects of Good and Bad Government**. In a style that is as lively as it is as natural, the artist combined the noble and doctrinal tones inherent to allegorical painting with the detailed narrative style which he supported with great fervour and thus created a work that is predominantly didactic with scenes that are variously amusing or poetic. Not only was it unique in medieval times, in that its inspiration was totally profane, but it is also of inestimable artistic value and its documentary interest is priceless.

Good Government (*wall facing the window*) is represented by a noble old man dressed in the colours of Siena. Beside him are seated the cardinal virtues – Temperance, Justice, Fortitude and Prudence with Magnanimity and Peace; the room takes its name from Peace, one of the finest figures in the fresco, shown dressed in white. Above are the Theological Virtues – Faith, Hope and Charity. Justice is shown a second time, majestically seated on a throne (*extreme left of the scene*). At her feet is Concord, with a plane in her lap, an allusion to the equality that must reign between the citizens depicted on the fresco in rows. They are all holding ropes, the symbol of agreement, running down from the scales of Justice.

The effects of *Good Government* (*above the door*) can be seen in town and country. Against the backdrop of Siena as it was in the Middle Ages with many towers, are a number of elegantly dressed men and women on horseback. A tavern scene shows young men playing and young girls dancing. A clog-maker is at work in his workshop. Masons are building a house. The fields are depicted at the two best seasons of the year (spring and summer). The peasants are busy in the fields while noblemen set off to hunt wild boar.

Bad Government (*on the wall opposite the door*), the most severely damaged fresco, shows figures representing the Vices surrounding Lucifer, who is sowing discord in the town where citizens are being arrested or killed. The countryside appears as it is in the dead seasons of the year (autumn and winter).

The **Sala dei Pilastri** (**11**) contains works by Sienese artists from the 13C, 14C and 15C including a *Maestà* by Guido da Siena (*right-hand wall*) and a surprising *Massacre of the Innocents* by Matteo di Giovanni (*opposite the door*).

From the corridor between the Balìa Room (**7**) and the Risorgimento Room (**6**), a flight of 51 steps leads up to a superb **Loggia** containing the original fragments of the Fonte Gaia. From the loggia, which looks down on the marketplace below, there is an extensive view southeast of the countryside, which penetrates into the city between the urban districts of Santa Maria dei Servi (*left*) and San Agostino (*right*).

Torre del Mangia

🕐*Open mid-Mar–Nov daily 10am–7pm; rest of the year 10am–4pm.* 👁€6, €10 joint ticket with Palazzo Pubblico. 📞0577 29 22 26. www.comune.siena.it/museocivico. *Access from the courtyard; visitors are not allowed to spend more than 20min at the top.*

From the top of the **tower** there is a superb **panoramic view**★★★ of the entire city and the surrounding countryside filled with gently rolling hills.

Two Great Saints

St Catherine was born in Siena in 1347. She was the daughter of a dyer-fuller who had 25 children. According to tradition, she decided at the age of seven to devote her life not to a human but to a heavenly husband and she entered the Dominican Order when she was 16. Her mystical marriage with Christ was a favourite subject with artists. She should not be confused with St Catherine of Alexandria to whom a wedding ring was given, not by the adult Christ but by the Child Jesus. The golden legend of St Catherine of Siena is one of the most eventful in the hagiography. She had numerous visions and ecstasies and received the stigmata in Pisa in 1375. She also wrote a religious treaty. In 1377 she assisted in the return to Rome of the papal court, which had been resident in Avignon since 1309. She died in Rome in 1380.

In the same year **St Bernardino** was born in Massa Marittima. He too is greatly venerated by the Sienese. He gave up his university studies in order to help plague victims in the hospital of Santa Maria della Scala in Siena, of which he took charge. At the age of 22 he entered the Franciscan Order. He founded the Congregation of Observants who complied strictly with the Rule laid down by St Francis and made the monastery of Osservanza to the north of Siena into a major centre for his teaching. St Bernardino was an eloquent reformer who travelled throughout Italy preaching sermons filled with a degree of caustic sarcasm. Two of them, which he preached in Siena, have remained famous to this day. He died in 1440 in L'Aquila.

Cathedral Precinct★★★

2hr

Piazza del Duomo

Cathedral Square, dominated by the famous cathedral, is situated at the top of the hill. The southwest side is lined by the long façade of the hospital of Santa Maria della Scala dating partly from the 13C. Its name, St Mary of the Steps, is derived from the steps (*opposite*) leading up to the main entrance to the cathedral. On the two short sides are (*northwest*) the neo-Gothic Archbishop's Palace and (*southeast*) the 16C Prefecture.

Antico Ospedale di Santa Maria della Scala

This former hospital houses various exhibitions and an interesting Etruscan museum. Among the most interesting rooms is the 14C **Sala del Pellegrinaio**★, which is decorated with frescoes, most of which are attributed to Vecchietta (c. 1412–80) and to Domenico di Bartolo (1428–47). Note the scaffolding in the *Alms of the Bishop* or the detail in the most famous fresco, *Government and the Cure of the Sick*.

Duomo★★★(Cathedral)

⚭*See floor plan on following pages.*
🕑*Open mid-Mar–Oct 7.30am–7.30pm; rest of the year 7.30am–1pm and* 2.30pm–5pm (Sun to end of Mass). 𝄞0577 28 30 48. www.operaduomo. siena.it.

The history of the **cathedral** is complex. The present building was begun in the middle of the 12C but was not completed until early in the 14C. The final work was mainly due to the Cistercian monks of San Galgano, who sought inspiration in the design of their own abbey. In the 14C, when Siena was at the height of its prosperity, the citizens decided to create a much larger church in honour of the Virgin Mary, a cathedral which would be larger than the one in the rival city of Florence. The existing building would have become simply the transept of the new edifice. The work began in 1339 and was proceeding with great speed when it was suddenly interrupted in 1348 by the outbreak of the Plague.

Siena lost much of its manpower and decided to abandon the vast project. Some of the new building was deemed dangerous since the ground had been insufficiently prepared to take its weight and it was demolished. In the last quarter of the 14C, therefore, work began on the completion of the original cathedral – the upper section of the west front, raising the roof level of the nave, construction of the apse. The only relics of the grandiose 14C project are the arches of the nave and what was to be the façade of the new building (*south side of the present cathedral*).

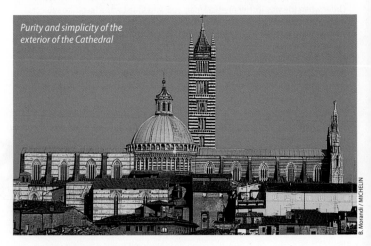

Purity and simplicity of the exterior of the Cathedral

B. Morandi / MICHELIN

Pavement of the Duomo

1. Hermes Trismegistus (1481 – 1498)
2. Coat of arms of Siena and 12 other towns (mosaic)
3. Imperial altar
4. Allegory of Fortune (Pinturicchio)
5. Wheel of Fortune (Marchese d'Adamo, 1406)
6-15. Sibyls (1481 – 1498)
16. The Seven Ages of Man (c. 1450)
17. The theological virtues – Faith, Hope and Charity – and Religion
18. Story of Jephthah (1481 – 1498)
19. Story of Eli and Ahab (Beccafumi 1518 – 1547) (certain scenes were repainted in 1878 by Alessandro Franchi)
20. Moses smiting the rock to bring forth water (Beccafumi 1518 – 1547)
21. Moses on Mount Sinai (Beccafumi between 1518 and 1547)
22. Emperor Sigismond (1434)
23. Death of Absalom (1443)
24. Battle of Samson against the Philistines (c. 1425)
25. Moses and the tablets of the Law (c. 1425)
26. Goliath the giant (c. 1425)
27. David singing psalms (c. 1425)
28. Young David armed with his sling (c. 1425)
29. Joshua (c. 1425)
30. Hanging of the five Amorite kings (c. 1425)
31. Abraham's sacrifice (Beccafumi 1518 – 1547)
32. Prudence (Marchese di Adamo, Early 15C)
33. Temperance (Marchese di Adamo, Early 15C)
34. Mercy (Marchese di Adamo, Early 15C)
35. Justice (Marchese di Adamo, Early 15C)
36. Fortitude (Marchese di Adamo, Early 15C)
37. Judith liberating Bethulia (1473)
38. Massacre of the Holy Innocents (Matteo di Giovanni, 1481– 1495)
39. Herod losing his throne (1481 – 1498)

DUOMO
Piazza San Giovanni
0   10 m

35 34 33
36 CHŒUR 32
31
C 29 25
30 27 24
28 26
★★★ Chaire 21 22 23
37 20
38 18
TRANSECT
19
B 39 16 17 A
Libreria
Piccolomini 15 5 10
14 4 9
13 NEF 8
3
12 2 7
11 1 6
N
Piazza del Duomo

Although somewhat lacking in unity, the **West Front** is attractive for its rich ornamentation and the gentle colouring in its marble. The lower section is Romanesque but shows signs of the impending Gothic style. It was designed by Giovanni Pisano, who worked on it from 1285 to 1296 and decorated it with statues that have now been replaced by copies (*originals in the Cathedral Museum*).

The upper section, which was built a century later and was strongly influenced by the west front of the cathedral in Orvieto, shows the full exuberance of the Gothic style. The mosaics on the gables date from the end of the 19C. The **Campanile** (bell tower), completed in 1313, is austerely Romanesque.

The most characteristic and breathtaking features of the **Interior** are the densely alternating horizontal bands of light and dark marble, the short but very broad transept, the rectangular apse, and the large number of pillars which provide an infinity of different perspectives in the transept and chancel.

The **Pavement**★★★ is unique. It is composed of 56 marble panels depicting figures from mythology (Sibyls, Virtues and allegories) and scenes from the Old

Geometry of the interior of the Cathedral

M. Gurfinkel/ MICHELIN

Testament, all of them outstanding for their intricacy and liveliness.

They were produced between 1369 and 1547 by some 40 artists, including Matteo di Giovanni, Pinturicchio and Beccafumi. The designs for 35 of the panels are due to Beccafumi's remarkable talent for drawing and decoration. Some of them have been restored; others have been replaced by copies.

60% of the pavement is protected from excessive wear by a temporary floor which is moved from time to time so that all the panels can be admired in succession.

The oldest panels were made using the *graffito* technique. They consist of white outlines on a black background and the details and reliefs are engraved in the marble then blackened using asphalt. From 1518 onwards, when Beccafumi took over the work, he used inlay techniques with different coloured marbles.

The Baroque **Cappella della Madonna del Voto** (A) contains (*flanking the door*) marble statues of *St Jerome* (*right*) and *St Mary Magdalen* (*left*) carved by Bernini in the 17C. He also produced the altar and the two angels above it.

The right-hand wall in front of the entrance is covered with votive offerings, including a few caps hung there by jockeys (*fantini*) after the Palio (*see above*). The superb 16C marble altar in the **Sanctuary** has a fine bronze tabernacle, made c1470 by Vecchietta, and four candlesticks at the corners, made

a few years later by Francesco di Giorgio Martini (the two lower candlesticks) and Giovanni di Stefano. The back panels of the choir **stalls**★★ are a fine example of woodcarving with marquetry. The ones at the end of the chancel date from the 16C; the ones on the sides, which are the finest, date from the 14C and were further embellished by wonderful marquetry panelling by Fra Giovanni da Verona (1503). The circular stained-glass window in the sanctuary (recently restored) depicts the *Annunciation*, the *Coronation* and the *Burial of the Virgin* Mary. It was made in 1288 to designs by Duccio di Buoninsegna.

The **Cappella di Sant'Ansano** (B) was dedicated to the first patron saint of Siena. Set in its pavement is the gravestone of Bishop Pecci carved by Donatello (1426); against the wall is a marble Gothic tomb (1318) by Tino di Camaino and his father, Camaino di Crescentino.

The splendid carved marble **Pulpit**★★★ is a masterpiece by Nicola Pisano made from 1266 to 1268, six years after the one in the Baptistery in Pisa, with the assistance of Giovanni, his son, and a few other pupils such as Arnolfo di Cambio. The pulpit bears a resemblance to the earlier one but shows greater compliance with the Gothic tradition in its light design and flowing sculptures.

The artist has used seven panels to depict episodes from the Life of Christ with the same sense of grandeur and power as on the pulpit in Pisa but with heightened drama – (*left to right*) the *Nativity*, the *Adoration of the Magi*, the *Flight into Egypt* and the *Presentation of Jesus in the Temple*, the *Massacre of the Innocents*, the *Crucifixion* and the *Last Judgement* (*two panels*). The various panels are separated by statues of prophets and angels. On the sill is a lectern shaped like an eagle, the emblem of St John. Between the trefoiled arches are seated female figures representing the Virtues. The pulpit is supported by nine marble, granite and porphyry columns.

Shaped like a rotunda, the Renaissance **Cappella di San Giovanni Battista** (C) contains a statue of St John the Baptist by Donatello (1457) in a niche (*below the* *window*). The frescoes (restored) are by Pinturicchio.

A highly decorative marble doorway flanks the entrance to the **Libreria Piccolomini**, a very famous room, which was built c. 1495 on the orders of Cardinal Francesco Piccolomini to contain the library of Enea Silvia Piccolomini, his uncle, who had become Pope Pius II.

On the floor and in the friezes round the ceiling is the Piccolomini emblem, the crescent moon set on a blue background. All of the walls were painted by Pinturicchio. In the **frescoes**★★ that he produced between 1502 and 1509 he used his light, attractive narrative talents to illustrate the main episodes in the life of the Pope.

The series of ten panels shows (*starting right of the window and going clockwise*) his departure from Genoa to attend the Council of Basel, his return from the Council, his meeting with James I of Scotland, his consecration as a poet by Frederick III, his submission to Pope Eugene II, Enea at the betrothal of Emperor Frederick III and Eleonora of Aragon near the Camollia Gate, Pope Calixtus III presenting him with the Cardinal's hat, his election as Pope, his decision to go to war against the Turks taken at the Congress in Mantua, the canonisation of Catherine of Siena, the welcome extended to the Christian fleet on its return from Turkey. The ceiling is richly decorated with allegories, mythological scenes and grotesques. A fine marble group representing the *Three Graces*, a 3C Roman sculpture showing the influence of the Greek tradition, stands in the centre of the room. The display cases beneath the frescoes contain 15C psalters. Outside the Libreria (*on the right*) is the impressive **Piccolomini Altar**, a late 15C work with statues attributed to Michelangelo.

Museo dell'Opera Metropolitana★★ (Cathedral Museum)

Piazza del Duomo 8. Entrance beneath the great arch facing the south transept of the cathedral. ⊙*Open Mar–Nov daily 9.30am–7pm; rest of the year daily* 10am–5pm. ⊙*Closed 1 Jan, 25 Dec.* ⊛*€6, €10 joint ticket (valid for 3 days) with Libreria, Battistero, Oratorio S. Bernardino.* ✆*0577 28 30 48. www.operaduomo.siena.it.*

The **cathedral museum** is housed in what was to be the south aisle of the new cathedral.

On each side of the **Ground Floor** gallery are statues by **Giovanni Pisano**, originally designed to decorate the west front of the cathedral. They include prophets, sages of Antiquity and Sibyls. Just beyond the gates in this room is the great roundel (*tondo*) of the *Madonna and Child* by Donatello. Near the entrance are the bull and the lion – symbols of the Evangelists – and the She-wolf suckling Romulus and Remus, the emblem of Siena, also by Giovanni Pisano. In the centre of the room is a superb **relief** representing the Virgin Mary, St Anthony Abbot and a cardinal; it was carved by Jacopo della Quercia in the year of his death (1438).

On the **First Floor**, admirably highlighted against the ambient gloom, is the famous **Maestà**★★★ (Virgin Mary in Majesty) painted by Duccio towards the end of his life for the high altar in the cathedral. The now-separated reredos, commissioned by the city in 1308 for 3 000 gold florins, had narrative panels on both sides. The artist worked on it for almost three years, after which the *Maestà*, which has remained his greatest masterpiece, was carried with much pomp and ceremony through cheering crowds from the painter's studio to the cathedral. The work is of outstanding interest for its effect on Sienese painting in later years. The Virgin Mary is set against a golden background, in accordance with medieval Byzantine tradition, and is pictured from the front, her face absolutely devoid of expression. Yet the work shows a certain flexibility, which is a precursor of Gothic art.

The reverse side of the reredos (*left of the entrance*) originally consisted of some 40 panels which were sold off in 1771; some of them are now in London and New York. The 14 panels here depict episodes from Christ's Passion, with an

Reverse side of the Maestà by Duccio

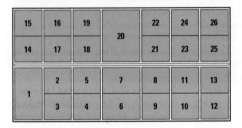

1. Christ's entry into Jerusalem
2. Christ washing the Disciples' feet
3. The Last Supper
4. Jesus taking leave of the Apostles
5. Judas' pact
6. Jesus praying on the Mount of Olives
7. The kiss of Judas
8. Jesus before Annas, the High Priest
9. Peter denies Christ
10. Jesus before Calaphas, the High Priest
11. Jesus being mocked
12. Jesus brought before Pontius Pilate
13. Pontius Pilate's response to the Jews
14. Jesus before Herod
15. Jesus brought before Pontius Pilate again
16. Jesus being scourged
17. The Crown of Thorns
18. Pontius Pilate washing his hands
19. The climb to Calvary
20. The Crucifixion
21. The deposition from the Cross
22. The entombment
23. The Descent into Hell
24. The women at the tomb
25. Christ appears to Mary Magdalen
26. The pilgrims on the road to Emmaüs

exceptionally rich narrative style and a charming sense of observation.

In his work the *Birth of the Virgin Mary* (*against the wall to the right of the door*) Pietro Lorenzetti used a triptych to depict a single scene. Beside it is the *Madonna and Child* by Duccio.

The most outstanding items displayed in **Cathedral Treasury** (*mezzanine and second floor*) are the bellcote-shaped reliquary containing the head of St Galgano (*centre of the room*), a fine piece of *repoussé* silver-gilt work dating from the late 13C and decorated with scenes from the saint's life, the "Golden Rose Tree" (*display case against the end wall*) given by Pope Alexander VII Chigi in 1658 to the cathedral in Siena, his native city, and a superb 15C **altarcloth** (*against the left-hand wall*) embroidered in gold and silver thread with scenes from the *Life of Christ*; the *Annunciation, Christ's Entry into Jerusalem*, and the *Last Supper* are particularly fine.

In the room opposite the head of the stairs on the **Third Floor** are some fine works by the Primitives including (*in the centre*) the **Madonna dagli occhi grossi** (*Madonna with the Large Eyes*) which gave its name to the room.

This is one of the earliest Sienese paintings (early 13C) . There is also a *St Bernardino* by Sano di Pietro flanked by two scenes representing the saint preaching to the crowds in Piazza del Campo and Piazza San Francesco in Siena.

The other room (*right of the head of the stairs*) is hung with works by 16C–17C Italian artists including a *St Paul* by Beccafumi in which the background shows the saint's conversion on the road to Damascus and his beheading.

At the far end are the steps (*about 150*) up to the top of the façade of the unfinished nave of the abandoned cathedral. From the top there is a magnificent **panoramic view**★★.

Battistero San Giovanni★

⏱Open Mar–Nov daily 9.30am–7pm; rest of the year daily 10am–5pm.
🚫Closed 1 Jan, 25 Dec. ⊛€3, €10 joint ticket (valid for 3 days) with Museo dell' Opera, Libreria, Oratorio S. Bernardino. ℘0577 28 30 48. www.operaduomo. siena.it.

The unfinished 14C Baptistery of St John, beneath the apse of the cathedral, has a white marble façade (1382) and was built in a more austere Gothic style than the cathedral.

The interior is vaulted and has three aisles. It was decorated with frescoes in the 15C. In the centre stands the 15C **font**★★. It consists of a hexagonal basin decorated with gilded bronze panels capped by a delightful marble tabernacle. Said to have been designed by Jacopo della Quercia, it is one of the most successful pieces of Tuscan sculpture from the transitional period between Gothic and Renaissance.

Several masters worked on the panels round the basin depicting episodes from the life of St John the Baptist: *Zachariah being expelled from the Temple* (*beside the altar*) was also by della Quercia; *The Birth of St John the Baptist* (*next on the right*) was by Turino di Sano; *The Preaching of St John the Baptist* was by Giovanni di Turino, one of Jacopo della Quercia's pupils; *The Baptism of Jesus* and the *Arrest of St John the Baptist* were carved by Lorenzo Ghiberti, who designed the Paradise Door in the Baptistery in Florence; and *Herod's Feast* was by Donatello. Donatello also carved two of the statues of the *Virtues of Faith and Hope* placed at each of the corners of the basin.

Pinacoteca★★★
(Picture Gallery)

2hr. Palazzo Buonsignori, Via San Pietro 29. ♿⏱Open Tue–Sat 10am–5.15pm, Mon, Sun and Hols 8.30am–1.15pm. 🚫Closed 1 Jan, 1 May, 25 Dec. Bookshop. ⊛€4. ℘577 28 11 61. www.comune.siena.it.

The **picture gallery** is housed in the **Buonsignori Palace**★ (mid-15C). Although it contains very few works by Sienese masters Duccio and Simone Martini, it is of outstanding interest for its extensive collections showing the development of Sienese painting from the 13C to the 16C.

The **Second Floor** is devoted to the Primitives. The painted *Crucifixes* in **Rooms 1 and 2** used to decorate the Romanesque churches in the region, and were the only pictures in existence in the late 12C and early 13C. The first room contains two examples of these works, both of them of Byzantine inspiration, obvious in their hieratic character and brilliant colouring. Christ is shown in triumph and not in suffering, as was the case in later years. The first known artist from Siena was Guido da Siena.

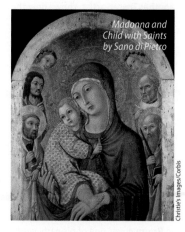
Madonna and Child with Saints by Sano di Pietro

Christie's Images/Corbis

The three scenes from the Life of Christ (*wall opposite the door*) are among the earliest works on canvas attributed to his school.

The second room is almost entirely concerned with this great master, Guido da Siena. His works were all markedly Greek in style. The figures are shown from front view, although the heads are sometimes bent or seen from three-quarter view; the volume is suggested in the lines – the systematic emphasis of the ridge of the nose, the concentric lines used to

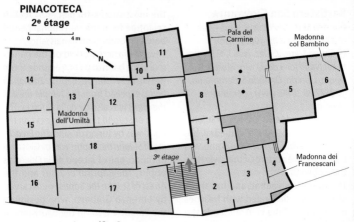

PINACOTECA
2e étage

Via San Pietro

suggest volume in the cheeks – and the folds or creases in the clothes are very marked and emphasised in dark colours or gold. The painting of *St Francis* (*right of the door*) by Margaritone d'Arezzo, another Tuscan artist, shows how the Byzantine influence continued until the second half of the 13C.

In some cases the end of the 13C was marked by a development in artistic techniques: facial shapes were more gentle, the attitudes more natural and fabrics given greater volume. Niccolo di Segna, in **Room 3**, sought to accentuate the natural features of his figures; the eyes are no longer heavily outlined and the hair and beards are softer. His large painting of the *Crucifixion* (*opposite the window*) shows a suffering Christ. Duccio is the supreme representative of the great period of Sienese painting. The delicate little **Franciscan Madonna** in **Room 4** was one of his early works and it shows the solemnity and rigidity of expression typical of Byzantine art. There is, however, a foretaste of the flowing, graceful lines that were to characterise the Sienese School in later years in the slight bend in the Virgin Mary's body and the curl along the hem of her cloak.

Room 5 contains paintings by Luca di Tommè and Bartolo di Fredi, who worked during the second half of the 14C, in the same style as the great masters (Simone Martini and the Lorenzetti brothers) but

with additional refinement. An *Adoration of the Magi* by di Fredi (*right-hand wall*) shows brilliant narrative skill and exquisite command of colouring.

Simone Martini (d. 1344) is represented in **Room 6** by his **Virgin and Child** painted with a softness and purity rarely equalled. There is also his attractive polyptych of the *Blessed Agostino Novello*. The Madonnas painted by Lippo Memmi, his closest pupil, show something of his elegance and grace but they lack the vibrant lyricism that characterised the works of the great master of Sienese painting.

Room 7 room is also of outstanding interest for its remarkable series of works by the Lorenzetti brothers, who died of the plague in 1348. The great **Pala del Carmine** (*right of the door to Room 8*) was a reredos commissioned from Pietro, the elder brother, in 1329 by the Carmelites of Siena. Although the severe and impressive *Virgin Mary in Majesty*, shown full face and sitting very straight, is still rather stiff, the scenes on the predella depicting the history of the Carmelite Order show a very lively sense of narrative, supplemented by the landscapes and architectural perspectives. The exquisite little *Virgin Mary in Majesty* (*opposite*) by Ambrogio, Pietro's brother, is a more precious and more refined piece of work which is also more tender, like his other representations of the Madonna, several of which are in the same room. Ambrogio also painted two charming little views of a *Town overlooking the Sea* and a *Castle on the Shores of a Lake* in which his Gothic grace is expressed in the extreme detail of the towers above the town and the graceful curve of the boat on the lake.

The golden *Assumption*, a work of unrivalled affectedness, was painted by the Master of Monte Oliveto who was strongly influenced by the monumental character of Pietro Lorenzetti's works. Most of the works on the left-hand side of the room are by this artist and by Paolo di Giovanni Fei.

In **Rooms 11 to 13** are examples of works from the last Sienese Primitives to work in the late-Gothic style in the 15C. Taddeo di Bartolo (*Room 11*), who died c. 1425 is represented here by an *Annunciation* (*right-hand wall*). In Room 12 is the *Assumption of the Virgin Mary surrounded by four Saints* by Giovanni di Paolo (c. 1403–82), whose Mannerist tendencies are obvious – the flowing garments, the slight bend in the knees of John the Baptist and the very obvious veins and the almost excessive suffering of the *Ecce Homo* and saints on the predella. The artist's delightful **Virgin of Humility** (*Room 13 – left of the door*) is exquisitely unreal, with a long and sinuous outline, separated by a poetic curtain of rose trees from a minutely detailed background.

Rooms 14 and 15 contain Sienese works that have been influenced by the Renaissance masters. In the 15C Sienese art was open to the innovations of the Renaissance while at the same time retaining the grace that is natural to the city of the *Palio*. In his religious paintings, Francesco di Giorgio Martini (1439–1502) shows the beginnings of the Florentine influence and in his descriptive landscapes there is an obvious fondness for Mantegna. Matteo di Giovanni (c. 1430–95) had a vigourous drawing technique and he willingly accentuated and varied the attitudes and expressions of his figures; he produced a number of paintings of the *Madonna and Child* (*Room 14*) and an *Adoration of the Shepherds* (*Room 15*).

Sano di Pietro (1406–81), represented in **Rooms 16 and 17**, was a very prolific but not very innovatory artist. It was he, however, who remained most faithful to the Gothic style during this period. His great polyptych (*Room 16 – right-hand wall*) shows a *Madonna and Child with Saints* in brilliant, refined colours; the drawing is of good quality. He also was the author of a number of exuberant polyptychs (*Room 17*) in the Gothic style.

The aesthetic innovations of the Florentine Renaissance are also evident in **Room 18** in works by Vecchietta (c. 1400–80) whose great coffered panel (*centre of the room*), originally part of a reliquary chest (*arliquiera*), shows a very obvious sense of perspective. In works by Girolamo di Benvenuto and Benvenuto di Giovanni, this new style is accompanied by a certain harshness.

The **Spannocchi Collection** on the **Third Floor** contains paintings from the 16C–17C of Flemish, Dutch and German origin (*St Jerome* by Dürer); from Venice (works by Paris Bordon, *Nativity* by Lorenzo Lotto) and from Lombardy, Emilia and Rome.

Room 23 (*2nd room to the right beyond the courtyard*) contains a roundel (*tondo*) of *The Holy Family with the young St John* by Pinturicchio set against a background of gentle countryside suffused in the characteristic light of Umbrian skies.

The other two artists whose personality marked Sienese painting in the 16C, Beccafumi and Il Sodoma, are well represented. Among the outstanding works by Beccafumi is a **Birth of the Virgin Mary** (*below Room 13 on the 2nd floor*) in which the colours are daringly graduated; the main subject is set against a fairly dark background that seems to absorb the colours because of the unreal lighting. Il Sodoma painted the pathos-filled **Christ on the Column** (*below Room 15*) which is an amazingly beautiful work in aesthetic terms. The following room contains his large *Deposition from the Cross* on which the clothes look like sails swirling in the wind and the colours are rich and shimmering.

Other Sights

Basilica di San Domenico★

Piazza San Domenico.

It was in this convent **church** near her home (☞*see below*) that St Catherine of Siena experienced her ecstasies. The church was built from the 13C–15C in a powerful and austere Gothic style.

The T-shaped interior is spacious and well-lit, with a wide nave and very small chancel.

At the east end of the nave and on a slightly higher level is the Cappella delle Volte, a chapel which contains (*above the altar*) the only authentic portrait of the Saint, painted by one of her contemporaries, the Sienese artist, Andrea Vanni.

In **St Catherine's Chapel** (*mid-nave – right*) is the Renaissance marble **taber-nacle**★ carved in 1466 by Giovanni di Stefano, another Sienese artist, which contains the Saint's head. Il Sodoma painted the famous **frescoes**★ (*end wall and left-hand wall*) which depict scenes from her life: St Catherine in Ecstasy, St Catherine receiving the Stigmata, St Catherine helping a Condemned Man. The modern stained glass windows in the chancel were made in 1982 by B Cassinari.

The tabernacle and two angels (*high altar*) were carved in the 15C by Benedetto da Maiano. The delightful triptych of the *Madonna and Child surrounded by Saints* (*first chapel to the right*) is by Matteo di Giovanni, who also painted an exquisite *St Barbara between two Angels and two other Saints* (*second chapel to the left*). In the lunette (*right-hand wall*) is an *Adoration of the Magi*.

Santuario Cateriniano (St Catherine's Birthplace)

Costa di Sant'Antonio, entrance Via Santa Caterina.

The birthplace of St Catherine of Siena, which was turned into a sanctuary in 1465, now consists of a group of super-imposed chapels, surrounded by other buildings. On the lower floor (*staircase left at the end*), on the site of the dyeshop belonging to Catherine's father, there is now a church dedicated to the Saint. On the upper floor are two chapels. The one (*left*), on the site of the former kitchen, is richly decorated with wooden panel-ling decorated in blue and gold and a superb majolica pavement dating from the 17C. The other (*right*) contains the 13C painted Crucifix to which the Saint is said to have been praying in Pisa when she received the stigmata.

Fonte Branda★

Via di Fontebranda.

Downhill from the basilica church of San Domenico is the unusual brick-built **Branda Fountain**, the oldest in the city. It was already in existence in 1080 but it was in 1246 that it acquired its present form, similar to the façade of Siena's Gothic mansions with its crenel-lated top and three arches as wide as doorways.

Basilica di San Francesco

Piazza San Francesco.

On the very top of one of the three hills on which Siena is built stands the basilican **church** dedicated to St Fran-cis, designed in the Gothic style but extensively restored (19C west front). It was in front of this church in 1425 that **St Bernardino**, a Franciscan monk, preached one of his sermons, hence the small **chapel** (*right of the church*) bear-ing the three initials IHS on its façade. The basilica always flies the colours of the *contrade*. The building has a single, magnificently wide **nave**★, in which the painted decor imitates the alternating black and white marble of the cathedral, and a chancel, flanked by small chapels. The church is lit by particularly fine nar-rative stained-glass windows.

Pietro Lorenzetti painted the fresco (*first chapel to the left of the altar*) represent-ing the *Crucifixion*, and other frescoes (*third chapel*) are by his brother, Ambro-gio, depicting (*right-hand wall*) *St Louis of Toulouse*, great-nephew of St Louis and brother of Robert of Anjou, King of Naples, in front of *Boniface VIII* and (*opposite*) the *Martyrdom of the Francis-cans in Ceuta*. This was the church cho-sen by Verdi for the first performance of his *Requiem*, with a choir of 400 singers, as is recorded on the plaque (*east end of the nave – left-hand side*).

Sant'Agostino
Prato di Sant'Agostino.
This **church**, which is dedicated to St Augustine, dates from the 13C but has a Baroque interior (18C) redesigned by Vanvitelli.
The admirable **Adoration of the Crucifix**★ (*second altar to the right*), set against a superb landscaped background, was painted in 1506 by Perugino. The Piccolomini Chapel (*door immediately beyond the altar*) contains some interesting **paintings**★: a remarkably fresh fresco of the *Madonna with the Saints* by Ambrogio Lorenzetti and an *Adoration of the Magi* by Il Sodoma (*above the altar*).

Santa Maria dei Servi
Piazza Manzoni.
The **church** presents an unfinished and rustic façade of brick at the top of a short avenue of cypress trees. Above

it is an attractive Romanesque-Gothic bell tower. From the top of the steps in front of the church, there is a magnificent **view**★★★ of the steeply sloping hill on which the cathedral is built and of the rear of the Palazzo Pubblico.
The interior of the church is an unusual combination of Gothic and Renaissance styles but it also contains some outstanding **works of art**★: a *Virgin Mary in Majesty* (1261) by the Florentine artist Coppo di Marcovaldo who was taken prisoner at Montaperti and is said to have painted this work (*second altar on the right*) in exchange for his freedom; a highly expressive *Massacre of the Innocents* by Matteo di Giovanni (*fifth altar*); frescoes by Pietro Lorenzetti (*second chapel on the left of the chancel*) depicting *Salome's Dance* and the *Death of St John the Baptist* (*right*); an *Adoration of the Shepherds* (1404) (*above the altar*) by Taddeo di Bartolo. A very gentle *Virgin Mary of Misericord* by Lippo Memmi (*end of the north transept*) is incorporated into another painting.

Walking Tour
Map p283

Stroll through the streets of Siena, starting from the Piazza Banchi di Sotto, from the **Loggia del Papa** (*right*) is a building with huge Renaissance arches supported by Corinthian columns. Its name recalls that it was built at the request of Pope Pius II Piccolomini.

Via Banchi di Sotto★
East from the junction of Via di Città and Via Banchi di Sopra.
This **street**, which skirts the north side of the mansions facing Piazza del Campo, includes the historic university of Siena (*left*). Opposite is the white travertine façade of the **Palazzo Piccolomini**★. It was very probably Bernardo Rossellino, the architect of the Palazzo Ruccellai in Florence, who drew the plans for this fine Renaissance build-

ing and gave it its Florentine features – façade with light rustication becoming even less marked towards the top, small cornices emphasising the various levels, projecting roof with the coat of arms of the Piccolomini (crescent moon) set between the consoles. It houses the city archives.

◗ *Take Via Banchi di Sopra.*

Via Banchi di Sopra★

◗ *North from the junction of Via di Città and Via Banchi di Sotto.*

On the west side of Piazza Tolomei stands **Palazzo Tolomei**, dating from the early 13C, which now houses the Cassa di Risparmio di Firenze. This is the oldest privately owned mansion in Siena. Its façade is built entirely of stone and has two rows of Gothic double-bay windows over an unusually high ground floor. It gives an impression of austerity but also of elegance. Robert of Anjou, King of Naples, stayed here in 1310.

Piazza Salimbeni★ is one of the most noble squares in Siena and is lined on three sides by buildings in which three different styles of architecture are represented. On the east side is 14C **Palazzo Salimbeni**, which was extensively restored in 1879. It has a light-coloured stone façade with a row of Gothic triple-bay windows, each capped by a pointed arch. It was named after an influential medieval Sienese family of merchants and bankers.

Building began on the **Palazzo Spannocchi** (*south side*) in 1470 to designs by the Florentine architect Giuliano da Maiano, for the treasurer to Pope Pius II Piccolomini. Its Renaissance façade with double bays and three rows of smooth rustication flanked by cornices is similar to the mansion built during the same period in Florence.

The **Palazzo Tantucci** (*north side*) was designed almost a century later by the Sienese architect, Riccio. All three house the departments of the famous **Monte dei Paschi**, a very ancient Sienese credit institution founded in 1472; its very existence was closely linked to the prosperity of Siena. Its name comes from the pastures (*pascoli* or *paschi*) in the Maremma region of Tuscany which in those days were owned by Siena. The income from the pastures guaranteed the financial viability of the credit institution. The Monte dei Paschi is now one of the foremost banks in Italy.

▷ *Take Via della Sapienza and turn left into Via della Galluzza.*

Via della Galluzza

▷ *Northwest from Piazza del Campo.*

This narrow, steeply-sloping **street** is one of the most picturesque medieval thoroughfares in Siena. It is lined with old brick houses incorporating unremarkable doors and windows and has eight arches, one of which includes an attractive triple bay.

▷ *Walk towards the Duomo. At the Piazza, take Via del Capitano.*

Via del Capitano★

▷ *From Piazza del Duomo southeast to Piazza Postierla (also known as Quattro Cantoni).*

This **street** is one of the finest in Siena. **Palazzo Chigi alla Postieria** (*left no 1*) is a 16C building attributed to the Sienese architect Riccio.

The late 13C **Palazzo del Capitano del Popolo** (*left nos 15–19*), which was extensively restored in the 19C, is a fine Gothic building of stone and brick in the Sienese style. The powerful and austere lower level has only three tall doorways and contrasts sharply with the top of the building, which is relieved by a long row of Gothic double-bay windows, a cornice above tiny arches containing coats of arms and a row of merlons.

▷ *Turn into Via di Città.*

Via di Città ★

▷ *From Piazza Postierla (south of Piazza del Duomo) to Via Banchi di Sotto (north of Piazza del Campo).*

This **street**, like most in the historic city centre, is a pedestrian precinct. Together with Via Banchi di Sopra, it constitutes the main shopping area in Siena.

Both streets are narrow and winding, cobbled and without pavements but they are lined with patrician houses and superb **palaces**★.

In **Via di Città** (*about half way from the southern end*) beyond several brick mansions is (*left*) Palazzo Piccolomini, also known as **Palazzo delle Papesse**, which now houses the offices of the Banco d'Italia. It was probably designed by Bernardo Rossellino and built of light-coloured stone in the second half of the 15C on the orders of Catherine Piccolomini, the sister of Pope Pius II (Enea Silvia Piccolomini). On the lower section of its stone façade it has marked rustication in the style of the Florentine Renaissance.

Almost opposite is the long and slightly curved Gothic façade of the **Palazzo Chigi-Saracini**, which was partially rebuilt in the 18C. The combination of stone and brick, the two rows of elegant triple-bay windows and the merlons along the top of the wall are all reminiscent of the Palazzo Pubblico. The building houses the *Accademia Chigiana*, a famous academy of music. It was from the top of its tower, since truncated, that the victory of Montaperti is said to

have been proclaimed to the citizens. At the north end of the street (*Croce del Travaglio*) is the **Loggia dei Mercanti** (*right*), the Merchants' Loggia, which was the seat of the Commercial Court. It was built at the beginning of the 15C. Its architecture is Renaissance but its decoration – niches with statues – still bears traces of the Gothic style. Marble benches carved with low reliefs representing philosophers and generals from the days of ancient Rome run along two of its sides. The upper storey was added in the 17C.

Excursions

CONVENTO DELL'OSSERVANZA

3km/2mi NE of Siena by S 408 (to Montevarchi). After the level crossing, follow the yellow signs to Basilica Osservanza.

The **Observants' Monastery**, which was founded by St Bernardino (♿ *see p285*), stands on a hilltop from which there is an attractive view of Siena.

The brick basilica, which was rebuilt in its 15C style after being destroyed in 1944, contains some interesting **works of art**★ – a terracotta *Coronation of the Virgin Mary* by Andrea della Robbia (*second chapel on the left*); a triptych of the *Madonna and Child* by Sano di Pietro (*first chapel on the left*); a fine *Pietà* (*second chapel on the right*) carved by the Sienese sculptor, Giacomo Cozzarelli (1453–1515).

Inside the monastery is St Bernardino's cell containing his personal effects and a cast of his face made in 1443, one year before his death.

ASCIANO

21km/13mi SE by S 438.

Asciano is separated from Siena by a line of hills. It is an old medieval fortified town on a rise overlooking the Ombrone river. The Corso Matteotti runs through it from one end to the other.

The 12C Romanesque **Basilica di Sant'Agata** (St Agatha's Basilica), built

entirely of travertine marble, has a Gothic façade approached by a wide flight of steps. The nave, with its bare rafters, has a wonderful fresco of the *Madonna and Child* attributed to Girolamo del Pacchia.

Left of the basilica is the **Museo di Arte Sacra** (✆*0577 71 95 10*). The museum of sacred art houses a collection of paintings and sculptures by the Sienese School, dating from the 14C and 15C, including an *Annunciation* by Taddeo di Bartolo, a *Birth of the Virgin Mary* by Sassetta and a polyptych by Ambrogio Lorenzetti with *St Michael Slaying the Dragon* (central panel).

On Corso Matteotti is the **Museo Archeologico** (🕐*open mid-Mar–Jun;* 🕐*closed Nov–mid-Mar;* ✆ *€4.50;* ✆*0577 71 95 10*), an Etruscan archaeology museum, housed in the tiny Church of San Bernardino. It contains exhibits (ceramics, urns) dating from the 5C to 1C BC from the neighbouring Etruscan cemetery in Poggio Pinci.

The **Museo Amos e Giuseppe Cassioli** (🕐*open Apr to mid-Oct daily (except Tue afternoon) 10am–noon and 3pm–6pm, Sat–Sun and Hols 9.30am–12.30pm; rest of the year open mornings only;* ✆*€4;* ✆*0577 71 95 10*) is devoted to the works of Amos Cassioli (1832–92), who was famous in his day for his portraits and historical paintings, and of Giuseppe Cassioli (1865–1942), his son.

ADDRESSES

🏠 STAY

Campeggio Colleverde – *Strada di Scacciapensieri 47, 2.5km/1.5mi N of the city centre; follow the signs FS. ☎0577 28 00 44. Fax 0577 28 10 41. Closed 10 Nov to 21 Mar. ⌖ ☒. 200 places.* Situated among the green hills surrounding Siena but not far from the historic centre, this campsite has a restaurant, mini-market and swimming pool. Fine view of the towers particularly at night.

Ostello Guidoriccio – *Via Fiorentina 89, 6km/4mi N of the city centre; Florence –Siena motorway, Siena nord junction, 500m towards the centre. ☎0577 52 212. ▣. 120 beds. ☒.* This is a good address for people travelling by bus or car as there is a bus stop a few yards from the door and a car park opposite. The rooms are simple and furnished with wash basins and bunk beds. Buffet breakfast served in a large diningroom.

Bed & Breakfast Casa per Ferie Convento San Francesco – *Piazza San Francesco 5/6. ☎0577 22 69 68. Fax 0577 22 69 68. Closed 20 days in Jan. ♿. 16 rooms. ☒.* This small hostel is part of the basilica complex and reflects the simplicity of the Franciscan order. The rooms are modern and functional with one bathroom between two.

Fattoria di Cavaglioni – *Via del Poggetto 4, loc. San Rocco a Pilli, 53018 Sovicille, 9km/6mi SW of Siena, on S223 towards Grosseto. ☎0577 34 77 23. www.anfamtos.com. Closed 2 months in winter. 7 rooms. ☒.* This property consists of a 17C house and a little hamlet offering peace and simplicity. The surrounding countryside may entice you to take healthy walks but you can enjoy a well-earned rest in the relaxing atmosphere.

Il Ficareto – *53018 Ancaiano, 13km/8mi SW of Siena towards Sovicille-Ancaiano on the SS 73. ☎0577 31 10 20. Fax 0577 31 10 20. ⌖ ♿.* Off the usual tourist track, this farmhouse is ideal for a relaxing stay close to nature. The owners, a friendly couple, handle all matters with care and passion.

Palazzo Ravizza – *Piano dei Mantellini 34. ☎0577 28 04 62. www.palazzoravizza.it. ▣. 33 rooms. ☒.*

Restaurant ☒☒☒. A Renaissance mansion with coffered ceilings and frescoes, redolent of the austere Tuscan elegance and appreciated for its turn of the 19C atmosphere and contemporary furniture. The shady garden is a strong point in summer.

Villa Scacciapensieri – *Via di Scacciapensieri 10, 2km/1.2mi N of the city centre. ☎0577 41 441. www.villascacciapensieri.it. Closed 5 Jan–11 Mar. ▣☒. 27 rooms. ☒. Restaurant ☒☒☒☒.* This elegant 19C manor house in a commanding setting among the surrounding hills has a comfortable family atmosphere. Strong points are the common space with its great chimney-piece, its Italian garden and its extensive and luxuriant park.

Hotel Palazzo di Valli – *V. E. S. Piccolomini 135. ☎0577 22 61 02. www.anticatorresiena.it. 11 rooms, 2 apartments. Closed Nov-Mar.* This 16C villa, 800m from the Porta Romana, has been recently restored with care to preserve the frescoed, vaulted ceilings and terracotta flooring. A lovely feature is its Italian garden, an ideal respite for famlies with children.

Hotel Santa Caterina – *V. E. S. Piccolomini 7. ☎0577 22 11 05. Fax 0577 27 10 87. ▣. 22 rooms.* A few metres from the Porta Romana, this villa is decorated in the Tuscan style. You can have breakfast or admire the sunset in its small garden. Sophisticated, familial atmosphere.

🍴 EAT

Osteria la Chiacchiera – *Costa di Sant'Antonio 4. ☎0577 28 06 31.* In summer the time spent waiting to be served is considerably shortened thanks to the tables set up in the little side street between Santa Caterina and the Piazza del Campo. In winter, be patient if you wish to savour the traditional Tuscan dishes served in this perenially crowded restaurant.

Hosteria Il Carroccio – *Via Casato di sotto 32. ☎0577 41 165. Closed Wed, 20 days in Jan and Feb.* This unpretentious restaurant near the Piazza del Campo attracts the locals with its authentic Sienese cooking, which includes traditional dishes and delicious salads.

◎◎ **Antica Trattoria Papei** – *Piazza del Mercato 6. ℘0577 28 08 94. Closed Mon except Hols, and 20–30 Aug.* There is a lively atmosphere in this simple and well-kept restaurant. In summer the tables are set out in the crowded square against the backdrop of the Torre del Mangia. Good value for money.

◎◎ **Ristorante Gallo Nero** – *V. del Porrione 65-67. ℘0577 28 43 56. www. gallonero.it.* This restaurant's ambience, service and cuisine are inspired by the Middle Ages. Choose from several set menus.

◎◎ **Trattoria Fòri Porta** – *V. C. Tolomei 1. ℘Fax 0577 22 21 00. Closed 20 Jul–10 Aug, Sun in Jul and Aug.* Next to the Porta Romana, this simple restaurant is the place to try true Sienese fare. Attached to the trattoria is a wine shop and grocery where you can purchase local products before or after your meal.

◎◎◎ **Medio Evo** – *Via dei Rossi 40. ℘577 28 03 15. Closed Thu, Jan and 15–31 Aug.* This restaurant, located in a 13C mansion is not far from the Piazza del Campo. Here you can taste the traditional flavours of Sienese cooking in an appropriate old world setting.

◎◎◎◎ **Antica Trattoria Botteganova** – *Strada statale 408, per Monte-varchi. ℘0577 28 42 30. Closed Mon, 3–20 Jan, 20 Jul–7 Aug. Resevations suggested.* This restaurant is considered one of the best eating places in Siena and, although it is away from the centre, it is well worth the journey. Local dishes, including fish, are served with care and attention in the elegant country-style dining room.

🚃 TAKING A BREAK

Piazza del Campo – It is difficult to choose among the many cafés in this vast square. It is best to select those with tables on the terrace and enjoy the warmth and comfort of the sun while savouring a drink, a gelato or a piece of the traditional Sienese sweet (*panforte*).

Nannini – *Via Banchi di Sopra 22/24. ℘577 23 60 09. Open 7.30am–midnight.* This, the most famous café in the city, has become the ambassador of Sienese specialities in Italy and abroad. Indulge in a cake or an ice cream; it will be an experience you will never forget.

Panforte

B. Morandi / MICHELIN

Caffè Novo – *Non Solo Caffè, Via Camporegio 13. ℘0577 28 74 74. Closed Sun summer, Mon winter.* This café, with its warm and friendly bar and great view of Siena, is more than just a café. Moreover it serves the most delicious hot chocolate.

Pasticceria Bini – *Via dei Fusari 9/13. ℘0577 28 02 07. Closed 1.30pm–3030pm and Mon.* Opened in 1943, this patisserie is one of the best in Siena, offering all the local specialities at one go: *panforte margherita* (with candied citron peel), *panforte oro* (with candied melon), *panforte copate* (little white cornets) or *cannoli* (flaky pastry rolls filled with almonds).

La Costarella – *Via di Città 31/33. ℘577 28 80 76. Closed Wed and Thu Sept–Jun.* This home-made ice cream establishment contains a cosy, elegant tea room overlooking the Piazza del Campo. It is a good place in which to take refuge from the searing heat or the freezing cold.

🍷 WINE BARS

Enoteca Italiana – *Fortezza Medicea. ℘0577 28 84 97. www.enoteca-italiana.it. Open Mon–Sat noon–1am (8pm Mon). Closed 10 days in Jan.* The Siena wine warehouse is housed in the fortifications of the 16C Medici fort. It stocks over 1 000 Italian, particularly Tuscan, wines selected for their quality. Tasting and talks given by well-known winemakers.

The austere atmosphere of Siena is also reflected in its province, which extends south over cypress-dotted hills towards Lazio until reaching a pinnacle at Monte Amiata, the highest peak south of the River Arno. This land is characterised by its medieval-era structures, found in the the abbeys at Monte Oliveto Maggiore and Sant'Antimo and in San Quirico d'Orcia and Montalcino, two cities ringed by high walls. But there are also rich reminders of the Renaissance: in Pienza, the "ideal" city conceived by Pope Pius II and realised by Bernardo Rossellino, and in Montepulciano, a picturesque hill town known worldwide for its excellent *vino nobile*. The solemn Sienese hills also provide the backdrop for Chianciano Terme, a delightful spa town popular since Roman times, but fully equipped for the 21C.

Monte Amiata

Patrick Dieudonne/Robert Harding

The land south of Siena that now constitutes its province has been inhabited since the days of the Etruscans, who established a stronghold at Chiusi (Porsenna), once part of the League of Twelve Cities.

The Etruscans also built an impressive villa at Poggio Civitate, near the town of Murlo, and several Etruscan burial grounds are located in the environs of Pitigliano. Romans also walked these lands, especially along the Via Francigena, the ancient pilgrimage road to Canterbury that slices through the Orcia Valley near the cities of Chianciano Terme and San Quirico d'Orcia. During the Middle Ages, Siena fought for and won custody of the cities in this territory. San Quirico d'Orcia and Montalcino, with their positions near the Roman roads of Via Cassia (today's SS 2) and Via Francigena, were especially prized.

Siena's province has a strong cultural and artistic heritage, from the cultivation of vines in Montalcino and Montepulciano (two cities whose names are synonymous with the superb red wines that they produce) to exemplary Renaissance architecture. Of particular note is Pienza, the village formerly known as Corsignano, which was reconstructed into an ideal Renaissance town at the behest of native son Aeneas Piccolomini (Pope Pius II). Outside Montepulciano, itself a lovely Renaissance town with many palazzi, stands the Chiesa della Madonna di San Biagio, considered the masterpiece of architect Antonio da Sangallo.

This pocket of Tuscany, long known as a place of refuge, is mostly undiscovered by tourists. Its abundance of tranquil spaces include numerous monasteries, such as those built by the Olivetan and Augustinian Orders; serene spas at Chianciano and Saturnia, which are fed by natural hot springs; and Monte Amiata, from the top of which visitors can glimpse the province's many treasures.

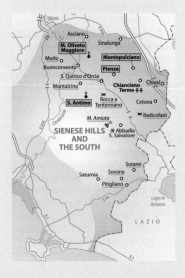

Monte Amiata★
and Abbadia San Salvatore

This old volcano, the highest mountain in Tuscany south of the Arno, is the source of several rivers and springs that supply water to Siena and Grosseto. The mountain also has numerous deposits of mercury and antimony, which were already well known in the days of the Etruscans and Romans. Nowadays, this is a pleasant place for winter sports.

AROUND THE MOUNTAIN

A winding road (13km/8mi) runs round the mountain (recommended access from Abbadia San Salvatore, brown signs for "Vetta Amiata"), providing a number of impressive views.

From the south side, the most attractive, the road runs up to the summit marked by an iron cross (22m/72ft high) at the top of a paved path (*15min there and back on foot*) flanked by a ⛷ chair-lift and ski lifts.

ABBADIA SAN SALVATORE✳

The small town of Abbadia San Salvatore is a summer and winter holiday resort at the foot of Monte Amiata. It has a large **medieval quarter**, a labyrinth of arched streets and alleyways and a fortress.

It takes its name from an abbey which was once the wealthiest monastery in Tuscany.

Chiesa Abbaziale – The **abbey church** is all that remains of the monastery founded in AD 743 by Rachis, a Lombard king converted to Christianity. Building work on the church was completed in the 11C; slight alterations were made in the 16C. The austere façade contains a large bay with colonnettes; the tall bell tower is crenellated.

The interior has a nave but no aisles. The chancel, raised above the level of the nave, has rounded arches painted with Renaissance friezes. The transept was decorated with frescoes in the late 17C and early 18C. A large 12C painted wooden Crucifix adorns the south wall of the nave.

🦶 **Michelin Map:** Michelin Atlas p 44 and Map 563 – N 16 or Map 735 S of Fold 15.

🗎 **Info:** Via Adua, 25, 53021 Abbadia San Salvatore (Siena), ☎0577 77 58 11. www.amiataturismo.it.

▷ **Location:** Mount Amiata (alt 1 738m/5 649ft) rises beside the Via Cassia not far from the Umbria Pass at the heart of Apennines.

◉ **Don't Miss:** The crypt at Abbadia San Salvatore and Radicofani's medieval fortress.

Beneath the chancel is the **crypt**★ (8C) of the original church. It was built in the shape of a Cross (one of the arms has been reconstructed) and is supported by a profusion of columns with decorated capitals. Beside the church are the traces of the cloisters.

RADICOFANI★

Fort Radicofani is perched on a natural promontory (over 800m/2 600ft high). It dominates the whole of the surrounding countryside and is easily recognisable for its mighty tower standing out proudly against the skyline.

The village of Radicofani, built in the same dark brown stone as the fortress above it, has medieval houses and steep streets nestling up against the fortress

Tower of Fort Radicofani

photooale - Fotolia.com

walls. To the left of the main street is a tiny square in which stand two churches, opposite one another.

From the adjacent public park, there is a fine **view**★ of Monte Amiata and the surrounding countryside dotted with the sharp bare peaks of the **Orcia Hills**. The main street then leads to the 16C Palazzo Pretorio, decorated with coats of arms, and to the **fortress**★ itself (*car park nearby*). The fortress was built in the 13C, altered in the 16C and destroyed by an explosion in the 18C. Its majestic ruins were shored up early in the 1990s.

Chianciano Terme⳥⳥

and Chianciano Vecchia

Chianciano Terme is a large, elegant spa town delightfully situated at the foot of the old hilltop village of Chianciano Vecchia, overlooking the fertile Chiana valley to the west. The mineral water here has a high sulphate and calcium content; the hot springs were known to the Etruscans and Romans, and were mentioned by Horace.

SPA TOWN

Chianciano is divided into two distinct towns. The upper village (Chianciano Vecchia) is set within medieval walls (⳥*see opposite*). The spa town, or Terme, lies in the valley below the old town. Though the curative waters of the area had been known for centuries, Chianciano Terme's spa facilities, many of which were built in the neoClassical style, were not fully developed until the 19 and 20C. Notable visitors to Chianciano Terme include author Luigi Pirandello and director Federico Fellini.

Today the spas in Terme offer all of the modern comforts and many wellness and fitness courses. Each thermal facility also has its own therapeutic speciality: Acqua Santa and Acqua Fucoli for gastrointestinal and liver health; Acqua Sillene for the skin; and Acqua Sant'Elena for the kidneys.

ADDRESSES

🏠 STAY

⊖⊖ **Azienda Agrituristica Il Poggio** – *53040 Celle sul Rigo, 30km/19mi SW of Chiusi by S478.* ℘*0578 53 748. www.ilpoggio.net.* 🖃. ⌁. *5 rooms half board only.* This attractive farm, which is also an approved equestrian centre, offers authentic traditional cooking and horse riding in the quiet Sienese country. Additional activities include swimming and archery.

▶ **Population:** 7,203
🕭 **Michelin Map:** Michelin Atlas p 44 and Map 563– M 17 and Map 735 Fold 15.
🛈 **Info:** Piazza Italia 67; ℘0578 63 648. www.chincianotermeinfo.it.
◖ **Location:** There are four separate thermal establishments, (Acqua Santa, Acqua Fucoli, Acqua Sillene and Acqua Sant'Elena). The resort has ultra-modern hotels and treatment centres and a number of beautiful, shady parks. The main street, Viale Roma, is the most elegant in the resort. Chianciano is on S 146, which links Montepulciano and Chiusi.

Museo Civico Archeologico delle Acque★

In Via Dante, in front of the Biblioteca Comunale 🕒*Open Apr–Oct Tue–Sun 10am–1pm and 4pm–7pm; rest of the year open Sat, Sun and Hols only.* ⊖⊖€4. ℘*578 30 471. www.chincianotermeinfo.it.*

The Archaeological Museum houses items that date back to when the area was an Etruscan settlement. On the ground floor are relics unearthed from the nearby necropolis at Tolle and a fine collection of jewellery.

Another section of the museum contains a reconstruction of two rooms from an Etruscan farmhouse, the Poggio Bacherina. Note the boot-shaped vases for crushing grapes.

The museum has items from the Selene temples excavations, recognisable by the symbols of a dolphin and the moon.

EXCURSION
Chianciano Vecchia
2km/1mi NE.

The entrance to the old town from the spa town is the Rivellini Gate. The first part of the main street is dominated by the clock tower, decorated with the coat of arms of the Medici.

Further on, there is a superb view (*left*) over the Chiana Valley before reaching a square flanked by the Palazzo del Podestà, decorated with a few coats of arms, and (*opposite*) the Palazzo dell'Arcipretura. The **Museo della Collegiata** (Collegiate Church Museum), which is housed in the latter building, contains mainly Sienese paintings and gold or silverware from the 13C to 19C, including a **Virgin Mary of Humility**★ by Lorenzo di Niccolò. ◔*Open Jun–Oct Tue–Sun 10am–noon and 4pm–7pm; rest of the year by appointment.* ◔*Closed Mon.* ◠€1.50. ✆057 83 03 78.

Chianciano Terme
Stefano Caporali / Tips Images

Further along the main street stands the **Collegiate Church**, which has an austere travertine façade decorated with a delicate Romanesque portal.

From Via della Croce (*turn right*) there is a fine view of the surrounding countryside.

Slightly further on (*left*) is the Porta del Sole, leading to the late 16C **Church of La Madonna della Rosa**, built entirely of brick and stone. From the Porta del Sole, Via Garibaldi skirts the town walls and returns to the entrance.

ADDRESSES

🏠 STAY

◠ **Golf Hotel** – *Via Veneto 7.* ✆*0578 63 321. Fax 0578 63 352. Closed Dec–Mar.* ⌂*. Restaurant* ◠◔. A shady garden in a residential district is the setting for this modern hotel, decorated and furnished in a simple uncluttered style. It is close to the spa and has a pleasant panoramic terrace.

◠◔ **Hotel Montecarlo** – *Viale della Libertà 478.* ✆*0578 63 903. www.hotel-montecarlo.it. Closed Nov–Apr. 41 rooms.* ⌂*. Restaurant* ◠◔. This hotel, with modern, simply furnished rooms, is situated on the avenue which leads to the town centre. The panoramic

terrace on the roof has a solarium and swimming pool. The kitchen can cater for special diets.

🍽 EAT

◠◔◔ **Il Buco** – *Via della Pace 39.* ✆*578 30 230. Closed Wed and Nov.* The atmosphere is welcoming and the fare simple – pizzas, home-made pasta, red meat and, in season, mushrooms and truffles.

☕ TAKING A BREAK

Centro Storico – *Via A Casini 22.* ✆*578 31 444. Closed Mon in winter.* This tea room and patisserie is in the town centre opposite the clock and has a tiny terrace overlooking the roofs of the old town and the Chianciano Valley.

Chiusi★

and around

Now a quiet, friendly little town, Chiusi was built on an easily defended hilltop, as it was once one of the 12 sovereign towns of the Etruscan confederation. It derived its prosperity not only from the farmland in the surrounding fertile plain but also from its control of the Chiana, then a tributary of the Tiber, which linked the town to Rome and to the sea.

▶ **Population:** 8,664

🍴 **Michelin Map:** Michelin Atlas p 44 and Map 563 – M 17 or Map 735 Fold 15.

ℹ **Info:** Piazza XX Settembre 1. ℘0578 22361. www.comune.chiusi.siena.it.

🕐 **Location:** Chiusi is on the boundary with Umbria on S 71 between Chianciano Terme and Città della Pieve.

A BIT OF HISTORY

In 507 BC **Porsenna**, the powerful King of Chiusi, attempted to reimpose on Rome the domination that had endured for over a century under three Etruscan kings, before the Romans set themselves free by instituting a republic. Once Rome regained its freedom, it gradually gained in power and finally allied itself to Chiusi, which rallied to Rome in the 4C BC and began a period of Romanisation. These links also explain why, in the early days of Christianity, so many of the people of Chiusi were converted to the new religion.

TOWN

The streets of Via Porsenna and Via Pietriccia meet in the town centre at Largo Cacioli, where most attractions are located.

Museo Archeologico Nazionale ★

🕐 Open 9am–8pm (7.30pm last admission). 🕐 Closed 1 May, 25 Dec, 1 Jan. ▥€4. ♿. ℘0578 20 177. www.archeologia.beniculturali.it/pages/atlante/S52.html.

The **National Archaeological Museum** contains numerous artefacts excavated in local graveyards and presented in a display illustrating Etruscan art and civilisation as it existed in the Chiusi region.

The anthropomorphic, earthenware **funeral urns**, also known as canopic jars, date from the Villanovan period and were first used in the 7C BC. In the

6C BC they were replaced by carved busts made of stinkstone, a local limestone that gets its name from the unpleasant odor it gives off when being carved. From the 2C BC onwards Chiusi became famous for its high output of clay urns with moulded decoration. Realist art forms and Etruscan fantasy were expressed in architectural terracotta ornaments for temples and mansions, in bronze sculptures and utensils, gold jewellery, lamps, glassware, clay votive offerings and decorated tableware.

Chiusi was a major producer of buccheroware, the glazed black pottery which in the 6C BC was decorated with low-relief motifs and from the 5C BC was produced without any decoration.

The museum has a collection of Attic black-figure and later red-figure vases, which were initially imported but later made locally by Greek artists who settled in Etruria.

Painting, an art form that was rare in the north of Etruria, is represented here by the reconstitution of a tomb (*tomba delle Tassinaie*), which dates from after the mid-2C BC and is thought to have been decorated by artists from Tarquinia.

🕐 A museum warden will accompany visitors who have a car to see a few of the tombs found along the Lake Chiusi road (3km/2mi).

Visitors are usually shown two tombs: the **tomba del Leone** (tomb of the lion), which was originally painted and in which the burial chambers are set out in the shape of a Cross around a central area, and the **tomba della Pellegrina** (tomb of the pilgrim) at the end of a corridor (*dromos*) and containing 3C and 2C BC urns and sarcophagi decorated with reliefs drawn from Greek mythology or, on later artefacts, the war between the Galatians and the Romans.

Cattedrale di San Secondiano
The earliest **church** on this site, a 4C–5C palaeo-Christian basilica, was destroyed by the Goths and rebuilt in the 6C by Bishop Fiorentino. After being destroyed again during the Barbarian invasions, it was rebuilt to an identical design in the 12C. The nave and aisles are separated by 18 ancient but dissimilar columns, revealing the re-use of Roman material from various sources. In the 17C the body of St Mustiola was interred in the south transept.

Campanile
The bell tower (*campanile*) was built in the 12C as part of the town's system of defence. The upper section was converted into a bell tower in the 16C.

Museo della Cattedrale
Open Jun–mid-Oct daily 9.30am–12.45pm and 4pm–7pm; rest of the year 9.30am–12.45pm, Hols 3pm–6pm. Closed Easter, 25 Dec. Museum €1.50; Etruscan remains, Porsenna Labyrinth and Roman well €2.50; Christian catacombs €3. (using your own vehicle). 0578 22 64 90.
On the ground floor of this **museum** are Etruscan, Roman and palaeo-Christian

remains discovered beneath the cathedral. From the gardens, there is a view of part of the Etruscan wall dating from the 3C BC. On the first floor, the museum displays a collection of furniture, religious ornaments and reliquaries, including two magnificent 15C chests from the Embraschi workshops. There is a valuable collection of illuminated antiphonaries, psalters and graduals dating from the 15C and 16C; they were brought here from the Abbey of Monte Oliveto Maggiore (*see Abbazia di MONTE OLIVETO MAGGIORE*).

EXCURSIONS
Catacombe di Santa Mustiola e di Santa Caterina
On the lake road. Open Jun–mid-Oct daily 11am and 5pm; rest of the year 11am. Closed Easter and 25 Dec. €3. 0578 22 64 90.
These **catacombs**, the only ones known to exist in Tuscany, were discovered in 1634 and 1848 respectively. They were built in the 3C and were still in use as burial places in the 5C. The earliest catacombs, where St Mustiola was buried, consist of an extensive network of galleries bearing a large number of inscriptions; the second catacombs are smaller and owe their name to the tiny chapel dedicated to St Catherine of Alexandria which was built above them.

Torri Beccati Questo e Beccati Quello
3km/2mi E.
Translating roughly as "Take This and Take That", these towers stand only a

---

Porsenna Labyrinth

Excavations have revealed a complex system of underground galleries used originally by the Etruscans and later by the Romans to supply the town with water. Pliny the Elder records that the famous Porsenna "was buried beneath the town of Chiusi, in a monument with a square base (90m/300ft long) enclosing a maze". It is tempting to imagine that these galleries could be part of the tomb of the Etruscan king.

The tour of this ancient water system starts in the Museo della Cattedrale and finishes in the Etrusco-Roman water tank (2C–1C BC); the tank was probably used as an emergency water supply in the event of fire. Visitors exit at the bottom of the medieval tower which has been used as a bell tower since the end of the 16C.

few yards apart. The first tower stands in Umbria and the second in Tuscany, recalling the former rivalry between the two regions. The octagonal Tuscan tower is dominated by the Umbrian tower which is square and slightly taller.

Lago di Chiusi
5km/3mi N.

This **lake** is a quiet spot offering boating, rowing and angling. Fish from the lake are used in the traditional dishes of Chiusi including pike (*brustico*) cooked directly on reeds from the lake, and **tegamaccio**, a kind of fish stew consisting of lake fish cooked in tomato sauce and served on slices of garlic toast.

Sarteano
6.5km/4mi NW.

This spa resort consists of three swimming pools filled with warm, mineral-rich water. The 24ºC water comes from a thermal spring known to the Ancient Romans. The village is dominated by an 11C hilltop fortress, which was altered in the 15C by the Sienese; its walls and mighty square tower with machicolations are well preserved.

The **Church of San Martino** has a single nave and contains a number of interesting paintings: (*left*) a large **Annunciation**★★ by Beccafumi; a *Madonna and Child between St Roch and St Sebastian* by Andrea di Niccolò; a *Visitation* by Vanni; and two works by Giacomo di Mino del Pellicciaio: a *Madonna and Child,* signed and dated 1342, and a triptych.

Cetona
9km/6mi N.

During the Middle Ages Cetona lay on the border between the Republic of Siena and the Papal States and was fiercely possessed or angrily coveted by both parties. A fortress from that era crowns the hilltop. The village has been extensively restored since becoming fashionable with the Italian jet set, many of whom have holiday homes here.

The **Collegiata** church dates from the 13C and contains a fresco of the Assumption. The **Museo Civico per la Preistoria del Monte Cetona** (◷open Jun–Sept

Tue–Sun 9am–1pm and 5pm–7pm; rest of the year Tue–Fri 9.30am–12.30pm, Sun and Hols 9.30am–12.30pm; museum ⊗€2, Museum and park ⊗ €2.50, Archaeological museums of Chianciano and Sarteano ⊗€5; &; ℘0578 23 76 32; www.archeo logiatoscana.it) is housed in the town hall and has exhibits illustrating the geology of Monte Cetona (◷see below). There are also items proving the existence of prehistoric settlements from the Palaeolithic era to the end of the Bronze Age.

Monte Cetona
5.5km/3.5mi SW of Cetona by car; 500m/547yd on foot to the summit.

The summit of the bare rocky mountain (*1,148m/3,731ft*) provides a superb **panoramic view**. Humans have settled the natural caves in these slopes since the Palaeolithic era. However, the major period of population growth took place in the middle of the second millennium BC. Around **Belverde** (*signs*) some of these ancient **caves** have been made accessible and electricity has been installed. ◷Open Jul–Sept Tue–Sun 9am–1pm and 4pm–7pm; rest of the year by appointment. Cetona Museum ⊗€2.50, park only ⊗ €2.

ADDRESSES

⌂ STAY

⊗⊗⊜ **Residenza Re Porsenna** – *Via Ermanno Baldetti 37. ℘0578 21 922. Fax 0578 22 43 82. 6 double rooms. ⊠.* A mansion house in the old town offering B&B. It is furnished with fine antiques. The common eating room, shared by guests and hosts, adds to the charm. Excellent and generous breakfast.

♀/ EAT

⊗⊜ **Osteria La Solita Zuppa** – *Via Porsenna 21. ℘0578 21 006. Closed Tue, 15 Jan–10 Mar. Reservations required.* The owners of this large, country-style osteria take pleasure in putting their guests at ease. The fare is Tuscan, with soups and simple dishes on offer.

Montalcino★

and Buonconvento

The hillside town of Montalcino still has part of its 13C walls and its fortress (*rocca*) built in 1361. It was ruled by Siena for several centuries and served as a refuge for the members of the government of the Republic of Siena when their town was captured by Charles V in 1555. Each autumn during the Thrush Festival (Sagra del Tordo) the four districts of the medieval town recall the past with a procession in period costume; they also compete against each other in an archery contest. Montalcino is known throughout Italy for its excellent red wine, Brunello, a very high-quality vintage from a restricted wine-growing area. Brunello is the local name for the Sangiovese grape grown here.

TOWN

The Rocca, at Piazzale Fortezza, is at the top of this hilltown. Go down the hill (heading north) to visit the town's other sights.

Rocca★★

Piazzale Fortezza. ◷*Open Apr–Oct Tue–Sun 9am–8pm (6pm Nov–Mar).* ☞€2, €5 *combined ticket with Museo Civico e Diocesano.* ℘*0577 84 93 31. www.prolocomontalcino.it.*

This fine example of a 14C **fortress** has been remarkably well preserved despite the fact that the development of artillery in the following century made this type of defensive system vulnerable to attack. The high walls, complete with a parapet walk and machicolations, form a huge pentagon in which the population could seek refuge.

In the interior are the remains of a basilica and the keep (*mastio*) designed to house officials and noblemen in times of siege. There is **wine-tasting** (*ground floor*) and the standard of the Republic of Siena painted by Il Sodoma (*second floor*). From the **parapet walk** there is a vast panoramic **view** over the town and surrounding countryside.

▶ **Population:** 5,099

⌖ **Michelin Map:** Michelin Atlas p 44 and Map 563 – M 16 or Map 735 Fold 15.

▤ **Info:** Via Costa del Municipio 8. ℘0577 84 93 31. www.prolocomontalcino.it.

◐ **Location:** Montalcino sits not far from the Via Cassia between Siena and San Quirico d'Orcia.

⊛ **Don't Miss:** Montalcino's 14C fortress (Rocca).

Palazzo Comunale★

The 13C building overlooking Piazza del Popolo is flanked by a 14C–15C arcaded loggia and surmounted by a tall belfry.

Sant'Egidio

Piazza Garibaldi, behind the town hall. The church has a nave with wooden rafters and is divided by three arches. Near the entrance is a gilded 16C tabernacle.

Museo Civico e Diocesano

Via Ricasoli. ◷*Open Tue–Sun 10am–1pm and 2pm–6pm.* ☞€4, €5 *combined ticket with la Rocca.* ♿. ℘*05777 84 60 14. www.prolocomontalcino.it.*

The **Civic and Diocesan Museum** contains a number of prehistoric and Etruscan remains, 13C–18C ceramic ware from Montalcino, 14C–15C paintings and polychrome wooden statues by the Sienese School and a two-volume Bible and a Crucifix, both dating from the 12C, from the nearby abbey of Sant'Antimo.

EXCURSION
Buonconvento

14km/9mi N of Montalcino.

Buonconvento stands at the confluence of the Arbia and Ombrone rivers, on the Via Cassia, the Roman road between Siena and Rome. The centre of a small farming community, the town is built entirely of brick and enclosed within 14C town walls. Emperor Henry VII, in whom Dante placed his hopes of a unified, pacified Italy, died here in 1313. On the north side of the fortifications stands the great **Porta Senese** (Siena Gate), topped with small relieving arches and battlements, from which Via Soccini traverses the town. In a small square to the left is the **Church of SS Pietro e Paolo** (St Peter and St Paul) which has a façade in the Jesuit style. Further on is the **Palazzo Pretorio** surmounted by an elegant tower based on Siena's.

Museo d'Arte Sacra della Val d'Arbia★

Via Soccini 17. ⏱*Open mid-Mar–Oct.* ⊚*€3.* ♿*.* ℘*0577 80 71 81. www.museoartesacra.it.*

This **museum of sacred art** presents 14C to 17C paintings by the Sienese School, as well as church plate, liturgical vestments and reliquaries from the Buonconvento and the Arbia Valley.

ADDRESSES

🏨 STAY

🍴 **Il Poderuccio Girardi** – *53020 Sant'Angelo in Colle, 10km/6mi SW of Montalcino towards Grosseto.* ℘*0577 84 40 52. Fax 0577 84 40 52. Closed Dec–Easter.* 🍴 ⚒. *13 rooms.* ⚒. Here among vineyards and olive groves you will find repose for body and soul without having to give up the pleasure of a dip in the swimming pool. For the more energetic there are various sporting activities nearby.

🍴 **Fattoria Pieve a Salti** – *53022 Buonconvento, 15km/9mi N of Montalcino by the Via Cassia and then the road towards Buonconvento.* ℘*0577 80 72 44. www.pieveasalti.it.* 🍴 ⚒. *16 rooms.* ⚒. This country estate in the Sienese Hills is ideal both for visitors wishing to relax and those who want to indulge in horse riding, mountain biking, tennis, swimming and fishing, all of which are available within the inn's Centro Benessere (health centre).

🍴 **Agriturismo Le Ragnaie** – *3km/2mi SW of Montalcino.* ℘*0577 84 86 39. www.leragnaie.com. Closed Apr–Oct.* 🍴 ⚒. *10 rooms.* ⚒. *Restaurant* 🍴🍴. A relaxed family atmosphere reigns in this rustically furnished farmhouse. The restaurant menu is also typical of the locality, and includes wild boar (*cinghiale*) and rabbit (*lepre*).

🍴 EAT

🍴 **Locanda di Piazza Padella** – *Piazza Garibaldi 9.* ℘*0577 84 60 54. Closed Mon, Feb. Reservations suggested.* On a stool at the counter or at one of the

tables in the two small rooms you can try regional dishes in season. The wines are representative of this famous region; some are served by the glass.

🍴🍴 **Taverna dei Barbi** – *Fattoria dei Barbi, località Podernovi, 5km/3mi S of Montalcino by S2.* ℘*0577 84 12 00. Closed Tue, Wed evening and 7–31 Jan. Reservations suggested.* Surrounded by elegance and rusticity you can explore all aspects of country life by visiting this property and its historic cellar. You can taste, then buy, the authentic tasting products of the Barbi farm.

🚌 TAKING A BREAK

Enoteca La Fortezza – *Piazzale Fortezza.* ℘*0577 84 92 11. www.enotecalafortezza.it. Open summer daily 9am–8pm. Closed Mon in winter.* The former guardroom with its terrace in the couryard of the old fortress now houses this superb cellar and wine bar. On display beneath the great red brick vaults are wines and produce from the Montalcino region.

Caffè Fiaschetteria Italiana – *Antica Cantina del Brunello, Piazza del Popolo 6.* ℘*0577 84 90 43.* The period furnishings – yellow marble tables, velvet seats and old mirrors – add to the fascination of this historic wine bar, which was founded in 1888 by Ferruccio Biondi Santi, the original vintner of Brunello.

Circolo Arci – *Via Ricasoli 2.* ℘*0577 84 82 12. Closed Mon.* At the back of a courtyard, embellished by a handsome old well, the Associazione Ricreativa e Culturale Italiana brings together young and old for passionate discussions or a game of cards over glasses of Brunello or grappa.

Abbazia di
Monte Oliveto Maggiore★★

The huge pink brick buildings of this famous abbey nestle among the cypress trees in a landscape of eroded hills. Monte Oliveto is the mother-house of the Olivetians, a congregation of Benedictine monks founded in 1313 by Blessed Bernardo Tolomei of Siena. A fortified tower with terracotta decorations by the Luca della Robbia School leads into the monastery grounds.

- **Michelin Map:** Michelin Atlas p 44 and Map 563 – M 16 and Map 735 Fold 15.
- **Info:** ℘0577 70 76 11. www.ftbcc.it/monteoliveto.
- **Location:** Monte Oliveto is in the heart of the area known as Toscana della Fede not far from the abbeys of San Galgano, Sant'Antimo and Farneta. It is about 10km/6mi from the Via Cassia and about 30km/18mi SE of Siena.

MAIN CLOISTERS

Open daily 9am–noon and 3.15pm–6pm (5pm winter).

The cloisters were decorated with a superb series of 36 **frescoes**★★ recounting the life of St Benedict. They were painted by Luca Signorelli from 1498 onwards and by Sodoma between 1505 and 1508.

The cycle (*left to right*) begins near the church door with the main arch on which are paintings of *Christ at the Pillar* and *Christ carrying the Cross*, both of them masterpieces by Sodoma. Like the frescoes on the north side, the first 19 scenes, starting with *St Benedict leaving his Father's House*, are by the same painter. They are followed by a fresco by Riccio and then eight frescoes by Signorelli.

Sodoma, who is portrayed in the third fresco facing the viewer, was a man of refinement and a genius, who was influenced by Leonardo da Vinci and Perugino. He was not particularly pious and was mainly attracted by the aesthetic portrayal of human types, landscapes and picturesque detail, as shown in the 4th fresco in which St Benedict receives the hermit's habit, the 12th fresco (*first on the south side*), where the saint welcomes two young men in the midst of a crowd of characters in varying poses, and the 19th fresco (*last on the south side*), in which lascivious courtesans are sent to tempt the monks.

The work of **Signorelli** is distinguishable by the sculpture-like power of his figures and the dramatic settings in which the landscapes are reduced to a mere suggestion of space. This is evident in the 24th fresco where St Benedict restores to life a monk who has fallen from the top of a wall.

The cloisters give access to the 15C refectory which is decorated with frescoes dating from the same period (*Last Supper*).

ABBEY CHURCH

The interior has been refurbished in 18C Baroque style but the stained glass windows are of modern design.

The chapel (*left of the entrance from the exterior*) contains a wooden Crucifix brought to the abbey by its founder in 1313. The nave is lined by magnificent **choirstalls**★★ (1505) by Fra Giovanni da Verona; they include marquetry inlays of birds, architectural vistas, tabernacles and musical instruments etc. A staircase to the right of the chancel leads to the crib.

Abbazia di Monte Oliveto Maggiore

puck - Fotolia.com

Montepulciano★★

Montepulciano is an attractive little town typical of the Renaissance period. It occupies a remarkably picturesque setting★★ on the top of a tufa hill separating two valleys. The town was founded in the 6C by people from Chiusi fleeing the Barbarian invasions. They named it Mons Politianus, which explains why people from the town are known as Poliziani. Poets have long sung the praises of its ruby-red wine (*vino nobile*). Antonio da Sangallo the Elder, one of the two senior members of the famous family of Renaissance sculptors and architects, bequeathed some of his most famous works to Montepulciano.

▶ **Population:** 13,890

Michelin Map: Michelin Atlas p 44 and Map 563 – M 17 or Map 735 Fold 15.

Info: Via di Gracciano nel Corso 59/a. ℘0578 75 73 41. www.monte pulciano.com.

Location: Montepulciano is between San Quirico d'Orcia and Chiusi on S146.

Don't Miss: The Palazzo Comunale affords splendid views of the countryside Further afield, the church of San Biagio is a fine example of Renaissance architecture in a lovely rural setting.

🐾 WALKING TOUR

The walk lasts about 1hr 30min
Within Porta al Prato, a fortified gate bearing the Tuscan coat of arms, and beyond the Florentine lion (*Marzocco*), the main street lined with numerous interesting **mansions**★ and churches climbs uphill. At the end of the first section (Via Roma) the street divides in two to enclose the main historic landmarks.
The splendid Palazzo Avignonesi (*no 91 Via Roma*) dates from the late Renaissance period (16C) and is attributed to Vignola. The mansion (*no 73*), which belonged to the antique dealer Bucelli, is decorated with engraved Etruscan and Roman stones. Further along (*right*) is the church of Sant'Agostino (restored) with its Renaissance **façade**★ designed by Michelozzo of Florence in the 15C. The Jack-o'-the-clock on the tower (*opposite*) is none other than Mr Punch.

▶ *Turn left at the Logge del Mercato (Corn Exchange) into Via di Voltaia nel Corso.*

The Palazzo Cervini (*no 21*) was designed by **Antonio da Sangallo the Elder** and is a fine example of Florentine Renaissance style, with its rustication and rounded and triangular pediments.

▶ *Continue along Via dell'Opio nel Corso and Via Poliziano.*

Poliziano was born at no 1 Via Poliziano. At the end of the street stands the **Church of Santa Maria dei Servi**, which contains a *Virgin and Child* by Duccio di Buoninsegna.

Piazza Grande★★

The **main square** at the top of the town is the central landmark. Its irregular layout and the different styles of façade avoid architectural monotony and combine to give an overall sense of harmony.

Palazzo Comunale★

West side. The Gothic **town hall** includes 15C alterations by Michelozzo. It is reminiscent of the Palazzo Vecchio.
From the top of the **tower** there is an extensive **panoramic view**★★★ of the town and its outskirts including the Church of the Madonna di San Biagio (*west*) and the Tuscan countryside embracing Mount Amiata (*southwest*), Pienza (*west*), Siena (*northwest*), Cortona (*northeast*) and Lake Trasimeno (*east*). On the other side of the square stands **Palazzo Contucci**, which was begun in 1519 by Sangallo the Elder but was not completed until the 18C.

Palazzo Nobili-Tarugi★
North side. This majestic Renaissance **mansion** opposite the cathedral is attributed to Sangallo the Elder. Six Ionic columns set on a very high base support the pilasters of the first floor. It features a portico and huge doorway with semicircular arches. The bay windows with their rounded pediments are set on small consoles. On the left above the central doorway, note the window from which the occupants of the palace could watch visitors arriving. The loggia (*left*) used to be open but has been walled up. Next to Palazzo Tarugi is the Palazzo del Capitano (*north side*).

Well★
This picturesque well is made especially charming by the two lions supporting the Medici coat of arms.

Duomo
South side. The **cathedral** was built in the 16C–17C, though the façade never received its marble cladding. The interior, consisting of nave and two aisles, is austere and stylistically pure. Beside the central doorway (*left*) is the recumbent statue of Bartolomeo Aragazzi, Secretary to Pope Martin V; the statue was formerly part of Aragazzi's tomb, designed by Michelozzo (15C) and dismantled in the 17C. The two elegant statues flanking the high altar and the low-relief sculptures on the first two pillars were also originally part of the tomb.

The 14C Baptistery is surmounted by a fine piece of terracotta by Andrea della Robbia. One of the pillars in the north aisle bears a portrait of the Madonna painted by Sano di Pietro in the 15C. Behind the high altar is a monumental **reredos**★ painted in 1401 by Taddeo di Bartolo, the Sienese artist, depicting the *Assumption*, the *Annunciation* and the *Coronation of the Virgin Mary*.

◗ *Continue north down the main street.*

Piazza San Francesco
The **square** provides a fine view of the surrounding countryside and the church of San Biagio below.

◗ *Continue down Via del Poggiolo. Turn right into Via dell'Erbe to return to the Logge del Mercato (Corn Exchange).*

EXCURSIONS
Chiesa della Madonna di San Biagio★★
Below the town (west); off S 146 to Pienza.
An avenue of cypress trees leads to this magnificent **church**, dedicated to Our Lady of San Biagio and built of pale golden stone, which stands in a delightful setting in the middle of a grassy stretch of flat land high above the valley. It is the masterpiece of Antonio da Sangallo the Elder and was inaugurated in

San Biagio, Montepulciano

PH. Benet, R. Hozbachova / MICHELIN

1529 by Pope Clement VII, a member of the Medici family. As Sangallo's building was strongly influenced by Bramante's plan for the reconstruction of St Peter's in Rome which, owing to the artist's death, was not carried out as planned, it is a valuable reminder of the designs drawn by the architect for the Pope. Although somewhat simplified, San Biagio copies the notion of the central plan in the form of a Greek cross with domed roof, the main façade being given greater emphasis by two bell towers set in the recesses of the cross. One is incomplete; the other includes the three orders – Doric, Ionic and Corinthian. The south transept extends into a semicircular sacristy. The harmonious lines and skilful design of the architectural motifs enhancing the structural features convey a sense of majestic solemnity, which continues into the interior. Note (*left of the entrance*) an *Annunciation*, painted in the 14C, and the impressive marble high altar (1584). The elegant building with a portico (*opposite*) is the canon's residence (*Canonica*).

Sinalunga

21km/13mi N of Montepulciano.
The old town stands high above the Chiana Valley, an area, which used to be full of swamps and where malaria was rife. Since land improvement and the building of the railway, Sinalunga has expanded into the plain. In the vast main square, **Piazza Garibaldi**, there

are three 17C and 18C churches. The **Collegiata di San Martino**, at the top of a large flight of steps, was begun in the late 16C, on the site of the old fortress, using the stone from the castle. Inside (*right of the chancel*) the *Madonna and Child surrounded by two Saints and two Angels*, set on a golden background, is signed Benvenuto di Giovanni (1509). From Piazza XX Settembre (*right of the church*) Via Mazzini leads to the historic town centre and the **Palazzo Pretorio**, decorated with coats of arms of the *Pretors* and of the Medici family who gained possession of the town in 1533; it has been altered on several occasions.

Trequanda

7km/4mi SW of Sinalunga.
This is a small hilltop village which has retained some sections of its crenellated walls and a few remains of Cacciaconti Castle, including one huge round corner tower. The 13C **Church of San Pietro** has a very unusual rustic façade with an alternating checkerboard design of white travertine and brown-ochre local stone. The interior presents an *Ascension* by Il Sodoma (*right-hand wall*) in a frame of carved and gilded *pietra serena*. Above the altar is a triptych by Giovanni di Paolo.
The **Museo Civico** in Via Ricci displays a superb collection of glazed terracotta ware by Andrea della Robbia, Luca's nephew. There are also Etruscan exhibits and 13C–18C paintings.

ADDRESSES

STAY

⊖⊖ **Agriturismo Relais Ai Battenti** – *Via dell'Antica Chiusina 23, 1,5km/1mi S of Montepulciano.* ℘*0578 71 70 09. Fax 0578 71 70 09. Closed 10 Jan–20 Mar.* ⊟. *4 rooms.* ⊊. There is a pleasant family atmosphere in this farmhouse, particularly at breakfast which is laid out on a long wooden table in a room with a large fireplace. Each of the comfortable rooms, furnished with country furniture, has its own bathroom, although it may not be en suite.

⊖⊖ **Albergo Meublé Il Riccio** – *Via Talosa 21.* ℘*0578 75 77 13. www.ilriccio. net. Closed 1st 2 weeks Jun and Sept.* *6 rooms.* ⊊. This converted medieval palazzo offers simple, functional rooms and a sitting room, furnished in country style, with two terraces and a ravishing view of Montepulciano, the valley and nearby lakes.

⊖⊖⊜⊜ **Agriturismo Le Colombelline e Il Morone** – *Via delle Colombelle, 3.5km/2mi NW of Montepulciano, after 700m on S327 turn left.* ℘*0578 61 199. Fax 0578 62 021.* ⊟ ⊅⊛. *9 rooms.* Breathtaking views of Montepulciano and San

Biagio and large, comfortable rooms (4–6 people) are what you'll find at these two nicely restored farm buildings. There are two swimming pools or you can rest in the extensive gardens.

⫿ EAT

🍽🍽 **Borgo Buio** – *Via Borgo Buio. ☎0578 71 74 97. www.borgobuio.it. Closed Mon. Reservations suggested.* This restaurant, appreciated as much for its "sinful savoury treats" as for its meals, has a great choice of dishes accompanied by an appropriate wine in a rustic, yet elegant setting.

🍽🍽🍽 **La Grotta** – *Località San Biagio, 1km/0.6mi SW of Montepulciano by S146. ☎0578 75 74 79. Closed Wed, Jan–Feb.* Under the splendid vaulted ceiling of a 16C palazzo you can taste the typical flavours of Tuscan cooking. In summer, meals are served in the cool of the well-tended garden.

TAKING A BREAK

Caffè Poliziano – *Via Voltaia nel Corso 27/29. ☎0578 75 86 15.* Since 1868, artists such as Pirandello, Malaparte and Fellini have frequented this beautiful café. The great panoramic room is an ideal place to try one of the 30 types of hot chocolate or to savour the excellent red wines of Montepulciano.

Cantina Avignonesi – *Via di Gracciano nel Corso 91. ☎0578 72 40 08. Closed Mon–Sat 1pm–3pm and Sun.* Ettore Falvo was one of the main agents in the rehabilitation of the Montepulciano vineyard. His elegant shop reflects the quality of the wine he produces. Try the Vin Santo "Occhio di Pernice".

⫿ GOING OUT

Il Caffè degli Archi – *Vicolo San Cristofano 2. Closed 5am–7.30pm (9pm winter).* Every evening this cocktail bar organises concerts of jazz and blues under its superb vaulted ceilings. If, like the owner, you are fond of music and the cinema, you are in for a pleasant evening.

Murlo★

The tiny medieval village of Murlo consists of several buildings in a single row of houses backing onto the town walls. From the 11C to the 18C it belonged to the Bishops of Siena. Today it is famous for the Etruscan archaeological discoveries made in Poggio Civitate, not far from Vescovado (north of Murlo).

▶ **Population:** 1,912
Ⓒ **Michelin Map:** Michelin Atlas p 44 and Map 563 – M 16 or Map 735 Fold 15.
▯ **Info:** ☎0577 81 40 50. www.comune.murlo.siena.it.
▷ **Location:** Murlo is 24km/15mi S of Siena, between S 223 and the Via Cassia.

VILLAGE
Antiquarium di Poggio Civitate★★

🕓*Open May–Sept Tue–Sun 10am–1pm and 3pm–7pm (9pm Jul–Aug); rest of the year Tue–Sun 10am–1pm and 3pm–5pm. ☎0577 81 40 99.*
The **museum** is housed in the former bishop's palace (*palazzone*) and contains the remains of a patrician residence (7C–6C BC) discovered in Poggio Civitate. This early Etruscan quadrangular villa formerly had a central porticoed courtyard. It gives a rare insight into domestic architecture, including the roofing structure which has remained almost intact. The reconstructed roof and its rich terracotta decoration demonstrate the importance of this architectural feature, which was a reflection of the family's social status. The ridge is adorned with a series of statues (over 1.50m/5ft high), consisting of some 20 animal and human figures, including a man wearing a wide-brimmed hat and boasting a Pharaonic beard. The roof was further emphasised by a border of antifixae representing

Gorgon heads and a large frieze decorated in the Greek style with banqueting and horseracing scenes.

In addition to this exhibit, there are also some fine ceramic vases imported from Greece and locally-produced bucchero ware, crockery used in the kitchen or by servants, and ivory and bronze decorative objects and jewellery, giving an insight into the life of an aristocratic Etruscan family from the mid-7C to the late 6C BC.

Pienza★★

Pienza, located in Val D'Orcia, is a perfect example of Renaissance town planning. It was commissioned by Pope Pius II, a scholarly man who wanted to build the ideal town, and who was born (1405) when the village was known as Corsignano. Florentine architect Bernardo Rossellino is the designer responsible for realising the Pope's perfectly-proportioned city.

▸ **Population:** 2,258
🖝 **Michelin Map:** Michelin Atlas p 44 and Map 563 – M 17 or Map 735 Fold 15.
🖪 **Info:** Via Casenuove 22. ✆057 87 48 072. www.pienza.info.
▸ **Location:** Pienza lies on S146 between San Quirico d'Orcia and Montepulciano.

PIAZZA PIO II★★

In the city centre, off Corso Rossellino.
This tiny **square**, named after Pope Pius II, is the earliest example of a real town planning policy and it is flanked by the main monumental buildings constructed by Rossellino. It was designed so as to reflect the balance between the civil and religious authorities through architectural harmony.

On the south side stands the cathedral. Opposite is the Palazzo Comunale with an open loggia on the ground floor. On the east side is the Bishop's Palace, with simple 15C restorations. On the west is an aristocratic mansion, surmounted by an architrave bearing the Piccolomini coat of arms.

A walk round the outside of the cathedral gives an opportunity to enjoy a picturesque **view**★ of the Orcia Valley.

Duomo★

The **cathedral**, completed in 1462, has a simple yet grand Renaissance façade. The restored interior is Gothic in style and consists of a nave and two side-aisles of equal height and an apse with five radiating chapels. It contains some major 15C works by the Sienese School, including altarpieces (*south aisle*) by Giovanni di Paolo and (*south transept*) by Matteo di Giovanni. The most

The Humanist Pope, Aeneas Sylvius Piccolomini (1405–64)

Aeneas undertook numerous diplomatic missions before becoming Pope under the name of Pius II in 1458. He was famous for his intellect and writings and in 1442 Emperor Frederick III appointed him Poet Laureate. As he was also an art lover, he released Filippo Lippi and Lucrezia Buti from their vows. Shortly after his election as Pope, he commissioned **Bernardo Rossellino**, the Florentine architect and pupil of Alberti, to undertake the rebuilding of his native village, Corsignano. It was later renamed Pienza in memory of the papal name of its most famous citizen.

View of Pienza and the Orcia Valley

B. Morandi / MICHELIN

remarkable works, however, are the *Madonna and Saints* by Sano di Pietro (*north transept*) and **Vecchietta's** masterpiece (north apse) depicting the **Assumption**★★ of the Virgin Mary between Popes Pius and Calixtus, St Catherine of Siena and St Agatha, who bears a cup containing her breasts, which had been cut off by her torturer. Note the golden backgrounds, the impression of relief, the delightful use of colour and the accuracy of the drawing. The chancel contains a Gothic lectern and stalls with the Piccolomini coats of arms.

Museo Diocesano

⊘*Open mid-Mar–Nov Wed–Mon 10am–1pm and 3pm–7pm; rest of the year Sat–Sun and Hols 10am–1pm and 3pm–6pm.* ✆€4. ♿. ☎0578 74 99 05.
The top floor of the **museum** contains 14C–15C paintings by the Sienese School, 15C–16C Flemish tapestries, a 14C panel with 48 painted compartments depicting scenes from the Life of Christ, and an extraordinary 14C cope decorated with narrative embroidery given to Pius II by an Eastern prince.

Palazzo Piccolomini★

⊘*Open mid-Mar–mid-Oct Tue–Sun 10am–6.30pm; rest of the year Tue–Sun 10am–4.30pm.* ⊘*Closed Feb 15–28.* ✆ €7. ☎0577 53 00 32. www.palazzo piccolominipienza.it.

This building, Rossellino's most accomplished work, was much inspired by the Palazzo Rucellai in Florence. The three façades overlooking the town are identical in appearance. Their most characteristic feature is the well-ordered harmony created by the vertical pilasters and the horizontal entablatures. The courtyard owes its elegance to the slender Corinthian columns. The interior contains an armoury, early printed books in the library and a Baroque bed in the papal chamber.

This was the first mansion purposely designed to look out over a wide expanse of countryside and it enjoys a view over the Orcia Valley from its three-storey loggia and hanging gardens on the south side.

Streets of Love

At the end of the 19C some of its street names of Pienza were changed, particularly those to the east of the main square. In a quest for the ideal, the names were taken from games of chance and inspired by love rather than war. The streets on the right of the main thoroughfare are named after Fortune (Via della Fortuna), Love (dell'Amore), the Kiss (del Bacio) and Darkness (Via Buia) and lead to the city walls and a panoramic view.

Romanesque church, Pieve di Corsignano

Agenzia turismo Chianciano Terme - Valdichiana/ Fototeca ENIT

EXCURSIONS
Pieve di Corsignano
1km/0.5mi W along the south side of Pienza past the town walls.

This was the old village church before Pienza was built. It is an 11C–12C Roman-esque building standing alone at the foot of the town. The façade, built of pale golden stone, is decorated with a carved doorway and a window with a column in the form of a statue. Beside it is a short cylindrical bell tower.

Monticchiello
10km/6mi E.

This medieval hillside village, sur-rounded by walls dotted with crenel-lated towers, is riddled with lanes and little squares steeped in charm. The vil-lage church has a pentagonal staircase leading up to its austere Gothic door-way. From the car park at the entrance to the town, there is a superb **view**★ of the Orcia Valley. On the right is Pienza with a foreground of arid hilltops, a char-acteristic feature of the landscape south of siena, and (left) the summit of Monte Amiata (see *MONTE AMIATA*).

ADDRESSES

🏠 STAY

☞☞ **Camere in Pienza** – *Corso Rossellino 23. ℘0578 74 85 00. ✉. 4 rooms.* ⌂. These modest but comfortable accommodations, located in an old palazzo near Pienza Cathedral, have iron bedsteads and old wooden furniture.

☞☞ **Agriturismo Santo Pietro** – *Località Santo Pietro 29, 5km/3mi NE of Pienza by S146. ℘0578 74 84 10. Fax 0578 74 84 10. Closed mid-Nov–Feb. ✉ ⌂. 8 double rooms.* ⌂. Here is a dream farmhouse in the heart of the fertile Sienese countryside: each room is decorated in an individual rustic style; authentic cooking using the local farm produce… and a pony for the children.

🍴 EAT

☞☞ **La Porta** – *Via del Piano 3, località Monticchiello, 7km/4mi SE of Pienza. ℘0578 75 51 63. www.osterialaporta.it. Closed Thu, 15 days in Nov. Reservations suggested.* Relax on the splendid terrace admiring the "postcard" view of the surrounding hills dotted with cypress trees and savouring the speciality of the day. Good wine list and sale of regional produce.

☞☞ **La Buca delle Fate** – *Corso Rossellino 38/a. ℘0578 74 82 72. Closed Mon, 7–30 Jan, 15–30 Jun.* The 15C Gonzaga palazzo, in the town centre, has large rooms and vaulted brick ceilings decorated in an elegant country style. It serves traditional food at reasonable prices.

🍷 TAKING A BREAK

L'Enoteca di Ghino – *Via del Leone 16. ℘0578 74 80 57. www.enotecadighino.it. Closed Nov–Mar, Wed.* This wine merchant, former wine waiter and maitre d'hôtel, has no need to make a name for himself in the district. He has tasted everything he sells – and the oldest vintage is from 1898. With over two thousand labels in stock, prices range from five euros to thousands.

La Taverna di Re Artu – *Via della Rosa 4. Closed Fri.* The phrase from a famous French drinking song – "Taste and see if the wine is good" – could be the motto of this wine bar, where it may be difficult to make your way through the throng of regulars.

Pitigliano★

Sorano, Sovana, Saturnia

The town was an Etruscan settlement before being colonised by the Romans. From the 13C to the early 17C, it belonged to the Aldobrandeschi family and later to the Orsini family, before being annexed to the Grand Duchy of Tuscany. From the late 15C until the early 20C, Pitigliano had a large Jewish population and became known as "Little Jerusalem". Its synagogue in Via Zuccarelli was built in 1598.

As Pitigliano is a small town it is a pleasant place for a walk. From Piazza della Repubblica there is a fine view of the valley below.

- ▶ **Population:** 4,232
- **Michelin Map:** Michelin Atlas p 49 and Map 563 – O 16–17 or Map 735 Fold 25.
- **Info:** Via Roma 6. ℘0564 61 44 33. www.comune. pitigliano.gr.it.
- **Location:** Pitigliano stands in a picturesque setting high above the confluence of the Lente and Meleta rivers.
- **Don't Miss:** There is an impressive **view**★ of the town by the church of the Madonna delle Grazie on the southern outskirts (S74).

MEDIEVAL TOWN

The town is traversed by cobbled streets lit by old lanterns, and the streets are linked to each other by covered alleyways or flights of steps.

At the lower end of the town stands the small **Church of San Rocco** (12C), which has a Renaissance west front and a bell tower decorated with arcading and tracery. The left wall incorporates an 11C low relief depicting a man with his hands in the mouths of two dragons.

Palazzo Orsini

This vast square building retains its 14C appearance with crenellations, machicolations and an austere loggia with two arches of unequal size. In the 16C alterations were made at the rear, including a courtyard with a well bearing a coat of arms. Along one side of the courtyard is a wing with arcades supported by Ionic columns. The other wing has a delicately carved Renaissance entrance.

Duomo

The 18C Baroque façade of the **cathedral** forms a sharp contrast with the fortified bell tower, the old medieval belfry. Nearby is a travertine column (1490) carved with coats of arms and surmounted by a bear, the emblem of the Orsini family.

EXCURSIONS
Sorano★

9km/5.6mi NE of Pitigliano.

Medieval Sorano is picturesquely set above the superb wooded limestone **Lente Gorge**★ dotted with natural or man-made caves (Etruscan tombs). In the Middle Ages it belonged to the Aldobrandeschi family before passing, in 1293, into the hands of the Orsini family, and finally becoming part of the Grand Duchy of Tuscany in 1608.

The town is dominated by the half-ruined Orsini Fortress, built in the 15C. The 18C district, *Masso Leopoldino*, built on a flattened rock platform, provides a breathtaking view down into the gorge. In the modern district there is a pleasant public park built in terraces from which

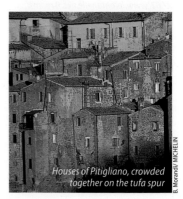

Houses of Pitigliano, crowded together on the tufa spur

B. Morandi/ MICHELIN

317

Lente Gorge, Sorano

ROMA-OSLO/ iStockphoto

there is an interesting view of the gorge, the town and the citadel.

Sovana★

8km/5mi N of Pitigliano.

Sovana was the birthplace of **Pope Gregory VII** (Ildebrando di Sovana), who was born c. 1020 and elected Pope in 1073. Although it is now a sleepy village, Sovana still boasts some interesting reminders of its glorious past.

The church of **Santa Maria** (12C) has a typically Romanesque interior and some 16C frescoes. The intricately carved **ciborium**★ dates from the 9C. At the west end of the same street stands the **cathedral**★, a large Romanesque and Gothic construction.

The **Etruscan Graveyard** (*1.5km/1mi W of Sovana towards San Martino*) contains numerous Etruscan graves (7C–2C BC), the main ones of which are reachable by footpaths or narrow **gorges**★ (*tagliate*) cutting into the cliffs. Visitors can see several tombs, such as the **Tomba Ildebranda**, which consists of a majestic set of terraces and caves surmounted by a temple, within view of Sovana Cathedral.

Saturnia

30km/19mi NW of Pitigliano.

Saturnia, famous for its Etruscan and Roman remains, has a number of excavated burial grounds, including the 7C BC **necropoli del Puntone** (*sign-posted*). The 15C **castle** (*cassero*), built in the days of Sienese control, has been reduced to a few remains. Remains of the **Roman baths** are visible on Piazzale Bagno Secco.

The town is now popular with people taking the waters in **Terme di Saturnia**♨♨, where the sulphur-rich water rises from the spring at a temperature of 37°C/98.6°F. It is particularly effective in the treatment of skin diseases and respiratory disorders.

ADDRESSES

🛏 STAY

🍴 **Agriturismo Le Fontanelle** – *Località Poderi di Montemerano, 58050 Montemerano, 3km/2mi S. ℘0564 60 27 62. www.lefontanelle.net. 8 rooms.* 🛏. Ideal for nature lovers, this quiet and simple farmhouse lies in wooded country beside a little lake inhabited by wildfowl. The owners are welcoming and the bedrooms comfortable.

🍴🍴 **Hotel La Taverna Etrusca** – *Piazza del Pretorio 16, 58010 Sovana. ℘0564 61 61 83. Closed Jan–Feb. 9 rooms.* 🛏. *Restaurant* 🍴🍴🍴. Hotel and restaurant in a converted 13C palazzo. A steep staircase leads up to the bedrooms, which are decorated in retro style. The rustic-style restaurant serves local specialities.

🍴 EAT

🍴 **Osteria Passaparola** – *Via del Bivio 16, 58050 Montemerano, 23km/14mi SW of Pitigliano by S322 towards Manciano, then Montemerano-Saturnia. ℘0564 60 28 27. Closed Thu, Feb and Jul.* Choose between traditional dishes at the osteria and more elaborate cuisine in the elegant restaurant, at the other end of the village. You can also find a comfortable room at the inn of the same name.

🍴🍴 **Trattoria del Orso** – *Piazza San Gregorio VII 64. ℘0564 61 42 73. Closed Thu in winter. Reservations suggested.* You can enjoy the local cooking – Tuscan crostini, pasta (*pici*) and sausages – in one of the two little eating rooms or, in fine weather, in the picturesque square, Piazza San Gregorio.

San Quirico d'Orcia★

and the Val d'Orcia

This old town set on a small rise still has its 12C walls and its huge gates. Very early in the Middle Ages, San Quirico gained importance because it straddled Via Francigena, which passed through the Orcia Valley linking Rome and the north of Italy. In 1154 Frederick I of Swabia, better known as Frederick Barbarossa, received ambassadors from Pope Adrian IV here. Every year the town commemorates the event in the "Festa del Barbarossa" (third Sunday in June).

TOWN WALKING TOUR
The walk begins at the Collegiate Church.

Collegiata ★★
This admirable Romanesque-Gothic **collegiate church** was built in the 12–13C. On the elegant but simple façade, beneath a row of arcading, is a fine carved rose window, emphasising the richness of the majestic **Romanesque portal**★. Its columns and its lintel, which is carved with monsters in confrontation, are set in a great arch supported by entwined columns resting on lions' backs. On the right-hand side of the church are **two Gothic portals**, the wider of the two flanked by statue-columns supported by lions and of a more complex design than the Romanesque portal on the west front. Note also the kneeling, smiling Telamones supporting the division in the double bay to the right.

The most notable features of the interior are (*between the last two pillars to the left of the nave*) the recumbent statue of Count Henry of Nassau, who died in San Quirico in February 1451 when returning from a jubilee in Rome, (*chancel*) the early 16C carved wood panelling with marquetry inlays (*north transept*) and, most outstanding of all, a **reredos**★ painted by Sano di Pietro (15C), consisting of a triptych depicting the

Virgin Mary, the Child Jesus and four saints against a golden background; in the lunette is the Resurrection and Descent into Hell; the predella is decorated with scenes from the Life of the Virgin Mary.

Palazzo Chigi
One side of Piazza della Collegiata is filled by this 17C **mansion**. Despite its poor state of repair, its past majesty is apparent in the regular disposition of the doors and windows and the magnificent coat of arms which include the six hummocks of the Chigi family and the crown of oak leaves of the Della Rovere family.

Porta ai Cappuccini
Along the right side of the Palazzo Chigi is Via Poliziano, a narrow, medieval street leading to Porta ai Cappuccini, a 13C **gate** in the form of a polygonal tower.

DRIVING TOUR

Val d'Orcia
1hr 30min without visiting Rocca a Tentennano – about 10km/6mi from San Quirico to Castiglione and Rocca d'Orcia.

From San Quirico take the Via Cassia (S2) south towards Rome.

The road descends gently into the Orcia Valley between undulating hillsides. On the nearest hill is the mighty Rocca d'Orcia (fortress); in the distance

Population: 2,444
Michelin Map: Michelin Atlas p 44 and Map 563 – M 16 or Map 735 Fold 15.
Info: Piazza Dante Alighieri 31. ☎0577 89 72 11. www.portalevaldorcia.it.
Location: San Quirico d'Orcia is situated on the Via Cassia, about 40km/25mi S of Siena.

Collegiata di San Quirico

B. Morandi/ MICHELIN

the Orcia Valley, including the fortress at Tentennano, to the rich Sienese Salimbeni family. In 1419 the Republic recovered all the land when Cocco Salimbeni was forced to capitulate in a struggle against his native town.

The traingular main square, **Piazza Vecchietta**, was named after Lorenzo di Petro, also known as the Vecchietta, who was said to have been born in Castiglione c. 1412. In the centre of the piazza is a 17C travertine well. Little remains of the fortress, **Rocca Aldobrandeschi**, above the village. From the esplanade above the outer wall (*access by a flight of steps*) there is a view of the castle ruins and a panoramic view of Monte Amiata and the Orcia Valley.

is Monte Amiata and the fortress at Radicofani.

▷ *Before crossing the River Orcia, turn right towards Bagno Vignoni.*

The road climbs steeply along the sheer-sided river valley, giving a fine view of the nearby fortress.

Bagno Vignoni

This hamlet is popular for its spring water which was reputed for its effectiveness in the treatment of arthritis and rheumatism as far back as Roman times.

The houses cluster round an old bathing pool flanked, on one side, by St Catherine's Portico, a reminder that the saint is said to have come here at the end of her life.

Opposite the large neighbouring car park is the Rocca d'Orcia, set high above part of the Orcia Gorge, which in the Middle Ages provided a means of communication with the Maremma region.

▷ *Return to the bridge and cross the River Orcia. After 350m/380yd turn right into the Castiglione road.*

Castiglione d'Orcia

Castiglione used to belong to the Aldobrandeschi family but in the early 14C it passed to Siena. A few years later Siena sold the village and other property in

▷ *Follow the signs to Rocca a Tentennano; car park below the fortress.*

Rocca a Tentennano★

🕐*Open summer daily 10am–1pm (also Sun and Hols 2.30pm–4.30pm); rest of the year Sat only 10am–1pm and 2.30pm–4.30pm.* ✆€1.50. ✆*0577 88 73 63.*

The promontory, which overlooks Via Francigena and the Orcia Valley, is said to have been occupied and built on in the 9C. The fortress was designed by Tignoso di Tentennano and it remained in the hands of the Tignosi until the middle of the 13C when the Republic of Siena took possession of it.

The fortress was restored in the 1970s, and the missing sections were replaced by brick.

The **tour** of the fortress not only provides splendid views of the Orcia Valley and Monte Amiata but also reveals the medieval system of defence. The pentagonal fortifications enclose a military parade ground and a polygonal tower.

Rocca d'Orcia

Accessible on foot from the fortress.

This medieval town was built up against the walls of the Rocca a Tentennano on which it was dependent, hence its name. The narrow streets, which are still partly cobbled, meet around a huge polygonal water tank capped by a well.

Abbazia di
Sant'Antimo★★

The former abbey of Sant'Antimo lies at the foot of the village of Castelnuovo dell'Abate and has preserved its solitude in the depths of the delightful Tuscan landscape★ composed of hills planted with olive and cypress trees.

ABBEY

🕐 *Open Mon–Sat 10.30am–12.30pm and 3pm–6.30pm, Sun and Hols, 9.15am–10.45am and 3pm–6pm. Services sung to the Gregorian chant.*
📞 *0577 83 56 59. www.antimo.it.*
Founded in the 9C, the abbey reached the peak of its prosperity and influence in the 12C. The **church** (12C) is a particularly fine example of Romanesque Cistercian architecture. The Burgundian style is evident in the ambulatory with radiating chapels; on the other hand the porch and pilaster strips decorating the bell tower and various walls are typically Lombard in style.

The interior is spacious and austere. The raftered nave is separated from the rib-vaulted aisles by columns crowned with superb alabaster capitals. Note the graceful proportions of the ambulatory, the light apse with its double window, the frescoes dating from the 14C–17C, and the capitals (the capital on the second column to the right is attributed to

Michelin Map:
Michelin Atlas p 44 and Map 563 – M 16.
Location: The abbey of Sant'Antimo is situated 19km/12mi S of Montalcino. It is a short drive south from Siena by the Via Cassia, turning off at Montalcino.

Maestro di Cabestany and depicts Daniel in the lions' den).

The abbey is now dedicated to spiritual retreats and prayer (**Gregorian chant**) and is run by a community of Augustinian monks affiliated to the order founded in the 12C by St Norbert in Prémontré.

ADDRESSES

🏠 STAY

Foresteria dell'Abbazia di Sant'Antimo – *Località Sant'Antimo 222, 53020 Castelnuovo dell'Abate.*
📞 *0577 83 56 59. www.antimo.it. Prices available at the house.* Staying here is like going back in time to the Middle Ages. The view of the abbey and the sound of the Gregorian chant will remain in the memory for many years. Only for those who are looking for a true retreat as silence is a must.

Abbazia di Sant'Antimo

G. Bludzin / MICHELIN

From elegant sun-drenched enclaves lined with umbrellas and cafés to private coves, the Tuscan coast has a beach for every visitor's budget and hobby. The best known beaches are those of Versilia, which includes; Viareggio, where the summer season kicks off during the city's Carnevale, Italy's most popular after that of Venice; and Forte dei Marmi, a resort town frequented by the jet set. Further south, between the harbours of Livorno and Piombino, lies the Etruscan Riviera, a largely natural landscape consisting of pine woods interspersed with quiet beaches and scattered Etruscan ruins. Tuscany also boasts its own archipelago, of which Elba, Napoleon's exile island, is the largest and most famous. Here you will find excellent diving, windsurfing and hiking.

Tuscany's coastline stretches from the north, where the Apuan Alps tumble into the Tyrrhenian Sea, to the south, where the Promontorio dell'Argentario juts out from the mainland. In the north is the Riviera Versilia where many Florentines and Pisans spend their summers. It includes family beaches, such as Marina di Carrara, the closest shore to marble centre Carrara, Pietrasanta and Viareggio, as well as sophisticated resorts, such as Forte dei Marmi and Torre del Lago, adopted home of Giacomo Puccini.

Below Versilia, sandy, crowded beaches give way to both busy ports and more natural landscapes. Harbour town Livorno (Leghorn), one of the largest cities on the Tuscan coast, is home to an Italian naval academy and an American military outpost. Between here and Piombino, where ferries to Elba and other islands disembark, is the Etruscan Riviera, dotted with archeological sites, such as Populonia.

The final, southern section of the coastline includes the Maremma, one of Tuscany's wildest landscapes. This massive sub-region consists of pine forests, sea coves and preserves for flora and fauna. The Parco Naturale della Maremma, one of Italy's first nature preserves, has a stunning array of indigenous wildlife. At the Promontorio dell'Argentario are views of, and ferries to, Isola del Giglio.

Tuscan
Archipelago★★

The Tuscan Archipelago is a string of seven islands, of which Elba is the largest. Giglio, Capraia, Montecristo, Pianosa, Giannutri and Gorgona are mountainous, with a rich unspoiled natural environment that is seen at its best during the seasons when the climate is mild and the coastline free from crowds of tourists.

ISOLA D'ELBA★★

Elba, island of seahorses, is the largest island in the Tuscan Archipelago. It is popular with tourists for its solitary beauty, its silence, its mild climate, its untamed nature and its varied landscapes.

The Isle of Elba was part of the Tyrrhenian continent that was partially submerged beneath the sea in the Quaternary era, leaving behind the islands of Corsica, Sardinia, the Balearics, Elba and two mountain ranges on the French Riviera (Les Maures and L'Estérel). Elba is a mountainous island; its highest peak is Monte Capanne (1,018m/3,308ft). It has a jagged coastline consisting of natural, well-sheltered coves with small beaches. Professional fishermen regularly catch

- ⚑ **Michelin Map:** Michelin Atlas pp 36, 42 and 48 Map 563 – L, M 11 and N, O, P 12, 13, 14; Map 735 Folds 14, 24, 25.
- ▷ **Location:** From north to south, the small islands of the Tuscan Archipelago are: Gorgona, Capraia, Pianosa, Montecristo, Giglio and Giannutri.
- ⊘ **Take Note:** Gorgona, Montecristo and Pianosa cannot be visited.
- ℹ **Giglio Info:** Via Umberto 1, Giglio Porto, Isola del Giglio. Via Assunzione, Capraia. www.arcipelago.turismo.toscana.it.
- ℹ **Elba Info:** Calata Italia, 26, 57037 Portoferraio, ✆0565 91 46 71, www.arcipelago.turismo.toscana.it.
- ▷ **Elba Population:** 28,482
- ⏱ **Elba Timing:** Elba is more of a holiday resort than a place for a day excursion, but it is possible to tour the island in two days, either in one's own car or in a rental car available in Portoferraio.

GETTING THERE

BY SEA: Elba is easily reached from Piombino, port of departure for ferries going to Portoferraio and Rio Marina. Contact: Navarma–Moby Lines, Via Giuseppe Ninci 1, 57037 Portoferraio, ✆0565 91 81 01, www.mobylines.it; Toremar, Calata Italia 22, 57037 Portoferraio, ✆0565 91 80 80, www.toremar.it.

BY BUS/TRAIN: Buses and trains go only as far as Piombino (⚑see above). Piombino Marittima train station (✆0848 888 088, www.trenitalia.it) is reachable from all major cities (transfer at Campiglia Marittima). SITA buses (Via L. da Vinci 13, 57025 Piombino, ✆0848 580 028, www.atm.li.it) have routes to

Piombino Porta and a direct bus from Florence.

BY AIR: Direct flights operate from Pisa and some international destinations to La Pila airport (✆0565 97 71 50; www.elbaisland-airport.it).

GETTING AROUND

BY CAR: You can take your car from the mainland to Elba via a car ferry. Otherwise, you can hire a car (multiple options available at port).

BY BUS/TAXI: ATL operates intra-island bus routes as well as city routes in Portoferraio (Viale Elba 20, 57037 Portoferraio, ✆0565 91 47 83). For taxi service from the port or elsewhere in Portoferraio, call ✆0565 91 51 12.

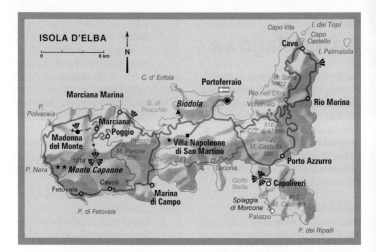

tuna fish and anchovies along the island's rocky shores.

Elba is perhaps best known as the place of exile for Napoleon from 1814 to 1815. From his homebase in Portoferraio he commanded a small court and initiated several public works projects.

Portoferraio ⚓

The capital of Isola d'Elba lies on the shores of a beautiful bay, protected by the remains of outer walls and two fortresses.

In the upper part of the town overlooking the sea (*north*) is the **Museo Nazionale della Palazzina dei Mulini** (Mill House), a simple house with a patio and garden, where Napoleon lived during his brief period of sovereignty (*access from the town centre; follow signs by a fatiguing climb on foot up a long flight of steps or by car up a rough narrow road*). The house contains the **Museo Napoleonico** (🕐 *open Mon and Wed–Sat 9am–8pm (7pm last admission), Sun and Hols 9am–1.30pm (1pm last admission);* 🕐 *closed 25 Dec, 1 Jan;* 🎫€4.50; joint ticket with Palazzina dei Mulini (valid 3 days); 🎫€7.75; ☎0565 91 46 88; www.ambientepi.arti.beniculturali.it and www.elbaisola.com*) consisting of the officers' mess, Napoleon's library, his bedroom and the antechamber; from the first floor there is a fine view of the garden and the sea; downstairs are the WC, the servants' room, Napoleon's salon, his

study and the door to the garden, where one can take a stroll.

The **road**★ west from Portoferraio to Marciana Marina is particularly recommended for the views it provides of Procchio and Procchio Bay.

🚗 DRIVING TOUR

THE WEST★
70km/44mi – about 5hr anti-clockwise from Portoferraio, following the route indicated on the map.

Biodola
This is a vast, beautiful sandy beach.

Marciana Marina ⚓⚓
This is a harbour protected by two jetties, one of which holds the ruins of the Medici Tower (*torre Medicea*).

▷ *West of Marciana Marina and the sea front, the road climbs through the woods on the northern slopes of Monte Capanne.*

Poggio
Small resort perched on a spur of rock.

▷ *The road continues to climb through the trees. To the left, on the outskirts of Marciana, is the lower station for the cable-car to the summit of Monte Capanne.*

Napoleon, Sovereign of the Isle of Elba

After signing the Act of Abdication in Fontainebleau, the deposed French Emperor lived on Elba from 4 May 1814 to 26 February 1815.

Napoleon had with him a small court governed by Bertrand, the Grand Marshal of the Palace. He also commanded about 1,000 soldiers, of whom 300 had accompanied him at the outset, together with 100 grenadiers and infantrymen from his imperial guard, and 600 more came to join him, including Polish lancers under the orders of Drouot and Cambronne. He also had his own navy consisting of one brig, *L'Inconstant*.

During his short stay he directed Cambronne's men to build roads, and the Polish lancers developed mines, made improvements to farming methods and modernised the road network in Portoferraio.

Monte Capanne★★
15min by cable-car. ⏱*Operates Easter–Jun daily 10am–12.15pm, 2.30pm–5.30pm.* 👁*€6.50 return.* ✆*0565 90 10 20.*
From the rocky summit (*15min on foot from the top station*), there is a superb panoramic view★★ over the entire island of Elba, (*east*) to the coast of Tuscany and (*west*) to the east coast of Corsica.

Marciana
The village lies at the foot of its ruined castle on the eastern slopes of Monte Giove, providing a wonderful **view**★ of Poggio, Marciana Marina and Procchio Bay.
The small **Museo Archeologico** (Archaeological Museum) has exhibits dating from the Iron and Bronze Ages and a collection of Greek pottery. ⏱*Open May–Sept Thu–Tue 9.30am–12.30pm and*

4pm–8pm (May and Sept 3pm–7pm). ⏱*Closed Oct–Apr.* 👁*€2.* ✆*0565 90 12 15. www.comune.marciana.li.it.*

Madonna del Monte
Alt 627m/2,037ft. 45min there and back on foot from the road to the castle above Marciana.
A rocky path runs through the trees at the beginning of the walk but later provides panoramic views as it climbs to the 16C chapel built on the north slope of Monte Giove. Near the chapel is a strange semicircular fountain dating from 1698 and the "hermitage" where Napoleon lived with Maria Walewska for a few days in the summer of 1814.
From the adjacent rocks the **view**★ embraces the creeks on the north coast, Marciana Marina and Procchio Bay, and the villages of Marciana and Poggio.

Portoferraio

Stefano Photography / iStockphoto

Semi-precious Stones

Where the Isle of Elba is not green with vegetation, it is red with iron ore in the east and white with granite in the west. It's a good hunting ground for minerals; golden or silvery pyrites in various shapes, cubes, and dodecahedrons and octahedrons can be found near Rio Marina. You can look for light blue beryls, the famous aquamarines, in the granite of Monte Capanne, the Oggi cave, Fonte del Prete, Speranza and Gorgolinato. The island mines are no longer in operation, but there are many minerals in the old workings. The local pyrite is likely to be found near deposits of hematite, which is reddish or brown, and the velvety black ilvaite, which is also known as lievrite – the name Elba is derived from the Latin *ilva*. A search for aquamarines may turn up a piece of tourmaline.

The road continues along the west coast passing the beaches of Sant'Andrea and **Fetovaia**. East of Fetovaia the road reaches **Cavoli**, a seaside resort with a sandy beach.

Marina di Campo

Marina di Campo lies on the edge of a plain dotted with olive trees and vineyards and is popular for its superb beach. Fishermen make the delightful little harbour a bustling place.

◐ *Take the road that runs up the Galea Valley, bordered to the right by the uninhabited Lacona region, to return to Procchio. From Procchio take the road towards Portoferraio; in San Martino, turn right to Villa Napoleone.*

Museo di Villa San Martino★

⊙*Open Tue–Sat 9am–8pm (7pm last admission), Sun and Hols 9am–1.30pm*

(1pm last admission; also summer Sat 9am–11pm. ⊙Closed 25 Dec, 1 Jan. Joint ticket with the Palazzina dei Mulini (valid 3 days) ⊗€7.75. ℘0565 91 46 88. www.ambientepi.arti.beniculturali.it or www.elbaisola.com.

The silent hillsides planted with oak trees and vineyards have not changed since Napoleon's day; nor has the view, except for the neo-Classical palace built by Prince Demidoff. Above it stands the modest house used by Napoleon as his summer residence; the interior decoration has been restored to what it was during Napoleon's occupation. From the terrace, there is a pleasant view of Portoferraio Bay.

THE EAST★

68km/42mi – about 3hr–clockwise from Portoferraio following the route indicated on the map. From Portoferraio take the road south; after 3km/2mi turn

Marciana marina, Isola d'Elba

Masterlu / Dreamstime.com

Isola del Giglio

left towards Porto Azzurro. The road skirts Portoferraio harbour before bearing south across the the narrowest part of the island. It then crosses the Monte Calamita peninsula.

▷ *Turn right to Capoliveri.*

Capoliveri
On the western outskirts of this small town, the point known as **Three Seas Panorama**★★ offers views of three bays: Portoferraio Bay (*north*), Stella Bay (*west*) and Porto Azzurro Bay (*east*); below (*south*) is the beach at Morcone. Out to sea (*southwest*) are the islands of Pianosa and Montecristo.

▷ *Return to the road to Porto Azzurro.*

Porto Azzurro☖☖
This town faces a delightful harbour commanded by a fortress that is now a prison. The vegetation consists mainly of cacti and agaves.
The road then winds north across the eastern slopes of Monte Castello and Cima del Monte.

▷ *Before reaching Rio nell'Elba turn right to Rio Marina.*

Rio Marina
This fine village and mining harbour is protected by a small tower with merlons. The **coast road**★ to Cavo provides a number of attractive views of the tiny rocky islands of Cerboli and Palmaiola in the Piombino Strait and of Follonica Bay and the mainland.

Cavo
This is a pretty little harbour, the nearest to the mainland, protected by Cape Castello.

▷ *Take the road via Rio nell'Elba towards Porto Azzurro. At the crossroads, turn left and then first right.*

The **Volterraio road**★★ runs high above the sea, providing a number of breathtaking views of the ruins at Volterraio and Portoferraio Bay.

OTHER ISLANDS IN THE ARCHIPELAGO
Isola del Giglio★
🛈*Via Umberto 1, Giglio Porto, Isola del Giglio.*
The mountainous island of Giglio (Lily Island) lies just off Monte Argentario. There are only three villages – **Giglio Porto**, where the boats from the mainland dock, **Giglio Castello**, the medieval village encircled by the walls of its fortress, and **Campese**, a village with accommodations, which overlooks a delightful bay fringed with a sandy beach. The sheer, rugged coast carpeted with scrub blends harmoniously with the natural beauty of the wild and emo-

327

tive environment, which is the product of the very dry climate. A range of sports is available including sub-aqua, windsurfing and riding.

Capraia

Capraia lies nearer the northern tip of Corsica than Italy. The western side is mountainous; the eastern side is gentler and more hospitable. The natural environment is rugged, and only the centre and harbour are inhabited. It is this untamed nature that makes the island a paradise for walkers who come to admire the tiny lake (*laghetto*) in an old volcanic crater.

Sailors like to view the island from the sea and admire the nesting birds and the deep colours of the Cala Rossa (Red Creek). The coastline is perfect for sub-aqua and windsurfing activities.

ELBA ADDRESSES

🏠 STAY

🛏️🍽️ **Hotel Residence Villa Giulia** – *Località Lido di Capoliveri, 57036 Porto Azzurro, 7.5km/5mi NW of Capoliveri towards Portoferraio.* 🕿*0565 94 01 67. www.villagiuliahotel.it. Closed mid-Oct– Easter. 35 rooms.* 🛆. The comfortable rooms, in four separate buildings, have cane furniture and a balcony or small garden. In summer meals for residents are served on the terrace overlooking the sea.

🛏️🍽️ **Da Giacomino** – *Capo Sant'Andrea, 57030 Marciana, 6km/4mi NW of Marciana.* 🕿*0565 90 80 10. www.hoteldagiacomino. it. Closed Nov–Easter. 33 rooms.* 🛆🛆. *Restaurant* 🛏️🍽️🍽️. The ideal place for a holiday – set in a magnificent garden, against the steep cliff, with a fine view of the sea. The rooms are light and pleasant, and the owners are charming.

🛏️🍽️ **Hotel Dino** – *57031 Pareti, 4km/ 2.5mi S of Capoliveri.* 🕿*0565 93 91 03. www.hoteldino.com. Closed Nov–Easter. 30 rooms.* 🛆. *Restaurant* 🛏️🍽️. All the rooms at this value-priced hotel are spacious with a view of the sea and far enough (although not too far) from the noise of the beach. The hospitality of the staff will add to your enjoyment.

Isola di Giannutri★

Giannutri, which lies southeast of Giglio, is privately owned but open to visitors for a few hours every day (🚫 *no camping or picnics*). There are traces of a 1C Roman villa which may have belonged to Domitian Enobarbus.

Gorgona, Pianosa and Montecristo

🔒 *Not open to visitors.*

There are prisons on **Gorgona**, which lies offshore from Livorno (Leghorn), and on **Pianosa**, which is south of Elba. **Montecristo**, south of Pianosa, is a granite island dominated by Monte Fortezza (645m/ 2 096ft), classified as an uninhabited nature conservancy zone.

The island is famous as the setting chosen by Alexandre Dumas (1844) for his novel *The Count of Monte Cristo.*

🛏️🍽️ **Hotel Brigantino** – *Via Di Gualdarone 9, 57030 Campo all'Aia, 15km/9mi E of Marciana.* 🕿*0565 90 74 53. www.hotelbrigantino.com. Closed 21 Oct–22 Mar. 45 rooms.* 🛆🛆. *Restaurant* 🛏️🍽️. The best feature of this hotel is the vast and shady garden a few yards from the sea. The rooms are spacious and adequately furnished. Meals are served outside under a thatched shelter.

🛏️🍽️🍽️ **Casa Rosa** – *57037 Biodola, 9km W of Portoferraio.* 🕿*0565 96 99 31. Closed Nov–Mar. 38 rooms.* 🍴🛆🛆. *Restaurant* 🛏️🍽️. The luxuriant greenery is not so abundant as to spoil the panoramic view. This is a good place for enjoying the celebrated beach at Biodola without paying a fortune.

🍴 EAT

🛏️🍽️ **Sarabanda** – *Località Molino 11, 57031 Capoliveri, 1km/0.6mi N of Capoliveri.* 🕿*0565 93 52 77. Closed 15 Sept–29 Jun. Reservations required.* Multicoloured lights, the rhythm of the salsa music and the waiters' ponchos and sombreros create a lively ambience at this restaurant that serves Mexican dishes and exotic drinks. There are fine views from the terrace.

⊜⊜ **Da Pilade** – *Località Marina di Mola, 57031 Capoliveri, on the road to Capoliveri. ℘0565 96 86 35. www.hotel dapilade.it. Closed mid-Oct–Easter. Reservations required.* Not far from the sea, this hotel restaurant specialises in grilled Angus steak and a huge choice of delicious hors d'œuvres.

⊜⊜⊜ **La Lanterna Magica** – *Via Vitaliani 5, 57036 Porto Azzurro. ℘565 95 83 94. Open daily Jun–Sept. Rest of the year closed Mon and Dec–Jan.* This restaurant is built partly on stilts with wide windows overlooking Porto Azzurro. Elban dishes are on the menu, as are locally produced wine and the olive oil of first-class quality.

⊜⊜⊜ **Affrichella** – *Via S Chiara 10, 57033 Marciana Marina. ℘0565 99 68 44. Closed Wed. Reservations required.* This little restaurant near the Cathedral is known for its fish specialities and extensive wine list. Also on the menu are various hot and cold hors d'œuvres. Ideal in summer for romantic candle-lit dinners in the adjoining square.

⊜⊜⊜⊜ **Publius** – *Piazza XX Settembre 6/7, 57030 Poggio, 3km/2mi E of Marciana. ℘0565 99 208. Closed Mon in winter.* Choose a table on the veranda to enjoy splendid views of Marciana, the hills and the sea. The cooking is authentic with an emphasis on fish.

🏃 SPORT AND LEISURE

🏊 **Centro Club Corsaro** – *57031 Pareti Capoliveri. ℘0565 93 50 66. Reservations required. Open 8am–9.30pm. Closed Nov–Mar.* Experienced divers can explore the subterranean fauna off the south coast of Elba with this scuba club. Nocturnal excursions are also available.

🐎 **Centro Ippico L.E. Farms** – *57030 Procchio, south of Procchio towards Marina di Campo. ℘0565 97 90 90. Reservations required.* The horses in this small riding school are well cared for and the local rides (on the beach or in the country) are most agreeable. Excursions are organised by day or by night (*1hr, 3hr or all-day; picnic or restaurant meal included*).

⚓ **Centro Velico Naregno** – *Spiaggia di Naregno, NW of Capoliveri, 57031 Capoliveri. ℘0565 96 87 64. www.centro veliconaregno.it. Open 8am–8pm. Closed mid-Oct–Mar.* Naregno sailing school provides courses and craft for hire: surf boards, catamarans, F J boats, Hobie Cat and scooters.

⚓ **Nautilus Bagni Lacona** – *Spiaggia Grande, 57031 Capoliveri. ℘0565 96 43 64 or 337 70 23 10 (mobile). Reservations required. Closed Nov–25 Apr.* This submarine provides a pleasant way to see the marine flora and fauna without having to dive. Motor boats, sailing boats, canoes and paragliding available.

GIGLIO ADDRESSES

🏨 STAY

⊜⊜⊜ **Hotel Campese** – *Località Campese, 58012 Isola del Giglio. ℘564 80 40 03. www.hotelcampese.com. Closed Oct–Easter. 39 rooms. 🛏. Restaurant ⊜⊜.* The hotel, which overlooks its private beach, is a quiet family-run hotel and has recently been refurbished.

🍴 EAT

⊜⊜⊜ **La Vecchia Pergola** – *Via Thaon de Revel 31, Giglio Porto, 58013 Isola del Giglio. ℘0564 80 90 80. Closed Tue and Nov–Feb .* Hovering on stilts above the water, this restaurant's peaceful island village atmosphere is ideal for seaside dining.

⊜⊜⊜ **Da Maria** – *Via della Casa Matta, Località Castello, 58012 Isola del Giglio. ℘0564 80 60 62. Closed Mon and Jan–Feb.* This restaurant, possibly the most typical of the island, is located in the picturesque centre of medieval Castello, with a panoramic view from the terrace of Campese Bay. Local specialities, such as fish and seafood, are served in a simple setting.

Carrara

Massa and the Quarries

This town, whose name comes from the Ligurian root "kar" meaning "stone", is world-famous for its exceptionally pure, fine-grained white marble. Carrara marble (marmo) has been quarried since Roman times, and Michelangelo used to come to the local quarries to choose blocks of stone for his masterpieces. In 1769 Maria Teresa Cybo Malaspina (the last of the aristocratic family which controlled events in Massa and Carrara for many centuries) set up an Academy of Fine Arts, which still provides teaching in techniques and artistic skills.

▶ **Population:** 65,564

Michelin Map: Atlas P 32 and Map 563 – J 12 and Map 735 Fold 14.

Info: Viale Vespucci 24, 54037 Marina di Massa. ℘0585 24 00 63. www.aptmassacarrara.it.

▶ **Location:** Carrara lies in a delightful valley on the edge of a ruggedly spectacular limestone mountain range, the Apuan Alps, which are so white that they seem to be covered in snow. It is easily reached by the Genoa–Livorno (Leghorn) Motorway.

Don't Miss: Fantiscritti.

TOWN
Duomo
The **cathedral** was built (11C–14C) in the Romanesque-Gothic style with a façade in the Pisan style, pierced by a rose window, decorated with superb marble tracery and flanked by an elegant 13C bell tower. The interior contains a number of interesting statues including a wooden *Crucifix* and a marble *Annunciation*, both dating from the 14C.

Beside the cathedral is a huge 16C fountain decorated with a statue by Baccio Bandinelli (1493–1560).

Museo del Marmo★
1km/0.5mi from town centre, on the right in the avenue linking the town to Marina di Carrara. ◔*Open Jun–Sept Mon–Sat 10am–8pm; May and Oct 10am–5pm; Nov–Apr, 8.30am–1.30pm.* ◔*Closed 16 Jun.* ⊜€3. ☞*Call for guided tour and information* ঙ. *℘0585 84 57 46; www.comune.carrara.ms.it.*
Marble and its uses from Antiquity to the present day, is presented in five different sections. The first explains how marble was quarried during the days of the ancient Romans, information that has been obtained from archaeological excavations. The second section, the **Marmoteca**★, is a "library" including more than 300 samples of marble and

granite from the largest seams in the world. The third section deals with quarrying techniques from the 17C to the early 20C. The fourth concerns various aspects of the use of marble and the final section consists of a collection of modern sculptures.

MARBLE QUARRIES★
The untamed scenery, the white scree slopes and the gigantic scale of the work undertaken by man are an amazing sight. Beside the road stand small platforms which provide a view (*during working hours*) of the machinery in operation. To extract the marble, the quarrymen use a "diamond wire", a steel wire containing small cylinders covered with diamond dust which acts as a high power abrasive.

The blocks of stone are then taken down to the plain where they are divided in stone-cutting plants; after being processed in marble works, the stone is exported from the harbour in **Marina di Carrara**.

Fantiscritti Quarries★★
4 or 5km/2.5 or 3mi NE beyond Miseglia. This is the most impressive of all the quarry sites because of its ruggedness and terracing. The site is reached by a

Carrara Marble

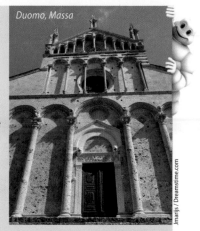
Duomo, Massa

Jmarijs / Dreamstime.com

The marble seams in the Apuan Alps extend over several square miles but the largest of all is in Carrara. It is famous for its translucent whiteness and fine grain, qualities which are highly prized in statues, hence its title – *statuario*. Once polished, it acquires the pearly sparkle that is its characteristic quality. Carrara also produces veined or coloured marbles (dark red, green, grey-blue, orange). The colours result from the presence of mineral salts (or other elements) in the original limestone which, after crystallising for several million years, has turned into marble.

On this side of the Apuan Alps, quarrying has been in progress for some 2,000 years. Quarrying is now concentrated in three valleys – Colonnata, Fantiscritti and Ravaccione. Over the centuries, quarrying has undergone constant expansion and the industry now produces 800,000 tonnes of marble a year. This has been made possible, since the 19C, by new techniques and the opening, in 1876, of a railway linking the quarries to the sea, thereby facilitating the transport of the stone.

From the reign of Caesar Augustus until the 5C, Imperial Rome obtained three-quarters of its building stone from Carrara. Thereafter, Carrara marble was used for such prestigious works as the main staircase in the Hermitage in St Petersburg, London's Marble Arch and the Kennedy Center for the the Performing Arts in Washington, DC. Since the Renaissance many sculptors – Michelangelo, Giambologna, Bernini, Canova and Henry Moore – have come to the quarries in the vicinity to choose the stone for their work.

Carrara marble continues to be a sought-after building material. Today, the Carrara Marmotec exhibition takes place every two (even-numbered) years and attracts builders and architects from around the world.

Marble quarry in the Apuan Alps

L. Pessina/ MICHELIN

Marina di Massa

proim/Fotolia.com

particularly steep road, which crosses three viaducts known as the *Ponti di Vara*; they were built in the 19C for the railway and have been converted into road bridges.

Colonnata Quarries★

8km/5mi E via Bedizzano or Carrara along the valley floor. These quarries are more easily accessible than the others; the road mounts from one level to the next, passing several stone-cutting plants. The setting is less grandiose but more attractive owing to the greenery.

CAMPO CECINA ROAD★

20km/12mi N of Carrara by the Fosdinovo road (S 446d) to the viewing point.
The road climbs above a wooded valley and passes through Gragnana and Castelpoggio. The first view (*left*) is over the final outcrops of the Apuan Alps and down to the sea, including the beach at Marina di Carrara and the promontory at Montemarcello.

▶ *Turn right into the winding Campo Cecina road which is used by the large trucks transporting the marble from the quarries.*

The road runs along the south-facing, pine-clad slopes of Monte Pizza. There are more views (*right*) over the Carrara area. A picturesque trip along a road cut into

the bare marble hillsides of Monte Uccelliera, interspersed with forest sections, leads to **Piazzale dell'Uccelliera**, from which there is a magnificent **view**★★ of the Torano quarries, the beaches at Marina di Massa and Montignoso, the islands in the Tuscan Archipelago and the peaks in the Southern Alps.

MASSA

In the plains at the foot of the Apuan Alps, 4km/2.5mi inland from the Riviera.
This provincial capital is a modern town whose squares are adorned with large fountains and marble sculptures. There are also numerous white marble façades owing to the proximity of Carrara. Two important **historic buildings** have survived from the 15C–18C, when the town belonged to the powerful Malaspina family. Their 15C–16C Renaissance **castle**, Castello Malaspina, is incorporated in the half-ruined medieval fortress (*Rocca*) on the stony hillside overlooking the town; their 16C–17C family residence, **Palazzo Cybo Malaspina**, now houses the Prefettura (*Piazza Aranci in the town centre*). From Piazza Aranci take Via Dante Alighieri to see the **cathedral** (*duomo*). It has a modern marble façade and contains a number of interesting works of art, including a a *Madonna* by Pinturicchio (*above the altar*), and (*in an underground chapel*) the Malaspina family tombs.

Livorno
and Casciana Terme

The commercial harbour of Livorno (Leghorn) is one of the main ports on the Mediterranean, shipping mainly wood, Florentine craftwork, marble, rough-cut or crafted alabaster and cars. The local fishing trade has given rise to two culinary speci-alities: fish soup (*cacciucco*) and red mullet (*triglie*).

PORT

The hub of city life in Livorno centres on **Via Grande**. Near its harbour end is **I Quattro Mori**★. The **Four Moors Monument** in Piazza Micheli is dedi-cated to Ferdinando I in memory of a victory over the Moors by the Knights of St Stephen. The bronze statues of the Four Moors were produced in 1626.

Via Grande extends from the harbour to the elliptical-shaped Piazza della Repub-blica. To the southeast of the piazza is the **Mercatino Americano** (American Market). Originally set up to sell Ameri-can army surplus clothing and camp-ing equipment, the American Market in Piazza XX Settembre is one of Livorno's best-known sights. It has since diversi-fied to include other goods.

Adjacent to the northwest end of the Piazza della Repubblica is the Fortezza Nuova (New Fortress). In Piazza Guer-razzi near the New Fortress stands the

- ▶ **Population:** 161,673
- ⏱ **Michelin Map:** Michelin Atlas p 36 and Map 563 – L 12 or Map 735 Fold 14. Town plan in the Michelin Guide italia.
- ℹ **Info:** Piazza Cavour 6. ℘0586 89 81 11. www. costadeglietruschi.it.
- ▶ **Location:** The city can be reached by the A12 Genova-Livorno major road, the A11 Florence-sea coast major road or the motorway (superstrada Firenze–Livorno).

Cisternino (small tank) built in 1837 by Poccianti. It never fulfilled its original function as a water tank and in the 1950s it was converted into an arts centre which now hosts figurative art exhibitions.

Between the New Fortress and the Fortezza Vecchia (Old Fortress), lies the **Venezia Nuova district**, founded in 1629 by the Medici. Resembling a lit-tle Venice, its main features are canals, bridges and narrow lanes.

The **Viale Italia** runs south from the town centre to the district of Ardenza, providing sea views and passing close to the **Terrazza Mascagni**, a broad board-walk of black and white marble tiles, and

Port, Livorno

Sokol25 / Dreamstime.com

the **Accademia Navale** (Italian Naval Academy) ⏱*Closed for refurbishment.*

Museo Civico G Fattori

Villa Mimbelli, Via Jacopo in Acquaviva. ⏱*Open Tue–Sun 10am–1pm and 4pm–7pm.* ⏱*Closed 1 May, 15 Aug.* ⬤€4. ♿. ☎*0586 80 80 01.*
The **Fattori Museum** displays paintings by **Giovanni Fattori** (1825–1908), leading exponent of the Macchiaioli movement, and by his Macchiaioli colleagues, among them Telemaco Signorini, Giovanni Boldini, Silvestro Lega and Vittorio Corcos.

Museo Mascagnano

The **Pietro Mascagni Museum** (⏱*Closed for restoration at time of writing.* ☎*0586 26 45 28*) houses a collection of the scores, instruments and memorabilia of this composer (1863–1945) who is best-remembered for his opera *Cavalleria Rusticana.*

EXCURSION
Casciana Terme ⚕

15km/9mi S of Pontedera, on the axis of the Florence-Leghorn Motorway. Population: 3,462.
Casciana Terme is surrounded by hills planted with vines and peach and olive trees. This ideally quiet yet varied holiday town is perfect for taking the waters, before exploring nearby towns on daytrips.
The springs in Casciana were known in the days of Caesar Augustus, and they have been famous since the 11C. Legend has it that **Matilda of Canossa** (1046–1115), Marchioness of Tuscany, saw, from the window of her castle in Casciana, a blackbird heal its swollen foot in these waters. The springs are strongly recommended for the treatment of circulatory disorders, hypertension, arthritis, rheumatism, asthma and bronchitis. The treatment takes the form of baths, mud baths, inhalations or consumption of water.

ADDRESSES

🛏 STAY

⬤▨ **Mini Hotel** – *Via Buontalenti 57.* ☎*0586 88 72 82. mini.hotel@wooow.it. 17 rooms.* ☲. After a tiring visit to the heavily laden stalls of the covered market, you can stay in this small family hotel, which has well-proportioned rooms with bathrooms en suite. Breakfast is served in a pretty little garden. Good value for money.

🍴 EAT

⬤▨ **Da Galileo** – *Via della Campana 20.* ☎*0586 88 90 09. Closed Wed, Sun evening and 16–30 Jul.* Near the fortress and far from the noise of Via Garibaldi, this trattoria has a long-established clientele of the famous and less well known. Here in old-fashioned surroundings you can taste the most authentic Livorno specialities, such as fish soup and red mullet.

⬤▨▨ **L'Antico Moro** – *Via Enrico Bartelloni 59. ☎0586 88 46 59. Closed Wed, 1st two weeks in Sept and 27 Dec–4 Jan. Reservations required.* In the past

this restaurant was the meeting place for local artists. The tiny dining room with its original decor usually attracts local customers who come to eat the fresh fish prepared in the traditional way.

🍴 TAKING A BREAK

Bar Civili – *Via del Vigna 55.* ☎*0586 40 13 32. www.barcivili.it. Open Mon–Sat 8am–1am. Closed 1–20 Aug.* For over a hundred years the young and less young have been meeting here for a glass of one of the best "Livorno punches" – not to be missed.

Chalet Mauri – *Viale Italia 22.* ☎*0586 80 44 08. Open Tue–Sun 7.30am–4am.* Who would refuse a cocktail on the seafront? This is what is offered by this pleasant tea room with a terrace.

La Baracchina Rossa – *Viale Italia 106.* ☎*0586 50 21 69. Open daily 6am–2am.* Within a beautiful garden of flowers, this great red building has been converted into an ice cream parlour. It is one of the rare buildings to have survived the war. The warm welcome and the 19C paintings make this a favourite address among the Livornese.

La Maremma★

Region

This huge sub-region of Tuscany is particularly old in geological terms, and includes a range of hills, marshes, lakes and coastal dunes (*tomboli*), which act as natural dams. It is notable for its natural heritage, particularly the vast Parco Naturale della Maremma, one of Italy's first nature preserves.

A BIT OF HISTORY

The Etruscans, who founded Populonia, Roselle and Vetulonia, were the first to attempt to drain this marshy area, but the first major hydraulic work was undertaken during the Pax Romana. After the decline of the Roman Empire, the communication routes fell into disuse. The region returned to its natural state and the land reclaimed as a result of these first drainage projects was lost. Malaria became rife in the wild marshland areas.

In 1826 the Dukes of Lorraine, especially Leopold II, resumed land reclamation and the work continued during the period of Italian Unification and under the Fascist regime. The territory was finally drained and agriculture is now its main source of income.

GROSSETO

The capital of La Maremma lies on the Aurelian Way in the fertile Ombrone plain 13km /8mi from the sea. The city is a modern provincial capital. The old centre is enclosed within huge hexagonal brick ramparts fortified with bastions, built by the Medici in the late 16C. The heart of the old town is the area around Piazza Dante Alighieri, flanked by the cathedral and the provincial palace, a Gothic-Renaissance pastiche.

The 13C Gothic church of **San Francesco** has a number of small frescoes by the Sienese School (14C–15C) and a painted Crucifix attributed to Duccio di Buoninsegna (c. 1255–c. 1318). In the adjoining cloisters is a portico-covered well dating from the days of the Medici (1590), which is known as the buffalo well

- **Michelin Map:** Michelin Atlas pp 43, 48 and Map 563 – N/O 15 and Map 735, folds 24-25.
- **Info:** Viale Monterosa 206, Grosseto. ℘0564 46 26 11. www.lamaremma.info. www.gol.grosseto.it.
- **Location:** The Maremma is usually divided into three areas: the Pisan Maremma; the Grossetan Maremma; and the Latin Maremma stretching from Tarquinia to Cerveteri. It also reaches inland as far as the western flanks of the Metalliferous Hills.
- **Don't Miss:** Exploring the flora and fauna of the Parco Naturale della Maremma.
- **Timing:** Allow at least one day for Grosetto and at least a day per driving tour.

because animals from the Maremma, including buffalo, came to drink there. The **Museo Archeologicoe d'Arte della Maremma★** (*open May–Oct Tue–Sun 10am–1pm and 5pm–8pm; rest of the year Tue–Sun 9am–1pm and 4pm–6pm; closed 1 Jan, 1 May, 25 Dec; €5; ℘0564 48 87 50; www.gol.grosseto.it*) has five sections tracing the history of Roselle, the Maremma and the Grosseto. The Diocesan Museum section is rich in works by Sienese artists.

Herdsmen with Maremma horses and cattle

B. Morandi / MICHELIN

335

🚗 DRIVING TOURS

1 COUNTRYSIDE, PINE FORESTS AND SEA

135km/84mi – 1 day

The Grosseto province, generally considered the most typical of the Maremma region, consists of a plain which rises from below sea-level along the coast to rolling countryside further inland. The hills are planted with olive trees and vines and interspersed with farmland. Near the sea the colours can be intense and vary with the changing seasons. Along the coast the fine sandy beaches are fringed with pine forests.

Ruins of Roselle

Not far from Grosetto, on the top of a hill north of Roselle, are the **Rovine di Roselle** *(10km/6mi NE of Grosseto on S223;* ⏰*open daily May–Aug 9am –7.30pm, rest of the year daily 9am– 5.30pm;* ⏰*closed 1 Jan, 1 May, 25 Dec;* ⚫*€4;* 📞*0564 40 24 03).*

These are the ruins of one of the most illustrious towns in northern Etruria. The ancient Etrurian town was separated from Vetulonia (*west*) by a lake, Lacus Prilius. According to Livy, the Etruscan town of Russel (*Russelae* in Latin) was colonised by the Romans in 294 BC. It fell into decline after the fall of the Roman Empire and was almost abandoned after 1138 when it ceased to be a bishopric. **Gli scavi** (the **excavations**) begun in 1942 and still in progress, have revealed a wall (over 3km/2mi long and up to 2m/6ft high) built of polygonal blocks of stone. In front of the wall was an outer line of fortifications built of rough bricks, probably dating from the 7C BC.

The wall itself was built to the north in the 6C and to the west in the 2C BC. Only three huge gateways have been discovered but it is likely that there were more roads leading into the town. Archaeologists have also uncovered various Roman buildings such as an amphitheatre and imperial forum, as well as cobbled streets and a villa dating from the days of the Empire with a mosaic floor, and a residential district with houses and craft workshops dating from the late 6C.

▶ *After crossing S1 (Via Aurelia), continue towards Buriano. The road crosses the plain south of Vetulonia on the hillside and climbs along a series of terraces to the burial ground and*

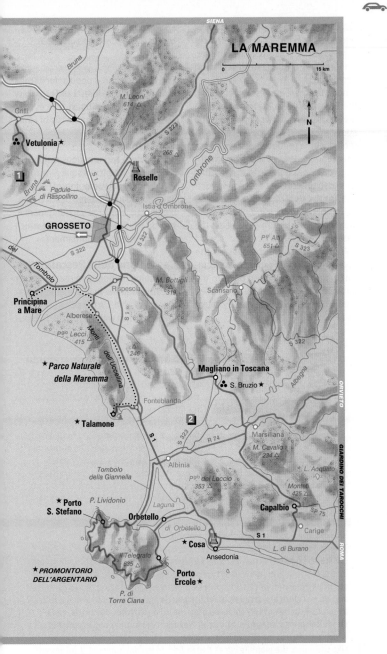

the site of an archaeological excavation before reaching the village.

Necropoli di Vetulonia★

Vetulonia lies a few miles from the motorway between Livorno and Grosseto, dominating the Grosseto plain. On arrival follow the signs for Tombe etrusche; the unsurfaced track (800m/866yd long) is rough but passable.

The huge walls of Vetulonia, which used to be one of the largest towns in northern Etruria, are the only relics of the original citadel (6C–5C BC). The present town stands on the site of its Etruscan predecessor and has an interesting necropolis.

Among the most interesting remains is the **Tumulus della Pietrera** (7C BC), a grave consisting of two chambers, one above the other. The upper chamber is roofed with a pseudo-dome and has a quadrangular layout; the lower chamber, which has a pillar in the middle, was probably circular when first built. The **Tombe del Diavolino** (Little Devil's Tomb) has a quadrangular chamber beneath a pseudo-dome; it still has the base of its central pillar.

The excavations in progress on the Greek and Etruscan-Roman town (*northeast of the village*) are also open to the public. They have uncovered a paved road which used to be lined by shops and houses.

▷ *To reach Follonica either take the road through Gavorrano or take S1.*

Follonica⚘
This seaside resort is popular for its mild climate, fresh pine forests and proximity to places of artistic interest. It faces west across Follonica Bay to the Isle of Elba.

Punta Ala⚘⚘⚘
This modern and luxurious residential resort is set in a picturesque pine forest on the southern promontory of Follonica Bay. The superb sheltered beach is complemented by a large yachting marina, sports facilities and a golf course which hosts international tournaments.

Castiglione della Pescaia⚘⚘
The fishing harbour and seaside resort of Castiglione was built as a canal port at the foot of a hill. On the slope is a walled medieval town with steep paved streets,

Flora and Fauna of the Maremma

M. Dewynter/ MICHELIN

The **wild boar** is the symbol of the Maremma and its most popular denizen, the quarry during the hunt (*cacciarella*), a traditional event bringing together hunters, hounds and beaters. Also typical of the region are the **Maremma ox**, a huge beast with lyre-shaped horns, and the **Maremma horse**, a small and very sturdy animal, probably descended from the Berber horse. Herdsmen (**buttero**), similar to the cowherds of the Camargue region in southern France, carry out their ancient and taxing task on horseback. The highlight of the year is the branding of the cattle (*merca*) which takes place on 1 May in **Alberese**.

The **fallow deer** is another common inhabitant of the region; its hide is reddish-brown dotted with white in the summer and grey-brown in the winter.

The woods are also home to **roe-deer**, **porcupine** and **badgers**. Indeed, porcupine and badgers often share the same set. As for the **fox**, it is the undisputed lord of Maremma, at home in all types of natural environment, whether fields of crops, pastureland, woods, rocky areas, pine forests, marshes or dunes. The area also boasts **wildcats**, **stone martens**, **weasels** and other mammals, as well as a multitude of beautifully coloured birds including **falcons**, **buzzards**, **owls**, **shoveller ducks**, **seagulls**, **hoopoes**, **herons**, **cormorants** and **kingfishers**, which are of great interest to bird-watchers.

Like the fauna, the plantlife varies depending on the environment. **Juniper** and **lentiscus** can be found growing between the **marine lilies** of the coastal dunes and the pine forest. The rocks are covered with **thyme** and **red valerian**, while the hills are overrun by scrub and **heather**. Among the many other species native to the region are the **dwarf fan-palm**, **rosemary**, **asphodel**, **broom**, **yellow poppies** and **orchids**.

The Buttero and the Merca

Although the work of the herdsman (*buttero*) has undergone fundamental changes, it still requires a daily effort governed by the rhythms of nature. In the past the Maremma herdsman's day began at dawn when he selected his horse, and was followed by a range of different tasks, including the supervision and sorting of the cattle and pens and helping any cow having difficulty giving birth. While still inside the cow the calf was hitched to the horse and then pulled out. The high point of the herdsman's working year is the **merca**, a ceremony rather than a practice, in which cattle are branded to indicate ownership. To facilitate the branding and ensure more rapid healing, the job is done in spring when the animals have lost their winter hide. This exhausting and hazardous work used also to be seen as a form of entertainment. As the saying goes: "Anyone whose heart has not been seared by the *merca* could not really have been there." The cowherds were not the only people involved in the day's events. The glorious finale was entrusted to the women of the farm, who spent several days preparing pasta, meat and cakes, and served up a meal fit for a king.

houses with barred windows, covered passageways and fortified gates. From the castle-capped summit there is an interesting view of the canal port and the fine sandy headland beaches.

South of Castiglione the road skirts the umbrella pines of Pineta del Tombolo.

Principina a Mare ⚓

This peaceful seaside town lies in the heart of the pine forest that stretches south along the coast from Follonica. There are some splendid walks beneath the pine trees or along the long beach of fine sand.

② UCCELLINA HILLS

160km/100mi – 1 day. From Grosetto take the S1 (Via Aurelia) to the Alberese exit. In Alberese,, park by the visitor centre (centro-visite), to buy tickets or to get on a coach tour of the park.

Parco Naturale della Maremma★

Piazza del Combattente, 58010 Alberese. 🕐*Open mid-Mar–Oct daily 8am–5pm; rest of the year 8.30am–1.30pm.* ⊛*€3–€19 depending on tour.* ✆*0564 40 70 98. www.parco-maremma.it.*

The **park** consists almost entirely of the **Monti dell'Uccellina** (almost 4 000ha/9 884 acres), an area of forest (Mediterranean scrub), running parallel to the coastline between Principina a Mare and Talamone. The many species of local flora

and fauna are influenced by the varied climate that includes features typical of continental, Mediterranean and, in certain cases, desert conditions.

There is much evidence of the first human settlements from the Palaeolithic era through the Bronze Age up to the days of the Romans. Man has been able to hunt here since ancient times, owing to the great mammals which have always been a characteristic feature of the Maremma region. In the past, however, the coastal areas were infested with mosquitoes carrying malaria and it was impossible for people to settle there permanently.

There are guided or self-guided tours along the theme-based itineraries designed to include the various differ-

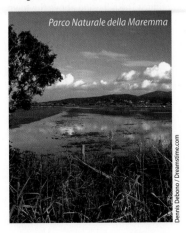
Parco Naturale della Maremma

Dennis Debono / Dreamstime.com

A Troubled History

The promontory had an eventful history both in the Middle Ages, when it belonged to the Aldobrandeschi and Orsini families, and in the 16C when it passed out of the hands of the Republic of Siena and became a Spanish fortress. In the 18C it passed to the Austrians, then to the Bourbons and later to the Grand Duchy of Tuscany before being annexed to the Kingdom of Italy in 1860.

ent aspects of the park (forest, wildlife and panoramic views).

Also available are the "Parkland" itineraries (guided tours in summer; self-guided tours along the paths in winter) of San Rabano (5hr – one departure per day) and delle Torri (tour of the Towers – 3hr – two departures per day) or a tour of the outlying area around Alberese concentrating on the flora and fauna.

Continue south to rejoin S1.

Fonteblanda

This town at the Talamone road junction is famous for its spa, **Terme dell'Osa**.

Talamone⚬⚬

Talamone is a typical little fishing harbour, overlooked by a 15C fortress. The town has both Etruscan and legendary origins. The hill rising above the town is said to be the burial mound of Telamon, who took part in the Argonauts' expedition to Colchis in search of the Golden Fleece. In 225 BC two Roman consuls, Emilius Papus and Attilius Regolus, won a major victory over the Gauls in the nearby plain of Campo Regio.

③ PROMONTORIO DELL'ARGENTARIO★

43km/27mi – about 2hr

Argentario was once called Promontorio Cosano (after the neighbouring Etruscan town of Cosa) and is said to owe its present name to the shiny, silvery appearance of its rocks, although its name may also be an allusion to the activities of its former owners who were bankers (*argentarii*). This former island is linked to the mainland by ancient sand spits, Tombolo di Feniglia and Tombolo di Giannella. It consists of the small limestone range known as Monte Argentario (635m/2 064ft high). The headland is approached by three causeways and served by a picturesque coastal road. To reach Argentario take the Via Aurelia and turn off at Albinia or at Orbetello.

Orbetello

Piazza della Repubblica 1, Orbetello, ℘0564 86 12 26.

The town lies on the middle causeway which crosses the lagoon and carries the main access road to the peninsula (S 440). In the past the town was known by the Latin name of *Urbis Tellus* (literally territory of the City, ie of Rome), perhaps because in AD 805 it was given by Charlemagne to the Abbey of the Three Fountains in Rome.

The fortifications date from the days of Sienese then Spanish occupation, when Orbetello was the capital of the Garrison State. The **cathedral** stands on the site of an ancient Etruscan-Roman temple. According to an inscription on the architrave on the central portal, the late Gothic façade was altered in 1376 under the direction of Nicolo Orsini. The two aisles date from the days of the Spanish occupation. The Lombard-style chancel rail is decorated with entwined vine shoots.

Between the edge of the lagoon and Porto Santo Stefano, the road (S 440) runs uphill along the north coast of the peninsula between hedgerows, villas and hotels, finally providing a view of the Talamone headland on the mainland and Porto Santo Stefano on the island.

Porto Santo Stefano⚬⚬

The main town on the peninsula is the embarkation point for boat trips to Giglio (see ARCIPELAGO TOSCANO). The houses are built on the hillside, flanking the 17C Aragonese fortress (*Rocca*) from which there is a superb **view**★ north over the harbour and Talamone Bay.

Porto Santo Stefano

Vito Arcomano / Fototeca ENIT

○ *From Porto Santo Stefano take the scenic route (Strada Panoramica) north.*

Beyond the headland at Lividonia, there is a succession of views over the west coast and the island of Giglio.
The corniche road descends between cypress trees, passing above Cala Grande Bay, distinguished by the tiny island of Argentarola, and the small seaside resort of Cala Piccola and its bay. Further south the island of Giannutri is visible.

○ *Beyond the junction with a road running across country to Porto Santo Stefano, the road continues to twist and turn as it runs downhill; there is no retaining wall.*

At high altitude, there are several **views**★★ of the rocky creeks along the southwest coast, the island of Rossa (consisting of reddish rocks) and of the terraced fields and peaks of Monte Argentario. One part of the road (*unmetalled for 3km/2mi*) looks down on the rugged headland of Torre Ciana (crowned by a tower), the south coast and then on the island of Isolotto and Fort Stella. The road then passes Rocca Spagnola, a 16C bastioned citadel, before reaching Porto Ercole.

Porto Ercole⌂⌂
The seaside resort stands at the foot of the Rocca Spagnola, to which it is linked by two parallel walls capped with bat-

tlements. A medieval gate leads into the old town. Piazza Santa Barbara is flanked by the arcades of the former Governor's Palace (16C); from the square there is a view of the yachting marina, the bay and the two old Spanish fortresses, opposite on Monte Filippo.

○ *The road completes the round tour by skirting the eastern slopes of the Argentario promontory where it soon runs at water level between the headland and the Levante lagoon before joining (right) the road (S 440) to Orbetello.*

4 RUINS, VINES AND OLIVE TREES
After visiting the ruins of Cosa, the final section of the tour runs north of Carige from Capalbio to Magliano through rolling hills planted with vines and olive trees.

Rovine di Cosa★
11km/7mi SE of Orbetello, at the base of the tombolo meridionale.
On the top of a promontory north of **Ansedonia** ⌂ overlooking the Laguna di Orbetello and the Argentario peninsula stand the **ruins** of Cosa. A Roman colony from the 3C BC until the 4C AD, Cosa was built beside the **Via Aurelia**. In the town there is a **Museo Archeologico** (○*open daily 9am–7pm; excavations: 9am–dusk;* ○*closed 1 May, 25 Dec, 1 Jan;* ∞€2; ⌂; ℘0564 88 14 21).

Historical Perspective

The first document to mention Capalbio dates from 1161. In the 14C the Aldobrandeschi family gave the village to the Republic of Siena and thereafter the destinies of the two places were linked. In 1555 Capalbio, like Orbetello, was invaded by the Spaniards (allies of the Medici). In the 18C and 19C the town suffered from the neglect of the surrounding farmland which had been allowed to return to marsh, causing malaria and the general impoverishment of the whole area. Not until the 20C did Capalbio see an increase in its population, due to a revival of farming.

The **excavations** (*scavi;* ⏰*open daily May–Sept daily 9am–7pm, Oct–Apr 9am–1.30pm; museum* ⬤⬤*€2; archaeological zone no charge;* ☎*0564 88 14 21*) reveal two distinct centres of interest, even though they are only a few hundred yards apart. On the top of the promontory is the acropolis, its outer walls consisting of huge blocks of stone enclosing the surviving walls and columns of the capitol, a temple and other smaller buildings. Further north is the town itself – paved streets intersecting at right angles, foundations of the buildings within the forum (basilica, temples, curia, shops), numerous water tanks and houses. The massive north gate (Porta Romana) is still standing.

Capalbio

Population: 3,867. Michelin Atlas p 48 and Map 563 – O 16 and Map 735 Fold 25. ⓘ*Palazzo Collacchioni 2;* ☎*0564 89 66 11. www.capalbio.net.*
Capalbio occupies a favourable position on a hilltop (209m/679ft above sea level), overlooking a varied and fertile landscape of undulating hills to the south of the Tuscan Maremma, not far from the sea. Dominated by a crenellated tower, Capalbio's medieval appearance is visible from all directions. These days, the town is favoured by the jet set and plays host each summer to Capalbio Cinema, a festival of short films.
There are two gates, Porta Senese (Siena Gate) and Porticine (Little Gate), into the walled medieval village. Within stands the Romanesque Church of San Nicola which contains 14C frescoes (*chapels on north side*) and 15C frescoes (*chapels on south side*). The bell tower, pierced by twin bays, dates from the 12C. Nearby is the Aldobrandeschi fortress (*Rocca*).
Outside the walls, in Piazza Provvidenza, the Oratorio della Provvidenza is decorated with a 15C fresco based on works by Perugino and Pinturicchio.

Magliano in Toscana

30km/19mi approximately N of Orbetello.
Magliano stands at the top of a hill covered with olive trees and is half concealed by its 14C and Renaissance walls. The main street, Via di Mezzo, contains two churches: San Giovanni Battista, which has a Renaissance façade and San Martino, which dates from the Romanesque period. Originally there was an Etruscan town nearby; its **necropolis** is still visible. The town later became a Roman colony under the name of **Heba**. *For information* ☎*0564 59 22 97 (Sig. Vellati Vasco) and* ☎*0564 59 24 80 (Signora Marianelli Simona).*
Ruins of San Bruzio★ – Just beyond the village beside the road to Magliano da Marsiliana (*left*) are the remains of a 12C church standing solitary in the middle of a vast field.

Ruins of San Bruzio

fioredicampo - Fotolia.com

ADDRESSES

🛏 STAY

CAPALBIO

Azienda Agrituristica Ghiaccio Bosco – *Strada della Sgrilla 4, 4km/3mi N of Capalbio. ℘0564 89 65 39. www.ghiacciobosco.com. Closed Jan–Mar. 10 rooms.* This large farm, with classic decor, is set in the heart of the Maremma countryside, but not far from the sea. Home-made cakes and jam make for an ample breakfast.

CASTIGLIONE DELLA PESCAIA

Agriturismo La Rombaia – *Località Rombaia, 58043 Castiglione della Pescaia, 4km/2.5mi NE of Castiglione della Pescaia; after 2km/1.2mi driving towards Grosseto, turn left. ℘0564 94 40 12. www.larombaia.it. 10 rooms.* Each room at this farmhouse is carefully decorated according to an agricultural theme and provides comfort and tranquillity.

ORBETELLO

Azienda Agraria Grazia – *Via Aurelia Km 140,100, 58016 Orbetello, 7km/4mi E of Orbetello at 140km on the Via Aurelia towards Rome. ℘0564 88 11 82. www.agriturismograzia.com. 3 suites.* Set in a wildlife reserve where deer, sheep and wild boar roam freely, this farmhouse is ideal for those who enjoy the outdoors and riding. Rooms are comfortable, well-lit and well-appointed.

Antica Fattoria La Parrina *Località Parrina, 58010 Albinia, 5km/3mi N of Orbetello Scalo at 146km post on Via Aurelia towards Firenze. ℘0564 86 55 86. www.parrina.it. Weekly rates from €775. Restaurant.* Stay in the country in grand style in this working farm which offers accommodation in its 19C house, furnished in period style. In summer, breakfast and dinner are served on the beautiful veranda – the wine, olive oil and cheese are home-produced.

TALAMONE

Talamone International Camping Village – *Via Talamonese, 58010 Talamone, 1km/0.5mi E of Talamone towards Fonteblanda. ℘0564 88 70 26. www.talamonecampingvillage.com. Closed 30 Sept–31 Mar. 300 sites. Restaurant.* In addition to the view of the bay and of Talamone, this campsite is equipped with a swimming pool, a restaurant and a private beach. The huge site, which runs down to the sea, provides the campers with a certain amount of privacy.

🍴 EAT

CAPALBIO

Tullio – *Via Nuova 27. ℘0564 89 61 96. Closed Wed, 5–20 Nov.* If you are weary of the seaside but too lethargic to move far, this traditional family restaurant is for you. The menu concentrates on local Maremma dishes; meals are served on the terrace in summer.

CASTIGLIONE DELLA PESCAIA

Osteria nel Buco – *Via del Recinto 11, 58043 Castiglione della Pescaia. ℘0564 93 44 60. Closed Mon (except Jul and Aug), 15 Nov–15 Dec, Jan, Feb. Reservations required.* Known for its typical dishes as much as for its energetic owner, who entertains his guests with musical interludes, this restaurant is situated in the ramparts street which encircles the village.

FOLLONICA

La Osteria – *Vi Santini 4, 58022 Follonica. ℘0566 42 142. Reservations required.* Situated on the road to the sea, this pleasant and intimate hostelry has a limited number of seats which are much in demand. The owner/chef prepares various original recipes with a good selection of antipasti vegetarian dishes.

GROSSETO

Il Canto del Gallo – *Via Mazzini 29. ℘0564 41 45 89. Closed Sun and evenings, 2 weeks in Feb. Reservations required suggested, particularly at noon.* This restaurant, situated near the ramparts, has chosen the cockerel as its decorative theme and boasts over 300 china figures from all over the world. It uses organic produce and serves many vegetarian dishes. There's no surprise that its speciality is chicken (*galletto alla diavola*).

🍴🍴 **Buca San Lorenzo (da Claudio)** – *Via Manetti 1.* 📞*0564 25 142. Closed Sun, 10–26 Jan, 1–15 Jul. Reservations required.* Within the old ramparts is the town's best known restaurant, which offers traditional cooking served by candlelight.

PROMONTORIO

🍴🍴🍱 **Il Cavaliere** – *Strada Statale (major road) 440 39/41, 58016 Orbetello Scalo, after the railway bridge.* 📞*0564 86 43 42. Closed Wed and 10–25 Nov. Reservations suggested.* Far from the crowds of tourists, this family restaurant serves its local clientele in a simple setting, although it is sometimes rather noisy because of the passing trains. Hors d'œuvres and fish specialities.

🍴🍴🍱 **Il Moresco** – *Via Panoramica 156, Cala Moresca, 58019 Porto Santo Stefano, 5.5 km/3mi SW of Porto Santo Stefano.* 📞*0564 82 41 58. Closed Tue, Wed afternoon, Jun–Sept and Feb .* From its unique position on a cliff top, the restaurant, specialising in traditional fish dishes, enjoys a panoramic view of the isle of Giglio.

🍴🍴🍱🍱 **La Fontanina** – *Loc. San Pietro, 58019 Porto Santo Stefano, 3 km/ 1.9 mi south of Porto Santo Stefano.* 📞*564 82 52 61. www.lafontanina.com. Closed Wed, two weeks in Jan and Nov 5–30. Reservations suggested.* This friendly seafood restaurant provides an elegant, bucolic break away from the typical beach-going lifestyle.

🤸 SPORT AND LEISURE

For cycle tourism and horseback riding in the Maremma, see:

🚴 *www.maremmainbici.it*
🐎 *www.viaequestregrossetana.it*

🚃 TAKING A BREAK

Bar Bagianni – *Piazza Garibaldi 8, 58015 Orbetello.* 📞*0564 86 81 34. Open Mon–Sat 7am–1am, Sun 7am–1pm and 3pm –1am.* This place is a bar, an ice cream parlour, a cyber café and a tea room. Its terrace overlooking the main square is a lively meeting place.

Baretto – *Lungomare Andrea Doria 41, 58018 Porto Ercole.* 📞*0564 83 26 54. Open Jul–Aug 8am–3pm; closed Wed Sept–Jun and for a month in winter.* The Baretto with its terrace occupies the most central location in the port. Its warm welcome and delicious fruit juice cocktails make it the first choice among the youth of Argentario.

Pietrasanta★

Since the 1960s Pietrasanta has attracted painters and sculptors from all over the world because of the marble of Versilia and the Carrara basin, as well as the famed skill of the local craftsmen who work in stone and, perhaps more surprisingly, in bronze. The 100 or more local workshops also produce copies and undertake the restoration of works of art.

▶ **Population:** 24,436
🧭 **Michelin Map:** Michelin Atlas p 32 and Map 563 – K 12 and Map 735 Fold 12.
ℹ **Info:** Piazza Matteotti 29. 📞 0584 79 53 42. www. comune.pietrasanta. lu.it/turismo/.
◐ **Location:** Pietrasanta is located in the hinterland of Versilia, 11km/7mi S of Massa.

A BIT OF HISTORY

Pietrasanta stretches out at the foot of its fortress, the **Rocca di Sala** (13C). Like its neighbour Camaiore, it was built in 1255 as an outpost for Lucca, in an attempt to define and protect a route to the sea. The town also kept watch over the Via Aurelia which, in this region, more or less coincided with the Via Francigena leading to France. Like all free towns founded between the 11C and the 13C Pietrasanta had a mainly military function and its original rec-

Botero, the Adopted Son

Born in Columbia in 1932, the painter and sculptor Fernando Botero combines a knowledge of pre-Columbian art and the South American Baroque with his passion for the Italian Renaissance. This led him to settle in Pietrasanta where he now works. His paintings display vivid, cheerful colours and intricate detail reminiscent of his original culture. Italy has taught him the skill of drawing and the traditional techniques of marble sculpture, bronze casting and oil and fresco painting. A master of round voluptuous forms, he brings grace and lightness to obesity, artificial naïveté to sensuality and humour to solidity. His imagination often conveys a sense of sometimes rather wry satisfaction that is seldom found in contemporary art.

tangular layout, which is still perfectly visible today, had the rigourous grid appearance of a Roman encampment, with four rows of houses separated by three roads intersected in the centre by a large square.

The town walls were built in the early 14C and were connected to the fortress by two crenellated curtain walls, of which a few stretches have survived.

TOWN
Piazza del Duomo

The main historic buildings are located in this large rectangular square. The **cathedral, Duomo di San Martino**, has a white tripartite marble façade. In the centre is a huge rose window surmounted by the coats of arms of the Medici and the Papacy (Pietrasanta came under Florentine rule in the 16C).

To the left of the cathedral are a large brick **bell tower**, the Renaissance **Palazzo Moroni** at the top of a double flight of steps and, in the corner, the church of **Sant'Agostino**. At this end of the square stand a monument to Grand Duke Leopold II and the Marzocco column bearing the Florentine lion, erected in 1513. Inside the Palazzo Moroni is the **Museo Archeologico** (Ground floor of the Palazzo Moroni; ⏰ opening times vary; ℘0584 79 55 00), which provides an insight into life in Upper Versilia from prehistoric times to the period when the area was under the control of Genoa, Lucca, Pisa or Florence, from the Middle Ages to the 18C.

To the right of the cathedral, beyond the 14C **Palazzo Pretorio** and the **clock tower** dating from 1560, the square is closed by the limited remains of the **Rocchetta Arighina** (also Porta Pisa) decorated with small overhanging arches.

Frescoes in the Church of San Biagio e Sant'Antonioa (also della Misericordia)
Via Mazzini. South of the Piazza del Duomo

Two frescoes (opposite sides of the nave) by Fernando Botero depict the **Gateway to Paradise** and the **Gateway to Hell**. The influence of the Renaissance masters is apparent in the choice of technique, subject matter and composition, such as the cherubs, landscape or the moulding on the frame, but the whole work is enhanced by the imagination of an artist confronted with the modern world and his country's history. This has led him to include numerous details such as Mother Teresa, Hitler, the Italian flag and a conquistador. Perhaps by way of a signature, a modest self-portrait can be seen at the bottom of Hell, where he can be recognised by his goatee beard.

Piazza Matteotti
North entrance of the town.

Opposite the town hall (*Municipio*) stands Botero's bronze statue of a naked, armed **Warrior**★ in the Classical style but displaying the roundness that is characteristic of the artist.

Etruscan **Riviera**

Region

The Etruscan Riviera, the strip of land along the coast between Livorno and Piombino, is rich in natural features, archaeological remains and literary associations. On its southern border lie the parks of the Val di Cornia – Parchi costieri della Sterpaia e di Rimigliano, Parco Archeologico di Baratti e Populonia, Parco Archeominerario di San Silvestro, Parco Naturale di Montioni and Parco Forestale di Poggio Neri.

- ☺ **Michelin Map:** Michelin Atlas p 36 and 42 and Map 563 – I/M 13 or Map 735 Fold 14.
- ▣ **Info:** Piazza Cavour 6, Livorno. ✆0586 20 46 11. www.costadeglietruschi.it.
- ◖ **Location:** The towns of the Riviera degli Etruschi are accessible via the SS1 motorway (Via Aurelia).

🚗 DRIVING TOUR

◖ *Begin in Castiglioncello, 21km/13mi S of Livorno. Take the motorway to Piombino; go inland to Castagneto Carducci, Bolgheri, Campiglia Marittima.*

Castiglioncello ♨

This is an elegant seaside resort on the Etruscan Riviera, well known for its delightful beaches sheltering in creeks in the shade of pine woods. The resort has an excellent climate owing to its ideal situation, protected by a headland and by hills descending to the water's edge.

Rosignano Marittimo

The remains of the medieval centre are in the upper part of the village. The **Museo Archeologico** (Archaeological Museum; ◷ open Mon–Sat 9am–1pm (also 5pm–10pm summer); ◷ closed 1 Jan, 1 May; ⊜€2.50; ♿; ✆0586 79 92 32; www.comune.rosignano.livorno.it) in the castle provides an insight into local history from the Etruscan period to the Middle Ages. *Via del Castello 24.*

Cecina

Cecina is a farming and industrial town which was founded in the mid-19C following local land improvement. It is set at the heart of Etruscan Riviera, which extends to the coast as **Marina di Cecina**, a seaside resort sheltered by a wonderful pine wood that contains numerous Etruscan remains still being studied by archaeologists.

The **Museo Archeologico** (Archaeological Museum) contains Etruscan buccheroware, Greek vases decorated with painted figures dating from the Classical and Hellenistic periods, urns dating from the 6C BC and funeral items from the days of imperial Rome. *Villa Guerazzi.* ◷Open Tue–Sun 6pm–10pm. ⊜€4. ✆0586 26 08 37. www.comune.cecina.li.it/museo. archeologico.

Marina di Castagneto-Donoratico

This is a seaside resort with a long sandy beach sheltered by attractive pine woods.

Castagneto Carducci

The town, attractively situated on a hilltop in a landscape of olive trees, used to belong to the Counts della Gherardesca. All that remains of their castle are the ruins of one tower (*torre di Donoratico, 3.5km/2mi S*) where the infamous Ugolino della Gherardesca, having been accused of treachery by Pisa after the Battle of Meloria (1284), is said to have found temporary refuge before suffering the terrible punishment of starving to death with his children in 1289.

Castagneto had belonged to Pisa since the 12C but it came under Florentine jurisdiction in 1406. The village, however, has a claim to fame that is rather more literary than historic. It is named after the Italian poet **Giosuè Carducci** (born in 1835 in Valdicastello; died in 1907 in Bologna), who stayed in the vil-

Long avenue lined with large cypress trees leading to Bolgheri

Carp71 / iStockphoto

lage during his youth and wrote poetry in honour of the beautiful Tuscan countryside. His life and work is recalled in the **Museo Archivio** (○*open Mon–Fri 10am–1pm, Sat–Sun 3pm–6pm;* ℘*0565 76 50 32*) in the Palazzo Municipale (town hall). *Via G. Carducci 1.*

Bolgheri

This is the village in which Carducci lived from 1838 to 1848. The long avenue lined with large cypress trees leading to the village from San Guido (*west*) was described by the poet in his elegiac work, *In Front of San Guido*, a work well known to Italians.

Campiglia Marittima

Campiglia developed on a hilltop (210m/ 682ft above sea level) in what was once the Pisan section of the Maremma district. The village consists of a strange collection of stone-built houses surrounded by walls that were once impregnable. The village must be very old as a document dating from 1004 states that Count Gherardo II della Gherardesca granted ownership of the town to a monastery near Chiusdino. From 1259 onwards the community was governed by a captain from Pisa, and this form of local government continued even after 1406, when Pisa was conquered by Florence. In the 16C it declined in military power and from then on it was ruled by influential families.

▷ *From Piazza della Repubblica, the street climbs to Palazzo Pretorio.*

Palazzo Pretorio

The building is decorated with the coats of arms of the captains who lived here until 1406. The column to the left was used as the base of the cage in which wrongdoers were exposed to public ridicule.

▷ *Follow Via Cavour to Porta Fiorentina (Florentine Gate).*

Rocca

Overlooking the Florentine Gate, which bears coats of arms from the four rulers of Campiglia, are the remains of the **fortress**, built in the 12C–13C, probably on the site of an earlier 8C fortress.

▷ *Via Roma leads to Porta a Mare and Piazza della Vittoria, from which there is an extensive view of the coast.*

Pieve di San Giovanni

In the cemetery. This parish **church** was built in the 12C in the shape of the Greek letter *tau* (T) and has two particularly interesting features. Beneath the side portal is a low relief depicting *The Boar Hunt in Meleagre*.
Beneath the roof of the side chapel is an inscription of the mysterious **magic square** which dates from the beginning of the Christian era, if not from earlier

"An Avenue of Cypress Trees Standing Tall and Slim from San Guido to Bolgheri"

Walking down the long avenue or touring in the gentle Maremma countryside may bring to mind these words by Giosuè Carducci (1835–1907) that celebrate his boyhood spent in Tuscany and reflect an intimate link between man and nature, a yearning for the values of liberty, justice, patriotism and brotherly love. They are reinforced by a fervent adherence to the classical ideals expressed to perfection by Rome, a city which the poet held to represent a superior civilization. The classical myths conferred a certain nobility on the austere verses of Carducci, who wished to avoid romantic effusions. His true inspiration is perhaps revealed in his nostalgic love for the luminous quality of a way of life which is destined to be extinguished at death. His awareness of the transience of existence, which he acknowledged boldly, made his aspiration to supreme ideals more poignant and sounded a sad note in his verse.

times. The five words are set out in a square of five lines which read the same both backwards and forwards and up and down –

```
S A T O R
A R E P O
T E N E T
O P E R A
R O T A S
```

Although its meaning remains obscure, it seems to have been used as a magic spell to ward off evil spirits.

Parco Archeologico di San Silvestro

🕐Open Jun–Sept Tue–Sun 9am–8pm (also Jul–Aug Mon); rest of the year Mon–Fri by appointment, Sat–Sun and Hols 10am–dusk. 🕐Closed 24–25 and 31 Dec,

Wine Road

The Etruscan Riviera has been an agricultural district since the 15C; the two main local wines are the Cabernet Sassicaia and the Ornellaia.

The Wine Road begins in Rosignano Marittimo and finishes in Piombino. It is a good route (160km/99mi) for cycling and we would recommend the stages between Bibbona, Bolgheri and Castagneto Carducci.

🔹 **Consorzio Strada del Vino** – Costa degli Etruschi, Loc. San Guido, 45 Bolgheri, Castagneto Carducci. ✆0565 74 97 05. www.lastradadelvino.com.

1 Jan. 🚭€10, €6.20 (partial tour). ✆0565 83 86 80. www.parchivaldicornia.it.
In the hills north of Campiglia Marittima is an archaeological mining site (450ha/ 1 112 acres) laid out with waymarked routes illustrating mining techniques in the Etruscan period. **Rocca San Silvestro**, which dates from the 10C, is a village devoted to the extraction of minerals (copper, lead and silver) and to the making of alloys. (♿museum only).

Populonia★

🕐Castello open Jun–Aug Tue–Sun 9am–8pm (also Mon in summer); rest of the year Mon–Sat 9am (10am Sat) to dusk. 🕐Closed 24–25 and 31 Dec, 1 Jan. Guided tour by appointment. ✆0565 29 002. 🚭€10, €6.20 (partial tour). www.parchivaldicornia.it.
The **necropolis** of the Etruscan town of *Pupluna* stands below the acropolis overlooking the sea. It dates from the Iron Age (9C–8C BC), when Baratti Bay was the site of all the great burial grounds. Economic activity was probably based on the mineral mines on the Isle of Elba and in the hills around Campiglia (northeast).
From the 4C BC, when people began to mine iron on the island, the burial grounds were gradually covered with scoria and waste from the kilns. They remained concealed until the beginning of the 20C.
Different types of graves were excavated – pits, ditches and chambers (being the oldest) and oriental-style barrows.

Etruscan necropolis of Populonia

B. Morandi / MICHELIN

Among the tumuli with cylindrical bases are the **Tomb with Funeral Beds** (*letti funebri*) and the **Tomb with the Pear-Shaped Urn** (*a small Grecian urn*). The **Funnel Tomb** (*dei colatoi*) has a tall barrow; the **Fan Tomb** (*dei flabelli*) and **Goldware Tomb** (*delle oreficerie*) are the only tumuli to have remained intact; the **Small Bronze Offering Tomb** is a tomb with aedicule and was named after the bronze fans found among other funeral items.

The **Museo Gasparri** (☀️ *open Tue–Sun 9am–6.30pm;* 🕐 *closed 24–25 and 31 Dec, 1 Jan;* ℘ *0565 29436*), in the village of Populonia, displays funeral urns, fibulae, wine jars and other Etruscan objects found in the locality.

Piombino

Population: 34,449. Michelin Map: Michelin Atlas p 42 and Map 563 – n 13 or Map 735 Fold 24. 🚩 *Via Ferruccio 4;* ℘ *0565 63 111. www.turismopiombino.it.*

Piombino lies midway down the coast of ancient Etruria and was built on a promontory which has been the site of three successive harbours since Antiquity – the Etruscan port of Baratti, the port of Marina (12C–early 20C) and the old Falesia harbour, now known as Portovecchio. Little is known of Piombino's historical and artistic aspects. The town is best known as Italy's leading passenger ferry port and is the port of embarkation for the Tuscan Archipelago (🕐 *see*

TUSCAN ARCHIPELAGO for information on ferries).

Piazza Verdi is the starting point for walks through the town centre. The buildings in the square include the Rivellino (1447), Piombino's old main gate, and the Torrione, a massive tower built in 1212.

South of the square on Corso Vittorio Emmanuele, is the **Palazzo Comunale**. This town hall was built in 1444 and comprehensively restored in 1935. The 13C **Casa delle Bifore** (nearby in Via Ferruccio) contains the municipal archives. At the far southern end of Corso Vittorio Emmanuele is Piazza Bovio, a square shaped like a ship's prow, with a fine **view**★ of the Tuscan Archipelago. From Piazza Bovio turn right towards the tiny port of Marina to see the **Fonti dei Canali**. These 13C public marble **fountains** are attributed to Nicola Pisano and have provided the local water supply for almost seven centuries.

Head west from Piazza Verdi on Via Leonardo da Vinci to see the bastions of the town walls. At the end of the road is the citadel, built between 1465 and 1470 on the orders of Jacopo III Appiani. It is remarkable for its marble **reservoir**.

Head southeast from Piazza Verdi (*Piazza del Castello*) for the 13C–16C castle (*cassero*) and the fortress (*fortezza*), just off Via Giordano Bruno, built in 1552 on the orders of Cosimo I.

ADDRESSES

🛏 STAY

🍴 **Podere la Cerreta** – *Località Pian delle Vigne, 57020 Sassetta, 8km/5mi S of Castagneto Carducci on S325 towards Sassetta.* ✆*0565 79 43 52. www.lacerreta.it.* 🏊♿. *11 rooms.* ⊠. *Restaurant* 🍴. Only a few miles from the sea, in the heart of the Maremma, this farm offers traditionally furnished rooms in converted farm buildings, food produced on the farm – honey, yoghurt, oil and meat – and an authentic experience of the country.

🍴🍴 **Albergo Miramare** – *Via Marconi 8, 57012 Castiglioncello.* ✆*0586 75 24 35. www.albergo-miramare.it. Closed Oct–Easter.* 🅿. *47 rooms.* ⊠. Historic names such as Churchill, Pirandelli and some of the Macchiaioli are on the visitors' list of this coral coloured mansion. The beautiful grounds looking out over the bay extend to the promenade and the beach. The rooms are pleasant and some have a sea view. Half or full board according to choice.

🍴🍴 **Hotel Massimo** – *Via Zaccaria 3, 57023 Cecina Mare.* ✆*0586 62 02 16. www.hotelmassimo.it.* ♿. *34 rooms.* ⊠. *Restaurant* 🍴🍴. Only 150yds from the beach and a short walk from the pine grove, this hotel is the ideal place for a peaceful seaside holiday. The rooms are funished in a modern style; some have a balcony. There is also a large garden for relaxation.

🍴🍴🍴 **Casa Vacanze Il Chiostro** – *Piazza della Cisterna, 57028 Suvereto, 12km/8mi NE of Campiglia Marittima by S398.* ✆*0565 82 87 11. www.vacanzeilchiostro.it. 17 suites.* ⊠. Located in the old town, this property has spacious rooms and small apartments with kitchenettes decorated in rustic style. The rooms are light with a fine view of the town and the valley.

🍴 EAT

🍴 **La Gramola** – *Via Marconi 18, 57022 Castagneto Carducci.* ✆*0565 76 36 46. Closed Nov–Mar except at Christmas and 1 Jan.* This restaurant enjoys a splendid position with a breathtaking view of the valley running down to the sea. Inside

or outside on the terrace you can eat pizzas, sandwiches made of delicious slightly salty bread (*schiacciatine*), salads and traditional regional dishes (wild boar, hare, mussels and clams).

🍴 **Tarabaralla** – *Via Curtatone 19, 57023 Cecina.* ✆*0586 68 42 38. Closed Mon evening. Reservations suggested.* Here you can enjoy innovative, but traditional cooking while you dine by candle light in the garden or in small rooms.

🍴 **Osteria del Contadino** – *Via Don Sturzo 69, 57010 Guasticce.* ✆*0586 98 46 97. Closed Sun, Sat at noon, 15–31 Aug, 1 week at Christmas. Reservations suggested.* From the starter to the dessert, the dishes here are prepared with first-class ingredients and are served with flair. The pleasant and relaxing atmosphere is particularly evident in the "cantina" room.

🍴 **Il Canovaccio** – *Via Vecchio Asilo 1, 57021 Campiglia Marittima.* ✆*0565 83 84 49. Closed Tue except in summer, Nov and Jan. Reservations suggested.* This restaurant serves light dishes made of only vegetables or seafood. Meals can be enjoyed in the small dining room or on the veranda looking out over the square.

🍴🍴🍴 **Ristò la Gattabuia** – *V. A. Gramsci 32, 57016 Rosignano Marittimo.* ✆*0586 79 97 60. www.gattabuia.it. Closed Tue, Jan. Reservations suggested.* Traditional dishes prepared with original touches are served in the elegant dining room and, in summer, in a well-maintained garden.

🍽 TAKING A BREAK

PIOMBINO

La Vera – *Piazza Giovanni Bovio. Open Apr–Oct daily 9am–2am (8.30pm rest of the year).* This is an unpretentious place for a drink on the tourist route, overlooking the sea and offering one of the best views in Piombino.

La Pergola – *Località Baratti 23.* ✆*565 29 596. Open daily 9am–11pm. Closed Nov–Mar.* This small bar has a delightful terrace overlooking Baratti Marina. While it is short distance from Piombino centre, it is quiet and restful.

Versilia★

Versilia is a district with a mild climate lying between the sea coast and the mountains, which form a natural barrier against the north wind. Along the coast lies a string of superb resorts boasting fine sandy beaches (up to 100m/108yd wide) that slope gently into the sea and are ideal for families with young children. The gently rolling hills give way to a lush coastal plain that was formed in the Quaternary Era by the alluvium deposited by the streams tumbling down from the mountain peaks. In the distance is the Apuan Alps National Park, including Camaiore, Pietrasante, Seravezza and Stazzema.

- **Michelin Map:** Michelin Atlas p 32, 36 and Map 563 – j 12-K 12/13 or Map 735 Fold 14.
- **Info:** Viale Carducci 10, Viareggio. ✆0584 96 22 33.www.aptversilia.it.
- **Location:** Versilia is easily accessible from the Genoa-Livorno motorway or from the motorway from Florence to the sea.

⊳ DRIVING TOURS

1 THE RIVIERA
28km/17.5mi

Viareggio♨♨♨
This is the main seaside resort in Versilia and one of the most popular in the whole of Italy. The small fishing and shipbuilding village was transformed in the early 19C into a seaside resort by Marie-Louise de Bourbon, who made sea-bathing fashionable. The unemployed shipwrights turned their hand to building and gradually **Viale Regina Margherita** was lined with a series of single-storey wooden pavilions comprising cafés, bathing houses or shops. In October 1917, however, a terrible fire ravaged the famous seaside promenade. The sole survivor of this era is the **Chalet Martini**.
As the rebuilding of Viale Regina Margherita and its prolongation, Viale Guglielmo Marconi, was accomplished in a short time, the two streets provide fine examples of the architectural style of the late 1920s, somewhere between art nouveau and art deco, such as the splendid **Gran Caffè Margherita**, with high coloured Baroque cupolas.
The resort has a long broad beach of fine sand; certain sections are reserved

for the residents of the seafront hotels. There is also a fairly busy fishing harbour. The carnival in Viareggio is internationally famous for the procession of allegorical papier mâché floats, traditionally caricatures of Italian and international political figures.

▷ *North of Viareggio the coastline consists of an almost unbroken line of seaside resorts facing the Gulf of Genoa.*

Lido di Camaiore♨♨
Lido di Camaiore is more modern and more of a family resort than Viareggio, its prestigious neighbour, but they are so close that they tend to run into one another. It has the same fine sandy beach, the same pine woods and a delightful esplanade along the front.

Marina di Pietrasanta♨♨
Like Lido di Camaiore, this part of the shoreline, which includes the towns of

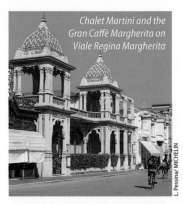
Chalet Martini and the Gran Caffè Margherita on Viale Regina Margherita

L. Pessina/ MICHELIN

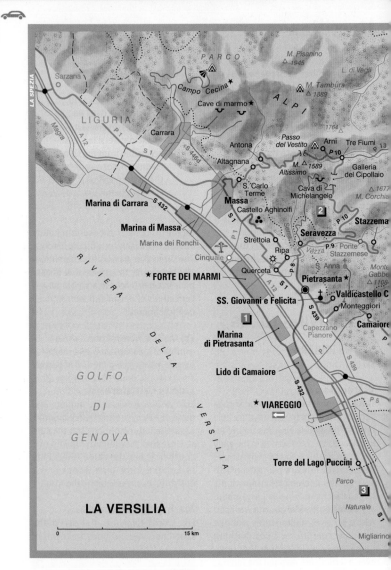

LA VERSILIA

0	15 km

Focette, Motrone, Tonfano and **Fiumetto**, is named after the village situated inland at the foot of the mountains. The seaside resort has a long beach (over 5km/3mi), delightful paths through the pine woods, ideal for walking or cycling, and a wide range of sports amenities. There is also excellent nightlife.

On the outskirts of Marina di Pietrasanta, on the other bank of the Fiumetto, set slightly back from the beach, is **Versiliana Park** (about 80ha/198acres of woodland). The park is traversed by pleasant paths and in summer it plays host to various cultural events.

Forte dei Marmi🏠🏠🏠

This particularly elegant resort is popular with artists and the Italian jet set. The beach has regular rows of delightful little cabins painted different colours.

▶ *To the north the mountains of Liguria turn west towards the coast and plunge into the sea, marking the end of the gentle Versilian coastline.*

Marina di Massa and Marina di Carrara

A somewhat deserted stretch of coast precedes these two resorts, which have a number of fine late 19C/early 20C buildings. Between them is the harbour from which marble is exported with huge marble warehouses on the quayside.

② THE APUAN ALPS

Tour of 84km/52mi – 3hr.

This route through Upper Versilia skirts **Monte Altissimo** in the heart of the Apuan Alps. It has been known for its excellent marble since the days of the Etruscans and Romans. Quarrying was abandoned in the Middle Ages but began again in the Renaissance with the encouragement of Pope Leo X, who entrusted the enterprise to Michelangelo.

Michelangelo worked here from 1515 to 1518 and one of the quarries still bears his name. He selected the routes leading to the quarries from Seravezza and those for transporting the quarried marble down into the valley.

Pietrasanta★
(*see PIETRASANTA*)

▷ *Take the main road (S1) northwest towards Massa. In Querceta turn inland. In Ripa turn left to Strettoia.*

Further on is a mountain pass on which stand the ruins of the **Castello Aghinolfi**, a castle said to have been commissioned by the Lombard king, Agilulfe, c. 600.

Beach Huts, Forte Dei Marmi

N. Bosqués / MICHELIN

353

The Versilian Pievi

The Versilia district used to belong to Lombardy until it was annexed in the Middle Ages by Lucca which was seeking an outlet to the sea to facilitate its exports. The Romanesque churches (*pievi*), built in the 12C–13C, were therefore subject to Luccan influence as regards their structure and carved ornamentation. Their main features are their harmonious austerity, their smooth façades defined within a square, and their interiors with rafters.

From the road, there is a fine view of the coast.

▷ *Beyond Capanne the road rejoins Via Aurelia (S1) to Massa.*

Massa

(& see CARRARA)

▷ *From Massa take SP4 east inland towards S Carlo.*

The road passes through **San Carlo Terme, Altagnana** where there is a particularly superb view of the Apuan Alps, and **Antona**. Beyond the mountain pass (**Passo del Vestito**) the road runs close by Arni.

▷ *At the junction (left to Castelnuovo di Garfagnana) bear right into SP10 to Seravezza and Pietrasanta.*

In **Tre Fiumi** there is a succession of marble quarries. South of the **Galleria dei Cipollaio** (tunnel – about 1km/0.5mi long) the road is flanked (*right*) by **Monte Altissimo** (*alt 1 589m/5 213ft*), the mountain that contains Michelangelo's famous quarry.

▷ *At the junction by the River Vezza turn left; after 2km/1mi, in the main square in Ponte Stazzemese, turn right onto a narrow and winding road to Stazzema (5km/3mi).*

Stazzema

The summit of Monte Procinto casts its shade over the winding streets and flower-decked balconies of this village (*alt 440m/1,444ft*), a popular holiday resort. Near the entrance to Stazzema stands the Romanesque church (*left*) of **Santa Maria Assunta**, which has a wonderful 14C ceiling.

▷ *Return downhill. In Ponte Stazzemese bear left and continue west down the Vezza Valley to Seravezza.*

Seravezza

This village grew up at the confluence of the Serra and Vezza Rivers, hence its name. Since the early 16C its history has been closely linked to the quarrying of marble. When the Medici revived interest in this activity, Grand Duke Cosimo I commissioned a mansion, **Palazzo Mediceo**★ (1561–65).

In the centre of the splendid inner courtyard is a delightful well carved out of a single block of marble to represent a trout; it is said to be a copy of the fish caught by Marie-Christine of Lorraine in the River Vezza in 1603.

In the centre of Seravezza stands the **Cathedral Church of Santi Lorenzo and Barnaba**. Construction began in 1422 and the cathedral was consecrated in 1569. It was badly damaged by bombs during the Second World War but has retained the early 16C marble font carved by Stagio Stagi, a local artist.

▷ *South of Seravezza the road runs along the north bank of the River Vezza; turn left over the river into S439 to return to Pietrasanta.*

③ FROM THE APUAN ALPS TO THE MIGLIARINO-SAN ROSSORE-MASSACIUCCOLI PARK

Tour of 38km/24mi

Pietrasanta★

(& see PIETRASANTA)

▷ *Take S439 south towards Lucca; on the outskirts of Pietrasanta turn left.*

Pieve dei Santi Giovanni e Felicità

Left. Among the olive trees stands the oldest church (9C) in the Versilia region.

▷ *Continue up the valley to Valdicastello Carducci.*

Valdicastello Carducci

It was here that the poet Giosuè Carducci was born. His **birthplace** (*casa natale*) houses a small museum with exhibits relating to his life. ○*Open Jun–Sept Tue–Sun 5pm–8pm; rest of the year Tue 9am–noon, Sat, Sun 3pm–6pm. ℘0584 79 55 00. www.comune.pietra santa.lu.it.*

▷ *Return to S439. After 3.5km/2mi turn left (shortly before Capezzano Pianore) towards S Lucia and Monteggiori.*

The road climbs through olive groves and cypress trees to **Monteggiori**, a medieval village clinging to the mountainside.

▷ *Continue by car to Camaiore towards S Anna di Stazzema (left at the first road junction) and Camaiore (right at the second junction).*

Camaiore

This Roman village (Campus Major) is now a major farming and commercial centre at the foot of Monte Prana (alt 1 220m/3 965ft). It has few reminders of its medieval past: one such is the **Romanesque church of Santa Maria Assunta** (1278) flanked by a solid 14C campanile in Piazza S Bernardino da Siena.

Beyond the 14C gate (*Follow signs to Badia and Cimitero; 1km/0.5mi from the centre*) stands the church of an 8C Benedictine abbey (*badia*).

▷ *From Camaiore take the road east towards Lucca. At the T-junction by a river, turn right to Massarosa. Continue for 5km/3mi.*

In a bend (*right*) stands the 11C Church of San Pantaleone di **Pieve a Elici**. Immediately beyond Pieve a Elici there is a view of the former Massaciuccoli Marshes.

▷ *In Massarosa take S439 south to Quiesa. Turn right to Massaciuccoli.*

Massaciuccoli★

This village, which gave its name to the neighbouring lake, has retained some links with the Roman era. At the entrance to the village is the **Antiquarium** which displays the various ceramics found on the site. ○*Open Mar–Oct Tue–Sun 9am–noon and 3pm–7pm; rest of the year 9am–noon and 4pm–6pm. ○Closed 1 Jan, Easter, 25 Dec. ℘0584 97 92 82.*

The impressive ruins of the **Roman baths★** are set on a hilltop amid the olive trees (*left of the road; access on foot only along a path signposted Zona Archeologica*). From in front of the church of San Lorenzo (*first on the left after the villa*) there is a fine **view★** downhill over the baths and the lake to the sea.

▷ *Continue south and west; turn right into Via Aurelia (S1) N towards Viareggio; left to Torre del Lago.*

This road crosses part of the **Migliarino-San Rossore-Massaciuccoli Country Park** including the lake, the Massaciuccoli Marshes and the remains of the ancient Pisan Forest.

Torre del Lago Puccini

It was here that **Puccini** (1858–1924), who was born in Lucca, composed most of his works: *La Bohème, Tosca, Madame Butterfly*. On the shores of the pleasant **Massaciuccoli Lake** stands his house, **Villa Puccini** (○*open Tue–Sun 10am–12.30pm and 3pm–6.30pm (5.30pm winter);* ○*closed Nov, 25 Dec;* ✆€7; *℘0584 34 14 45; www.giacomopuccini.it*), containing memorabilia relating to the composer, who is also buried here.

▷ *Return to Pietrasanta via Viareggio and Lido di Camaiore (tour B).*

ADDRESSES

🛏 STAY

Hotel Grande Italia – *Via Torino 5, a Tonfano, 55044 Marina di Pietrasanta.* *℘0584 20 046. Fax 0584 24 350. Closed 20 Sept–May.* 🚭 🅿. *23 rooms.* 🚱. *Restaurant* 🍽. This hotel will please all those who like early 20C architecture. The simple family atmosphere and the neighbouring pine trees contribute to the pleasure of staying here.

Hotel Sylvia – *Via Manfredi 15, 55043 Lido di Camaiore.* *℘0584 61 79 94. www.hotelsylvia.it. Closed mid-Oct–Apr.* 🅿. *21 rooms.* 🚱. In a quiet location, not far from the sea, surrounded by a lovely garden, this family-run hotel has large light rooms and home cooking. Guests may use the library on the ground floor.

Hotel Arcangelo – *Via Carrara 23, 55049 Viareggio.* *℘0584 47 123. www. hotelarcangelo.com. Closed Oct–Easter. 19 rooms.* 🚱. *Restaurant* 🍽. Although it is in one of the side rooms leading off the promenade, this converted house standing in its own garden is quiet and relaxing. The public rooms are well maintained and the bedrooms are simply furnished in the 1950s style.

Hotel La Pergola – *Via Verdi 41, Località Poveromo, 54039 Ronchi, S of Marina di Massa.* *℘0585 24 01 18. Fax 0585 24 57 20. Closed mid-Sept–Easter.* 🅿. *25 rooms.* 🚱. *Restaurant* 🍽. This is a simple and pleasant hotel only a short walk from the sea, with a large garden (equipped with children's games).

Albergo Dei Cantieri – *Via Indipendenza 72, 55049 Viareggio.* *℘0584 38 81 12. Fax 0584 38 85 61. Closed 20–30 Nov.* 🚭. *7 rooms.* 🚱. South of the town on the edge of a pine wood are two well-converted outbuildings of the manor house. In fine weather you can breakfast in the gazebo in the garden.

Hotel Miramare – *Via Donati 34/36, 55042 Forte dei Marmi.* *℘0584 78 72 32. www.miramarehotel.org. Closed Nov–Feb.* 🅿🚲. *18 rooms.* 🚱. This hotel is located in a residential district, a few miles from the famous Forte dei Marmi. The atmosphere is restful and welcoming and the prices are reasonable. Some of the rooms have a small terrace.

Hotel Pardini – *Viale Carducci 14, 55049 Viareggio.* &. *℘0584 96 13 79. www.hotelpardini.com. Closed 20 days in Nov. 14 rooms.* 🚱. This family-run hotel on the promenade at Viareggio is close to the beaches, restaurants and shops. A good place for a quiet stay in spacious, modern, simply furnished rooms; attentive and considerate service.

🍽 EAT

Rino – *Via della Chiesa 8, 55040 Bargecchia, 4km/2.5mi S of Camaiore.* *℘0584 95 40 00. Closed Tue (Oct–May).* In the middle of the village is a traditional restaurant known as much for its furnishings as for its culinary choice – fresh pasta and grilled meat. In summer meals are served in the beautiful garden.

Mokambo – *Viale della Repubblica 4, 55042 Forte dei Marmi.* *℘0584 89 446. Closed Wed.* After a day at the seaside, it would be pleasant to stop by this spacious restaurant, which is as popular with young people as with families. The menu includes pizzas or the traditional option, *pane arabo*, sandwiches or a complete meal based on fresh fish.

Osteria alla Giudea – *Via Barsanti 4, 55045 Pietrasanta.* *℘0584 71 514. Closed Mon. Reservations suggested.* From the eating room you can see the owners in the kitchen, preparing the daily dishes. The wrought–iron marble-topped tables are reminiscent of a French bistro but the food is in the pure Tuscan tradition.

Lombardi – *Via Aurelia 127, 55048 Torre Del Lago Puccini.* *℘0584 34 10 44. Closed Tue.* This place is over 100 years old and looks as though it is a coaching inn for riders and their horses. Within is an elegant restaurant in the classic style. The menu reflects the seaside location; game is served in winter but has to be ordered in advance.

Il Puntodivino – *Via Mazzini 229, 55049 Viareggio.* *℘0584 31 046. Closed Mon, Tue noon (Jul–Aug), 25 Dec–25 Jan.* Here is a trendy and appropriate place for a quick meal. In the evening the choice is greater with interesting gastronomic menus. Good wine list.

Da Cecco – *Belvedere Puccini, 55048 Torre Del Lago Puccini. ☎0584 34 10 22. Closed Sun evening, Mon and 20 Nov–15 Dec.* This family-run restaurant, situated at the beginning of the lakeside promenade, next to the Puccini's house, serves seafood and local produce, with game in winter. Among the house specialities are eel and frogs' legs.

Il Centro Storico – *Via Cesare Battisti 66, 55041 Camaiore. ☎0584 98 97 86. Closed Mon.* A simple trattoria owned by a family who offers typical local dishes and specialities based on truffles and mushrooms "cooked in all the sauces."

Trattoria al Porto – *Via Coppino 319, 55049 Viareggio. ☎0584 38 38 78. Closed Sun, Mon at noon, 15 Dec–15 Jan. Reservations suggested.* It is best to make a reservation a few days in advance if you wish to eat in this always crowded restaurant. The waiter will announce the classic seafood specialities, which are made with very fresh ingredients.

🚅 TAKING A BREAK

Pasticceria Bar Fappani – *Viale Marconi, Lungomare, 55049 Viareggio. ☎0584 96 25 82. Open Tue–Sun 8am–midnight.* The large terrace facing the sea is a good place for eating sticky cakes. This patisserie has been offering a warm welcome and a relaxing atmosphere since it started in 1921.

🎭 ENTERTAINMENT

Discotheques in Versilia – *Seaside promenade between Lido di Camaiore and Forte dei Marmi – 55042 Forte dei Marmi.* Every evening the seafront is transformed into a dance floor. From Viareggio to Forte dei Marmi there is a chain of discotheques, each one different. The oldest, founded in 1970, is **La Bussola**, which has given Versilia is reputation for a lively nightlife. The 25 to 30 year olds prefer **Seven Apples**, with its pool, or **La Capannina**, which has orchestral evenings. **Faruk**, **Agorà**

and **Midho** (which has a special room, the **Kupido**, for techno music) are favourites with the younger age group. On the edge of Forte dei Marmi, is **La Canniccia**, favoured by the over 30s, with 4 dance floors and a large garden.

Agorà – *Viale Cristoforo Colombo 666, 55043 Lido di Camaiore. ☎0584 61 04 88. Open Wed, Thu and Sat 9pm–4am.*

Faruk – *Viale Roma 53/55, Tonfano, 55044 Marina di Pietrasanta. ☎0584 21 57 8/ 05 84 21 744. Open Thu–Sat midnight–4am.*

La Bussola – *Viale Roma 44, Focette, 55044 Marina di Pietrasanta. ☎0584 22 737. Open Thu–Sun 10pm–4am.*

La Canniccia – *Via Unità d'Italia 1, Uscita A 12 Versilia, 55044 Marina di Pietrasanta. ☎0584 23 225/ 0584 74 56 85. Open Fri–Sun 11pm–4.30am.*

La Capannina – *Viale della Repubblica 18, 55042 Forte dei Marmi. ☎0584 80 169. Open Fri–Sat 5.30pm–5am.*

Midho' e Kupido – *Viale Achille Franceschi 12, 55042 Forte dei Marmi. ☎0584 89 114. Open Fri–Sat and Tue 11.30pm–4am.*

Seven Apples – *Viale Roma 109, Focette, 55044 Marina di Pietrasanta. ☎584 20 458/ 0584 22 433. Open Fri–Sun 8.30pm–4am.*

SHOPPING

Laboratorio di Cartapesta – *Via Morandi, 55049 Viareggio. Guided tours. Information Piazza Mazzini.* This workshop produces huge masks made of papier mâché for the Viareggio Festival; here you can see the craftsmen at work and buy an interesting souvenir.

Zona Darsena – *Via Coppino, 55049 Viareggio.* La Darsena, where the largest boatyards for yachts are concentrated, is the place for anything to do with sailing – clothes, sails and fittings. If you are looking for something decorative or for a present, come and browse and admire the superb yachts moored in the marina.

PISA★★★

Pisa's iconic buildings are a lasting reminder of its long and illustrious history. The city is more spacious than Florence and less austere – thanks to its yellow, pink or yellow-ochre house fronts – but it shares the same river, the Arno, which bisects the city here in a majestic meander. Pisa has the atmosphere of a minor capital that has lost some of its hustle and bustle, but the city's charm is in its aristocratic air and genteel Mediterranean lifestyle. Pisa is almost totally encircled by walls and is traversed from north to south by a main street lined with shops. On the south bank the thoroughfare is called Corso Italia. On the north bank, the road narrows and is flanked by arcades, known as Borgo Stretto. The noble, yet cheerful appearance of the winding Via Santa Maria, linking Piazza del Duomo to the Arno, is characteristic of the city. The interesting streets on the north bank flank the busiest district in the city, full of shops and restaurants.

THE CITY TODAY

Modern Pisa has a decidedly youthful atmosphere, thanks to the University of Pisa, one of Italy's largest and best universities. In fact, among students and contemporary art lovers, one of the city's most popular monuments is a giant mural (*near the train station*) by the American pop artist Keith Haring. When school is not in session, Pisa's population is supplemented by millions of tourists, who flock to see the Leaning Tower, perhaps one of the world's most distinctive architectural structures.

A BIT OF HISTORY
Maritime Splendour

When it was founded c. 7C BC, Pisa was on the coast. The shoreline soon receded some distance from the city because of the accumulation of alluvium at the mouth of the Arno.

The city was occupied by the Etruscans and was an ally of Rome for many years. From 180 BC onwards it was colonized by the Romans who took advantage of its geographical location on the banks of the Arno only a few miles from the sea, and turned it into a naval base free from the risk of attack by pirates. Pisa continued to fulfil the role of a naval base until the fall of the Roman Empire in the West in AD 476.

In AD 888 the city became an independent republic but did not begin to take advantage of its geographic location to encourage economic development until the Middle Ages. Like Genoa and Venice, the city was one of the powerful maritime republics that resisted Mus-

Piazza dei Miracoli

G. Bludzin / MICHELIN

lim domination; its "merchant-warriors" fought stubbornly throughout the Mediterranean Basin. Pisa took possession of Sardinia in 1015 and later of Corsica, over which it exercised absolute control in the last quarter of the 11C. In 1114 it captured the Balearic Islands then expanded its conquests into Tunisia and began to set up trading posts in the eastern Mediterranean as far as Syria.

Pisa developed into a very active port in the 11C and reached the peak of its prosperity in the 12C and first half of the 13C. Its ships plied the Mediterranean carrying arms, wool, furs, leather and timber from the Apennines to the Orient, together with iron mined on the Isle of Elba: they returned with spices, silk and cotton. This period was marked by the construction of the finest buildings and the founding of the university, which still has a reputation for excellence.

When a major quarrel, the Investiture Controversy, broke out between the Papacy and the Empire in the late 11C, Pisa, a resolutely Ghibelline city, rallied to the Emperor's camp. At sea it successfully resisted the threat of Genoa, its main maritime rival for commercial supremacy in the Mediterranean. On land it withstood its two Guelf rivals, Lucca and Florence. When Pisa was deprived of the support of Emperor Frederick II (d. 1250) and of King Manfred (his son who was killed in 1266), the city began to fall into decline. In August 1284 at the great **Battle of Meloria** (a small island off Livorno), the Pisan fleet was wiped out by Genoese ships. The city was forced to transfer all its rights in Corsica to Genoa and to give up Sardinia. It was unable to prevent the collapse of its commercial empire in the East as it was cut off from its trading posts by the loss of its fleet. The city was also undermined by internal strife and was eventually taken over by Florence in 1406.

The Medici dynasty was particularly interested in Pisa. Lorenzo the Magnificent reorganized its university and began to build a new one. In the 16C Pisa was incorporated into the Grand Duchy of Tuscany and Cosimo I founded the Order of the **Knights of St Stephen** in the city. During this period the city enjoyed a renewal of its influence, mainly in the sciences.

PISAN ROMANESQUE

An innovative artistic style emerged between the 11C and the 13C, while Pisa was increasing in economic prosperity and political power. It had a marked effect on both the city's architecture and sculpture.

GETTING THERE
BY AIR: Galileo Galilei International Airport (℘050 50 07 07) is linked to the city centre (2km/1.2mi) by the bus (15min, no 3, every 12min). There is a shuttle train between the airport and Florence (Santa Maria Novella Station, every hour).
BY TRAIN: Pisa **Central Railway Station** (**Piazza della Stazione**) is linked to Genoa (Genoa-La Spezia-Pisa line), Rome (Pisa-Livorno–Grosseto–Rome line), Lucca and Florence; change at Empoli for Siena.
BY CAR: Pisa is approached by road from Florence by the express route Florence–Pisa–Livorno and from north or south by the coastal motorway A12 which runs north–south between Pisa and the sea.

GETTING AROUND
TRAFFIC AND PARKING: Driving in Pisa is difficult owing to the pedestrian precincts and the one-way system designed to take traffic away from the city centre. The larger car parks are outside the town walls (**near Piazza dei Miracoli**). There are numerous small car parks or parking spaces in the streets or along the banks of the Arno in the centre near the main sights; wait for the attendant who will issue a ticket and collect payment when you leave.

Architecture

Pisan religious architecture differed in style from other forms present in Italy during the Romanesque period. It reached its heyday in the 13C and spread throughout Tuscany, to towns such as Lucca, Pistoia and Arezzo. It also left its mark on churches in Sardinia and Corsica, both then Pisan possessions.

The style became known as Pisan Romanesque and it brought together a pleasing combination of several influences, most markedly the architecture of Lombardy. To it was added a wealth of decoration inspired by the shapes and motifs of articles brought back from the Orient or the Islamic world by the Pisan fleet. This trend led to buildings of outstanding elegance and unity of which the cathedral in Pisa is the most rigorous and solemn example. The west front, side walls and apse are all skillfully faced with green and white marble, a costly building material that was as popular in Pisa as it was in other Tuscan towns, in particular Florence. Whereas the architects of Florence emphasised the geometric divisions on the façades of churches by framing them in marble, the craftsmen of Pisa made extensive use of relief – tall but shallow blind arcading running all round the building and galleries with colonnettes, a feature that is discreetly present in Lombard architecture but used in Pisa with great exuberance, marking off the upper section of the gable and dappling it with light and shade. Rose windows, diamond shapes and other small motifs picked out in marble marquetry show Oriental inspiration in their use of colour.

In the second half of the 11C and early 12C the architects whose names are inextricably linked with the great buildings of Pisa were **Buscheto**, **Rainaldo** his direct successor who was a contemporary of **Diotisalvi**, and **Bonanno Pisano**, architect and sculptor. **Giovanni di Simone** was the main architect working in the second half of the 13C.

Sculpture

Medieval Pisan sculpture has pride of place in the history of Italian art.

Local artists such as Bonanno Pisano and **Fra' Guglielmo**, or Lombards such as **Guido da Como**, worked on the decoration of the Romanesque churches of Pisa in the 12C and early 13C. It was, however, Nicola Pisano, a sculptor thought to have come from Apulia, who is credited with paving the way for a whole succession of artists in the second half of the 13C. In their eyes Pisa was the birthplace of Italian Romanesque and especially of Gothic sculpture.

These sculptors, who were also architects and interior decorators, were responsible for the creation of huge and unusual pulpits, veritable masterpieces owing to their harmonious structure, their intricate decoration and the aesthetic beauty of their carvings.

Nicola Pisano (born c. 1220, died shortly after 1280) studied classical sculpture. He assimilated its majesty and power but added to it the sense of humanity and the realism seen in the paintings of his contemporary, Giotto. His main works are the pulpit in the Baptistery in Pisa and in the cathedral in Siena. With the assistance of his son, Giovanni, who worked with him in Siena, he also built the Fontana Maggiore in Perugia. One of his pupils was Arnolfo di Cambio, the architect of the cathedral in Florence.

Giovanni Pisano (born c. 1250, died c. 1315–20) was undoubtedly the greatest of all the sculptors. He had a more flexible technique and was more concerned with the expression of dramatic intensity. He worked with his father until the latter's death. His art form developed towards the creation of compositions that were increasingly complex with figures that were more and more tormented, although they were also filled with an outstanding intensity that gave them a wonderful life-like quality. It was his genius that created the splendid pulpit in the Siena cathedral and in Sant'Andrea in Pistoia. He was also the first person to direct work on Siena cathedral, which he wanted to cover with huge statues like the Gothic cathedrals in France that he had visited c. 1270. Giovanni was the last member of the first Pisano dynasty and his death marked the end of the great period of powerful and monumental Gothic sculptures in Tuscany. His most able pupil was Tino di Camaino, from Siena.

Andrea da Pontedera, named after a town near Pisa and also known as **Andrea Pisano**, was born at the end of the 13C and worked mainly in Florence where one of his major works was the first bronze door for the Baptistery. His elegant and refined style (which he developed while training as a goldsmith), and his attractively drawn scenes, were not inspired by his Pisan predecessors. He also sculpted some powerful high reliefs used to decorate the bell tower by Giotto in Florence.

Andrea's son, **Nino Pisano**, who died c. 1365–70, preferred to work in the round. He was a past master in the art of relief and he created graceful Madonnas including a famous *Madonna del Latte* (🏛 *San Matteo National Museum*). This second Pisano dynasty, which also included **Tommaso**, Nino's brother, enjoyed a reputation in the late 14C that made their workshop an obligatory training ground for a number of great Sienese and Florentine sculptors in the early 15C, including Lorenzo Ghiberti and Jacopo della Quercia.

PISAN FESTIVALS

Historical Regatta of the Maritime Republics (May/June)

Since 1956 the Regatta of the Four Maritime Republics (Amalfi, Genoa, Venice and Pisa) has been held in each city in turn. The festivities begin with a costumed pageant: the procession of pages, damsels, captains and men-at-arms, all dressed in period costume, makes its way through the city, together with historical figures whose costumes are designed according to the information available in old documents. Costumes include Kinzica de' Sismondi in pink, the heroine whose courage saved Pisa when besieged by the Saracens; the Duke of Amalfi in a gold costume; Guglielmo Embriaco from Genoa; the Doge of Venice accompanied by Caterina Cornaro. The regatta itself is a boat race in which the old rival republics compete.

The *"Luminara" di San Ranieri*

The "Luminara" di San Ranieri (16 June)

On the banks of the Arno, on the evening before the Feast Day of St Rainier the patron saint of the city, the Lungarno Mediceo and Lungarno Galilei quays are lit with hundreds of tiny lanterns outlining the windows, architectural lines of mansions, parapets along the quays and the architecture of Santa Maria della Spina. The lanterns are reflected in the Arno where other tiny lights float on the water. This festival of light is best seen at sunset when the sky turns red, followed by spectacular fireworks.

Historic Regatta in Honor of San Ranieri (17 June)

In the afternoon a regatta is held on the Arno with historic boats. Four of the city's historic districts (*Rioni*) compete against each other in a race (2km/1mi) against the current; the rowers are dressed in traditional costume.

Il Gioco del Ponte (last Sunday in June)

Based on the game of *mazzascudo* played at least as far back as the 12C, the *Gioco del Ponte* is said to have been played for the first time on 22 February 1569. The Pisans have always been very proud of their game and they would not permit it to be copied in any of the territories they conquered, as shown in a

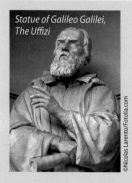

Statue of Galileo Galilei, The Uffizi

©Nicolas Larento/Fotolia.com

Eppur si muove!

Galileo Galilei was born in 1564 into a well-educated family in Pisa. He abandoned his medical studies in favour of physics and astronomy.

He was only 19 when, watching a swinging lamp in the cathedral in his native town, he realised that the oscillations always took the same amount of time whatever their range. From this observation he developed the principle of the pendulum and decided to apply the measurement of its movement to the measurement of time. He used the Leaning Tower of Pisa to study the laws of falling bodies and uniformly accelerated motion. He also built one of the earliest known microscopes.

Galileo invented the telescope that now bears his name and began to study the stars, measuring the height of relief on the moon's surface, discovering Saturn's ring and Jupiter's satellites, and observing sun spots.

He was a strong supporter of Copernicus' theory of the movement of the planets around their own axes and around the sun, in particular the theory of the double rotation of the Earth. This led to problems with traditionalist scholars who had him summoned before the Inquisition in 1633. After a trial lasting 20 days, sentence was passed and he was forced to recant on his knees. According to tradition, as he rose to his feet, he added in desperation a remark that has remained famous to this day – *Eppur si muove!* (Yet it does turn!). He was 70 years old at the time. He retired to a villa near Florence where he spent the last years of his life under the watchful eye of the Inquisition, under a form of house arrest. He died, blind, in 1642.

decree dated 1318 concerning Sardinia. The various districts of the town are organised in two groups reflecting the two parts of the city that are divided by the Arno – the north bank (*Tramontana*) and the south bank (*Mezzogiorno*). They compete on the Middle Bridge (*Ponte di Mezzo*), which is divided into two equal sections where the teams take up their positions. The aim is to gain control over the entire bridge. Over the centuries the rules have remained unchanged but the game has been altered to make it less violent. The *Mazzascudo*, literally a bludgeon-shield, had one narrow end designed for attack and one broad end for defence. For the game (*Gioco del Ponte*) it was replaced by a limewood or poplar shield (*targone*), which had more or less the same shape, that of a small oar, but was less dangerous despite its length (1m/3.28ft) and its weight (2.5kg/5.5lb). Nevertheless the hand-to-hand struggles between men in armour continued to be violent and so, since the Second World War, the competition has consisted of pushing the other team backwards across the bridge using a 7-tonne cart mounted on a central rail. A flag drops automatically as soon as the entire cart has crossed into the other camp. The six districts in each of the two halves of the city compete against each other in groups of two. The overall winner is the team which has obtained at least four victories in the quarter- and semi-finals.

Before the game the two "armies", each bearing their local colours, parade along the quaysides in two processions of more than 300 people dressed in ornate 16C costumes and armour. The procession of magistrates, which has some 60 participants, is separate and neutral. On the following Sunday the pennant (*palio*) is formally handed over to the winning team in the Palazzo Comunale. Festivities are held in the victorious districts.

Piazza dei Miracoli★★★

(Miracles Square) *Allow 3hr.*

This prestigious **square**, which is also known as **Piazza del Duomo** (Cathedral Square), contains four buildings which constitute an exceptionally beautiful sight, one of the most famous in the world. It resembles a vast enclosure, lined on two sides by a slim wall of red brick to which crenellations were added in the mid-12C. Within are the dazzling white marble mass of the baptistery and the cathedral with its famous bell tower, known as the Leaning Tower of Pisa. In the background is the cemetery (*Camposanto*). This succession of buildings is best seen from **Porta Santa Maria** and it is also from this point that the angle of the Leaning Tower is most spectacular.

Leaning Tower★★★

🕐*Open Apr–Sept daily 8.30am–8.30pm, Mar and Oct 9am–6pm. Rest of the year 10am–5pm. Last entry 30 min before closing. By reservation only.* ⊛*€15, €17 online reservations (at least 15 days in advance).* ℘*050 56 05 47. www.opapisa.it.*

The **Torre Pendente**, the bell tower (58m/189ft high) of the cathedral, is the pre-eminent symbol of the city. Its famous angle (approximately 5m/16ft off the vertical) has made it one of the most popular tourist attractions in the world. Its angle is caused by the alluvial soil, which is not compact enough to bear the weight of the building.

The building work was begun by Bonanno Pisano in 1173 and had reached the first floor when the first subsidence occurred. The architect, however, ignored it and another two storeys were built. When the second subsidence occurred, work stopped and did not start again until a century later when another architect, Giovanni di Simone, tried to correct the angle of slope by ensuring that the side which was sinking into the ground carried less weight. He died at the Battle of Meloria before his work was completed. The top of the bell tower was added in 1350.

The peculiarity of the tower cannot conceal the beauty of its architecture. It was built as a cylinder, like the towers in Byzantium, and has six floors of galleries which seem, because of the angle of incline, to be unwinding in an ethereal spiral.

On the lower level, in the purest of Pisan Romanesque styles, is the circle of blind arcading decorated with diamond-shaped motifs.

Cathedral backed by the leaning Tower

B. Pérousse / MICHELIN

363

"Long live the tower of Pisa, which leans and leans but does not fall…"

Since 1178, when the tower was first observed to lean, over 8,000 projects have been drawn up to remedy the problem, with varying degrees of success. The tower was closed to the public in 1990 because of the inherent danger of collapse and a committee was formed to debate how best to find a long-term solution to the problem. In 1992 two stainless steels rings were placed around the first floor.

In 1991 the tower was attached to the ground by 18 steel cables and in 1993 the foundations were strengthened with a reinforced concrete sheath containing 670 tonnes of lead (1m/3.28ft in length) to counterbalance the lean.
The progression of the lean was effectively stopped for several years.

Early in 1994 it was noted that the tower had moved back towards the vertical by 9mm/0.036in but the work was then stopped owing to a lack of funds.

Another restoration attempt in September 1995 ended in disaster when the tower shifted 2.5mm/1 inch in one night, double the annual rate. Engineers dumped lead on the base of the north side, and the tower was prevented from falling. No further restoration work took place until 1998, when steel-cable "braces" were attached to the tower. They were removed in 2001 when the tower had moved a further 40cm/1.3ft towards the vertical, returning the tower to the angle it was at in 1838. The tower was reopened to the public later that year. From the top there is a superb view★ of the square and the city spread out below. In fine weather the view extends across the countryside to the coast. In this prestigious university town, however, it is worth recalling the age-old curse that is well known to Italians – "Any student hoping to graduate should never risk the climb to the top."

Duomo★★

🕐Open Apr–Sept daily 10am–8pm, Oct and Mar 10am–6pm; rest of the year daily 10am–1pm and 2pm–5pm. ⊕€2, €10 joint ticket for 5 museums. 📞050 56 05 47. www.opapisa.it.
The two architects of the **cathedral** were Buscheto, who began the building work in 1063, and Rainaldo, who completed it towards the middle of the 12C.
It was the fabulous booty brought back to the city after major victories over the Saracens in Sicily that provided the funds required for the construction of this lavish building.
Pisa Cathedral is a vast building in the shape of a Latin Cross and it gives an impression of being wonderfully well-balanced with its long nave, huge transept and boldly projecting apse. To counterbalance this solemnity, a light touch is created by the rows of galleries on the west front, the blind arcading, the three rows of windows flanked by pilasters round the building and the

bonding with alternating light and dark marble string-courses. All these features formed the major characteristics of the Pisan Romanesque style.
Set in the **west front**★★★ decorated with elegant geometric motifs picked out in marquetry and mosaics of marble and multi coloured glazed terracotta is the tomb of Buscheto (*first arch on the left*).
Bronze **doors**★ cast in 1602 to designs by Giambologna replaced the original doors which were destroyed by fire in the late 16C. They depict the Life of the Virgin Mary (*centre*) and the Life of Christ (*sides*). The most famous of the doors is the one named San Ranieri, which opens into the south transept opposite the Leaning Tower. Cast in the late 12C, its admirable Romanesque bronze **panels**★★ were designed by Bonanno Pisano. Using a rigorous economy of figures but showing prodigious inventiveness, he depicted the Life of Christ in 20 small tableaux in a manner that

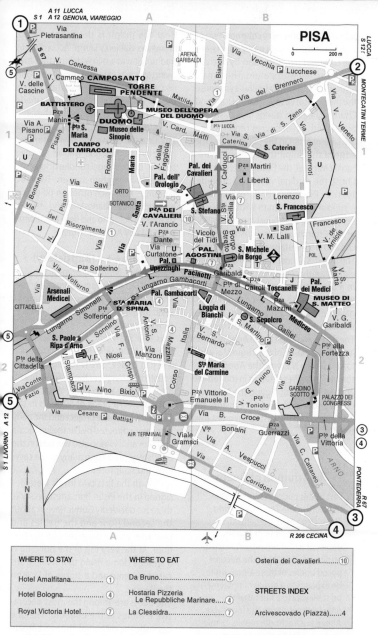

was highly stylised and gracefully naïve (⌖ *it is difficult to see the work because of the constant flow of visitors*).

The **Interior** of the building (best seen from the end of the nave) is less uniform than the exterior. It is a very impressive sight with its nave (100m/325ft long), four aisles, deep apse, triple-bay tran-

sept and slightly oval dome. The 68 columns, each carved out of a single block of stone, provide an amazing variety of perspectives.

The splendid **pulpit**★★★ on which **Giovanni Pisano** worked for almost ten years (1302–11) is a masterpiece of strength and delicacy. The pulpit itself is supported by porphyry columns, two of which stand on lions, a motif taken from the Lombard tradition, and by five pillars decorated with statues. The female figures on the central pillar symbolise the theological virtues – Faith, Hope and Charity. The pillar stands on a base decorated with small figures representing the Liberal Arts. On the pillars round the edge of the pulpit the carvings represent St Michael, the Evangelists carrying Christ, the cardinal virtues – Fortitude, Justice, Prudence and Temperance – supporting a woman with a baby at her breast, an allegorical representation of the Church being nourished by the Old and New Testaments, and Hercules. The pulpit is almost circular owing to the eight slightly convex carved panels.

In a set of tumultuous carvings filled with human figures Giovanni Pisano gave full vent to his talent for expressiveness and his sense of the dramatic. The first panel depicts the Annunciation and the Visitation of the Virgin Mary, followed by the Nativity, the Adoration of the Magi, the Presentation in the Temple and the Flight into Egypt, the Massacre of the Innocents, Christ's Passion, the Crucifixion and the Last Judgement (*two panels*).

The Triumph of Death

Part of this painting is taken from the story of the *Three Living and Three Dead Men*, a legend known throughout Europe. St Macaire is depicted (*left*) holding an unrolled scroll and pointing to the decomposed bodies of three kings, while he explains to a group of noblemen on their way to a hunt that the only reality is death, the inevitable. Above are Anchorite monks calmly preparing for death as they go about their daily business. Death (*right*) is ignoring a group of beggars pleading for his attention (*in the centre*) and preparing instead to swoop down triumphantly on a party of carefree young people in a delightful orchard.

Near the pulpit is the bronze lamp, known as Galileo's Lamp. According to tradition it was while watching the lamp swing as it was lit by the sexton that Galileo was inspired to develop his famous theory. In fact Galileo had already made his discovery a few years before the lamp was placed in the cathedral.

The Crucifix above the high altar was made by Giambologna, who also created the two bronze angel candlesticks at the corners of the choir screen. Two 16C paintings face each other on pillars on each side of the chancel – (*right*) *St Agnes* by Andrea del Sarto and (*left*) a *Madonna and Child* by Antonio Sogliani.

Battistero★★★ (Baptistery)

🕐*Open Apr–Sept daily 8am–8pm, Mar and Oct daily 9am–6pm; rest of the year daily 10am–5pm.* ∞€5, €10 joint ticket for 5 museums. ♿. ✆*050 56 05 47. www.opapisa.it.*

This is a majestic, circular building (almost 110m/358ft in circumference and just under 55m/179ft high) almost equal to the height of the Leaning Tower. It took 250 years to build. Work began in 1153, with a break of 50 years in the 13C, until 1400. The project and the early work were directed by Diotisalvi. Nicola and Giovanni Pisano also worked on the Baptistery, producing many of the carvings and sculptures.

Although the first two levels were designed in the Pisan Romanesque style, there is a decidedly Gothic flavour about the second floor and the gables and pinnacles above the arches on the first floor. At the very top of the building is a strange dome rising to a small, truncated pyramid and a statue of St John the Baptist.

The doors are among the most decorative features in the building. The one opposite the cathedral, the most ornate of the four, is flanked by columns carved with foliage in the 13C. On the lintel, carved in a Byzantine style, are episodes from the Life of St John the Baptist; above is a representation of Jesus between the Virgin Mary and St John with the four Evangelists on either side, alternating with angels. On the jambs are illustrations of the work of the 12 months of the year (*left*) and carvings of the apostles (*right*). The **Interior** (35m/114ft in diameter) is impressive for its tall rows of arcading, its deep dome, its striking majesty and the amount of light that floods into it. A remarkable echo can be heard in the Baptistery.

The alternating strips of light and dark marble create an austere form of decoration. Elegant monolithic columns with attractively carved capitals alternate with huge pillars to form a uniform peristyle on the lower level with a wide gallery above which is open to visitors (*staircase left of the entrance*). The effect of the near-perfect spatial layout can be seen at its best from the gallery. The circular building, articulated by the ring of columns and pillars, converges on the superb octagonal **font**★. It was designed in 1246 by Guido Bigarelli, an artist from Como and was used for christenings.

The Baptistery also has an admirable **pulpit**★★, carved by Nicola Pisano who completed it in 1260. It is more austere than the one produced for the cathedral by his son, Giovanni, and it stands on plain columns. In retracing the Life of Christ, the artist sought inspiration in the classical sculptures seen on the Roman sarcophagi in the Camposanto. This influence is particularly strong in the first two pulpit panels representing the Nativity and the Adoration of the Magi in which the Virgin Mary resembles a Roman matron. The following panels depict the Presentation in the Temple, the Crucifixion and the Last Judgement; the face of Lucifer (*bottom right-hand corner*) is reminiscent of the masks used in Classical theatre).

Camposanto★★

○*Open Apr–Sept daily 8am–8pm, Mar and Oct daily 9am–6pm; rest of the year daily 10am–5pm.* ⊕€5, €10 joint ticket for 5 museums. & ℘050 56 05 47. www.opapisa.it.

The cemetery is almost as famous as the other buildings in Piazza del Duomo. Building began in 1277 under the direction of Giovanni di Simone, the second architect to work on the bell tower, but was interrupted by the war against Genoa which ended in the Battle of Meloria (1284). The cemetery was not finished until the 15C.

Originally designed like an unroofed cathedral nave, this huge graveyard now resembles vast cloisters, as the tall Romanesque arches were converted in the 15C into wonderfully light four-bay Gothic windows. In the middle is the **Sacred Field** (*Camposanto*) which is said to have been laid out using earth brought back from Golgotha in the early 13C by the Crusaders. The earth was said to have the power to reduce dead bodies to skeletons in a few days. The galleries are paved with 600 tombstones and contain several superb Greco-Roman sarcophagi, most of them re-used in the Middle Ages for the burials of Pisan noblemen.

The walls used to be covered with admirable **frescoes** painted in the second half of the 14C and in the following century by artists such as Benozzo Gozzoli, Taddeo Gaddi, Andrea di Buonaiuto and Antonio Veneziano. In July 1944 artillery caused a fire which melted the lead roof, destroying or badly damaging most of the frescoes. Some of them, however, were saved and restored, including the famous fresco depicting the *Triumph of Death*, attributed to **Buffalmacco**, who also painted the *Last Judgement, Hell* and the *Story of the Anchorites in the Thebaid*.

▷ *Walk round the Camposanto anticlockwise.*

The **North Gallery**, now totally bare like the South Gallery, is lined by a number of rooms containing the most remarkable of the frescoes.

Beyond a small chapel, containing the St Rainier Altar carved by Tino di Camaino, is a room containing a photographic reconstruction of the frescoes as they were originally. In the centre of the room is a very fine Attic marble urn (2C BC) carved with Dionysian scenes in light relief. The great chamber beyond contains the **Fresco Room**. Among the frescoes

Sinopia

Although frescoes (*see INTRODUCTION TO TUSCANY*) can withstand the passage of time and the effects of the elements, they must be painted on a fresh base. They therefore have two main disadvantages – they have to be completed quickly and, once dry, cannot be touched up. In order to overcome these disadvantages, artists used to draw a sketch called an underdrawing (*sinopia*) on the wall, after the initial base had been prepared. This type of sketch got its name from a town, Sinope, on the shores of the Black Sea which provided the reddish-brown pigment usually used to draw them. Once the scene had been roughly sketched in, the artist could take his time to produce the final work, preparing the base only for the area he wanted to paint on a particular day. Many of these underdrawings have come to light over the past few decades as frescoes have been removed from walls for restoration.

(*left wall*) is the **Triumph of Death**★★, one of the most interesting examples of 14C Italian painting. This is an edifying work, probably painted shortly after the plague epidemic of 1348, and it illustrates themes that were very popular in western Europe at that time – the vanity of earthly pleasures and the shortness of life.

The two magnificent frescoes covering the end wall of the room and part of the next wall represent the **Last Judgement**★★ and **Hell**★. These were originally part of the same cycle as the previous fresco. The *Story of the Anchorites in the Thebaid* (*beyond*) depicts various details of the hard, lonely and ascetic life led by the early Christians who sought refuge in Egypt from persecution.

On the last wall (*right of the entrance*) are *Satan's pact with God* and *The Sufferings of Job* by Taddeo Gaddi.

The **West Gallery** was the first one to be filled with the lavish tombs of Pisan noblemen from the 16C onwards. Each tomb was placed symmetrically in relation to the others. The **East Gallery** was organised in the same way. In the 18C the custom became so popular that the tombs began to spread into the longer North and South Galleries.

In 1807 Carlo Lasinio was appointed Curator and he introduced the ancient sarcophagi which had lain along the sides of the cathedral and in the many monasteries and churches in Pisa.

Museo delle Sinopie★

Open Apr–Sept daily 8am–8pm, Mar and Oct daily 9am–6pm. Closed rest of the year. €5, €10 joint ticket for 5 museums. 050 56 05 47. www.opapisa.it.

This **museum**, formerly a hospice built in the 13C and 14C, contains the underdrawings of the Camposanto frescoes. Most of the underdrawings displayed on the **Ground Floor** were sketched in the 15C and are very rough since it was customary for artists to work at their studies on paper and only the main lines of the work were sketched on the wall.

During the restoration work on the frescoes, which had been damaged in 1944 the underdrawings were also removed and restored. They are now skilfully displayed in a high-ceilinged chamber covering two floors.

On the **Upper Floor** a series of platforms (*staircase at the end of the room*) gives a panoramic view of the gigantic underdrawings created before the completion of the most famous frescoes in the Camposanto. At the end of the room is the underdrawing for the *Crucifixion*, the first fresco to be painted c. 1320–30 by Francesco di Traino, who was the most important artist in Pisa in the 14C. The grandiose compositions used for the *Triumph of Death*, the *Last Judgement* and *Hell* and the *Story of the Anchorites in the Thebaid* show the remarkable drawing talents, especially in the facial expressions.

Two higher galleries provide different views of the works.

Museo dell'Opera del Duomo★★

🕐 *Open Apr–Sept daily 8am–8pm; Mar and Oct daily 9am–6pm; rest of the year daily 10am–5pm.* 👛*€5, €10 joint ticket for 5 museums.* ♿. ☏*050 56 05 47.* *www.opapisa.it.*

The works in the **museum** come from the buildings in Piazza dei Miracoli. Room 1 gives visitors a view of the buildings, in the form of 19C models, before seeing the sculptures and furnishings.

The first pulpit on the **Ground Floor** produced (1158 to 1162) for the cathedral (*Room 2*) was carved by **Guglielmo**, the architect and sculptor who was in charge of the building work. In 1310 it was replaced by the pulpit carved by Giovanni Pisano and given to Cagliari Cathedral in Sardinia. Copies of the pulpit are shown here and its structure was such that it became a prototype for future creations throughout Tuscany.

The foreign works (*Room 3*) are part of the cathedral's furnishings and the shapes imported from distant lands enrich the early, mainly Classical, Romanesque architecture. Most of the additions were from the Islamic world with which the Pisans were well acquainted owing to their maritime trading links. New geometric and iconographic motifs were introduced, with a taste for polychrome marble inlay, a craft form which was already known through Byzantine art and architecture. Sculptures from Provence – a head of David – and Burgundy – a wooden statue of Christ – prove that there were links with French Romanesque artists.

The other buildings in the square – the tower (*Room 4*) and the Baptistery (*Rooms 5 and 6*) – are celebrated together with their glorious Pisan sculptures. The nine busts (*in the cloister gallery*), which adorned the top of the Baptistery loggia, were the work (1269–79) of **Nicola Pisano** and his son, **Giovanni Pisano**. The latter also created (1302–10) the second pulpit (*Room 5*) and some other works (*Room 7*).

The Sienese sculptor **Tino di Camaino** (*Room 8*), who worked in Pisa for many years, was one of the most famous sculptors of funeral monuments in the 14C. The statues of the Emperor, four of his advisers, an *Annunciation* and two angels (1315) come from his mausoleum for Henry VII of Luxembourg, who died in 1313.

Nino Pisano (*Room 9*) also created a number of the tombs in the cathedral in the second half of the 14C. The tomb of Archbishop Giovanni Scherlatti so delighted Archbishop Francesco Moricotti that he asked Nino to create an identical one for him.

The main figure in the 15C art world was the Florentine, **Andrea di Francesco Guardi** (*Room 10*), a pupil in Donatello's workshop. His main piece of work was Archbishop Pietro Ricci's tomb.

The cathedral **treasury** (*Room 11*) displays some of the oldest and most precious items – an 11C ivory chest a small 12C silver gilt Crucifix known as the "Pisans' Cross", two Limoges reliquaries (12C), and six fragments of the cathedral girdle (*cintola*) dating from the 13C and 14C. The 15C–18C paintings and sculptures on the **First Floor** (*Rooms 13–14*) are followed by (*Room 15*) the marquetry decorating the choir stalls in the cathedral. The three panels depicting *Faith, Hope* and *Charity* were made by Baccio and Piero Pontelli to drawings by Botticelli. The panels by Guido da Seravallino show 15C views of the quays in Pisa.

Among the illuminated manuscripts and antiphonies (*Room 16*) are two 12C–13C "*Exultet*". On one side of these rolls was a transcript of the liturgical chant sung on Easter Saturday while on the other were the paintings seen by the congregation, representing scenes from the mystery of the Resurrection.

The vestments (*Rooms 17 to 20*) provide an opportunity to admire fabrics and embroideries dating from the 15C to 19C.

The final part of the museum deals with archaeology – Egyptian, Etruscan and Roman remains collected from the various churches and monasteries in Pisa in the 19C by Carlo Lasinio, the curator of the Camposanto. With his son, he also produced a series of etchings based on the Camposanto frescoes.

Cavalieri to the Arno

Piazza dei Cavalieri★

This spacious, tranquil **square** lies in the heart of the medieval town and is now frequented by students. It has remained one of the most majestic and best-preserved areas in Pisa and it was here, in 1406, that the end of the Pisan Republic was proclaimed.

The square was totally transformed when Cosimo I de' Medici commissioned his architect, Vasari, to erect the buildings designed for the **Knights of St Stephen** (Cavalieri di Santo Stefano). This holy, military Order, which was subject to the Rule of St Benedict, was founded in 1562 to lead the fight against the Infidel, its main task being to capture the Muslim pirates who infested the Mediterranean. The brotherhood died out in 1860.

The square is lined by 16C and 17C buildings and dominated by the **palazzo dei Cavalieri** on which the long, unusual, slightly curved **façade**★ is decorated with grotesque figures and foliage. The upper storeys are separated by a frieze of niches containing the busts of the six members of the Medici dynasty who were Grand Dukes of Tuscany. Their coat of arms – six balls – is visible in several places, as is the Cross of the Knights who were given instruction here. The build-

ing is currently the seat of the university founded during the days of Napoleon Bonaparte. In front is a statue of Cosimo I made in 1596 by Francavilla.

The Church of **Santo Stefano** dates from 1569 but its white, green and pink marble west front, including the Medici coat of arms and the Cross of St Stephen, was built some 40 years later.

The **Palazzo dell'Orologio** (Clock House), also known as the **Gherardesca**, was reconstructed by Vasari in 1607 on the site of two older buildings. He incorporated the remains of a tower (Torre della Fame) in which, following the defeat of Pisa in 1284 at the Battle of Meloria, Count **Ugolino della Gherardesca**, the commander-in-chief of the Pisan fleet, was accused of treason and sentenced to death by starvation with his children. Dante described this episode in his *Inferno* (*Divine Comedy, Song XXXIII*).

Santa Caterina

Leaving the Piazza Cavalieri to the east you come to the Via Carducci. Go left to see the elegant **facade**★ of Santa Caterina, built of white marble discreetly marked with lines of darker marble. It consists of a harmonious combination of austere, wide Romanesque blind arches on the lower level and two successive rows of graceful Gothic columns and multifoiled arches on the upper sections. The interior contains two white marble tombs facing one another. Nino

Historic Regatta in Honor of San Ranieri goes past Santa Maria della Spina

APT Pisa, Pisa Tourism Board

Pisano sculpted the left tomb, as well as the two sculptures of the *Annunciation* flanking the chancel.

San Michele in Borgo

Head south towards the river from Piazza dei Cavalieri and you will find the **façade**★ of this **church**; a remarkable example of the transition between the Romanesque and Gothic periods in Pisan architecture. It has three rows of galleries with trefoiled pointed arches and colonnades decorated with masks, which contrast sharply with the more robust lower section where, unlike most of the churches in Pisa, there is no blind arcading.

Museo Nazionale di San Matteo★★

Piazza San Mateo in Soarta (Lungarno Mediceo). ⓒ*Open Tue–Sat 9am–7pm, Sun and Hols 9am–2pm.* ⓒ*Closed 1 Jan, 1 May, 25 Dec.* ◉€4. ♿. ☎*050 54 18 65. www.liberologico.com.*

Turn left along the river from San Michele in Borgo to get to this **museum**, which is set out around the cloisters in the former St Matthew's Monastery (15C). The rooms contain an extraordinary collection of sculptures and paintings, from Pisan churches and monasteries, by local artists, all showing the extent to which the city was a major centre of artistic creativity from the 13C to 15C.

The first door at the end of the **Ground Floor** gallery gives access to the collections of **ceramics**. Pisa acquired a large quantity of Islamic ceramics and was also famous in the 13C–17C for its original work. From the 14C onwards production was exported throughout the Mediterranean basin from Spain to Turkey, including Provence, Corsica and Greece. It was used locally as an unusual feature in the architectural decoration of churches (ⓒ*see San Piero a Grado below*). From the mid-13C, Pisan workshops, which were among the largest in Tuscany, succeeded in making their ceramics waterproof by coating them in pewter-based vitreous enamels. The main feature of this "early majolica" is its brown and green painted decoration.

From the 15C onwards the designs were etched into the ceramics and usually highlighted by a brown ochre tint. The item itself could be left white or uniformly painted in pale yellow, yellow ochre or green. These incisions (*a stecca*) later developed into the decorative style known as "peacock's feather eye". The following rooms contain ceramics imported from Liguria, southern Italy, Islamic countries or the Middle East. The collection of 10C–13C Islamic items is especially extensive.

The upper gallery in the **First Floor** cloisters contains pieces of architectural sculpture, of which the oldest date from the 12C.

The tour of **Pisan painting** begins in the room (*left at the top of the staircase*) with works dating from the 12C–13C. The huge Crucifixes are characteristic of this period, which was still strongly influenced by Greek and Byzantine works. 14C works (*right of the staircase*) show the extent to which Pisa was open to new artistic trends. The great freestanding polyptych, which is painted on one side with the glory of Saint Ursula and on the other with the glory of Saint Dominic, is by Francesco di Traino (1344). At the end of the room is a magnificent polyptych of the *Virgin and Child*, painted c. 1320 by Simone Martini for the church of Santa Caterina.

The room at the end on the right is filled with examples of **Pisan sculptures** from the 14C, a period that was dominated by the workshop of Andrea Pisano and his sons, Nino and Tommaso (ⓒ*see above*). Note the delightful marble *Madonna and Child* by Nino Pisano and, more particularly, the **Madonna del latte** on which the Virgin Mary is depicted gracefully leaning over with a serene smile on her face.

The tour of the world of painting continues in the room opposite (*and in the cloister gallery at right angles to it*). Although the outbreak of plague in 1348 interrupted the flow of commissions and caused a break in the choice of subject matter, Pisa remained a major centre of creativity even after that date. The other rooms reveal the level of artistic activity in Pisa in the 15C. After coming under Florentine control in 1406, Pisa saw an influx of prestigious artists from the Tuscan capital. In the corner of the cloister gallery, there is a *Virgin Mary of Humility* by Gentile da Fabriano and, in the first room in this same gallery, a **St Paul** who is stupefyingly life like. This was once part of a polyptych painted in 1426 by Masaccio. There is also a *Madonna and Child* (*stucco low relief*) by Michelozzo, a delightful *Madonna and Child* by Fra Angelico and a gilded bronze bust of St Rossore by Donatello. The following room contains a number of works by Benozzo Gozzoli and a *Holy Conversation* by Ghirlandaio.

In the same gallery are life-size sculptures in painted and gilded wood; most are by **Francesco di Valdambrino**, who learned his craft from the Pisano family of artists. These mainly feminine figures used to decorate Pisa's convents.

Lungarni

The Lungarni are the streets that run parallel to (along) the Arno River.

Lungarno Pacinotti

From Piazza Solferino and the bridge of the same name, there is a view east along the **quays** of a bend in the Arno, with Monte Pisano in the background. To the west is the tall brick tower of the old citadel. The slender, white church of Santa Maria della Spina stands out on the south bank. The **Palazzo Upezzinghi** (no 43) was built in the early 17C and is now part of the university. Its façade flanks a large gateway, surmounted by a window opening onto a balcony, above which is a huge coat of arms decorated with a lion. The 15C **Palazzo Agostini**★ (nos 28–25) has a decorative façade built entirely of brick including two rows of Gothic windows. On the ground floor is the famous **Caffè dell'Ussero** (Hussars' Café) established in 1794 and frequented by the writers of the Risorgimento. On the other side of the bridge (*Ponte di Mezzo*), in close proximity to each other, are the 17C **Loggia di Banchi** that used to house the linen market and the austere **Palazzo Gambacorti**, the late 14C town

hall built of grey-green stone decorated with a few rows of pink stone. Its three storeys include double windows set in semicircular arches.

Lungarno Mediceo

The superb **Palazzo Toscanelli** (no 17) has a majestic Renaissance façade. Byron wrote part of his *Don Juan* there between the autumn of 1821 and the summer of 1822. The **Palazzo dei Medici** (now the Prefettura) dates from the 13C–14C but has undergone much alteration since that time. Its most famous guest was Lorenzo the Magnificent of Florence.

Religion on the Arno

San Sepolcro

Like the Holy Sepulchre in Jerusalem, this **church** of the same name is built to a similar layout. Its octagonal design with pyramid-shaped roof was created in the 12C by Diotisalvi. The **interior**★ consists of an ambulatory and majestic central chancel around which very tall, mighty pillars support high arches surmounted by a deep dome surrounded by brick bonding.

Santa Maria della Spina★★

Standing alone, white and ethereal on the banks of the Arno, this tiny marble Romanesque-Gothic **church** looks like a reliquary with its spires, gables, pinnacles, niches and rose windows. For many years, it contained one of the thorns (*spina*) from Christ's Crown, hence its name. It was built in the early 14C on a level with the river but was demolished in 1871 because of the damage caused by the proximity of the water. It was then rebuilt on the spot where it stands today. Several of the statues that decorated the exterior, created by the Pisano School, have been replaced by copies. The plain rectangular room forming the nave and chancel is lit, on the side facing the Arno, by an almost unbroken row of Gothic double windows beneath a Romanesque arch. The church contains a graceful *Madonna and Child* by Nino Pisano.

San Paolo a Ripa d'Arno

As its name suggests, this 11C and 12C church stands on the bank of the Arno.

Its attractive **façade**★ with three rows of columns, its alternating rows of black and white marble and the blind arcading decorating the sides are all typical of the Pisan Romanesque style.

Excursions

Cascina
21km/13mi SE.
The town specialises in the small-scale and mass production of furniture, hence its size. Before 1364 it was controlled by Pisa, but after the **Battle of Cascina** it fell to Florence. Michelangelo chose it as the subject of a major fresco that was never painted; however, the battle remained famous because of the artist's magnificent cartoon. It was designed for the Hall of Five Hundred in the Palazzo Vecchio in Florence where it would have appeared opposite Leonardo da Vinci's fresco of the Battle of Anghiari. Michelangelo, who was fascinated by the anatomy of the human body, chose to illustrate this episode which allowed him to depict Florentine soldiers bathing naked in the Arno when they were subjected to a surprise attack by Pisan troops. The old town, laid out in a grid pattern, is traversed by Corso Matteotti, a street lined with arcades. At one end, there is a clock tower containing a small bell; this is all that remains of the walls which encircled the town in the Middle Ages. At the other end is the Oratory of San Giovanni (late 14C) which has a *Crucifixion* by Martino di Bartolomeo (1398) above the altar, including (*top right*) the beginning of a cycle of frescoes on Genesis. Set back from the Corso Matteotti and flanked by two other churches is the **Santa Maria**, a 12C church with a typically Pisan **façade**★.

⊷ DRIVING TOURS

ARNO TO THE SEA
30km/19mi. From Pisa take the road along the south bank of the Arno and follow signs for Mare and Marina di Pisa and then for San Piero.

The 12C **Cappella Sant'Agata** behind the apse is a strange little octagonal brick chapel with a pyramid-shaped roof that is usually attributed to Diotisalvi.

San Piero a Grado
The 11C Romanesque **basilica**★ of San Piero a Grado (St Peter's on the Quay) is said to stand on the old quayside in the Roman port of Pisa where St Peter is believed to have landed. The 14C frescoes in the interior, depicting the life of St Peter, are said to be copies of the ones that decorated the original basilica of St Peter's in Rome.
Tirrenia ⌂ (*second turn to the right after the basilica*) is an elegant resort famous for its extensive pine woods, its white sandy beach and its film studios.
Marina di Pisa is a popular beach at the mouth of the Arno. There is a view of Livorno (*south*). Nearby is the vast pine wood on the **San Rossore** estate which belonged to the Medici family and then to the House of Savoy. It is now part of the Migliarino-San Rossore-Massaciuccoli country park.

MONTE PISANO★
60km/38mi round trip – about 2hr 30min . From Pisa take S12 (blue signs to Lucca) and A11 (green signs to Firenze).
This small outcrop of the Apuan Alps, lying between Pisa and Lucca, rises to a peak in Monte Serra (917m/2,980ft).

San Giuliano Terme
This small **spa** town was once frequented by such famous 19C figures as Byron and Shelley. In the distance is a large yellow ochre portico with five arches, which marks the entrance to the pump rooms.

▷ *Turn left before a small bridge to return to the village (no signs). The road runs beside a stream before crossing the first bridge on the right.*

The pump rooms stand in a small square where Shelley took lodgings. The two hot springs, famous since Roman times, produce water at temperatures of 38°C /100°F and 41°C/106°F.

▷ *Turn right opposite the pump rooms to rejoin S12. Turn right to return to the original crossroads and turn left into the road to Calci.*

At the junction where the left turn leads to Agnano, Monte Pisano comes into view. The small "Verruca" hill, site of a now-ruined 13C Pisan fortress, is the final promontory before the descent.

▷ *8km/5mi from San Giuliano, beyond a petrol station (right), turn left to Calci and Montemagno. After 1km/0.5mi of bends the road leads to Calci church.*

Calci
The 11C parish **church** (**Pieve**) has a fine Pisan Romanesque west front. The interior contains a 12C christening font.

▷ *Continue; straight at the lights (700m/ 758yd) to the charterhouse.*

Certosa di Calci★
⏱*Open Tue–Sat 8.30am–6.30pm (12.30pm Sun and Hols).* ⏱*Closed 1 Jan, 1 May, 25 Dec.* ♿€4. ☎050 93 84 30.
The first stone of the impressive set of buildings that is the **Calci Charterhouse** was laid in 1366. The daily routine of the Carthusian monks alternated between their solitary cells and the church; these buildings form part of a harmonious group, which includes the **Great Cloisters★** and the prior's lodgings.
In the 18C the buildings resounded less to the murmur of monks at prayer and more to the voices of the guests in the Grand Duke's apartment. The monks, whose numbers had dwindled, left in 1973.
The sense of abandonment is enhanced by a tour of the buildings, which passes from the pharmacy to the monks' chapels, to the cemetery and past the monks' gardens to the refectory. The monks were mainly vegetarian, although their rule permitted them to eat fish. One wing of the monastery houses a

natural history museum (⏱*Open Mon–Fri 9am–1.30pm, Sat 9am–6pm, Sun and hols 10am–7pm; www.msn. unipi.it*) run by the University of Pisa. The highlight of the collection is a magnificent gallery of cetacean skeletons.
From the grounds there is a view of the surrounding mountains and the ruins of the Verruca fortress.

▷ *Return to the crossroads in Calci and go right at the lights to Monte Serra.*

The Arno Plain is visible (*right*) with the river winding majestically through the countryside at the foot of the mountain range. There is a superb **view★** from a layby (*5.3km/3mi from the crossroads in Calci*). At the Y-junction the road (*left*) continues to climb Monte Serra; the other road, (*right*) to Buti, soon crosses to the opposite side of the range where the scenery becomes less rugged.

▷ *In Buti take the road to Pontedera. At the T-junction, opposite the river, turn right; first left, cross the bridge; bear left. At the fork, turn left uphill. At the end, Vicopisano and its keep come into view.*

Vicopisano
The Pisan Romanesque church (12C–13C) contains a rare woodcarving of the **Deposition from the Cross★** (11C). The old village still has some picturesque traces of its medieval walls, including three towers. At the top of the hill stands the crenellated keep and the Palazzo Pretorio.

▷ *Take the road along the north bank of the Arno to return to Pisa.*

Near **Uliveto Terme** the road skirts the rugged slopes of Monte Pisano. As it approaches Caprona, the outpost of the fortress on Verruca comes into view high above a quarry which produces the yellow-ochre veined stone known as *verrucano*.

▷ *Follow signs; take S67 to Pisa.*

ADDRESSES

🏨 STAY

Hotel Amalfitana – *Via Roma 44. 📞050 29 000. Fax 050 25 218. 21 rooms.* A 15C mansion, a few steps from the Piazza dei Miracoli in the Santa Maria university district – could you ask for more? This a comfortable, small, family-run hotel where you will find attention to detail, courteous service and reasonable prices.

Hotel Bologna – *V. Mazzini 57. 📞050 50 21 20. Fax 050 43 070. www. hotelbologna.pisa.it. 64 rooms.* 🅿 *paid parking.* *Shuttle to the Duomo or airport: € 7.* Located in the Sant'Antonio quarter, close to the train station, not far from the airport and within walking distance of the city centre, this hotel is situated in a beautifully restored palace that offers every comfort.

Royal Victoria Hotel – *Lungarno Pacinotti 12. 📞050 94 01 11. Fax 050 94 01 80. 48 rooms.* 🅿 *paid parking.* On the bank of the Arno, this hotel, housed in a restored 14C palace, has been managed by the Piegaja family since 1837.

🍴 EAT

Osteria Dei Mille – *Via dei Mille 32. 📞050 55 62 63.* This is a typical osteria, about 5min from the Piazza dei Miracoli, serving Tuscan cooking and a good choice of vegetarian dishes. The copper pots on the walls add a cheerful touch to the decor.

La Clessidra – *Via Santa Cecilia 34. 📞050 54 01 60. Closed Sat noon, Sun, 27 Dec–8 Jan and 5–25 Aug. Reservations suggested.* This simple but pleasant restaurant is in one of the most elegant and best preserved districts of Pisa. The chef will give you a taste of the typical flavours of the Tuscan region as well as one or two interesting variations of his own.

Osteria dei Cavalieri – *Via San Frediano 16. 📞050 58 08 58. Closed Sat midday, Sun and Aug.* This family-run trattoria, a local favourite, offers a reasonably priced menu of standard dishes served with care and a touch of originality. The warm welcome and attentive service are an added attraction.

Hostaria Pizzeria Le Repubbliche Marinare – *Vicolo Del Ricciardi 8. 📞050 20 506. Closed Mon and 7 Jan-7 Feb. Reservations suggested.* This little restaurant is an oasis of tranquility on a pretty square in the Sant'Antonio quarter. Pizza and fish specialities.

Da Bruno – *V. Luigi Bianchi 12. Porta a Lucca. 📞050 56 08 18. Fax 050 55 06 07. Closed Mon eve, Tue.* A few steps from the Piazza dei Miracóli, this is an ideal restaurant in which to sample Tuscan and Pisan specialties.

La Mescita – *Via Cavalca 2. 📞050 54 42 94. Closed Mon. Reservations suggested.* In the heart of the city, this restaurant is subdivided into two warm and comfortable rooms, and serves a menu that reinterprets traditional dishes. Reliable service in a pleasant atmosphere.

🍽 TAKING A BREAK

Caffè dell'Ussero – *Lungarno Pacinotti 27. 📞050 58 11 00. Open Sun–Fri 7.30am–9pm. Closed Aug.* This café, founded in 1794, is situated beside the Arno on the ground floor of the Palazzo Rosso. First it was frequented by intellectuals, then it became a musical café and then a cinema. Now it is a cosy tea room.

Pasticceria Federico Salza – *Borgo Stretto 46. 📞050 58 02 44. Open 7am–8pm. Closed Mon from Easter–Aug.* This café is divided into a cosy bar and a large and light tea room. Its charming terrace under the arches looking onto a picturesque street attracts many customers.

🎭 ENTERTAINMENT

Cagliostro – *Via del Castelletto 26/30. 📞050 57 54 13. Open Wed–Mon 12.45pm–2.30pm and 8pm–2am.* This combined bar, wine bar and art gallery is unlike any other café in Pisa with its metal and copper decor. The winter garden is a good place for relaxing and tasting one of the 300 bottles of wine and liqueurs.

INDEX

INDEX

INDEX

🏨 STAY

🍷 EAT

MAPS AND PLANS

COMPANION PUBLICATIONS

Michelin map 563 Italia Centro
a map of central Italy on a scale of 1:400
000 with an index of place names and
town plans of Florence and Rome

Atlas Italia
a practical, spiral-bound atlas on a
scale of 1:300 000 with an index of
place names and maps of 70 cities and
conurbations

Michelin map 735 Italia
a practical road map on a scale of
1:1 000 000 which provides an overall
view of the Italian road network

www.ViaMichelin.com
The www.ViaMichelin.com website
offers a wide range of services and
practical information for motorists in
43 countries, including route planning,
maps and a selection of hotels and
restaurants from the red-cover
Michelin Guide.

Sports and recreation

	Racecourse
	Skating rink
	Outdoor, indoor swimming pool
	Multiplex Cinema
	Marina, sailing centre
	Trail refuge hut
	Cable cars, gondolas
	Funicular, rack railway
	Tourist train
	Recreation area, park
	Theme, amusement park
	Wildlife park, zoo
	Gardens, park, arboretum
	Bird sanctuary, aviary
	Walking tour, footpath
	Of special interest to children